West African Culture Dynamics

World Anthropology

General Editor

SOL TAX

Patrons

CLAUDE LÉVI-STRAUSS
MARGARET MEAD†
LAILA SHUKRY EL HAMAMSY
M. N. SRINIVAS

MOUTON PUBLISHERS · THE HAGUE · PARIS · NEW YORK

West African Culture Dynamics:

Archaeological and Historical Perspectives

Editors

B. K. SWARTZ, JR.
RAYMOND E. DUMETT

MOUTON PUBLISHERS · THE HAGUE · PARIS · NEW YORK

ISBN 90–279–7920–0
Indexes by Society of Indexers, Great Britain
Jacket photo by permission of ABC Press, Amsterdam
Photo by W. W. Manley
Cover and jacket design by Jurriaan Schrofer
Phototypeset in V.I.P. Times by
Western Printing Services Ltd, Bristol
Printed in Great Britain

General Editor's Preface

The understanding of West Africa's past by Euro-American scholars has been clouded by the shadows of both colonialism and racism. In recent years it has helped that Eastern and Southern Africa were discovered to be the birthplace of the genus *Homo*. And with independence, North Africa has been restored to its continent by scholars who had turned the homeland of Hannibal, the Pharoahs, and Shakespeare's moors into the south shore of a European Mediterranean Sea. The rescue of Africa from popular ignorance and prejudice concerning "the Dark Continent — where there was no literature, no political systems, no history" by the participation of African scholars has been increasingly evident. The present book is a significant addition to the growing enlightenment: it is a significant result of a remarkably representative gathering of anthropologists and other scholars from throughout the world.

Like most contemporary sciences, anthropology is a product of the European tradition. Some argue that it is a product of colonialism, with one small and self-interested part of the species dominating the study of the whole. If we are to understand the species, our science needs substantial input from scholars who represent a variety of the world's cultures. It was a deliberate purpose of the IXth International Congress of Anthropological and Ethnological Sciences to provide impetus in this direction. The *World Anthropology* volumes, therefore, offer a first glimpse of a human science in which members from all societies have played an active role. Each of the books is designed to be self-contained; each is an attempt to update its particular sector of scientific knowledge and is written by specialists from all parts of the world. Each volume should be read and reviewed individually as a separate volume on its own given subject. The set as a whole will indicate what changes are in store for anthropology as scholars from the developing countries join in studying the species of which we are all a part.

The IXth Congress was planned from the beginning not only to include as many of the scholars from every part of the world as possible, but also with a view toward the eventual publication of the papers in high-quality volumes. At previous Congresses scholars were invited to bring papers which were then read out loud. They were necessarily limited in length; many were only summarized; there was little time for discussion; and the sparse discussion could only be in one language. The IXth Congress was an experiment aimed at changing this. Papers were written with the intention of exchanging them before the Congress, particularly in exten-sive pre-Congress sessions; they were not intended to be read aloud at the Congress, that time being devoted to discussions -- discussions which were simultaneously and professionally translated into five languages. The method for eliciting the papers was structured to make as represen-tative a sample as was allowable when scholarly creativity -- hence self-selection -- was critically important. Scholars were asked both to propose papers of their own and to suggest topics for sessions of the Congress which they might edit into volumes. All were then informed of the suggestions and encouraged to re-think their own papers and the topics. The process, therefore, was a continuous one of feedback and exchange and it has continued to be so even after the Congress. The some two thousand papers comprising *World Anthropology* certainly then offer a substantial sample of world anthropology. It has been said that anthropology is at a turning point; if this is so, these volumes will be the historical direction-markers.

As might have been foreseen in the first post-colonial generation, the large majority of the Congress papers (82 percent) are the work of scholars identified with the industrialized world which fathered our tradi-tional discipline and the institution of the Congress itself: Eastern Europe (15 percent); Western Europe (16 percent); North America (47 per-cent); Japan, South Africa, Australia, and New Zealand (4 percent). Only 18 percent of the papers are from developing areas: Africa (4 percent); Asia-Oceania (9 percent); Latin America (5 percent). Aside from the substantial representation from the U.S.S.R. and the nations of Eastern Europe, a significant difference between this corpus of written material and that of other Congresses is the addition of the large pro-portion of contributions from Africa, Asia, and Latin America. "Only 18 percent" is two to four times as great a proportion as that of other Congresses; moreover, 18 percent of 2,000 papers is 360 papers, 10 times the number of "Third World" papers presented at previous Congresses. In fact, these 360 papers are more than the total of *all* papers published after the last International Congress of Anthropological and Ethnologi-cal Sciences which was held in the United States (Philadelphia, 1956).

The significance of the increase is not simply quantitative. The input of scholars from areas which have until recently been no more than subject matter for anthropology represents both feedback and also long-awaited theoretical contributions from the perspectives of very different cultural, social, and historical traditions. Many who attended the IXth Congress were convinced that anthropology would not be the same in the future. The fact that the Xth Congress (India, 1978) was our first in the "Third World" may be symbolic of the change. Meanwhile, sober consideration of the present set of books will show how much, and just where and how, our discipline is being revolutionized.

This is one of at least five "Africa" volumes in the *World Anthropology* series which readers of the present book will wish to consult. In addition, most of the volumes in the series which cover general topics in a comparative way include papers on Africa and by African authors. These volumes include a range of topics from human evolution and cultural development from earliest to contemporary times to discussions of colonialism and the politics of anthropology.

Chicago, Illinois SOL TAX
August 21, 1979

Preface

The essays in this volume are based in part on papers presented in the session West African Culture Dynamics at the IXth International Congress of Anthropological and Ethnological Sciences. Because I believed it necessary to extend the range of papers beyond those originally presented at the rather brief session, approximately half of the papers, and particularly those in the history section, were solicited by the editors after the Congress. In addition, several papers presented at the Congress were substantially revised to meet challenging questions raised by commentators both at the Congress and after. Several of the papers presented at the Congress were not included in the final volume. Members of the original panel included, in addition to the editors, R. G. Armstrong, S. J. S. Cookey, Hassan Fekri, Peter Fuchs, T. R. Hays, A. U. M. Obayemi, John A. Rustad, and Peter Skalník. Although we decided not to include a separate section of comments based on tapes of the original Congress session, edited portions of some discussion have been included. The essence of many of the remarks by discussants has been included in the editors' introductions.

The topics included in this anthology range over broad areas of recent work in the archaeology and history of West Africa. Obviously no single volume of this type could encompass the totality of recent research trends in both of these disciplines, but it has seemed worthwhile to bring to the attention of general readers and scholars in other fields of specialization some of the more significant new research areas and some of the highlights of findings in prehistory, protohistory, and recorded history of West Africa. One of the clear-cut improvements in perspectives on Africa in recent years — whether one is dealing with limited tool assemblages or broad cultural patterns or, in parallel, with small-scale societies or great kingdoms and empires — is that Africanists can no longer be content to analyze data in statis, but must take cognizance of both long-term and short-term change. Technological, environmental, cultural, social, political, and economic themes are emphasized, and bases for cross-cultural comparison are suggested. Among the topics included in Part One are the origins of occupation, the development and diffusion of plant domestication and iron technology, and the occurrence of ceramics. In Part Two, the papers deal with such diverse topics as elements in state formation in the Guinea forest zone, patterns of ethnic migration and conquest, influence of Islam, the *modus vivendi* for both trading and pastoral societies of the Western Sudan. Other papers in the history section touch on the impact of the slave trade and slave raiding, the influence of Islam, changes in the status of kings and chiefs from precolonial through colonial rule, and the impact of European imperialism and the origins of West African nationalism in the nineteenth and early twentieth centuries.

B. K. SWARTZ, JR.

ACKNOWLEDGMENTS

The editors would like to thank the following persons for advice and assistance in the preparation of this collection: John Flint, Stephen Baier, George Brooks, Charles Bird, J. O. Hunwick, Enya Flores-Meiser, and Jack Whitehead, for comments on specific papers; Jack Harlan and his coeditors Jan de Wet and Ann Stemler, for consenting to the reprinting of three papers (Flight, David, and Munson) first published in *Origins of African plant domestication* (Mouton 1976); Norman Bennett, for permitting reprinting in revised form of Bruce Mouser's "Landlord-strangers: a process of accommodation and assimilation," first published in *International Journal of African Historical Studies* 8 (1975). Finally, we express our deep appreciation to Sol Tax, President of the IXth International Congress of Anthropological and Ethnological Sciences and General Editor of the *World Anthropology* series, and to Karen Tkach and Barbara Metzger for their support and meticulous attention to detail in seeing the volume through to publication.

Table of Contents

XII   *Table of Contents*

PART TWO: HISTORY

PART ONE

Archaeology

Introduction: Some Formulations on the Prehistory of West Africa

B. K. SWARTZ, JR.

Three general works deal with broad aspects of West African archaeology (Mauny 1961; Davies 1964, 1967). Only the last of these can claim comprehensiveness, and it has serious faults as to approach and interpretation. I hope that this presentation can serve as a brief introduction to the subject. It is organized as follows: (1) general summaries of contributions, sometimes with supplementary data, (2) a few general conclusions, and (3) a short developmental synthesis, by general stage, of West African prehistory.

Bassey W. Andah's paper "Processes of Coastal Evolution in West Africa during the Quaternary" underscores the disparity in Quaternary time control between West Africa and East Africa. As organizer of this volume I am delighted to have this study as a general chronological framework for West African archaeology, but as the author of the paper that follows it I reject the idea that a valid deduced subcontinental approach to West African geochronology is possible, though Andah presents a well-studied account.

He proposes a set of four alternating Atlantic transgressions and regressions in the last 10,000 years. The telescoping of the sequence suggests, however, that minor fluctuations are more and more masked through time. The regressions seem associated with dry conditions and the transgressions with wet conditions. Andah suggests that this pattern is caused by alternating temperatures of the Benguela current. When the current flows west–southwest, it produces cold offshore water, causing land aridity, and vice versa. He attributes inland transgression of rivers to a northeastern drift of precipitation patterns.

As commentator, and realizing no other satisfactory time-placement method is available, I consider none of the archaeological identifications mentioned with associated terraces to have been demonstrated as valid.

One effect of my paper on the status of Guinea Coast paleoarchaeo-logical knowledge is to counterbalance and place in perspective the neces-sary tenuousness of Andah's introductory overview. I make two points: (1) no satisfactory geochronology exists in the area, and (2) the only demonstrated "paleoarchaeological" materials on the Guinea Coast are residual and late. In regard to the second, it might be added that this absence of paleoarchaeological remains extends from the Guinea Coast north into the trans-Senegambia.

Andah's report on his excavations at Rim, Upper Volta, is, as he states, paleoecology, not archaeology. Working in an area where no previous paleoanthropological research has been done, Andah has employed as many approaches as were available to him to work out an environmen-tally altering time framework for the north-central Upper Volta region. He initially presents discussions on topography, geology, geomorpho-logy, soils (pedology), and "bioclimatology" (a composite of climatology, plant geography, and, in the latter part, land settlement). The significant contribution is the sediment analysis. Soil-column samples were collected and analyzed to discover discordances of deposits in the region. Mechani-cal variations, such as granularity (sorting, skewing), density, and cumulative weight, were examined. Chemical variables such as pH, car-bon, organic phosphorus, iron, and nitrogen were measured. From this analysis it was possible to define a valid series of soil horizons. Efforts to extract further environmental information through the recovery of plant materials by flotation were less successful. It is work of this nature that is needed to construct the valid inductively derived areal, regional, and subcontinental geochronologies I have advocated in the preceding paper.

Though Andah's research focus is paleoecological, the results have allowed him to identify discrete archaeological occupations in the area, thereby establishing an initial regional sequence. Each occupation is apparently sealed by a recognizable soil formation. Rim I is a living-floor surface overlain by a yellow sand deposit. The materials represented can best be described as a blade/flake industry. The commonest tool in the assemblage is the microlith. Large scrapers are present, but polished and ground stone and pottery are absent. The dominant manufacturing material is metavolcanic chert, though quartz is present, especially for microlith manufacture. This occupation is undated, but Andah believes the overlying eolian deposit represents the Saharan arid phase of about 5,000 B.P. Overlying the eolian deposit is the Rim II occupation, repre-sented by living areas that indicate the presence of structures. Microliths disappear, and scrapers and choppers become less common. Coarse igneous rock is commonly selected for manufacturing various ground and polished tools. Andah dates this occupation from 3,630 to 2,840 B.P. The final occupation, Rim III, overlies a red sand deposit. Iron (but no evidence of smelting) and pot burials appear. Igneous and metamorphic rocks are intensively used. Scrapers and choppers are rare. Andah dates this occupation at 1,900 or 1,500 to 1,000 B.P. There is, clearly, a shift from a hunting-and-gathering subsistence pattern to a settled cultivating subsistence pattern from rim I to Rim II. Rim I conforms to the standard LSA (Later Stone Age) pattern in sub-Saharan Africa developmental-stage terminology.

The four following papers deal in some way with food production, a topic that has yet to be presented in print as an integrated study for West Africa. D. G. Coursey reiterates his previous (1967) conclusions that *Dioscorea rotundata*, the white Guinea yam, was domesticated in West Africa and that this process took place gradually during the LSA, 11,000 to 5,000 B.P. He specifies the area of domestication as the savanna fringe of the West African forest belt, possibly with a secondary center of development in the central Congo basin. He argues that *D. alata* was introduced into West Africa by the Portuguese and *D. esculenta* in colonial times. He stresses that tuber domestication is by nature a gradual, evolutionary process, unlike Childe's revolutions tied to drama- tic grain-domestication activity.

Historically, Anglophone scholars have distinguished *D. rotundata* from *D. cayenensis*, the yellow yam, while Francophone scholars have referred to both under the latter name. There is no consensus as to whether the difference is specific or subspecific. *D. rotundata*, unlike *D. cayenensis*, is a true cultigen — there are no wild forms — and is similar to the Asiatic *D. alata*. Therefore, both forms are probably hybrids. Varia- tions in distribution and crop history have produced subtle differences between the West African forms. Coursey's view of the sequence of West African yam domestication may be summarized as in Table 1.

Colin Flight places, his zooarchaeological research in the broader perspective of West African cultural development. He observes that Kintampo materials (date estimated at 1400 B.C.) reveal no direct evi-

Table 1.   Sequence of West African yam domestication according to Coursey

Dates (B.P.)	Technicultural[a] evidence	Practice
post-2,500	Iron tools, further forest penetration	Intensification of cultivation
5,000–2,500	Stone axes, forest clearance	Introduction of African grains
11,000–5,000		Savanna expansion, yam "proto-culture"[b] (selected planting), hybridization of cultigens
45,000–11,000	Sangoan and Lupemban "picks," hoes (?)	Yam conservation
pre-60,000–45,000		Discovery of fire, yam gathering

[a] My term, after Osgood (1942:33).
[b] Not to be confused with Hallowell's (1956) use of this term.

dence of plant domestication. Flight is not convinced by Davies's identification of Kintampo *"Pennisetum*-rouletted" pottery. These people did have, however, cattle and domesticated dwarf goats, and Flight entertains the idea that settled-village farming in West Africa evolved from pastoralism rather than from incipient cultivation as proposed by Braidwood. He does not rule out Coursey's early vegecultural subsistence pattern based on yams, but he argues that both tubers and grains were originally cultivated in overlapping mosaic forest-savanna areas after a pastoral stimulus. Finally, Flight pleads for studies of the history of crop cultivation in sub-Saharan Africa and suggests that they can be easily accomplished with existing and recently developed archaeological techniques.

On the basis of research at Dhar Tichitt, south-central Mauritania, Patrick J. Munson has established an eight-phase local sequence ranging from about 2000 to 400 B.C. The major thrust of his paper is an examination of plant cultivation in the sixth of these, the Chebka phase, radiocarbon-dated at 1000–900 B.C. Munson infers, on the basis of 121 pottery grain impressions (61 percent in relation to other species), that *Pennisetum* (bulrush millet) was intensively cultivated at this time. He proposes a series of alternative hypotheses for plant cultivation at Dhar Tichitt: (1) local development, (2) introduction from the south (Guinea Coast), (3) introduction from Ethiopia (Murdock's hypothesis), (4) introduction from the Sahara, where cultivation may have begun independently or as a result of stimulus diffusion from the Near East via Egypt. Munson believes that the last alternative is the most reasonable.

David V. Ellis's "Comments on the Advent of Plant Cultivation in West Africa," essentially a critique of Munson's study, is a broad synthesis of the results of recent research on West African cultivation. Ellis proposes an alternative sequence for the development of cultivation in West Africa based on Munson's data and indirect artifactual and speculative environmental evidence. He suggests that the demographic pressures needed for experimentation with plant cultivation commenced not around 1000 B.C. at Dhar Tichitt, as Munson has proposed, but during the desiccation of the Sahara around 3000 B.C. in arid locales still to be discovered. He argues that Munson "has provided too much time for the impact of the environmental deterioration to have its predicted consequences and too little time for the later cultural developments of West Africa."

Though not mentioning Munson and unaware of Ellis's studies, David, in his "History of crops and peoples in North Cameroon to A.D. 1900," further supports the idea of a northern intrusion of Saharan grain cultivators into West Africa in Neolithic times. He believes that there was cultivation in the Chad basin by Neolithic peoples but knows of no direct evidence to support this contention. Cattle, at Daima, indicate pastoral activity in addition to fishing. He is less convinced of (grain?) cultivation by Neolithic populations farther south. On the basis of ethnohistorical reconstruction, he lists 15 North Cameroon Neolithic cultigens. These seem to be part of Murdock's Sudanic complex of plant domestication or local adaptations and include *Disocorea*, *Sorghum*, and *Pennisetum*. *Eleusin* (finger millet) is introduced after A.D. 500 and *Digitaria* (fonio) and *Gossypium* (cotton) between A.D. 1000 and 1600. Other cultigen species were then rapidly added, particularly after A.D. 1750. Grain recovered by Connah at Daima is identified as *Sorghum caudatum* by Stemler, Harlan, and de Wet (1975:177–178) and dated at A.D. 900.

T. R. Hays discusses the presence of pottery among sedentary pre-agriculturalists in the nearby central Sahara before 6000 B.C. Quite rightly, in my opinion, he relates the development of pottery to sedentism, not, as has been done in the past, to plant domestication, though Smith (1974) reports the use of pottery by cattle-herding nomads in the Tilemsi Valley, Mali, by 2000 B.C. Central Saharan "Sudanese Neolithic" pottery antedates currently dated Near Eastern (including Egyptian) pottery by as much as 2,000 years and appears to have evolved independently. Hays's study does not include the Guinea Coast, but Shaw (1972b) has reported the presence of pottery at Iwo Eleru, southwestern Nigeria, at 3620 ± 60 B.C. (Hv–1510), and Hartle, in this volume, summarizes his finds at Ezi-Ukwu Ukpa, southeastern Nigeria, at 2935 ± 140 B.C. In Ghana, Smith (1975) reports a radio-carbon date of 3420 ± 100 B.C. (N-1805) from Bosumpra cave.

Donald D. Hartle's paper is a survey of preliminary field data and previously published accounts of southeastern Nigeria archaeology. An unpublished LSA excavation is the Ezi-Ukwu Ukpa rock shelter near Afikpo. A series of ten radiocarbon dates ranging from 2935 B.C. to A.D. 15 recovered from the thirteen-foot occupation depth are presented. The 2935 ± 140 (GX-0938) figure dates the earliest known human occupation of southeastern Nigeria. At least two occupations are present at the site. The earlier is represented by Afikpo Red Ware, which is "light brown-reddish" in color, grit-tempered, fired at low temperature, and, in general, "crude." In association is one of only two known lithic complexes in the area. Tools include hoes, celts, disks, spheres, querns, grinding stones, and hammerstones manufactured from argillite, sandstone, quartzite, quartz, and quartz crystals. Curiously, microliths are absent. The later occupation is represented by Afikpo Gray Ware, which is dark-colored and/or grit-tempered and fired at higher temperature. The other significant site described is Igbo-Ukwu. It is dated by Shaw at A.D. 850, but Lawal (1973) questions this date on the basis of the presence of European-type high-lead manillas, beads, and highly perishable archaeological remains. He suggests that the "aberrant" single radiocarbon date of A.D. 1445 ± 70 is the valid one. These finds are fascinating because of the sophisticated non-Ife, non-Benin true bronze

figures extensively described by Shaw in various recent publications. The
introduction to Cookey's paper in Part Two deals with much of the same
material, and the reader might consider reading it immediately after
Hartle's for comparison of outlook.

Oliver Davies's paper is a site report of a Kintampo culture occupation
in north-central Ghana radiocarbon-dated between 1630 and 1240 B.C.
The Kintampo culture is, essentially, the occurrence of a distinctive
coarse pottery ware with comb-impressed decoration, often over all or
much of the vessel surface, and stone "rasps" with scored decoration
found within a larger polished-stone (Neolithic?) context (see Table 2 for
a comparison of the terms used here with those of Davies and Flight).
Flight adds to this corpus the following traits: celts, stone rings, grooved
stones maufactured from broken "rasps" or sandstone, grinding and
pounding stones, and wood- and pole-impressed daub chunks (structure
remains). Davies probably would also include perforated disks
(1967:222). The two major investigations of this culture are at Kintampo
(actually three sites) and Ntereso, though the unique "rasps" have also
been found at Mumute, Chukoto, and other Ghanaian sites (Agorsah
1975).

Davies simultaneously describes over a three-component sequence
two pottery traditions at Ntereso, a coarse ware (similar to Kintampo K6)

Table 2.   Variations in Kintampo terminology

Davies	Flight	Swartz
Kintampo Neolithic[a]	Kintampo culture	Kintampo culture[b]
Phase	—	Component
Terracotta (and stone) "cigars"	Stone rasps	"Rasps"[c]
Reticulated and scored pottery	Comb-impressed pottery	—[d]
Stone arm-rings	Stone bracelets	Stone rings[e]
Celts	Axe-blades	Celts[f]
Arrowheads	—	Points
Types	—	Classes[g]

[a] I differ from Flight and Ellis in believing that Davies is justified in defining the African
Neolithic on a technological basis, viz., the appearance of polished stone tools, if he wishes
to do so. This is an easier diagnostic to identify from archaeological evidence than economic
features such as settled villages and plant/animal domestication. Indeed, it was Lubbock's
original definition of the term.
[b] "Culture," rather than "phase," since manifestations occur in various areas and have
been excavated at two separated sites — Kintampo and Ntereso.
[c] Ideally, some morphological descriptive term other than "cigars" should be found or their
function discovered. Here I follow Agorsah (1975), who suggests that they may have been
stamps. "Terracotta" should be used as an adjective only when appropriate.
[d] Here I follow Flight. More specifically, some is stamped, as is mentioned by Davies and
Flight elsewhere.
[e] Function is assumed by Davies and Flight. These rings may have been worn on legs or used
for some unknown and unrelated purpose.
[f] Axes are grooved or holed.
[g] Types must have demonstrated spatiotemporal variations.

and a fine, thin ware. Coarse ware may be comb-impressed, often over the whole vessel surface. Forms include bowls with incurvate rims and jars with rounded bases. Thin ware is often painted in the earliest component, though outlining with paint seems to have been avoided. Two intrusions of different pottery are also described. The early intrusion has a unique black polished pottery with banded cord impressions, pointed rims, distinct necks, and carinated shoulders. The late-intrusion pottery is hard and wide-lipped, jars and colanders being common forms. Similar pottery is found in the Gonja region.

Davies also describes five classes of bifacially flaked points (none are tanged), net weights, unbarbed ivory fishhooks, and bone harpoons. He, like Ellis, believes this material has a northern source.

John A. Rustad's paper on the emergence of iron technology in West Africa is built around the implications of Bernard Fagg's (1967) discovery of a Nok iron-smelting complex at Taruga, Benue Valley uplands, Nigeria. The foundations and partial walls of ten to twelve smelting furnaces occur in association with tuyeres, wrought-iron objects, and slag. This complex has been radiocarbon-dated within a range of 440 to 280 B.C., the earliest acceptable date being 440 ± 140 B.C. (I-2960). Nok iron has also been reported by Angela Fagg (1972) at the Nok site of Samun Dukiya, radiocarbon-dated at 210 ± 95 B.C. (I-4913). A date of 3190 ± 120 B.C. (SR-61) associated with iron at Ntereso, Ghana (Davies 1968:238) is not considered by Rustad and is now rejected by Davies himself (see his paper, this volume).

Rustad poses three hypotheses for the origin of Nok iron technology: (1) diffusion from Anatolia via the Nile Valley and Meroe, (2) diffusion across the Sahara from Carthage or allied Phoenician settlements, and (3) autonomous local development. His basic argument against the diffusion hypotheses is that neither copper nor bronze was introduced into West Africa before iron, though knowledge of their lower-temperature smelting processes antedates iron. Using the evidence that at Ngwenya, western Swaziland, thirty-four tons of iron ore were extracted in MSA (Middle Stone Age) times, 28,000 B.C. (Dart and Beaumont 1969), he makes the significant point that mining of an ore is not necessarily dependent on prior knowledge of the nature of metal. Provocative as the interpretation may be, I am not sure that these observations necessarily discredit diffusion hypotheses. Pristine iron smelting in Nigeria may be traceable to the absence of copper ores in the Guinea Coast (Herbert 1973:179–180) rather than to an "inverted development" due to the vagaries of contact with iron smelters. A point Rustad misses in this regard is A. Fagg's mention of iron beads and bracelets at Samun Dukiya (1972:77), indicating that smelting was more than just a hardening process for utilitarian objects. Rustad also notes that metal is not a prerequisite for iron-smelting paraphernalia. Granite can be used for anvils and hammers.

Battered quartz rocks were present at Taruga. Wood can be used for tongs. Also, preexisting technology can be adapted to metallurgy; for example, pottery kilns can be improved for use as smelting furnaces.

The strongest arguments against the diffusion hypotheses are (1) the short time interval for the diffusion supposed to have taken place — one and two centuries respectively — and (2) the absence along the diffusion route of dated evidence of iron smelting in the Sahara and the scarcity and questionable nature of such evidence in the Sudan, the latter not associated with Meroe remains (Daima, etc.).

In addition, since the dynamics of urbanization, social stratification, craft specialization, and centralization of authority are present in both southwestern Asia and West Africa at the time iron technology emerges, why is it possible to conclude that this technical process was independently invented in each area? Rustad, however, never unequivocally embraces his third hypothesis. High-temperature carbon steel smelting in natural draft furnaces in sub-Saharan Africa for 1,500 to 2,000 years has recently been demonstrated by Schmidt (1977; Schmidt and Avery 1978; Swartz 1978).

R. M. A. Bedaux describes ritual pottery from central Mali characterized by a bowl on a disk base with tetrapodal or quadripodal support. These bowls occur with other forms of pottery in the Tellem culture, Phase 1, dated from A.D. 1000 to 1200. Iron bracelets, rings, voluted pins and points, carnelian beads, and quartz lip-plugs are also part of this ritual complex. Bedaux's material was recovered from two sites, both associated with large burial caves in the Bandiagara bluff. Similar bowl forms occur in the trans-Timbuktu Niger basin.

Atherton's study is a superb example of what can be done with protohistorical (or, in the New World, ethnohistorical) resources to interpret the techniculture (Osgood 1942; the specific techniques and uses of objects) of archaeological remains. I cannot improve on the author's own abstract:

This paper discusses three classes of prehistoric archaeological materials from *Sierra Leone* in an attempt to determine their original uses and their interrelations with aspects of *prehistoric* material culture in contiguous areas. A careful examination of the pieces is combined with a study of relevant *archaeological, historic, ethnographic*, and *material culture* studies to make a preliminary assessment of possible functional attributes.

Flaked and polished stone celts and various forms of flaked quartz artifacts have been recorded from four archaeological excavations and scattered surface finds in Sierra Leone. Evidence points toward their having been used primarily for woodworking and occasionally for work on other materials such as ivory and soapstone. Rare unused miniature polished celts may have had "religious" uses.

"Bored stones" and large bifacially worked implements found during mining operations in southeastern Sierra Leone are felt to have been used in quarrying — possibly for gold.

Carved soapstone figures from the southern part of the country, usually known as *nomoli*, appear to have been representations or intermittent abodes of one or more types of supernatural entities. Recent research on these pieces has provided more information on their probable use as well as the processes used to manufacture them.

Atherton's study makes it clear that not only ethnologists and historians but also archaeologists, have use for protohistorical methods.

Perhaps the overriding issue which emerges from the archaeological papers in this volume is the question: Was West Africa a major primary center of plant domestication? The strongest supporters of the hypothesis that it was are those scholars who consider vegeculture a major factor in the domestication of plant food resources. Coursey argues for an early major center of yam domestication on the basis of botanical evidence. Davies (1960, 1968) makes the same argument on the basis of archaeological evidence. Others deemphasize tubers and view West Africa as a secondary or derivative region for the development of eastern Sudanic (Murdock 1959) or Nile Valley grain domestication. A number of leading scholars, including some whose papers appear in this volume (for example, Munson, Ellis, and David), stress grain cultivation as the primary causal force, though they are not necessarily opposed to the possibility of early yam cultivation. Flight, on the other hand, seriously questions the antiquity of yam domestication in West Africa but does not seem enamored with grain theories as an alternative; he concludes by making a plea for further work on the problem.

By a simple remark Flight alludes to a related secondary issue: How was the knowledge of grain cultivation introduced to West Africa? The commonly accepted assumption is that the cultivators themselves migrated to West Africa (and resettled? or practiced transitory nomadism?). Stimulus diffusion is sometimes invoked, but while this might explain the acceptance of a crop it scarcely explains the acceptance of an entire pattern of subsistence. Hays mentions the possibility of sedentary "incipient" cultivators in the central Sahara on the basis of early pottery finds. Such groups would certainly have been highly receptive to the introduction of effective cultivation practices and new plants. Flight, on the other hand, infers from early, pre-millet occurrence of domesticated goats and cattle that West African agriculture may have evolved from pastoral nomadism.

On a less pervasive issue, I differ from Andah in believing that a unified West African geochronology can be established only by proceeding inductively — that is, by excavating, recording, compiling, and interpreting soil profiles site by site until regular variations can be perceived. Andah, by contrast, adheres to the traditional approach and extrapolates from various data, especially terracing, to construct a general geochronological model for West Africa. My position may be viewed by some as self-defeating, but it may be argued that the absence of an acceptable geochronological sequence for West Africa will stimulate proper research in the area.

To examine the dynamics of West African culture change, I have ordered the material presented here and elsewhere in a developmental sequence. The units proposed are a compromise between current chronological terminology and descriptive developmental headings, not terminological taxa.

Original Populating. "Original populating" is a useful neutral term for the first developmental stage of West African culture dynamics. I have indicated in my paper that no evidence exists for the occurrence of "Classic Acheulean" in the Guinea Coast subarea of West Africa, though a late, attenuated Acheulean may have penetrated to the ocean along the Akwapim–Togo–Atakora corridor. Shaw (1972a:47), noting Soper's (1965) observations, states that Classic Acheulean does occur in sub-Saharan West Africa: "the Jos Plateau and the high ground to the north of it formed a sort of promontory of habitable land projecting southwards from Air and the main Saharan Acheulian area north of 16° N. For nowhere in West Africa is such good Acheulian material found as on the Jos Plateau. . . ."

The extensive work by the French clearly establishes an elaborate Classic Acheulean throughout much of the Sahara. Intensive and systematic excavation and study of pre-Acheulean pebble (including chunk or flake) tool complexes of Villafranchian times has not been undertaken, but such remains may very well exist. The biostratigraphic opportunities afforded by Olduvai Gorge may distort our perceptions of human origins, being restricted to the recently amassed East African data. Arambourg (1950) has found faceted stones (bolas?) associated with Villafranchian deposits at Aïn Hanech in the Maghreb. A craniofacial skull fragment identified as a *H. habilis* form was found by Coppens (1967) in deposits of the latest Villafranchian age in the Yao area of the Lake Chad basin.

To summarize, sub-Saharan West Africa was probably originally populated from the Sahara (Figure 1), the earliest intruders being the makers of the Acheulean tool assemblages.

Intermediate Stone Age (50,000 to 10,000 B.C.). The "Intermediate" Stone Age is defined here by adding my ESA–MSA transition (this volume) of Clark's (1963) First Intermediate to the conventionally defined Middle Stone Age (MSA). Essentially it represents a specialization in technology and geography of the "Great Hand Ax Tradition" which, on the basis of a single tool class, might be called the "Equatorial Pick Sub-Tradition," often simplistically referred to by the industrial-complex term Sangoan. Materials of this subtradition are clearly established in eastern West Africa.

Shaw (1972a:49) argues that during First Intermediate times "San-

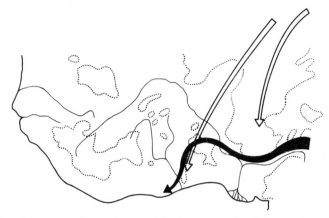

Figure 1. Original populating of West Africa (open arrows) and Intermediate Stone Age penetration according to Shaw (1972a) (solid arrow)

goan" man came to West Africa along well-watered corridors, especially river valleys — perhaps down the Benue Valley, up the Niger into northern Dahomey, and then down the Atakora–Togo–Akwapim corridor into Ghana. It should be added that he probably continued along the Gold Coast shore (see Figure 1).

In the later portion of this developmental stage, as I note in this volume, there is in Ghana "a shift in tool manufacture from massive heavy tools, such as picks and choppers, to materials that include a sizable 'microlithic' component, with such forms as gravers, crescents, lunates, 'trapezes,' backed blades, and microcores." Development along this line is sometimes referred to as Lupemban in the Congo basin.

Two variations of the standard West African Intermediate Stone Age can be noted. A faceted-butt technique reminiscent of the North African "Middle Palaeolithic" seems to protrude into West Africa along the Jos "peninsula," the same region in which the original Acheulean occupation occurred (Soper 1965:188–190). On the basis of a single artifact form, the tanged point on a blade, Davies (1964:122–123; 1967:130, Figure 28:135) suggests that a variant of the "Aterian" industrial complex of North Africa penetrates the Atakora–Togo corridor (again an area of earlier "Acheulean" occupation) into eastern Ghana, but not to the coast. This distribution is termed by Davies "Guinea Aterian."

Later Stone Age (10,000 to 3000 B.C.). Throughout the latter portion of the Intermediate Stone Age, miniaturized worked flakes, or microliths, appear to increase in frequency. The Later Stone Age (LSA) is the climax of this development. These flakes were hafted onto composite tools. Inventoried collections attributable to this stage in various regions of West Africa are published elsewhere. In this volume Andah reports crescents, curved back pieces, triangular and trapezoidal retouched pieces, scrapers, choppers, becs and burins and irregular flake cores and discoidals from Rim I, dated 10,000 to 3000 B.C.

From Nigerian evidence Daniels (1969:25) argues that the LSA subsistence was based on hunting. Compositely hafted bows and arrows were used, and rock shelters at cave mouths, often containing rock paintings of hunting and living scenes, were the preferred living areas.

A skeleton from Iwo Eleru rock shelter, about fifteen miles northwest of Akure, southwestern Nigeria, has been dated by radiocarbon at 9250 ± 200 B.C. and an associated deposit at 7200 ± 150 B.C. (Shaw 1965). No artifacts were in association, and no generalizations as to racial affiliation of the remains have been attempted. These are the earliest known human remains discovered in tropical West Africa to date. A radiocarbon date of 4440 B.C. has been run on material from the classic Asselar find, about 100 miles north of the bend of the Niger River, northern Mali (R. Mauny 1966, cited in Oakley and Campbell 1967:34). The investigators state that the Asselar remains display Negroid features. From those remains it can be concluded that man, during this stage, is fully neoanthropic.

Sedentism-nomadism (3000 B.C. to A.D. 300). This developmental stage embraces the conventionally termed archaeological periods of "Mesoneolithic," Neolithic, and Iron Age. Fundamental changes can now be detected that override technological innovations, and it is these that must be stressed to understand the dynamic cultural processes of West Africa.

Sedentism was brought about by the accumulation of a food surplus (Braidwood and Reed 1957). The surplus was probably created by the intensification of a yam-centered vegetative pattern that had begun in the preceding stage fused with an agricultural pattern of seed crops largely introduced from the east. In the Sahara the significant shift may have been from hunting and gathering to nomadism rather than sedentism. Pottery is present in the Sahara prior to 3000 B.C. (see Hays, this volume) but may not have penetrated to the Guinea Coast until near the end of this stage. Ground/polished stone and iron technology appear, also, near the end of this stage. A result of sedentism is the probable developmental continuity of populations into recorded history. (For a contemporary analysis of this economic pattern, see Baier's paper in Part Two.)

REFERENCES

AGORSAH, KOFI
   1975   [Untitled.] *Nyame Akuma* 7:24–25.
ARAMBOURG, C.
   1950   Traces possible d'une industrie primitive dans un niveau Villafranchian de l'Afrique du Nord. *Bulletin de la Société Préhistorique Française* 47:348–350.

BRAIDWOOD, ROBERT J., CHARLES A. REED
1957   The achievement and early consequences of food production: A consideration of the archaeological and natural-historical evidence. *Cold Spring Harbor Symposia on Quantitative Biology* 22:19–31.

CLARK, J. DESMOND
1963   *Prehistoric cultures of northeast Angola and their significance in tropical Africa.* Subsídios para a História, Arqueologia e Etnografia dos Povos da Lunda, Publicacões Culturais 62, part one.

COPPENS, Y.
1967   "L'hominien du Tchad." *Actas del Quinto Congreso Panafricano de Prehistoria y del Estudio del Cuaternario*, 329–330.

COURSEY, D. G.
1967   *Yams*. London: Longmans Green.

DANIELS, S. G. H.
1969   "The Middle and Late Stone Age," in *Lectures on Nigerian prehistory and archaeology*. Edited by Thurstan Shaw, 25–29. Ibadan: Ibadan University Press.

DART, R. A., P. BEAUMONT
1969   Evidence of iron ore mining in southern Africa in the Middle Stone Age. *Current Anthropology* 10:127–128.

DAVIES, OLIVER
1960   The Neolithic revolution in tropical Africa. *Transactions of the Historical Society of Ghana* 4:14–20.
1964   *The Quaternary in the coastlands of Guinea*. Glasgow: Jackson.
1967   *West Africa before the Europeans*. London: Methuen.
1968   The origins of agriculture in West Africa. *Current Anthropology* 9:479–482.

FAGG, ANGELA
1972   Excavations of an occupation site in the Nok Valley, Nigeria. *West African Journal of Archaeology* 2:75–79.

FAGG, BERNARD
1967   Radiocarbon dates for sub-Saharan Africa. *Journal of African History* 8:513–527.

HALLOWELL, A. IRVING
1956   The structural and functional dimensions of a human existence. *Quarterly Review of Biology* 31:88–101.

HERBERT, EUGENIA
1973   Aspects of the use of copper in pre-colonial West Africa. *Journal of African History* 14:179–194.

LAWAL, BABATUNDE
1973   Dating problems at Igbo-Ukwu. *Journal of African History* 14:1–8.

MAUNY, RAYMOND
1961   *Tableau géographique de l'Ouest africain au moyen âge d'après les sources écrites, la tradition et l'archéologie*. Mémoires de l'Institut Français d'Afrique Noire 61.

MURDOCK, GEORGE PETER
1959   *Africa: its people and their culture history*. New York: McGraw-Hill.

OAKLEY, KENNETH PAGE, BERNARD GRANT CAMPBELL, *editors*
1967   *Catalogue of fossil hominids*, part one: *Africa*. London: British Museum (Natural History).

OLIVER, ROLAND, BRIAN M. FAGAN
1975   *Africa in the Iron Age c. 500 B.C. to A.D. 1400*. Cambridge: Cambridge University Press.

16   B. K. SWARTZ, JR.

OSGOOD, CORNELIUS
1942   The Ciboney culture of Cayo Redondo, Cuba. Yale University Publications in Anthropology 25.
SCHMIDT, PETER R.
1977   "Steel production in prehistoric Africa: insights from ethnoarchaeology in Buhaya, Tanzania." Paper presented at the Eighth Pan-African Congress of Prehistory and Quaternary Studies, Nairobi.
SCHMIDT, PETER R., DONALD H. AVERY
1978   Complex iron smelting and prehistoric culture in Tanzania. *Science* 201:1085–1089.
SHAW, THURSTAN
1965   Excavations at Iwo Eleru, 1965. *West African Archaeological Newsletter* 3:15–16.
1972a   "The prehistory of West Africa," in *History of West Africa*, volume one. Edited by J. F. A. Ajayi and Michael Crowder, 33–77. New York: Columbia University Press.
1972b   "Finds at Iwo Eleru rock shelter, western Nigeria." *Actes du Sixième Congrès Panafricain de Préhistoire et de l'Etude du Quaternaire*. Edited by H. J. Hugot, 190–192. Daker.
SMITH, ANDREW B.
1974   Preliminary report of excavations at Karkarichinkat-Nord and Karkarichinkat-Sud, Tilemsi Valley, Republic of Mali, Spring, 1972. *West African Journal of Archaeology* 4:33–55.
1975   Radiocarbon dates from Bosumpra cave, Abetifi, Ghana. *Proceedings of the Prehistoric Society* 41:179–182.
SOPER, R. C.
1965   The Stone Age in northern Nigeria. *Journal of the Historical Society of Nigeria* 3:175–194.
STEMLER, A. B. L., J. R. HARLAN, J. M. J. DE WET
1975   *Caudatum* sorghums and speakers of Chari-Nile languages in Africa. *Journal of African History* 16:161:183.
SWARTZ, B. K., JR.
1978   Prehistory and Quaternary studies in Africa. *Current Anthropology* 19:206.

Processes of Coastal Evolution in West Africa During the Quaternary

Throughout the Quaternary, and even earlier, a host of factors acted in various ways and to varying degrees to mold the present-day coastline of West Africa. These factors include the rate of influx of land-derived sediments, the volume of beach material, tidal current systems, climate, the relative movements of land and sea, the type of waves, and the geological composition of the coastline. Some of the resultant features, present in different parts of the West African coast, are relict beaches, remnant barrier spits, lagoons, buried' river valleys and channels, sea cliffs, and deltas. The origin and time of formation of several of these features, especially the nature of the balance between climate and geology (e.g., lithology and tectonics), are far from well understood. In this paper these problems are critically examined. First, the character of the West African coastline is examined and its principal features are demarcated. Then I discuss how these features may have been formed and set out what is currently known of the sequence of Pleistocene events in the different areas.

As used in this context, the term "coast" refers to both present and past shorelines and to those shallow sections of the sea bed whose relief is produced by waves at given sea levels (submarine beach slope zone). "Beach," on the other hand, refers to an accumulation of loose materials around the limit of wave action consisting of coarse-grained sand, shingle, or shelly materials (Morgan and Pugh 1969). The definition of "continental terrace" is as outlined by Lewis (1974): the sediments and rock underlying the coastal plain, continental shelf, and continental slope. "Continental shelf" and "Continental slope" refer only to the interface between continental terrace and water. The sediments beneath the continental rise, which is the gently inclined portion of the sea bed at the base of the continental slope (Heezen 1959), are excluded from the continental terrace but included in the "continental margin." At many places the coastal plain is difficult to delimit, but the continental terrace extends as far landward as the most landward shore-line of Holocene age.

The present West African coastline stretches some 3,860 kilometers (2,400 miles), from Cape Verde to Mount Cameroon, and may be divided into three principal sections. From west to east, these are a zone of submergence, a smooth, almost featureless central stretch, and another zone of submergence.

The first zone of submergence stretches from Cape Verde to Cape St. Anne (1,050 kilometers; 650 miles); it has narrow coastal plains, high tidal amplitudes, and rocks folded more or less at right angles to the coast. The River Senegal, with its vast estuarine bars and fringe mangrove swamps, belongs to this section, along with a short stretch of cliffed sediments south of Dakar, raised beaches in the peninsular area of Sierra Leone, and the muddy estuaries of westward-flowing rivers, which occupy a considerable area of Gambia, southern Senegal, Guinea, and Sierra Leone. (The most important of these rivers are the Saloum, the Gambia, and the Casamance.)

The second zone — the smooth, almost featureless stretch — extends from Cape St. Anne to the Benin River. It is characterized by wide, almost flat coastal plains and river outlets frequently deflected by long-shore drift moving from southeast to northwest. It has continuous coastal dunes backed by seasonal swamps or longitudinal and transverse lagoons. Between Cape Three Points and the Volta, low plateaus approach the coast, and dunes are present across estuaries and valley mouths.

The other zone of submergence stretches from the Benin River to Mount Cameroon (640 kilometers; 400 miles). Present here are the submerging Niger delta, which has several openings into the sea; wide, shallow, continually changing bars formed by an eastward coastal drift; and, finally, estuaries lined with continuous mangrove swamps (e.g., the Cross River and Rio del Rey).

Different kinds of features reflecting environmental changes during the Pleistocene are to be found in the different parts of this coast. Outstanding among these are relict beaches which are present in three areas: a short stretch south of Dakar, the peninsular area of Sierra Leone, and the rocky coast of Ghana. In the areas of the Saloum and the Casamance, the Volta and the Niger are various other kinds of geomorphic features: remnant barrier spits, buried river valleys and channels, sea cliffs, estuarine deposits, and deltas. Widespread along the entire coastline but especially characteristic of the smooth zone are lagoons of various shapes and sizes, and high erosional surfaces, some capped by active and fossilized dunes.

Such relict features clearly indicate that the West African coast was not directly affected by glaciation in the Quaternary. Rather, it experienced alternations of erosion and deposition. The periods of extensive erosion appear to be marked by exposed remnants of erosion surfaces found on lateritic scarps and plateaus, especially in the dry, open areas of the coastal stretch. In some places they are capped by extensive deposits of active and fossilized dunes, while in others they are cut by belts of active faulting and subsidence. This latter fact greatly complicates the question of the origin and dynamics of some of these erosional features.

Distinctly different kinds of Pleistocene deposits are found in the different depositional environments. Generally these deposits consist mostly of dissected bodies of alluvium, marine sands and silts, and colluvium. Since they are usually confined to particular localities, investigators have been unable to carry out regional correlations by tracing features in the field. Further, it has been all the more difficult to separate the roles played by tectonics and isostasy. There is in fact so much variation in the heights of raised beaches and reefs along some stretches of the coast as to suggest warping or other height modifications resulting from tectonics. It seems that ancient surfaces near the coast have experienced repeated monoclinal downwarping, which in turn has led to rejuvenation of southward-flowing streams and a greater degree of dissection of the low plains behind the coast than of the high plains of the interior. The downwarping has given much of the coast a drowned character, the lower parts of valleys being flooded to produce estuaries such as those from Sierra Leone to southern Senegal in the west and that of the Cross River in the extreme east. Between these two localities, the same features are frequently found on the north side of coastal lagoons separated from the sea by sand-ridge systems (Zenkovitch 1967). The irregularity of sea-level heights which these remnant features reflect calls for more care in the study of the nature and content of raised beach materials and cautions against depending solely on height variations to demarcate eustatic transgressions. It has nonetheless been possible to elicit certain important points from a careful review of research work carried out to date in various parts of this coastline.

For instance, there seems to be a close interaction between climate, the energy system of the Atlantic, and coastal morphology and dynamics in both present and past times. The energy system governing the Atlantic and largely determining the present-day climate and the nature of the currents, waves, and tides experienced in the coastal areas of West Africa was apparently also operative during the Quaternary. It comprises two principal high-pressure systems (the Azores anticyclone to the north and the St. Helena to the south), which shift south and north with the seasons, and an intertropical low-pressure belt to the east which modifies the impact of these systems. The overall impact of this energy system probably varied, as it does today, according to the coastal alignment and altitude of the locality.

Generally, a humid stable air mass blows into the coastal and forest belts of West Africa, giving rise to two wet seasons with a short dry spell in between. The currents and waves generated by this high-energy system of the Atlantic are strong, and their force lessens eastward from the source. There are, however, variations on this general pattern. A north–south coastal alignment backed by a high plateau north of Cape Palmas prolongs the monsoonal influence as far as Guinea, and consequently marine trade winds are strong, waves powerful, and shore drifts and tidal range great. Where there is very open water along the coast, forces combine to smooth the shores (e.g., between the Saloum estuary and northern Gambia). In estuaries adjacent to a comparatively wide continental shelf, as in southern Senegal, Guinea, and Sierra Leone, mud flats have resulted. Where the tidal range diminishes significantly and the coast is sheltered, as in the Senegal and Saloum estuaries and in southern Sierra Leone and Liberia, sand spits have been formed. In the Niger delta region, similar coastal alignment in relation to the effective high-energy system and the arresting influence of the Cameroon Mountains results in long periods of heavy rainfall (the mean annual rainfall on the slopes of Mount Cameroon is 762 centimeters), which in turn nourish year-round swamps. The strong swell of the South Atlantic currents in the general direction south-southwest to north-northeast helps to divert the sediments brought into the sea by the rivers, distributing them widely along the coast and thus preventing the formation of a bird's-foot type of delta.

Variation of tidal amplitude from about one meter in the Benin River to more than three meters in the valley of the Cross River affects the water level of rivers and also has a physicochemical effect caused by the salt-water wedge penetrating upstream underneath the fresh water. Finally, the anomalous dry zone between Accra and the Nigerian border and several lagoons are related to change in coastal orientation, a change which results in the movement of winds away from Cape Three Points. More specifically, the available evidence suggests first that the principal estuaries and deltaic deposits on the coast advanced into the sea faster during regressive phases and secondly that spits, lagoons, raised beaches, and reefs were at least initiated when sea level stood higher in relation to the land than it does today but were left as relics when that sea retreated. Wide continental shelves were apparently cut by waves during periods of low sea level, as were extensive coastal alignments of active and fossilized dunes. It has been reasonably well established that changing sea levels brought about separately by eustacy and tectonics result in the accumulation of different kinds of materials in spits, beach platforms, and continental shelves (McMaster et al. 1970a). Tectonics-initiated deposition appears to contain more terrigenous material, while deposition in stable areas resulting from eustacy contains more calcareous material. Study of shelf sediments from Senegal, Guinea, and Sierra Leone provides only a few examples.

There is also evidence (e.g., in Senegal and Ghana) that the tropical character of the environments encouraged the development of a deeply weathered slope mantle during Pleistocene low sea levels. Ample evidence of this is observable on stretches of raised beaches at Accra and Tema in Ghana. In some parts of the West African coast, however, some of these deposits were reworked during rising sea levels and incorporated into continental shelf sediments, thus further complicating the picture.

Because of their geology, certain parts of coastal Senegal, Sierra Leone, and Ghana were marked by terracing during the Pleistocene. In most other parts of the coast, however, incisional and depositional activities were prevalent around river deltas and estuaries, and these are highlighted by the diversity of geomorphic features in the Guinea–Sierra Leone area and of the estuarine and deltaic deposits of the Senegal and the Niger. This variety of environmental features was variously caused by sea-level changes and earth movements, singly or in combination, with erosion and valley cutting occurring during real retreats of sea level at glacial maxima and/or apparent drops in sea level initiated by local tectonic subsidence. Because of the progressive lowering of sea level in the coastal areas, some valleys were cut into earlier terraces so that the remaining older terraces lie at higher topographic levels than the younger ones.

The Senegalo–Mauritanian sequence of raised beaches is the best-known because, unlike those to the east, these strandlines present a regular succession. Some of the levels have been dated, and there has been some success in separating the role of tectonics from those of other variables (Michel 1966). It has been demonstrated that from late Pleistocene times to the present there have been two transgressions: the Upper Inchirian, which dates to between 40,000 and 30,000 years B.P., and the Nouakchottian, which lasted from 5,500 to 4,500 B.P. Prior to these, a previous high-water mark, the Lower Inchirian seems to have occurred around 100,000 B.P. Earlier transgressions, as yet undated, were the Aroughian and Tafaritian. It appears that sections of the lower stretches of the Senegal and neighboring rivers were blocked by dunes during the periods between the transgressions. One of these phases of sea regression and dry conditions in the area occurred somewhere in the time interval between 5,500 and 30,000 B.P.

In Sierra Leone there is definite evidence for only two raised beaches, at sixty-six meters and thirteen to fifteen meters, but Gregory (1962) reports a possible intermediate level between twenty-six and thirty-five meters and a more recent phase which seems to have suffered submergence. Thus it is possible that four major transgressions also affected the Sierra Leone stretch of the coast. In the absence of archaeological/faunal/dating associations to relate the Sierra Leone and Senegal beaches however, nothing definitive can be said.

In Ghana, raised beaches are known, and some of these appear to have archaeological associations. This fact notwithstanding, the situation is probably more confused here than anywhere else. Davies (1964, 1967) has claimed the presence of six beaches (at sixty to fifty-five meters, around twenty-three meters, fifteen to twelve meters, eight to six meters, and six to two meters). Bruckner and Anderson (1957), however, recognize only three; they rightly point to the tectonic factor and suggest that the several levels between six and fifty meters belong to one former shoreline subsequently broken up and tilted differentially.

There is unquestionable evidence that the coastal area of Ghana is strongly fractured, and in many places along the coast a complicated fault pattern is demonstrable (Burke 1969a). Some of these faults are still active, as earth tremors in the Accra area have shown. They include the Akwapim series, running along the southeast margin of the Akwapim range and Accra, and major faults which are more or less parallel to the present coastline in the western and eastern coastal regions of Ghana and experience downthrows of several thousands of meters of seaward blocks. Burke (1969b) has noted evidence of structural features off the Guinea Coast which may indicate where some Atlantic fracture zones reached the continental margins of Africa. First, the edge of the continental shelf south of Accra runs nearly straight for 200 kilometers, striking almost northeast and sloping very steeply, falling 4,000 meters in fifty kilometers. Secondly, the 1906 and 1939 Accra earthquakes indicate epicenters near the edge of a fault-controlled shelf. Thirdly, evidence obtained variously from drilling gravity observations and seismic contours shows substantial Neogene sedimentary thickening across the line of the shelf edge under the Volta delta, which continues in the northwestern margin of the Dahomey basin. The occurrence of an isolated seismic area near Accra with recently active faults indicates differential movements across the fracture zone which, though geologically small, were probably extremely significant for the present irregular character of Quaternary beaches on the Ghana coast.

Unfortunately, it is not known exactly when these differential movements occurred and therefore which raised beaches were affected and to what extent. All that is known at present is that the Sehoue, Lokossa, and Akwapim faults, which form an angle of about twenty degrees with the shelf edge, indicate left lateral motion as on the chain fracture zone; the thrust of the Akwapim fault and the intensity of the Accra earthquakes decrease into the continent, and there is no evidence of faulting at distances greater than 300 kilometers inland along the trend of the fracture.

The beaches themselves hardly fare better as regards dating. Only the two-to-six-meter Takoradi beach has been dated — to around 5,600 B.P., a date which ties up with the Nouakchottian and strengthens the impression that the transgressions and regressions for which there is evidence on the Senegal coast must have been west-coastwide. Archaeological material contained within the beach deposit has been described by Davies (1967) as Late Middle Stone Age, but a reassessment based on reexamination of the beach deposit and the archaeological material contained in it is called for. The twelve-to-fifteen-meter beach apparently contains an industry described as evolved Acheulean.

Excavations by this author and others at Asokrochona, off the coast of Ghana at Accra, and observations of beach sections in various parts of the Ghana coast have revealed a depositional sequence similar to that reported by Russell and McIntire (1965) for many summer beaches. The basal sediments, apparently deposited after wave energy begins to decline, usually include considerable variations in particle size and are poorly sorted. Above this basal layer appear the coarsest and heaviest deposits in the sequence, and large shells, where these are present (as in places between Labadi and Osu beaches at Accra), form the next layer. Upward in the sequence is a gradation from coarser to finer sediments, reflecting progressive decline of wave energy and turbulence.

Drillings at various points off the coast of Ghana have also uncovered evidence of buried valleys and submerged beach levels. Buried valleys are clearly attested at minus twenty-two meters and minus eighteen meters; these as well as the several lower submerged beach levels probably testify to former phases of regression, if they are not the result of local tectonics. As with the raised beaches, however, an acceptable sequence has yet to be worked out.

Most of the remaining sections of the West African coastline are characterized by depositional and other forms of geomorphic features. Morphological features preserved in the Guinea–Sierra Leone area, in the valley and delta of the Lower Senegal, and in the Niger delta and the Volta are easily the most spectacular. The present geomorphic pattern of the continental shelf off the Guineas and Sierra Leone includes remnant barrier spits, barrier island lagoons, sea cliffs, drowned channels, and shelf-edge deltas, all of which appear to record Pleistocene sea-level fluctuations, particularly of the Würm transgressive–regressive sequences.

McMaster et al. (1970a) and McMaster, DeBoer, and Ashraf (1970b) envisage that during low sea-level stands of the Würm, Portuguese Guinea streams cut deeply into older deltaic material and carried sediments to the shelf edge. In the central region, subparalleled channels, now drowned, were actively linked to what are now relict shelf-edge deltas which led into submarine canyons in the south. Remnant barrier spits, a barrier island lagoon complex, and sea cliffs at minus ninety-, eighty-, fifty-five-, forty-five-, thirty-five-, and twenty-five-meter levels reflect a pre-Holocene transgression. The cliff features certainly represent stillstands either of a falling or of a rising sea. A coral discovered on an algal rock broken from -130 to -111 meters yielded a date of 18,750 B.P. and also indicated the presence of shallow water at this level around this time. Thus, whatever the nature of the stillstands these cliffs represent, 18,750 B.P. was a crucial date, since it marks the terminal date for a steadily falling sea level and/or the commencement point for a rising one. Apparently a regression of the sea which probably commenced around 30,000 B.P. was succeeded (or superseded) by a transgression, at least on this part of the coast, at around 19,000 B.P. This transgression may have in itself been minor or may have continued with only minor interruptions until 5,500–4,500 B.P.

The prevalence of lagoons and longshore barriers on the present coastline of West Africa seems to be related to this most recent transgression. As a result of the transgression, most shores, seas, and oceans show clear signs of submergence. The large amount of sand contained in the bars indicates that the whole width of the submarine slope, now under water too deep for the waves to be able to move sand, was formerly available to supply sand to the barriers.

A study by Bruckner and Morgan (1964) of sea-bottom samples taken along a line across the continental shelf of Accra reveals that they were made up of opaque minerals derived from the hematite limonite of the Quaternary mantle as well as nonopaque heavy minerals from the Dahomeyan rocks east of Accra. The alignment of the opaque heavies further indicates west-southwest transport, opposite to the west to east flow of the Guinea current which predominates on the surface but in the same direction as the cold Benguela current, which replaces the Guinea current from time to time. As the coastal zone around Accra has only minor streams, which usually deposit their load in lagoons, the clastic material deposited on the beach and inner shelf is almost exclusively provided by wave erosion of the coastal cliffs, on which outcrops of bedrock alternate with stretches exposing only the Quaternary mantle.

In northwestern Africa, on the other hand, it would seem that modern shelf facies are found where the shelf is narrow and the sediment supply ample. Apparently bottom turbulence and action (in the Canary Islands and Guinea) are not strong enough to keep the outer shelf free of fine sediment accumulation. Where the shelf is wide, modern fine sediments are being deposited in estuaries, and on the inner shelf, a calcareous sediment type is found where the shelf has been tectonically stable and sediment supply inadequate. Finally, very low carbonate values (less than 5 percent) occur where a modern shelf facies is being deposited or where, as in the Guinea–Sierra Leone regions, it is possible that, at several stillstands during the late pre-Holocene regression, beach and dune materials lithified, followed by differential erosion of the submerged shoreline forms with contemporaneous or subsequent algal growth on favorable exposures.

Young and Hollister (1974) have attempted to determine from piston cores the effect of late Quaternary climatic changes upon the sediments and sedimentation processes on the northwestern African continental rise between the Strait of Gibraltar and Cape Blanc. They conclude that these climatic fluctuations (1) induced periods of local Alpine glaciation of the Rif and Atlas mountain ranges; (2) produced solifluction layers in soils of the ranges at elevations 700–1,000 meters lower than at present; and (3) created, intermittently, pluvial conditions resulting in deposits of red silt beds on currently dry floodplains. They also note that Tertiary and early Quaternary shelf sediments were actively eroded during periods when sea level was lowered and circulation was most active (Butzer 1964; McMaster and La Chance 1968, 1969; Robb 1971; Summerhayes, Nutter and Tooms 1971). Lithology, mineralogical composition, sedimentation rates, and sedimentary structures in the study area were, however, apparently not much affected, and sedimentation on the northwestern African continental rise remained relatively uniform during late Quaternary times.

It is not known whether pluvial and glacial conditions were concurrent in northwestern Africa, but since there was greater runoff Young and Hollister argue that deposition of relatively greater amounts of terrigenous sediments on the adjacent continental margin and continental rise should be expected. If this is so, then the absence of such sediments there would mean either that they were eroded after being deposited or that they were deposited elsewhere. Summerhayes, Nutter, and Tooms (1971) propose that since mid-Tertiary times the locus of deposition has been the continental slope, while Young and Hollister note that one likely site for the deposition of continental sediments brought to the continental margin during the Quaternary would be the trough formed by Canary-Island/Conception-Bank/Dacia-Bank chain of seamounts and islands and the opposing continental slope. This basin probably acted as a trap for much of the sediment eroded from the adjacent continent throughout the Cenozoic.

The results of deep-sea drilling show that the dominant sedimentary facies since the Eocene have been pelagic carbonate oozes interlayered with pelagic carbonate volcanic turbidites, the sediment types still accumulating on the continental rise. On the other hand, core lithology indicates that sedimentation processes and mineralogy (carbonate abundance) remained unchanged during the late Quaternary climatic fluctuations which apparently increased erosion on the adjacent African continent. Terrigenous sediments or shallow-water fossils were absent in turbidites on the continental rise, apparently because they had been trapped along the slope and the upper continental rise in basins formed by islands or seamounts in this area. The high rate of pelagic productivity apparently accounts for the abundance of calcium carbonate in the continental-rise sediments. Most quartz silts and kaolinite clays were probably supplied by eolian sources and montmorillonite clays by the diagenesis of volcanic rocks. Faunal analysis and radiocarbon dating indicate a sedimentation rate of 2.3 centimeters per thousand years during the later Quaternary (a radiocarbon date of 27, 420 ± 900 B.P. has been obtained for the first appearance of dinoflagellates at seventy-two to seventy-five centimeters in cores).

Core data and bottom photographs thus suggest that (1) turbidity currents, distinguished by their lack of shallow-water fossils and terrigenous minerals, were an important process on the northwestern African continental rise and (2) reworking of bottom sediments has been principally by benthic organisms and occasionally by turbidity currents. These bottom currents are no longer active on the northwestern African continental rise and are apparently unimportant in basins deeper than 2,000 meters in this area.

The Niger delta coast is a classic example of a section of the West African coastline which has been subsiding since late Pleistocene times. In contrast to the generally rocky shore off Ghana, but like sections of the Senegal stretch, it is sandy. The present environment (see Short and Stauble 1967:Table 1) comprises a terrestrial or topset aspect (the Benin formation), a marine or bottomset section (the Akata formation), and a forest environment in which marine and terrestrial deposits interfinger (the Agbada formation). The sedimentary environments, as mapped by Allen (1965a:557), distinguishable in the delta today are depicted in Table 1.

The base of the Pleistocene in this region may be loosely correlated with first appearance of pollen attributable to *Podocarpus milanjianus* (Burke and Durotoye 1970a) a wind-borne form characteristic of high altitudes whose appearance is suggested to be related to the formation of mountains along the Cameroon line. Although this event may be a few million years older than the base of the Quaternary, the *P. milanjianus* surface gives a rough measure of the shape and depth of the sub-Quaternary surface. About 400 meters of sediment overlie the surface at the present coastline, and 40 meters offshore it is buried to a depth of more than 1,000 meters. All of this strongly suggests that during the Quaternary, the Niger delta continued, as it had for the past 70,000,000 years to push forward into the Gulf of Guinea. Like other stretches of the West African coast, it has special features related mainly to ice-controlled oscillation in sea level. It would appear that the Niger was able to build such a large delta because it has been spilling deposits into the ocean both laterally and vertically for more than 40,000,000 years (Maron 1969). The river and its tributaries drain for a very large area; moreover, both

Table 1.   Sedimentary environments in the Niger delta after Allen (1965a:557)

Subaerial delta	Upper floodplain
	Lower floodplain
	Mangrove swamp
	Beach
Marginal barrier island lagoon	Beach
	Channel and creek
	Lagoon
	Lagoon delta
	Marginal swamp
Marginal estuary	Marginal swamp
	Open water
Continental shelf under delta influence	River-mouth bar
	Delta front platform
	Pre-delta slope
	Open shelf
Continental slope	
Nondepositional	

the Niger and the Benuc flow for consideiable distances over sediments which are physically softer than the basement rocks. In addition, drillings offshore have revealed formations of continental sands below recent marine deposits. These indicate that accumulation of ice on the poles during the Ice Ages resulted in extreme regressions of the sea and a very fast delta advance to lines far beyond the present coastline, but more recently the sea advanced during the Holocene transgression, when the ice on the polar caps melted.

Little is known as yet of the older Quaternary in the Niger delta, but the more recent Quaternary has been studied in detail by Allen and others (Allen 1964, 1965a, 1965b; Allen and Wells 1962; Oomkens 1974). They have found three major cycles of Quaternary deposits (the details of which are set out in Table 2). The sediments exposed on this continental margin divide into two: older and younger. The older sands, largely concealed by the younger, constitute a sheetlike body of quartz sand which has been traced (Allen 1964) over most of the continental shelf and was deposited during the late-Pleistocene-to-earlier-Holocene transgression. The surface of the sheet consists of three terraces (outer, middle, and inner) and two rises (outer and inner). If, as Allen (1964) thinks, the rises represent barrier beach or island complexes, it would seem that these features were formed twice, together with crosscutting tidal channels, during the transgression.

Of the three major cycles of Quaternary deposits preserved, the earliest was apparently deposited when the sea was shallow, the next when it

Table 2.   Quaternary deposits in the Niger delta

Younger Suite (Holocene)	Sands, silts, and clays of modern delta and associated barrier island lagoon and estuary complex.
Older Sands (Late Pleistocene to Early Holocene)	Quartzose sands with shell debris and "glauconite" deposited during rise of sea level following last glaciation. Upper surface of unit forms a flight of gently sloping platforms or terraces divided by more steeply inclined rises ending locally on low ridges parallel to the edge of the shelf. Three terraces are separated by two steeper sections — inner and outer rises — interpreted as drowned barrier island beach-ridge complexes formed during the transgression, when sediment supply temporarily exceeded the rates of subsidence and sea-level rise. The outer terrace — average depth forty-five fathoms, width twenty kilometers (at lat. 6° 11' N, long. 3° 46' E) — is dated from calcareous algae at not less than $11,500 \pm 150$ B.P. Minimum age of the sands straddling the outer limit of the terrace due west of Fernando Po is $12,250 \pm 450$ B.P. (composite sample of shell from depths of one hundred to seventy-five fathoms). The outer rise, in fifteen to seventy fathoms of water, is two to sixteen kilometers wide. A date from shells in a core on the rise west of the Pennington River at a depth of one hundred meters is $10,750 \pm 250$ B.P. The middle terrace has not been dated. The inner terrace has produced a local minimum date of $1,190 \pm 150$ B.P. between the Bonny River and Cape Formosa and a date off Lagos, on shells from depths of seven to nineteen fathoms, of not younger than $3,380 \pm 150$ B.P.
Depositional break (regression)	
Pre-Older Sands (earlier than Late Pleistocene)	Plant-bearing clays, silts, and sands; some (?) soils, especially at the top, poorly consolidated. Deposited on shore and in shallow water prior to Late Würm/Wisconsin low sea level (approximately 20,000 B.P.).

Sources: Allen (1964, 1965a, 1965b); Allen and Wells (1962); Oomkens (1974).

was much deeper; the youngest represents two stages of deltaic material brought to the coast from inland by river action. Allen (1965a) has attributed this sequence to an alternation from regressive incision to transgressive aggradation and finally a regressive deposition when the sea was retreating and the delta subsiding. The dates for the most recent regressive phase indicate that it immediately follows the Nouakchottian/Takoradi Holocene transgression and had brief stillstands at 3,000 and 4,000 B.P. Such evidence further suggests a possible correlation between the late Pleistocene and Holocene events of the entire West Coast.

Two groups of coral thickets on the shelf mapped by Allen and described by Allen and Wells (1962) appear to have been formed during the brief stillstands and at the same time as an inner terrace. They are ahermatypic corals whose growth has been controlled by the existence of a thermocline forty-five meters down at which water temperatures fall from about twenty-six degrees to nineteen degrees. The deeper group is about 4,000 years old and the shallower about 3,000 years old. As they now lie in considerably deeper water than the present thermocline, they also provide a measure of the amount of subsidence since their formation.

Depth changes for the coral thickets and the terraces and rises of the older sands are generally similar, and the present depth variation of the latter appears to have resulted from the gradual combined tectonic and compactional subsidence of the continental margin as the transgression proceeded. Allen (1964) considers it likely that, prior to the transgression, the margin of the sea lay close to the shelf edge and that the rivers which drained across the shelf deeply entrenched themselves by supplying sediment to form turbidity currents; the streams at this time may have facilitated the erosion of canyons and larger gullies on the continental slope.

The transgression was reversed into a regression only when the above relation between sediment supply, subsidence, and sea-level change was also substantially reversed. This reversal led to the deposition of the younger sands, a deposition (regression) that is continuing at present in the area, and saw the growth of the Niger delta in its modern form. This suite of sands consists of sand near shore, silt at moderate depths, and clay on the deep shelf and slope. The sediments appear to be thickest where subsidence was greatest. Their surface of deposition comprises many river-mouth bars and an inshore terrace and rise. A widespread sand sheet was found near the coast at shallow depths in the younger suite, and Allen (1964) infers from this that the regression has thus far occurred in at least two stages.

If this coastal stretch were stable, one would expect that marine processes would be dominant only where there was pronounced longshore drift or frequent exposure to high-energy swell or wave occurrence and that the delta front would assume a comparatively simple coastal outline. In contrast, alluvial processes would be dominant and the front characterized by an intricate pattern of advancing distributaries, some of which became subordinate to others, where the above factors were absent or of little consequence.

The relation between advance and retreat of delta shorelines is primarily dependent on the ratio of supply to removal of sediment (by distributaries, waves, tidal and nontidal currents, winds, ice, vegetation, and fauna) and on the rate and direction of base-level variations. Some deltaic areas are at present inactive, while others are active. The amount of sediment transported by the delta-building rivers is of vital importance for the rate of advance and development of deltas. In large rivers like the

Niger and the Mississippi, the transportation of sediment may reach very imposing dimensions. The average annual sediment load of the Mississippi, for example, is of the order of 500,000,000 tons. However, the average areal rate of advance of the Mississippi and Niger deltas is rather slow in relation to that of other deltas with a sediment supply of a corresponding order of magnitude, primarily because of rapid subsidence within the deltaic area caused by downwarping, isostatic lowering, and compaction and consolidation of sediment and partly because of the rather small grain size of the sediment supplied.

The topography of the basin also influences the rate of delta advance. Deltas that are built out into deep basins usually advance rather slowly, while in shallow basins the rate of advance may be very high, especially if the base level is sinking. The rate of advance or retreat also usually varies considerably between different parts of the delta front. It may be high at the mouths of the larger active distributaries, but between these the removal of sediment by beach drift and longshore drift may exceed the supply. With increasing length of the distributaries, the slope of the energy gradient will decrease, the limit of backwater will retreat upstream, and the exposure to wave and current action may increase. This favors shifts in the position and activity of the distributaries and the formation of subdeltas. The direction of principal advance may therefore shift to places where the slope of the energy gradient is greater or there is less exposure to wave and current action, and formerly advancing parts may instead retreat.

The sediment supply may thus shift to another part of the deltaic area, and the abandoned part may be modified by and coupled with wave and current action. According to Scruton (1960), a delta cycle therefore consists of constructional and destructional phases. The constructional phase will end when erosion by waves and currents begins to dominate. During the destructional phase, compaction of sediment goes on, the sorting process may be rather active in shallow water, finer-grained material may be removed, and coarser-grained residual may be concentrated into thin veneers, beach ridges, and barrier islands. Large deltas are often built up in a step-by-step manner, local delta construction being followed by partial destruction and later by another construction phase (Scruton 1960:82).

The maximum transgression of the sea which resulted in the deposition of the older sands has been neither mapped nor dated, but Burke and Durotoye (1970a, 1970b) were able to obtain some idea of the extent of the transgression from the mouths of the Oshun, Ogun, and Ona, three rivers on the western flank of the delta near Ijebu-Ode, which appear to have fed a valley heading toward the head of a submarine canyon, Avon's Canyon, in times of low sea level. The oldest beach bars in the area outline the shape of an estuary at the mouth of the three rivers and mark the maximum extent of the transgression. In the delta proper, the oldest beach ridges are those farthest inland, but erosion of old ridges is taking place in the mangrove swamps, and relicts of the oldest barrier islands are probably no longer preserved. The barrier island complex is wider on the delta flanks than on the nose, suggesting that the transgression progressed farther where sediment supply was lower.

Rocks marking a regressive episode during which the delta advanced onto the older sand form a diachronous assemblage which falls into two major divisions: a submarine division on the shelf (Allen's younger suite, with average depth of ten meters and maximum depth of over forty meters) and a subaerial division in the delta. This latter, on which regressive sediments are being deposited (see table), divides into upper and lower floodplains. These are freshwater swamps with coarse layered sediments being deposited in river channels, point bars, levees, back swamps, and mangrove swamps (in which large tidal creeks separate into creek flats drained by smaller creeks of very complicated pattern) as well as beaches characterized by ridges with wider and narrower spacings (Webb 1958).

Off West Africa, then, deltas have added some three to ten kilometers to the two-hundred-kilometer-wide continental shelf during the Quaternary, and in all instances these show a maximum of three phases of outbuilding in any one profile. The postulations of the various workers notwithstanding, however, it is not certain that each phase can be correlated with a glacial age, since deltas are apt to change their direction and locus of growth. Moreover, the coastlines in West Africa have proved to have been subject to Continental flexure in the sense, as proposed by Bourcart (1938, 1949), that the boundary between the ocean and continent acts as a hinge line or zone resulting in an uplift of the continent and a downwarping of the shelf. Jessen (1943) gathered much material to show such continental flexure off Angola, while Allen and Wells (1962) have presented evidence for the Niger delta. What is certain, however, is that the edge of deltas formed since the last major rise of sea level forms a shelf break at less than ten meters deep. In the Niger delta in particular, the seaward edge of young coral reefs forms a shelf break at sea level.

Watercourses such as the Gambia, Senegal, Volta, and Niger which flow into the sea have fluviatile terraces, some intimately associated with sand-dune deposits. There even seems to be a similarity in the alternation of periods of erosion and aggradation observed in the river valleys. In nearly every case (Michel 1966), successive series of terraces are known. It is, therefore, hardly surprising that some workers have proceeded to correlate these with the marine cycles. As Biberson (1963) has pointed out, however, even where a four-phase terrace sequence clearly exists, climate and marine cycles appear to have intermingled in such a complex way as to preclude easy establishment of a chronological parallel between

the series of different regions. Indeed, except in the Lower Senegal region
it has not been demonstrated that the periods of maximum accumulation
corresponded exactly with the periods of maximum regression as is often
suggested.

Very little is known about the prehistoric association of these terraces.
The only regions which have yielded some information are Senegambia
and the Lower Volta of Ghana, and what is known suggests possible
connections between some terraces in the two regions. For instance, the
middle terrace of some tributaries of the Senegal and the Gambia is
described as containing a Middle Acheulean. Davies (1967), on the other
hand, has described the artifacts contained in a middle terrace of the
Volta as Chellean (or early Acheulean), although unfortunately the
Volta terrace artifacts are mostly rolled. The low terraces of the
Senegambia rivers and the Volta both contain material more evolved
than Middle Acheulean. Michel (1966) reports that the artifacts from the
low terrace of the Senegal are considered to fit into the end of the
Acheulean and the beginning of the Levalloisian, while Davies classes the
artifacts from the Volta low terrace as later Acheulean/Sangoan. Bessac
(1953) collected tools described as Mousteroid *in situ* in the upper mantle
of gravels near Richard Toll. Davies's Volta basal-gravel inner-silt
materials are similarly Middle Stone Age in character.

The attempt to correlate river terraces on the basis of their archaeological content at best gives us only a doubtful relative time scale because of
the virtual absence of radiocarbon determinations for these occurrences.
So far only one fluvial deposit has yielded a date. This is the basal-gravel
inner silts of the Volta described by Davies as containing Late Middle
Stone Age material, and its date of 5,500 B.P. suggests a connection with
the Nouakchottian/Takoradi transgression.

Present evidence, at least for Late Pleistocene and Holocene times,
shows a coincidence of regressive phases with the onset of drier conditions and transgressive phases with wetter conditions. Therefore it seems
reasonable to envisage much longer-term shifts in the energy system of
the Atlantic. If this were the case, it would mean that the retreat of the sea
coincided with a southwestward shift of the energy system. During these
periods, the cold Benguela current, moving west to southwest, probably
shifted to the north, affecting the eastern stretch of the West African
coast between Dahomey and Ghana, which runs west-to-southwest. Such
changes would have led in turn to a general southward retreat of the
forest areas, an expansion of the grassland in the Dahomey gap region,
and downward incision at the mouths of some coastal rivers in an effort to
achieve equilibrium with the fallen sea level. On the other hand, a
transgression inland may have coincided with a northeastward shift of the
ocean's energy system. This shift would probably have led to more
rainfall and less evaporation on a substantial part of the coast and inland,

a northward extension of forest vegetation, the contraction and sometimes virtual disappearance of the Dahomey gap grassland, and, finally,
the extension of coastal river courses by cutting through sand deposits in
their middle and upper reaches. At the same time, substantial deposits of
silt would have accumulated at their mouths as the rivers sought equilibrium with the rise in sea level.

The above suggestion does not discount the known fact that tectonics
and subsidence affected various sectors of the coast. Seismic profiling on
the coast suggests that the phases of earth disturbance recorded during
Late Pleistocene and Holocene times were localized and did not act in
isolation but mostly further complicated the effects of transgression and
regression. Perhaps seismic profiling on a regional scale (and the oil
companies who have carried out or commissioned most such studies to
date are probably best placed to continue this) can reveal a lot more about
the recent climatic and environmental history of the West African coast.
We need, for instance, to know more about the lateral and vertical
magnitude and direction of downthrow or upthrow and about where and
when shelf edges were faulted, volcanic rocks intruded on the continental
slope, and coastal slopes crept seawards.

At present it appears that the climatic evidence in the affected areas is
either superimposed on that of tectonics or vice versa. Following this line
of reasoning, a tentative model of the sequence of events on the West
African coast is set out in Table 3. It should be noted that most of the
sequence so far studied lacks proper archaeological association. Only
through the recovery of such associated evidence and more precise separation of erosion deposition cycles stimulated by tectonics can a better
understanding of the sequence of events be achieved. Sediment analysis,
useful as it has been, can only help indicate where the influences of the
two variables are inextricably mixed and where they are not. It cannot
date these events.

Table 3.   Tentative model of the sequence of Pleistocene events on the West African coast

Event and date	Coast	Inland
Regression and slight coastal subsidence, 2,000–5,000 B.P., with stillstands at 3,000 and 4,000 B.P.	Senegal, Ghana, Niger delta younger lower deltaic plain continental facies (sandy alluvial deposit); dune formation	Downcutting of coastal rivers
Transgression, 5,000–6,000 B.P.	Nouakchottian (Senegalo-Mauritanian), Ghana (Takoradi-Asokrochona?-Tema?), Niger delta sub-marine facies (fine sand, silt, and clay with associated marine fauna)	Volta fluvial deposits; Jos Plateau second alluvial with Middle Stone Age? Senegambia alluvial cycle

Table 3. (*continued*)

Event and date	Coast	Inland
Regression, 19,000 B.P.	Red (Ogolian) dunes; Senegalo-Mauritanian, Niger delta holomarine facies; shelf-edge delta formation within central region of Guinea-Sierra Leone shelf; lagoon complexes; sea cliffs at minus ninety, eighty, fifty-five, forty-five, thirty-five, and twenty-five meters, Guinea-Sierra-Leone shelf	Downcutting of coastal rivers; Senegambia alluvial cycle
Transgression, 30,000–40,000 B.P.	Upper Inchirian (Senegalo-Mauritanian); twelve-to-fifteen meter beach at Asokrochona with Later Acheulean; remnant barrier spits	Jos Plateau first alluvial deposit
Regression	Niger delta, Senegal-Guinea deltas and estuaries advance into sea; dune formation but no longer existent?	
Transgression, 100,000 B.P.	Lower Inchirian (Senegalo-Mauritanian)	
Regression		
Transgression	Arougian (Senegalo-Mauritanian)	
Regression		
Transgression	Tafaritian (Senegalo-Mauritanian)	

REFERENCES

ALLEN, J. R. L.
1964   The Nigerian continental margin: bottom sediments, submarine morphology, and geological evolution. *Marine Geology* 1:289–332.
1965a   Late Quaternary of the Niger delta. *Bulletin of the American Association of Petroleum Geologists* 49:547–600.
1965b   Coastal geomorphology of eastern Nigeria: beach ridge barrier islands and vegetated tidal flats. *Geologie en Mijnbouw* 44:1–21.
1970   "Sediments of the modern Niger delta: a summary and review," in *Deltaic sedimentation*. Edited by James P. Morgan, 138–157. Society of Economic Paleontologists and Mineralogists Special Publication 15.
ALLEN, J. R. L., J. W. WELLS
1962   Holocene coral banks and subsidence in the Niger delta. *Journal of Geology* 70:381–397.
BESSAC, H.
1953   Découverte du Paléolithique évolue à Richard Toll (Bas Sénégal). *Notes Africaines* 55:65–67.

BIBERSON, P.
1963   "Human evolution in Morocco in the framework of the palaeoclimatic variations of the Atlantic Pleistocene," in *African ecology and human evolution*. Edited by F. C. Howell and F. Bourlière. Chicago: Aldine.

BOURCART, J.
1938   La marge continentale: essai sur les regressions et transgressions marines. *Bulletin de la Société Géologique de France* 8:393–474.
1949   *Géographie du fond des mers*. Paris: Payot.

BRUCKNER, W. D., M. M. ANDERSON
1957   "Note on raised shorelines of the Gold Coast." *Proceedings of the Third Pan-African Congress on Prehistory*. Edited by J. D. Clark, 86–92. London: Chatto and Windus.

BRUCKNER, W. D., J. P. MORGAN
1964   "Heavy minerals on the continental shelf of Accra," in *Developments in sedimentology*, volume one: *Deltaic and shallow marine sediments*. Amsterdam: Elsevier.

BURKE, K.
1969a   The Akwapim fault: a recent fault in Ghana and related faults of the Guinea Coast. *Journal of Mining and Geology* 4(1–2).
1969b   Seismic areas of the Guinea Coast: where Atlantic fracture zones reach Africa. *Nature* 222:655–657.

BURKE, K., B. DUROTOYE
1970a   The Quaternary in Nigeria: a review. *Bulletin de l'Association Sénégalaise pour l'Etude du Quaternaire Ouest-Africaine* 27–28:70–96.
1970b   Late Quaternary climatic variation in south-western pediment deposits. *Bulletin de l'Association Sénégalaise pour l'Etude du Quaternaire Ouest-Africaine* 25:79–96.

BUTZER, K. W.
1964   *Environment and archaeology*. Chicago: Aldine.

DAVIES, O.
1964   *The Quaternary in the coastlands of Guinea*. Glasgow: Jackson.
1967   *West Africa before the Europeans*. London: Methuen.

GREGORY, S.
1962   The raised beaches of the peninsular area of Sierra Leone. *Transactions of the Institute of British Geographers* 31.

HAYWARD, D. F.
1968   A note on the evolution of Sakumo Lagoon, western Accra. *Bulletin of the Ghana Geographical Association* 13:48–50.

HEEZEN, BRUCE C., MARIE THARP, MAURICE EWING
1959   *The floors of the oceans*. New York: Geological Society of America.

JESSEN, O.
1943   Die randschaften Wellen der Kontinente. *Petermanns Geographische Mitteilungen* 241:1–205.

LEWIS, K. B.
1974   The continental terrace. *Earth Science Review* 10:37–71.

MARON, P.
1969   Stratigraphical aspects of the Niger delta. *Journal of Mining and Geology* 4(1–2).

McMASTER, R. C., T. P. LA CHANCE
1968   Seismic reflectivity studies on the northwestern African continental shelf, Strait of Gibraltar to Mauritania. *Bulletin of the American Association of Petroleum Geologists* 52:2387–2395.

1969 Northwestern African continental-shelf sediments. *Marine Geology* 7:57–67.

McMASTER, R. L., T. P. LA CHANCE, A. ASHRAF, J. DE BOER
1970a Continental shelf geomorphic features of Portuguese Guinea, Guinea, and Sierra Leone. *Marine Geology* 9.

McMASTER, R. L., J. DE BOER, A. ASHRAF
1970b Magnetic and seismic reflection studies on the West African continental shelf. *Bulletin of the American Association of Petroleum Geologists* 54:158–167.

MICHEL, P.
1966 Le Quaternaire dans les bassins de flueves Sénégal et Gambiae. *Bulletin de Liaison, Association Sénégalaise pour l'Etude du Quaternaire Ouest-Africaine* 3:19–21.

MORGAN, W. B., J. C. PUGH
1969 *West Africa.* London: Methuen.

OOMKENS, E.
1974 Lithofaces relations in the Late Quaternary: Niger delta complex. *Sedimentology* 21.

ROBB, J. M.
1971 Structure of continental margin between Cape Rhir and Cape Sim, Morocco, Northwest Africa. *Bulletin of the American Association of Petroleum Geologists* 55:643–650.

RUSSELL, R. J.
1967 Aspects of coastal morphology. *Geografiska Annaler* 49A (2–4):299–309.

RUSSELL, R. J., W. G. Mc INTIRE
1965 Beach cusps. *Bulletin of the Geological Society of America* 76:307–320.

SCRUTON, P. C.
1960 "Delta building and the deltaic sequence," in *Recent sediments, northwest Gulf of Mexico.* Edited by F. P. Shepard, 82–102. Tulsa, Okla.: American Association of Petroleum Geologists.

SHORT, K. C., A. J. STAUBLE
1967 Outline of the geology of the Niger delta. *Bulletin of the American Association of Petroleum Geologists* 51:761–779.

SUMMERHAYES, C. P., A. H. NUTTER, J. S. TOOMS
1971 Geological structure and development of the continental margin of Northwest Africa. *Marine Geology* 11:1–25.

WEBB, J. E.
1958 The ecology of Lagos: the lagoons of the Guinea Coast. *Philosophical Transactions of the Royal Society of London* B241:307–318.

YOUNG, R. A., C. D. HOLLISTER
1974 Quaternary sedimentation on the Northwest African continental rise. *Journal of Geology* 82:675–689.

ZENKOVITCH, V. P.
1967 *Processes of coastal development.* London: Oliver and Boyd.

The Status of Guinea Coast Paleoarchaeological Knowledge as Seen from Legon

B. K. SWARTZ, JR.

The purpose of this paper is to place in perspective the existing knowledge of the earlier Stone Age occupation of the Guinea Coast[1] of Africa. "Paleoarchaeology," though an etymological redundancy, is used here for artifactual evidence not historically connected to extant populations in, or from, the region of excavation, e.g., the ESA (Earlier Stone Age) and MSA (Middle Stone Age) (Ozanne 1971:37). The term "paleo-anthropology" is more appropriate for evidence that includes fossil hominid remains (none of which has been discovered on the Guinea Coast).

It is dangerous policy in archaeological reporting to assume that negative evidence is ultimate; often intensive study of a region reveals the unexpected. On the other hand, one must not assume the existence of anything before it is found. The assumption of the existence of an ESA on the Guinea Coast is an instance of premature speculation. For example, it has recently been shown that the Yapei "pebble tools" are not artifacts (Swartz 1972). Also, Davies's "Chellean" materials can be explained as selected tools of the later "Sangoan." Davies himself states (1964:85), "Objects may be assigned to [the Chellean] . . . only if they are found in a suitable geological horizon; crude techniques are no proof of the Chellean, because they continued in use from the Acheulian and especially the Sangoan."

On the basis of the distributions of general morphological forms, it seems tenable that the lowland Guinea Coast through the Akwapim–Togo–Atakora corridor was inhabited by later ESA–early MSA popula-

[1] "Guinea Coast" is Herskovits's Great Bend or Guinea subculture area (1930), the West Adamawa Highland tropical belt of West Africa. The west coast of southern-hemisphere tropical Africa is sometimes referred to as a part of the Guinea Coast. "Upper Guinea Coast" is unsatisfactory in that it may refer to Herskovits's unit or only a portion of it.

tions, though a clear "Middle Acheulean" occupation is not demonstrated. The absence of an Acheulean is noted for lowland Nigeria by Daniels (1969:18), for the Ivory Coast by Mathew Hill (personal communication, 1973), and for Liberia and Sierra Leone by John H. Atherton (personal communication, 1971). It is interesting to speculate on the MSA habitat correlation. MSA does not seem to penetrate areas that now have tropical-rainforest vegetation cover. It is hoped that future continental distribution maps will be revised in the light of existing evidence.

I know of only four central Guinea Coast MSA sites with itemized tool classes: Achimota (Davies 1954:267), Hohoe (Swartz 1974:68–69, Table 2), the Yellow Sandy Clays deposit at Manprobi (Sordinas 1971), and the Aeolian Sands deposit at Asokrochona (Nygaard and Talbot 1976:17). The latter three are associated with specific deposits. A comparison of these assemblages indicates that during the Guinea Coast MSA there is a shift in tool manufacture from massive heavy tools, such as picks and choppers, to materials that include a sizable "microlithic" component, with such forms as gravers, crescents, lunates, "trapezes," backed blades, and microcores. Despite Davies's extensive publications on the subject, at present this is all that can be said about the Guinea Coast MSA from stratigraphic evidence.

The following changes through time can be noted from the local stratification at Hohoe, eastern Ghana: quartz replaces quartzite; core scrapers, blades, microliths, and possibly hammerstones occur late; and cortex flakes in debitage occur late and may be tied to the manufacture of circular blanks with retouched surfaces (Swartz 1971a, 1971b, 1974).

Davies (1956) has attempted to establish a chronometric sequence for the "coastlands of Guinea" and then base this on the correlation of beach terraces with those of Morocco and South Africa (Davies 1961a; 1964:33–35; 1967:38–41) and with the classic East African pluvial sequence. He even offers correlations of the European glacial sequence with inland river terraces (Davies 1960, 1961a, 1961b). Few scholars today would attempt transcontinental comparison of beach terraces, and Davies himself admits (1964:32–33; 1967:38–41) that the Moroccan and South African sequences are complex, warped, and altered by tectonic movements. Cooke (1958) and Flint (1959a, 1959b) have repudiated the East African pluvial sequence and stress that chronology must be built up by the establishment of local stratigraphic units. The identification of various lithic tool agglomerations in "water-worn gravels" as specific cultural assemblages, a standard procedure of Davies's for correlating archaeological data with river terraces, has been seriously questioned by Cahen and Moeyersons (1977) from experimental studies of post-Acheulean remains at Gombe Point, Kinshasa, Zaïre.

Davies's work shows possible lines of future investigation, but until time markers are established for specific Guinea Coast sequences the only time-placement possibilities are broad geographic comparisons of basic artifact forms with areas for which there is better time control. Even here, preconceived evolutionary schemes and magnitudes of time lag must be considered.

REFERENCES

CAHEN, D., J. MOEYERSONS
    1977   Subsurface movements of stone artefacts and their implications for the prehistory of Central Africa. *Nature* 266:812–815.

COOKE, H. B. A.
    1958   *Observations relating to Quaternary environments in East and Southern Africa.* Geological Society of South Africa 60, supplement.

DANIELS, S. G. H.
    1969   "The Early Stone Age," in *Lectures on Nigerian prehistory and archaeology.* Edited by Thurstan Shaw, 14–22. Ibadan: Ibadan University Press.

DAVIES, OLIVER
    1954   The Sangoan culture in Africa. *South African Journal of Science* 50:273–277.
    1956   The raised beaches of the Gold Coast and their associated archaeological material. *Quaternaria* 3:91–93.
    1960   The climatic frame of prehistoric chronology. *Bulletin of the Ghana Geographical Association* 5:1–12.
    1961a "The correlation of the African seven-metre beach with the sequence of interglacials." *Report of the Sixth International Congress of the Quaternary Association, Warsaw*, volume one, 270–283.
    1961b "The attempted correlation of the African pluvials with European glaciations." *Fünfter Internationale Kongress für Vor- und Frühgeschichte, Hamburg, 1958*, 223–230.
    1961c Geological and archaeological evidence for the Late Quaternary climatic sequence in West Africa. *Ghana Journal of Science* 1:69–73.
    1964   *The Quaternary in the coastlands of Guinea.* Glasgow: Jackson.
    1967   *West Africa before the Europeans.* London: Methuen.

FLINT, R. F.
    1959a On the basis of Pleistocene correlation in East Africa. *Geology Magazine* 96:265–284.
    1959b Pleistocene climates in eastern and southern Africa. *Bulletin of the Geological Society of America* 70:343–374.

HERSKOVITS, MELVILLE J.
    1930   The culture areas of Africa. *Africa* 3:59–76.

NYGAARD, SIGNE, M. R. TALBOT
    1976   Interim report on excavation at Asokrochona, Ghana. *West African Journal of Archaeology* 6:13–19.

OZANNE, P. C. M.
    1971   "Ghana," in *The African Iron Age.* Edited by P. L. Shinnie, 36–65. Oxford: Clarendon.

SORDINAS, AUGUSTUS
    1971   "Problems of stratigraphy in West Africa: the Stone Age of Manprobi,

Accra, Ghana," Paper presented at the First Meeting of Africanist Archaeologists, Urbana, Ill.

SWARTZ, B. K., JR.

1971a "A field report on archaeological survey and excavation of Stone Age sites in the upper Dayi Valley, Volta region, Ghana." Unpublished manuscript, Ghana National Museum, Accra.

1971b "Survey and excavation of Stone Age sites in the upper Dayi Valley, Volta region, Ghana." Paper presented at the First Meeting of Africanist Archaeologists, Urbana, Ill.

1972 An analysis and evaluation of the Yapei pebble tool industry, Ghana. *International Journal of African Historical Studies* 2:265–270.

1974 A stratified succession of Stone Age assemblages at Hohoe, Ghana. *West African Journal of Archaeology* 4:57–81.

Excavations at Rim, North-Central Upper Volta: A Paleoecological Study

BASSEY W. ANDAH

Between September 1970 and July 1972, I conducted an archaeological investigation into the prehistory (Stone Age) of Upper Volta, an investigation focused especially on the transition from hunting and gathering to food production. Rim, the subject of this paper, is by far the most important site so far investigated in this connection. A paleoecological approach was adopted, which in essence meant attempting to understand (reconstruct) past environmental settings and how man adapted to them.

REGIONAL TOPOGRAPHY

Rim (13° 43' north latitude, 20° 31' west longitude) lies eighteen kilometers northwest of Ouahigouya, in the north-central region of Upper Volta (Figure 1). This region is characterized physiographically by a gently undulating surface dominated by tabular high lateritic surfaces and iso-

In carrying out the field geomorphological and geological studies here outlined, I relied greatly on the help and collaboration of Shiona Archibald, at the time of the Geology Department, University of Legon, and to a lesser extent on that of Pierre Mar-chelle, a geographer attached to the Office de la Recherche Scientifique et Technique Outre-Mer, Ougadougou, and Ouétian Bognounou, the botanist at the Centre Voltaïque de Recherche Scientifique, Ougadougou. Miss Archibald also kindly took charge of the mechanical aspects of the laboratory analysis, while Chief Technician Mabey of the Food and Nutrition Science Department of the University of Legon performed the chemical study of the sediments. John Hall and J. M. Lock of the Botany Department analyzed the organic materials. I am grateful to these persons and to others not mentioned by name, without whose help in the field or the laboratory this piece of work would not have been possible. Lawrence Knowa kindly typed the manuscript; Messrs Ahenaki and Danquah (Legon) and Osoba (Ibadan) helped with photographs, while Charles Knutchuga drew the maps. My thanks are due also to J. Desmond Clark, G. Ll. Isaac, and Merrick Posnansky for their constructive help and supervision and to the National Science Foundation of Washington, D.C., which financed this project.

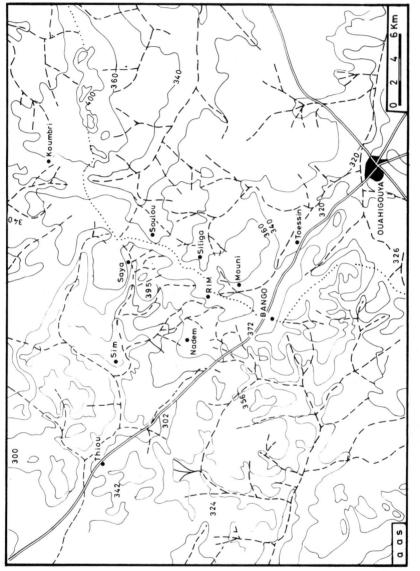

Figure 1.   Rim and neighboring sites of Ouahigouya district

lated hills and ridges. In the Ouahigouya district, one observes today a near rhythmic alternation from broad valleys to two successive levels of ancient lateritic units, as well as block ridges, all of which trend from south to north. The open-air prehistoric site of Rim lies in such a setting directly northwest of the village and at the extreme northern end of the White Volta basin. In marked contrast to the situation in the far south, the Volta rivers are no more than seasonal streams in their upper courses. In the case of the White Volta, the first definite evidence of it today lies far south of Rim, directly north of the village of Kirsi, but several valley profiles containing seasonal streams to the north of this point, of which Rim is one, indicate that the stream regime extended farther north at some time in the past.

GEOLOGY

The hard rocks of Rim are Birrimian metasediments and metavolcanics of the Precambrian basement into which dolerites are intruded, apparently conformably. These rocks are overlain unconformably by Quaternary cuirasse (Figure 2). Both the Birrimian and the dolerites have undergone metamorphism and faulting. The Birrimian rocks have been folded and now dip seventy-five to eighty degrees east. It is uncertain whether the dolerites were intruded pretectonically or posttectonically, but their structural relations suggest the former — that is, that they were intruded into the Birrimian and the two folded together.

The metamorphism is stronger in the metasediments and metavolcanics between the dolerites, which exhibit a poorly developed slatey cleavage and are completely recrystallized to yield rocks of the quartz-albite-muscovite-chlorite subfacies of the greenschist facies (Winkler 1967). The metavolcanic rocks outcropping adjacent to the dolerites show relict igneous texture, while the dolerites, which appear to have acted as a competent member during the deformation, are the least metamorphosed.

The faulting offsets the Birrimian rocks and the dolerites but does not affect the cuirasse. Thus it postdates the folding of the Birrimian rocks and dolerites and pre-dates the development of the cuirasse. The cuirasse is a residual deposit which results from an extensive period of tropical weathering. The older cuirasse forms isolated erosional remnants rising from the level surface of the younger.

These rocks are nonpermeable and therefore water-retentive, a fact which helps to explain the abundance of groundwater in the area. This water is relatively near the surface, for Rim people obtain their water entirely from wells of an average depth of twenty-five meters. Wells fewer than fifty meters deep dry up during the dry season, but their existence

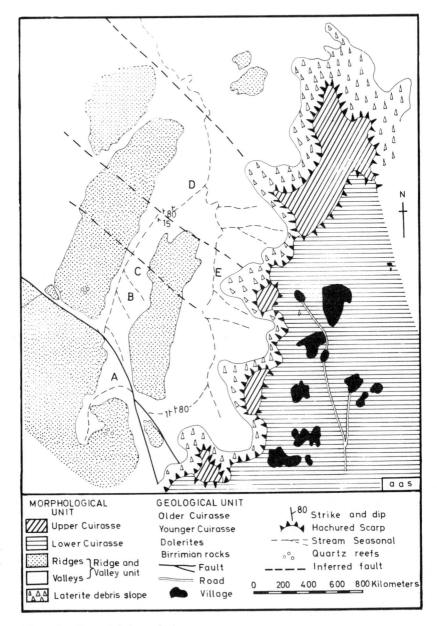

Figure 2.   Geomorphology of Rim area

may reflect a water table which was much higher in the recent past than it is at present.

GEOMORPHOLOGY

The site of Rim lies mainly within the eastern portion of a shallow valley approximately four kilometers long and one-and-a-half kilometers wide, but with sections intersected in several places by Birrimian ridges and the two cuirasse scarps. This valley contains naturally accumulated sediments and occupation deposits, actively dissected in places by gullies and channels. Altitude grades from 380 meters above sea level at the crest of the younger cuirasses to 360 meters for the older cuirasse on which the village of Rim is located to about 340 meters in the valley bottom.

The geomorphology may therefore be considered in two units — the lateritic plateaus and the ridge and valley unit — which are closely related to the geological structure (Figure 3). The younger cuirasse stands above the ridge and valley unit and forms an even, slightly undulating surface.

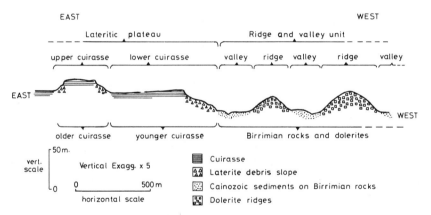

Figure 3.   Section illustrating geomorphological and geological elements

The older cuirasse occurs as isolated residual hills. The lateritic plateaus terminate abruptly in a scarp which is composed of a free face and debris slope of varying importance. The scarp is twenty to thirty meters high west of Rim. These two cuirasses represent remnants of formerly very extensive formations believed to date back to Tertiary and Early Pleistocene times. Lateritization appears to have been followed by a phase of intensive weathering and erosion, resulting in the substantial retreat of lateritic units (Figure 4).

The ridge and valley unit is being exposed by the recession of the cuirasse scarps. The ridges correspond to metadolerites and the valleys to

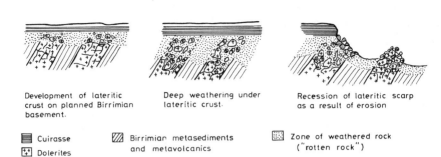

Development of lateritic
crust on planned Birrimian
basement.

Deep weathering under
lateritic crust.

Recession of lateritic scarp
as a result of erosion

▤ Cuirasse

▦ Birrimian metasediments
    and metavolcanics

▨ Zone of weathered rock
    ("rotten rock")

⊞ Dolerites

Figure 4. Suggested pattern of development of the geomorphology

metasediments and metavolcanics. Thus the linear element in the topography parallels the Birrimian trend (020° magnetic). The two elements
of this unit will be discussed separately in view of their differing histories.

The ridges are steep-sided, almost devoid of soil; the slopes consist of
loose blocks with isolated solid outcrops occurring near the crest.
Remnants of cultivation terraces are found on the flanks of some of the
ridges, mainly the less steep lower sections. These ridges extend
unchanged in character to merge with the debris slope of the cuirasse
scarp and finally pass under the lateritic crust. Nowhere are their crests
higher than the younger cuirasse; hence it is suggested that their form is a
result of deep weathering under a lateritic crust and the removal of the
weathered material since exposure, following the recession of the
cuirasse scarp (Figure 4). Isolated blocks of laterite on the crests of the
ridges are evidence of the previous extent of the lateritic surfaces.

The junction between the ridge and valley elements is relatively sharp.
There is a break of slope at the foot of the block slopes, and the extension
of "ridge debris" onto the valley floor is restricted to a few small water-
laid fans. The valley floor is undulating, with several distinctly upraised
areas; it also trends from south to north, sloping down approximately
eleven meters in the same direction. The valleys contain a sandy fill
sediment which appears to have been partly transported and partly
residual in origin. This horizontally to subhorizontally layered sediment
lies with a marked unconformity on the Birrimian rocks. The valley floor
itself may be considered as consisting of two hydrological units: (1) the
area of sheet and rill wash and (2) the area of gullying.

The area of sheet and rill wash is undergoing erosion by infiltration,
excess overland flow and two runoff patterns are observed. The first is
"normal" drainage, from the break of slope at the foot of the ridge toward
the gullies. The second is "reversed" drainage, toward the break of slope
and away from the main valley channel. This second pattern seems
abnormal and may have resulted from human activities. In the area of
sheet and rill wash are patches of lateritic gravel, typically sited on
interfluves between minor channels and thickest at the downslope limit of

the area. These are probably residual deposits. A residual deposit of cultural debris, resulting from soil erosion and deflation, is also present in this area.

Two main gullies, trending south to north, are situated at the western and eastern ends of the valley. Ridges of the Birrimian stand out to the west of the western gulley, while the lower cuirasse flanks the eastern gulley to the east. At the southern end of the valley, the two gullies lie nearly half a kilometer apart, with a Birrimian ridge running in between, but they converge immediately to the north of this ridge to contain a succession of deposits which on close inspection reveals affinities with the valley deposits.

SOILS

Soil differences noted in the region are related partly to differences in parent material and partly to the spread of weathering and erosion products across the topographic sequence. The catena existing here is repeated, in part or wholly, over wide areas of north-central Upper Volta (Boulet 1968). On the slopes of the laterites and ridges, exposure (i.e., orientation) and slope gradient constitute additional crucial soil-forming factors.

A gravelly red soil is typical on the virtually level to gently undulating lateritic surfaces. These generally are deep, with concretionary ironstone in the lower profiles, and are underlain by massive laterite. The soils present on the slopes appear to be directly related to gradient. Slopes with a very steep gradient are covered by little more than crust fragments and debris, whereas slopes with relatively gentle gradients are characterized by the formation of young, sometimes slightly evolved encrusted soils over thin beds of debris. The slopes and valleys on basic outcrops have a fine, silty water-retentive soil packed with loose blocks of rocks, whereas areas in which argillaceous schists outcrop rather abruptly carry lithosols or regosols, depending on the hardness of the rock. Finally, soils found in the valley bottom range from a red (ferruginous), loose, sandy type, very mottled and porous, to a more compact sandy loam showing zones of different colors.

BIOCLIMATE

Rim is set within the Sahelo–Sudanese zone, which has a very dry climate. This fact is reflected in the very short duration of the rainy season, the scanty rainfall, the long dry season and its high temperatures, the moderately strong winds, and the very sparse vegetation cover. The wet season runs from mid-July to the beginning of October, with a maximum in

July–August. Average rainfall is around 700 millimeters. From November through to March, strong dry winds called harmattans (average speed ten kilometers per hour) blow from the northeast or east-northeast. These winds, which are very cold, are largely responsible for a sharp drop in temperature, especially at night and in the early morning, at this time of year. From May to October, monsoon winds blow from the south-southwest, often changing abruptly into storms of high speed (fourteen kilometers per hour). Temperature falls significantly during the rainy season and attains a maximum in the dry season, except in December and January.

The length (nine months) and the intensity of the dry season are two critical factors limiting plant growth in the region. Other factors are soils and human activities. Although generally vegetation consists of shrub land interspersed with woody trees, there is a distinct zonation of vegetation from upland to lowland areas. Important elements of the vegetation include thorn plants such as *Tribulus terrestris* and plants possessing rubbery leaves such as *Pergularia daemia*. Also common are herbaceous elements such as *Portulacia olacera*, *Waltheria indica*, and *Leptadenia hastata*.

The most characteristic form of vegetation on the thin gravelly soils capping the lateritic surfaces and their slopes is a discontinuous cover of low thickets generally about one meter high and a scatter of isolated trees. Predominant elements are *Combretum* sp. (*microntum* and *aculiatum*); the tree *Celtis integrifolia* is common near the cuirasse. Sections of the slopes of the ridges are characterized by clayey, water-retentive soils which are apparently preferred to other microenvironmental situations by several *Acacia* species (*albida*, *sieberiana*, and *senegal*). Also present here are *Dalbergia melanoxylon*, a plant possessing distinctive pods, and *Sclerocarya birrea*.

In relatively inaccessible sites, particularly gullies with deep soils, the vegetation contains elements which are rarely found in the more open and degraded terrain. Important elements are woody species such as *Euphorbia balsamifera*, *Balanites aegyptica*, and *Anogeissus leiocarpus*. The presence of these tree elements may testify to the widespread existence in the area at some time in the past of wooded savanna. Although the climate is severe, it appears to be adequate to support a woody savanna vegetation. That this kind of vegetation is no longer characteristic is attributable to other limiting factors, especially the effect of slope on soil cover and interference by man and animals.

There are several elements present today in the vegetation of Rim which apparently first came into existence as larger and more permanent features of the vegetation as a result of cutting and burning by man and animal grazing. These include *Guiera*, *Boscia senegalensis*, and *Bauhinia refuscens*.

A wide-ranging survey indicated that the Rim valley is the most pronounced of those cut through faultlines and schist rocks in tributaries of the Upper White Volta. The valley is also unique ecologically, for it combines the vegetable, soil, and water resources of the valleys and hillsides with the relatively more abundant faunal resources of the cuirasse uplands and hilltops, as well as prominent outcrops of igneous and metavolcanic rocks suitable for the manufacture of a great variety of stone tools. These circumstances contributed to the almost uninterrupted occupation of this valley by hunter-gatherers and later farmers from at least Late Stone Age times to the present.

The present inhabitants of Rim are Mossi and settled here at least eight generations ago. Their settlements are located at the edge of the younger lateritic surface directly facing the valley. According to oral tradition, they chased away the former inhabitants, who apparently occupied the same highland area or the slopes of the cuirasses facing the valley. The present population comprises five clans which occupy distinct sections of the village and claim to have come from different places. Settlement is nucleated and very compact, and society is polygamous and patrilineal; Islam and animism constitute the main religions.

The people subsist primarily by cultivating large- and small-grained varieties of millet and raising animals, principally goats, sheep, cattle, guinea fowls, chickens, and dogs. This is supplemented, especially in periods of scarcity, by a little hunting and a substantial degree of collecting. The abundance of hunting dogs suggests that hunting may have been more important in the past than it is today. At present, in any case, Rim inhabitants recognize at least four resource zones: (1) the central sections of valley, employed mainly for cultivating large-grained millet and for some animal grazing in the dry season; (2) the gentle slopes of the ridges and cuirasses, on whose soils small-grained millet is cultivated, with the help of terraces, but where grazing animals are given greater latitude; (3) the cuirasse crests, hardly used except for hunting and the obtaining of lateritic crust; and (4) the high plains directly east of the younger cuirasse, which serve principally as loci for settlement and, despite its very poor soil cover, for cultivation.

Examination of this valley's rich surface scatter of artifacts and study of soil character using a soil auger pointed to suitable places to sink test pits and enabled us to delimit five areas in the eastern valley, designated A, B, C, D, and E, containing distinct and differentially distributed populations of cultural items (Figures 5, 6, 7); quarry sites on the slopes and foothills of the eastern stretch; and an archaeological assemblage in a valley stretch to the far west which had no proper stratigraphic reference. During five separate seasons between September 1970 and July 1972, Areas B and D were extensively excavated, test pits were sunk in the slightly uplifted sections of Area A, and an extensive survey was carried out of factory and

☒ Ground and polished stone tools

▤ Workshop sites

⊙Z Quartz outcrops

0 1 2 3 4 500 m

Figure 5. Surface distribution of artifacts

◎   Burial sites

▨▨▨   Surface distribution of pottery

WW   Factory locations

0 1 2 3 4 500 m

Figure 6.   Surface distribution of artifacts

Concentration of percussion flaked artefacts

Rock fragments

Iron tools

⊕ Few iron slag remnants

0 1 2 3 4 500 m

Figure 7.   Surface distribution of artifacts

other sites in the valley. Stratigraphic sounding and subsequent excavations in Areas A, B, and D revealed three archaeological occurrences, labelled Rims I, II, and III, which represent three different time periods and reflect important changes from Late Stone Age subsistence to food production first without and subsequently with a knowledge of iron tools. They also showed that the site has been severely affected by erosion on various occasions in the past, particularly before the earliest occupation period and immediately following the most recent one, and that during the most recent period the people occupying the valley buried some of their dead in pot complexes.

The cultural data recovered from Rim and other excavations in Upper Volta are comprehensively dealt with elsewhere (Wai-Ogosu 1973). Here only summary statements of cultural and chronological sequences (Tables 1 and 2) are included as an aid to better appraisal of the results of the paleogeographic study of the site.

Table 1.   Cultural sequence at Rim

Archaeological occurrence	Main artifact types	Dates
Rim I (lower level at Site B)	Microliths, especially crescents, curved backed pieces, triangular and trapezoidal retouched pieces Scrapers Choppers Becs and burins Variety of irregular flake cores and discoidals	12,000–5,000 B.P.
Rim II (lower level at Site D)	Flaked axes Rubbing and/or grindstones Scrapers Core axelike and picklike tools from associated factory sites Roulette-decorated and stamped pottery	3,630–2,840 B.P.
Rim III (upper levels at Sites A, B, D)	Polished axes Flaked axes Ribbing/hammerstones Grindstones Scrapers *Outils esquillés* Core axelike and picklike tools at associated factory sites Roulette- and comb-decorated, stamped, plant (cob)-impressed pottery Pot burial complexes	1,500–1,000 B.P.

Table 2. Radiocarbon chronology at Rim

Date (B.P.) based on 5,730 half-life	Lab. No.	Field	Site and layer	Cultural stratigraphic entity	Notes	Date (B.P.) based on 5,568 half-life
1,000 ± 195	N 1204	J-2-71	Site D, top of Layer b, 20 cm from datum point	Rim IIIb	Charcoal from test pit	970 ± 190
1,110 ± 105	N 1157	S-1-71	Site D, top of Layer b, 20 cm from datum point	Rim IIIb	Charcoal from excavation unit E6	1,080 ± 100
1,030 ± 105	N 1168	S-2-71	Site D, Layer b (coarse red-brown sand), 40 cm from datum point	Rim IIIb	Charcoal from E6, lower sections of Rim IIIb	1,000 ± 100
1,400 ± 90	N 1261	F-2-72	Site D, Layer b (coarse red-brown sand), 40 cm from datum point	Rim IIIb	Charcoal from E6, lower sections of Rim IIIb	1,360 ± 85
1,560 ± 225	N 1260	F-1-72	Site B, pot burial associated with Layer a, 30 cm below datum point	Rim IIIa	Human bone sample from pot burial	1,510 ± 220
1,910 ± 115	N 1203	J-1-71	Site B, upper section of Layer b, 60 cm below datum point	Rim IIIa	Dispersed charcoal from uneroded remnants of coarse red-brown sands in excavation unit R10, 30 cm below unit's surface	1,860 ± 110
2,920 ± 85	N 1263	M-1-72	Site D, top section of cultural deposit, 55–60 cm below datum point	Rim II	Burned wood from hearth in unit D7	2,840 ± 80
3,230 ± 85	N 1264	M-2-72	Site D, main section of cultural deposit, 60–65 cm below datum point	Rim II	Charcoal from unit D7	3,130 ± 80
3,730 ± 125	N 1250	J-3-71	Site D, basal section of cultural deposit, 70–80 cm below	Rim II	Charcoal from test pit	3,630 ± 120

STRATIGRAPHY AND CHRONOLOGY

Geological and cultural succession within the valley fill were obtained by excavations in Areas A, B, and D and observation of gulley cuttings and profiles. Sections of test cuttings at these various localities are illustrated in Figures 8 and 9.

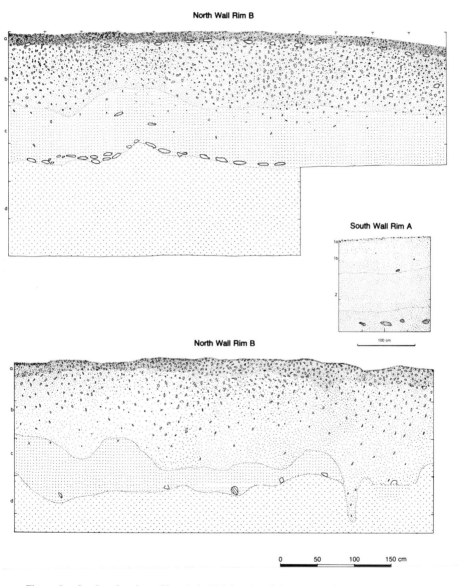

Figure 8.   Section drawings, Sites A (*middle*) and B (*above and below*)

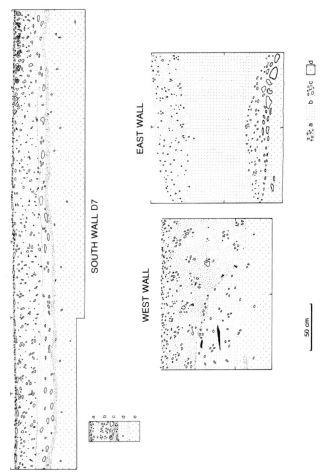

Figure 9.   Section drawings, Site D (*above*) and gulleys northeast (*below, left*) and east (*right*) of it

Sections at Site A reveal a very hard, crusty reddish yellow earth, overlain disconformably by a thin band of relatively fine yellow-brown sand which interdigitates in places with a reddish brown coarse sand containing limonitic pebbles. Several rock fragments and some stone tools were present at the junction (apparently a former land surface) between the two deposits.

At Site B, bedrock, which is schistose and was reached only in the test trench, is overlain by a very thick and compact sterile yellow sand. In all excavation units, the yellow sand directly underlies a lens of fine brown sand which is separated disconformably from a coarse, bright red-brown sand containing several pebbly concretions. In places, the entire sequence is capped by a very thin brown sandy topsoil. Two archaeological occurrences were discerned at this site. The older (Rim I) lies on a disconformable surface mostly sandwiched between the fine brown and the yellow sands but in a few sections found within the fine brown sands. The younger (Rim III) occurrence directly overlies and extends into the upper sections of the coarse red-brown sands.

Bedrock was not reached at any section of Site D. Nevertheless, the natural sequence revealed, especially in the test pit, was similar in some respects to that at Site B: thin topsoil, a dark red-brown coarse sand, a fine brown sand, and a basal yellow sand that is especially mottled in the lower sections. Although two archaeological occurrences were also present here, only one, the younger (Rim I), occurs in the same stratigraphic position as its counterpart at Site B. The older (Rim II) occurrence is found between the coarse red-brown and fine brown sands. The succession of natural deposits noticed in gulley sections, from the schistose bedrock upward was also similar to sections at Sites B and D.

SEDIMENT ANALYSIS

Red-brown, fine brown, and yellow sands were thus the principal deposits found in the Rim valley. Field observations suggest that these had distinct characteristics and may have either formed or accumulated after exposure to different sets of environmental conditions. To describe them better and to determine the pattern of variation through the soil-sedimentary column, we subjected samples to granulometric and mechanical analysis, measuring particularly the degree of sorting and skewness of the deposits, and also examined soil pH and the vertical distribution of organic phosphorus, carbon, organic matter, iron, and nitrogen.

Individual samples were sieved dry for twenty minutes. The weight of the sample retained on each sieve was measured and this calculated as percentage of the total weight of the sample and as a cumulative percentage (summing from coarse to fine). The cumulative percentage values were plotted semilogarithmically by conversion of the size parameters to the scale ($\log_2$ [size in millimeters]). From these graphs the Q_1 (first quartile, 25 percent of the sample larger than this value), MD (median diameter, 50 percent of the sample larger than this value), and Q_3 third quartile, 75 percent of the sample larger than this value) were obtained.

For each sample these values were used to calculate (1) the sorting coefficient, $S_o = Q_1/Q_3$ (with $S_o = 1$ indicating a very well-sorted sediment and $S_o < 1$ one less well-sorted) and (2) the skewness of the sample, $S_k = \sqrt{Q_1 \cdot Q_3}/MD^2$, a function of the sigmoid form of the curve; curves may be positively or negatively skewed if $(MD - Q_1) > -Q_3 - MD)$ or $(MD - Q_1) < (Q_3 - MD)$ respectively (see Table 3).

Table 3. Results of mechanical analysis of sediments from Rim

Site	Depth in centimeters	Q_1	MD	Q_3	S_o	S_k	$MD - Q_1$	$Q_3 - MD$
A, test pit	topsoil	2.3	2.83	3.2	0.847	0.92	0.53	0.37
	20–30	1.45	2.35	3.0	0.695	0.789	0.90	0.65
	S.W. 25	2.175	2.65	3.33	0.812	1.032	0.475	0.68
	40–50	1.15	1.98	2.75	0.646	0.802	0.73	0.77
	80–90	0.9	1.98	3.25	0.535	0.744	1.08	1.27
B, test pit	0–10	1.5	2.4	3.1	0.696	0.850	0.9	0.7
	35–55	2.3	2.83	3.15	0.862	0.906	0.53	0.32
	70–80	2.3	2.97	3.51	0.802	0.915	0.67	0.54
	110–130	2.25	2.85	3.1	0.852	0.860	0.6	0.25
	140–160	2.05	2.57	3.2	0.890	0.994	0.52	0.63
	200–220	2.55	2.95	3.28	0.882	0.961	0.4	0.33
	240–260	2.5	2.72	3.15	0.891	1.063	0.22	0.43
B, R10A$_2$	0–10	1.22	2.07	2.90	0.649	0.79	0.85	0.83
	20–30	1.7	2.22	2.87	0.770	0.98	0.52	0.65
	30–40	1.47	2.2	2.93	0.713	0.891	0.73	0.73
	40–50	1.6	2.33	3.13	0.716	0.94	0.73	0.80
	50–60	1.58	2.29	2.88	0.741	0.868	0.71	0.59
	60–70	1.49	2.2	2.85	0.723	0.878	0.71	0.65
	70–80	1.8	2.35	2.8	0.802	0.979	0.55	0.45
	80–90	1.64	2.28	2.83	0.761	0.803	0.64	0.49
	90–100	1.65	2.34	2.88	0.757	0.867	0.69	0.54
	100–110	1.55	2.18	2.72	0.748	0.886	0.63	0.54
D	0–10	2.15	2.65	3.2	0.820	1.195	0.50	0.55
	0–5	2.0	2.51	3.06	0.809	0.971	0.51	0.55
	5–15	2.1	2.62	3.17	0.814	0.970	0.52	0.55
	15–25	2.0	2.52	3.01	0.815	0.948	0.52	0.49
	25–35	1.91	2.40	2.97	0.802	0.985	0.49	0.57
	40–50	2.0	2.43	2.87	0.835	0.972	0.43	0.44
	50–60	1.88	2.34	2.75	0.827	0.944	0.46	0.41
	60–70	1.96	2.43	2.91	0.820	0.966	0.47	0.48
	70–80	1.96	2.50	2.91	0.820	0.912	0.54	0.41
	80–90	1.82	2.35	2.86	0.798	0.942	0.53	0.51
	90–100	1.62	2.37	2.87	0.751	0.828	0.75	0.50
	110–135	1.70	2.35	2.92	0.763	0.899	0.65	0.57
	135–160	1.76	2.20	2.65	0.815	0.963	0.44	0.45
	160–190	1.83	2.43	2.90	0.794	0.899	0.60	0.47

The pattern shown on the graph plotting S_o and S_k against depth for Test Pit 1 of Rim Site A (Figure 10) is one of decreasing sorting with increasing depth. The surface sample is, however, markedly better sorted than the subsequent levels. This may be due to winnowing by the wind, duststorms being prevalent in this area today. Sites B and D (Figures 11 and 12) both show complex profiles with well-defined discordances in S_o and S_k values at 70–80 cm (120–130 cm from the reference point in the lower sections) at Site B and at 90–100 cm at Site D. Both discordances coincide with the level of fine brown sands located between the red-brown and yellow sands. Moreover, these values are strikingly similar to those obtained for the eolian deposit forming today at Site A. These results and the site stratigraphy suggest that the discordances represent windblown sands which have been intermixed, possibly as a result of the action of soil fauna, with the adjacent horizons. A less well-defined discordance was observed 20–30 cm from the surface level of one of the excavation units in Site B (and 70–80 cm from the reference point), but as this appears different in character from the others on the graphs no equivalence is suggested.

The deposits directly overlying major discordances at both sites are probably derived, while those underlying it may be residual. The relationship of the profile at A to those at B and D is unclear, but the values of the sorting coefficient and the stratigraphy suggest that A is a residual deposit formed on a different kind of bedrock from those at B and D.

Limited heavy-mineral analysis showed up rutile, garnet, and iron ore as the most important minerals present at Site B. Iron ore values are relatively high in the red-brown and yellow sands, while dropping signifi-

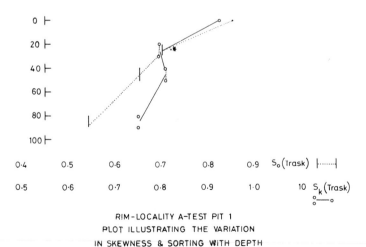

RIM-LOCALITY A-TEST PIT 1
PLOT ILLUSTRATING THE VARIATION
IN SKEWNESS & SORTING WITH DEPTH

Figure 10.   Variation in skewness and sorting with depth, Site A, Test Pit 1

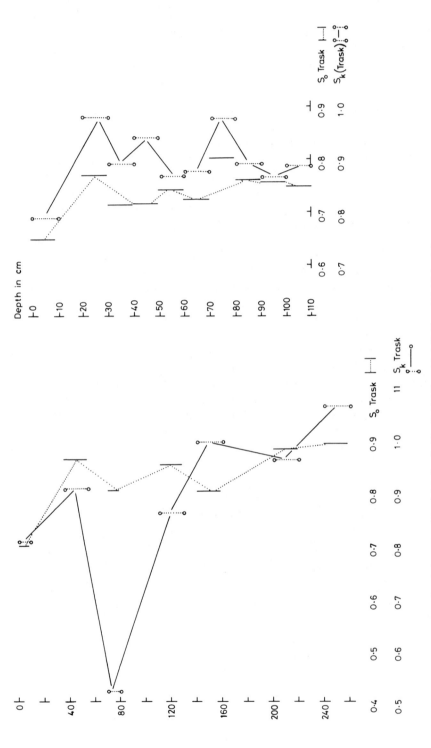

Figure 11.   Variation in skewness and sorting with depth, Site B, N7 Test Pit 1 (*left*) and R 10 (*right*)

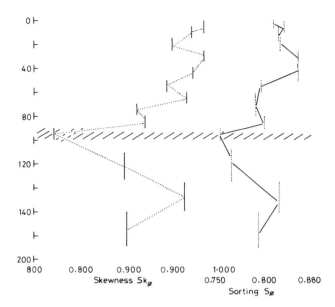

Figure 12.   Variation in skewness and sorting with depth, Site D

cantly in the fine brown zone. Garnet, on the other hand, is uniformly distributed throughout the levels, while rutile percentage increases markedly in the zone of discordance. The presence of garnet and rutile suggests a source area with strongly metamorphosed rocks, a feature indeed characteristic of the valley of Rim.

Chemical analysis reveals rather slight differences between the principal deposits at B and D (Table 4). In fact, the slight variation in calcium, phosphorus, iron, and pH values throughout the profile probably reflects present soil conditions more than the conditions which existed at the time the deposits were formed. In the latter respect, mechanical and granulometric analysis would seem to have been more useful. The fact that the red-brown sands at the top and the yellow sands at the bottom of the stratigraphic section were about equally coarse and poorly sorted and contained more iron ore suggests formation under similar sets of environmental conditions. That the brown sands are much finer and better sorted and have relatively little iron ore reflects a distinctly different type of environment. It is in fact reasonable to infer that the red-brown and yellow sands reflect moderately humid periods while the fine brown sands reflect a moderately arid phase.

In an effort to retrieve organic material at Rim, a simple basin flotation method and subsequently an elaborate seed machine made available through the courtesy of Andrew Smith of Berkeley were utilized to screen selected soil samples from occupation deposits. The material obtained was subjected to microscopic analysis. Considering the effort put into this

Table 4.   Results of chemical analysis of sediments from Rim

Site	Depth in centimeters	Nitrogen	pH	Organic matter	Calcium	Phosphorus	Iron
B, R10	0–5	0.025	5.65	2.39	0.10	0.003	1.30
	5–15	0.021	5.75	2.22	<0.05	<0.001	1.70
	15–25	0.007	5.95	2.15	0.45	0.002	1.20
	25–35	0.007	5.95	2.22	0.10	0.001	1.20
	35–45	0.014	6.05	1.87	0.40	0.002	1.10
	45–55	0.011	6.20	1.74	0.15	0.002	0.90
	55–65	0.014	6.20	1.69	0.45	0.003	0.80
	65–75	0.007	6.25	1.90	0.35	0.003	0.70
	75–85	0.007	6.30	1.58	0.05	0.003	0.93
	85–95	0.011	6.40	1.93	0.20	0.003	0.93
D, E6	0–5[a]	0.018	6.00	2.00	0.30	0.003	1.00
	5–15	0.018	5.90	2.14	0.10	0.003	0.95
	15–25	0.018	6.10	2.40	0.15	0.003	1.25
	25–35	0.021	6.05	2.09	0.45	0.002	1.90
	40–50	0.014	5.95	2.28	0.10	0.002	0.95
	50–60	0.014	6.00	1.73	0.10	0.003	0.75
	60–70	0.007	5.90	1.64	0.05	0.003	1.00
	80–90	0.011	5.80	1.68	0.10	0.002	1.25
	90–100	0.014	5.80	1.61	0.15	0.002	1.15
	110–135	0.007	5.80	1.75	0.25	0.002	1.00
	135–160	0.007	6.05	1.27	<0.05	0.002	0.80
	180–190	0.011	6.25	1.29	<0.05	0.001	0.60

Results are expressed as percentage of dry matter.
[a] 0 is just over 11 meters below main reference point at B.

exercise, the amount of carbonized material recovered was extremely small. No plant material was obtained from the two levels uncovered at Site D. At Site B, plant material was recovered only from the thin brown/yellowish brown sandy deposit directly overlying and encasing the lower occupation material. This plant material included seeds of *Acacia* and *Cassia* sp. Cyperaceae, Gramineae, Papilionaceae, and *Crotalaria*. Details are set out in Table 5.

Several factors make it difficult to determine what useful information, if any, the identifications contain with respect to vegetation and/or food plants of the level from which the plant materials are derived. First, the deposits are very porous and permeable and appear to constitute parts of actively weathering soil profiles. Secondly, and related to the first, the several remains of termites, ants, and beetles as well as grass awns and rootlets strongly suggest substantial disturbance of deposits by burrowing animals. One side effect of the influence of such factors would be the introduction of plant seeds such as those belonging to species of *Acacia, Cassia,* Euphorbiaceae, and Paniceae into much older deposits.

Table 5.   Organic material from Rim Site B

Area	Plant	Nonplant
R6F	*Fimbristylis* seed (Cyperaceae) Grass awns and rootlets Many seeds of *Panicum* sp. Seeds of Papilionaceae	Remains of termites and ants
R8	Two seeds of *Fimbristylis* sp. Three seeds of Paniceae (Graminae)	Large numbers of heads of termites of various types
P5	Two seeds of *Acacia* (?) *sieber-* *iana* (relatively recent) One seed of *Acacia* (?) *albida* (relatively recent) One seed of Papilionaceae, small species	
P6	Two seeds of one species of Papilionaceae and one of another species	
Bulk between Pits 3 and 4	Grain of sorghum (cultivated) Seeds of *Crotalaria* Fecal pellet (recent)	
Bulk between Pits 3 and 5	Three seeds of *Acacia* sp. (*albida* or *sieberiana*) One seed of (?) *Crotalaria*	
R10A$_{11}$	One small spherical seed ([?]Euphorbiaceae) One small legume seed, possibly a small *Cassia* sp. (A) One small legume seed, possibly a small *Tephrosia* sp. (B) One larger legume species (C)	One insect head (Coleoptera) Two insect bodies (Tene- brionidae, typical of detritus)[a]
R10B	Four legume seeds of Type A Six legume seeds of Type B Three larger legume species, Type C One small ribbed seed (D)	Two fragments of small-mammal molar One fragment of pale blue-green glass
R10B$_2$, R10C$_1$	One seed of Type C One small seed One triangular seed, probably *Ipomoea* sp.	

[a] Specimens are quite old, but cannot be further identified (D. Leston, personal communication).

PALEOHISTORY

Excavations at Sites A, B, and D revealed a succession of natural events with three distinct phases in which the area was occupied by people with distinctly different cultures, especially at least with regard to subsistence and settlement traits (Rim I, II, and III). Except for a short while between Rim I and Rim II when conditions may have been slightly more arid than at present, environmental conditions were either not markedly different from what they are today or else slightly less arid.

Rim I directly overlies the yellow sands, whose formation depended much on weathering of the largely schist bedrock of the valley bottoms during a relatively humid phase. It comprises a living floor located on a discomformable surface and strewn with a relatively thick concentration of lithic artifacts. It is primarily (35 percent) a microlithic assemblage lacking in pottery and ground and polished elements, but it also contains a variety of large scrapers, a very low proportion of knives and pointed tools (becs and burins), and a few flaked axes. It is essentially a blade/flake industry employing a cherty metavolcanic rock and a little quartz. The industry in fact reflects the efforts of people who were conversant with or experimenting in blade manufacture but found the available cherty metavolcanic rock difficult and sometimes impossible to adapt to blade flaking methods. The high proportion of microliths suggests a special emphasis on hunting. The overall impression is one of a narrowly specialized industry probably associated with a terminal phase of intensive food collecting. No radiocarbon dates were obtained for this level or for the eolian deposits overlying it but dates obtained for the level overlying the eolian phase (Table 2) reveal that the eolian period predates 4,000 B.P. and probably belongs to the Saharan arid phase of ca. 5,000 B.P. If so, this microlithic (Later Stone Age) industry is much older than 5,000 B.P.

Rim II is found only at Site D, where it directly overlies the eolian unit. It is characterized by a lithic assemblage strikingly different from that at Rim I and dating to between 2,840 B.P. and 3,630 B.P. Present in the tool kit are several new tool elements, especially flaked axes, rubbing stones, polished and/or lower grindstones, and pottery. Tools such as scrapers and choppers become much less important, and microliths are entirely absent. Moreover, whereas only cherty metavolcanic rock and quartz were used for Rim I, a variety of medium- to coarse-grained igneous rocks were additionally used, especially for the ground and polished tools. Floor remains were encountered which suggest the presence and use at this time of some form of dwelling structure possessing floors hardened with pebbly lateritic earth. Thus, not only did the Rim II folk occupy a greater part of the valley than the Rim I people, but the artifacts suggest that they were beginning either to make use of a different set of resources or to make different use of some of the old resources. The shift in artifact assemblage in fact suggests an important shift in subsistence techniques not incompatible with changeover from hunting and gathering to cultivating.

Evidence for Rim III was obtained primarily from the upper levels at Sites B and D, where it directly overlies the derived red-brown sands, but the occurrence also extended through to Sites A, C, and E. This cultural level, which is very near the surface, was extensively eroded and disturbed at Site B (Rim IIIa), especially where the land slopes steeply. However, radiocarbon dates from associated burials and from Rim IIIb (at Site D) indicate a time span from around 1,500 B.P. (possibly extending back to 1,900 B.P.) for Rim IIIa and 1,400 to 1,000 B.P. from Rim IIIb. Viewed artifactually, Rim III has many traits in common with Rim II. Both contain mainly ground and polished elements; except for the singular presence of cob impressions in Rim III, pottery decoration is also similar, being mainly rouletting and comb impression. In contrast to Rim II, however, igneous and metamorphic rocks were more intensively used; polished axes and large anvil stones are more numerous and choppers, scrapers, and other flaked tools much less so. At Rim IIIa and parts of Sites A and C, there are elaborate pot burials. One of those opened contained an iron object. This, together with several iron tools collected particularly from the surface of Site A, indicates knowledge and use of iron at some time during Rim III. There is, however, no evidence to suggest that these iron tools were made anywhere on the site.

Although excavations did not provide any direct evidence for dietary practices, the artifactual evidence indicates drastic differences between Rim I and associated quarry sites, on the one hand, and Rim II and III, on the other, which are suggestive of a correlative change in mode of livelihood. If such changes in fact reflect a change to a food-producing economy, they are more likely the result of early cultivation than of pastoral activities. This event appears to have commenced about 4,000 years ago in the valley and surrounding hilly flanks of Rim.

REFERENCES

BOULET, R.
   1968   *Etude pédologique de la Haute-Volta région: Centre Nord.* Ougadougou: ORSTOM.
WAI-OGOSU [ANDAH, BASSEY W.]
   1973   "Archaeological reconnaissance of Upper Volta." Unpublished Ph.D. dissertation, University of California, Berkeley.
WINKLER, H. G. F.
   1967   *Petrogenesis of metamorphic rocks* (second edition, revised). (Translated from the German by N. D. Chatterjee and E. Froese.) New York: Springer.

The Origins and Domestication of Yams in Africa

D. G. COURSEY

Although yams are among the most important of African plant domesticates, the origin of the edible yam in Africa and, indeed, elsewhere is a much misunderstood subject. Numerous misconceptions have appeared recently in the writings of Africanists and others concerned with the history of early agriculture, although as early as the publication of Watt (1890) it was recognized that the practice of yam cultivation was indigenous to Africa as well as to Asia and tropical America. This concept was also tacitly accepted in various writings of Burkill (1921, 1939, 1960) and in some of the earliest writing of Chevalier (1909). It has even been implied in otherwise responsible works (Dumont 1966) that yams were introduced in cultivation to Africa from America along with cassava and other crops. The view, expressed in some detail by Murdock (1959), that yam cultivation developed in West Africa only as part of the "Malaysian plant complex" (of yams, aroids, sugar cane, and bananas), reaching West Africa later than 2,000 B.P., has gained wide acceptance, in spite of the above-mentioned works of Burkill and Chevalier, those of Davies (1960, 1967, 1968), and my own more recent publications on the subject (Coursey 1967; Coursey and Alexander 1968; Alexander and Coursey 1969). A recent review on the subject of the history of West African agriculture (Havinden 1970) makes no substantial reference to indigenous yam cultivation and appears uncritically to accept Murdock's Malaysian hypothesis of the origin of yam cultivation in the continent. Proper understanding of the subject has been further complicated by differences in the taxonomic systems used for West African yams, there being a consistent difference in this matter between Francophone and Anglophone authors.

In considering the origins of the yams as domestic plants, it is necessary to realize that while some yams were brought into cultivation in the

African continent, other species of yams were domesticated at other places in the world; today, yams of Asiatic origin are grown to a substantial degree in most parts of tropical Africa. In the Caribbean area, where African yams are extensively cultivated, these same Asiatic species are also grown. Yams are thus at the same time both African and non-African domesticates. The domestication of the yam has been described from a global point of view in a previous publication (Alexander and Coursey 1969), where it is shown that different species of *Dioscorea* were brought into cultivation independently in three areas of the world: (1) in Southeast Asia, (2) in West Africa, (3) in pre-Columbian tropical America. Different species were involved in these three areas, and thus no single center of origin of domestication, in the Vavilovian sense, can be ascribed to the yams.

In view of the complexity of the situation, it may be useful briefly to discuss the botany and taxonomy of the yams before proceeding to the main theme.

BOTANY AND TAXONOMY

The yams we are concerned with here are members of the genus *Dioscorea*. This is the type genus, and also by far the largest genus, of the family Dioscoreaceae. It contains several hundred species which occur throughout the tropics, with a few members in temperate and montane regions. The Dioscoreaceae are themselves the principal family of the order Dioscoreales, recently reestablished by Ayensu (1972), although they were formerly (Burkill 1960; Coursey 1967) classified with the Liliales (Table 1). The Dioscoreales are monocotyledons (although they show many features normally associated with dicotyledons, and some species have a nonemergent second cotyledon) which exhibit a number of primitive features compared with most of the angiosperms, for example their inconspicuous flowers.

The Dioscoreales may well have been among the earliest angiosperms to have evolved, and their original appearance may thus have been in what is now Southeast Asia as early as the late Triassic or early Jurassic, the location and time regarded by Axelrod (1970) as that of the origin of the angiosperms. Origin in this area, though at a rather later date (early Cretaceous), is suggested by Burkill (1960). Though no fossil records of the genus are available prior to the Eocene, indirect evidence indicates that ancestral forms of *Dioscorea* had achieved pantropic, if not worldwide, distribution before the end of the Cretaceous. In any case they are widely distributed, especially in the tropical regions of the world, and achieved that distribution long before the advent of man. Fairly early in their evolution in geological time, they were subjected to ecological

Table 1.   Classification within the order Dioscoreales (after Ayensu 1972)

Order	Family	Genus
Dioscoreales	Dioscoreaceae	*Avetra*
		Dioscorea
		Rajania
		Stenomeris
		Tamus
	Trichopodiaceae	*Trichopus*
	Roxburghiaceae	*Croomia*
		Stemona
		Stichoneuron

pressures which resulted in the development of an organ of dormancy (usually a tuber, but a rhizome in some of the more primitive species) and a climbing vine which is almost always of an annual nature.

The plant exists entirely as the dormant subterranean organ through the inclement period of the year, which, in the tropics, is equated with the dry season. The substantial reserves of food and water contained in the organ of dormancy predispose the plant to attack by both animals and man. For this reason, most species of *Dioscorea* have some form of protection for their tubers, which may take the form of alkaloidal or steroidal toxins, spinous development of the stems or even of the roots, or the habit of burying the organ of dormancy deeply in the ground so as to be inaccessible to rootling animals. For more detailed botanical information reference may be made to Waitt (1963), Coursey (1967), Coursey and Martin (1970), Burkill (1960), Ayensu (1972), and Coursey (1976).

The genus *Dioscorea* occurs today throughout the tropical regions of the world. There are substantial differences related to separation early in the evolutionary history between the New and Old World species. Within the Old World there are also differences between Africa and Asia; but these are considerably less, reflecting the much more recent evolutionary separation of the species of these two continental areas, which is believed to have occurred in the Miocene when desiccation of what is now southwestern Asia was occurring. Old World species, apart from a few aberrant exceptions, have chromosome numbers based on ten, whereas the *Dioscorea* of the New World have chromosome numbers based on nine.

The yams which are of economic importance as food crops today, whether Asian, African, or American, have the following general characteristics: The plant grows during the rainy season as a twining vine which extends often for many meters through trees or undergrowth. In cultivation the vines are usually trained on stakes, strings, or wires. These vines, which are annual, bear racemes of inconspicuous white, greenish, or yellowish flowers; the male and female flowers are always separate and nearly always occur on separate plants. The female flowers are followed by dehiscent trilocular capsules, each loculus containing two seeds which are winged for dispersal by wind. At the end of the season of active growth, i.e., the rains, the vine dies down, and the plant persists through the dry season in the form of dormant tubers. It is these tubers, the natural storage organs of the plant which enable it to survive the dry season, that are economically useful to man. In all the edible yams these tubers are annually renewed organs. In other species of *Dioscorea* which have not been used by man as food, the tuber is perennial and becomes large and progressively more lignified from year to year, while, as already mentioned, some primitive *Dioscorea* have rhizomatous organs of dormancy. In modern agricultural practice throughout the world, edible yams are propagated vegetatively by means of tuber cuttings or sets which are either small tubers or fragments of tubers. Millennia of vegetative propagation in cultivation have reduced the sexual fertility of many of the cultivars so that they flower comparatively seldom and set fertile seed even less frequently.

In Table 2 are listed the principal species that have been brought into cultivation by man in the three main areas of the world where yams are cultivated. Numerous other *Dioscorea* have occasionally been utilized as food by man in various parts of the world but are of much less importance: most of these are discussed to some extent by Coursey (1967).

COURSES TOWARD DOMESTICATION IN ASIA AND AMERICA

Before considering the processes by which domesticates of the genus *Dioscorea* arose in Africa, it may be well to review what is known from other parts of the world, especially Southeast Asia, a region which has been fairly intensively studied. This area has been regarded by several ethnobotanists since Sauer (1952) as a most important area of plant domestication. It is also the area in which some of the *Dioscorea* species now grown in Africa originated.

The principal species of yam of importance in tropical Southeast Asia and those areas, such as Indonesia and the Pacific, which have acquired their agricultural heritage from Asia are *D. alata* and *D. esculenta*. The origins of these species in cultivation have been discussed in considerable detail by Burkill (1924, 1951). Geographically, the ideas put forward are entirely acceptable, but the comparatively recent chronology, suggesting the beginnings of systematic cultivation little more than 2,000 B.P., needs considerable revision: the writer did not appreciate the extreme antiquity of vegetative agriculture in Southeast Asia. Recent archaeological evidence (Chang 1967, 1970; Chang and Stuiver 1966; Gorman 1969) has indicated that non-grain-using Mesolithic cultures, which were related to

Table 2.   Major food yam species (after Coursey 1967; Alexander and Coursey 1969)

	Africa	Asia	America
Major economic spp.	*D. rotundta* Poir[ab] *D. cayenensis* Lam.[b]	*D. alata* L.[a] *D. esculenta* (Lour.) Burk.	*D. trifida* L. f.
Secondary spp.	*D. bulbifera* L.[c]	*D. bulbifera* L.[c]	*D. convolvulacea* Cham. et Schlecht.
	D. preussii Pax.	*D. hispida* Dennst.	
	D. praehensilis Benth.	*D. pentaphylla* L.	*Rajana cordata* L.
	D. sansibarensis Pax.	*D. nummularia* Lam.	
	D. dumetorum (Knuth) Pax.	*D. opposita* Thunb.[d] *D. japonica* Thunb.[d]	

[a] These species are true cultigens, unknown in the wild.
[b] Some authors regard *D. rotundata* as only a subspecies of *D. cayenensis* (Note 2).
[c] *D. bulbifera* is the only species common to both Africa and Asia. The African form is, however, quite distinct and is sometimes regarded as a separate species, *D. latifolia* Benth.
[d] These are often together known as *D. batatas* Decne and are temperate species native to China and Japan.

the Hoabinhian ceramic traditions and possessed some knowledge of cultivation, existed in the region of domestication of these *Dioscorea* species at dates around 10,000 B.P. Harrisson (1963) has suggested even greater antiquity for Stone Age cultures which had some form of systematic crop utilization in the area.

The most important of the Asiatic yams, *D. alata*, is a true cultigen, unknown in the wild state. It is believed (Burkill 1924, 1951) to have been derived by human selection from wild forms of common origin with *D. hamiltonii* Hook. and *D. persimilis* Prain et Burk., species whose natural ranges overlap in the northern-central parts of the Malaysian peninsula. As has been pointed out by this author, the yams likely to be most useful to man as food will be those native to regions with a fairly prolonged dry season, as these will tend to have the largest tubers — tubers which become dormant most deeply and for the longest period and therefore have the greatest suitability for storage. In comparison, because of their almost continuous period of growth, equatorial *Dioscorea* species have little dormancy and, therefore, have much less tuberous development. In a more recent publication the same author (Burkill 1960) follows Haudricourt and Hedin (1943) and Sauer (1952) in supposing that the original cultivation of vegetatively propagated root crops in this area was undertaken by littoral peoples whose staple economy depended on fishing. This may perhaps be true of the Araceae, such as *Colocasia*, which are adapted to cultivation under extremely moist conditions; but, as has been pointed out by Barrau (1965a), the vegecultural civilizations which are based on the Southeast Asian development of cultivation contrast fundamentally the production of such aroid crops under littoral or other moist conditions with the production of yams, which is associated more with dryland conditions. The introduction of crops, whether vegetatively propagated or otherwise, into cultivation on such a basis has also been criticized by Heiser (1969). In view of this, and also in view of the facts indicated by Burkill (1924, 1951) that yam cultivation in Southeast Asia tends to be associated with upland rather than littoral or riverine peoples, it could be suggested that yam domestication was originally brought about inland, rather than at waterside areas. However, Chang (1970) considers that the cord-marked Hoabinhian ceramics indicate the association of these cultures with littoral or riverine habitats, and the distribution of archaeological material is certainly suggestive of this.

In a more recent publication, Barrau (1970) draws attention to the observation made by Burkill (1953) of the significance of the ritual protection which is afforded to certain *Dioscorea* by the Andaman Islanders — people who within the ethnographic present were without any conventional form of agriculture. On the basis of this and observations of other practices recorded among preagricultural peoples in the Southeast Asian area and among the Australian Aborigines, it was suggested that the cultivation of crops such as yams derived initially from ritual protection afforded by gatherers to wild food plants.

After having been brought into cultivation, this species of yam was carried by man far out into the Pacific by the Polynesian migration, which probably originated in southern China and Indochina about 3,500 B.P. (Suggs 1960), and later, around 2,000 B.P. or more recently, to Madagascar and the East African littoral.[1] As we have indicated elsewhere (Coursey and Alexander 1968; Alexander and Coursey 1969), there is

[1]   So little is known of the prehistory of Madagascar that it is virtually impossible to make any useful statement about the origins of agriculture on the island, whether in connection with yams or other crop plants.

It is generally assumed that the island was uninhabited at the time of the Malaysian colonization ca. 2,000 to 1,500 B.P. It is clearly established that these settlers carried *D. alata* with them as one of their principal food plants. It was an important crop there in 1516 and in 1638 according to historical evidence and until living memory, although now it is largely displaced by cassava (Burkill 1951). It is likely that *D. esculenta* and the Asiatic form of *D. bulbifera* were also brought to Madagascar from Asia.

The indigenous flora of Madagascar is in many ways distinct from that of continental Africa. In particular, the genus *Dioscorea* in Madagascar contains a substantial number of species unknown elsewhere (Jumelle 1922; Jumelle and Perrier de la Bathie 1910; Perrier de la Bathie 1925), and many were formerly used as food. Although some were highly

no reason to suppose that this species traveled across Africa in cultivation, contrary to the opinion expressed by Murdock and others. Its distribution in Africa has been mapped by Prain and Burkill (1939), showing that there are substantial areas in the central parts of the continent where it is not known. It was, however, carried in cultivation to West Africa by the Portuguese at an early date after the paleocolonial expansion into the Indian Ocean, as there are definite records of it from São · Tomé by approximately the end of the sixteenth century (Burkill 1938).

The other principal Asiatic species, *D. esculenta*, appears to have followed roughly the same path to domestication and, subsequently, in cultivation. However, most varieties being less adapted for storage than *D. alata*, it was not so much favored by seagoing people; though it possibly reached Madagascar at an early date with *D. alata*, it was not introduced to West Africa in substantial quantities until late in the colonial era (Miège 1948).

Various other species of yams of lesser importance in Asia have been considered by Barrau (1965a, 1965b, 1970) and by Haudricourt (1962, 1964).

Although the genus is more widely speciated in tropical America than in any part of the Old World, few of the American *Dioscorea* attained any great importance as crop plants in pre-Columbian America. However, a number of species (notably *D. trifida*) were utilized by Amerindians (Chevalier 1946). This comparative neglect of the genus as sources of food by the Amerindians is probably associated with the abundance of alternative root and tuber crops in the New World (Hawkes 1970), especially cassava and sweet potatoes, which are more ecologically flexible and less seasonally yielding than most of the *Dioscorea*. Most of the yams cultivated in tropical America today are of Asiatic or West African origin. Although *D. trifida* is still grown to some extent and is greatly favored, it is regarded more as a vegetable relish than as a staple.

As has been pointed out by Burkill (1960), there has been a general east-to-west movement of the yams in domestication. Thus, Asiatic yams have been transferred in cultivation to both Africa and the New World, African species also being taken to the New World; but there has been little movement in cultivation in the reverse direction. The statement that the American *D. convolvulacea* has been taken in cultivation to West Africa (Dalziel 1937) has not been substantiated. It is believed that *D.*

---

esteemed, none appears to have been greatly ennobled in cultivation, and most retain deeply burying tuber forms. As in mainland Africa, many species are toxic but can be rendered edible by maceration and soaking.

Some of the most important indigenous species are: *D. analalavensis* Jum. et Perr.; *D. antaly* Jum. et Perr.; *D. bemandry* Jum. et Perr.; *D. mamillata* Jum. et Perr; *D. ovinala* Baker; D. *soso* Jum. et Perr. The last two of these were formerly most favored, being nontoxic and of good flavor. The island is also within the range of the African form of *D. bulbifera.*

trifida has been grown on a small scale in Ceylon (Waitt 1963), but this is comparatively insignificant. African and American yams have recently been cultivated to a limited extent in New Caledonia and the New Hebrides (Dominique Bourret, personal communication, 1972).

COURSES TOWARD DOMESTICATION IN AFRICA

The Indigenous Origin of the Domesticates

It has already been indicated that the genus *Dioscorea* was of pantropic distribution long before the advent of man, or even of the primates, and that by the Miocene, at the latest, the African members of the genus were isolated genetically from those of the New World and Asia — the desert areas of Arabia and southwestern Asia forming as effective a barrier as the Atlantic Ocean (Burkill 1960).

The majority of the yams grown in Africa today are improved or selected forms of recognizable African species which are known in the wild state in that continent and nowhere else. Asiatic species, mainly *D. alata*, but also to a lesser extent the Asiatic form of *D. bulbifera* and to a much lesser degree *D. esculenta*, are grown, but there is no evidence to suggest that these reached East Africa before the Indo-Malaysian contacts around 2,000 B.P. or West Africa prior to paleocolonial Iberian contacts later than 500 B.P. — in spite of such statements as those of Chevalier (1909) that "elle parait cultivée en Afrique depuis une très haute antiquité," or, more recently (1936), "les Noirs, lors de leur migration vers le continent Africain, apportaient avec eux ... les Ignames de cette espèce," referring to *D. alata*. The range of cultivars of these species found in Africa is extremely limited, compared with what is known in Southeast Asia or the Pacific. The only African cultivated yam unknown in the wild except as an escape is *D. rotundata*, which is a true cultigen, and even this is closely related to known wild African species. It is clearly of African affinity, being so close to *D. cayenensis* that it is sometimes regarded as a subspecies.[2] Yam domestication in Africa

---

[2]   A word is needed here on the taxonomic history of the main West African yams, *D. rotundata* and *D. cayenensis*. Confusion initially arose from the unfortunate coincidence that both species were originally described botanically from cultivated material being grown in tropical America, that is, in locations and ecologies remote from their natural habitats. The former species was rather incompletely described by Poiret from Jamaican material in 1813 and the latter from material in Guiana (the specific is derived from the town of Cayenne) by Lamarck in 1789. Subsequently, in 1864, *D. rotundata* was reduced by Grisebach to subspecific status within *D. cayenensis*. This reduction was accepted by Prain and Burkill (1919) and has subsequently been maintained by Francophone writers such as Chevalier (1936) and Miège (1952, 1969). French authors, when referring to *D. cayenensis*, may thus often be discussing material that Anglophone authors would know as *D. rotundata*. In another publication (Burkill 1921), *D. rotundata* was restored to specific status and

depended, therefore, upon indigenous yam species and not upon plant introduction. Similarly, in view of what is now accepted as to the history of man in Africa (G. Clark 1969; J. D. Clark 1970; Shinnie 1971), it need not initially have depended upon external cultural contacts, although ideas derived from the grain-based agriculture of southwestern Asia influenced the later stages of its progress (J. D. Clark 1962; Alexander and Coursey 1969). To quote from Burkill (1939), "To the African himself is entirely due the invention of *D. cayenensis* as a crop plant."

Geographical Centers of African Yam Domestication

Wild African *Dioscorea* which are botanically close to the modern cultivated forms are widely distributed in the continent between the Sahara and the arid zones of southern Africa. Maps of the distribution of some of the principal species are given by Burkill (1960). Apart from some differentiation between high-rainfall-adapted forest species and others adapted to drier conditions, there is no very great localization within this very large area.

Nevertheless, at the present time, within the ethnographic present, and within the few hundred years that written history has existed in most of Africa, the use of cultivated yams as the principal food crop has been restricted to a comparatively limited part of Africa. This is the area of

---

its identity with the white Guinea yam established, the taxon *D. cayenensis* being restricted to the yellow yam, on the basis of examinations of material in experimental cultivation in Singapore. In his major (1939) study of the African *Dioscorea*, Burkill discusses the species under the general heading of *D. cayenensis*, although in his final major work (1960) he again refers to it as a separate species. This separation has also been adopted by Dalziel (1937) and has been fairly generally accepted by Anglophone workers in West Africa. It should be pointed out, however, that a distinction based merely on the color of the tuber flesh is not reliable, as some yellow-fleshed forms of *D. rotundata* and some almost white-fleshed forms of *D. cayenensis* exist. The entire spectrum of cultivated forms as grown in the West Indies has been grouped under *D. occidentalis* Knuth, but this taxon is not valid. Recently, Ayensu (1970) has shown that there are differences in the vascular anatomy of cultivated material of the two types and considers that this warrants a formal separation. Biochemical differences involving the nature of the polyphenolics present in cultivated forms have also been pointed out by Bate-Smith (1968).

Although *D. cayenensis sensu stricto* is widespread in the wild state in West Africa and other parts of the continent, *D. rotundata* appears to be a true cultigen, unknown in the wild state, like the Asiatic *Dioscorea alata* which it closely resembles. Similarly, it must be presumed to be of hybrid origin. The great similarity in tuber form between some cultivars of *D. alata* and some cultivars of *D. rotundata* has been a further cause of confusion (the growing plants can be readily distinguished by the alate stems of the former and the spinous stems of the latter) as has the fact that both are often referred to simply as "white yam".

Attention needs to be paid to an early and frequently overlooked work of Chevalier (1909) in which a relationship between cultivated yams of the *D. rotundata* type of the West African savanna and the wild species *D. praehensilis* is indicated. In his major African work (1939) Burkill also indicates the probability of *D. rotundata*'s being a hybrid form between *D. cayenensis* and *D. praehensilis* or perhaps *D. abyssinica* Hochst.

West Africa between the Bandama River of the central Ivory Coast in the west and the Cameroon Mountains in the east, and from the sea, or the coastal lagoons or swamps, in the south to the northern climatic limit of yam cultivation (roughly, the 800-millimeter isohyet). This is the ethnobotanical domain originally described by Miège (1954) as "la civilization de l'igname" in contrast to "la civilization du riz" to the west, where the upland rice *Oryza glaberrima* Stapf. was traditionally the main nutritional basis of the diet. I have investigated further the concept of the "yam zone" (Coursey 1965, 1966, 1967; Alexander and Coursey 1969; Coursey and Coursey 1971; Ayensu and Coursey 1972) and the association of the zone with ethnic boundaries, with the area occupied by people speaking languages of the eastern Kwa linguistic group (Murdock 1959), and with the highest indigenous cultures of the forest areas of Africa, such as the Akan states, Ife, Benin, and Igbo-Ukwu (see Figure 1). Today, this comparatively limited area of Africa produces more than 90 percent of the yams grown in the continent. This may in part be a reflection of the high population densities in much of the yam zone, which, in turn, may well be associated with a long tradition of yam-based agriculture (Shaw 1976). The fact remains that outside the yam zone, yams are proportionately quite minor crops.

On the basis of present-day distribution of cultivation, I have earlier (Coursey 1967) suggested a center of origin of yam cultivation, in the Vavilovian sense, "on the fringe of the West African forest belt, either within the savannah, or possibly in the Dahomey gap," and that there "may have been a subsidiary center near or in the Congo basin." The

---

Today, *D. rotundata* is by far the most important of the African food yams, and it exists in a profusion of cultivars, most of which have never been properly documented. However, a substantial number of Nigerian cultivars have been described by Waitt (1965) and some others from the Ivory Coast by Miège (1952). In situations such as this where a large number of vegetatively propagated clonal cultivars exist which have arisen by spontaneous processes in cultivation, it is questionable whether strict Linnaean concepts of taxonomy can be applied. The classificatory approaches adopted for two other food crops which are of great antiquity in vegetative cultivation — that of Simmonds (1966) for the banana or the statistical taximetric approach used by Rogers (1967) for cassava — may well be appropriate. On this philosophy perhaps the most satisfactory way of considering the cultivated forms of the Guinea yams is to regard them simply as members of the *rotundata/cayenensis* group without commitment as to whether this currently represents one or two species, but acknowledging that at least two wild species have contributed to their ancestry. The contributions of the two (or more) wild species vary from one cultivar to another so that the whole corpus of cultivated material represents in fact a spectrum of forms ranging at one extreme from selected forms of *D. cayenensis sensu stricto* to something approaching pure, but again selected, *D. praehensilis* at the other extreme. The more that the former species has contributed to the ancestry of a particular cultivar, the more it is adapted to forest rather than savanna conditions, that is, to a short dry season and a longer period of vegetative growth; the converse is also true. Further experimental work on this hypothesis is needed, however, in the form of chemotaxonomic studies on a large number of the cultivated forms, preferably in conjunction with work on the photoperiodic response of the same cultivars, which may be indicative of their latitude of origin (Ayensu and Coursey 1972).

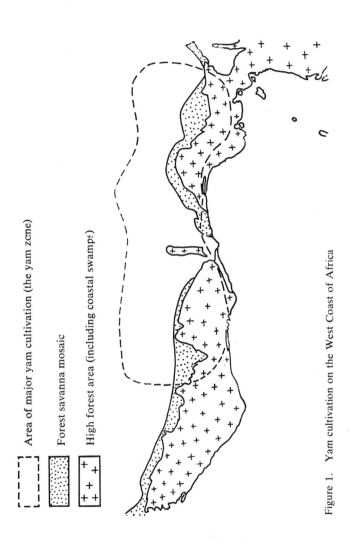

Area of major yam cultivation (the yam zone)

Forest savanna mosaic

High forest area (including coastal swamps)

Figure 1. Yam cultivation on the West Coast of Africa

first and more important of these would at least approximately coincide with the West African center proposed for various other African crops (Murdock 1959; Wrigley 1960; Portères 1962; Morgan 1962). No comment on the geographical centers of origin of yam cultivation in Africa had been made by either Vavilov or de Candolle.

It has been proposed recently (Harlan 1971) that the concept of a geographically compact center of origin is only applicable to grain-crop and similar domesticates of the temperate or subtropical regions and that the vegetatively propagated crop plants of the humid tropical or equatorial regions were domesticated over much larger, diffuse areas or "noncenters." The African yams, on the basis of this concept, originated in cultivation merely somewhere within the African "non-center."

The use of yams as food is, to a limited extent, certainly a feature of most of the area covered by Harlan's African "noncenter," but the intense concentration of the cultivation of yams, especially of the *rotundata/cayenensis* group, in the West African yam zone needs some further explanation. The use of the more highly ennobled cultivars toward the *rotundata* end of the hybrid spectrum (cf. fn. 2) is largely confined to this part of Africa. These yams, in common with other members of the section Enantiophyllum of *Dioscorea*, are nontoxic; the wild forms have tubers which penetrate deeply into the ground and also often have spinous stems, which protect the plants from attack by rootling animals. Most of the yams commonly used in other parts of Africa (apart from recent non-African introductions) belong to other sections — for example, *D. dumetorum*, Lasiophyton; *D. preussii*, Macrocarpeae; *D. bulbifera*, Opsophyton; and *D. sansibarensis*, Macroura — which secrete alkaloidal or steroidal toxins to a greater or lesser extent. Such toxins are comparatively simply removed by extraction of water — usually the running water of a stream, after some form of grating, shredding, or slicing — but nevertheless need the conscious application of a detoxification process. It may well be that there is a contrast between separate courses toward domestication that were followed more widely by the toxic yams and the nontoxic Enantiophyllum yams in a more restricted area.

In the case of the *rotundata/cayenensis* group of yams, although it may be incorrect to define a strictly Vavilovian center of origin of cultivation, progress toward domestication, the formation and ennoblement of clonal vegetative cultivars, and the emergence of cultigens appear to have taken place in a fairly limited area. If it is accepted that the yams of this group are of hybrid origin, with both forest species (*D. cayenensis sensu stricto*) and savanna species (*D. praehensilis* and/or *D. abyssinica*) contributing to their ancestry, they could only have arisen at the ecotone between forest and savanna, along with what could be termed an "axis of origin" generally running in an east to west direction but dipping southward in the Dahomey gap.[3]

The use of other species of yam is fairly well diffused over the whole of the African "noncenter," but nowhere else are they of such importance. It has been suggested on linguistic grounds that the cultivation of yams was formerly more widespread, at least in East Africa, and that they have been displaced by other crops, but the evidence is by no means clear (Posnansky 1968; Coursey 1969). It is certain, however, that in times of famine even the most highly toxic yams are used as emergency foods in many parts of Africa, even where yams are not normally cultivated today (Burkill 1939; Coursey 1967). The importance of yams in African cultural history appears, however, to be greatest in West Africa, and most of the discussion here refers to this area.

The Antiquity of Yam Domestication in Africa

Most of what can be said chronologically concerning the domestication of yams in Africa is necessarily highly speculative in view of the limited archaeological data that are available in the relevant parts of Africa, especially with regard to pre-Iron Age times. Not only has comparatively little systematic excavation been undertaken, but both soil and climate are unfavorable to the preservation of archaeological material; and neither parts of yam plants themselves, nor the wooden digging sticks that even today are often used in their cultivation, are likely to be preserved (Alexander 1970; Posnansky 1969).

Until recently, a general impression existed that all African agriculture was fairly recent and was derived largely from external influence. It has been suggested that penetration of the forest zone for permanent settlement was impossible before the introduction of iron tools (J. D. Clark 1962) and even that modern human populations reached the coastal areas of West Africa only within the last millennium (Ward 1969). It is now becoming established, however, that there is some continuity of cultural

---

[3]   Shaw (1976) has suggested that the dense populations in the southeastern parts of the yam zone — approximately the present-day Igbo-speaking areas — are associated with a great antiquity of controlled yam and oil palm exploitation in those areas. Further, there are some rather tenuous indications that at the other end of the zone the western limit of intensive yam cultivation has been moving farther westward in comparatively recent times (less than 1,000 B.P.) into the area where rice is the dominant staple. It has been pointed out by Harris (1972) that vegecultural systems do not normally expand at the expense of grain-based cultures.

Taken together, these considerations would be consistent with the concept that the earliest domestication of yams occurred at the eastern end of the forest-savanna axis of West Africa rather than elsewhere. It must be emphasized, however, that this is highly speculative and is contrary to the ideas on population movements in West Africa put forward by Flight (this volume).

tradition in the forest areas of West Africa extending back at least to the Mesolithic (Willett 1971; Ozanne 1971), the introduction of iron around 2,500 to 2,000 B.P. merely rendering the process of forest clearing more efficacious. It has been established (Gray 1962) that African Neolithic stone axes are quite effective tools for felling moderate-sized trees, while larger areas could be cleared by firing. Evidence from other parts of the humid tropics, such as New Guinea (Powell 1970), shows that forests were cleared effectively by people with only stone tools and fire at least 5,000 B.P. Yam cultivation on a systematic basis obviously antedates the historic period on the West African coast. One of the earliest Iberian explorers (Pacheco Pereira 1505) mentions not only the cultivation of yams at various points, but an established trade in yams between Bonny in the eastern Niger delta and yam-growing areas "hundred of leagues" inland at the time of his visits, nearly 500 B.P. From then on there are frequent references to yams by European visitors to West Africa, many of whom emphasize the importance of the crop. The prohibition on the use of iron tools at certain rituals associated with yam cultivation is at least suggestive that it antedates the introduction of iron, but as the West African Iron Age is little more than 2,000 years old, this suggestion provides no indication of a very great antiquity of yam domestication. Indeed, it has been suggested (Baker 1962) that the yams "need not be assumed to have any great antiquity as cultivated plants." A conventional approach based on the views of J. D. Clark (1962, 1964) is that cultural diffusion from southwestern Asia via Egypt and the Sudan introduced grain-crop agriculture to the West African savanna, sorghum and millet replacing the wheat and barley of Asia and Egypt. The concept of agriculture was then transmitted to hunter-gatherers already inhabiting the northern fringes of the forest, who adopted yams and other tubers (such as *Solenostemon* [*Coleus*], *Anchomanes,* and *Sphenostylis*) into cultivation rather than grains. This contact would be dated around 5,000 to 4,000 B.P.

There is little doubt that such culture contacts and the introduction of iron tools two or three thousand years later played a major part in the development of yam cultivation in West Africa to its present level of sophistication. Somewhat comparable cultural interactions appear to have taken place in all three main areas of the world where yams are cultivated, at approximately the same time, 5,000 to 4,000 B.P. (Alexander and Coursey 1969).

These interactions can be regarded, of course, as taking place between the differing cultures of Harlan's "noncenters" with their corresponding centers. It has already been seen that in the Southeast Asian "noncenter" there is direct archaeological evidence for Mesolithic cultures based on some systematically controlled exploitation of economic plants. Thus, prior to cultural interactions with grain-crop agriculturalists, the inhabitants of the "noncenter" had progressed substantially beyond the basic hunter-gatherer level toward a symbiotic relationship with their food plants. Even in the absence of archaeological evidence, this is a more satisfactory hypothesis than one based on contact between relatively advanced agriculturalists and primitive hunter-gatherers. Most historic experience of such contacts indicates that they are associated with such severe cultural shock as to lead to the destruction or near destruction of the latter groups or to their assimilation almost without trace, whereas, in fact, in both Asia and Africa high cultures based on vegeculture have emerged (Coursey 1972). Although there is, at present, no clear evidence in Africa of Mesolithic horticultural civilizations comparable to those discussed by Chang (1970) in Asia, similar considerations may well apply, and African yam cultivation can be accepted as having its origins in a culture that developed initially without significant contacts from outside the "noncenter."

In the case of Southeast Asia, Barrau (1970) relates the emergence of symbiotic relationships between man and plant to religiously sanctioned concepts of protection of edible wild plants, citing Burkill's discussion (1953) of the Andamanese ritual control of the collection of their main food yam, *D. glabra* Roxb., and other important vegetable foods from the wild. These ritual sanctions served to encode culturally the empirically acquired knowledge of the factors necessary to ensure the survival of the food plant species, while continuing to utilize it as a source of human food.

We have used an approach which is virtually identical, even in making reference to Burkill's concepts (1953), in an analysis of the West African New Yam Festival (Coursey and Coursey 1971). This festival is, or was within living memory, the major socioreligious event in the year in the West African yam zone, being the equivalent at once of the New Year and the Harvest Festival in the grain-crop-oriented cultures of temperate western Eurasia. It was held to mark the time when yams of the new crop could first be eaten, that is, the end of the period of ritual prohibition of their consumption, that period which corresponds to the phase of active growth of the yam plant, during which it is highly susceptible to damage and, at the same time, would give only a very small yield of tubers. We have suggested that it is a social survival from extremely remote times when the inhabitants of the area were at the gathering stage of development but were beginning to develop some concept of protecting their wild food resources by ritual sanctions comparable to those of the Southeast Asian region (Barrau 1970; Coursey and Coursey 1971). It was also suggested that this concept of protection as a first phase of domestication might date back as far as the end of the terminal Pleistocene, when the contraction of the habitable environment, caused by the expansion of the Sahara, was placing a strain on the reserves of of wild vegetable foods — of which yams would have been a most important element.[4]

There is, to date, no rigorous archaeological proof for this hypothesis, but what evidence is available is not inconsistent. Through much of the Congo basin and West Africa, artifacts are found which are described as hoes and as being suitable for the digging of yams and similar subterranean plant materials (Davies 1960, 1967, 1968) deriving from the Paleolithic Sangoan and Lupemban cultures, dating from 40,000 B.P. or even earlier.

Evidence is now beginning to appear (Willett 1971) for the development of microlithic industries within the yam zone at dates around 10,000 B.P. — industries which are indicative of an increasing degree of cultural sophistication. Most of the artifactual material found so far is associated with hunting rather than plant-food-collecting activities, but the same applies to the material possessions of hunter-gatherer cultures within historic times, even though such people usually derive a substantial part of their nutrition from vegetable foods.

THE PROCESS OF DOMESTICATION OF YAMS IN AFRICA

In discussing the antiquity of yam utilization in Africa, we have already given some indication of the processes involved in the early stages of domestication. As has been indicated by Harris (1967, 1969, 1972), the domestication of vegetatively propagated crops such as yams should not be regarded as a sudden cultural change comparable to the "Neolithic Revolution" of southwestern Asia (Childe 1951, 1952), but rather as a gradual evolutionary process.[5] More detailed examination of this process indicates that it can be divided into the following phases:

1. Hunter-gatherer man from the earliest times, or at least after he had established the controlled use of fire (before 60,000 B.P.), utilized yams of many species collected from the wild in those parts of Africa where they grow.

[4]   The concepts put forward here were originally developed on the basis of the assumption that the initial stimulus toward domestication of yams in West Africa was provided by the increasing desiccation of the environment at the close of a pluvial period and the corresponding southward shift of the desert-savanna and savanna-forest ecotones. However, it should be pointed out that not dissimilar pressures on human populations could alternatively have arisen from the northward spread of the forest into the previously inhabited savanna at the onset of a pluvial. Recently developed ideas on the pluvial history of West Africa (van Zinderen Bakker 1976) need to be considered in this content. The rest of the thesis presented here, however, remains unchanged by this alternative concept.
[5]   In the case of the cereal crops the first major step in the domestication process can simply be identified with a genetic factor — the appearance of the nonshattering rachis. No such simple distinction can be made in the case of the yams. It must also be borne in mind that the domestication process must be much more gradual than with the seed-propagated crops, as

2. In the period of the Sangoan and Lupemban Paleolithic industries (45,000 to 15,000 B.P.), large stone hoes or picks were developed, apparently especially for the excavation of hypogeous plant foods including yams.

3. During this period the first concepts of protecting wild food resources by ritual or other sanctions started to develop. It should be noted that even preagricultural peoples, such as the present-day Bushmen (Schapera 1930), have concepts of protection of wild plant food resources, some of which are systematized in magico-religious concepts. Further, it is established (Campbell 1966) that even Neanderthal man had begun to sublimate individual demands to the needs of the community, again using ritual sanctions as regulators of individual behavior.

4. Beginning around 11,000 B.P., the evidence from Lake Chad (van Zinderen Bakker 1976) suggests that there may have been a contraction of the West African forest and savanna environments which favored both man and yams. At about the same time the diffusion of more modern types of man (the proto-Negro) of the Kanjeran genetic stock into the West African savanna began (Brothwell 1963). These new human types were associated with the appearance of microlithic industries which may be regarded as indicative of the emergence of a more sophisticated level of interaction between man and his environment (but see fn. 4).

5. From the human point of view this process of interaction involved the increasing regularization of the exploitation of plant food resources. At the same time, man was modifying the natural ecosystem and thereby creating new ecological niches, prominent among which would have been middens and the cleared areas around habitations — situations comparable to the "dump-heaps" proposed by Anderson (1952) as the sites of many early plant domestications. In these artifactual environments and, especially, subject to the interest and protection of man, spontaneous hybrid or mutant plant forms were able to survive which would have been eliminated by natural-selection processes in the undisturbed natural envi-

---

sexual reproduction is only involved in the initial stages when the plant is still close to the wild form. Once a particular yam has been taken into domestication, it is propagated entirely clonally, and the opportunity for sexual recombination rarely if ever takes place. All plants of a single yam clone are essentially isolated fragments of the same individual plant and should therefore be genetically identical. It is well known, however, that yams are extremely plastic in cultivation, and it is possible that somatic mutation plays a part in this. The only criteria of domestication that can so far be suggested for the yams are (1) the partial or complete loss of the natural defense mechanisms — toxicity, spinous development of stem or root, or deep-burying habit in the tuber; (2) loss of sexual fertility; and (3) a high degree of polyploidy. None of these, however, is entirely satisfactory. The degree of ploidy has not yet been studied in a sufficient variety of cultivated forms for definitive statements to be made with confidence, although very high polyploids are known. The loss of sexual fertility may be at least in part associated with the juvenility of form that is artificially maintained by the practice of continuous vegetative propagation from small tuber fragments.

ronment. This was of special relevance in the case of the nontoxic Enantiophyllum yams, ancestral to the yams cultivated today in West Africa.
The human populations using wild or semi-wild yams originally lived
mainly on the savanna between the forest and the Sahara; as this environment contracted and, at the same time, the human populations
increased, they increasingly penetrated the forest fringes. Such clearings
provided suitable locations for interspecific crossing between savanna
species — *D. praehensilis* and *D. abyssinica* — and the forest *D. cayenensis* and for the survival, under protection, of forms superior to both as
food plants but less adapted to survival in the wild — the ancestral *D.
rotundata*. A parallel exists between this concept of a major step toward
domestication occurring as part of human penetration of a nonoptimal
environment and the Flannery-Binford model that has been used (Wright
1971) in connection with cereal domestication in southwestern Asia
(Shaw 1976).

6. As the greater control of food resources permitted the further
expansion of human populations and, simultaneously, as the move into
the less congenial forest environment encouraged closer association for
mutual protection within a human group, individual human settlements
tended to increase in size. This generated further needs for regular food
supplies concentrated into limited localities, and the domestication process moved forward from the simple, ritual protection of natural "stands"
of food plants (some of which were already in man-created ecological
niches such as middens and disturbed ground) to the removal of wild
plants to more convenient, accessible, or advantageous locations in or
near settlements. Such an operation has actually been observed within
the ethnographic present (Chevalier 1936) with *D. dumetorum* in the
Ubangui-Shari: plants were collected for food from the wild, and those
not immediately required were replanted near the settlements. This
process was described as "protoculture."

7. With increasing regularization of production, yams, by now of partially ennobled forms, became capable of supplying needs sometimes in
excess of immediate requirements. The yam tuber, as the dormant phase
of the entire plant, is inherently well adapted for storage, and tubers could
therefore be reserved for future use. Once the concept of planting had
been developed in connection with removal of wild plants to better
locations, the idea of replanting a stored tuber which had begun to sprout
at the end of the endogenous period of dormancy would not be a difficult
one to develop.

8. By 5,000 to 4,000 B.P., after an intervening pluvial period, another
period of desiccation occurred, causing further population movements
out of the Sahara belt. These were now Neolithic grain-crop agriculturalists, already influenced by southwestern Asian cultural patterns. Interaction between these peoples and the yam "protoculturalists," who were

fairly sophisticated by now, was possible on a basis of approximate equality, and cross-fertilization of ideas took place leading eventually to the development of a yam-based agriculture in something approaching the present form.

9. With the introduction of ironworking into West Africa around 2,500 B.P., penetration deeper into the forest was facilitated. As this human penetration into increasingly humid areas progressed, yams were increasingly favored ecologically at the expense of grain crops. The yam-using ethnic groups were thus able to evolve to higher cultural levels, as they had a more adequate, reliable, and generally superior nutritional basis. The more complex societies thus developing, with varying degrees of socioeconomic specialization within a culture, gave opportunities for increased conscious development of yam-growing practices; the elaboration of associated philosophical notions, enriching the nonmaterial culture; further ennoblement of cultivars; and the exchange of cultivars between groups, facilitating the spread of optimal forms.

SYNTHESIS

The domestication of the yam in Africa may thus be viewed as an essentially indigenous process based on wild African species. Only in its later stages was it influenced by external factors through cultural interactions — southwestern Asian Neolithic culture, the use of iron tools, and the introduction of non-African genetic material.

The initial moves toward domestication consisted, not of any traumatic changes comparable to the "Neolithic Revolution" of southwestern Asia, but rather of the gradual evolution of a symbiotic relationship between man and yam. At the same time this involved a realization of the physiological nature of the yam plant as needing protection from exploitation at certain stages of its growth cycle and an increasing communalization of control over plant food resources, subordinating immediate individual needs to long-term social ones. These two factors were eventually encoded into a complex of ritual socioreligious sanctions which regulated the behavior of man toward the yam plant in such a way as to facilitate the emergence of stable cultivars and cultigens. A "protocultural" system was elaborated capable of assimilating major external cultural influences when these occurred. The consequence was a complete agricultural complex.

These crucial processes occurred along an axis at the forest-savanna ecotone in the eastern part of West Africa corresponding to the present-day "yam zone." It is suggested that the emergence of this symbiotic relationship is chronologically associated with the appearance of microlithic industries in a dry phase ca. 10,000 B.P. This crucial stage in the interrelationship of man and yam could thus be linked with the beginnings of the evolution and diversification of the ancestors of the Negro races.

REFERENCES

ALEXANDER, J.
  1970   "The domestication of yams: a multidisciplinary approach," in *Science and archaeology*. Edited by D. R. Brothwell and E. Higgs. London: Thames and Hudson.
ALEXANDER, J., D. G. COURSEY
  1969   "The domestication of the yams," in *The domestication and exploitation of plants and animals*. Edited by P. J. Ucko and G. W. Dimbleby. London: Duckworth.
ANDERSON, E.
  1952   *Plants, man, and life*. Boston: Little, Brown.
AXELROD, D. I.
  1970   Mesozoic paleogeography and early angiosperm history. *Botanical Review* 36:277–319.
AYENSU, E. S.
  1970   Comparative anatomy of *Dioscorea rotundata* Poir and *Dioscorea cayenensis* Lamk. *Journal of the Linnean Society (Biol.)*, supplement one, 63:127–136.
  1972   *Anatomy of the monocotyledons*, volume six: *Dioscoreales*. Edited by C. R. Metcalfe. Oxford: Clarendon.
AYENSU, E. S., D. G. COURSEY
  1972   Guinea yams. *Economic Botany* 26:301–318.
BAKER, H. G.
  1962   Comments on the thesis that there was a major centre of plant domestication near the headwaters of the River Niger. *Journal of African History* 3:229–233.
BARRAU, J.
  1965a   L'humide et le sec. *Journal of the Polynesian Society* 74:329–346.
  1965b   Histoire et préhistoire horticoles de l'Océanie tropicale. *Journal de la Société des Océanistes* 21(21):55–78.
  1970   La région indo-pacifique comme centre de mise en culture et de domestication des végétaux. *Journal de l'Agriculture Tropicale et de Botanique Appliquée* 17:487–504.
BATE-SMITH, E. C.
  1968   The phenolic constituents of plants and their taxonomic significance. *Journal of the Linnean Society (Bot.)* 60(383):325–356.
BROTHWELL, D. R.
  1963   Evidence of early population change in central and southern Africa: doubts and problems. *Man* 63(132):101–104.
BURKILL, I. H.
  1921   The correct botanic names for the white and yellow Guinea yams. *Gardens' Bulletin, Straits Settlements* 2:438–441.
  1924   A list of Oriental vernacular names of the genus *Dioscorea*. *Gardens' Bulletin, Straits Settlements* 3:121–244.

1938   The contact of the Portuguese with African food-plants which gave words such as "yam" to European languages. *Proceedings of the Linnean Society London* 150:84–95.

1939   Notes on the genus *Dioscorea* in the Belgian Congo. *Bulletin du Jardin Botanique de l'Etat, Bruxelles* 15:345–392.

1951   The rise and decline of the greater yam in the service of man. *Advancement of Science* 7(28):443–448.

1953   Habits of man and the history of cultivated plants in the Old World. *Proceedings of the Linnean Society, London* 164:12–42.

1960   The organography and the evolution of the Dioscoreaceae, the family of the yams. *Journal of the Linnean Society (Bot.)* 56(367):319–412.

CAMPBELL, B. G.

1966   *Human evolution: an introduction to man's adaptations.* Chicago: Aldine.

CHANG, K-C.

1967   The Yale expedition to Taiwan and the South-East Asian horticultural evolution. *Discovery* 2(2):3–10.

1970   The beginnings of agriculture in the Far East. *Antiquity* 44:175–185.

CHANG, K-C., M. STUIVER

1966   Recent advances in the prehistoric archaeology of Formosa. *Proceedings of the National Academy of Sciences* 55:539–543.

CHEVALIER, A.

1909   Sur les Dioscoréas cultivés en Afrique tropicale et sur un cas de sélection naturelle relatif à une espèce spontanée dans le forêt vierge. *Comptes Rendus Hebdomanaires de l'Académie de Sciences, Paris* 149:610–612.

1936   Contribution à l'étude de quelques espèces africains du genre *Dioscorea. Bulletin du Musée National d'Histoire Naturelle, Paris*, second series 8:520–551.

1946   Nouvelles recherches sur les ignames cultivées. *Revue Internationale de Botanique Appliquée et d'Agriculture Tropicale* 26(279–280):26–31.

CHILDE, V. G.

1951   *Man makes himself.* New York: Mentor.

1952   *New light on the most ancient East.* London: Routledge and Kegan Paul.

CLARK, G.

1969   *World prehistory: a new outline.* Cambridge: Cambridge University Press.

CLARK, J. D.

1962   The spread of food production in sub-Saharan Africa. *Journal of African History* 3:211–228.

1964   The prehistoric origins of African agriculture. *Journal of African History* 5:161–183.

1970   *The prehistory of Africa.* London: Thames and Hudson.

COURSEY, D. G.

1965   The role of yams in West African food economies. *World Crops* 17(2):74–82.

1966   The cultivation and use of yams in West Africa. *Ghana Notes and Queries,* no. 9, 45–54.

1967   *Yams.* London: Longmans, Green.

1969   Yams in East Africa. *Uganda Journal* 3:86.

1972   The civilizations of the yams. *Archeology and Physical Anthropology in Oceania* 7:215–233.

1976   "Yams," in *Evolution of crop plants.* Edited by N. W. Simmonds, 70–74. London: Longmans.

COURSEY, D. G., J. ALEXANDER
  1968   African agricultural patterns and the sickle cell. *Science* 160 (3835):1474–1475.
COURSEY, D. G., CECILIA K. COURSEY
  1971   The New Yam Festivals of West Africa. *Anthropos* 66:444–484.
COURSEY, D. G., F. W. MARTIN
  1970   "The past and future of yams as crop plants." *Proceedings of the Second International Symposium on Tropical Root Crops, Hawaii*, volume one, 87–93, 99–101.
DALZIEL, J. M.
  1937   *The useful plants of west tropical Africa*. London: Crown Agents.
DAVIES, O.
  1960   The Neolithic revolution in tropical Africa. *Transactions of the Historical Society of Ghana* 4(2):14–20.
  1967   *West Africa before the Europeans*. London: Methuen.
  1968   The origins of agriculture in West Africa. *Current Anthropology* 9:479–482.
DUMONT, R.
  1966   *False start in Africa*. London: Deutsch.
GORMAN, C. F.
  1969   Hoabinhian: a pebble-tool complex with early plant associations in South East Asia. *Science* 163(3868):671–673.
GRAY, R.
  1962   A report on the conference. *Journal of African History* 3:195–209.
HARLAN, J.
  1971   Agricultural origins: centers and noncenters. *Science* 174:468–474.
HARRIS, D. R.
  1967   New light on plant domestication and the origins of agriculture. *Geographical Review* 57:90–107.
  1969   "Agricultural systems, ecosystems and the origins of agriculture," in *The domestication and exploitation of plants and animals*. Edited by P. J. Ucko and G. W. Dimbleby. London: Duckworth.
  1972   The origins of agriculture in the tropics. *American Scientist* 60:180–193.
HARRISSON, T.
  1963   100,000 years of Stone Age culture in Borneo. *Journal of the Royal Society of Arts* 112(5091):174–191.
HAUDRICOURT, A. G.
  1962   Domestication des animaux, culture des plantes et civilization d'autrui. *L'Homme* 2:40–50.
  1964   Nature et culture dans la civilization de l'igname, origine des clones et des clans. *L'Homme* 4:93–104.
HAUDRICOURT, A. G., L. HEDIN
  1943   *L'homme et les plantes cultivées*. Paris: Gallimard.
HAVINDEN, M. A.
  1970   The history of crop cultivation in West Africa. *Economic History Review* 23:532–555.
HAWKES, J. G.
  1970   The origin of agriculture. *Economic Botany* 24:131–133.
HEISER, C. B.
  1969   Some considerations on early plant domestication. *BioScience* 19:228–231.

JUMELLE, H.
    1922   Ignames sauvages et ignames cultivées à Madagascar. *Revue Internationale de Botanique Appliquée et d'Agriculture Tropicale* 2(9): 193–197.
JUMELLE, H., H. PERRIER DE LA BATHIE
    1910   Fragments biologiques de la flore de Madagascar. *Annales du Musée Colonial Marseille*, second series, 8:373–468.
MIÈGE, J.
    1948   Le *Dioscoréa esculenta* Burkill en Côte d'Ivoire. *Revue Internationale de Botanique Appliquée et d'Agriculture Tropical* 28(313–314): 509–514.
    1952   L'importance économique des ignames en Côte d'Ivoire. *Revue Internationale de Botanique Appliquée d'Agriculture Tropical* 32(353–354):144–155.
    1954   Les cultures vivrières en Afrique occidentale. *Cahiers d'Outre-Mer* 7(25):25–50.
    1969   "Dioscoreaceae," in *Flora of west tropical Africa*, volume three, part one, 144–154. First edition edited by J. Hutchinson and J. M. Dalziel, revised second edition by F. N. Hepper.
MORGAN, W. B.
    1962   The forest and agriculture in West Africa. *Journal of African History* 3:235–239.
MURDOCK, G. P.
    1959   *Africa: its peoples and their culture history*. New York: McGraw-Hill.
OZANNE, P.
    1971   "Ghana," in *The African Iron Age*. Edited by P. L. Shinnie. Oxford: Clarendon.
PACHECO PEREIRA, D.
    1505   *Esmeraldo de situ orbis*. Lisbon. (Translated into English and published by the Hakluyt Society, London, 1937.)
PERRIER DE LA BATHIE, H.
    1925   Ignames cultivées et sauvages de Madagascar. *Revue Internationale de Botanique Appliquée et d'Agriculture Tropical* 5:417–428.
PORTÈRES, R.
    1962   Berceaux agricoles primaires sur le continent africain. *Journal of African History* 3:195–210.
POSNANSKY, M.
    1968   Yams. *Uganda Journal* 32:231–232.
    1969   Yams and the origins of West African agriculture. *Odu* 1:101–111.
POWELL, JOCELYN M.
    1970   The history of agriculture in the New Guinea highlands. *Search* 1:199–200.
PRAIN, D., I. H. BURKILL
    1919   *Dioscorea sativa. Annals of the Royal Botanical Gardens, Kew* no. 9, 339–375.
    1939   An account of the genus *Dioscorea*, part two: Species which turn to the right. *Annals of the Royal Botanical Garden, Calcutta* 14:211–528.
ROGERS, D. J.
    1967   "A computer-aided morphological classification of *Manihot esculenta* Cranz." *Proceedings of the First International Symposium on Tropical Root Crops, Trinidad*, volume one, part one, 57–80.

SAUER, C. O.
1952   *Agricultural origins and dispersals*. New York: American Geographical Society.

SCHAPERA, I.
1930   *The Khoisan peoples of South Africa*. London: Routledge.

SHAW, T.
1976   "Early crops in Africa: a review of the evidence," in *Origins of African plant domestication*. Edited by Jack R. .Harlan, Jan M. J. de Wet, and Ann B. L. Stemler, 107–154. World Anthropology. The Hague: Mouton.

SHINNIE, P. L., *editor*
1971   *The African Iron Age*. Oxford: Clarendon.

SIMMONDS, N. W.
1966   *Bananas*. London: Longmans, Green.

SUGGS, R. C.
1960   *The island civilization of Polynesia*. New York: Mentor.

UCKO, P. J., G. W. DIMBLEBY, *editors*
1969   *The domestication and exploitation of plants and animals*. London: Duckworth.

VAN ZINDEREN BAKKER, E. M.
1976   "Paleoecological background in connection with the origin of agriculture in Africa," in *Origins of African plant domestication*. Edited by Jack R. Harlan, Jan M. J. de Wet, and Ann B. L. Stemler, 43–63. World Anthropology. The Hague: Mouton.

WAITT, A. W.
1963   Yams, *Dioscorea* species. *Field Crop Abstracts* 16:145–157.
1965   "A key to some Nigerian variations of yam (*Dioscorea* spp.)." Memorandum 60. Ibadan: Federal Department of Agricultural Research.

WARD, W. E. F.
1969   *A history of Ghana* (fourth edition). London: Allen and Unwin.

WATT, G.
1890   *A dictionary of the economic products of India*, volume three. London: Allen.

WILLETT, F.
1971   "Nigeria," in *The African Iron Age*. Edited by P. L. Shinnie. Oxford: Clarendon.

WRIGHT, G. A.
1971   Origin of food production in southwestern Asia: a survey of ideas. *Current Anthropology* 12:447–477.

WRIGLEY, C.
1960   Speculations on the economic prehistory of Africa. *Journal of African History* 1:189–203.

The Kintampo Culture and Its Place in the Economic Prehistory of West Africa

COLIN FLIGHT

The Kintampo culture is the only prehistoric culture in Ghana to have been at all adequately defined (cf. Flight 1972). It has sometimes been called the Kintampo Neolithic, but the name Kintampo culture has priority (Davies 1962) and is preferable in any case. In spite of the recommendations of Bishop and Clark (1967), I do not propose to start calling cultures "industrial complexes."

Rather less than twenty sites are known which can be assigned with confidence to the Kintampo culture. Some were discovered by the Geological Survey many years ago: the first two sites to be recorded were found in 1916, one near Jema and the other near Tolundipe (Kitson 1916). However, the majority have been discovered within the last twenty years, mostly by Davies, who was responsible for recognizing and initially defining the culture (Davies 1962, 1964, 1967).

Some sites have been excavated (these I later mention individually), but the collections we have to work with are mostly small, consisting, at best, of a few dozen pieces picked up off the surface. As far as it is possible to tell, however, the sites all seem to be very similar in content. The Kintampo culture is apparently so distinctive, so unlike any other prehistoric culture in Ghana, that sites belonging to it can be recognized easily. Only when the collection is very small does doubt sometimes arise.

In order to qualify for inclusion in the Kintampo culture, a site ought to possess all or most of the following characteristics: a good number (say three or more) of the enigmatic objects which Davies describes as terracotta cigars, but which I would prefer to call stone rasps (certainly they are not of terracotta); polished stone axe blades, polished stone bracelets; grooved stones made either from broken rasps or else from sandstone; grinding and pounding stones; pottery of a distinctive style (but shards exposed on the surface are often too badly weathered to be diagnostic);

This paper was written in 1974 and revised for publication in 1975. It has not been brought up to date.

and chunks of burnt daub which sometimes bear the impression of wooden poles.

Even twelve years ago, before any of the sites had been excavated, enough was known about the Kintampo culture for it to seem likely, on indirect evidence, that the economy was one of village farming. Thus it was possible to cite evidence for durable structures of some kind (the burnt daub), for trade in essential equipment as well as luxuries (the axe blades and bracelets), for land clearance (the axe blades again), and perhaps for the processing of seeds (the grinding stones). Until recently, however, there was no direct evidence either for cultivated crops or for domestic animals.

The distribution map (Figure 1) needs to be read with care, but it does show more than just the distribution of archaeological effort. A few of the blank spaces may well be filled in by future work (sites are surely awaiting discovery, for example, on the other side of the Ghana-Ivory Coast border), but some of the patterning in the map can probably be relied on.

A clear distinction can be made, in terms of geography at least, between upland and lowland sites; it remains to be seen whether there is any corresponding difference in material culture. The upland sites occur in relatively dense concentrations: one in the Banda Hills and another on the high ground around Kintampo, not far from the edge of the forest. The lowland sites occur more sparsely in the open woodland of the inner Volta Basin, and most of them are in riverain locations.

Rather surprisingly, the Kintampo culture also turns up in the Accra plains, a long way farther south. The site excavated by Davies (1964:244) at Christians Village was unstratified, and it seems to me that the material from it is very mixed. However, there are many stone rasps, and some of the pottery can also be ascribed to the Kintampo culture on grounds of fabric and decoration. Another site may possibly exist at Somanya, where a few rasp fragments have been collected. It is likely that this gap in the distribution will sooner or later be bridged. Access to the Afram plains is difficult, and they are almost unknown archaeologically. One large fragment of a stone rasp, presented to the Department of Archaeology at Legon some years ago, was reported to have been found near the remote village of Adiemmra; this is as yet the only hint we have of a Kintampo culture site in that region.

On the other hand, the absence of sites in the forest is very probably genuine. Some rasp fragments admittedly do occur — for instance, there is one from an eighteenth-century site at Mampongten, and a few were found at a site on the University campus at Kumasi (Nunoo 1969). Such finds serve only to confirm what is known from evidence elsewhere, that stray fragments do turn up occasionally on later sites, and sometimes well outside the range of the Kintampo culture. (By the same token, of course, we should not rely much on that single fragment from Adiemmra.)

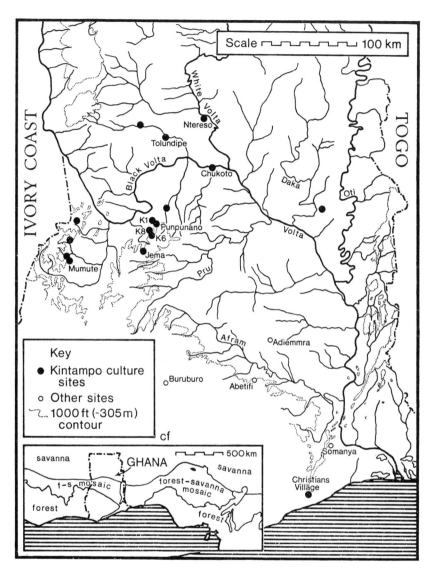

Figure 1.   Distribution map of the Kintampo culture

In broad outline, therefore, the distribution pattern is as follows: Kintampo culture sites do not occur, as far as we know, in the forest. There are many sites on the edge of the forest, concentrated on high ground, and a few farther north, mostly near rivers. Farther north again there are none. The Kintampo culture is thus confined within the zone described by some (e.g., Clark 1967: Map 5) as forest-savanna mosaic; but when that is said, the question at once arises whether it may not be thoroughly misleading to superimpose the distribution map of a prehistoric culture on a map of the modern vegetation. Can we afford to ignore the possibility of environmental change? For the time being, and with some qualifications, I think that we can (but this is a question I shall need to return to later).

It was suggested at one time by Davies that the Kintampo culture began in about 500 B.C. The argument was never convincing, but criticism seems superfluous now that we know from the evidence of radiocarbon dates that the conclusion was mistaken. The Kintampo culture turns out to have been much earlier than was supposed.

We know nothing for certain of the contemporaneous cultures which, presumably, must have existed in the forest and in the far north of Ghana. Perhaps we may guess that they were of an undistinguished "later Stone Age" character.

Two of the lowland sites had been excavated before I began work at Kintampo, and I will comment briefly on both.

A site at Chukoto on the Black Volta was investigated by Mathewson in 1965 as part of the program of rescue excavation carried out by the Volta Basin Research Project. Chukoto gave us, for the first time, a large and representative collection of pottery and stone artifacts from a site belonging without argument to the Kintampo culture (Mathewson 1967). Organic material, unfortunately, was not preserved, and even the pottery is in bad condition.

The controversial site at Ntereso, not far from the White Volta, was excavated by Davies in 1961 and 1962. Most of the differences which were claimed to exist between this and other "typical" sites of the Kintampo culture have disappeared, perhaps predictably, now that the Kintampo culture is better known. Ntereso has become famous for the iron objects which were allegedly found in association with the Kintampo culture material. I say nothing of these, since Davies (1969) has asked for time to reconsider. It is my opinion that only the stone arrowheads, unique to this site as far as we know and thoroughly Saharan in appearance, require some special explanation. Ntereso is nonetheless an important site. Organic material was well preserved. Shells and fish bones occur in quantity, proving the economic importance of aquatic resources that was already implied by the location of the site on a low ridge overlooking the river and by the occurrence of bone harpoons and fishhooks. The animal bones are mostly from wild species — from antelopes especially — but dwarf goats are represented as well (Carter and Flight 1972). More relevant is the claim that ears of *Pennisetum* were used as roulettes for decorating some of the pottery. This identification does not seem to have been authenticated by a specialist, however, and I would rather reserve judgment. None of the pottery from my own excavations is decorated in this way, as far as I can tell. Three radiocarbon dates suggest that the Ntereso site was occupied around 1300 B.C. These dates are in good agreement with those obtained more recently from sites near Kintampo itself, in spite of being very much earlier than Davies had expected.[1]

The research which I carried out around Kintampo in 1967 and 1968 was intended to determine more satisfactorily the date and character of the Kintampo culture in the area where it had first been recognized. This is very different terrain from that in which the lowland sites occur — a dissected sandstone plateau bounded on the west by a steep and sometimes precipitous scarp. Rainfall is higher here, the dry season shorter, the vegetation lusher. We concentrated our attention entirely on the many caves and rock shelters in the hope of finding organic material better preserved than is generally the case on open sites. The Kintampo culture had not been found in a rock shelter before, but some of the sites already known in the area — like Jema, the first ever to be discovered, or Punpunano, the first to be discovered by Davies — were in close proximity to sandstone inselbergs. This encouraged the hope that some use might have been made of the available rock shelters. In the event, our hopes were justified. At several of the shelters which we investigated, there had indeed been occupation by Kintampo culture communities. Preservation was bad in some but in others it was excellent. We were thus able to make some progress in defining the date and character of the culture and in placing it for the first time in a local cultural-stratigraphic sequence.

Work began with the excavation — by Philip Rahtz in 1966 and myself on a smaller scale in 1967 — of a rock shelter (K1) ten kilometers north of Kintampo (Rahtz and Flight 1974). During 1967 I also made trial excavations at three other shelters (K2–4) in the same inselberg as K1; at three shelters (K5–7) in an inselberg four kilometers to the south of Kintampo; and finally at a shelter (K8) in a cliff one kilometer to the west. In 1968 I returned to K6, which had produced by far the most promising results, and enlarged the original excavation. For much of this second season I had the help of Peter Schmidt, then of Northwestern, now of Brown University. (Some account of the work has been given in interim reports: Flight 1972, 1968; cf. Calvocoressi 1970: 71–73; Willet 1971:352–353.)

The cultural sequence, as far as it can be pieced together at present, is described in the forthcoming K1 report. Here I am concerned only with what happen to be the two best-documented parts of the sequence — the Kintampo culture itself and the immediately preceding but altogether

---

[1]   I may add that an upland site belonging to the Banda Hills group has been discovered and excavated by Joanne Dombrowski since this paper was written.

different Punpun phase. For the break between the two, a date of 1450 to 1400 B.C. is likely on the evidence of six radiocarbon dates, and neither seems to be of more than a few centuries' duration.

Occurrences of the Punpun phase (to which I referred initially as the "Buobini culture") have been found at three sites in the Kintampo area, but nowhere else. The distinctive pottery turned up first in small quantities at K1, and quite substantial middens were excavated later at K6 and K8. These middens are full of snail shells, seed husks of *Celtis* sp., and animal bones from a wide variety of species. Here we seem to be dealing with camp sites occupied at least during the wet season — for that is when the snails appear and the hackberries ripen — by groups of hunter-gatherers; I believe that this population was then displaced by the immigrant communities which are represented in the archaeological record by the Kintampo culture. I have no special liking for hypotheses of invasion, but in this case the differences are so pronounced in almost every respect that no other explanation seems possible.

The Kintampo culture is present at the same three sites overlying the Punpun-phase occurrences and also at two others (K4 and K7). It is only at K6, however, that the material is both abundant and well preserved. A study of the pottery suggests that the Kintampo culture in this area can be divided into two phases, but the distinguishing characteristics need not be considered here. Solid structures were being built at K6 during the second phase at least. Unluckily none were found in the excavated area, but large quantities of burnt daub had been dumped repeatedly in this part of the shelter in the later stages of the Kintampo culture occupation.

The evidence from K6 throws light on two main aspects of the economy; one is trade, the other subsistence.

The importance of trade is worth emphasizing. Except for grinding stones, which may have been made from local rock, all of the stone equipment must have been imported. Axe blades occur by the hundred, many being made of Birrimian rocks, the nearest outcrops of which are in the Banda Hills. Traffic in stone rasps and bracelets can also be inferred, though it is not possible yet to pinpoint the sources. I suspect that a small proportion of the pottery was traded as well. One surprising find was a shell of the brackish-water species *Tympanotonus fuscatus*, which must somehow have traveled northward from the coast, perhaps beginning its journey at one of the Kintampo culture sites in the Accra plains.

The evidence relating to subsistence is of more immediate interest. Animal bones were disappointingly few, but Carter has identified as many of them as possible and arrived at some valuable conclusions (Carter and Flight 1972). Domestic animals are certainly present — dwarf goats and a small breed of cattle as well. The remaining bones are mostly from various antelopes. These were presumably hunted, except perhaps for the tiny nocturnal species, the royal antelope (*Neotragus pygmaeus*), which would, I suppose, more probably have been caught in traps. Snail shells occur, though not in the same large quantities as in the Punpun-phase middens. For the recovery of carbonized vegetable remains we used the flotation technique described by Struever (1968). No detailed study of this material has yet been made, but cowpeas (*Vigna unguiculata*) and seed husks from the oil palm (*Elaeis guineensis*) are both easily identified and very common. Also recognized were a few seed husks from the tree *Canarium schweinfurthii*, which has edible fruit. *Celtis* husks, being largely composed of carbonate, come out in the heavy fraction. They are much less common than in the Punpun phase.

The question of possible cultivation hardly arises except in the case of *Vigna*. With regard to *Celtis, Canarium*, and (probably) *Elaeis*, it is to be presumed that the trees grew wild. There is no proof that the cowpeas were cultivated, but in view of their abundance I regard it as likely that they were. Whether they were domesticated in the sense of having pods which did not burst when ripe is unknown.[2]

Evidence for the cultivation of cereals is still only indirect and circumstantial. It might reasonably be argued, however, that indirect evidence carries greater weight in this environment than it would, say, in the southern Sahara. I would go so far as to suggest that it is pedantic, knowing what we do about the Kintampo culture, to insist on waiting for direct evidence. Of course I regret not being able to prove that cereals were grown; but it irks me more that I cannot say which cereals they were. If I were asked to guess, my first choice would be sorghum.

There is no direct evidence to show that yams were cultivated or even that they were used as food, likely though this would seem. It is a serious question, however, whether yams can be expected to survive at all in a recognizable form.

Clearly the evidence is not as complete as might be wished. In spite of that, I think we are justified in some conclusions which do not altogether fit the conventional picture of later African prehistory.

I am convinced by Munson's work in Mauritania (Munson, this volume) that environmental change is an important factor in the prehistory of the southern Sahara during the last few thousand years B.C. Farther south I see no reason to think that it had much effect. The evidence from K6 is roughly what we might expect of a village-farming site placed in a forest-savanna setting not greatly different from the modern environment. We can point to the royal antelope, for example, as proof of forest not far away; but the existence of more open vegetation, too, is implied by

[2]   A careless remark of mine to the effect that the cowpeas are small has been quoted by Calvocoressi (1970:72). This, though true, need not be significant: it may be simply due to shrinkage during carbonization.

the presence of other antelopes, as well as by the occurrence of oil palms and cowpeas. What attracted human settlement was, I suppose, precisely this ecological diversity. Forest and savanna do not merge; they become interspersed. Thus it seems to me that the evidence from Kintampo is consistent with the conclusion reached by Morgan and Moss (1965:293), who say, with reference to the forest-savanna mosaic, "Diversity is not the product of human intervention; it is an inherent property of the pattern."

It is also significant, I think, that this is an area where today both yams and cereals are grown. According to the conventional view of the origins of African agriculture, such a combination of crops would be regarded as a secondary development, resulting from an overlap between the two primary complexes — a vegecultural complex in the forest and a seed-agricultural complex in the savanna. Even if it were true, however, this would not be a sufficient explanation. It does not explain why people should choose to grow yams and cereals in combination: it suggests how the opportunity to do so might have arisen, but it does not explain why the opportunity should ever have been taken. The combination ought instead to be seen as an attempt to solve the problems posed by one specific environment — as a strategy which aims to achieve the maximum yield with the minimum risk.[3] This particular solution will only work where in most years there is neither too much rain for cereals nor too little for yams; and those limits coincide very nearly with the limits of the forest-savanna mosaic. It is within this zone, in Ghana and perhaps elsewhere, that the earliest village-farming settlements we know of are found. I am led to suggest that the yam-cereal combination may not be a secondary development at all, but the primary form of agriculture in sub-Saharan Africa. The K6 evidence is admittedly inconclusive, but it points in the right direction. Yams have not been recognized, but at least we have proof of the oil palm; cereals have not been identified, but at least we have found the cowpeas.

I doubt whether any close relationship exists between the Kintampo culture and the various aspects of "late Neolithic" in the southern Sahara. It would be easy to exaggerate the significance of the arrowheads from Ntereso. They are, as I have said, anomalous: they require some special explanation. Perhaps it is not coincidental that they occur only at one of the most northerly Kintampo culture sites.

In summary, then, I visualize the Kintampo culture spreading eastward along the edge of the forest as small groups of people moved on in search

[3] I originally referred at this point to an article by Gould (1963), believing it to be an empirical study (cf. Haggett 1965:173–174; Clarke 1968:492–496). Having read the article again, I realize that I was mistaken. Gould makes it quite clear that his example is imaginary, intended only to illustrate the application of game theory to a problem in geography. I apologize for adding to the confusion, but still think that my argument is valid.

of land. They bring with them their cattle and goats; they make clearings where they can build their villages and plant their crops; they hunt, they set traps, they gather snails and fruit from the forest; they trade with their neighbors. Mostly they settle in upland areas where patches of forest are juxtaposed with patches of savanna. Other groups move northward into more open country, which is less attractive on the whole but where by way of compensation they can fish in the rivers and collect shellfish during the dry season.

The Kintampo culture is already developed when it makes its appearance around Kintampo in 1400 B.C. or a little earlier. It had taken shape elsewhere, perhaps in the Banda Hills but I think more probably farther west, perhaps in Ivory Coast. In Ghana it seems to represent a rather brief episode, not lasting for more than a few hundred years at most. What happened afterward is obscure. Were it not for the evidence of a few sherds from K1, it could be thought that the area was entirely uninhabited during the first millennium B.C. Possibly the Kintampo culture survived in some form, but not in the rock shelters where we were looking for it.

This is a paper written mainly for archaeologists. I hope that they may find the information of value and the ideas of interest. Any botanist who has read this far, now that he sees the end approaching, will realize that there is little in it for him. Not much has been added to the stock of archaeobotanical evidence — evidence which is at the same time archaeological and botanical — relating to the history of crop cultivation in Africa. Shaw (1976) has drawn up a list of all the direct evidence available to us; the list is embarrassingly short. And yet, by looking for sites where preservation is good and by using the very efficient recovery techniques which have now been developed, the evidence we need should not be hard to come by.

REFERENCES

BISHOP, W. W., J. D. CLARK, *editors*
  1967 *Background to evolution in Africa.* Chicago: University of Chicago Press.
CALVOCORESSI, D.
  1970 Report on the Third Conference of West African Archaeologists. *West African Archaeological Newsletter* 12:53–90.
CARTER, P. L., C. FLIGHT
  1972 A report on the fauna from the sites of Ntereso and Kintampo rock shelter 6 in Ghana, with evidence for the practice of animal husbandry in the second millennium B.C. *Man* 7:277–282.
CLARK, J. D., *editor*
  1967 *Atlas of African prehistory.* Chicago: University of Chicago Press.
CLARKE, D. L.
  1968 *Analytical archaeology.* London: Methuen.

100   COLIN FLIGHT

DAVIS, O.
  1962 "Neolithic cultures of Ghana." *Actes du Quatrième Congrès Panafricain de Préhistoire*, volume three. Edited by G. Mortelmans and J. Nenquin, 291–301. Tervuren: Musée Royal de l'Afrique Centrale.
  1964 *The Quaternary in the coastlands of Guinea*. Glasgow: Jackson.
  1967 *West Africa before the Europeans*. London: Methuen.
  1969 On radiocarbon chronology of the Iron Age in sub-Saharan Africa. *Current Anthropology* 10:230.
FLIGHT, C.
  1968 Kintampo 1967. *West African Archaeological Newsletter* 8:15–20.
  1972 "The prehistoric sequence in the Kintampo area of Ghana." *Actes du sixième Congrès Panafricain de Préhistoire et de l'Etude du Quaternaire*. Edited by H. Hugot, 68–69. Chambéry: Imprimeries Réunies.
GOULD, P. R.
  1963 Man against his environment: a game theoretic framework. *Annals of the Association of American Geographers* 53:290–297.
HAGGETT, P.
  1965 *Locational analysis in human geography*. London: Arnold.
KITSON, A. E.
  1916 The Gold Coast: some considerations of its structure, people, and natural history. *Journal of the Royal Geographical Society* 48:369–392.
MATHEWSON, R. D.
  1967 "Chukoto," in *Archaeology in the Volta Basin, 1963–1966*. Edited by R. N. York, R. D. Mathewson, D. Calvocoressi, and C. Flight, 26–27. Legon: Volta Basin Research Project and Department of Archaeology.
MORGAN W. B., R. P. MOSS
  1965 Savanna and forest in western Nigeria. *Africa* 35:286–293.
NUNOO, R. B.
  1969 "Buruburo factory excavations." *Actes du Premier Colloque International d'Archéologie Africaine*. Edited by Y. Coppens, 321–333. Fort-Lamy: Institut National Tchadien pour les Sciences Humaines.
RAHTZ, P. A., C. FLIGHT
  1974 A quern factory near Kintampo, Ghana. *West African Journal of Archaeology* 4:1–31.
SHAW, T.
  1976 "Early crops in Africa: a review of the evidence," in *Origins of African plant domestication*. Edited by Jack R. Harlan, Jan M. J. de Wet, and Ann B. L. Stemler, 107–153. World Anthropology. The Hague: Mouton.
STRUEVER, S.
  1968 Flotation techniques for the recovery of small-scale archaeological remains. *American Antiquity* 33:353–362.
WILLETT, F.
  1971 A survey of recent results in the radiocarbon chronology of western and northern Africa. *Journal of African History* 12:339–370.

Archaeological Data on the Origins of Cultivation in the Southwestern Sahara and Their Implications for West Africa

PATRICK J. MUNSON

Since 1959 perhaps no single subject has more occupied the attention of West African cultural historians and ethnobotanists than the question of the origins of plant cultivation in this area. Most of this interest and controversy have resulted, directly or indirectly, from a hypothesis presented by Murdock (1959:64–70). In the total absence of relevant archaeological and paleobotanical data from this area, Murdock relied upon modern ethnographic, linguistic, and ethnobotanical material to construct an argument that some twenty-five food and fiber plants, including such seed crops as bulrush millet (*Pennisetum typhoideum*), sorghum (*Sorghum vulgare*), fonio (*Digitaria exilis*), and African rice (*Oryza glaberrima*), had been brought under domestication, independent of external influences, in the Sudanic zone around the headwaters of the Niger River and that this had occurred around 4500 B.C.

Chevalier (1938), some two decades previously and on the basis of plant geography, had presented a somewhat similar hypothesis. He argued that during a wetter period at an unspecified time in the past sorghum, bulrush millet, African rice, *Eleusine, Echinochloa, Panicum, Dactyloctenium*, cotton, the jujube (*Zizyphus* spp.), and possibly the date palm were all originally domesticated at the southern edge of the Sahara. Vignier (1945) presented a rather similar argument for the domestication of sorghum. Using plant geography, ethnographic data, and some indirect archaeological considerations, Portères (1950, 1951a) argued for the domestication of African rice in the central delta of the Niger prior to 1500 B.C.

It is the "Murdockian hypothesis," however, which has commanded the greatest attention, at least among Anglophone scholars; and although at least one ethnobotanist seems to have accepted Murdock's position almost in its entirety (Anderson 1967:175), the great majority of botanists and archaeologists have raised very serious objections (e.g., Wrigley 1960; Baker 1962; Clark 1962). These counterarguments, however, share one basic weakness with Murdock's position, as well as with the earlier and somewhat similar hypotheses put forward by the French plant geographers. They are all based primarily on modern botanical distributions and to a lesser extent on modern ethnographic material rather than on direct archaeological data, which until the last few years has been nonexistent, at least as directly relevant to this question and for this area.

During the winter months of 1966–1967 and 1967–1968, I carried out a program of archaeological research which had as one of its major objectives the testing of the hypothesis that there was an early, independent center of origin of seed-crop agriculture in the general West African Sudanic-Sahelian zone. Several significant alterations were made, however, in the hypothesis as presented by Murdock. The first alteration took into account the fact that archaeological research in the Near East and in Mexico had adequately demonstrated that seed-crop agriculture emerged not around the relatively lush oases and river valleys, but rather in marginal areas which were steppe or semi-desert in climate; only subsequently did agriculture move into the oasis-valley areas. The headwaters of the Niger, being near the southern and wetter margin of the Sudanic zone, would not compare environmentally with known seed-crop hearths. Second, there has been increasing evidence that from ca. 5500–5000 B.C. to ca. 2500–2000 B.C., during the so-called Neolithic Wet Period, the Sahara enjoyed significantly more precipitation than it does at present; and if comparable changes in annual rainfall had occurred in areas farther south, the Niger headwaters region during this period may well have been rainforest.

Accordingly, the modified hypothesis to be tested was that if seed-crop cultivation did emerge at a relatively early date in the general West African area, this occurrence would have been in the steppe (or Sahelian) zone; and if it had occurred early enough to qualify as an independent hearth, its emergence would have coincided with a period of increased rainfall which would have pushed the Sahelian zone northward into areas that are now Saharan, or near-Saharan, in climate.

The region chosen to test this hypothesis was the Dhar Tichitt region of south-central Mauritania, a region which today has a mean annual rainfall of about 100 millimeters and thus straddles the boundary between Sahara and Sahel as defined. This area had several qualifications for this kind of program. Numerous dry lake beds which occur in this region showed evidence of existing as freshwater lakes in the not too distant past, and their existence would have considerably modified the overall environment. The area is also at or near the northern boundary of distribution of a number of wild grasses that are related to several of the African cultigens, namely *Pennisetum, Digitaria, Sorghum*, and *Echinochloa*, thus perhaps qualifying as a "nuclear zone" as defined by Braidwood (1963:106). Several brief archaeological surveys in this region (e.g., Mauny 1950) had recorded the existence of large, well-preserved, stone-masonry "Neolithic" villages in this area, thus suggesting a relatively high level of cultural achievement here in the past presumably based upon effective food production. And finally, pottery collected from the surfaces of some of these sites and stored at the Institut Fondamental d'Afrique Noire was found to bear numerous and clear grain and chaff impressions.

THE ARCHAEOLOGICAL SEQUENCE OF DHAR TICHITT

The Later Stone Age occupation that was discovered and investigated in this area can be conveniently divided into a sequence of eight phases. The earliest sites, from the Akreijit phase, are not numerous. They are small, thin, and nonarchitectural and are located just behind the highest of the three beach ridges of the now extinct freshwater lakes. Associated artifacts include ground stone axes and gouges, chipped stone geometric microliths (none of which show evidence of use as sickle blades), projectile points, scrapers, a few small milling stones, and pottery decorated with stamped and incised patterns similar to ceramics found over a considerable portion of the western Sahara. Rock art of the so-called Ethiopian megafauna style, heavily emphasizing giraffes and other

Table 1.　Date subsistence, and environment of the Tichitt phases

Date B.C.	Phase	Subsistence	Environment
400–700	Akjinjei	Herding cultivation limited collecting and hunting	Invasion of desertic species, rainfall less than x1.5
700–900	Arriane		Lakes gone, decreasing rainfall
900–1000	Chebka	Herding, cultivation, collecting, limited hunting	
1000–1100	Naghez	Herding, collecting, limited hunting and fishing, incipient cultivation?	Shrinking lakes, decreasing rainfall
1100–1200	Nkhal		
1200–1400	Goungou	Herding, fishing, limited collecting and hunting	Large lakes, rainfall greater than x1.75
1400–1500	Khimiya		
Hiatus			Very dry
2000?	Akreijit	Hunting, fishing, limited collecting	Large lakes, rainfall greater than x2.0

Sahelian-Sudanic wild animals, is apparently associated. Unfortunately, no sites with subsurface deposits could be found. No bone was preserved on the sites, nor did the pottery bear recognizable grain impressions. The consequence is that we have little "hard" data on the subsistence pattern of the peoples of this phase. The total emphasis on wild animals in the apparently associated rock art and the high incidence of projectile points on the sites, however, suggest some considerable emphasis on hunting. Furthermore, the sites' locations, immediately adjacent to the lakes, suggest at least some utilization of aquatic resources probably including fish; and the presence of the small milling stones, albeit in limited numbers, argues for at least some utilization of hard seeds. The absence of depictions of domesticated animals in the rock art and the scarcity of milling stones, on the other hand, argues against the presence of food production. A single radiocarbon determination on aquatic shells collected from near the surface of the beach which was apparently contemporary with this phase yielded the surprisingly late date of 1750 B.C. ± 130 (GX-1890). Although this date is earlier than the determinations for the following phase, it must still be viewed with suspicion, since comparable data, both archaeological and environmental, from elsewhere in the western Sahara would suggest a date at least several hundred years earlier.

Following the Akreijit phase, there is a hiatus in the cultural chronology which coincides with a period of extreme dryness — perhaps as dry as today or even drier. The lakes at this time shrank drastically, possibly almost drying up completely; and the human population of the area either followed the receding shorelines of the lakes (and their sites, if they exist, have been buried by the silts of a subsequent rise in lake levels) or the people migrated southward into more hospitable regions. There is some slight archaeological support for this latter possibility in the form of artifactual similarities from sites near Nioro, just south of the Mauritania-Mali border (Vaufrey 1947) and from the rock shelter of Kourounkorokalé near Bamako, Mali (Szumowski 1956).

As dated by several satisfactory radiocarbon determinations, another period of increased rainfall commenced about 1500 B.C. or slightly earlier, and the lake basins again partially refilled. The area was then reoccupied by peoples who, on artifactual grounds, seem to have been the descendants of the earlier Akreijit phase or a culturally closely related group. This second phase, the Khimiya and the two following phases, Goungou and Nkhal, represent a cultural continuum which, dated by six radiocarbon determinations, spans the period from just before 1500 B.C. to about 1100 B.C. Each of these phases can readily be separated from the others on the basis of changing artifactual styles. Also, site locations vary with time: sites of the Khimiya phase are located on low dunes immediately behind the beach of the middle of the three lake stages,

Goungou-phase sites are located directly on the middle beach, and Nkhal-phase sites are situated directly on the lowest of the three beaches. Despite these differences, however, subsistence patterns, for which considerable data exist for interpretation, are essentially identical.

Domesticated cattle and goats, as evidenced by numerous bones and as identified by Turnbull (1971), are presented in numbers from the beginning; their appearance and adoption in the general region obviously occurred during the hiatus between the Akreijit and Khimiya phases (i.e., some time prior to 1500 B.C. but probably not earlier than about 2000 B.C.). The numerous fish bones on and in the sites indicate that fishing was an important activity. Hunting also played some role, but since bones of wild animals occur in a much lower percentage than do bones of domesticated animals, it appears that this was a relatively minor part of the subsistence pattern. Of greatest importance for purposes of the problem at hand, however, are the relatively abundant recovered plant remains, in the form of both mineralized hackberry seeds (*Celtis integrifolia*) and identifiable impressions of grains and chaff upon the pottery (Jacques-Félix 1971).

A total of sixty-seven identifiable impressions were found on the ceramics recovered from sites of these phases. Of these, sixty-six (99 percent) are seed coverings of the grass "kram-kram" (*Cenchrus biflorus*), a species which, because of the burry nature of the seed head, has probably never been considered a candidate for cultivation. Where it occurs in the wild state today, however, it is widely collected, particularly as a famine food (e.g., Chapelle 1957: 192; Dalziel 1937: 522). The remaining impression (1 percent) is of the genus *Pennisetum*, which is of particular interest since this is the same genus as the modern cultigen bulrush millet. Unfortunately, however, it has not been possible to determine if this impression represents a wild or a domesticated form. There are, however, a number of reasons for arguing that the peoples of these phases were not cultivators: the very low percentage of even potential cultigens, the fact that wild species of *Pennisetum* exist even today just south of the Tichitt region, the limited occurrence and small size of associated milling stones, and the paucity (relative to subsequent phases) of grain impressions.

The following Naghez phase, dated by three radiocarbon determinations to about 1100 to 1000 B.C., clearly derived from the preceding Nkhal phase. It does, however, represent a point of inflection from preceding patterns in at least several respects. Villages, like the villages of the ancestral Nkhal phase, are still located on or just behind the lowest of the three beaches, but the sites for the first time are of stone-masonry construction. Furthermore, and rather surprisingly, they are quite large; the site of Glaib Tijat is 500 meters square, and the site of Naghez is approximately 1,200 meters long by 300 meters wide.

Although the sites of this phase are still located adjacent to the lake basins, all indications are that the lakes had almost dried up again by this time. Consequently, the fish potential was much reduced, and emphasis on fishing was much more limited than in preceding phases. Apparently as a substitute for this diminishing resource, the peoples turned to a heavier emphasis on plant foods, as indicated by the greatly increased numbers of milling stones (which are also quite large at this time and which take a variety of shapes), by the increased numbers of associated small collecting stations, by the increased numbers of grain impressions on the pottery, and by the greater variety of species represented by these impressions. Herding of cattle and goats continued in its apparently rather significant role, and limited hunting continued to be practiced.

A few hackberry seeds were recovered, which certainly represent collecting, and of the thirty-two identifiable grain and chaff impressions found on the pottery twenty-four (75 percent) are of the wild *Cenchrus biflorus*. *Panicum laetum*, another wild seed plant widely collected today as a food source, makes its appearance in limited numbers (9 percent), as does *Brachiaria deflexa* (12 percent), and *Pennisetum* sp. increases slightly (3 percent). Here again it has not been possible to determine if the *Pennisetum* represents a wild or cultivated variety; but in view of the increased attention the peoples of this phase were giving to plant foods, the possibility of cultivation of this species, albeit only to a very limited degree, would seem to be enhanced. Furthermore, the *Brachiaria deflexa* might be of some interest in this regard; although seeds of this plant are today fairly commonly collected in the wild state and despite the fact that the Naghez phase specimens seem in no way different from modern wild varieties, there is, nevertheless one contemporary record for the cultivation of this species in West Africa (Portères 1951b). Whatever the status of *Pennisetum* and *Brachiaria deflexa* (as wild or domesticated) in this phase, the much higher incidence of the definitely wild *Cenchrus biflorus*, plus *Panicum laetum* and *Celtis*, both also wild, indicates that most plant foods were still derived from collecting.

The following Chebka phase, dated by two radiocarbon determinations to the period from about 1000 B.C. to 900 B.C., represents still another point of inflection because *Pennisetum*, much of it now showing definite characteristics of a domesticated variety, "jumps" to a position of 61 percent of the 121 identifiable grain impressions for this phase. This happens despite the fact (or perhaps *because* of the fact) that all indications are that the climate of the region was becoming even drier. Some collecting continued to be practiced and apparently still played a rather significant role, since *Cenchrus biflorus* occurs as 34 percent of the total. However, it is the *Pennisetum*, much or all of it cultivated, which formed the bulk of the plant food. Also noteworthy is the fact that *Brachiaria deflexa* persists (although in a much reduced percentage), and one

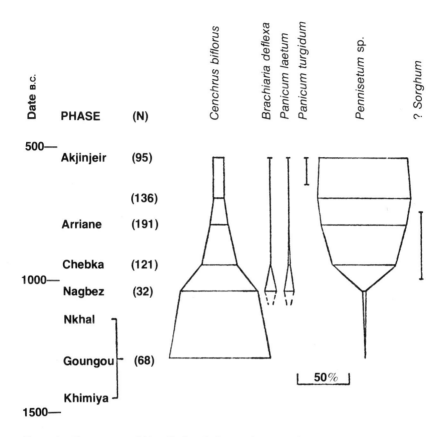

Figure 1.   Percentages of identified grain impressions per phase

impression was found which might be sorghum. Herding also continued to play an important role, and limited hunting was still practiced.

Villages of the Chebka phase, although similar in construction, plan, and size to the villages of the preceding Naghez phase, differ in that they are about four times more numerous (reflecting, one might suspect, an increase in population resulting from the increased potential from an almost fully food-producing subsistence pattern). Sites are also no longer placed immediately adjacent to the lake basins, but rather are placed along the lip of the sheer, 100-meter-high escarpment which transects this region. Movement away from the margins of the lake basins is explained by the fact that the lakes had ceased to exist as permanent features by this time. The placement of the villages at the top of the escarpment, however, is best explained in terms of defense, an explanation much strengthened by the presence of many clearly defensive structures associated with these villages; each village is entirely encircled by a high, thick masonry wall, and each approach to the village is lined with masonry "archer's redoubts." All indications are, however, that the warfare that was occurring was of an internal nature, probably village against village and very possibly representing conflict over the limited arable land which exists in this region.

The subject of arable land leads us, at this time, to a consideration of how cultivation was practiced in this area. Today, with mean annual rainfall only about 100 millimeters and surface deposits consisting of little more than sand and rock, cultivation is, at best, extremely marginal and is limited to a few hand-watered gardens. From studies based on the wild plant and animal remains associated with the Chebka phase, it can be inferred, however, that mean annual rainfall at that time was probably somewhere between 150 and 175 millimeters. Today in the vicinity of Tidjikja, some 200 kilometers to the west of Tichitt, where annual rainfall averages about 155 millimeters, fairly intensive cultivation is practiced utilizing the *décrue* system, a system whereby a low dam is placed across a shallow wadi and, after a pool collects during the brief rainy season, crops are planted in the moist soil at the margins (Toupet 1958:87). It seems unlikely, however, that an identical practice was employed prehistorically in the Tichitt area, since there is no evidence of the necessary dams. But a variation of the *décrue* system is also found today in the central valley of the Niger. Here, natural basins in the floodplain are filled yearly by the flooding of the river, and as the trapped water evaporates, crops are planted in the moist, newly exposed silt deposits (Drouhin 1944; Harlan and Pasquereau 1969). The internally drained lake basins in the Tichitt area would have filled in a comparable manner during the rainy season, particularly if rainfall was greater than today; and because the lake beds had only recently been exposed after centuries of existence as lake bottoms, it seems likely that they would have been blanketed with deep, rich silt deposits.

Returning to the archaeological sequence, the Arriane phase, which derived from the Chebka phase, can be dated by extrapolation from radiocarbon determinations for preceding and following phases to about 900 to 700 B.C. The evidences of warfare which were so common in the preceding phase are now gone, indicating that the sources of conflict had somehow been resolved. Villages are somewhat smaller but are much more numerous, reflecting still greater increases in population. Evidence of cultivation involving *Pennisetum* and possibly very limited amounts of sorghum (and perhaps also *Brachiaria deflexa*) are even more numerous; of the 141 identifiable impressions found on the pottery recovered from sites of this phase 82 percent are *Pennisetum*. Herding also continued in its important role, and collecting of wild plant foods and hunting were still practiced to limited extents.

The terminal Neolithic phase of this region, Akjinjeir, is dated by two radiocarbon determinations to the period from about 700 B.C. to 400 B.C.

With a sample of 231 identifiable impressions from the associated pottery, *Pennisetum* climbs still further to about 90 percent, despite the fact
that the peoples of this phase were experiencing considerable stress from
two quarters. For the first time since the end of the Akreijit phase, we find
evidence of true Saharan species (addax, jerboa, *Panicum turgidum*)
indicating that mean annual rainfall had probably dropped below 150
millimeters. And there is considerable archaeological evidence that the
area at this time was invaded by very mobile, horse-riding Libyco-
Berbers from North Africa who were equipped with metal weapons.
Under the combined weight of these two pressures the presence of
Neolithic cultivators in this region came to an end about 400 B.C.

THE ORIGIN OF CULTIVATION IN THE TICHITT AREA

For our purposes here the major concern is with the middle portion of the
Tichitt sequence, from the Nkhal phase, dating just prior to 1100 B.C.
(with no evidence of cultivation and only limited collecting of wild seeds),
to the Naghez phase, dating from ca. 1100 B.C. to 1000 B.C. (with intensive
seed collecting and possibly some incipient seed cultivation), and to the
Chebka phase, dating ca. 1000 B.C. to 900 B.C. (with abundant evidence of
rather intensive cultivation of *Pennisetum*). The question now is what the
source of this complex was: (1) Was it basically an *in situ* development,
perhaps without benefit of external stimulation? (2) Was it the result of
diffusion of the idea and the species of cultivation from a still earlier (and
possibly independent) agricultural hearth to the south of the Tichitt
region? (3) Was it the result of diffusion of ideas and crops westward
across the Sudanic zone from an earlier hearth or center of dispersal in
the general Ethiopian area? (4) Or was it the result of diffusion of the idea
and perhaps the domesticated plants from earlier agricultural groups
dwelling to the north or northeast?

Independent, In-place Development?

If one disregards the absolute chronology for the Tichitt sequence, it
would appear to represent a "classic" pattern of agricultural emergence,
the peoples progressively changing from a limited collecting system utilizing only a small range of wild species to intensive collecting and experimentation with a large number of wild species and finally to the selection
of one or perhaps several of the more promising of these species to be
brought under full domestication, with all of these events occurring
during a period of demonstrated environmental deterioration. The problems in this picture emerge, however, when one places this sequence of

events within a dated chronology. First, the date of ca. 1100 to 1000 B.C. for the initial appearance of cultivation makes it extremely difficult to argue that this was an invention totally independent of external influences, since cultivation was present at least 3,500 years earlier in northeastern Africa. Furthermore, domesticated cattle and goats had appeared in the Tichitt area at least 500 years prior to the first evidence of cultivation, and these species were unquestionably domesticated initially in the Near East. Second, in the two independent seed-crop hearths of the world which have been adequately investigated, the Near East and Mexico, the cultural transition from collecting through incipient cultivation to intensive cultivation, plus the botanical transmission from a totally wild species to a fully domesticated form, is measured in millennia, whereas in the Tichitt sequence this transition seems to have occurred in only a little over one century. Perhaps the Near Eastern and Mexican situations do not represent a universal pattern; and some of my botanist colleagues inform me that a morphological transition such as that seen in the prehistoric Tichitt *Pennisetum* might very possibly have occurred in a hundred years (a century, after all, does represent a hundred generations for an annual). Nevertheless, one might legitimately feel uncomfortable in arguing for this sequence to represent an independent development.

Diffusion From an Earlier Hearth to the South?

Those who are enamored, wholly or in part, of Murdock's hypothesis of an early center of origin of seed-crop agriculture in the West African savanna zone will perhaps be tempted to see the Tichitt seed-crop complex as a deriving from earlier developments to the south. Since 1959, a few scattered pieces of archaeological data have accumulated for West Africa which bear directly on this problem. The earliest, but by no means conclusive, hint of cereal cultivation comes from Iwo Eleru rock shelter in southwestern Nigeria, where microlithic trapezoids with silica gloss (indicating their use as sickle blades) were recovered in levels dating only shortly after 3000 B.C. (Daniels 1969:27). Unfortunately, however, sickle blades, like milling stones, digging-stick weights, and hoes, although sometimes associated with cultivation, are not confined to use as agricultural implements.

The next two earliest suggestions of cultivation in this area both come from Ghana. Davies (1968:481) has found "what are almost certainly impressions of *Pennisetum* cobs" on shards from the northern Ghana site of Ntereso, and this site has three radiocarbon determinations ranging from 1240 B.C. ± 120 to 1630 B.C. ± 130. Assuming that these impressions do represent *Pennisetum* and that it is a domesticated variety, this would then precede the Tichitt material. However, in previous articles we find not only that the radiocarbon determinations are contrary to the stratigraphy of the site, but also that there was iron in some of the levels (Davies 1967a: 116; 1967b: 238–239) which, if it is not intrusive, would suggest a date of ca. 500 B.C. at the earliest. Equally nebulous, but for different reasons, is material from the Kintampo rock shelter in central Ghana, where Flight (1970) recovered carbonized remains of oil palm (*Elaeis guineensis*) and cowpeas (*Vigna* sp.) in levels dating after 1400 B.C. but prior to the introduction of iron. Both of these species are domesticated today, but it has not been possible to determine if the early Kintampo materials represent cultigens.

The earliest definite evidence of plant cultivation in West Africa, excluding the Tichitt material, comes from the site of Daima in north-eastern Nigeria and is surprisingly late. Here, in levels radiocarbon-dated to about A.D. 500, "actual carbonized grains [of sorghum] were discovered" (Connah 1969:34). Lower levels of this site (which extend back to ca. 500 B.C.) produced no evidence of cultivation. If the archaeological absence of cultigens in these lower levels is "real" and not simply the result of preservation factors and/or recovery techniques, and if the lower levels of the site do not result from specialized and/or seasonal occupations, then the absence of cultigens in this area until a very late period would seem highly significant.

In view of the relative paucity of archaeological research directed toward recovery of data bearing upon Later Stone Age subsistence patterns in West Africa, however, the negative evidence for early cultivation is far from conclusive. But, given the absence of evidence for cultivation prior to ca. 1100 to 1000 B.C. in the relatively well-investigated Dhar Tichitt sites, and given the validity of my initial postulate that seed-crop cultivation would appear earlier in areas environmentally marginal to West Africa, I do not now find it all surprising that cultivation in West Africa proper does not seem to have begun much earlier than about 1000 B.C.

The reasons for this position involve in large part the consideration of *why* peoples become food producers in any case, and, even more specifically, why the first steps in this direction were more likely to occur in environmentally marginal areas. The most convincing explanation has recently been presented by Binford (1968), who has modified certain aspects of Childe's propinquity theory (1951:23–25) and incorporated White's (1959:284) concept of equilibrium systems. The argument (Binford 1968:327) is that in areas with large resources of wild foods, peoples at a hunting-and-gathering level of subsistence would establish an equilibrium system with their resources:

If we recognize that an equilibrium system can be established so that populations are homostatically regulated below the carrying capacity of the local food supply, it follows that there is no necessary adaptive pressure continually favoring means of increasing the food supply.

Therefore, in seeking the origins of food production (or any other change in subsistence), "we are forced to look for those conditions which might bring about disequilibrium and bring about selective advantage for increased productivity" (p. 328). Binford goes on to suggest two ways in which disequilibrium might have occurred: (1) a change in the physical environment which reduced the available food resources or (2) an increase in population density which strained the carrying capacity (p. 332):

... it is in the context of such situations of stress in environments ... that we would expect to find conditions favoring the development of plant and animal domestication. Such situations would be characterized by disequilibrium between population and resources which, in turn, would offer selective advantage to increases in the efficacy of subsistence technology.

In neither the Tichitt area nor West Africa in general do we have evidence of increased population densities preceding the establishment of food production. But, at least in the Tichitt area, there were two well-documented episodes of environmental deterioration. Prior to the first of these, during the high-lake-level period, the peoples of the Akrei-jit phase had apparently established an equilibrium at a hunting-fishing-limited-collecting level of subsistence. It was only during the period following, beginning around (?) 2000 B.C. with a reduction in rainfall and the resultant near-disappearance of the Tichitt lakes, that a new element of subsistence was added: the people adopted herding of cattle and goats (probably via pastoral peoples who had been forced out of the central Sahara by the same environmental factors). With a return to moister conditions around 1500 B.C. a new equilibrium was established, now based on herding, fishing, limited collecting, and limited hunting, and the population stabilized at a higher density. By about 1100 B.C., however, the lakes began drying up once again, thus reducing (and eventually eliminating) the fish potential. Hence a new disequilibrium resulted, and if the people were to maintain themselves at the same density in this area, a new food source had to be substituted for the fish. The solution was the adoption of cultivation of seed plants.

The relevance here to cultivation farther south in the West African savanna is twofold. If cultivation had been present in West Africa during the earlier of these two periods of environmental stress, why did the peoples of the Tichitt region not adopt it at that time? They did adopt herding, and there is evidence of contacts with the more southern regions. Second, and more important, if the above model is a valid explanation for changes in subsistence patterns, what would have been the motivation for peoples to the south to have changed earlier? It would have been in the environmentally marginal areas, such as southwestern Mauritania, that stress would have appeared earliest and with the greatest intensity. In short, I would argue that the source of seed-crop cultivation in the Sudanic zone of West Africa was from cultivators (or at least the idea of cultivation) expanding into that area from the drier, more sensitive margins.

Was It Diffusion from an Earlier Hearth in Ethiopia?

This possibility would seem to be considerably stronger than either of the other two just considered. Numerous botanists have argued for many years that Ethiopia was a major center of origin and/or dispersal for many African seed crops, including finger millet (*Eleusine coracana*), teff (*Eragrostis abyssinica*), sorghum, and bulrush millet (Snowden 1936; Vavilov 1949–1950; Wrigley 1960; Portères 1962; Doggett 1965; Simoons 1965). Furthermore, at least some antiquity for seed-crop cultivation can be demonstrated for this region. There is fairly good historical evidence for the cultivation of teff, and probably millet, sorghum, wheat, and barley, in the northern Ethiopian highlands prior to 1000 B.C. (Simoons 1965:9), and both archaeological and linguistic evidence from India suggests that finger millet, sorghum, and possibly bulrush millet had spread to that area, presumably from Ethiopia, prior to 1500 B.C. (Allchin 1969:325; Doggett 1965:61–62; Portères 1962:204). Furthermore, Portères (1962:205) and Wrigley (1960:193), on the basis of Egyptian archaeology and cotton genetics respectively, have argued for the presence of cultivation in this area prior to 3000 B.C.

Assuming a fair antiquity for seed-crop cultivation in Ethiopia (the question of its origin in this area is essentially irrelevant in regard to West Africa), the next question is, did it spread across what someone has called "the easiest of all corridors," the savanna zone bordering the southern edge of the Sahara, and if so, when? It would seem entirely possible that it did spread by this route, moving relatively slowly and taking perhaps 2,000 years to complete its "journey" to the western margins. However, the only piece of archaeological evidence that might be brought to bear upon this hypothesis does not lend support; the site of Daima, located near the Sudanic-Sahelian boundary in northeastern Nigeria and about equidistant between Ethiopia and Tichitt, produced evidence of cultivation only in levels dated some 1,500 years later than its appearance on the western margins. A single excavated site, of course, can hardly be considered conclusive; but still there is another possibility for the source of the prehistoric Tichitt cultigens, and it is one for which there is (at least yet) no detracting evidence.

Was the Tichitt Cultigen Complex Diffused from the North or Northeast?

Direct archaeological evidence for cultivation in the Sahara proper is, at best, only slightly better than that for sub-Saharan Africa, but such evidence as exists suggests an initial date for cultivation much earlier than anywhere to the south (with the possible exception of Ethiopia). Perhaps indirectly relevant as well, however, is the presence of Near Eastern plant domesticates in Egypt by about 4500 B.C. and the presence of Near Eastern domesticated animals in the northeastern quarter of the Sahara perhaps as early as (or earlier than) 5000 B.C.

The earliest evidence for cultivation in the Sahara comes from the site of Amekni in the Ahaggar (Hoggar), near the center of the Sahara, where Camps (1969:186–188) recovered two pollen grains which, because of their size and shape, seem to represent a domesticated variety of *Pennisetum*. The zone from which these pollen grains were recovered is bracketed by radiocarbon determinations from about 6100 B.C. to 4850 B.C. Somewhat comparable although later evidence comes from the site of Méniet, also in the Ahaggar, from which Pons and Quézel (1957:27, 35) identified two pollen grains which appear to represent a cultivated cereal, and this site has been radiocarbon-dated to about 3500 B.C. Hugot (1968:485) not only accepts the Méniet pollen as indicative of cultivation in this area at this date, but also goes on to suggest that it represents the cultivation of wheat.

Additional but much less conclusive evidence for seed-crop cultivation in this area comes from the rock shelter of Sefar — located in the Tassili and radiocarbon-dated about 3100 B.C. — where paintings seem to depict cultivation (Lhote 1959:118), and from some linguistic evidence which suggests a considerable antiquity for the cultivation of sorghum in the central Sahara (Camps 1960:79).

Assuming that seed-crop cultivation was being practiced, at least to some extent, in the central Sahara prior to 3000 B.C., two other questions arise which have some relevance to the origins of cultivation in the Tichitt area and areas farther south in West Africa: one question regards both the intensity and extent of cultivation in this region, the other the origin of both the idea and the crops.

Today, in the higher plateaus and mountainous regions of the Sahara, as well as around the scattered oases, a fairly wide range of seed crops is cultivated, including bulrush millet, sorghum, wheat, and barley (Nicolaisen 1963: 184; Gast and Adrian 1965). The intensity of cultivation today, however, is often not great; the Tuareg of Aïr and Tassili n'Ajjer, for example, simply sow seeds upon the moist beds of wadis following the rainy season and then leave the area until harvesting time (Nicolaisen 1963:184). The important aspect for our concern, however, is not the intensity, but rather the simple presence, of cultivation in this area today. If it can be practiced here in modern climates it could also have been possible at any period in the past where rainfall was as high as today, and in periods of increased rainfall it would have been easier and could have been more widespread.

The other question regards the origin of this central Saharan crop complex. The majority opinion, and the one perhaps easiest to defend, is that it represents stimulus diffusion from the Near East via Egypt. Near Eastern domesticated crops were demonstrably present in Egypt by 4500 B.C., and Near Eastern domesticated animals were introduced into the central Sahara at a very early date, perhaps prior to 5000 B.C. Thus the "lines of communication" were present. Furthermore, with only slightly wetter conditions (which certainly existed in the central Sahara between 5000 B.C. and 3000 B.C.), it seems likely that wild *Pennisetum*, as well as perhaps wild *Sorghum*, would have been present at least in the higher, better-watered regions of the central Sahara. Therefore, the peoples of this region, possessing knowledge of cultivation but confronted with the difficulty of growing the winter-rainfall-adapted Near Eastern crops in this summer-rainfall zone, began experimenting with such wild, summer-rainfall-adapted local species as *Pennisetum*.

Neat as this picture is, however, there is still another hypothesis for the origin of Saharan cultivation which at least deserves serious consideration. In the vicinity of the Dungal and Dineigil oases in southwestern Egypt, Hobler and Hester (1969) have discovered a preceramic complex with numerous milling stones and sickle blades, and this complex dates at least as early as 6000 B.C. and may extend back as early as 8300 B.C. The associated artifacts, plus the fact that this complex is restricted to the vicinity of now-dry silt basins, argue that these peoples were at least intensive seed collectors and possibly that they were incipient seed-crop cultivators. This position is considerably strengthened by the results of recent research in the Nubian region of the Nile, only a few hundred kilometers to the south, in a context dating perhaps as early as 13,000 B.C., which has revealed the existence of a complex with numerous sickle blades and milling stones, plus associated spores of smut and fungi which today are most commonly associated with wheat (Wendorf 1968:935–946). Probably no one would argue that this early Nubian complex represents cultivation, even incipient cultivation. However, it clearly represents a heavy orientation toward wild seeds as a source of food, which can be considered a prerequisite to actual cultivation, and this complex predates by at least 3,000 years evidence for comparable activities in the Near East.

In viewing this evidence, Hobler and Hester (1969) and Hester (1968) have suggested that incipient cultivation, including perhaps wheat, sorghum, and millet, may have been present in this Nubia-southwestern Egypt region as early as (or earlier than) 6000 B.C. and then go on to suggest a route of dispersal of this complex to other areas of the Sahara. The plateaus and mountains of Darfur, Ennedi, Tibesti, Tassili, Ahaggar, Aïr, and Adrar des Iforas form a broad arc from the southeastern Sahara to the central Sahara and then down to the southwestern Sahara. Gebel Oweinat and Gilf Kebir in extreme southwestern Egypt represent a northeastward extension of the highlands. Today, these higher areas receive considerably greater precipitation than do other portions of the Sahara, and most present cultivation of the Sahara is confined to these regions. Hester and Hobler then argue that developments in cultivation which arose in the Dungal-Dineigil-Nubian region jumped the few hundred kilometers which separate these areas from Gebel Oweinat and Gilf Kebir and from there spread through this highland "Saharan Fertile Crescent."

Whether the crops of the Sahara were domesticated independently in the eastern Sahara or as a result of stimulus diffusion from the northeast, the most relevant aspect in regard to West Africa is that the tip of the southwestern horn of this "fertile crescent" is Adrar des Iforas. The great bend of the Niger is only a few hundred kilometers to the southwest of Adrar des Iforas and connected to it by the valley of the Tilemsi. The Niger bend, in turn, lies only 500 kilometers east-southeast of the southeastern edge of Dhar Tichitt-Oualata. Consequently, any pressure in the central Sahara, either in terms of environmental deterioration or population density, could well have forced cultivators in that region southwestward into Adrar des Iforas and beyond into the central Niger region; and from that area there would be no major geographical problem for ideas and plants to be transmitted to the Tichitt region.

In this regard, it would be extremely interesting to have some data on the subsistence patterns of the peoples at sites such as Karkarichinkat-Sud (Mauny 1952), located in Adrar des Iforas and recently radio-carbon-dated to 1360 B.C. ± 110 (Fagan 1969: 150), or of late prehistoric groups in the vicinity of Timbuktu. My guess is that as one moves eastward from Tichitt to Timbuktu, and then northeastward from Timbuktu, the earliest date for the occurrence of seed-crop cultivation (particularly *Pennisetum*) will become progressively earlier, and conversely, as one moves south and southwestward form Timbuktu (or southward from Tichitt) the date of initial occurrence will become progressively later.

SUMMARY

Archaeological research in the Dhar Tichitt region of south-central Mauritania has revealed the existence of an eight-phase Later Stone Age sequence. Subsistence data from this well-dated sequence not only shed considerable light on the question of late prehistoric food production in this specific vicinity, but also serve as the basis for testing previous hypotheses and presenting new ones dealing with the origins of seed-crop cultivation in the general West African Sahelian-Sudanic zone.

The late prehistoric sequence in the Dhar Tichitt region begins with the Akreijit phase, coinciding with a substantially wetter period with extensive lakes and probably dating prior to 2000 B.C. Subsistence data for this phase are limited but suggest an orientation toward hunting, fishing, and limited plant collection and a total absence of food production. Following a sizable hiatus in the cultural sequence, which coincides with a very dry episode, the sequence resumes about 1500 B.C. with the Khimiya phase, sites of which are located around the refilled lake basins. The abundant data for this phase suggest a subsistence pattern based upon extensive herding (cattle and goats) and fishing combined with limited hunting and seed collecting (with almost total collecting emphasis on the wild grass *Cenchrus biflorus*). The following Goungou and Nkhal phases show a continuation of this pattern, but by about 1100 B.C. the lakes once more began to dry up, reducing and eventually eliminating the fish potential. In apparent response to this environmental stress, the peoples at this time (the Naghez phase) turned to intensive collecting of a wide range of wild seeds including *Cenchrus biflorus, Panicum laetum, Brachiaria deflexa,* and *Pennisetum* sp. There is at least a possibility that some limited cultivation of *Pennisetum*, as well as possibly *Brachiaria deflexa*, was beginning to be practiced at this time, but as yet this cannot be demonstrated with certainty. In the following Chebka phase, however, beginning by or only shortly after 1000 B.C., *Pennisetum* increases to over 60 percent of the recovered and identifiable food-plant remains, and much of this shows definite characteristics of a domesticated variety. One grain impression very tentatively identified as *Sorghum* was also found associated with this phase, and *Brachiaria deflexa* continued to be present. The following Arriane phase reflects an intensification of this agricultural pattern, as does the still later, terminal Neolithic Akjinjeir phase, which came to an end, at least in this specific region, about 400 B.C. under combined pressures from desiccation and an invasion of horse-mounted raiders from North Africa.

In view of the lateness of appearance of cultivation in this area (ca. 1000 B.C.) and since the cultural transition from limited seed collecting to intensive seed-crop cultivation encompassed little more than a century, the hypothesis that this represents an independent, *in situ* development of plant domestication can probably be rejected. Furthermore, if our model explaining why food production was developed or adopted is valid, the hypothesis that there was an earlier agricultural hearth to the south in the savanna zone of West Africa can also be rejected. This position is strengthened by the absence of archaeological evidence for cultivation in that area at a period earlier than its appearance in the Tichitt area.

The possibility of Ethiopia's being an early center of domestication and of the dispersal of cultivated plants from that area ultimately to the Tichitt-West Africa region is also examined. Although this hypothesis suffers no serious flaws in terms of available evidence, there is, nevertheless, still another model which seems more satisfactory. There is some evidence for seed-crop cultivation, including *Pennisetum*, in the highlands of the central Sahara prior to 3000 B.C. Its ultimate origins are probably very early, possibly independent seed-crop domestication in the eastern Sahara or stimulus diffusion from earlier developments in the Near East via Egypt. Pressure in the central Sahara, from population increases resulting from this increased food base and/or environmental deterioration, might well have pushed some of these cultivators southwestward into such southern Saharan highland areas as Aïr and Adrar des Iforas and from there down such corridors as the Tilemsi Valley into the central valley of the Niger in the vicinity of Timbuktu. From that point there would be no geographical barriers to the movement of both the ideas and the already domesticated plants anywhere in the Sahelian-Sudanic zone of western Africa.

REFERENCES

ALLCHIN, F. R.
  1969   "Early cultivated plants in India and Pakistan," in *The domestication and exploitation of plants and animals*. Edited by Peter Ucko and G. W. Dimbleby, 323–329. Chicago: Aldine.
ANDERSON, EDGAR
  1967   "The bearing of botanical evidence on African culture history," in *Reconstructing African history*. Edited by C. Gabel and N. Bennett, 167–180. Boston: Boston University Press.
BAKER, H. G.
  1962   Comments on the thesis that there was a major centre of plant domestication near the headwaters of the River Niger. *Journal of African History* 3:229–233.
BINFORD, LEWIS R.
  1968   "Post-Pleistocene adaptations," in *New perspectives in archeology*. Edited by Sally R. Binford and Lewis R. Binford, 313–341. Chicago: Aldine.
BRAIDWOOD, ROBERT J.
  1963   *Prehistoric men* (sixth edition). Popular Anthropology Series 37. Chicago: Chicago Natural History Museum.
CAMPS, GABRIEL
  1960   *Aux origines de la Berbérie: Massinissa ou les débuts de l'histoire*. Libyca (sér Archéologie-Épigraphie) 8(1).
  1969   *Amekni: Néolithique ancien du Hoggar*. Mémoires du Centre de Recherches Anthropologiques, Préhistoriques et Ethnographiques 10.
CHAPELLE, JEAN
  1957   *Nomades noires du Sahara*. Paris: Plon.

CHEVALIER, A.
1938   Le Sahara, centre d'origine de plantes cultivées. *Mémoires de la Société de Biogéographie* 6:307–322.

CHILDE, V. GORDON
1951   *Man makes himself.* New York: Mentor.

CLARK, J. DESMOND
1962   The spread of food production in sub-Saharan Africa. *Journal of African History* 3:211–228.

CONNAH, GRAHAM
1969   "The coming of iron: Nok and Daima," in *Lectures on Nigerian prehistory and archaeology*. Edited by Thurstan Shaw, 30–36. Ibadan: Ibadan University Press.

DALZIEL, J. M.
1937   *The useful plants of west tropical Africa.* London: Crown Agents.

DANIELS, S. G. H.
1969   "The Middle and Late Stone Age," in *Lectures on Nigerian prehistory and archaeology*. Edited by Thurstan Shaw, 23–29. Ibadan: Ibadan University Press.

DAVIES, OLIVER
1967a Timber-construction and wood-carving in West Africa in the second millennium B.C. *Man*, n.s., 2:115–118.
1967b *West Africa before the Europeans.* London: Methuen.
1968   The origins of agriculture in West Africa. *Current Anthropology* 9:479–482.

DOGGETT, H.
1965   "The development of the cultivated sorghums," in *Essays on crop plant evolution*. Edited by Sir Joseph Hutchinson, 50–69. Cambridge: Cambridge University Press.

DROUHIN, M. G.
1944   Le Niger central: ses possibilités agricoles et économiques. *Bulletin de la Société de Géographie et d'Archéologie d'Oran* 65:7–34.

FAGAN, BRIAN M.
1969   Radicarbon dates for sub-Saharan Africa 6. *Journal of African History* 10:149–169.

FLIGHT, COLIN
1970   Excavations at Kintampo. *West African Archaeological Newsletter* 12:71–72.

GAST, MORCEAU, JEAN ADRIAN
1965   *Mils et sorgho en Ahaggar: étude ethnologique et nutritionnelle.* Mémoire du Centre de Recherches Anthropologiques, Préhistoriques et Ethnographiques 4.

HARLAN, JACK R., JEAN PASQUEREAU
1969   *Décrue* agriculture in Mali. *Economic Botany* 23:70–74.

HESTER, JAMES J.
1968   Comment on: Origins of African agriculture, by Oliver Davies, H. J. Hugot, and David Seddon. *Current Anthropology* 9:497–498.

HOBLER, PHILIP M., JAMES J. HESTER
1969   Prehistory and environment in the Libyan desert. *South African Archaeological Journal* 23(92):120–130.

HUGOT, H. J.
1968   The origins of agriculture: Sahara. *Current Anthropology* 9:483–488.

JACQUES-FÉLIX, H.
1971   "Grain impressions," Appendix K in The Tichitt tradition: a late pre-

historic occupation of the southwestern Sahara, by Patrick J. Munson. Unpublished Ph.D. dissertation, University of Illinois, Urbana.

LHOTE, HENRI
1959   *The search for the Tassili frescoes.* New York: Dutton.

MAUNY, RAYMOND
1950   Villages néolithiques de la falaise (dhar) Tichitt-Oualata. *Notes Africaines* 50:35–43.
1952   "Les gisements néolithiques de Karkarichinkat (Tilemsi, Soudan français)." *Actes du Deuxième Congrès Panafricain de Préhistoire.* Edited by L. Balout, 616–629. Paris: Arts et Métiers Graphiques.

MURDOCK, GEORGE P.
1959   *Africa: its peoples and their culture history.* New York: McGraw-Hill.

NICOLAISEN, JOHANNES
1963   *Ecology and culture of the pastoral Tuareg.* Nationalmuseets Skrifter, Etnografisk Rœkke 9. Copenhagen: National Museum.

PONS, A., P. QUÉZEL
1957   Première étude palynologique de quelques paléosols sahariens. *Travaux de l'Institut de Recherches Sahariennes* 16(2):15–40.

PORTÈRES, ROLAND
1950   Vieilles agricultures de l'Afrique intertropicale: centres d'origine et de diversification variétale primaire et berceaux d'agriculture antérieurs au XVIe siècle. *L'Agronomie Tropicale* 5:489–507.
1951a Géographie alimentaire, berceaux agricoles et migrations des plantes cultivées en Afrique intertropicale. *Comptes Rendus de la Société de Biogéographie* 239:16–21.
1951b Une céréale mineure cultivée dans l'Ouest africain (*Brachiaria deflexa* C. E. Hubbard var. *sativa* nov. var.). *L'Agronomie Tropicale* 6:38–42.
1962   Berceaux agricoles primaires sur le continent africain. *Journal of African History* 3:195–210.

SIMOONS, FREDERICK J.
1965   Some questions on the economic prehistory of Ethiopia. *Journal of African History* 6:1–12.

SNOWDEN, J. D.
1936   *The cultivated races of sorghum.* London: Adlard.

SZUMOWSKI, G.
1956   Fouilles de l'abri sous roche de Kourounkorokalé (Soudan français). *Bulletin de l'Institut Français d'Afrique Noire* B18:462–508.

TOUPET, CH.
1958   La vallée de la Tamourt en Naaj. Tagant: Problèmes d'aménagement. *Bulletin de l'Institut Français d'Afrique Noire* B20:(1–2):68–110.

TURNBULL, PRISCILLA F.
1971   "Mammalian fauna," Appendix L in The Tichitt tradition: a late prehistoric occupation of the southwestern Sahara, by Patrick J. Munson. Unpublished Ph.D. dissertation, University of Illinois, Urbana.

VAUFREY, RAYMOND
1947   Le néolithique para-toumbien, une civilization agricole primitive du Soudan. *La Revue Scientifique* 85(3267):205–232.

VAVILOV, N. I.
1949–1950   *The origin, variation, immunity, and breeding of cultivated plants.* Chronica Botanica 13.

VIGNIER, P.
1945   Les sorghos à grains et leur culture au Soudan français. *Revue*

Internationale de Botanique Appliquée et D'Agriculture Tropicale 25:163–230.

WENDORF, FRED
1968 "Late Paleolithic sites in Egyptian Nubia," in *The prehistory of Nubia*, volume two. Edited by Fred Wendorf, 791–953. Dallas: Fort Burgwin Research Center and Southern Methodist University Press.

WHITE, LESLIE A.
1959 *The evolution of culture*. New York: McGraw-Hill.

WRIGLEY, CHRISTOPHER
1960 Speculations on the economic prehistory of Africa. *Journal of African History* 1:189–203.

Comments on the Advent of Plant Cultivation in West Africa[1]

DAVID V. ELLIS

In 1950, Portères proposed that West Africa, particularly the region around the central Niger River, constituted a major center of domestication of species of rice, millet, sorghum, and various oleaginous, tuber, and root crops. His theories were apparently ignored by most West Africanists until Murdock (1959:64–71) elaborated upon them and devised a list of twenty-nine species of plants which he concluded, largely on the basis of linguistic evidence, were originally cultivated near the headwaters of the Niger. Murdock's postulations spawned considerable and generally negative response, the attack being led by Baker (1962), Clark (1970), and Wrigley (1970). The work of botanists such as Burkill (1939: 368, 383), Anderson (1967:174–175), and Coursey (1967:8–11) tended to support the hypotheses of Portères. In addition, such noted researchers as Sauer (1952:34–36) and Harlan (1971:470–471) have agreed that rice and yams were domesticated at an early date in West Africa, but they do not state whether the cultivation of these plants was an independent development or the result of diffusion. Another blow to the concept of an independent center of domestication in West Africa was the rejection of the Vavilovian concept of centers of primary and secondary variation, upon which Portères based his approach (Harlan 1967; Isaac 1970:50–54).

The traditional hypothesis, as outlined by Davies (1960; 1967a:151–152), Gabel (1965:65–69), Clark (1967a, 1967b, 1970), Brentjes (1968), and others, would have agriculture diffusing from

[1] This paper was initially prepared for presentation in the Seminar in Old World Archaeology at the State University of New York at Binghamton, Spring 1973. I would like to thank the participants in the Seminar for their comments and criticisms in the early stages of the research. For their assistance and comments, I owe special thanks to Gene Sterud, B. K. Swartz, Jr., John Atherton, and Andy Smith.

southwestern Asia to Egypt and the Shaheinab-Khartoum region of the Upper Nile and thence into the central and southern Sahara during the so-called Makalian Wet Phase. The increased desiccation of the Sahara beginning around 3000 B.C. would have forced the Saharan pastoralists and cultivators southward, with a gradual adaptation of cultivation to the more southern savanna and forest.

In this regard, it should be noted that even Portères (1951:16–17) and Murdock (1959:66–67) believed that independent cultivation would have developed primarily in the savanna rather than in the forest. Portères, however, did agree (1950:500) that yam cultivation probably developed in the forest region of the Ivory Coast. Davies (1967a:118; 1968:479) has also proposed experimentation with yam cultivation in the forest as early as the Sangoan.

The controversy concerning the initial development of agriculture in West Africa still thrives, much of it continuing to make reference to the conflicting proposals of these researchers. Unfortunately, many of these earlier studies approached their subject matter in a hasty and haphazard fashion. Theoretical arguments have been erected on a base of highly questionable data. This problem is not peculiar to West Africa, but the extreme paucity of sound evidence in the region renders the foundation of the various theories even more fragile than in other areas of the world. The rapid developments in the last decade in theoretical and methodological approaches to the study of the processes of cultivation and domestication have left much of the earlier research behind. The research being conducted currently in West Africa demonstrates awareness of these advances but is still limited in scope.

Munson (1972) has recently presented a well-reasoned hypothesis concerning the advent of cultivation in West Africa which appears to utilize current methodological and theoretical paradigms of the development of agriculture. Rejecting the neolithic[2] lithic and ceramic evidence from Ghanaian and Nigerian sites as indicative of food-producing populations, Munson believes that the regions in the marginal savanna/Sahel zones would have been the West African areas initially engaging in food production. On the basis of the radiocarbon dates from his excavations at Dhar Tichitt (Mauritania), Munson places the introduction of cultivation in West Africa as no earlier than 1000 B.C. (p. 17). He argues (pp. 21–25) that agriculture diffused from southwestern Egypt

[2]   For the purposes of this study, the term "neolithic" is not capitalized when used as an adjective. It is defined, whether used as an adjective or as a proper noun, as the presence or possession of pottery, ground stone axes, and a microlithic industry. The probable domestication of plants and/or animals is implied in the term, as "preneolithic" is defined as the presence or possession of all or part of the "neolithic" lithic and ceramic assemblages but the absence of domesticated plants or animals. The scarcity of direct evidence of domestication at most West African neolithic sites precludes at this time use of the term consistent with current thought.

across the plateaus and mountains of the central Sahara to the western savanna zone.

This hypothesis was first advanced by Hester (1968:497–498) as a result of excavations at Dungul Playa in southwestern Egypt, which produced evidence of incipient cultivation as early as 6000 B.C. The series of plateaus stretching across the Sahara, termed the "Saharan Fertile Crescent," has its western terminus at Adrar des Iforas, which is ca. 650 kilometers east of the western edge of the Oualata-Tichitt region.

Some debatable evidence for cultivation in the Sahara is indicated at Méniet, in the Ahaggar (Hoggar), dated to 5,410 ± 300 B.P. (Sa-59; Fagan 1965:114), and at Amekni, also in the Ahaggar, with dates from 6100 to 4850 B.C. (Munson 1972:21). On the basis of this evidence, Munson postulates diffusion of plant cultivation across the "Saharan Fertile Crescent" during the 6000–3500 B.C. period of increased rainfall in the Sahara. As a result of either environmental deterioration or increased population density, cultivators moved southward through the western horn of the "crescent," eventually reaching the area of the central Niger River. From there diffusion to the Oualata-Tichitt region is comparatively easy.

This hypothesis places Munson in the camp of those who view West African agriculture as derived directly or indirectly from the classic southwestern Asian-Nile Valley agricultural "hearth." Adapting techniques adopted from Saharan populations to local plants, indigenous West African peoples did not become plant domesticators until the late date of 1000 B.C. Given the increasing evidence for the independent evolution of agriculture in different areas of the world and Binford's (1968:335) contention that "cultivation arose as a response to similar pressures many times and in many places," Munson's hypothesis appears to be a regression to Childean theory. In critically reviewing his proposals, it is necessary to examine both the quality of the archaeological evidence he has dismissed and the theoretical substructure he employs.

West Africa suffers from a paucity of archaeological research which is most apparent for the paleolithic and early neolithic periods. Munson (1966:1) noted that there was a "disproportionately high number of articles which synthesize, hypothesize and guess what the Neolithic occupations were like and what they were related to" but a noticeable lack of site reports in West African archaeology. Qualitatively, he could cite only five exceptions to the general mediocre trend of publications in the discipline. Clark (1967a:7–8), speaking of sub-Saharan archaeology in general, commented that whereas the different Iron Age and Neolithic pottery traditions could be clearly distinguished, virtually no information was available on the settlement patterns of the groups who practiced these traditions. In the years since these remarks were made, the situation has not substantially improved. Ghana is one of the few West African states in which extensive archaeological research has been undertaken. In their review of Ghanaian archaeology, however, Calvocoressi and York (1971:90–93) could cite only ninety-four excavations instituted between 1932 and 1969, among which only seven site reports had been published.

The scarcity of excavated sites constitutes another problem. Most of the archaeological material from West Africa consists of surface collections, often gathered during the colonial era, stored away, shuffled about, lost, mislabeled, etc. Among those few sites which have been excavated, the fieldwork has often consisted of improvised salvage operations. The lack of thorough research and fieldwork renders questionable (Swartz 1971: 1; Merrick Posnansky, personal communication) the data upon which Davies based his synthesis (1967a) of West African prehistory.

A third problem is the consequence of the small number of archaeologists working in West Africa. Researchers undertaking fieldwork have tended to limit their investigations to the archaeologically rich sectors of West Africa. As a result, many of the data available for the region below ten degrees north latitude are derived from Nigeria and Ghana. Although limited work has been inaugurated in Sierra Leone and Liberia, other areas such as Upper Volta and Benin are virtually unexplored. This bias gives West African archaeology a distinctly parochial aura.

Finally, except for Munson's material, there are no data from West African sites indicating the presence of domesticated plants before A.D. 500. This lack of palynological information is due to the acidic nature of West African soils, which inhibits preservation of both pollen and skeletal remains (Coon 1967:18; Merrick Posnansky, personal communication), and the failure until recently of West African archaeologists to collect the appropriate samples (Andrew Smith, personal communication). As a result, the definition of the Neolithic in West Africa is still reliant upon lithic and ceramic evidence. The presence of ground stone axes, perforated stones (interpreted as digging-stick weights), and stone hoes has served as an index of the existence of food-producing cultures (Davies 1967a: 190–201, 203, 205–208). The former two items cannot be considered representative only of cultivators, and even Davies (1968:480) admits to some reservations about the classification of certain shaped stones as "hoes."

It is for these reasons that both the Conference of West African Archaeologists (1966:48–49) and Clark (1967b:620–621) have urged that the Neolithic be redefined in terms of a new way of life. Archaeologists, however, continue to employ the old definition (e.g., Munson 1968:11; Kennedy 1968:499; Davies 1973:14).

The difficulties just summarized constitute a severe handicap in reconstructing a relatively accurate picture of the Neolithic in West Africa. Some archaeologists regrettably appear intent upon maintaining this burden by continuing to employ outmoded method and theory in the field, in the laboratory, and in print.

In an earlier analysis (Ellis 1973), twenty-five reports on twenty-one neolithic sites or site areas in West Africa (Figure 1)[3] were intensively reviewed. These reports include sites defined by both surface collections and excavations and representative of fieldwork from the early 1930's to the early 1970's. Eleven sites were situated in the Sahel and grassland savanna north of 10° north latitude; ten sites were located in the wooded savanna and forest south of 10° north latitude. In sum, the site reports can be considered characteristic of archaeological publications for the past forty years concerning neolithic sites throughout West Africa. Taking into account the different research orientations of the authors, these reports illuminate additional pitfalls awaiting the prehistorian.

The degree of thoroughness with which material recovered in field-work is reported varies. Atherton (1972), for example, quantifies in great detail the lithic finds at Kamabai rock shelter but provides no description of the pre-Iron Age pottery. Szumowski (1956), on the other hand, enumerates and exhaustively describes the pottery recovered at Kourounkorokalé but generally gives only a brief description of the lithic remains. Many reports are similar: complete descriptions are provided either for stone tools or for pottery, often of neither and seldom of both. Ten sources provide no data on ceramic materials, implying that none were recovered.

No standard terminology is employed by the various authors, and usually no definitions for terms are offered. It is possible in some instances to attempt visual comparisons of objects illustrated in the reports, but many sources provide no illustrations.

Radiocarbon dates are available only for a few selected sites excavated in the last decade. The Akreijit phase at Dhar Tichitt, which possesses the fullest complement of stone tools from the Tichitt sites, has been dated to 3,700 ± 130 b.p. (GX–1890). Munson (1972:5), however, believes that this date is too late and places the Akreijit phase around 2000 b.c.

---

[3] The northern sites or site areas and pertinent sources are those in the Dhar Tichitt area (Munson 1968, 1970, 1972); Taferjit and Tamaya Mellet, Niger (Kelley 1934); Chet Iler, near the Algeria-Mali border (Lhote 1941); the Ténéré area in Niger (Kelley 1951); the Tibesti region in Chad (Kelley 1951; Vita-Finzi and Kennedy 1965); Karkarichinkat, Mali (Mauny 1952); the Bamako area of Mali (Szumowski 1952); Kourounkorokalé, Mali (Szumowski 1956), the Akjoujt area of Mauritania (Mauny and Hallemans 1957); and the Outeidat region of Mali (Gallay 1966). The southern sites and sources are Kintampo (Davies 1967a:216–222; Flight 1968, 1970), Ntereso (Davies 1967b, this volume), the sites of the Buobini (Punpun) culture (Flight 1968, 1970), Abetifi (Shaw 1943:142–143; 1951:474–475), and Mumute (Dombrowski and Agorsah 1972), all in Ghana and representative of the Kintampo-Ntereso complex; Rop rock shelter, Nigeria (Fagg 1951; Eyo 1965); Achimota cricket-pitch, Ghana (Davies 1961); Old Oyo, Nigeria (Willett 1962); Ezi-Ukwu Ukpa rock shelter, Nigeria (Hartle 1967:139–140); and Kamabai rock shelter, Sierra Leone (Atherton 1972).

128   DAVID V. ELLIS

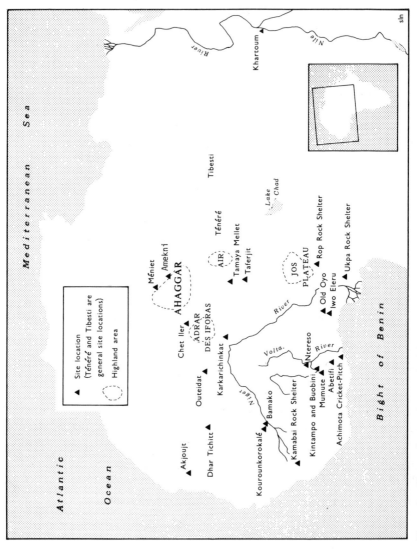

Figure 1.   Sites and natural areas cited in text

Three dates have been obtained from the main occupation at Ntereso, ranging from 3,580 ± 130 B.P. (SR–52) to 3,190 ± 130 B.P. (SR–61). However, the dates are reversed from the stratigraphic sequence, the oldest date coming from the uppermost level and the youngest date from the lowest level. Davies (this volume) believes that the primary site was occupied for only a 50-year period despite the 300-year range in the radiocarbon dates. He confidently dates the major neolithic occupation of Ntereso to 1300 B.C.

The coexistence of the preneolithic Buobini (Punpun) and neolithic Kintampo cultures is evinced by the dates from the three Kintampo sites. At K6, the Buobini has been dated to 3,570 ± 84 B.P. (Birm-29). Although no dates have been produced from the overlying Kintampo culture, Flight (1970:72), on the basis of dates from surrounding sites, places the replacement of the Buobini by the Kintampo culture at around 1400 B.C. At K8, the Buobini has been dated to 3,401 ± 74 B.P. (Birm-31). At K1, it has yielded a date of 3,630 ± 100 B.P. (I-2699), and the superior Kintampo levels have produced three dates: 3,560 ± 100 B.P. (I-2698), 3,339 ± 35 B.P. (Birm-30), and 3,220 ± 110 B.P. (I-2697).

Only a single date is available from the ten northern, non-Tichitt sites: Karkarichinkat has produced a date of 3,310 ± 110 B.P. (GSY-?; Fagan 1969:150).

Three of the other southern sites have been extensively dated. A series of dates running from 2935 B.C. to A.D. 15 has been obtained from Ezi-Ukwu Ukpa rock shelter (GX-0930, GX-0932-0938, GX-0940-0941; Fagan 1969: 152). The traditional neolithic lithic and ceramic assemblages are found throughout this site, including the oldest levels. In this context, it is interesting to note that the 0.50-to-0.65-meter level at Iwo Eleru in Nigeria has produced a microlithic industry with pottery and ground stone axes and has been dated to 3620 B.C. (Hv-1510; Fagan 1969:151). Kamabai rock shelter in Sierra Leone yields most of the standard neolithic elements in Level 10, dated to 2560 B.C. (I-3559; Atherton 1972:73).

It is significant that the sites at Dhar Tichitt and those of the Kintampo-Ntereso complex — at which we have some of the earliest evidence for plant and animal domestication in West Africa — lag from 500 to 2,000 years behind the dated classic neolithic levels at Kamabai and Ezi-Ukwu Ukpa rock shelters and at Iwo Eleru.

Munson has made use of the theoretical propositions of Binford (1968) in arguing the primacy of the Dhar Tichitt region in the development of West African agriculture. Binford (p. 328) has defined the two major stimuli for modification of a population's subsistence base as environmental deterioration and demographic pressure. This model posits a hunter-gatherer population in an environment which provides an abundant and regular food resource (or resources) permitting the population to adopt a sedentary or semisedentary life-style. In this environment, the population will establish itself in equilibrium with its resources. This equilibrium can be disturbed either by declining resource availability due to adverse environmental changes or by a substantial increase in population size. A cultural mechanism to reestablish homeostasis is the migration of segments of the population away from the parent settlement. Some of these daughter populations may be forced to emigrate to marginal environments in which resources are insufficient to support a sedentary population. Rather than abandon the sedentary life-style, Binford postulates, some of the migrants in marginal environments will experiment with controlling natural plant (or animal) populations, eventually achieving cultivation and domestication. On the basis of data from Mesoamerica, Meyers (1971:119–121) has proposed a modification in the Binfordian model to permit *in situ* development of agriculture as an alternative response to migration in a sedentary population.

Munson's hypothesis thus appears to rest upon a solid foundation. The poor quality of the archaeological evidence from other neolithic sites and the absence of direct evidence for plant cultivation or domestication from these same sites would appear to justify Munson's rejection of the data from these sites.

The first inhabitants of the Dhar Tichitt sites were probably migrants from the Saharan highlands. The relatively rich lacustrine environment would have permitted a sedentary or semisedentary existence without continued reliance upon a more labor-intensive agricultural (or horticultural) economy. Only with the desiccation of the Sahel environment would the Tichitt populations have been forced to revert to a subsistence based upon domesticated plants (or animals) in order to maintain their life-style. The environmental situation and history would thus satisfy the Binford-Meyers model.

Unfortunately, Munson's narrow focus on his Tichitt sites and his unwillingness to accommodate the lithic and ceramic data from the other West African sites in his hypothesis result in an inability to perceive the greater viability of alternative explanations. Although the artifactual material from neolithic sites in West Africa cannot demonstrate the presence of cultivating populations, it can be considered indicative of the presence of sedentary or semisedentary hunter-gatherer populations — as early as 3620 B.C. at Iwo Eleru, 2935 B.C. at Ezi-Ukwu Ukpa rock shelter, and 2560 B.C. at Kamabai rock shelter. Despite the oft-cited limited ability of the post-Pleistocene West African forest to support large populations (Murdock 1959:273; Clark 1967a:16; Davies 1967a:19), the forest could have provided the resources to support small sedentary populations. Assuming the presence of sedentary hunter-gatherer populations in the forest and savanna as early as 4000 B.C., the desiccation of the Saharan region and the subsequent influx of Saharan peoples southward commencing ca. 3000 B.C. would have been an example of Binford's "recipient open system" (1968:330–331). The intrusion of the Saharan migrants would

disturb the existing density equilibrium system and might raise the population density to the level at which we would expect diminishing food resources. This situation would serve to increase markedly for the recipient groups the pressures favoring means for increasing productivity. The intrusive group, on the other hand, would be forced to make adaptive adjustments to their new environment. There would be strong selective pressures favoring the development of more efficient subsistence techniques by both groups.

The initial deterioration of the Saharan environment, and of the savanna and forest zones to the south, would have been a gradual change. The move of cultivators and pastoralists to the south would also have been a leisurely migration of scattered populations. The savanna and forest ecosystems would have been able to assimilate these first migrants without significant disruption of ecological processes.

The Saharan migrants would have first faced the problem of adapting their agricultural systems to the savanna flora. The cereals cultivated in the central Sahara were winter-rain crops which cannot be grown in the tropical summer-rain environment (Davies 1967a:149; 1968:481–482; Aschmann 1968:494). The withdrawal to the south would have forced the abandonment of winter-rain cereals. In the savanna, the cultivators would have encountered indigenous millets and sorghums. The question is whether or not an attempt was initially made to domesticate these native plants. As Clark (1967a:10) and Davies (1967a:20) have noted, both wild plants and game are abundant in the wooded savanna. Depending upon their desire to maintain a sedentary life-style, the Saharan cultivators may have readily abandoned agriculture to "regress" to a hunting-gathering economy.

The situation is more complex, however. Experimentation with wild millet and/or sorghum forms may have occurred prior to the desiccation of the Sahara, either by occasional groups of cultivators moving into the savanna or by indigenous, sedentary hunter-gatherers. If retreating cultivators did not completely abandon cereal cultivation, they could have either domesticated millets and sorghums or adopted the cultivation of these plants from preexisting cultivating populations in the area.

As the Saharan populations continued to move south and the environment continued to degenerate, intense pressures on resources would develop in the forest and savanna. These pressures could be alleviated through several mechanisms: the institution or expansion of cultural controls on population size (e.g., infanticide, abortion, postpartum sex taboos, etc.), emigration to other areas, or systematic attempts to manipulate native plant and animal populations. It is probable that all three strategies were attempted, but the last is most likely to have resulted in the development of agriculture. It is also probable that these experiments occurred among both transplanted daughter groups in marginal environments and sedentary hunter-gatherer populations *in situ*. A proper interpretation of the Binford-Meyers model suggests that all three major environmental zones of West Africa — the sahel, the savanna, and the forest — were possible loci for early plant cultivation. The Dhar Tichitt region possesses no environmental precedence.

Munson's time perspective also is a vulnerable element of his hypothesis. Assuming that the deterioration of the Saharan environment commenced ca. 3000 B.C., the combined pressures of declining resource availability and increased population density would have stimulated systematic attempts to control plant development long before 1000 B.C. The mitigating factors of occasional respites from the desiccating trend (as manifested at Tichitt) and the relative abundance of resources in the savanna could have been offset by the familiarity of the Saharan emigrants with the processes of domestication.

A recent review of the evidence (Rustad, this volume) indicates that iron technology may have been introduced into West Africa as early as 1000 B.C. and was certainly established by 500 B.C. Although West African cultural developments should not be viewed from the perspective of traditional European and Mediterranean chronologies, it would be difficult to visualize a prehistoric culture's making the transition from a hunting-gathering subsistence to an agricultural economy and into the Iron Age almost simultaneously. From our perspective, Munson has provided too much time for the impact of the environmental deterioration to have its predicted consequences and too little time for the later cultural developments of West Africa.

It is not disputed that evidence for plant domestication does not appear in the archaeological record at the Dhar Tichitt sites until 1000 B.C. It is also conceded that the earliest direct evidence for plant domestication in West Africa is that at Dhar Tichitt. To argue, however, as does Munson, that plant domestication occurred nowhere else in West Africa prior to 1000 B.C. is premature. Our alternative hypothesis cannot be confirmed with the data at hand. However, it satisfies the Binford-Meyers model as well as Munson's proposition and utilizes the evidence from other West African neolithic sites — which Munson has chosen to ignore — while taking cognizance of the data from Dhar Tichitt.

Without a great deal of additional research in the field and in the laboratory, none of the difficulties and questions raised in this article or in Shaw's (1976) excellent review of the status of research on early crops in Africa can be resolved. Fortunately, most of the researchers in West Africa are aware of these needs and are working to correct the deficiencies in our data base. Theory building will be a pointless pursuit without the means for testing those theories.

This is not merely a matter of locating the appropriate sites but also of establishing the relationships between those sites. We cannot begin to answer the questions of the cultural processes which led to the development of agriculture without a knowledge of the interrelationships between populations throughout this region. The techniques developed in the last decade for the analysis of spatial relationships among archaeological phenomena (e.g., Hodder and Orton 1976) hold great promise of elucidating the interaction of the prehistoric cultures of West Africa. These methods in turn require the standardization of artifact types without imposing too much rigidity upon our exploitation of archaeological materials. In many ways West African archaeology has proceeded too quickly to explanatory levels, bypassing the lower, but nonetheless necessary, descriptive and analytical levels.

Finally, it must be emphasized that the ultimate goal of this research is not the "where" or "when" of the development of agriculture in West Africa, but the "how" and "why." As Higgs (1976) has cogently asserted, the cultivation and domestication of plants and animals should be viewed simply as phases on the continuum of man-plant and man-animal relationships. Given that the processes of domestication are gradual, to seek the "origins" of agriculture at specific times and places will be a sterile endeavor.

REFERENCES

ANDERSON, EDGAR
  1967 "The bearing of botanical evidence on African culture history," in *Reconstructing African culture history*. Edited by C. Gabel and N. Bennett, 167–180. Boston: Boston University Press.
ASCHMANN, HOMER
  1968 Comment on: Origins of African agriculture, by Oliver Davies, H. J. Hugot, and David Seddon. *Current Anthropology* 9:494–495.
ATHERTON, JOHN H.
  1972 Excavations at Kamabai and Yagala rock shelters, Sierra Leone. *West African Journal of Archaeology* 2:39–74.
BAKER, H. G.
  1962 Comments on the thesis that there was a major centre of plant domestication near the headwaters of the River Niger. *Journal of African History* 3:229–233.
BINFORD, LEWIS R.
  1968 "Post-Pleistocene adaptations," in *New perspectives in archeology*. Edited by Lewis R. Binford and Sally R. Binford, 313–341. Chicago: Aldine.
BRENTJES, B.
  1968 Comment on: Origins of African agriculture, by Oliver Davies, H. J. Hugot, and David Seddon. *Current Anthropology* 9:495.

BURKILL, I. H.
1939   Notes on the genus *Dioscorea* in the Belgian Congo. *Bulletin du Jardin Botanique de l'Etat Bruxelles* 15:345–392.

CALVOCORESSI, D. S., R. N. YORK
1971   The state of archeological research in Ghana. *West African Journal of Archaeology* 1:87–103.

CLARK, J. D.
1967a "A record of early agriculture and metallurgy in Africa from archaeological sources," in *Reconstructing African culture history*. Edited by C. Gabel and N. Bennett, 1–24. Boston: Boston University Press.
1967b "The problem of Neolithic cultures in sub-Saharan Africa," in *Background to evolution in Africa*. Edited by W. W. Bishop and J. D. Clark, 601–627. Chicago: University of Chicago Press.
1970   "The spread of food production in sub-Saharan Africa," in *Papers in African prehistory*. Edited by J. D. Fage and R. A. Oliver, 25–42. Cambridge: Cambridge University Press.

CONFERENCE OF WEST AFRICAN ARCHAEOLOGISTS
1966   Discussions on terminology. *West African Archaeological Newsletter* 5: 39–51.

COON, CARLETON
1967   Yengema cave. *Expedition* 9(3):8–18.

COURSEY, D. G.
1967   *Yams*. London: Longmans, Green.

DAVIES, OLIVER
1960   The Neolithic revolution in tropical Africa. *Transactions of the Historical Society of Ghana* 4:14–20.
1961   *Archaeology in Ghana*. Edinburgh: Thomas Nelson.
1967a *West Africa before the Europeans*. London: Methuen.
1967b Timber-construction and wood-carving in West Africa in the second millennium B.C. *Man* 2:115–118.
1968   The origins of agriculture in West Africa. *Current Anthropology* 9:479–482.

DOMBROWSKI, J., E. K. AGORSAH
1972   Mumute. *West African Trade Project Report on Research in 1972*, 6–10. Legon: University of Ghana.

ELLIS, D. V.
1973   The advent of cultivation in West Africa: a review of the evidence. Paper prepared for the IXth International Congress of Anthropological and Ethnological Sciences, Chicago, September 1–8.

EYO, EKPO
1965   1964 excavations at Rop rock shelter. *West African Archaeological Newsletter* 3:5–14.

FAGAN, B. M.
1965   Radiocarbon dates for sub-Saharan Africa 3. *Journal of African History* 6:107–116.
1969   Radiocarbon dates for sub-Saharan Africa 6. *Journal of African History* 10:149–169.

FAGG, BERNARD
1951   "Preliminary report on a microlithic industry at Rop rock shelter, northern Nigeria." *Comptes Rendus de la Première Conférence Internationale des Africanistes de l'Ouest*, volume two, 439–440. Paris: Librairie d'Amérique et d'Orient.

FLIGHT, COLIN
1968   Kintampo 1967. *West African Archaeological Newsletter* 8:15–19.
1970   Excavations at Kintampo. *West African Archaeological Newsletter* 12:71–75.
GABEL, CREIGHTON
1965   African prehistory. *Biennial Review of Anthropology* 7:40–83.
GALLAY, A.
1966   Quelques gisements néolithiques du Sahara malien. *Journal de la Société des Africanistes* 36:167–208.
HARLAN, JACK R.
1967   "Biosystematics of cultivated plants," in *Reconstructing African culture history*. Edited by C. Gabel and N. Bennett, 181–198. Boston: Boston University Press.
1971   Agricultural origins: centers and noncenters. *Science* 174:468–474.
HARTLE, DONALD D.
1967   Archaeology in eastern Nigeria. *Nigeria Magazine* 93:134–143.
HESTER, J.
1968   Comment on: Origins of African agriculture, by Oliver Davies, H. J. Hugot, and David Seddon. *Current Anthropology* 9:497–498.
HIGGS, E. S.
1976   "Archaeology and domestication," in *Origins of African plant domestication*. Edited by Jack R. Harlan, Jan M. J. de Wet, and Ann. B. L. Stemler, 29–39. World Anthropology. The Hague: Mouton.
HODDER, IAN, CLIVE ORTON
1976   *Spatial analysis in archaeology*. Cambridge: Cambridge University Press.
ISAAC, ERICH
1970   *Geography of domestication*. Englewood Cliffs: Prentice-Hall.
KELLEY, HARPER
1934   Collections africaines du Département de Préhistoire Exotique du Musée d'Ethnographie du Tracadéro. 1. Harpons, objets en os travaillé et silex taillés de Taferjit et Tamaya Mellet (Sahara Nigérien). *Journal de la Société des Africanistes* 4:135–143.
1951   Outils à gorge africaine. *Journal des la Société de Africanistes* 21:197–206.
KENNEDY, R. A.
1968   Comment on: Origins of African agriculture, by Oliver Davies, H. J. Hugot, and David Seddon. *Current Anthropology* 9:498–499.
LHOTE, HENRI
1941   Le gisement néolithique de l'oued Chet Iler (Tanezrouft n-Ahenet). *Journal de la Société des Africanistes* 11:125–140.
MAUNY, R.
1952   "Les gisements néolithiques de Karkarichinkat (Tilemsi, Soudan français)," *Actes du Deuxième Congrès Panafricain de Préhistoire*. Edited by L. Balout, 616–629. Paris: Arts et Métiers Graphiques.
MAUNY R., J. HALLEMANS
1957   "Préhistoire et protohistoire de la région d'Akjoujt." *Third Pan-African Congress on Prehistory*. Edited by J. D. Clark, 248–261. London: Chatto and Windus.
MEYERS, J. THOMAS
1971   "The origins of agriculture: an evaluation of three hypotheses," in *Prehistoric agriculture*. Edited by Stuart Struever, 101–121. Garden City: Natural History Press.

MUNSON, PATRICK J.
1966   An annotated bibliography of the literature pertaining to the Neolithic archaeology of West Africa, the Soudan and the Western Sahara. Unpublished manuscript, University of Illinois.
1968   Recent archaeological research in the Dhar Tichitt region of south-central Mauritania. *West African Archaeological Newsletter* 10: 6–13.
1970   Corrections and additional comments concerning the "Tichitt Tradition." *West African Archaeological Newsletter* 12:47–48.
1972   Archaeological data on the origins of cultivation in the southwestern Sahara and their implications for West Africa. Paper prepared for the Burg Wartenstein Symposium on the Origin of African Crop Domesticates, August 19–27.
MURDOCK, GEORGE P.
1959   *Africa: its peoples and their culture history*. New York: McGraw-Hill.
PORTÈRES, ROLAND
1950   Vieilles agricultures de l'Afrique intertropicale: centres d'origine et de diversification variétale primaire et berceaux d'agriculture antérieurs au XVIᵉ siècle. *L'Agronomie Tropicale* 5:489–507.
1951   Géographie alimentaire, berceaux agricoles et migration des plantes cultivées en Afrique intertropicale. *Comptes Rendus de la Société de Biogéographie* 239:16–21.
SAUER, CARL O.
1952   *Agricultural origins and dispersals*. New York: American Geographical Society.
SHAW, THURSTAN
1943   Archaeology in the Gold Coast. *African Studies* 2:139–147.
1951   "Prehistory and archaeology in the Gold Coast." *Comptes Rendus de la Première Conférence Internationale des Africanistes de l'Ouest*, volume two, 467–499. Paris: Librairie d'Amérique et d'Orient.
1976   "Early crops in Africa: a review of the evidence," in *Origins of African plant domestication*. Edited by Jack R. Harlan, Jan M. J. de Wet, and Ann B. L. Stemler, 107–153. World Anthropology. The Hague: Mouton.
SWARTZ, B. K.
1971   Exploration and excavation of earlier Old "Stone Age" sites in the southern portion of the Atakora-Togo-Akwapim corridor. Unpublished manuscript.
SZUMOWSKI, G.
1952   "La question de l'industrie microlithique aux environs de Bamako." *Actes du Deuxième Congrès Panafricain de Préhistoire*. Edited by L. Balout, 663–672. Paris: Arts et Métiers Graphiques.
1956   Fouilles de l'abri sous roche de Kourounkorokalé (Soudan français). *Bulletin de l'Institut Français d'Afrique Noire* 18B:462–508.
VITA-FINZI, C., R. A. KENNEDY
1965   Seven Saharan sites. *Journal of the Royal Anthropological Institute* 95:195–213.
WILLETT, FRANK
1962   "The microlithic industry from Old Oyo, western Nigeria." *Actes du Quatriéme Congrès Panafricain de Préhistoire et de l'Etude du Quaternaire*, volume three. Edited by G Mortrelmans and J. Nenquin, 261–272. Tervuren: Musée Royal de l'Afrique Centrale.

WRIGLEY, CHRISTOPHER
  1970   "Speculations on the economic prehistory of Africa," in *Papers in African prehistory*. Edited by J. D. Fage and R. A. Oliver, 59–73. Cambridge: Cambridge University Press.

History of Crops and Peoples in North Cameroon to A.D. 1900

NICHOLAS DAVID

My aims are (1) to summarize the few archaeological data available on the environment and prehistory of the Neolithic and later peoples and on the cultivated plants of North Cameroon; (2) to attempt, by a combination of linguistic, historical, and distributional approaches, to relate the archaeology of the area to its ethnohistory; (3) to present a tentative periodization of the establishment of crop plants in North Cameroon and suggest some features that may differentiate the Neolithic economies of the Chad and Benue basins; and (4) to point out some implications of relevance for the culture history of West and Central Africa.

North Cameroon extends from Lake Chad to the southern boundary of Adamawa department at 6° north latitude. The administrative departments correspond fairly closely with geographical regions and have been retained as the basis of the following brief description of the area (see Figure 1).[1]

The Upper Benue Basin Archaeological Project was supported by the National Science Foundation (GS-2236), by Ford Foundation Archaeological Traineeships and by the University Museum (University of Pennsylvania). In the writing of this paper I owe a particular debt of gratitude to George Jackson, with whom for a happy month I tramped around the Benue Valley and in the process assimilated a little African botany. He is not to be held responsible for my mistakes. I thank Philip Burnham for his many useful comments on an earlier draft and for generously allowing me to make use of his Gbaya data in advance of publication.

[1] In the absence of a satisfactory regional geography of Cameroon, this description is a patchwork of Billard's *Essai de géographie physique* (1963); Segalen's (1957) and Letouzey's (1958) sections on soils and phytogeography in the *Atlas du Cameroun* and the latter author's *Etude phytogéographique* (1968); the *Carte géologique de Cameroun*, published by the Direction des Mines et de la Géologie (1956); the Synthèse Régional pour la préparation du 3ᵉ Plan, 1971–76, put out by the Service Régional de l'Economie et du Plan, Région Administrative du Nord-Cameroun (1969); data kindly supplied by M. Letouzey and by the Direction de la Météorologie, Climatologie et Statistiques of the Ministère des Transports; and information culled from monographs and other sources cited below.

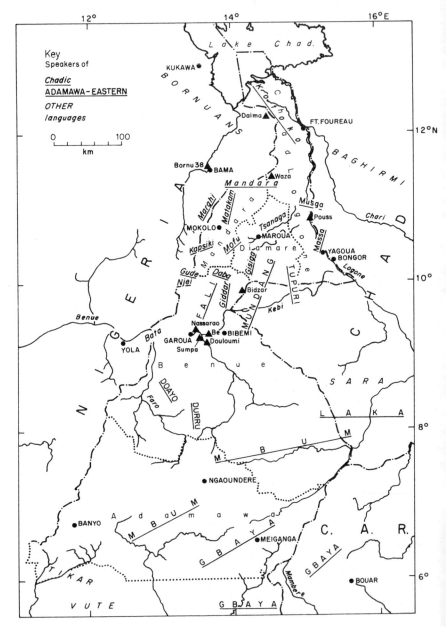

Figure 1.   North Cameroon: regions, towns, main sites, and peoples (omitting the Shuwa Arab pastoralists of the extreme north and the Fulani)

The Chad-Logone region (15,871 square kilometers) in the north and northeast comprises the Departments of Logone and Chari and Mayo (River) Danaï. In the Logone-Chari delta and on either side of the former river, which is at this point the eastern border of Cameroon, stretch seasonally inundated plains and marshes and higher patches of sandy soils that slope imperceptibly from 330 meters above sea level northward to Lake Chad at 282 meters. The rainy season (June-September) is short, and, as elsewhere in the area, evaporation greatly exceeds precipitation, which varies considerably from year to year. Average rainfall in the south is 900 millimeters, falling to about 400 millimeters in the extreme north. The average annual temperature at Fort-Foureau is 28° Centigrade. During the long dry season the mean of the maxima (MM) rises to 36° in April (42° at Yagoua), while in December the mean of the minima (Mm) falls to 20° (10° at Yagoua). South of the lake there are leached, sandy, ferruginous soils, locally hydromorphic or halomorphic; the central part of the region is blanketed by black tropical clays and silts, halomorphic in the north. South and west of Yagoua the soils are again sandy and ferruginous. Thorny acacia scrub grows on sandy soils above the level of the floods; tall grass savanna with *Echinochloa pyramidalis*, *Vetiveria nigritana*, *Oryza barthii*, and *Hyparrhenia* sect. *rufa* covers the inundated plains. The population density (1969) is 9.4 per square kilometer in the north, 32.0 in the south (17.4 overall).

The Mandara region (Department of Margui-Wandala; 7,433 square kilometers) is a raised block of Precambrian anatexites and ancient granites that have been pierced by igneous rocks. The plateau is at an altitude of 700–800 meters, with peaks rising to 1,450 meters. In the deeply incised valleys, streams and torrents run irregularly during the rains and are dry for much of the year. The rainy season (i.e., months with 100 + millimeters rainfall) lasts from May to September, with 967 millimeters average precipitation at Mokolo in the center of the plateau. March and April MM are between 41° and 42° Centigrade, but the nights are chilly in December and January (Mm = 8° Centigrade). The tropical ferruginous (fersiallitic) soils of the area are immature and, where not terraced by man, much subject to erosion. Sudan and Sudano-Sahelian dry savanna woodland with abundant *Isoberlinia doka* and grass including *Andropogon schirensis*, *Hyparrhenia rufa*, and *Loudetia acuminata* has been widely destroyed and replaced by a "domesticated" vegetation with *Acacia albida*, *Adansonia digitata*. *Celtis integrifolia*, *Ficus* spp., etc. The population density is 44.0 per square kilometer overall, but reaches over four times that figure locally.

The three remaining regions are effectively coincident with administrative departments and are named after them. The Diamaré (9,695 square kilometers) lies between the Chad-Logone and Mandara regions. The plain averages 400 meters above sea level and forms part of the Chad basin. Around Maroua and in tongues extending south to the indented border with Chad, northeast along the Mayo Tsanaga, and east along the Mayo Boula are the *harde* [black tropical clays] on which are grown durra races of sorghum; in the northwest and west are foothills and outliers of the Mandara Mountains. In the southwest, bands of embrechites, gneiss, and micaschists extend across the low Logone-Benue watershed to the Benue Valley; anatexites and granites reappear to the east. The pedology of the lithomorphic and sandy ferruginous soils reflects this geological diversity, while the climate is intermediate between those of the neighboring regions. Maroua receives an average of 850 millimeters rainfall. The vegetation, tree savanna and light savanna woodland, has been transformed by man and degraded by cultivation and use as pasture. There is a definite advance to the south of thorny Sahelian elements. The population density is 37.3 per square kilometer.

The Benue (61,754 square kilometers) and Adamawa regions lie mainly within the Atlantic drainage. The former region is roughly divisible into two geological zones. The Benue River flows in a geosyncline filled with Cretaceous rocks that extend some distance away from the river at a mean altitude of about 200 meters. Around this "trough" the ancient rocks reappear as a granitic and metamorphic peneplain broken up by inselbergs and outlying massifs of the Mandara and Adamawa highlands. The main tributaries, and the only ones that flow throughout the year, are the Mayo Kébi (which in the past and sometimes today serves to drain the overflow of the middle Logone) and the Faro, which flows north along the Alantika mountains to meet the Benue near the Nigerian border. During the rains (May-September), Garoua, the capital of North Cameroon, receives an average 980 millimeters of precipitation. The average annual temperature is 28° Centigrade, the MM 40° in March-April, the Mm 17° in December-January. Tropical ferruginous soils, often eroded and little affected by leaching, cover almost the entire region with the exception of the Benue and Kébi floodplains around and below their confluence, where there are black tropical clays and rich modern alluvium. The region falls within the Sudan savanna zone, varying from tree savanna to savanna woodland and open dry forest. The grass cover tends to consist mainly of *Hyparrhenia* spp.; characteristic woody plants include *I. doka, Monotes kerstingii*, and *Uapaca togoensis* on the slopes and in the valleys bordering the Adamawa. Toward the north the forests are characterized by *Boswellia odorata, Sclerocarya birrea*, and *Prosopis africana* but have for the most part been transformed into savanna bush with *Combretum* and *Terminalia* species and *Anogeissus leiocarpus*. North of the Benue, *Boswellia* and *Ficus* spp., *Prosopis, Sterculia setigera*, and *Acacia* spp. becomes more abundant. The population density is only 4.95 per square kilometer.

The Adamawa plateau (64,000 square kilometers), at an average altitude of 1,200 meters, with folded mountain ranges up to 2,450 meters, was formed by the uplifting of the Precambrian and granitic basal complex. Effusive igneous rocks, predominantly basalts, lie in a broad arc to the north of N'gaoundéré. The region is significantly cooler and wetter than those to the north. The rainy season lasts from April to October. At N'gaoundéré the average precipitation is 1,574 millimeters, average temperature 22° Centigrade, the MM only 29° in March, the Mm 16° in January. The pedology ranges from the poor ferrallitic soils of the northeast to thin, immature, mountain soils in the west. The remainder of the region is characterized by complex red ferrallitic savanna soils. Plantains grow in the derived savannas of the southern margins of the plateau (Letouzey's "Zone péri- ou postforestière"). Elsewhere, with the exception of some mountain communities and gallery forests, there is Sudan-Guinea grassland and shrub savanna with *Daniella oliveri* and *Lophira lanceolata*. The grass cover varies according to the intensity of its use as pasture, *Andropogon* spp., *H. rufa,* and *Panicum phragmitoides* becoming progressively degraded on eroded soils and replaced by *Urelytrum thyrsioides, Sporobolus pyramidalis*, and *Chloris pycnothrix*. On bare areas with some protection from fire, woody species may grow up to form thickets. Population densities, averaging 3.8 per square kilometer, are the lowest in North Cameroon.

The peoples and crops of the Tikar plain, administered as part of North Cameroon but in other ways more closely related to the south and west, are excluded from this study.

THE HOLOCENE ENVIRONMENTAL SEQUENCE

The Bame-Limani-Bongor ridge is an old shoreline formed between about 8000 and 1500 B.C. during stays of Lake Paleo-Chad at the 320-meter contour (Pullan 1969). Following a drop in the lake level to 300 meters, the lake divided into two parts, connected by the Bahr el-Ghazal. From that time the level of the lake in the Chadian "Pays-Bas" dropped more rapidly than that of Lake Chad. Neolithic sites in the Pays-Bas are clustered around the 320-meter contour but extend down to about 250 meters, whereas Lake Chad still stands at 282 meters (Schneider 1967). Thus, for much of the Holocene, the northern part of our area was denied to human habitation.

Hervieu (1969) has offered a tentative sequence for the area between the northern Adamawa and the borders of the Chad basin and has correlated his work with that of Pias (1967, 1968) on the southern Chad sequence. Hurault (1970) has studied the processes of gully erosion around Banyo in the Adamawa. In Table 1, I attempt to bring these sources together. The dates are taken from the Lake Chad sequence

Table 1. A tentative outline, with approximate dates, of the Late Pleistocene and Holocene sequences of North Cameroon after Hervieu 1969, van Zinderen Bakker 1972, and Servant and Servant-Vildary 1972

Dates	Phases	Inferred climate	Regions — Adamawa (Banyo)	Regions — N. Adamawa, Benue, Mandara	Regions — Lake Chad	Dates
A.D. 1900	Actuel	Tropical semihumid	Savanna grassland Forest destroyed by man; Partial regeneration of forest	Modern erosion and recent alluvium	282-meter lake Minor fluctuations	A.D. 1900
A.D./B.C.			Arid: open savanna	....	Lake above present level	
1500 B.C.	Sub-actuel	Recurrence of dry conditions		Low (1–2 meters) terraces	Lower lake levels	1500 B.C.
2500 B.C.		Humid	Humid		High lake 320 meters (?)	2500 B.C.
5000 B.C.		Tropical and more humid	Forest	Badlands erosion	Minor recession	5000 B.C.
5500 B.C.					320-meter lake Formation of Bama ridge	5500 B.C.
8000 B.C.		....	....		Recession	8000 B.C.
				Middle (4–8 meters) terraces and glacis accumulation and sheet erosion		9000 B.C.
10,000 B.C.	Later Bossoumian	Semiarid	Open savanna		Rising lake	10,400 B.C.
22,000 B.C.					Desert	
					Invasion	22,000 B.C.

(Schneider 1967; Servant and Servant 1970; van Zinderen Bakker 1976). A radiocarbon date of 8150 ± 230 b.c. (Gif-871) from a vertisol in the middle terrace of the Kébi (Hervieu 1969:17) would suggest that this was forming after the period of desert invasion during the first rise and subsequent recession of Lake Chad. Table 1 should be considered — at best — as a working hypothesis.[2]

As van Zinderen Bakker has demonstrated, our knowledge of the later Holocene geoclimatic sequence is rapidly improving, but vegetation patterns cannot yet be reconstructed. The fall in the level of Lake Chad that occurred at about 2000 b.c. may have been the result either of lowered rainfall or of higher temperatures and the consequent increased evaporation. Both alternatives, with their contrasting implications for the environment and for man, must still be entertained. The climatic changes of the time were, however, minor in comparison with those of the Late Glacial, and any shifts of vegetation belts are likely to have been correspondingly less marked. In this connection it is noteworthy that Hurault does not see the destruction of the Adamawa forest taking place until the last millennium b.c., by which time human intervention is by no means an impossibility.

A further obstacle to the reconstruction of vegetation patterns is our ignorance of the plant communities that would occur in the area today were it not for centuries of clearing and firing by man and the grazing and trampling of his cattle. Are edapho-climatic factors sufficient for the interpretation of man-land relationships in prehistory? Or must the modern flora be understood in climato-anthropo-edaphic terms (in which case both zonal shifts and the creation of quite new types of plant communities must be envisaged)? The work of Sillans (1958) on the ecology, origins, and development of the savannas of the Central African Republic is of the greatest relevance in this context. Sillans argues that the Central African savannas between 6° and 10° north latitude are an anthropogenic subclimax replacing, except in certain specialized habitats (as, for example, marshes and gallery forests), dense dry forest with tall trees forming a more or less closed canopy and with a virtual absence of grass cover. Clearing and cutting of the forest for cultivation are primarily responsible for savannization (pp. 258–259):

---

[2]   Dates of 18,000 and 15,000 b.p. are cited by Marliac (1971: vol. 2, p. 6) for paleosols identified by Hervieu as "Douroumien" and considered by him to be of the Middle Quaternary. If these dates are confirmed, substantial modifications, at least of the early part of the sequence, will be required.

It should also be noted that the arid period represented in the Chad sequence from ca. 2550 to 1550 b.c. is not recognizable in the Adamawa and that, conversely, the dry period commencing there at about the beginning of our era is not recorded in the north. Can the Banyo dates be misleading?

L'homme par la *Répétition Pluriséculaire de ses Techniques Culturales Primitives*, a détruit d'immenses étendues boisées dont la régéneration post-culturale *Malgré les Feux* semble avoir donné vraisemblablement naissance à toutes les formations savanisées oubanguiennes.

Fire acts to retard forest regrowth, but cannot alone degrade the forest and create savanna:

L'inexistence des stades de dégradation nous apparaît manifeste maintenant que nous croyons connaître le vrai processus évolutif des formations végétales centraficaines: *Forêt → Cultures → Savane → Forêt*. Insistons sur *L'origine Postculturale* des savanes . . . l'évolution actuelle de la végétation est commandée par les cultures, il en fut, de tous temps, la même chose. Depuis l'arrivée de premiers agriculteurs, l'évolution générale de la végétation oubanguienne tend vers le type savane, mais ces savanes, à leur tour, tendent manifestement vers le recrû forestier.

For Cameroon, Letouzey constantly emphasizes the effects of shifting agriculture, pasturage, and the cutting of trees for lumber and fuel, showing how these modify both the physiognomy and the species composition of the regional floras. He has shown how, in the zone of derived savanna around the forest and on the Adamawa plateau, fire alone cannot prevent forest regrowth and recolonization (1968:231–232). On the Sudano-Sahelian boundary, the 2,000-hectare Gokoro forest, thirty kilometers north-northeast of Mokolo, has been protected for some forty years from clearing and, theoretically, from use as pasture. During this period thorny scrub with some Sudanic elements has developed into more or less closed canopy forest. Grasses are being progressively displaced by various *Dioscorea* species, ferns, and tangles of *Acacia ataxacantha*. Fires lick around the margins but appear no longer able to penetrate. Although species will change, dense dry forest is already reestablished (Letouzey 1968:317–318; personal communication, 1973).

If these conclusions be accepted, they must radically influence our interpretation of the prehistory of large parts of the Central and West African savanna zone, for, in comparison with savanna ecosystems, dense dry forest must be of far less potential to men at the hunter-gatherer or Neolithic technological level. A probable greater variety of plant foods would not compensate for the lack of exploitable protein; game, and especially the preferred herd ungulates, would be scarce, and the forest itself would be irreducible without stone axes; with them the process would still proceed only slowly. Sillans (1958:246) describes a relict stand as composed of a large number of tree species, tall and straight-trunked in contrast to their often stunted and gnarled savanna habitus. Beneath the canopy there is a thick, impenetrable undergrowth of bushes and lianas. Before the introduction of iron technology the dry forest would appear singularly unattractive to human settlement.

It is unclear whether Sillans's conclusions can be extended north of the tenth parallel to the Sahelian-Sudanic zone of thorn scrub, with its reduced grass cover that disappears during the long dry season. From Nigeria and Cameroon there is, however, historical evidence concerning recent vegetation changes in regions that are comparable in latitude and rainfall. The "Great Forest" covering 6,000 square miles of Bornu was destroyed in less than fifty years after large-scale immigration began (Stenning 1959:26–27). Savanna has replaced forest in several other places south of Lake Chad that had been visited by the early explorers (e.g., Denham, Clapperton, and Oudney 1828: vol. 2, pp. 11, 24; Barth 1857: vol. 3, p. 161). Lestringant (1964:22) quotes Dizian and old native informants on the retreat of the forest in Giddar territory on the Benue-Diamaré border. He concludes, "Il importe donc d'avoir toujours à l'esprit que l'ensemble du pays, chaine du Mandara et bas-plateau, ont dû, voici plusieurs siècles, bénéficier d'un manteau forestier continu et épais."

These examples support Sillans by establishing both the presence of forest north of 10° north latitude in our area and that the manner in which it was destroyed was by clearing and burning, not by firing alone — with the implication that such clearance could not occur before the introduction of food production. Other authorities, including Aubreville (1949) and Trochain (in his preface to Sillans 1958), consider that fire is capable of degrading forest. The Central African savannas should, in their view, be considered as a fire subclimax. They could thus pre-date the origins of agriculture.

Edapho-climatic savannas unquestionably exist; the problem of savanna origins must be approached area by area and by ecologists, archaeologists, and botanists working in concert. Nevertheless, there is broad agreement that were it not for the intervention of man, the present savanna zone of the Central African Republic and neighboring regions of Chad and Cameroon would have a closed rather than an open vegetation cover. The same would hold under similar climatic conditions in the past, while the zone of present savanna *aspect*, although likely to be of botanically different composition, would be some distance north of the tenth parallel and, for edapho-climatic reasons, narrow from north to south and more in the nature of a transition between thorn scrub and dry forest than of a vegetation belt. If, as suggested above, climatic changes over the past 5,000 years have been of limited amplitude, then, if Sillans is correct, we might expect a shifting contrast between the northern and southern parts of our area. The Chad basin would be under either dry forest and savanna or thorn scrub and savanna, and in such times attractive to hunter-gatherers, cultivators, and pastoralists; dense dry forest is likely to have been more constant in the Benue basin and to have offered little inducement to settlement unless to farmers equipped with iron tools.

ARCHAEOLOGY

The Stone Age

Nothing is known of late Stone Age populations in the area until the Neolithic. The Bornu 38 site (11°32' north latitude, 13°40' east longitude), situated just within the Bama ridge, has given four dates ranging from 1880 ± 160 B.C. to 640 ± 170 B.C. (Libby half-life; laboratory numbers N-793 and N-796). These are the earliest dates for the Neolithic south of Lake Chad and agree well with dates from Bornu 70 and Daima (Connah 1970, and reported in Calvocoressi 1970). The earliest Chadian dates are 425 ± 150 B.C. (Gif-742) and 200 ± 135 B.C. (DaK-10) from Mdaga and 120 ± 180 B.C. (Gif-435) from Amkoundjo; both sites are located near Fort-Lamy at about 290 meters above sea level (Lebeuf 1969:8). The early occupants of Daima, the only site to have been published even in part (*Illustrated London News* 1967; Connah 1966, 1967), had cattle and were fishermen; there is no direct evidence of Neolithic agriculture. As the lake fell, the peoples of the area followed the retreating shoreline. No doubt there are many Iron Age mounds in the Chad-Logone region that have Neolithic components, but none have yet been excavated.

Several Neolithic axe factories from the mountains around Maroua have been described by Hervieu (1968) and Marliac (1971). Similar sites are known from Mount Balda on the Limani-Bongor ridge and, within the ridge, from Mount Waza. Although all are undated surface collections, Hervieu originally attributed some of them to the Lower Paleolithic on grounds of tool morphology and the virtual absence of polished stone tools. The archaic features are, however, characteristic of workshop materials and can be duplicated in the assemblages of several concentrations of stone tools excavated by Marliac and Quechon along 1,250 meters of the low terrace of the Mayo Tsanaga at Maroua. These are of undoubted Neolithic age. Although some fragments of pottery were found, decorated mainly by punctuations, the Mayo Tsanaga sites appear to be not settlements, but again factory or workshop areas. The lithic assemblages are composed largely of waste flakes and axe roughouts at varying stages of manufacture. Very rare pieces are ground or "semi-polished" (Marliac 1971: vol. 1). On the basis of Hervieu's suggested chronology, the low terrace is likely to have formed between the fourth and second millennia B.C. Marliac (personal communication, May 15, 1972) has kindly allowed me to cite a recently processed radiocarbon determination from one of the excavations. The date of A.D. 230 ± 90 (Gif-2232) is later than expected but still within the Neolithic period.

The discovery of ground and polished stone axes, which are lithologically similar to those from Maroua found in other parts of the Diamaré and in the Mandara region, suggests that Maroua pieces were widely distributed in an unfinished state. Other sources of raw material were also exploited (Hervieu 1968).

At Bidzar, a village south of Maroua, Buisson (1933) discovered simple abstract engravings on marble blocks. They are as yet undated and may be Neolithic or of the Iron Age.

There are no Neolithic sites with indisputable evidence of food production in the Benue region. A small cave at Sumpa (9°18′ north latitude, 13°31′ east longitude), located thirteen kilometers east of Garoua in a sandstone and conglomerate massif immediately west of the Benue-Kébi confluence, was excavated by Frank Bartell of the Upper Benue Basin Archaeological Project (UBBAP). He found 180 centimeters of deposits, the upper 80 centimeters somewhat disturbed by burrowing animals and the lower meter consisting largely of slabs fallen from the cave roof and rotting *in situ*. In, among, and just above the rockfall and below Iron Age levels were traces of an occupation that can best be designated Mesoneolithic. The assemblage included numerous quartz microliths, a little pottery with punctuations, and three upper grindstones. Two fragments of iron are likely to be intrusive. The microliths have not yet been studied but appear similar to the series from the upper (ceramic) level at Rop rock shelter in Nigeria (Rosenfeld 1972). Duiker has been identified from this level, but there were no identifiable vegetable remains.[3] Dating of the Sumpa cave series is problematic. A radiocarbon date in the sixteenth century A.D. for Mesoneolithic Level 3 is certainly too young, and others for Iron Age Levels 1 and 2 are reversed. The samples were in all probability contaminated by recent use of the cave as a stable. A thermoluminescent determination made on a sherd found beneath the rockfall of 6310 ± 400 B.C. is almost certainly too old, but it does suggest a considerable antiquity for the Mesoneolithic occupation.

A few undated pieces of Neolithic technology have been reported farther to the south and from the Adamawa (Alimen and Lecoq 1953; Pervès 1945; Jauze 1944).

The Iron Age

With the coming of iron, the northern and probably also the southern parts of the Chad-Logone region became relatively densely populated. Lebeuf's *Carte archéologique des abords du Lac Tchad* (1969) lists only eighteen Cameroonian sites outside this region as against 331 within it.

---

[3] Brian Fagan (University of California, Santa Barbara) has kindly undertaken the analysis of the faunal remains recovered by the UBBAP.

Only a minute proportion of the latter have been excavated and all of those before 1939. The sites, villages and town mounds, are attributed to the Sao; however, previous conceptions of the Sao phenomenon, as set forth for example in Lebeuf and Masson-Detourbet's *La civilisation du Tchad* (1950), require drastic modification due to recent excavations and dates from Nigeria and Chad that have raised major questions regarding the regional sequences and periodization (cf. Lebeuf 1962). Direct evidence of agriculture comes as yet only from Daima, where sorghum of the caudatum race was found in levels of the nine and tenth centuries A.D. (Connah 1967: 25; de Wet, Harlan, and Price 1976).

The most southerly mounds of any size on the left bank of the Logone are two at Pouss (10°51' north latitude, 15°4' east longitude); one of them was tested by the UBBAP. It began to form late in the first millennium A.D. While there are similarities, the pottery differs markedly from that of Sao sites to the north (cf. Griaule and Lebeuf 1948, 1950, 1951; Lebeuf 1962), and there is no reason to designate the inhabitants as Sao. Sedge nutlets (*Fimbrystylis* sp.) dated about A.D. 1200 have been identified from the site, and, according to George Jackson (personal communication, May 2, 1972), they were with other grains and suggest that *wild* grass seeds were collected from wet areas.[4] South of Pouss, one and sometimes two levels of pottery are visible in the bank of the Logone and extend with few breaks at least as far south as Yagoua. The Iron Age inhabitants would seem to have lived as the Massa do today, in long villages strung out along the levees.

Thirty-nine Iron Age sites, mounds, and mound complexes have been recorded by the UBBAP around the Benue-Kébi confluence, from Garoua in the west up the Kébi as far as Bibémi (and probably beyond) and up the Benue to Douloumi Lake. An open site of some antiquity was found farther up the Benue at Lagdo. Five small mounds were discovered in the Benue-Faro confluence area and another at Ndinkere on the Faro. Surface scatters of pottery have been collected from other sites in the region, but until typological analyses are completed, it would be unwise to suggest even approximate dates.[5] Some may well be as late as the Fulani

[4]   All provisional identifications of plant remains recovered by the UBBAP are by George Jackson (Botany Department, University of Ibadan), who also worked with the project on the ecology of the Benue-Kébi confluence area.

Dates for sites excavated by the project are based on radiocarbon readings calculated according to the 5,730-year half-life and corrected for changes in the atmospheric inventory of radiocarbon. They should thus correspond as closely as possible to calendar dates. They were run by E. K. Ralph and Barbara Lawn of the Museum Applied Science Center for Archaeology (University of Pennsylvania). Thermoluminescent determinations were made by Mark Han of the same institution. A full listing and brief discussion of all the absolute dates is to appear in a summary article by Colin Flight in the *Journal of African History*.

[5]   Frank Bartell is working up the pottery. His completed analysis will first appear as a Ph.D. dissertation (University of Pennsylvania).

incursion and conquest in the late eighteenth and early nineteenth centuries.

Excavations at Bé (9°18′ north latitude, 13°40′ east longitude) on the Mayo Kébi, one of the largest of the mound complexes, revealed over seven meters of occupation deposits. Two major phases (which can be further subdivided) are recognized on the evidence of the sequence of well-preserved structures. The first is characterized by round huts with beaten-earth floors and lasted from the first occupation of the mound in the ninth century to about A.D. 1300. In the second phase, which continued until the Fulani conquest of the Nyamnyam inhabitants in 1839, tessellated potsherd pavements, identical to those first reported from Nassarao I (David 1967, 1968; and reported in Calvocoressi 1970:69–70) and to modern examples made by the Fali (Lebeuf 1961:84), make their appearance. The oldest date for the Iron Age in the Benue region is from a village mound at Douloumi Lake (9°12′ north latitude, 13°39′ east longitude), where the earliest levels are of the sixth century A.D. As at Bé, two major structural phases are represented. Carbonized vegetable remains were recovered by flotation from these two sites and from the Iron Age levels at Sumpa cave. They are provisionally identified in Table 2.

Table 2. Carbonized vegetable remains

Plant remains	Date in centuries A.D.		
	Bé	Douloumi	Sumpa
Sorghum	11–12	9	–
Eleusine	9–10	–	17–18?
Setaria	13–14	–	–

The *Setaria* is unlikely to be a cultigen. As at Pouss, it forms part of a collection of wild grasses from wet places such as those that adjoin the site.

The ancient peoples of the Benue-Kébi confluence lived in permanent, nucleated villages on or very near light, sandy, terrace soils that they would have cultivated and in close proximity to rivers and lakes that they exploited intensively for fish. Domestic sheep/goats and cattle are represented in the sequences and were probably present throughout the Iron Age. The culture differs from that of the Sao in its pottery, in burial customs, and in the absence of figurine material. Nor is the pottery very like that of Pouss, where figurines were also lacking.

Gauthier (1972) has excavated at Fali and pre-Fali cemeteries in the massifs north of the Benue and has shown parallels in urn-burial practices between Ngoutchoumi-Dolu Koptu necropolis and a site in the Mayo

Kébi Valley northwest of Bibémi. Anthropomorphic figurines are present in the upland sites. A late sixteenth to early nineteenth century time range is suggested.

Nothing is known of the prehistoric Iron Age of the Mandara, Diamaré, or Adamawa. Across the border in the Central African Republic, Vidal (1969) has discovered a group of about a hundred megalithic structures. The sites are contained within a rectangle 130 kilometers long and about 30 kilometers broad, running southeastward from Mount Ngaewi on the Cameroon border to Bouar and beyond. They lie along the Chad-Congo watershed and are often situated near headwaters. Little is known about the builders; a few sherds, a smoking pipe, iron slag, and an iron bracelet were found in the megaliths and are believed contemporary. Two structures have been dated, one to 5490 ± 170 B.C. (Gif-1636) and another to A.D. 30 ± 100 (Gif-1637) (Willett 1971:353). The precise association of the dated material and the structures is unclear. It would appear improbable that megaliths were being built in that area in the sixth millennium B.C. and equally unlikely that the tradition persisted for over 5,000 years.

Speculations

Although there is a strong presumption of agriculture among the Neolithic peoples around Lake Chad, there is still no proof; farther to the south even the indirect evidence is unconvincing. Grindstones and rubbers have not been found *in situ* at the Maroua workshop sites, while miscellaneous pieces found elsewhere may be of Iron Age date. Only the rubbers from Sumpa are in stratigraphic context, but their date — although likely to be early — is unknown. So much is firm fact; the rest is speculation, but I hope useful.

Our prediction of a technologically and environmentally determined contrast between the northern and southern parts of the area is supported by the available evidence, such as it is. Thorough survey work throughout the area will provide confirmation or disproof. The full Neolithic appears to have been limited to the Chad basin and not to have extended south to the Benue drainage. The Diamaré and Mandara regions may at certain times during this period have had an open vegetation cover of thorn scrub and savanna and offered a more favorable habitat to peoples with a mixed farming, stock-breeding, and fishing economy than the dense dry forest, which I suppose to have covered the Benue region and, until very late, the Adamawa.

Except perhaps in the far north, the Iron Age of North Cameroon is unlikely to have begun before the fifth or sixth century A.D., after which there was an intensification of settlement in the Chad-Logone region and a local extension south into the Benue. Shortly afterward, according to our direct evidence, cultivation of sorghum and finger millet was taking place in the latter region. The heavy soils, vertisols, and silts of the floodplains were probably not cleared at this time. There is historical evidence that the Fulani under Ardo Bakari, ruler of Garoua 1855–1867, were the first to clear the Benue plain in order to plant dry-season *durra* sorghums (Bassoro 1965:67). Maistre (1895:244), passing through some thirty years later, described the valley much as it is today, "peu boisée et au sol fendillé." The nucleated Iron Age settlements are unlikely to have been a response to external political pressure, at least until the rise of the Jukun kingdom of Kororofa in the first half of the second millennium A.D. It may be that the mound dwellers desired to reserve the maximum area of light, sandy soils for cultivation — rational, "economizing" behavior if the region was indeed forested at the time. Over the centuries clearance for fields and pasture would have worked the transformation to savanna. The process may be reflected in the archaeology of Bé by the appearance of several small mounds, at least two of which have pottery pavements near their base, and a reduction in the area of occupation on the largest mounds.

LINGUISTICS AND ETHNOHISTORY

In this section I shall consider the linguistic affiliations of North Cameroonian peoples in conjunction with ethnohistoric data on their origins and migrations. The linguistic classification, which is that of Greenberg (1963), has not only a very real intrinsic value for the reconstruction of culture history, but also serves as an antidote to the sometimes quite wild theorizing of the ethnohistorians. The latter have been for the most part early travelers, colonial administrators, or ethnologists without special training in ethnohistoric techniques. Moreover, they have usually been concerned with only one group at a time and prone to attribute its origin to a distant area without proper consideration of whether this makes sense in the context of the distant area in question. It should also be borne in mind that many of the historical documents on which they rely, for example, those brought together by Palmer in his *Sudanese memoirs* (1928), were written at about the same time as antiquaries in England were assiduously tracing the Britons back to Troy — and they should be as critically received. Thus, while myths and legends indubitably reflect cultural values and contacts, they cannot be accepted as history in the absence of supporting evidence. As Meek (1931:24) once put it, "Any imaginative Muslim who can write is capable of manufacturing history for the benefit of the unlettered."

Over the past millennium North Cameroonian peoples have been the continual prey of powerful neighbors to the north, west, and east. These predations culminated in the eighteenth and nineteenth centuries with the influx and subsequent conquests of the Fulani, which drastically modified tribal distributions in the Adamawa and lowland Cameroon, except in the Chad-Logone region, which was suffering its own vicissitudes at the time and had, since the seventeenth century, been penetrated by ever-increasing numbers of Shuwa Arab pastoralists. The majority of ethnolinguistic groups are today an amalgam of units that have undergone episodes of fusion and acculturation under exterior pressures.

Les brassages et les influences réciproques entre ethnies de niveau technique équivalent sont anciens, ce qui rend difficile de caractériser les cultures traditionelles en présence et fournit un découpage géographique distinct selon les critères que l'on retient,

wrote de Garine (1964:22) of the Massa and their neighbors, but it is generally true. Tribal culture is a momentary constellation of traits; the Fali of A.D. 1600 were no doubt very different from those studied by Lebeuf (1961:20–44).

The peoples of the Chad-Logone region are speakers of Chadic languages, representing three of the nine groups recognized by Greenberg. These are Group 2, Kotoko dialects in the north; Group 7, Musgu in the center; and Group 8, Massa in the south. No other languages of these groups are spoken by geographically distant populations.

The traditions of the Kotoko and of their ancestors, the Sao, have been extensively studied over many years by several scholars (Griaule and Lebeuf 1948, 1950, 1951; Lebeuf and Masson-Detourbet 1950; Lebeuf 1962, 1969). The term "Sao" has been widely applied since antiquity in the general sense of "les hommes d'autrefois"; early traditions, such as that which situates Sao at Bilma in the seventh century A.D., must be regarded with suspicion. Ibn Hawqal mentions "fetishists" south of Lake Chad between the Komadugu Yobe (on the Nigeria-Niger border) and the Chari Rivers in A.D. 930. Various groups seem to have moved into the area at about this time and, after coalescing with earlier inhabitants, to have become the Sao-Kotoko. Most, driven by the rising power of Kanem, would have come from the north; others are thought to have migrated westward from Moïto and Lake Fitri (Lebeuf 1969:19). Over the next centuries the Sao peoples were harried and enslaved by the Sefawa and, following the loss of Kanem ca. A.D. 1380 and the removal of the dynasty to Bornu, forced into a contracting territory around the southern margins of the lake. Some Sao moved south to Logone Birni, Logone Gana, and other fortified mound towns; other remnants may have gone toward the Mandara, although traditions reflecting immigration to this and the Benue regions have received no archaeological support. By the death of *Mai* Idris Alooma in 1617 many Kotoko chiefs had accepted the suzerainty of Bornu. From then until the arrival of the French in 1900, their lands were ravaged and depopulated by wars and slave raiding by the forces of Bornu, Baghirmi, Wadai, and Rabeh.

A legend reported by Lebeuf and Masson-Detourbet (1950:33) locates Musgu at Minntour (Nigeria) south of the lake in the eighth century A.D. However this may be (and it is indeed likely that, after the fourteenth or fifteenth century, they were caught up in a general southward movement up the Logone and Chari), the Musgu would appear long established at about 11° north latitude between the Chari and Logone and locally farther west. From the sixteenth century they were irregular vassals of Bornu and, as such, conducted slave raids to the south. More recently they were shifting slowly west to escape Baghirmian depredations (Lembezat 1961:66–67). Their expansion along the Logone would have been one factor in the shunting of the Massa up and down the river. The latter, after establishing themselves by the assimilation of earlier inhabitants in the south of the region at an unknown date, were forced north of Pouss by the Tupuri, only to retreat upstream under northern pressure. From the eighteenth century, their return to the Yagoua area was accelerated by constant slave raiding (de Garine 1964:22).

Nevertheless, in spite of various intrusions and myriad local movements, the linguistic and ethnohistorical evidence suggests that these three peoples are autochthonous to the lake shores and "pays amphibie" of the lower Logone and Chari.

The Mandara peoples are also speakers of Chadic languages; the mountaineers are all, except the Matakam and Mofu (and conceivably the unclassified Bana), speakers of Bata-Marghi languages (Group 3), which extends across the Nigerian border (Marghi) and south to the Benue and Faro (Bata). The Mandara north of the mountains are placed in Group 6 with the Gamergu. Their dynasty claims a northern origin, but there is no reason to suppose that the bulk of the population is not indigenous to the northern fringes of the Mandara range. Since the sixteenth century, they have been heavily influenced by Bornu and were their allies against the Fulani in the early 1800's.

The mountains have long been considered a refuge area. Several peoples have traditions of eastern origins; the Matakam and Mofu extended down to the Diamaré plains before the Fulani incursion (Lembezat 1961:12). Nonetheless the weight of the evidence is in favor of a respectable antiquity in the region of its present peoples, perhaps augmented by Sao and other refugees.

The Gisiga and Daba of the Diamaré are both classed in Chadic Group 4 together with their erstwhile neighbors the Matakam and Mofu. There are now Daba groups in the Mandara, Diamaré, and Benue regions, the result of a recent history described by Lembezat as "assez confuse et 'bouscelée'." They are considered here as a people of the Diamaré on account of their close relationship to the Gisiga (Lembezat 1961:151–152), although the information on their crops was gathered at Mousgoy, over the border in the Benue region. Neither Daba nor Gisiga has been intensively studied, but they are known to have embraced a much larger portion of the plain in the past and to have been harassed by the Fulani.

The southern part of the region is occupied by the Mundang and the Tupuri, speakers of closely related Adamawa dialects of Group 2. Greenberg classified the Tupuri as Chadic, but his Tupuri are in fact the Kera, a neighboring people closely similar in many aspects of culture, who live over the Chad border south of Lake Tikem (de Garine 1973; Claus Schubert, personal communication, 1973). The Kera are speakers of Chadic Group 9, which includes Somrai and a number of other languages that have their center of distribution far to the east in southern Chad. This might suggest, in the light of the very little that is known of the earlier culture history of that area, that the Kera were displaced and became separated from their linguistic congeners by the westward movement early in this millennium of Sudanic-speakers, amongst whom were the Baghirmi.

The Tupuri claim to be autochthonous. Once extending up the Logone as far as Pouss, now Musgu territory, they have over the past five (?) centuries retreated south and west to the borders of the Chad-Logone and Diamaré regions. The Mundang, relatively recent immigrants into the Diamaré from a base on the upper reaches of the Kébi around Léré in Chad, claim, like so many other peoples, an eastern origin. Their linguistic affiliation is more suggestive of a local or ultimately southern derivation.

In the north of the Benue region, on its border with the Diamaré, live the Giddar, Chadic-speakers classed by themselves in Group 5. Lestringant (1964:79–80) insists upon the composite origin of the Giddar and neighboring peoples but does not suggest migrations from afar. In the northwest along the Benue and up the Faro, the Bata and related tribelets, who moved into the region from the Mandara Mountains in the eighteenth century, have replaced Chamba and other groups (Kirk-Greene 1958:17–18, 168–169). They are a Chadic intrusion into an otherwise Adamawa-speaking area.

Until the Fulani conquests of the early nineteenth century, the Benue Valley was the frontier between speakers of Chadic and Adamawa languages. The Adamawa-speakers are now either assimilated or confined to the massifs north of the Adamawa and to the Alantika Mountains. Outside our area they extend westward down the Nigerian Benue to 11° east longitude. In the massifs northeast of Garoua, the Fali are a reconstitution of divers groups, including some Bata, and speak the only language of Adamawa Subgroup 11. Lebeuf (1961) has demonstrated their mixed northern and southern characteristics, but it is hard to accept his suggestion that they were driven from the Kébi, a tributary of the Niger, in the fifteenth or early sixteenth century and thence via the Mandara to their present habitat.

The remnant populations, Mambay, Laka, and others on the Mayo Kébi and to the east of the Benue, are classed together with the Mundang and the Mbum in Adamawa Subgroup 6. West of the Benue, the Durru, Do Ayo or Namchi, and numerous smaller groups are placed in Subgroup 4, which is confined to this area. The ethnohistory of these fragmented tribelets is little understood; it is possible that the Ngewe, Nyamnyam, Oblo, Puri, and Duli, who lived around the Benue-Kébi confluence and who claimed an origin on the Logone (Mohammadou Eldridge, personal communication), may be identifiable with the mound dwellers of the second structural phase. If this is so, their migration might conceivably be correlated with the movements of the Tupuri and Mundang in the four-teenth and later centuries. Their linguistic affiliation is uncertain. The western part of the region must have been considerably influenced by the slaving and trading of the Jukun kingdom of Kororofa, which flourished on the Middle Benue from perhaps as early as the thirteenth century until its destruction by the Fulani in the nineteenth (Kirk-Greene 1958:16). Kororofa was at the height of its power in the seventeenth century, and its contacts with the Cameroon hinterland extended through the Benue to the Mbum of the Adamawa (Meek 1931:39–40).

The Mbum have lived in the Adamawa and adjoining portions of the Central African Republic for a very considerable period, during which some groups have split off and amalgamated with others to the southwest to form the Tikar, Bamum, and Vute, all speakers of Bantoid languages of Benue-Congo (Eldridge 1971:213 ff.). The Mbum language is related to Mundang and those of other peoples of the eastern Benue region. It is hard to credit the traditions reported by Eldridge (1971:146–173) that they derive ultimately from the Yemen or the Nile. The Gbaya, southern and eastern neighbors of the Mbum, are the only Cameroonian represen-tatives of the Eastern branch of Adamawa-Eastern and are recent immig-rants. Previously located in the Central African Republic north and west of the Ubangi River, they have been moving northwest throughout the nineteenth century, up the Mambere Valley to Cameroon (Burnham 1972:3 ch. 3 and appendix A). Under pressure from the Yangere at their backs, their immigration was facilitated by the disarray of the Mbum under Fulani attack and possibly by the supposed emigration southward from the Meiganga area of the "Pahouin" group of Bantu (Alexandre 1965).

The bulk of the ethnohistoric literature on North Cameroonian peoples emphasizes their peregrinations (cf. Lembezat 1961 for a summary of the dispersed information available). In recent years Eldridge has been performing invaluable work in collecting and compiling oral traditions, but their synthesis is incomplete. In its absence I have taken the view that traditions that have neither been subjected to modern critical analysis nor supported by archaeological data must, in cases of conflict, yield to the evidence of linguistics.[6] This is not to deny the very great value of oral tradition in revealing the direction and importance of culture contacts and influences within, between, and beyond the regions under consideration.

With exceptions noted above, the linguistic distributions suggest that population blocks have remained areally stable, although with shifting borders and internal movements, for a period sufficiently long for differentiation to have occurred at group and subgroup levels. This is most marked in the case of the Chadic subfamily of Afro-Asiatic. The peoples of the Chad basin form part of a broad belt of Chadic-speaking peoples that extends far to the east and west of North Cameroon. They have been subjected to influences mainly from the north, but also from the west and east, for at least a thousand years. The inhabitants of the Benue basin and Adamawa plateau are again a section of a chain of Adamawa-Eastern-speakers that reaches from the Azande in the east across to the Nigerian Benue. These regions have been less impinged upon from without.

We have to date no evidence that might indicate that speakers of early Benue-Congo languages such as pre-Bantu or proto-Bantu were ever occupants of our area. On the contrary, it would appear that the main linguistic groupings have been implanted since very ancient times.

THE CROPS

The distribution of cultivated plants by peoples can now be considered against the archaeological and ethnohistorical background sketched above, with a view to determining crop histories through age-and-area reconstruction (Kroeber 1948:561–571).

Few tribes received more than summary treatment by ethnographers, and fewer yet of the ethnographers have had any botanical competence, or even, like Barth, carried a copy of Hooker's *Flora Nigritia* in their pockets. Jacques-Félix's summary (1940) of crops grown at particular villages of various peoples is a valuable resource, especially for the Mandara region, but his listings are unlikely to be exhaustive. Other botanists, admirably precise on the crops, occasionally fail to make it

[6]   Greenberg has unfortunately not disclosed the genetic relationships *between* subfamilies and groups of languages. Thus, if the Kotoko group turns out to be more closely allied to Group 9 (Kera, Somrai, etc.) than to the Musgu group, our reading of the ethnohistory will require much revision.

clear who is growing them. I have been able to collect only limited and imperfect information, but at least one tribe of each region and of each linguistic grouping is represented, albeit often unsatisfactorily, and in two cases data are available for two time horizons. For the sake of comparison I have included material from southeastern Bornu, collected by Denham, Barth, and Nachtigal before 1900, from the Jukun, and from the Sara and the Gulla of Lake Iro in Chad. The Gulla are placed by Murdock (1959:136) in his Sara cluster, but the ethnography (Pairault 1966) leaves it uncertain whether the Gulla of Iro are in fact closely related to the Sara (Sudanic-speakers) or whether they are a Bua (Adamawa-Eastern) people.

Plants known to have been introduced since 1900, or of which the cultivation is said to be "récente" or "ne fait pas partie de l'agriculture traditionelle," are excluded from Table 3. Neither data nor available space permit the listing and discussion of protected species and semi-domesticates. These include the very common trees baobab, desert date, nettle tree, tamarind, etc. The useful plants that are commonly protected in and around Fulani villages in the Garoua area are noted in the appendix to this paper. Detailed botanical study of these plants, their distribution and history, would be of certain value to the culture historian.

In consulting Table 3 it should be remembered that the omission of a plant from the listings may only mean that it has not been reported.

Sorghum bicolor, present in the area by the ninth century A.D. and, inferentially, long before, is the staple of the Chadic-speakers.[7] Early-maturing sorghums of the *caudatum* race and subraces show the greatest variety and were the only sorghums cultivated by those Adamawa-Eastern-speakers not in close contact with Chadic groups. Later-maturing sorghums, mainly of the *guinea* and *caudatum* races and sub-races, are grown by most Chadic-speakers and in Bornu, while *bicolor* race sorghums are only reported for the Tupuri and Gulla, among whom there are many subraces. The severely limited data are in accordance with Harlan and Stemler's view (1976) that sorghums of *caudatum* race were developed from *bicolor* in the area extending eastward from Lake Chad. The date of the probable replacement of the early forms is uncertain, as is that of the arrival of *guinea* sorghums from the west. If my reading of the

[7]   Identifications of sorghums by species and variety are given only for the Massa, Gulla, and Tupuri. I received help in identification from the agricultural research station at Guétalé, but this extended only to the classification of the main groups. These identifications, of course, preceded Harlan and de Wet's (1972) new classification by race and subrace, which I have attempted to follow, referring where necessary to Doggett's modification of the Snowden key (Doggett 1970:41–48).
   The reader is referred to Purseglove (1968, 1972) and Coursey (1967) for the authorities for binomial names given in the text. Authorities are rarely cited in the sources, in which the names given are now in many cases incorrect. I have standardized to Purseglove and Coursey wherever possible, and in cases of doubt have allowed the author's term to stand or placed it in inverted commas.

Table 3. The distribution of crops by peoples. Crops *known* to have been introduced after 1900 have been excluded

Plant name (Binomial / vernacular)	Jukun	Gbaya (1968)	Gbaya (1914)	Mbum	Durru	Do Ayo	Fulani (1970)	Fulani (1900)	Fali	Giddar	Njei	Bana	Gude	Kapsiki	Mofu	Matakam	Daba	Mundang	Tupuri	Gulla of Iro	Sara	Massa	Musgu	Kotoko	S.E. Bornuans
		Ačamawa	*Ačamawa*	*Ačamawa*	*Benue*	*Benue*	*Benue*	*Benue*	*Benue*	*Benue*	*Mandara*	*Mandara*	*Mandara*	*Mandara*	*Mandara*	*Mandara*	*Diamaré*	*Diamaré*	*Diamaré*			*Chad-Logone*	*Chad-Logone*	*Chad-Logone*	
CEREALS																									
Sorghum bicolor Sorghum	+	+	+	+	+	+	+	+	+	+	+	+	+	+	+	+	+	+	+	+	+	+	+	+	+
Early-maturing sorghums, mainly red-grained and of *caudatum* race and subraces	?				+		+	+	+	+	+	+	+	+	+	+	+	+	+	+	+	+	+	?	+
Later-maturing sorghums, mainly of the *guinea*, but including *caudatum* and *bicolor* race and subraces																			+	+		+			+
Transplanted sorghums, mainly of *caudatum* race and subraces																			+						+
Transplanted sorghums, mainly of *durra* race and subraces																			+						
Pennisetum americanum Bulrush and pearl millet	+		+	+			+	+	+	+	+	+	+	+		+				+	+	+			
Eleusine coracana Finger millet				+					+	+	+	+	+	+	+	+		+			+	+			
Digitaria exilis Fonio										+					+	+	+				+	+		+	
Oryza sp. Rice	+					+	+	+							+								+	+	+
O. sativa Asian rice																								+	+
O. glaberrima African rice					+																				+
Zea mays Maize	+	+	+	+	+	+			+	+	+	+	+	+	+	+	+	+	+					+	
Triticum sp. Wheat							+	+																+	
Hordeum vulgare Barley								+																	
ROOT CROPS																									
Dioscorea sp. Yam	+	+	+		+	+	+	+	+	+		+	+	+	+					+					
D. bulbifera Potato yam		+	+	+																+					
D. dumetorum Bitter yam			+	+	+																				

D. abyssinica —
D. minutiflora —
D. rotundata   Guinea yam
D. cayenensis   Yellow yam
D. alata   Winged yam
Coleus dysentericus and/or Plectranthus
  esculentus   Hausa potato and/or rizga
Colocasia esculenta   Taro
Xanthosoma sagittifolium   Yautia
Ipomoea batatas   Sweet potato
Manihot esculenta   Manioc
Cyperus esculentus   Tiger nut

PULSES

Vigna unguiculata   Cowpea
V. sinensis
Cajanus cajan   Pigeon pea
Voandzeia subterranea   Earthpea
Arachis hypogaea   Groundnut

OIL-YIELDING

Sesamum indicum   Sesame
S. radiatum —
Ricinus communis   Castor
Jatropha curcas   Physic nut

VEGETABLES

Abelmoschus esculentus   Okra
Hibiscus sabdariffa   Guinea sorrel
H. cannabinus   Hemp-leaved hibiscus
Ceratotheca sesamoides —
Corchorus olitorius   Jew's mallow
Solanum melongena   Eggplant
S. incanum   Bitter tomato
S. aethiopicum —
Lycopersicum esculentum   Tomato
Capsicum spp.   Guinea peppers
Allium spp.   Onions, etc.
Physalis peruviana —

Table 3. *(continued)*

Plant name — *Binomial* vernacular	Jukun	Adamawa — Gbaya (1968)	Adamawa — Gbaya (1914)	Adamawa — Mbum	Benue — Durru	Benue — Do Ayo	Benue — Fulani (1970)	Benue — Fulani (1900)	Benue — Fali	Benue — Giddar	Mandara — Njei	Mandara — Bana	Mandara — Gude	Mandara — Kapsiki	Mandara — Mofu	Mandara — Matakam	Diamaré — Daba	Diamaré — Mundang	Diamaré — Tupuri	Gulla of Iro	Sara	Chad-Logone — Massa	Chad-Logone — Musgu	Chad-Logone — Kotoko	S.E. Bornuans
CUCURBITS																									
— Cucurbit																									
Lagenaria siceraria Gourd	+	+	+	+	+	+	+	+	+	+	+	+	+	+	+	+			+	+	+	+	+	?	+
Citrullus lanatus Watermelon	+		+	+			+	+	+	+						+			+	+	+	+			
Cucumeropsis edulis —			+	+					+										+			+			
Momordica balsamina / *M. charantia* } Balsam apple / Bitter gourd		?						?																	
Cucurbita pepo Pumpkin							+	+	+	+															
C. maxima Pumpkin							+																		
FRUITS																									
Musa paradisiaca Plantain and Banana		+	+				+	+		+												+			+
Citrus aurantiifolia Lime							+	+																	
Phoenix dactylifera Date		+					+	+																	
Carica papaya Pawpaw	+						+		+	+															
Passiflora foetida Stinking passion flower			+																						

OTHER

Tephrosia vogelii Fish poison bean	+	+				+	+	+	+		+	+	+	+		+	+	+	+	+
Gossypium spp. Cotton	+	+	+	+	+	+	+	+	+	+	+	+	+	+	+	+	+	+	+	+
Nicotiana spp. Tobacco	+	+						+	+	+	+	+	+	+	+	+	+	+		+
Indigofera arrecta Indigo												+	+	+			+			
Lawsonia inermis Henna												+	+	+			+			

Main sources:

General: Pelé and Le Berre 1966; Lembezat 1961.
Bornuans: Denham, Clapperton and Oudney 1828; Barth 1857; Nachtigal 1881.
Kotoko: Barth 1857; Nachtigal 1881; Jacques-Félix 1940.
Musgu: Jacques-Félix 1940.
Massa: Diziain 1954; de Garine 1964.
Sara: Chevalier 1907; Cabot 1965.
Gulla: Pairault 1966.
Tupuri: Diziain 1954; Guillard 1965.
Mundang and Daba: Diziain 1954.

Matakam: Jacques-Félix 1940; Boulet 1966.
Mofu: Jacques-Félix 1940; Vaillant 1947.
Kapsiki, Gude, Bana, Njei, Giddar: Jacques-Félix 1940.
Fali: Jacques-Félix 1940; Malzy 1956; Lebeuf 1961.
Fulani of Bé: N. David fieldnotes.
Do Ayo: Lembezat 1961.
Durru: Jacques-Félix 1940; Hata 1973.
Mbum: Jacques-Félix 1940, 1948.
Gbaya: Tessmann 1934; Burnham 1972.
Jukun: Meek 1931.

Kera immigration is correct, then it is conceivable that they reintroduced some *bicolor* strains from the east between A.D. 1000 and A.D. 1500, perhaps bringing with them the technique of transplanting *caudatum* sorghums. Transplanted sorghums of the *durra* race and subraces were introduced from Bornu to the Kotoko and western Musgu (Barth 1857:vol. 3, p. 186). Elsewhere they became established through Fulani agency, and until recently the Tupuri were alone in accepting them.

A sweet-stemmed *guinea-bicolor* sorghum (*S. mellitum* Snowden) is grown by the Gulla, and it may be this form that is known to the Fulani as *lakkawal* [the sorghum of the Lakka], which suggests that it was introduced from the east. The Fulani and other peoples grow *S. bicolor* var. *colorans* to obtain a red dye.

Pennisetum americanum, bulrush and pearl millet, is a less important but widespread crop. Five varieties are grown by the Massa and four by the Matakam. *Eleusine coracana*, finger millet, provisionally identified in the Benue in the ninth and tenth centuries A.D. and still grown there by the Fali, is second only to sorghum among the Mukhtele of the northern Mandara (Juillerat 1971:26). It is grown by all the Mandara peoples listed and also by the pagans of Dikwa Emirate in the former British Cameroons (White 1943). Farther to the east, it attains the status of a staple among some Kabalai, Gambai, and other riverine peoples of the Middle Logone (Cabot 1965:103–104). Fonio, *Digitaria exilis*, is reported from the Massa and Mundang and from the Mofu (Vaillant 1947).

The bulrush millets, domesticated to the north of our area, have long been cultivated in association with sorghum for variety and as insurance against a poor rainy season. The distribution of finger millet suggests that it was once more widely and extensively cultivated, but has been largely replaced (by *guinea* and, subsequently, *durra* sorghums?), except where it has been retained on account of its adaptability to a wide range of soil and moisture conditions. The rarity of fonio might indicate that it, too, was an early cultigen that subsequently dropped out of cultivation or, more probably, that it is a later introduction from the west.

The failure of the peoples living around Lake Chad to domesticate the wild African rice of the region is another indication of the antiquity of sorghum and millet as cereal staples. Wild rice (*Oryza barthii* ex. *breviligulata*) was collected in the nineteenth century and is still collected in times of scarcity by the Massa and the Fali, but the Kotoko only brought the local varieties under cultivation in the very late nineteenth or early twentieth centuries, perhaps to supplement the supplies of Asiatic rice that were imported from Hausaland (Denham, Clapperton, and Oudney 1828:vol. 2, p. 159). At the time of Barth's visit, rice was grown only in the western parts of Nigerian Adamawa, where there were close contacts with Hausa (Barth 1857:vol. 2, p. 481).[8] The cultivation of African rice (identified by S. Nakao, Osaka Prefectural University, Japan) by the Durru of the Benue is exceptional for this region (Hata 1973:98).

Maize (*Zea mays*) was already an important crop in Bornu in the late eighteenth century (Miracle 1965:42), but its introduction to the Massa is described as recent, suggesting that Bornu was a less important source of dissemination than Kororofa. The Jukun, who may have received it from Calabar, passed it on to the Adamawa-speakers probably in the first half of the eighteenth century (Meek 1931:39) Maize, the most important cereal on the Adamawa plateau, may have passed from there to the Gbaya, reaching northern Gabon only in the later nineteenth century (Miracle 1965:46). An alternative route or simultaneous diffusion of maize to the Gbaya could have come from the east via the Congo and the savannas of the Central African Republic (Tisserant 1953:226).

Barth (1857: vol. 2, p. 314) states that wheat (*Triticum* sp.) and onions (*Allium cepa*) reached Bornu across the Sahara about a hundred years before his visit. Denham's mention of barley (*Hordeum vulgare*; Denham, Clapperton, and Oudney, 1828, vol. 1, p. 216) is confirmed by Dalziel (1937:529). Neither was ever grown on a large scale in Bornu. The Fulani used to grow small quantities of wheat, which was used for ceremonial breaking of the fast, in watered plots. *Echinochloa colona* Link was raised in small quantities by the Banda and Gbaya of the Central African Republic to aid in the fermentation of beer (Tisserant 1953:241). This practice has not been reported from Cameroon. The floating millet cultivated by the Massa under the name of *ourlaga* is likely to be *Echinochloa stagnina*, while the Mundang are said to have grown small quantities of *Setaria pallidifusca* (R. Portères, personal communication).

Yams, long a staple of the Adamawa-speakers south of the Benue and much less important to the north, have been progressively replaced by sorghum, maize, and manioc. Pelé and Le Berre (1966) accord the Dioscoreaceae only a paragraph in their compendium of Cameroonian food plants. With the exception of the Durru, there are no firm identifications of the Guinea yam (*D. rotundata*). The yellow yam (*D. cayenensis*) and the winged yam (*D. alata*), nineteenth-century introductions to the savannas of the Central African Republic from the southwest (Tisserant 1953:229), were probably not in North Cameroon any earlier. *D. minutiflora*, found only among the Gbaya and native to the wetter parts of West Africa (Coursey 1965:57), may be another late arrival. *D. abyssinica*, native to Ethiopia and cultivated by the Durru, is perhaps the only species to have been transmitted from east to west along Murdock's "yam belt." The widely distributed potato yam (*D. bulbifera*) and bitter yam

[8] The rice of the Matakam is not identified as to species, but it is most unlikely to be *O. glaberrima* because their neighbors, the Mofu, grow the "Fulani variety" (Vaillant 1947:88).

(*D. dumetorum* [Kunth] Pax. and/or *latifolia* Benth.) may, on the other hand, have come under cultivation very early. *D. sansibarensis* Pax (= *D. macroura* Harms), which went out of cultivation only very recently in the Central African Republic (Tisserant 1953:229) and is still grown by the Banen of South Cameroon (Dugast 1944:43), should no doubt be added to this list. Jacques-Félix (1948) gives a Mbum name for *D. liebrechtiana* (= *cayenensis*?) and Gbaya terms for *D. "gribinguiensis"* and *D. lecardi* without stating specifically that they are cultivated.

The yams grown north of the Benue are identified as to species only in one instance, the bush yam (*D. praehensilis*) of the Massa. Raised only in minute quantities, sometimes even a single plant in a compound garden, they would repay study as possible relicts of an earlier phase of plant husbandry in a forest-savanna ecotone.

The spotty distribution of the Hausa potato (*Coleus dysentericus*) and apparent absence of rizga (*Plectranthus esculentus* = *Coleus dazo*) are best explained as the result of replacement. Both are grown to the east and west and were attributed by Portères (1962:207) to his central African cradle of agriculture. Portères has stated that he tends to agree with Harlan (1971:470) on an origin of the Hausa potato farther to the west between Guinea and Togo, although he has not excluded the possibility of independent domestication in more than one area. Yautia (*Xanthosoma sagittifolium*), recorded only from three Mandara peoples, the Durru, the Mbum, and the Gbaya of 1968, must be a colonial introduction, as its Mbum name, *Agô nasara*, implies. It has been known to the Banen only since around 1910 (Dugast 1944: 13). Taro (*Colocasia esculenta*) is not commonly cultivated in our area. According to Burkill (1938:95), it was transmitted to West Africa either from Egypt and North Africa across the Sahara by Arabs and Berbers or from the east coast "by infiltration along equatorial parts." Except perhaps in the extreme north, it is unlikely to have been established in Cameroon until after 1600. Sweet potatoes (*Ipomoea batatas*) are often known by corruptions of Hausa or Fulani names and are an introduction of the Fulani period. Their arrival in Bornu may be quite precisely dated between 1850 and 1880 (cf. Barth 1857: vol. 2, p. 315; Nachtigal 1881:533). Cassava or manioc (*Manihot esculenta*) was grown by the Fulani of Yola in 1850 (Barth 1857:vol. 2, p. 436) but had not yet reached the Adamawa plateau (p. 505). In the later nineteenth century it diffused rapidly from the southeast and west and by the 1880's had replaced the yam as a staple except among the Durru (Ministère d'Outre-Mer 1895:464).

Tiger nuts (*Cyperus esculentus*), known from ancient Egypt (Dalziel 1937:517), are grown in the Diamaré, Mandara, and Benue regions and are primarily associated with Chadic-speakers. In Bornu they appear to be escapes; Barth (1857: vol. 2, p. 381; vol. 3, pp. 31, 262) saw them dug up wild and says that there was also extensive use of their rhizomes (and/or those of *C. articulatus?*) for perfume. Their introduction must pre-date, perhaps very considerably, Islamic times.

Pulses are frequently mentioned by authors but rarely by their binomial name. The earthpea (*Voandzeia subterranea*) is ubiquitous and was until recently more important than the groundnut *(Arachis hypogaea)*, for the presence of which there is no certain evidence before the Fulani period.[9] The distributional and botanical evidence is in accord with the theory that the earthpea was domesticated near the Benue on the Cameroon-Nigeria border (Harlan 1971:471). On the other hand, I can find no report suggesting that the geocarpa bean (*Kerstingiella geocarpa*), also believed to have been domesticated in that region, has ever been cultivated in the area. Although not — or no longer — grown in the Central African Republic, a subspontaneous form, named *K. tisserantii* by Pellegrin, occurs in sandy places in the hills north of Bamberi (Tisserant 1953:235). Several varieties of cowpea (*Vigna unguiculata* and/or *sinensis*) are grown; it is ubiquitous and a very old cultigen.

The botanical and distributional evidence also favors a great antiquity for the cultivation of sesame (*Sesamum indicum*) in Cameroon. Sesame was a traditional oil-yielding plant before the advent of the groundnut, and is considered by Portères (1962:206–207) to have been domesticated between Lake Chad and Ethiopia. *Sesamum radiatum*, from the same general area, is, curiously, reported only from the Mbum. The oils of the castor plant (*Ricinus communis*) and physic nut (*Jatropha curcas*) are widely used in tropical Africa for specialized purposes, and the latter is often grown as a hedge plant (Dalziel 1937:160–163, 147–148). The castor plant, while utilized in the north of the area, is cultivated only in the south and by the Sara and tribes of the Central African Republic to the east. Of Ethiopian origin, it must have spread early along the savanna zone. I have no information on the physic nut, which is of New World origin.

In contrast to the majority of plants discussed above, which are commonly field crops, vegetables are usually produced in small gardens within and adjacent to the compound, on termite mounds, or in other special microenvironments. Some twenty years ago, Anderson (1952:136–150) pointed out the significance of such plots for experiments in cultivation. Harris (1973:400) has gone farther, postulating that "fixed plot horticulture preceded swidden cultivation." Unfortunately, on account of their biotic complexity and minor economic importance, gardens have received little attention. Of twenty-six vegetable species for which I have information, no less than fourteen are reported only from

---

[9]   Groundnuts are not called by corruptions of Fulani or Hausa names. They may have reached Bornu quite early. Barth (1857: vol. 5, pp. 334 ff., 447) reports that they had reached Baghirmi in his day, and Maistre (1895:176, 273) remarked that the Sara were already growing them in quantity in the late nineteenth century.

the Gbaya,[10] although many of these same species are collected by the Fulani of Bé and no doubt most other peoples. Philip Burnham has described to me how Gbaya will avoid chopping down useful leafy plants during swidden clearing, and may transplant them to their temporary garden plots. Such semidomestication would not "provide a genetic environment ideally suited to the emergence of domesticated variants through the selection and fixation of desirable characteristics" (Harris 1973:400) because selection, even unconscious, does not seem to occur. Plants are simply moved over short distances to more convenient locations, are replaced or not, as the case may be, from year to year, and are not taken along if the village is moved. Thus, although these plants may have a very long history of exploitation by man, they have not been ennobled.

So many wild and protected herbs, shrubs, and trees produce edible, even delicious, leaves that the only vegetables to have come under regular cultivation are those with other qualities. The bitter tomato (*Solanum incanum*) and okra (*Abelmoschus* [*Hibiscus*] *esculentus*) have sizable fruit; *Ceratotheca sesamoides* gives a mucilage that is used by the Fulani in plastering their walls; the *Hibiscus* species provide fiber. Guinea sorrel (*H. sabdariffa*) is a widely distributed and probably old domesticate with several cultivars. The hemp-leaved hibiscus (*H. cannabinus*) must be attributed to the Fulani period on the grounds that so many of its local names are corruptions of the Fulani *gabay*. Jew's mallow (*Corchorus olitorius*) appears to be an old cultigen, perhaps originally introduced as a fiber plant and now subspontaneous in much of North Cameroon. It was brought to Africa from the East in the first centuries A.D./B.C. (Murdock

---

[10]   Tessman (1934: 51–52) lists the following plants by their binomial and/or vernacular names, the latter translated here by reference to unpublished vocabularies prepared by P. Burnham and P. Vidal:

Tessman	Burnham (B) and Vidal (V)
mbōndó	*Justicia insularis* (B)
Amaranthus caudatus	Native terms given include *A. viridis* (V).
sáyumbá	*Gynandropsis gynandra* (V)
Composite (liló)	
Composite (mbuli, mbui-zam)	
"Abelmoschus moschatus"	
(?=*Hibiscus moschatus* L.)	
Polygonum species (mbanga-tàna)	
"Ocimum basilicum"	
(?=*O. americanum* L.)	
Solanum "dinklagei" (sōóle)	*S. nigrum* (B)
Solanum species (ngagō)	*S. nodiflorum* (B) or *S.* "distichum" (V) (?= *S. indicum* L. var *distichum* Thonning)
Asterocantha longifolia	*Vernonia cinerea* (V), presumably used medicinally.
gba-wuo	

According to Burnham's list, *Amaranthus* cf. *hybridus* and *Urena lobata* are also semidomesticates.

1959:207). Capsicum pepper (*Capsicum annuum* and *C. frutescens*) and *Allium* species were introduced relatively recently, the latter across the Sahara, the former probably by the Fulani (as many local names suggest) but also via Bornu, whence it was traded to Baghirmi in the 1850's (Barth 1857: vol. 3, p. 383). Birds may also have acted as agents of dispersal. Among the complex family of cucurbits, the extraordinarily wide distribution within and beyond Africa of the gourd (*Lagenaria siceraria*) and watermelon (*Citrullus lanatus*) argues for their very great age as cultigens. The botany of the multitude of local cultivars is little understood (Pelé and Le Berre 1966:6).

Although many native fruits were collected, none were ever regularly cultivated. The pawpaw (*Carica papaya*), of New World origin and yet of fundamental importance in Fali mythology, probably entered the area from Kororofa at the same time as maize. Tobacco may derive from the same source or have been introduced by the northern route. The plantain (*Musa paradisiaca*), which will not grow north of the southern Adamawa, and the banana (*M. paradisiaca* var. *sapientium*) seem to have diffused very late from the south. The lime (*Citrus aurantiifolia*) and date palm (*Phoenix dactylifera*) are Islamic imports spread by the Fulani.

Cotton (*Gossypium* spp.), grown as a perennial, is said to have been introduced into Kanem-Bornu between the tenth and the sixteenth centuries (Urvoy 1949:19). Although never grown on a large scale outside those areas where demand for woven clothing was stimulated by Islam, it was not limited to them. The Sara grew small quantities in 1900 (Chevalier 1907:267), and, although barkcloth made of the bark of figs or the roots of *Chlorophera excelsa* Benth. and Hook. was the preferred material in the Central African Republic, Tisserant (1953:249) considers cotton to be a very old savanna cultigen.[11] Indigo (*Indigofera arrecta*) had been carried into Kotoko territory and to Baghirmi from Bornu, often by immigrant Kanuri dyers, before the first European contact (Denham, Clapperton and Oudney 1828: vol. 2, pp. 19–20). The Fulani were responsible for its extension to the central and southern parts of the area and also for the introduction of henna (*Lawsonia inermis*), not mentioned by the early visitors to Bornu.

---

[11] Courtet and Chevalier give the following as species of cotton found in Bornu, Baghirmi, and Chad in the early years of this century (Chevalier 1907:731–732):

Gossypium hirsutum — from Nigeria
G. arboreum   — from Egypt
G. barbadense   — via the Congo to the Sara
G. anaomalum   — wild south of Kanem, along the Bahr el-Ghazal, and in the Dar el-Hadjer.

CONCLUSIONS: CROPS AND CULTURE HISTORY

The data on crop history are presented in summary form in Table 4. The table suggests that there were two main periods during which crop plants became established in North Cameroon: the Neolithic and Fulani periods. In the course of the intervening centuries, crops from East Africa and India and West African yams reached the area, but, except for finger millet, there is no direct evidence as to the date of their arrival. The question of pre-Islamic diffusion between central and eastern Africa (including the northeast) urgently requires investigation. Our polarized view of the process is almost certainly misleading, reflecting our ignorance of events within the long course of the Neolithic and of the agricultural economy of the Iron Age before A.D. 1600. The influx of New World crops after this date, even if less revolutionary than in the forests,

Table 4. The establishment of cultivated plants in North Cameroon: an attempted periodization.

Neolithic	Early Iron Age	Kanem-Kororofa	Kororofa-Bornu	Fulani	
?B.C.	A.D. 500	1000	1600	1750	1900
(Bicolor sorghums)		Cotton N	Maize W	Durra sorghums N	
Caudatum sorghums			Pawpaw W	Asian rice	
Pennisetum N			Tobacco W	African rice	
Earthpea				Wheat	
Sesame E				Barley	
Cowpea				Winged yam S	
Gourd				Yellow yam S	
Watermelon			Pigeon pea	Manioc S/W	
Guinea sorghums W	Finger millet E			Sweet potato W	
Bitter yam	Rizga			Hemp-leaved hibiscus W	
Potato yam	Castor plant E			*Musa* cultivars S	
Bush yam	Jew's mallow E			*Allium* spp. N	
Guinea sorre	Tiger nut N/E			Lime N	
C. sesamoides	Guinea yam W			Date palm N/W	
Bitter tomato	White yam W		Taro N/E	Henna W	
	D. abyssinica E		Indigo N	Pumpkin W	
		Fonio	Ground-nut W	Tomato N	
			D. minutiflora		

* Plants are placed in the column suggested by the weight of the various lines of evidence. When the period cannot be specified with confidence, the vertical lines indicate the likely time range; e.g., groundnuts were probably established between 1600 and 1750 but perhaps not until the Fulani period.

   The northern (mainly trans-Saharan Islamic), southern (from South Cameroon), eastern (along the Sudan zone), and western (from Nigeria) origins of introduced cultigens are indicated.

nevertheless transformed many aspects of savanna agriculture; nor should the accompanying diffusion of plants with a longer history of cultivation in Africa be forgotten. In thinking of the past we are perhaps overinclined to forget that "traditional" agriculture, even as described by early travelers, is a recent development. The supposedly conservative African cultivator has a remarkable record of innovation.

The crops listed as Neolithic are of three classes: (1) those for which botanical and in some cases archaeological evidence suggests domestication in or near North Cameroon (bicolor sorghums, caudatum sorghums, earthpeas), (2) those for which archaeological and/or botanical evidence would seem to indicate an early introduction from outside the immediate area (guinea sorghums, bulrush millet), and (3) residuals, that is, plants that are at home in the savanna zone, are widely cultivated (although often little ennobled), and for which there is no relevant botanical or archaeological evidence.

A fourth category, unlisted, should include crops that have fallen out of cultivation (e.g., most bicolor sorghums, and perhaps the geocarpa bean and *Dioscorea sansibarenis*). Without supposing that the list approximates a complete inventory of Neolithic cultigens, it may, in combination with other lines of evidence, be taken to suggest marked differences between Neolithic economies in the northern and southern parts of our area.

It can be inferred that the peoples of the Chad basin practiced a mixed economy of stock breeding and fishing combined with the cultivation of cereal staples and a variety of subsidiary crops. Hunting made some contribution to the diet, as almost certainly did the gathering of wild seeds (although according to Barth [1857: vol. 2, p. 312; vol. 3, pp. 29–30, 161, 274, 447] it was not the settled "black natives" but the pastoral Shuwa Arabs who exploited this resource). In the Benue basin there are few traces of Neolithic technology — let alone economy — and it is arguable whether food production was practiced south of the river before the Iron Age. Cereals were introduced from the north, while the Benue and Adamawa regions are marginal to the West African yam belt and are unlikely to have played a major role in yam domestication (Coursey 1967:22–25). The inhabitants, widespread although thinly scattered, must have relied far less on food production and on fishing than the northerners and more on hunting and gathering (cf. Sillans 1953) together with some plant husbandry. Their crops are likely to have included the earthpea, maybe their only significant achievement in domestication, and some of the more widely distributed yams. Because, as discussed above, there is no evidence of large-scale population replacements or immigration before the seventeenth and eighteenth centuries A.D., the practitioners of these contrasting economies may be provisionally identified as speakers of languages ancestral respectively to Chadic and Adamawa-Eastern.

I have attempted here to follow Murdock's (1959) example in making as systematic a use as possible of the evidence of crops for the reconstruction of culture history. The difficulties encountered in applying his approach even on a small scale help to explain the failure — howbeit stimulating and productive — of those sections of his continental synthesis that treat early developments in agriculture (Baker 1962; Portères 1962). The results of the present study are of relevance primarily to Cameroonian history, but because Cameroon occupies a strategic position near the center of the continent they may have wider implications.

The presence of the Chadic subfamily of Afro-Asiatic languages in sub-Saharan Africa is best explained by the hypothesis that the ancestral language originated in the southern Sahara, perhaps through the contact of its Neolithic pastoral population with peoples of the south (Olderogge 1956). With desertification in the last two to three millennia B.C., there would have been a tendency for some of these peoples to migrate southward, attempting thus to maintain their environmental adaptation. It is at this point that knowledge of the vegetation patterns of the day becomes crucial to an understanding of the processes of domestication. If there lay to the south the inexhaustible resources of the savanna, then, as Clark (1976) asks, why were they unable to maintain their broad-spectrum economy? If, on the other hand, they were hemmed into a narrow zone of scrub and savanna between the advancing desert and a less rapidly retreating forest, economic experimentation or specialization under population pressure becomes immediately comprehensible. In either case, competition for fishing rights along the few perennial rivers and retreating lakes is a probability. With the restriction of at least the fishing and perhaps also of the pastoral components, greater reliance would have been placed on other sectors of the economy. Specialization and the development of new exploitative techniques would have followed as responses to this difficult period. We cannot tell whether any differentiation of the Chadic languages occurred during the period of residence in the Sahara, but it would seem a strong possibility that the linguistic spread over much of its present wide distribution formed part and parcel of (1) the diffusion of a complex of successful economic adaptations to the peoples of the Sahel and northern Sudan zones and (2) a southward expansion of the complex and assimilation of forest hunter-gatherers as the edges of the dry forest were eroded by clearing and firing.

According to Murdock (1959:232), "the incidence and distribution of cultivated plants among the Eastern Nigritic [i.e., Adamawa-Eastern] peoples illuminate their culture history with exceptional clarity." Nothing, alas, could be farther from the truth; agreed that their present distribution suggests an overall, long-term movement eastward, agreed that this may have been stimulated by diffusion of Sudanic agriculture later supplemented by plants of the Malaysian complex, nevertheless the culture history of the Central African Republic and of the neighbor countries in which these languages are found is less well understood than that of any area of comparable size in the whole of Africa. There is no information about the date of their early movements, which may have commenced in the Neolithic or quite late in the Iron Age, or about their character; we do not know whether the spread of the languages was the product of migration or of diffusion of language along with a new economy or with iron technology. Any combination of dates and of these or other processes is possible.

North Cameroon may yet be implicated in the puzzle of Bantu origins, but no support has been found for the prevailing view that the *Ur-* or pre-Bantu homeland is to be sought in or to the east of our area (Johnston 1913:391; Guthrie 1962:281; Oliver 1966). The evidence, negative though it is, rather favors Greenberg's position, firmly restated in a recent article, "that the ultimate origin of Bantu should be approximately in the middle Benue area of Nigeria" (Greenberg 1972:192). There is a strong argument here for a concentration of archaeological research in Cameroon in Letouzey's (1959) "Zone péri- ou post-forestière," the man-made savannas still occupied by some Bantoid-speaking peoples (see above) that stretch south of the Adamawa from the Tikar plain across to Batouri.

None of these problems will be solved until much more archaeological and paleoecological information becomes available. The archaeological gaps are obvious enough but the contribution of archaeologists will very largely depend upon the success of paleoecologists in reconstructing past ecosystems.

Any human settlement has effects on its immediate environment. The present distribution of species on the Quaternary terraces of the Mayo Kébi is a human artifact (see appendix). There are few trees that are not encouraged or protected for their economic value, scarcely a shrub that is not in some way exploited, and the herbs are for the most part either weedy colonizers of the fields or used for thatch, matting, or fodder. (Two grasses are even said to have been introduced by the Nyamnyam.) The flotation technique, especially in its improved form (Higgs 1976), can be expected to provide the archaeologist with direct evidence of cultigens and of other plants growing in the environs of his sites. Interpretation of these data depends upon identification and, secondly, upon the "ethno-ecological" expertise necessary to infer from fragmentary evidence a complete system of man-land interrelationships. The difficulty of this task can be appreciated when we remember that "primitive" African agriculture has not been practiced these last 200 years.

A fundamental requirement for future culture-historical studies and research into crop plant evolution is a better knowledge of the Holocene environmental sequence and vegetation patterns. Prolonged swidden cultivation, especially if combined with stock breeding and the driving of game with fire, profoundly modifies plant communities, and not only in the immediate vicinity of settlements. Some modifications may be irreversible. Human agency is arguably paramount in the creation of the central African savannas from dense dry forest. Dry forest and savanna must require quite different adaptive strategies on the part of peoples with and without agriculture and with and without iron. Unless these strategies can be defined and recognized where and when they occur archaeologically, there is little hope of significant progress. Finally, I would ask the botanists to tell us what might have been the effects of savannization on the distribution of the wild ancestors of African domesticates and semi-domesticates. Is it not possible that ignorance of man-made vegetational changes that may in many areas go back no farther than the middle Iron Age is distorting our views not only of culture history but also of crop plant evolution?

APPENDIX

Useful plants found in and near settled Fulani villages in the Benue-Kébi confluence area of North Cameroon, a partial listing

Binomial name	Vernacular name	Use
Amaranthus spinosus L.	Spiny amaranth	Pot-herb
Asteroclina species		Pot-Herb
Brachiaria ramosa (L.) Stapf		Horse fodder
Cleome hirsuta Sch. and Thonn.		Pot-herb
C. cilata Sch. and Thonn.		Pot-herb
Cyperus cf. *articulatus*		Rhizomes burnt for fragrance
Dactyloctenium aegyptium Beauv.	Comb-fringe grass	Horse fodder
Echinochloa species		Horse fodder
Gynandropsis gynandra (L.) Briq.		Pot-herb
Hemarthria altissima (Poir.) Stapf and Hubbard		Thatch
Hyparrhenia species		Thatch
Pennisetum pedicellatum Trin.		Thatch
Polygonum species		Ashes as salt substitute
Trachypogon species		Thatch
Vetiveria nigritana Stapf		Zana matting
Adansonia digitata L.	Baobab	Multiple
Annona senegalensis Pers.	Wid custard apple	Fruit
Acacia albida Del.	Winter thorn	Fodder (dry season)
A. arabica Willd.	Egyptian thorn	Glue
A. polyacantha Willd. subsp. *campylacantha* (Hochst *ex* A. Rich.) Brenan	Catechu tree	Fence posts
A. senegal Willd.		Fodder, glue

APPENDIX (*continued*)

Binomial name	Vernacular name	Use
Balanites aegyptiaca Del.	Desert date	Multiple
Bombax costatum Pellegr. and Vuillet	Red-flowered silk-cotton tree	Mattress stuffing
Butyrospermum paradoxum (Gaetn. f.) Hepper subspecies *parkii* (G. Don)	Shea tree	Fruit
Capparis corymbosa Lam.		Arrow poison (root)
Cassia tora L.	Foetid cassia	Pot-herb
Ceiba pentandra Gaertn.	Silk-cotton tree	Mattress stuffing
Celtis intergrifolia Lam.	Nettle tree	Fruit, pot-herb
Commiphora kerstingii Engl.	African myrrh	Fodder, fence posts
Corchorus olitorius L.	Jew's mallow	Pot-herb
C. tridens L.		Pot-herb
Euphorbia unispina N. E. Br.		Arrow poison (sap)
Ficus gnaphalocarpa A. Rich.		Fruit, fodder
F. iteophylla Miq.		Fruit
F. platyphylla Del.	Gutta-percha tree	Fruit, fodder
F. polita Vahl		Fruit
Gardenia erubescens Stapf and Hutch.		Fence posts
Grewia tenax (Forsk.) Fiori		Wood for bows
G. mollis Juss.		Spice (bark)
Haematostaphis barteri Hook f.	Blood plum	Fruit
Hyphaene thebaica Mart.	Dum palm	Fruit, matting
Jatropha curcas L.	Physic nut	Hedge plant
Khaya senegalensis A. Juss	Dry-zone mahogany	Canoe wood
Kigelia africana Benth.	Sausage tree	Fence posts
Manihot glaziovii Muell Arg.	Ceara rubber	Glue, ornamental
Moringa oleifera Lam.	Horseradish tree	Drink (leaves)
Parkinsonia aculeata L.	Jerusalem thorn	Ornamental
Parkia clappertoniana Keay	Locust bean tree	Flavoring (seeds)
Prosopis africana Taub.		Smiths' charcoal
Ricinus communis L.	Castor plant	Oil
Securinega virosa (Roxb. *ex* Willd.) Baill.		Withies for beds and traps
Sterculia setigera Del.		String
Tamarindus indica L.	Tamarid	Drink (fruit pulp)
Vitex doniana Sweet		Fruit, wood for canoes
Ximenia americana L.	Wild olive	Fruit
Zizphus mauritiana Lam.	Jujube tree	Fruit, wood for bows
Z. mucronata Willd.	Buffalo thorn	Fruit

REFERENCES

ALEXANDRE, P.
   1965   Proto-histoire du groupe beti-bulu-fang: essai de synthèse provisoire. *Cahiers d'Etudes Africaines* 5:503–560.
ALIMEN, H., P. LECOQ
   1953   Une curieuse roche "gravée" des monts Alantika. *Bulletin de la Société Préhistorique Française* 50:345–351.
ANDERSON, E.
   1952   *Plants, man, and life.* Boston: Little, Brown.
AUBREVILLE, A.
   1949   *Climats, forêts et désertification de l'Afrique tropicale.* Paris: Editions Géographiques, Maritimes, et Coloniales.
BAKER, H. G.
   1962   Comments on the thesis that there was a major centre of plant domestication near the headwaters of the River Niger. *Journal of African History* 3:229–233.
BARTH, H.
   1857   *Travels and discoveries in north and central Africa: being a journal of an expedition undertaken under the auspices of H.R.M.'s Government in the years 1849–1855,* five volumes. London: Longman, Brown, Green, Longman, and Roberts.
BASSORO, M. H.
   1965   Un manuscrit peul sur l'histoire de Garoua. *Abbia* 8:45–76.
BILLARD, P.
   1963   *Le Cameroun Fédérale,* volume one: *Essai de géographie physique.* Lyon: Beaux Arts.
BOULET, J.
   1966   "Magoumaz: étude d'un terroir de montagne de pays mafa." Unpublished manuscript. Yaoundé: ORSTOM.
BUISSON, E. M.
   1933   Matériaux pour servir à la préhistoire du Cameroun. *Bulletin de la Société Préhistorique Française* 30:335–348.
BURKILL, I. H.
   1938   The contact of the Portuguese with African food-plants which gave words such as "yam" to European languages. *Proceedings of the Linnean Society, London* 150:84–95.
BURNHAM, P. C.
   1972   "Residential organization and social change among the Gbaya of Meiganga, Cameroon." Unpublished Ph.D. dissertation, University of California, Los Angeles.
CABOT, J.
   1965   *Le bassin du Moyen Logone.* Paris: ORSTOM.
CALVOCORESSI, D.
   1970   Report on the Third Conference of West African Archaeologists. *West African Archaeological Newsletter* 12:53–90.
CHEVALIER, A.
   1907   *Mission Chari-Lac Tchad 1902–1904, l'Afrique centrale française: récit du voyage de la mission.* Paris: A. Chellamel.
CLARK, J. DESMOND
   1976   "Prehistoric populations and pressures favoring plant domestication in Africa," in *Origins of African plant domestication.* Edited by Jack R.

Harlan, Jan M. J. de Wet, and Ann B. L. Stemler, 67–106. World Anthropology. The Hague: Mouton.

CONNAH, G.
1966   Summary of research in Benin City and in Bornu. *West African Archaeological Newsletter* 5:22–25.
1967   Progress report on archaeological work in Bornu 1964–1966. *Northern History Research Scheme, Second Interim Report*, 20–31. Zaria.
1970   Precursors of Daima? *West African Archaeological Newsletter* 12:91–92.

COURSEY, D. C.
1967   *Yams*. London: Longmans, Green.

DALZIEL, J. MC E.
1937   *The useful plants of west tropical Africa*. London: Crown Agents.

DAVID, N.
1967   "An archaeological reconnaissance in Cameroon and the Iron Age site of Nassarao I, near Garoua." *Actes du Sixième Congrès Panafricain de Préhistoire et de l'Etude du Quaternaire*. Edited by H. Hugot. Dakar.
1968   Archaeological reconnaissance in Cameroon. *Expedition* 10(3): 21–31.

DE GARINE, I.
1964   *Les Massa du Cameroun: vie économique et sociale*. Paris: Presses Universitaires de France.
1973   "Traditions orales et cultures au Mayo Kebbi (Tchad)," in *L'homme, hier et aujourd'hui: recueil d'études en hommage à André Leroi-Gourhan*, 421–433. Paris: Cujas.

DENHAM, MAJOR D., CAPTAIN CLAPPERTON, DR. OUDNEY
1828   *Narrative of travels and discoveries in northern and central Africa in the years 1822, 1823, and 1824* (third edition), two volumes. London: John Murray.

DE WET, J. M. J., J. R. HARLAN, E. G. PRICE
1976   "Variability in *Sorghum bicolor*," in *Origins of African plant domestication*. Edited by Jack R. Harlan, Jan M. J. de Wet, and Ann. B. L. Stemler, 453–464. World Anthropology. The Hague: Mouton.

DIZIAIN, R.
1954   "Densité de la population, démographie, économie rurale dans les subdivisions de Guider-Kaélé et Yagoua (Nord-Cameroun)." Yaoundé: IRCAM. Unpublished manuscript.

DOGGETT, H.
1970   *Sorghum*. London: Longman.

DUGAST, R.
1944   L'agriculture chez les Ndiki de population Banen. *Bulletin de la Société des Études Camerounaises* 8:9–104.

ELDRIDGE, M.
1971   "Traditions d'origine des peuples du centre et de l'ouest du Cameroun." Unpublished manuscript. Yaoundé: Ministère de l'Education, de la Culture et de la Formation Professionelle.

GAUTHIER, J. G.
1972   La civilisation Sao: recherches archéologiques en pays Fali (Nord-Cameroun). *Archéologia* 49:45–56.

GREENBERG, J. H.
1963   *The languages of Africa*. International Journal of African Linguistics 29 (1, pt. 2). Publication 25 of the Indiana Research Center in Anthropology, Folklore, and Linguistics.

1972   Linguistic evidence regarding Bantu origins. *Journal of African History* 13:189–216.
GRIAULE, N., J.-P. LEBEUF
1948   Fouilles dans la région du Tchad, 1. *Journal de la Société des Africanistes* 18:1–116.
1950   Fouilles dans la région du Tchad, 2. *Journal de la Société des Africanistes* 20:1–151.
1951   Fouilles dans la région du Tchad, 3. *Journal de la Société des Africanistes* 21:1–95.
GUILLARD, J.
1965   *Golonpoui: analyse des conditions de modernisation d'un village du Nord-Cameroun*. Paris, The Hague: Mouton.
GUTHRIE, M.
1962   Some developments in the prehistory of the Bantu languages. *Journal of African History* 3:273–282.
HARLAN, J. R.
1971   Agricultural origins: centers and noncenters. *Science* 174:468–474.
HARLAN, J. R., J. M. J. DE WET
1972   A simplified classification of cultivated sorghum. *Crop Science* 12:172–176.
HARLAN, J. R., A. B. L. STEMLER
1976   "The races of sorghum in Africa," in *Origins of African plant domestication*. Edited by Jack R. Harlan, Jan M. J. de Wet, and Ann B. L. Stemler, 465–478. World Anthropology. The Hague: Mouton.
HARRIS, D. R.
1973   "The prehistory of tropical agriculture: an ethnoecological model," in *The explanation of culture change: models in prehistory*. Edited by C. Renfrew, 391–417. London: Duckworth.
HATA, N.
1973   The swidden crops and the planting pattern of Dourou agriculture in North Cameroon. *Kyoto University African Studies* 8:93–115.
HERVIEU, J.
1968   "Contribution à l'étude des industries lithiques du Nord-Cameroun: mise au point et données nouvelles." Unpublished manuscript. Yaoundé: ORSTOM.
1969   "Le Quaternaire du Nord-Cameroun: schéma d'évolution géomorphologique et relations avec la pédogenèse." Unpublished manuscript. Yaoundé: ORSTOM.
HIGGS, E. S.
1976   "Archaeology and domestication," in *Origins of African plant domestication*. Edited by Jack R. Harlan, Jan M. J. de Wet, and Ann B. L. Stemler, 29–39. World Anthropology. The Hague: Mouton.
HURAULT, J.
1970   Les lavaka de Banyo (Cameroun): témoins de paléoclimats. *Bulletin de l'Association Géographique Française* 377–378:3–13.
Illustrated London News
1967   "Classic excavation in north-east Nigeria." *Illustrated London News,* section 2276, October 14.
JACQUES-FÉLIX, H.
1940   L'agriculture des noirs au Cameroun: enquêtes sur les plantes cultivées, sur les outils agricoles et sur les greniers. *Revue Internationale de Botanique Appliquée et d'Agriculture Tropicale* 20:815–838.

1948   Ignames sauvages et cultivées du Cameroun. *Bulletin de la Société des Études Camerounaises* 21–22:13–18.

JAUZE, J. B.
1944   Contribution à l'étude de l'archéologie du Cameroun. *Bulletin de la Société des Études Camerounaises* 8:105–123.

JOHNSTON, SIR H. H.
1913   A survey of the ethnography of Africa and the former racial and tribal migrations in that continent. *Journal of the Royal Anthropological Institute* 43:375–421.

JUILLERAT, B.
1971   *Les bases de l'organisation social chez les Mouktélé (Nord-Cameroun): structures lignagères et mariage.* Mémoires de l'Institut d'Ethnologie 8.

KIRK-GREENE, A. H. M.
1958   *Adamawa past and present: an historical introduction to the development of a North Cameroons province.* London: Oxford University Press for the International African Institute.

KROEBER, A. L.
1948   *Anthropology* (revised edition). London: G. C. Harrap.

LEBEUF, A. M. D.
1959   *Les populations du Tchad (nord du 10e. parallèle).* Paris: Presses Universitaires de France.

LEBEUF, J.-P.
1961   *L'habitation des Fali, montagnards du Cameroun septentrionale: technologie, sociologie, mythologie, symbolisme.* Paris: Hachette.
1962   *Archéologie tchadienne: les Sao du Cameroun et du Tchad.* (Postface 1969.) Paris: Hermann.
1969   *Carte archéologique des abords du Lac Tchad (Cameroun, Nigeria, Tchad).* Paris: CNRS.

LEBEUF, J.-P., A. MASSON-DETOURBET
1950   *La civilisation du Tchad.* Paris: Payot.

LEMBEZAT, B.
1961   *Les populations paiennes du Nord-Cameroun et de l'Adamawa.* Paris: Presses Universitaires de France.

LESTRINGANT, J.
1964   "Le pays du Guider au Cameroun: essai d'histoire régionale." Unpublished manuscript. Paris: CNRS.

LETOUZEY, R.
1959   "Phytogéographie camerounaise," in *Atlas du Cameroun.* Paris: Imprimerie Nationale.
1968   *Etude phytogéographique du Cameroun.* Encyclopédie Biologique 69. Paris: P. Lechevalier.

MAISTRE, C.
1895   *A travers l'Afrique centrale du Congo au Niger.* Paris: Hachette.

MALZY, P.
1956   Les Fali du Tinguelin. *Bulletin de la Société des Etudes Camerounaises* 51:3–37.

MARLIAC, A.
1971   "*La préhistoire du Cameroun*," two volumes. Unpublished manuscript. Yaoundé: ORSTOM.

MEEK, C. K.
1931   *A Sudanese kingdom.* London: Kegan Paul, Trench, Trubner.

MINISTÈRE D'OUTRE-MER, PARIS
1895   "Mission Ponel: relevé de carnet d'itineraire de Bania à N'gaoundéré, 31 Dec. 1892–17 Feb. 1893." Manuscript, 3, 14, Archives Gabon-Congo, Ministère d'Outre-Mer, Paris.
MIRACLE, M. P.
1965   The introduction and spread of maize in Africa. *Journal of African History* 6:39–56.
MURDOCK, G. P.
1959   *Africa: its peoples and their culture history*. New York: McGraw-Hill.
NACHTIGAL, G.
1881   *Sahara und Sudan: Ergebnisse sechsjähriger Reisen in Afrika*, volume two. Berlin: Weidmannsche Buchhandlung, Verlagshandlung Paul Parey.
OLDEROGGE, D. A.
1956   "The origin of the Hausa language." Paper prepared for the Vth International Congress of Anthropological and Ethnological Sciences, Philadelphia.
OLIVER, R.
1966   The problem of the Bantu expansion. *Journal of African History* 7:361–376.
PAIRAULT, C.
1966   *Boum-le-grand, village d'Iro*. Travaux et Mémoires de l'Institut d'Ethnologie 73.
PALMER, H. R.
1928   *Sudanese memoirs*. Lagos: Government Printers.
PASSARGE, S.
1895   *Adamaua: Bericht über die Expedition des deutschen Kamerun-Komitees in den Jahren 1893/4*. Berlin: Geographische Verlagshandlung Dietrich Riemer (Hoefer and Vohsen).
PELÉ, J., S. LE BERRE
1966   "Les aliments d'origine végétale au Cameroun." Unpublished manuscript. Yaoundé: ORSTOM.
PERVÈS, M.
1945   Notes de préhistoire africaine: Hoggar-Sahara occidentale-Cameroun. *Bulletin de la Société Prehistorique Française* 42:216–220.
PIAS, J.
1967   Quatre deltas successifs du Chari au Quaternaire (Républiques du Tchad et du Cameroun). *Compres Rendus Hebdomanaires de l'Academie des Sciences, Paris* 264 (série D):2357–2360.
1968   "Contribution à l'étude des formations sedimentaires tertiaires et quaternaires dans la cuvette tchadienne et des sols qui en derivent." Thèse Sc. ORSTOM (not consulted).
PORTÉRES, R.
1962   Berceaux agricoles primaires sur le continent africain. *Journal of African History* 3:195–210.
PULLAN, R. A.
1969   Geomorphology and pedological investigations in the south-central part of the Chad basin, Nigeria. *Palaeoecology of Africa* 4:49–51.
PURSEGLOVE, J. W.
1968   *Tropical crops: dicotyledons 1 and 2*, two volumes. London: Longman.

1972   *Tropical crops: monocotyledons 1 and 2*, two volumes. London: Longman.

ROSENFELD, A.
1972   The microlithic industries of Rop rock shelter. *West African Journal of Archaeology* 2:17–28.

SCHNEIDER, J.-L.
1967   Evolution du dernier lacustre et peuplements préhistoriques aux pays-bas du Tchad. *Bulletin de Liaison, Association Sénégalaise pour l'Etude du Quaternaire de l'Ouest Africain* 14–15:18–23.

SEGALEN, F.
1957   "Les sols du Cameroun," in *Atlas the Cameroun*. Paris: Imprimerie Nationale.

SERVANT, M., S. SERVANT
1970   Les formations lacustres et les diatomées du Quaternaire récent du fond de la cuvette tchadienne. *Revue de Géographie Physique et Géologie Dynamique* (2)12(1):63–76.

SERVANT, M., S. SERVANT-VILDARY
1972   Nouvelles données pour une interprétation paléoclimatique de séries continentales du Bassin Tchadien (Pléistocène récent, Holocène). *Palaeoecology of Africa* 6:87–92.

SILLANS, R.
1953   Sur quelques plantes alimentaires spontanées de l'Afrique centrale. *Bulletin de l'Institut des Études Centrafricaines* 5–6:77–100.

1958   *Les savanes de l'Afrique centrale: essai sur la physionomie, la structure et le dynamisme des formations ligneuses des régions sèches de la République Centrafricaine*. Encyclopédie Biologique 55. Paris: P. Lechevalier.

STENNING, D. J.
1959   *Savannah nomads*. London: Oxford University Press for the International African Institute.

TESSMAN, G.
1934   *Die Baja: ein Negerstamm im mittleren Sudan, part one: Materielle und seelische Kultur*. Stuttgart: Strecker and Schroeder.

TISSERANT, R. P. CH.
1953   L'agriculture dans les savanes de l'Oubangui. *Bulletin de l'Institut des Études Centrafricaines* 5–6:209–274.

URVOY, Y.
1949   *Histoire de l'empire de Bournou*. Mémoires de l'Institut Français de l'Afrique Noire 7.

VAILLANT, A.
1947   Une enquête agricole chez les Mofu de Wazam. *Bulletin de la Société des Etudes Camerounaises* 17–18:41–98.

VAN ZINDEREN BAKKER, E. M.
1972   Late Quaternary lacustrine phases in the southern Sahara and East Africa. *Palaeoecology of Africa* 6:15–27.

1976   "Paleoecological background in connection with the origin of agriculture in Africa," in *Origins of African plant domestication*. Edited by Jack R. Harlan, Jan M. J. de Wet, and Ann B. L. Stemler, 43–63. World Anthropology. The Hague: Mouton.

VIDAL, P.
1969   *La civilisation de Bouar: prospections et fouilles*. Recherches O. banguiennes 1. Paris: Firman-Didot Études.

WHITE, S.
1943   L'économie rurale des montagnes Kirdis de l'emirat de Dikoa au Cameroun sous mandat britannique. *Bulletin de la Société des Études Camerounaises* 3:77–86.
WILLETT, F.
1971   A survey of recent results in the radiocarbon chronology of western and northern Africa. *Journal of African History* 12:339–370.

The Sahara as a Center of
Ceramic Dispersion in Northern Africa

T. R. HAYS

Through the years the Near East has been considered the "cradle of
civilization," the area in which a sedentary Neolithic way of life began.
The Neolithic was first characterized in terms of the use of ground and
polished stone tools and the manufacture of pottery (Childe 1953). In
recent years prehistorians have modified this definition, making the
domestication of plants and/or animals also a prime consideration
(Bishop and Clark 1967:829) and recognizing that pottery may have
been a late addition to the Neolithic complex. Others, however, believe
that pottery is so interrelated with the other traits that its presence in a site
implies the presence of the others, particularly domestication (Camps
1969). Consequently, the techniques of pottery manufacture are believed
to have come to Africa from the Near East. The possibility that this
conclusion may be incorrect, however, led to an investigation into the
origin and dispersal of pottery in northeastern Africa (Hays 1971).

The idea of a Near Eastern origin for pottery has been supported by
arguments that the sedentary life made possible by domesticated plants
fostered the development of ceramic technology. The subsequent
appearance of ceramics in adjacent areas (e.g., the Nile Valley) has been
viewed as the result of the diffusion of a Neolithic trait complex. Thus, the
occurrence of pottery in northeastern Africa has been seen as a dispersal
of ceramic technology from the Near East (Baumgartel 1965; Kantor
1965). Recent excavations in the Sahara, however, challenge this explanation and suggest the need for a new one.

The proposal put forward here is that there was an indigenous
development of ceramics in the central Sahara and that the spread of
pottery from the central Sahara to the east met and mixed with Near
Eastern pottery-making ideas moving southward up the Nile Valley. To
test this postulate, the accuracy of the early dates for the ceramic sites in

the Sahara must be considered, the ceramic traditions of the Sahara and the Sudan need to be examined, and, finally, these ceramic traditions must be compared with those from Egypt and the Near East.

CHRONOLOGY

The oldest pottery in the Near East is dated at 6486 ± 102 B.C. from Level 9 at Çatal Huyuk in Anatolia (Mellink 1965:106). Among other sites dating from the seventh and sixth millennia are Ras Shamra 5C and Jericho Pottery Neolithic A and B (Watson 1965). Previously, the earliest pottery in North Africa was dated at 4850 ± 350 B.C. from Level 8 at Haua Fteah cave in Libya (McBurney 1967:271). The earliest pottery in Egypt, the Sudan, or Ethiopia is dated at 4441 ± 180 B.C. in the Fayum in Egypt (Libby 1955; Kantor, 1965:5), although a 3900 B.C. date may be more accurate (Wendorf, Said, and Schild 1970).

Until recently, all dates for Saharan ceramics have fallen within the fourth millennium B.C. A date of 3450 ± 300 B.C. is reported for Méniet (Hugot 1963), and Ténéré is dated at 3190 ± 300 B.C. (Tixier 1962). Recently, however, dates from the central and eastern Sahara point to a greater antiquity for the appearance of pottery which, significantly, has comb-impressed decoration. Pottery making in the central Sahara is now dated to the seventh millennium (6100 ± 80 B.C.) at Amekni (Camps 1969:207). In the Acacus (Tassili n'Ajjer), Mori (1965) has reported impressed ceramics at Fozzigiaren shortly after 6100 B.C. and at Ouan Tabu by ca. 5100 B.C. Two other dates in the sixth millennium have been reported from Titerast, ca. 5400 B.C. and Tiltekin, 5100 B.C. (Camps, Delibrias, and Thommenet 1968). At Fish Hill in Ténéré, pottery is dated before 5300 B.C. (Clark 1970), while in Ennedi, to the east, pottery in the lower level of Delebo cave is dated at 5230 B.C. (Bailloud 1966) (see Figure 1).

SEDENTISM

In the Near East, not all the criteria of the Neolithic occurred at the same time. Consequently, there are preceramic or aceramic Neolithic levels at, among other sites, Jericho, Hacilar, and Çatal Huyuk (Kenyon 1960; Mellaart 1965). Various explanations have been given for the development of pottery, but none is conclusive. In the prepottery Neolithic in the Near East, straw-tempered clay was used for bricks, floors, and figurines. In addition, straw-tempered unbaked clay vessels have been found at Çatal Huyuk and Suberde (Bordaz 1965).

In each case in the Near East, pottery development followed a long

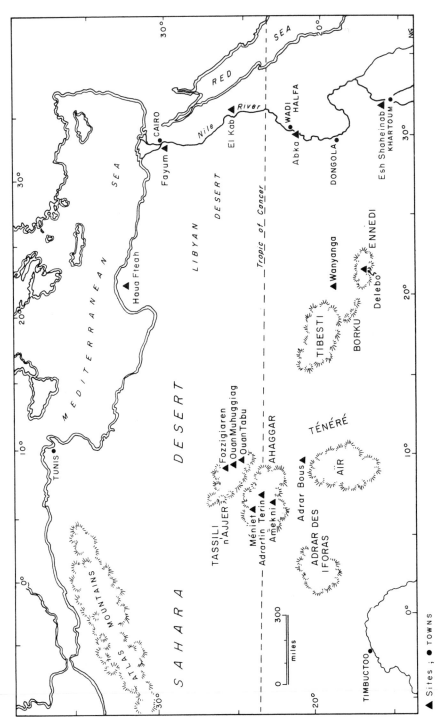

Figure 1. Sites with pottery in Saharan Africa

tradition of agriculture. Significantly, there is no evidence for a pre-ceramic Neolithic in Saharan Africa; pottery occurs in many areas before domestication. In some regions, where groups of people may have lived in ecological conditions unfavorable to the development of a Neolithic economy, domestication did not appear at all. These people maintained a Mesolithic (hunting-and-gathering) economy but developed certain technological artifact traits usually associated with the Neolithic.

When the criterion of domestication is utilized, the number of Neolithic sites in the Sahara is quite small, and these occur after the appearance of pottery. No grains of domesticated plants have been found in the Saharan sites. In fact, only the single pollen grain of a "cereal" identified at Méniet and dated after 3450 B.C. (Hugot 1963:156) and two pollen grains of cultivated millet recovered at Amekni (Camps 1969:205) can be presented as possible mainfestations of agriculture.

That agriculture is not a prerequisite for ceramics becomes obvious when data from other areas of the world are consulted. In Asia the earliest pottery is associated with Jomon fishing villages well before 6000 B.C. (Meggers, Evans, and Estrada 1965). In Europe, pottery occurs in Ertebølle fishing villages ca. 3600 B.C. (Schwabedissen 1962). In the New World, the earliest pottery occurs in fishing villages on the Pacific coast of South America (Meggers, Evans, and Estrada 1965) and on the Atlantic coast of North America by ca. 3200 B.C. (Phillips 1970). Thus, it is apparent from these data that a prerequisite for ceramic technology is not agriculture, but sedentism. Pottery occurs in settled villages, although their economic bases may be quite diverse.

The acknowledgment of a relationship between sedentism and the use of pottery is important in examining the data from Saharan Africa. The sites of Méniet and Amekni, in the Immidir region of the Ahaggar (Hoggar), have been described as "settlements" composed of more than one site (Hugot 1963: Camps 1969); all of these sites are located near large ancient rivers. Other sites in the Sahara include those located around old lakes at Ténéré and Wanyanga in the eastern Sahara. The sites at Wanyanga are primarily open sites (Arkell 1964), but Delebo is a cave and the Ténéré site is a rock shelter (Tixier 1962). All of these sites contain numerous grinding stones and bones of terrestrial and aquatic fauna. The small amount of evidence available regarding economic activities suggests that the inhabitants of northeastern Africa during the fifth and fourth millennia B.C. were engaged in intensive gathering, hunting, and fishing.

Thus the earliest utilization of pottery in the Near East seems to correlate with a settled way of life based primarily on the utilization of domesticated grains. On the other hand, in the New World, Asia, and Saharan Africa sedentism was based on other food sources. In the Sahara, ceramics could have been used to store wild grains. Modern pastoralists in the Sahara store grain for later use in ceramic containers at various locations in the desert (Lhote 1947). That this system was used prehistorically is attested by Hugot (1962) and Camps (1969) for the Ahaggar and Clark (1970) for Ténéré. In each case, however, only wild products (*Celtis* berries) were found. On the basis of these data, it is postulated that wild grains and aquatic fauna from the lakes and rivers of the Sahara were regular and predictable food sources. It has also been suggested that the year-round use of aquatic fauna, in addition to wild grains, would have made sedentary living possible in some areas in the Near East (Binford 1968). Thus, the economic basis of the Saharan populations could have permitted a certain amount of sedentism, making ceramic technology of value. Furthermore, the early dates of Saharan ceramic sites suggest that pottery making may have been independently invented both in the Sahara and in the Near East (cf. Camps 1969:210).

SAHARAN DATING

The implication that the Sahara was a locality of ceramic invention has raised some doubts as to the validity of the radiocarbon dates obtained there. If the dates are correct, they indicate a high degree of technological achievement which was not accompanied by other advances, such as domestication or large settled villages. In addition, recent work in the United States has indicated that dates from charcoal may be misleading because of the use of large dead trees as firewood; samples from differing depths of a large old tree trunk (such as that of a bristle-cone pine) can produce different dates (Libby 1963). These comments imply that the Saharan dates could be 2,000 years too early, and some evidence is available from the Sahara for trees' having such potential longevity (Hugot 1962; Clark 1970). On the other hand, other studies on large trees indicate a need to adjust radiocarbon dates because of variations in accumulation of carbon-14; the true age is often several hundred years older than the radiocarbon age (Suess 1970). In addition, such old trees occur at altitudes of 2,000 meters in the mountains of the Sahara. The use of these trees for firewood would have entailed considerable effort, since the settlements were situated near lakes and rivers at the base of the mountains.

In spite of some uncertainties, I assume that the early radiocarbon dates are correct. Significantly, there are several stratified sites in the Sahara which have produced similar sequences of early dates (Camps, Delibrias, Thommenet 1968). It is highly unlikely that these similar sequences could be attributed to chance or to the use of very old dead trees. Consequently, I conclude that the early dates for ceramic sites in the Sahara reflect the origin of ceramic technology in that area. Subsequently, this technology spread eastward across the southern Sahara toward the Upper Nile Valley.

THE NILOTIC SEQUENCE

The pottery from the Fayum is for the most part thick, unburnished, fiber-tempered, and undecorated. It is handmade, pots often being asymmetrical with straight rims. Bases show considerable variety, being rounded, flattened, knobbed, or ring-based. Pottery forms include small bowls, cups, and subrectangular dishes. A few pots have a red wash and are well burnished, although no incised, combed, or painted pottery occurs (Caton-Thompson and Gardner 1934).

The origin of Egyptian pottery is unknown, but influence from the Near East is strongly suspected (Frankfort 1956; Kantor 1965). Brunton and Caton-Thompson (1928:75) suggested that the Predynastic Egyptians were not indigenous, but possibly arrivals from the Red Sea area. This idea of the intrusion of people into the Nile Valley has also been voiced by later workers. The nonceramic microlithic assemblage at El Kab in Upper Egypt, dated at 6400 ± 160 B.C., shows little relationship with later Predynastic industries (Vermeersch 1970). Similarly, a restudy of the Fayum (Wendorf, Said, and Schild 1970) indicates that the nonceramic Fayum B industry, dated at 6150 ± 130 B.C., was not related to the later Fayum A Neolithic. Technological and typological differences between these two groups are of such magnitude that the authors consider it highly unlikely that Fayum A developed from the Terminal Paleolithic industry. Thus, it seems possible that new Neolithic peoples, not the descendants of the Paleolithic hunters and gatherers of the Nile, formed the cultural base from which Egyptian civilization was to emerge.

The origin of ceramics in the Sudan is equally unclear. Nonetheless, some information is available regarding the spread of ceramics and outside contacts. Pottery has been reported from Abka dated at 4000 ± 400 B.C. (Myers 1960:176). Other early pottery appearing at the Second Cataract is dated at 3650 ± 200 B.C. (Schild, Chmielewska, and Wieckowska 1968:757). The best-known ceramics from the Sudan are from Early Khartoum and Esh Shaheinab. The Khartoum Mesolithic is undated, but Arkell thinks 7000 B.C. is not too early (Arkell and Ucko 1965:148). The Saharan dates, however, would indicate a somewhat more conservative estimate. Similarly, the radiocarbon age of 3300 B.C. for the Shaheinab Neolithic is believed to be ca. 1,000 years too recent (Arkell 1953:107), although the Saharan evidence would not agree.

The origin of this pottery can be discerned by tracing certain connections outside the Sudan. One such connection, between Shaheinab and the Fayum (Arkell 1953:104), however, seems to me unjustified. Most of the proposed shared traits are hardly diagnostic: use of fire, absence of cemetries, use of stone celts and gouges, and burnished pottery. Both the stone industries and the ceramics are very different at these sites (Baumgartel 1965:156). The concave-based arrowheads and bifacially worked sickle blades of the Fayum are not present at Shaheinab, and shell fishhooks and stone labrets are absent from the Fayum. The inhabitants of these two sites may have been contemporary, but they should not be considered related. On the other hand, Arkell's view that the Shaheinab development was influenced from the west is supported by recent evidence.

Ceramics along the Nile in the Sudan show a change through time from rather thick, comb-impressed, unburnished pottery (Khartoum Mesolithic) through a thin, burnished, impressed ware (Shaheinab Neolithic) to a thin, burnished "ripple ware" with black tops (A-Group) (Arkell and Ucko 1965:149). Some sherds from Shaheinab are burnished after the combed decoration, a process somewhat similar to the rippling characteristic of Predynastic Badari in Egypt (Arkell 1953: Plate 33, Figures 10–11). This similarity at Badari has been interpreted as a result of diffusion from the Sudan (Arkell and Ucko 1965:151), but this position tends to disregard the radiocarbon dates. Ripple ware occurs in the Badarian prior to Nagada I, which is dated by radiocarbon ca. 3600–3800 B.C. (Kantor 1965:5), prior to Shaheinab. A ripple ware with black tops and conical (pointed) bases is also common in the Nubian A-Group which has been compared with the Shaheinab Neolithic (Nordstrom 1966: 64ff.). The similarities between the two pottery traditions involve mainly the treatment of the surface and the decoration, as many of the designs that occur in two A-Group sites at Saras have direct counterparts at Shaheinab (Nordstrom 1966:Figure 1). Decorations are frequently executed by pivoting impression with dentate stamps; pots usually have compacted (burnished or polished) surfaces and sometimes have a red ocher coating or wash. Similar sherds occur in close association with Egyptian pottery and other artifacts that clearly point to the Protodynastic period (Nordstrom 1966:65), dated ca. 3000 B.C. (Kantor 1965:5).

Nordstrom (1966:66) believes the similarities between the A-Group and the Shaheinab Neolithic to be a result of the two regions' belonging to the same cultural sphere. A better explanation, however, is that ceramic technology was invented in the Sahara and spread southeastward to the Sudan, while at the same time ceramics originating in the Near East spread to Egypt. Eventually, the two ceramic traditions met in the Nile Valley. As a result, the Badarian techniques of rippling and black-top are found in the Nubian A-Group later than at Badari. Moreover, the dotted-wolftooth design motif of the Shaheinab Neolithic is also evident in the A-Group.

THE SAHARAN SEQUENCE

Unlike the Nilotic sequence, that of the Sahara appears to be completely indigenous (Camps-Fabrer 1966:520). Even though the ceramic tradition of the Saharan sites remains virtually the same, some changes are evident from earlier to later assemblages. Pottery at Amekni (6100 B.C.) is primarily a thick, comb-impressed, unburnished, fiber-tempered fabric. The pottery of the latest Sudanese Neolithic assemblage at Adrar Tin Terin (2770 B.C.) is burnished, comb-impressed and stamped, and fiber-tempered (Camps 1969:206). Comparison of ceramics from the oldest assemblages with those of the latest reveals a widespread sequence of similar development. From the central Sahara to the Sudan, ceramics appear to change through time from an unburnished ware with comb-impressed designs to a burnished ware with stamped designs. Although the Saharan and Sudanese ceramic developments were similar, Saharan potters apparently were not influenced by any Egyptian traits.

While the central and eastern Saharan peoples appear to have had communication with the Nile Valley, there is little evidence for such a relationship with the northern Sahara. Early ceramic sites in northwestern Africa include Aïn Naga, dated at 5550 ± 80 B.C., and El Bayed, dated at 5350 ± 180 B.C. (Camps, Delibrias, and Thommenet 1968:27). Although ceramic technology probably derived from the Sahara, the two ceramic traditions were quite different. Numerous important stylistic differences exist between the Saharan Neolithic of Sudanese Tradition and the northern Neolithic of Capsian Tradition. Pottery in the north has conical bases and collars or necks (Aumassip 1967:157); pottery bowls in the Sahara have rounded bases. Decoration in the Sahara is characteristically by comb impression, with the design covering the entire pot; in the north, while comb impression does occur, the decoration is usually limited to the necks or to bands on the upper portions of the vessel (Camps-Fabrer 1966:427).

In the area between the Maghreb and Egypt. the earliest pottery is dated at 4850 ± 350 B.C. (McBurney 1967). The pottery in Upper Level 8 at Haua Fteah is thin, greyish buff in color, and burnished and contains a ground-shell temper. Decoration consists of four rows of subangular dot impressions below the rim (McBurney 1967:293). This pottery and the domestic goat or sheep are placed in Phase F, the Neolithic of Libyco-Capsian Tradition (5000–2700 B.C.). From the period of its full development, about 4500–3000 B.C., marked resemblance can be seen to the pottery of the Maghreb (McBurney 1967:328). There is, however, no resemblance to the Fayum pottery in Egypt, nor is there any important resemblance to the distinctive impressed ware characteristic of inland desert regions to the south.

CONCLUSIONS

Ceramic sites have been discovered in the central Sahara which have produced radiocarbon dates as early as the seventh millennium. These dates suggest that ceramic technology was present in the central Sahara at about the same time it was beginning in the Near East. An examination of the radiocarbon dates and the ceramic traditions indicates that ceramic technology originated both in the central Sahara and in the Near East. In both areas sedentism was a prerequisite for ceramics, although the subsistence bases of the settled life differed in the two areas. In the Near East, ceramics followed a long tradition of agriculture. In the Sahara, intensive gathering of wild grains, hunting, and fishing formed the economic basis.

The dispersal of ceramic technology into northeastern Africa came from both the central Sahara and the Near East. Consequently, three distinct zones of ceramic tradition can be delineated: (1) the central and southeastern Sahara, (2) the northwestern Sahara and the northern littoral, and (3) the northeastern Sahara and the Nile Valley. Ceramic technology spread from the central Sahara into North Africa and across the southern Sahara to the Upper Nile Valley in the Sudan probably by 5000 B.C. Knowledge of pottery manufacture from the Near East had arrived in the Fayum in Lower Egypt at least by 4500 B.C. These two ceramic traditions expanded along the Nile Valley until they met and combined in Nubia (Second Cataract area) around 3100 B.C. (Figure 2). Subsequently, this mixture of ceramic traditions from the east and west spread northward into Egypt and southward into the central Sudan.

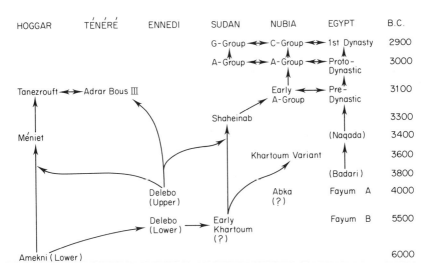

Figure 2.   Postulated cultural contacts in northeastern Africa

REFERENCES

ARKELL, A. J.
1953   *Shaheinab*. London: Oxford University Press.
1964   *Wanyanga*. London: Oxford University Press.
ARKELL, A. J., P. J. UCKO
1965   Review of Predynastic development in the Nile Valley. *Current Anthropology* 6:145–166.
AUMASSIP, G.
1967   Notes sur quelques dégraissants des céramiques néolithiques des Hoggar. *Libyca* 15:157–168.
BAILLOUD, G.
1966   "Le Néolithique," in *La nouvelle Clio, la préhistoire*. Edited by Robert Boutruches and Paul Lemerée, 157–203. Paris: Presses Universitaires de France.
BAUMGARTEL, E.
1965   Comment on: Review of Predynastic development in the Nile Valley, by A. J. Arkell and P. J. Ucko. *Current Anthropology* 6:156–157.
BINFORD, LEWIS R.
1968   "Post-Pleistocene adaptations," in *New perspectives in archaeology*. Edited by Lewis R. Binford and Sally R. Binford, 313–341. Chicago: Aldine.
BISHOP, W. W., J. D. CLARK, *editors*
1967   *Background to evolution in Africa*. Chicago: University of Chicago Press.
BORDAZ, J.
1965   Suberde. *American Journal of Archaeology* 69:137.
BRUNTON, G., G. CATON-THOMPSON
1928   *The Badarian civilization*. London: British School of Archaeology in Egypt.
CAMPS, GABRIEL
1969   *Amekni: Néolithique ancien du Hoggar*. Mémoires du Centre de Recherches Anthropologiques, Préhistoriques et Ethnographiques 10.
CAMPS, G., G. DELIBRIAS, J. THOMMENET
1968   Chronologie absolue et succession des civilizations préhistoriques dans le nord de l'Afrique. *Libyca* 16:9–28.
CAMPS-FABRER, H.
1966   *Matière et art mobilier dans la préhistoire nordafricaine et saharienne*. Mémoires du Centre de Recherches Anthropologiques, Préhistoriques et Ethnographiques 5.
CATON-THOMPSON, GERTRUDE, E. Q. GARDNER
1934   *The desert Fayum*. London: Royal Anthropological Institute.
CHILDE, V. G.
1953   *New light on the most ancient East*. New York: Praeger.
CLARK, J. D.
1970   "Preliminary report on an archaeological reconnaissance in northern Aïr and Ténéré." Unpublished manuscript.
FRANKFORT, H.
1956   *The birth of civilization in the Near East*. New York: Doubleday.
HAYS, T. R.
1971   "The Sudanese Neolithic: a critical analysis." Unpublished Ph.D. dissertation, Southern Methodist University.

HUGOT, H. J.
1962 *Missions Berliet Ténéré-Tchad*. Paris: Arts et Métiers Graphiques.
1963 *Recherches préhistoriques dans l'Ahaggar nord-occidental*. Mémoires du Centre de Recherches Anthropologiques, Préhistoriques et Ethnographiques 1.

KANTOR, H. J.
1965 "The relative chronology of Egypt and its foreign correlations before the late Bronze Age," in *Chronologies in Old World archaeology*. Edited by R. W. Ehrich, 1–46. Chicago: University of Chicago Press.

KENYON, K.
1960 *Archaeology in the Holy Land*. London: Ernest Benn.

LHOTE, H.
1947 La poterie dans l'Ahaggar. *Travaux de l'Institut de Recherches Sahariennes* 4:145–154.

LIBBY, W. F.
1955 *Radiocarbon dating*. Chicago: University of Chicago Press.
1963 Accuracy of radiocarbon dates. *Science* 140:278–280.

MC BURNEY, C. B. M.
1967 *The Haua Fteah (Cyrenaica) and the Stone Age of the southwest Mediterranean*. Cambridge: Cambridge University Press.

MEGGERS, B. J., C. EVANS, E. ESTRADA
1965 *Early Formative period of coastal Ecuador*. Smithsonian Contributions to Anthropology 1.

MELLAART, J.
1965 *Earliest civilizations of the Near East*. New York: McGraw-Hill.

MELLINK, M. J.
1965 "Anatolian chronology," in *Chronologies in Old World archaeology*. Edited by R. W. Ehrich, 101–132. Chicago: University of Chicago Press.

MORI, F.
1965 *Tadrart Acacus*. Turin: G. Einaudi.

MYERS, O. H.
1960 Abka again. *Kush* 8:174–181.

NORDSTROM, H. A.
1966 A-Group and C-Group in Upper Nubia. *Kush* 14:63–68.

PHILLIPS, P.
1970 *Archaeological survey in the lower Yazoo Basin, Mississippi, 1949–1955*. Peabody Museum Papers 60.

SCHILD, R., M. CHMIELEWSKA, H. WIECKOWSKA
1968 "The Arkinian and Shamarkian industries," in *Prehistory of Nubia*. Edited by F. Wendorf, 651–767. Dallas: Southern Methodist University Press.

SCHWABEDISSEN, HERMANN
1962 "Northern continental Europe," in *Courses toward urban life*. Edited by R. Braidwood and G. Willey, 254–267. Chicago: Aldine.

SUESS, H. E.
1970 "Bristlecone pine calibration of the radiocarbon time-scale 5200 B.C. to the present," in *Radiocarbon variations and absolute chronology*. Edited by Ingrid U. Olsson, 303–312. New York: Wiley.

TIXIER, JACQUES
1962 "Le Ténéréen' de l'Adrar Bous III," in *Missions Berliet Ténéré-Tchad*, by H. J. Hugot. Paris: Arts et Métiers Graphiques.

VERMEERSCH, P.
  1970   L'Ekabien. *Chronique d'Egypte* 45(89):45–67.
WATSON, P. J.
  1965   "The chronology of North Syria and North Mesopotamia from 10,000 B.C. to 2000 B.C.," in *Chronologies in Old World archaeology*. Edited by R. W. Ehrich, 61–100. Chicago: University of Chicago Press.
WENDORF, F., R. SAID, R. SCHILD
  1970   Egyptian prehistory: some new concepts. *Science* 169:1161–1171.

Archaeology East of the Niger: A Review of Cultural-Historical Developments

DONALD D. HARTLE

Archaeological research revealing the pre- and protohistory[1] of south-eastern Nigeria has yielded evidence of human habitation and exploitation of the environment since at least as early as 3000 B.C. Extensive survey and excavations demonstrate that this area is rich in cultural data that ultimately will relate to developments elsewhere in West Africa. The first excavations in this area were conducted by Thurstan Shaw in 1959 at Igbo-Ukwu (Shaw 1970). In 1961 and 1962 Philip Allison, then of the Federal Department of Antiquities, carried out a survey of the monoliths in the forests of the Middle Cross River (Allison 1968). During the period 1963 to 1967[2] I carried out extensive archaeological research in the then Eastern Region of Nigeria (Hartle 1965, 1966b, 1967). Four hundred sites were located and fourteen of these were excavated. At the present time (1972) we are again excavating the University Farm site on the Nsukka campus of the University of Nigeria and trying to sort out the thousands of sherds and stone tools which were scattered about the Laboratory of Archaeology and the University Museum during the recent civil war.

The prehistory of West Africa is less well known than that of most other parts of the African continent. Specialists have usually concentrated on the more spectacular biocultural phases of East and South Africa, on the assumption that little of archaeological interest would have been preserved in the heavily forested areas. The prehistory of southeastern Nigeria, except for the site of Igbo-Ukwu, has suffered a similar fate, most

[1] In this context, "prehistory" refers to the time prior to written documents; "protohistory" refers to the time during written history but before any particular areas were documented. In general, "history" refers to any evidence of man in the past.
[2] The survey was conducted under the auspices of the University of Nigeria at Nsukka and was further supported by a National Science Foundation grant in November 1964.

archaeological work until recently having been confined to the spectacular sites of the Nok culture, Ife, and Benin. During the last eight or nine years, however, considerable advances in prehistory have been made, particularly in Ghana and Nigeria, culminating in the first Conference of West African Archaeologists, held at Freetown, Sierra Leone, in June 1966. This report presents a review of the major sites excavated in southeastern Nigeria, emphasizing those significant in projections about the prehistory of West Africa as a whole rather than those of more limited or regional interest.

THE SITES

Sites recorded from various parts of southeastern Nigeria include caves, rock shelters, burials, shrines, forts, iron smelters, (?) war trenches, abandoned villages, and various others. The artifacts recovered from these sites, both habitation and work areas, include objects of stone, clay, iron, bronze, brass, shell, and glass. Our known chronology in southeastern Nigeria begins about 3000 B.C., in the Later Stone Age and the period of the beginnings of food production, and continues to present times. We do not have evidence of the earlier periods, such as the Acheulean, Sangoan, and Lupemban, which have been reported from northern Nigeria (Soper 1965).

The Ezi-Ukwu Ukpa rock shelter (see Figure 1), about a mile north of Afikpo, was extensively excavated in 1966. This is the earliest and perhaps the most important site excavated in the southeastern area; worked stone tools and pottery were excavated to a depth of thirteen feet (3.96 meters). A series of concordant radiocarbon dates (see Table 1) was obtained for this material, ranging between 4,885 ± 140 and 1,935 ± 80 B.P. (2935 B.C. and A.D. 15) (Hartle 1969). The following account of the excavations is tentative in that the data, including both the records and artifacts, were largely lost or mixed up during the recent crises. At present we are trying to reorganize and reconstruct these as well as other invaluable source materials.

This rock shelter is composed of heavy-grained sandstone embedded with quartz crystals and small pebbles as well as decomposed granite, and the opening faces a small valley three or four miles wide at this point. The site had an excellent protective and defensive location, since the innermost portion was usually dry and the mouth was ringed by a series of sandstone boulders. At least two separate cultural horizons are indicated. The upper levels, to about twelve inches (30.48 centimeters), contain what we have called Afikpo Gray Ware, which is dark, hard-fired, sand- or grit-tempered, and almost identical with modern Afikpo utilitarian ware. No significant stone tools were associated with this level. Below

Figure 1. Sites in southeastern Nigeria. *1*, Igbo-Ukwu; *2*, Isi Ugwu Obukpa rock shelter; *3*, Nsukka Okep Igara; *4*, University Farm; *5*, Ifeka Garden; *6*, Enugu Ukwu Farm; *7*, C.M.S. Mission; *8*, Garden; *9*, Ugwu Kabia; *10*, Ezi-Ukwu Ukpa rock shelter; *11*, Nwankwor

this, Afikpo Red Ware is much cruder pottery of a light brown-reddish color, poorly fired and heavy-grit-tempered. Although analysis is based on 2,500 sherds, there is still insufficient evidence of vessel shape apart from a few pieces that suggest pointed bases of some kind. Of great interest is the similarity of these sherds to those of the lower levels of almost all the sites excavated thus far in southeastern Nigeria. The techniques of manufacture, paste, and temper are remarkably similar for apparently long periods of time in sites more than 200 miles apart. One of the difficulties is the paucity of information about erosion and deposition

Table 1.　Radiocarbon dates for sites in southeastern Nigeria

Site	Depth (inches)	Radiocarbon date (B.P.)	B.C./A.D. date
Nwankwor			
1	18 24	1,145 ± 95	A.D. 805
2	66–72	minus 145	A.D. ?[a]
University Farm			
1	30–36	4,505 ± 130	2555 B.C.
2	36–42	3,410 ± 115	1460 B.C.[a]
Ezi-Ukwu Ukpa rock shelter			
1	18–24	2,045 ± 95	95 B.C.
2	42–48	2,055 ± 85	105 B.C.
3	60–66	1,935 ± 80	A.D. 15[b]
4	66–72	2,620 ± 380	670 B.C.
5	78–84	2,860 ± 65	910 B.C.
6	84–90	2,935 ± 85	985 B.C.
7	96–102	3,125 ± 95	1175 B.C.
8	102–108	3,930 ± 80	1980 B.C.
9	108–114	3,350 ± 95	1400 B.C.[b]
10	120–126	4,885 ± 140	2935 B.C.
Ifeka Garden			
1	18–24	4,550 ± 95	A.D. 1495
Igbo-Ukwu			
1 Burial chamber		1,100 ± 120	A.D. 850
2 Cistern		1,045 ± 130	A.D. 875
3 Disposal pit		1,110 ± 110	A.D. 840
4 Disposal pit		1,110 ± 145	A.D. 840
5 Disposal pit		500 ± 70	A.D. 1450[c]

Note: Except for Ifeka Garden, where wooden clappers and seeds were used, and Igbo-Ukwu, where wood was used, all dates are derived from charcoal samples.

[a] These are possible inversions. At Nwankwor, the sample was found in a garbage dump which had been used until fairly recently, and thus periodic pit turning may explain the date. At University Farm, rather irregular undulating pits were noticed while excavating which might be responsible for this inversion.

[b] These are minor discrepancies in a series otherwise concordant with the stratigraphy.

[c] This discrepancy is interesting in that it may correlate with the Ifeka Garden site.

rates for most of the area. With an annual rainfall of more than 100 inches in some localities and the resultant displacement of laterite deposits, the depths of the artifacts are most unreliable for comparative purposes of relative age determination. In other words, the pottery at Ezi-Ukwu Ukpa, considered alone, is not particularly significant or enlightening. It only becomes so when considered in relation to the stone artifacts excavated along with it and in comparison with pottery from other sites.

The association of Afikpo Red Ware and worked stone tools in the lower levels is the most significant aspect of the excavation, since this is the only stone industry thus far excavated in the southeastern area. Raw materials used were argillite, sandstone, quartzite, and quartz pebbles and crystals. There is little evidence of secondary flaking, ground tools are not well made, and whatever polish there is seems to be the result of use. The majority of the tools are on flakes, large and small, although core tools are well represented, too. An analysis of waste flakes was not very informative regarding traditions in the use of particular raw materials; the most that can be stated at present is that a flake industry of some sort is definitely present. Artifacts which have been identified include hoes, celts, disks, stone balls, querns, various grinding tools, and hammerstones, both spherical and oblong. Other tool types are present, but they had not been thoroughly categorized when we left the University in 1967. At present we are engaged in a detailed analysis of the stone materials and their association with the pottery types. Although this rock shelter would seem to belong to the same general period of cultural development as the rock shelters of Rop (Rosenfeld 1972), Iwo Eleru (Shaw 1968b), and Old Oyo (Willett 1962), it did not contain microliths such as were reported from these three sites.

The importance of the Ezi-Ukwu Ukpa rock shelter is that it may provide information about transitional periods between the Later Stone Age and the introduction of pottery and iron. The lower levels seem to characterize the initial period shortly after the addition of pottery to the stone assemblage. Very little iron was found, and that came from the top levels. It is possible, however, that iron was present earlier and has decomposed, a condition not uncommon in forested areas.

Three sites have been excavated in the Nsukka vicinity, in the northern part of the southeastern area. The Isi Ugwu Obukpa rock shelter produced fourteen samples of crudely worked stone associated with pottery found at some depth. The University Farm site, with radiocarbon dates of $4,505 \pm 130$ b.p. and $3,410 \pm 115$ b.p. (2555 b.c. and 1460 b.c.), is one of the earliest known pottery sites in southeastern Nigeria (Hartle 1966b). These dates are "inverted" (that is, the later materials were found at a greater depth because of intrusive pits), and no definable worked stone was found. Nsukka Okpe Igara, a "fort" located on the University campus, consisted of a ditch and wall encircling the top of a small hill and is one of eleven similar architectural features found along the Nsukka escarpment, from Unadu in the north to Ogurugu on the Anambra River, that may have been used for defense. It has also been suggested that they were used as "corrals" or temporary stopping places for slaves being shipped down the river to Onitsha (Hartle 1967).

The best-known site in southeastern Nigeria is Igbo-Ukwu, some twenty-five miles southeast of Onitsha (Shaw 1960, 1964, 1965, 1967, 1968a, 1970). This site produced the first known bronze in southeastern Nigeria and demonstrated that Benin and Ife are not the only sources of Nigerian bronze craftsmanship. Radiocarbon dates from Igbo-Ukwu,

200   DONALD D. HARTLE

particularly the date of 1,100 ± 120 B.P. (A.D. 850) from a stool in the burial chamber, prove that by the ninth century superb bronze artifacts were known in this area. It is particularly significant that these artifacts are of bronze, an alloy of copper, tin, and lead, rather than of brass, an alloy of copper and zinc. The Benin "bronzes" are actually brass. Obviously there are two traditions of bronze/brass casting in Nigeria — brass in the west and bronze in the east.

The importance of the Igbo-Ukwu burial, according to Shaw, is that it indicates a highly developed civilization, centered around some form of semidivine ruler, which was dependent upon the trans-Saharan ivory trade as well as trade in other articles including slaves and kola nuts. This site represents a fully developed Iron Age people exploiting a forest environment. It should be emphasized that there is no copper in Nigeria; therefore copper, which furnished the raw material from which the bronzes were manufactured (using the lost-wax technique), was probably a trade item.

Ifeka Garden, in Ezira, some fifteen miles east of Igbo-Ukwu, was also a burial site and included bronze and iron objects radiocarbon-dated at 455 ± 95 B.P. (A.D. 1495) (Hartle 1966a). The bronze artifacts included anklets, bracelets, earrings, caches of small and large bells, and several staff-like ceremonial objects. Iron gongs were found around the body and an iron sword or blade at its right side. The bronze artifacts contained decorations of exquisite fine lines like filigree or lace, indentations, cross-hatching, and elevated circles or ovals. They are in some respects stylistically similar to the artifacts from Igbo-Ukwu and appear to belong to a later development of the same tradition. Other bronzes have been reported from this general area. The sites of Igbo-Ukwu and Ifeka Garden indicate that in the near future estimates of the time of the introduction of bronze into the southeastern area will probably be drastically revised.

Nwankwor, near Bende, by tradition was occupied for about twelve generations, the present compound location being the third and last occupation by the same family (Hartle 1967). Records of any sort are rare in this part of eastern Nigeria, and old administrative reports, as well as local traditions, sometimes provide clues of archaeological interest. Thus, our object was to verify or refute this ethnohistory. Digging was confined to those portions that figured most prominently in the local traditions, including the *obu* [ceremonial enclosure], a garbage dump, and a drinking area. Materials excavated included pottery sherds, stone work, bits of iron, glass beads, palm kernels, and old gin bottles. In a general way, the excavations confirmed statements by the chief's son about the shape of the *obu*, the location of the altar, and other features referred to in village lore. Two radiocarbon dates were obtained from the garbage dump, 1,145 ± 95 B.P. and −145 B.P. (A.D. 805 and A.D.?)

DISCUSSION

The major archaeological problems in West Africa are synthesis of materials, development of chronologies, and the organization of a body of theory that will assist the direction of further research. We are still very much in the data collection phase in Nigeria, and consequently site reports rather than definitive analyses of archaeological horizons are offered. All of the archaeologists working in Nigeria have coordinated their efforts to define the cultural-historical outlines for the country as a whole and to make the best use of limited funds.

The most important archaeological investigations in Nigeria for some time to come will be the location and identification of sites and horizons and, even more, the dates in relation to other known cultural data for the determination of chronologies. An archaeologist is always pleased when he discovers something unique or different to add to our growing body of prehistoric cultural developments, and in southeastern Nigeria unexpected surprises seem to be forthcoming with each new set of radiocarbon dates. For example, the 2555 B.C. date at the University Farm site was much earlier than we had anticipated and provided our initial clue that pottery had been introduced into this area several thousand years B.C. Nwankwor, otherwise a rather routine excavation, provided a date of A.D. 805, which was some 150 years earlier than anticipated. The remarkable series of dates from the Ezi-Ukwu Ukpa rock shelter (2935 B.C. to A.D. 15) makes it abundantly clear that our previous conceptions of time depth in this area will have to be revised. Last but not least, the exquisite bronze antiquities associated with the burial at Igbo-Ukwu indicate a tremendous artistic achievement and offer some insight into the cultural heritage of the southeastern region at a very early date of A.D. 850.

Early pottery throughout southeastern Nigeria appears to be homogeneous as regards color, temper, texture, and method of manufacture. Decoration, essentially confined to the rim and neck, is extremely simple, usually in the form of geometric, incised patterns. This similarity is striking both at depth at any one site and between different sites at the lower levels. Color differences are probably attributable to clay sources and the length of time the sherds have been deposited in specific locations. Minor differences are insufficient, however, to establish broad types that can be grouped into contrasting cultural horizons or traditions. What is more interesting is the possibility, even probability, of a very long cultural continuum with little or no diffusion or influence from other areas. Pottery in the upper levels of all the sites is well-fired, the temper particles are small, and the incised decorations are numerous and finely executed. This is an abrupt change from the pottery in the lower strata, and there are no definable intermediate or transitional types.

Obviously more research and analysis are required before further generalizations can be made.

The stone tools from the Ezi-Ukwu Ukpa rock shelter are in part similar to those in other sections of Nigeria and from Dakar to Cameroon in West Africa. In very few cases, however, have actual comparisons been made or dating been established by geochronological methods. Most specimens are surface collections. At the Isi Ugwu Obukpa rock shelter, worked stone stools were recovered that resemble artifacts excavated from Ezi-Ukwu Ukpa. They may be more recent, but they were not clearly stratified, and no radiocarbon dates were obtainable. Further, the typological similarities are not enough to permit closer comparisons at present. Since these are the only two sites in southeastern Nigeria which have produced stone work, we obviously have not yet drawn analytical baselines, and further excavations are imperative. The few stone specimens found in most of the sites associated with pottery are grinding tools, and these sites are relatively recent. However, stone tools and pottery were found uniformly throughout the Ezi-Ukwu Ukpa rock shelter, and this presents a problem. Other rock shelters have been located in the Afikpo area, and the excavation of a selected few may help to clarify this problem.

A tentative chronology for southeastern Nigeria as related to the rest of the country can now be suggested. In the present state of knowledge, there are no very early archaeological horizons in this area. Cultural assemblages began sometime during the Later Stone Age, perhaps at the time when food production began to be developed. The Ezi-Ukwu Ukpa rock shelter, the oldest site excavated thus far, may characterize this period, which began much earlier than 3000 B.C. Probably related to this site in time is the Isi Ugwu Obukpa rock shelter. This is followed by the University Farm site, in which pottery was present but, with the exception of a few grinding tools, stone artifacts were absent. Perhaps by this time wooden artifacts had replaced stone. (This is pure conjecture, of course.) Nwankwor is next in the sequence, at A.D. 805, with its occupation continuing until about fifty years ago. Prior to this time, artifacts of iron and glass had diffused to the area. Somewhat later in the ninth century A.D., at Igbo-Ukwu, we have evidence of new cultural traits including ivory, beads, bone, copper, and bronze. The use of bronze continues at least until the end of the fifteenth century, as indicated by the excavations at Ifeka Garden. Allison (1968) suggests that the Ikom monoliths of the Nta were perhaps carved between the beginning of the sixteenth century and the beginning of the twentieth. The forts in the Nsukka area may date to the seventeenth or eighteenth centuries.

To summarize, the excavations of the several sites discussed have opened a new understanding of the cultural-historical depth in southeastern Nigeria. As research stands now, there are sites representing many phases of Nigerian history, from the very old to the very recent, and we can begin to sketch in the missing data with facts instead of speculation. It is worth repeating that the biggest problem is chronology. The schematic outline presented needs geochronological confirmation and further study by scholars in many related fields. Finally, it is suggested that some of the more fruitful areas for research into the earlier periods of southeastern cultural history will be found toward the east in the Cross River Valley. Only further work will test the validity of this hypothesis.

REFERENCES

ALLISON, PHILIP
   1968   *Cross River monoliths*. Lagos: Federal Department of Antiquities.
HARTLE, DONALD D.
   1965   An archaeological survey in eastern Nigeria. *West African Archaeological Newsletter* 2:4–5.
   1966a Bronze objects from Ezira, eastern Nigeria. *West African Archaeological Newsletter* 4:25–28.
   1966b Archaeology in eastern Nigeria. *West African Archaeological Newsletter* 5:13–17.
   1967   Archaeology in eastern Nigeria. *Nigeria Magazine* 93:134–143.
   1968   Stop press: radiocarbon dates from Nigeria. *West African Archaeological Newsletter* 9:73.
ROSENFELD, ANDRÉE
   1972   The microlithic industries of Rop rock shelter. *West African Journal of Archaeology* 2:17–28.
SHAW, THURSTAN
   1960   Excavations at Igbo-Ukwu, eastern Nigeria: an interim report. *Man* 60 (210):160–164.
   1964   Excavations at Igbo-Ukwu. *West African Archaeological Newsletter* 1:4–5.
   1965   Further excavations at Igbo-Ukwu: an interim report. *Man* 65(217):181–184.
   1967   The mystery of the buried bronzes. *Nigeria Magazine* 92:55–74.
   1968a Stop press: radiocarbon dates for Igbo-Ukwu. *West African Archaeological Newsletter* 4:41.
   1968b Radiocarbon dating in Nigeria. *Journal of the Historical Society of Nigeria* 4:453–465.
   1970   *Igbo-Ukwu: an account of archaeological discoveries in eastern Nigeria*. London: Faber and Faber for the Institute of African Studies, University of Ibadan.
SOPER, R. C.
   1965   The Stone Age in northern Nigeria. *Journal of the Historical Society of Nigeria* 3:175–194.
WILLETT, FRANK
   1962   "The microlithic industry from Old Oyo, western Nigeria." *Actes du Quatrième Congrès Panafricain de Préhistoire et de l'Etude du Quaternaire*, volume three. Edited by G. Mortelmans and J. Nenquin, 261–272. Tervuren: Musée Royal de l'Afrique Centrale.

The Ntereso Culture in Ghana

OLIVER DAVIES

In 1962 I excavated a habitation site at Ntereso in central Gonja (the most southerly region of Northern Ghana). To correct statements in preliminary reports written before the material was properly sorted, I present here a condensation of my final report, which is duplicated, and attempt to indicate the place of this site in the sequence of cultures in Ghana. There are still queries, because there has been little excavation, and of that little only a minimal fraction has been published and few dates have been obtained. The wide surface surveys which I carried out in Ghana between 1952 and 1966 have recorded many sites and given indications where to dig, but surface collections, even from stratified vertical faces, can provide neither the corpus of any culture nor satisfactory dating material older than recognizable European imports.

The lower basins of the Black and the White Volta have been more intensively surveyed than almost any other region of Ghana, and a good many excavations have been carried out under the salvage scheme of the Volta Basin Research Project (Davies 1971). Pending full publication, a summary (York et al. 1967) indicates that practically none of these sites is contemporary with Ntereso. In a wide region mostly south of the Black Volta, a culture which I have called the Kintampo Neolithic has been defined from my surface collections and those of the Geological Survey (Davies 1962, 1964b, 1967a) and from excavations (unpublished) by Flight (1968, 1970); it has been dated as lasting from rather before 1400 B.C.[1] to at least 900 B.C. (I-2707 from New Buipe; York 1966b;

In this condensed report it has been impossible to include plans and sections of the site, which have been inserted into the full duplicated report.

[1] It is just possible to fit the three dates for the Kintampo Neolithic (I-2697, I-2698, Birm-30) with the three dates of the preceding Buobini culture (I-2699, Birm-29, Birm-31)

Calvocoressi and York 1971). I will show that this culture contributed to
that of Ntereso, but another element has hybridized with it.

Ntereso lies in a wooded savanna on a ridge about two and a half
kilometers south of the White Volta and five and a half kilometers west
of Yapei Bridge (9°07′35″ north latitude, 1°12′35″ west longitude). The
annual rainfall is about 1,200 millimeters and the dry season lasts four
months. We found evidence for trees on the site both before and after its
occupation. Vegetable food would have been available, and the fauna
identified from the excavations shows that game and fish were once
abundant.

In the excavation I identified three Neolithic[2] strata above red sand
which had overlain the sandstone. Levels 1 and 2 had been destroyed by
conflagrations — probably bush fires, as there was no evidence of hostile
activity. There was no abandonment at the end of Level 1; at most, a few
days may have elapsed while the site was leveled and prepared; lateritic
wash beneath the floor of the rectangular house suggested a single
episode, a bush fire fanned by a tornado and followed by a downpour.
Most of the occupation earth and probably some subsoil was scraped
together to fill large pits. Level 2 ended in a similar fire, with again a layer
of lateritic wash ten centimeters thick among the burnt daub and one
posthole of the rectangular house. Level 3 yielded no structures except
two shallow pits and was much disturbed, so there was no indication how
it ended; scattered burnt daub in it suggests a conflagration. Because of
termites, timber houses in West Africa seldom last twenty years; it would
be reasonable to suppose that the whole Neolithic occupation did not
exceed half a century. There is very little evidence for cultural development during the whole occupation: hollow-based arrowheads of greenish
shale without denticulations are much commoner in Level 1 than higher,
and small lugs or knobs near pot rims become more abundant in the
higher levels.

From Level 1 there was little occupation earth, and parts of the site
seem to have been open and retained the original subsoil. I was able to
infer beneath the house of Level 2 an earlier rectangular house of which a
few postholes survived; it was roughly four meters square. The principal
remains of this stage were large pits. On the southwestern side, along a
slight depression which led to a pool, there was much pitting; the largest
pits were 175 and 145 centimeters deep below the base of Level 2. These
pits were almost certainly water holes, to collect drainage and store water

---

within a single statistical error. The latest date for the Buobini culture from site K8 is 3,401
± 74 B.P.; the date for the base of the Kintampo Neolithic from K1 is 3,560 ± 100 B.P. Other
dates for the Kintampo Neolithic are two or three centuries later. (All the dates mentioned
are uncalibrated.)

[2]   I am in this paper calling the primary site Neolithic because it yielded most of the classic
elements of Neolithic technology, without prejudice to the possible knowledge of metal.

for the dry season; perennial water may not have been available nearer than the White Volta, and peasants today can be seen scooping up the last drops of water in a muddy depression before they resign themselves to fetching it from a distance. Three other pit complexes, less well sited for collecting drainage but perhaps also used for water storage, were identified. Smaller pits which may belong to Level 1 may have been latrines or used for rubbish. The calcrete blocks in most of the pits are no indication of their use. They would be lime redeposited after dissolution of bones and shells in the fill by seepage over the course of centuries.

Level 1 had at least two phases. Two of the large pits were widened and the silted bases sealed, and one pit was filled before the final catastrophe. These improvements need not all be contemporary.

After the conflagration, the pits in Level 1 were filled with rubbish on the site and thickly sealed with daub from the burnt houses. On the leveled surface I traced the plans of two houses. One was rectangular and measured 4.3 by 3.4 meters, with a projecting porch at one corner and what appeared to be a screen separating the door from the interior (Davies 1967a: Figure 98; 1967b:117). The other was either circular or square, with rounded corners, 2.9 meters across; it probably had a central post. Near the west side of the site were two heaps of burnt daub 20 to 30 centimeters high, each with one posthole. Their purpose is uncertain; the single posts could not be parts of buildings but might indicate ritual. Four narrow cylindrical shafts, 67 to 155 centimeters deep and 32 to 45 centimeters wide, were probably wells, replacing the more irregular and wider waterholes of Level 1; it would not be possible to clamber down them, so water must have been drawn by means of a rope.

House architecture may be reconstructed from the burnt daub and the imprints on it. As the daub in the pits of Level 1 resembles that from the houses of Level 2, I presume that the houses of the two levels were similar. The occupation earth of the houses of Level 2 was covered by packed layers of daub thirty and fifteen centimeters thick. Outside the postholes of the walls these daub layers did not extend, though there was scattered daub. These remains imply flat roofs of horizontal poles, liberally plastered with mud. The postholes held vertical posts, set close together. The absence of heaps of daub along the wall lines shows that the walls were not plastered. They may have been covered with matting; more probably, chinks were stuffed with grass. Some pieces of daub from a pit of Level 1 are roughly shaped and have impressions of bundles of thin twigs or grass. These may be from one house in which the vertical posts were spaced and joined with crossbars of clay to which grass stuffing was attached.

Along the tops of the vertical posts there would have been architrave poles, probably resting on crutches formed by cutting the posts to forks. Several pieces of daub have impressions in two directions at right angles, and one has them in three dimensions which must represent crutch, architrave, and roof poles. The framework of the roof, on which daub was laid, was of contiguous cross-poles, interspersed with bundles of twigs, boards, and molded wood, the remains apparently of fine carpentry (Davies 1967b: Plates 6, 7). There were very few impressions of lianas for tying. The roofs were probably plastered outside only; the daub was applied semiliquid so that it penetrated the interstices and was smoothed with fingers. Few poles were as much as ten centimeters across; most had been barked, and rarely were there traces of termite runs in the baked clay.

As on nearly all sites, pottery was the principal material recovered from Ntereso. Owing to its abundance and variety, to lack of well-dated and properly published comparative material, and to the long survival of types of African pottery, it is difficult to classify. On the assumption that Level 1 nearly everywhere and Level 2 to a large extent were uncontaminated by later intrusion, I have distinguished certain types which do not seem to belong to the Neolithic site; these will be discussed later. There is, however, danger that this procedure may be circular.

On surface sites of the Kintampo Neolithic I have found small comb-impressed coarse sherds (Davies 1964b: Figures 114, 119). Flight (1968) seems to have found similar pottery at Kintampo K6; he specifies rolled rims, diagonal comb impressions, and what I have called scored reticulates on jar necks. It appears, therefore, that our abundant coarse jars, with rounded base and comb impressions often rampaging over the whole surface (Figure 1; Figure 11, 1 and 2; Davies 1967a: Figure 101) are akin to the Kintampo Neolithic; variations in the form of the rim may be unimportant. The increase in plain coarse sherds in Levels 2 and 3 suggests that overall comb impression went out of fashion. Its primary purpose was probably not aesthetic, but to permit a good grip.

Flight speaks also of bowls, apparently coarse, with plain incurved rim and probably rounded base. These also were abundant at Ntereso (Figures 2; 3, 1; 4), the rims being often thickened; they were commonest in Level 1.

Many jars, small bowls, and cups from Ntereso are of fine, thin ware, decorated with neat impressions of a fine comb in zonal bands and patterns of festoons and triangles (Figures 2; 3, 3; 5; 6; 7; 8, 1; 9, 2; Davies, 1967a: Figure 99). They are well polished and often painted red on the plain zones between the impressions and over the whole inside of the bowl. Paint was never used for designs against a background of the natural color of the clay. Fine ware was less common in Level 2 than in Levels 1 and 3, and paint was rare in Level 2; it may, however, have changed chemically in this level to a brown color which is undistinctive.

These fine wares, with their delicate decoration, had probably been introduced from the north. Comparable decoration occurs at Kobadi

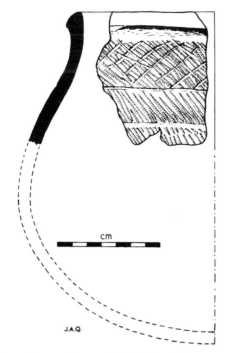

Figure 1.   Jar with comb impressions, red (M3eC, Level 3)

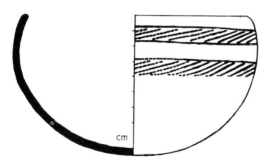

Figure 2.   Bowl, red-painted inside and on plain zones outside, outside brownish at base (Q7B, Level 3)

(Davies 1967a: Figure 85), a site on the Niger with similarities to Ntereso though its date is about 600 years later (Dak-56; Willett 1971:355). Pottery with bands of paint is reported from an early site at Aiguilles de Sisse in Tibesti (Vita-Finzi and Kennedy 1965:199). Painting seems to have been regularly practiced in the sub-Saharan area; it later developed patterns and again penetrated into Gonja as the Deber ware of the sixteenth century A.D. (Davies 1964a; Mathewson 1968).

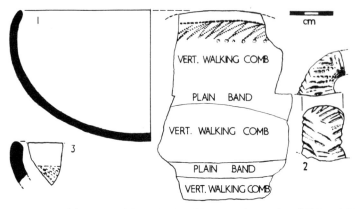

Figure 3.   *1*, bowl, light brown with bands of walking comb impressions (N2E and N2-1F); *2*, handle, red (N2E); *3*, bowl, brown, red-washed inside, with two zones of fine comb impressions and a plain zone 2.5 centimeters wide (N2-1F); all level 1b

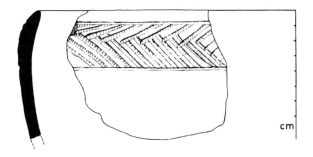

Figure 4. Bowl, red (P6D, Level 2)

Shallow bowls became commoner in the higher levels at Ntereso (Figure 8, *2* and *4*). They were probably made as lids, and some have molding on the rim or decoration on the outside which would be invisible if they were used as bowls. Originally ordinary bowls may have been used as lids. Chipped stone discs of roughly circular form also may have been jar lids.

Lugs and knobs near the rims of bowls (Figure 10) were rare in Level 1 but became commoner. There was one massive vertical handle (Figure 3, *2*) from a sealed pit which probably belonged to Level 1. Occasional cordons and animal figures in relief (Figure 9, *3*) were found in uncontaminated levels; they would have facilitated handling.

Nearly all vessels were round-bottomed (Figure 11, *4*). Very rarely, Neolithic pots have flat or ring bases (Figure 11, *3*); pedestals and pot stands seem intrusive.

The principal decoration was straight comb impressions, usually made with a notched stick; one notched piece of stone could have served the same purpose. The abundant walking comb and grooves were probably

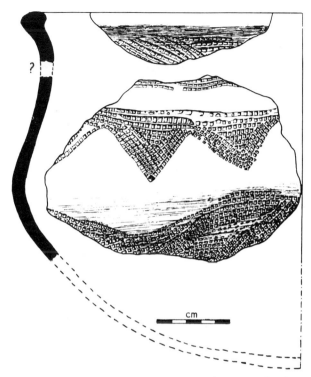

Figure 5. Bowl, yellow-brown, with comb impressions (R7-8H-L, fill of large pit, Level 1b)

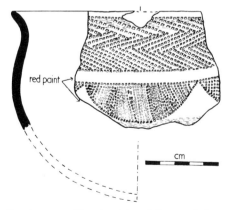

Figure 6. Bowl, yellow-brown, with red paint and fine comb impressions (R7-8D and R8D, Level 3 or 2)

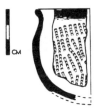

Figure 7.   Bowl, grey (R7-8D, Level 2–3)

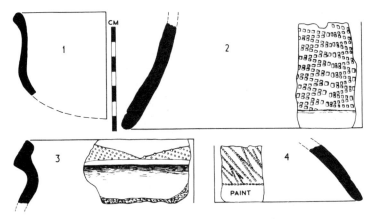

Figure 8.   *1*, bowl, fine grey ware (H3A); *2*, lid, yellow-brown (H3aS-B); *3*, bowl, whitish (H3aE-C); *4*, lid, painted inside (H3A); all Level 1 except *3*, which may belong to the first reoccupation

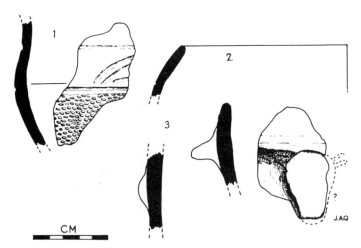

Figure 9.   *1*, brown bowl with possible cob impression (S7–8E, perhaps post-site; *2*, bowl, yellow-brown, with diagonal comb impressions on shoulder (S6nE, Level 2); *3*, cordoned sherds, red, possibly all from the same pot, one apparently representing a cow's head in relief S7E, Level 2)

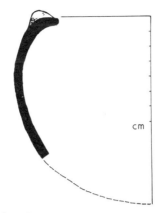

Figure 10.   Bowl with knob at rim, brown-black, diagonal walking comb impressions all over body below rim (R7-8P, top of Level 1a in large pit)

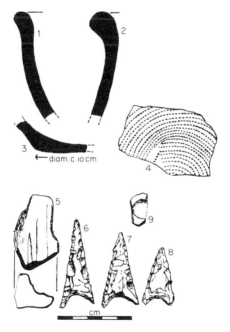

Figure 11.   *1*, bowl, yellow-brown, rough outside, external diameter twenty-five centimeters (N2-1F-G); *2*, jar, reddish, external diameter about thirty centimeters, diagonal walking comb impressions on neck (N2-1F); *3*, flat base, yellow-brown, diameter about ten centimeters (M1W-G); *4*, rounded base, brown, thirteen millimeters thick (N2E); *5*, (?) unfinished sandstone bracelet (N2-1F); *6–8*, hollow-based arrowheads with projecting barbs, greenish yellow shale (N2F, N2-1G); *9*, (?) bone spoon (N2-1G); all Level 1b

made with a curved stamp, possibly a serrated marine shell such as *Cardium edule* or *Arca senilis*, but there is no evidence for these from Ntereso. Blunt scorings were not uncommon and would have been made with a stick. The commonest were the reticulates on necks of coarse jars (Figure 1). Serpentine grooves were very rare (see Davies 1967a: Figure 100). Triangular jabs were rare and may possibly be derived from the Buobini ware (Flight 1968) which preceded the Kintampo Neolithic.

Eight or nine terracotta spoons were found. One occurred at the base of a pit of Level 1, others in uncontaminated collections from Level 2. Only the stubby handles were identifed, but it has been possible to calculate bowl diameters as nine to ten and a half centimeters. Some have comb impressions on the concave face (Figure 12, *1*; Davies 1966: Figure 3). I know no parallel from Neolithic contexts. Such spoons were much later adopted into Ashanti ritual furniture and have been found at the seventeenth-century site of Ahinsan. In another pit of Level 1 was what may be a small bone spoon (Figure 11, *9*).

In order to clarify my conclusions about Ntereso, I group the remaining

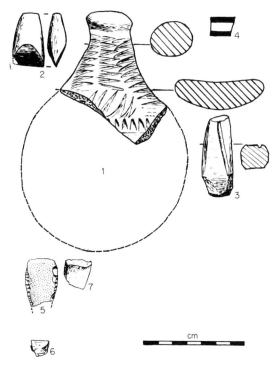

Figure 12.   *1*, pottery spoon, tight walking comb impressions also over back (N2C); *2*, polished stone axe (MOB); *3*, "cigar" rubbed down and grooved as polisher (M1C); *4*, terracotta bead (N2-3C); *5*, straight-based arrowhead, red shale (MOB); *6*, *7*, microliths on quartz pebbles, possibly transverse arrowheads (N2-1C, N2C); all Level 2 slightly mixed with 1

cultural material as probably northern derivatives and probably local objects.

Many biface arrowheads, nearly all of sandy shale, were found in all levels at Ntereso (Figure 13; Davies 1966: Figure 1; Davies 1967a: Figure 103). I have counted ninety-five pieces, including some that were unstratified and some unfinished or too broken to classify. I have distinguished five types:

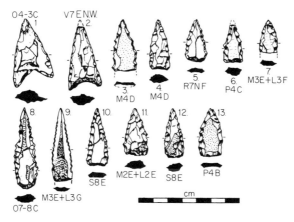

Figure 13.   Arrowheads *1, 2*, hollow-based with projecting barbs, greenish yellow shale; *3, 7*, broken toward the base; *4, 6, 10–12*, straight based, denticulated, red or yellow-brown sandstone; *5, 13*, narrow, round-based, with denticulations extending to the point; *8, 9*, slender, with denticulations ending below the point and either straight or rounded base, fine green or red sandstone; all Level 2

A. Fairly wide hollow-based pieces with projecting barbs (Figures 11, 6–8; 13, *1* and *2*), hardly ever denticulated and made of soft greenish yellow shale; common in Level 1 and rare higher.

B. Long, narrow, hollow-based arrowheads, denticulated; only two were found, in Level 3.

C. Straight-based arrowheads, usually denticulated if made of red or yellow-brown sandstone (Figures 12, *5*; 13, *4, 6*, and *10–12*); uncommon at any level.

D. Narrow arrowheads with rounded bases, denticulated if made of suitable material, denticulations extending to the point (Figure 13, *5* and *13*).

E. Long, slender arrowheads of fine green or red sandstone, with denticulations ending below the point and either straight or rounded base (Figure 13, *8* and *9*); rare at all levels.

There were no tanged arrowheads. Some microliths made on small quartz pebbles may be transverse arrowheads (Figure 12, *6* and *7*). This is a southern type and will be mentioned below.

One bifacial arrowhead was found by Cooper at Fiakwasa (recorded in the field notebooks of the Geological Survey; see Davies 1967a: 222), a site too inaccessible for archaeologists to reach; pieces collected by the geologists could belong to the Kintampo Neolithic or to the Ntereso culture. Six rough arrowheads of quartz were found at Bui, probably casual drops not associated with an occupation site (York 1966a). Otherwise, so far as I know, they have not been found in northern Ghana or in the savanna to the north. All my types are paralleled in Hugot's catalogue of Saharan arrowheads (Hugot 1957), but as his study was based on Algiers it lists very few from the southern Sahara and cannot be used to identify the region whence the Ntereso types are likely to have been derived.

Ntereso yielded five unbarbed fishhooks of ivory, grooved near the butt to attach a cord (Davies 1967a: Figure 43, *3–5*). Most came from the fill of the pits of Level 1, one from Level 2. These have been occasionally found on lakeside sites of the southern Sahara. The one barbed hook from Karkarichinkat-Sud, a site roughly contemporary with Ntereso (Balout 1958:165; Delibrias, Guillier and Labeyrie 1971:224), suggests that the Ntereso culture is not derived from the region of Gao.

Two unilateral harpoons and a barb were found together in a Level 1 pit (Davies 1967a: Figure 43, *1*). This association may mean that they had been the equipment of one household which had lived near this pit, all their rubbish having been swept into it after the conflagration. Another more doubtful and perhaps unfinished piece came from a pit outside the site (probably Level 1) and what may be an unfinished barb came from Level 3. They are made from slices of long bone by cutting and abrasion. One bilaterally barbed piece (Davies 1967a: Figure 43, *2*) was probably a harpoon, as it lacks adequate means of attachment to have been a fish spear.

None of the Ntereso harpoons were perforated, as was normal in the fairly numerous group from the middle Niger Valley and the lacustrine sites to the north of it. At Ntereso the cord was attached to a groove on the butt. No exact parallel is reported from the Sahara. Harpoons with shallow grooves around only part of the butt are known from Ishango on Lake Edward (Lake Idi Amin Dada), Early Khartoum (both sites much older than Ntereso), and Manga, Chad (undated) (de Heinzelin 1962). It would appear that the Ntereso type had been derived from the northeast but improved en route.

Ntereso yielded 480 small pebbles chipped on two edges to permit attachment of a cord (Davies 1964b: Figure 118, *11*). Such pebbles have been found on other riverine sites in Ghana (Chukoto, New Todzi) and without association close to rivers. In view of their distribution and the absence of evidence for vertical looms in Ghana, I regard them as weights for fishing nets. It is impossible to say if they were brought from the north or adopted locally. Chukoto, from surface finds, appears to belong to the Kintampo Neolithic and to be the only riverine site known of that culture, but Mathewson has not published his excavations. New Todzi (Davies 1968) lies far to the south but is undated and may be much later than Ntereso. Similar net weights are not known from the Niger Valley or the Sahara.

The slicer I regard as a northern tool. It is a fairly broad ground blade made on a thin slab of stone. Six were found at Ntereso (Figure 14). They occur near Bamako (Davies 1964b:184 n. 44 and Figure 97, *11*).

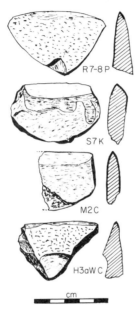

Figure 14.   Slicers; all Level 1

Stone tools, perhaps used for agriculture, are uncertain and atypical at Ntereso. There were two possible hoes, but none of the well-shaped hoes described from other parts of Ghana (Davies 1964b:203–218). A damaged rilled axe or hammer (Davies 1967a: Figure 65,*2*) from the base of a pit of Level 1 may be a northern type. A very blunt polished axe, ground on only one face to a slightly concave blade (Davies 1966: Figure 7, *1*), may also be a northern type and is paralleled particularly by pieces from the Soguinex mines of eastern Guinea.

The curious scored objects which I called "terracotta cigars" (Figure 15, *1–4*; Davies 1962: Figure 4; 1964b: Figures 115, 117; 1966: Figure 8; 1967a: Figures 72, 102) were found to the number of 313 at Ntereso. My name for them, though hardly scientific, does not prejudge their purpose; I dislike calling them rasps, because they would abrade if used for nuts or

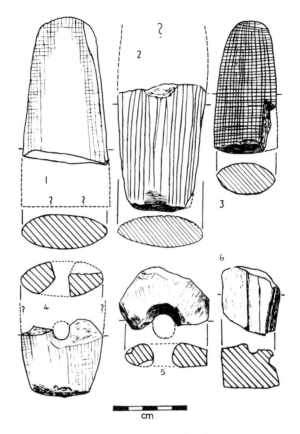

Figure 15. *1–4*, "terracotta cigars"; *1* has abraded face, *2* abraded underface (M4C, N2C, N2-3C, M4D); *5*, shale bracelet rough-out (MOB); *6*, sandstone bead-polisher (MOB); all Level 2

other food. Admittedly, however, many are not of terracotta. Twenty-two from Ntereso are of sandstone; others — I do not know how many or from where — have been found to be of some other stone.

They are slabs of flat-oval section, scored horizontally and vertically on both faces but usually not to the ends. Some taper slightly to both ends. The longest one, found complete near the base of a Level 1 pit, measures twenty-six and eight-tenths centimeters long and sixty to thirty-two millimeters wide. Others taper to one end and have a flat base. Attempts were made to perforate many of them after manufacture by pecking from both faces and then grinding when the hole was nearly through. The perforations which could be measured were ten to twenty-seven millimeters across. Many had broken before the perforation was complete, others after it was polished and therefore presumably in use. The perforations must have been for handles, either set at right angles or formed by a pronged stick on the same axis as the "cigar," with a peg to hold it in place.

Nearly all those found were fragmentary, suggesting vigorous usage. Few are worn at the end, including sandstone pieces which are not typical in shape. Many are worn on one or both faces, and the scorings have been partly erased. Theories as to their use — if they had a practical use — must take account of their fracture and wear. The suggestion that they were used in pottery manufacture does not. A smoothing tool would wear on the end; a stamp for impressions would not break. Nor do I conceive them as abraders for wood or rasps for nuts. On the whole, I would regard them as beaters for bark cloth. Stone pestles, scored on the ends, were found in eastern Guinea (Davies 1967a:201) and are thought to have had the same purpose.

Some were cut down for secondary purposes and grooved, probably for polishing shell beads or sharpening bone points (Figure 12, *3*).

These objects are typical of the Kintampo Neolithic and do not occur outside the complex of this and of the Ntereso culture. Stray pieces from Iron Age sites seem to have been collected as curiosities. They are not found north of Ntereso, and there are no close parallels outside Ghana. If they were for bark cloth, they would be useless north of the range of suitable trees in the gallery forests.

Most of the small polished stone axes from Ntereso (Figure 12, *2*; see Davies 1966: Figure 7) were of savanna types used in the Kintampo Neolithic and farther north. They are not numerous; the edge-ground axe, believed to be an early type in the forest, was not found.

Bracelets of shale and sandstone (Figures 11, *5*; 15, *5*; Davies 1966: Figure 6) will have been locally made and are paralleled in the Kintampo Neolithic. They were fifty to seventy millimeters across, implying small hands and gracile wrists. Two pieces of black-and-white (?) granodiorite were probably imported from a distant source. There were also two roughouts of bone bracelets.

Many microliths were found, made mostly from small quartz pebbles. The commonest were chisels, some perhaps transverse arrowheads (Figure 12, *6* and *7*); much less common were blunt-backed blades, tanged blades, awls, side- and endscrapers, and points. These types are common in the Ghana Mesoneolithic; there is no reason to suppose that any were introduced to Ntereso from the north.

Beads of riverine mollusc shell and grooved stones for polishing them (Figure 15, *6*; Davies 1966: Figures 4, 5) are undistinctive; so are pendants of *Etheria* shell, a perforated human incisor, bone points, chisels, and spatuae. Most of these types will probably turn up in the Kintampo Neolithic. Stone beads occur early both in the Sahara and in the south. Of the very few from Ntereso, some may be Neolithic, some are probably intrusive. A terracotta bead is Neolithic (Figure 12, *4*).

For food, the Ntereso people relied largely on hunting and fishing. A good variety of wild mammals, fish, and reptiles (turtle, tortoise, lizard, snake) has been recognized (Carter and Flight, 1972). They also collected *Etheria elliptica* (Volta oyster) and at least one other freshwater mollusc. The only domestic animal that Carter has recognized is dwarf goat. Cow was not found stratified, and Carter considers that two bovid bones which were stratified resemble buffalo. Flight's bovids from Kintampo K6 were probably domesticated. There is therefore no evidence that the Ntereso domestic animals did not derive from the Kintampo Neolithic.

Flight (1970) records from K6 oil palm (*Elaeis guineensis*) and cowpea (*Vigna unguiculata*); doubtless his final report will mention other wild and perhaps domestic seeds. The former would probably have grown wild near Kintampo; I have found kernels in a peaty stratum in the inner silt terrace upstream from Bui. At Ntereso we noticed no seeds or kernels. It is unlikely that such material would survive on an open site in the wooded savanna, with its long dry seasons. Although I did not have the opportunity of obtaining expert botanical opinion on the pottery impressions, I noticed sherds with impressions which seemed to be of cobs of maize and (?)*Pennisetum* (Figure 9, *1*). All but two of these came from squares and levels with Gonja intrusion (see below), and some are wares which on other grounds I consider Gonja. Of the two remaining (?)*Pennisetum* impressions, one was on a sherd which seemed to belong to the first (pre-Gonja) intrusion. The other came from a level probably uncontaminated, but I would not claim it as evidence for Neolithic cereal agriculture without an expert opinion.

On the other hand, Ntereso yielded fifty-three sandstone slabs, flat or slightly hollowed, which seem to be lower grindstones, used with a longitudinal motion, and twenty-six upper grindstones, used longitudinally, circularly, and in a wide groove. These were probably for grinding seeds, but there is no evidence whether the latter were wild or domesticated. There are also forty-two quartz pebbles with marks of pounding. Though it is likely that most of these were used in the preparation of food, they could have been used for breaking bones or pounding wild yams or nuts and are no evidence for domesticates.

To resume, the Ntereso culture seems to have derived some elements from the Kintampo Neolithic, which according to the dates given by Flight for its beginning at K6 (I–2697–8) would have been established two centuries before Ntereso was occupied. The principal southern elements are the coarse pottery and its commonest decoration, the "cigars," most of the stone axes, the shale bracelets, and apparently the quartz microliths. On the other hand, much of the Ntereso culture seems derived from the north or northeast, perhaps from the fringe of a Sahara which was becoming desiccated. Most obvious elements in this group are the bone fishing equipment, the biface arrowheads, the slicers, the decoration of the fine pottery and especially the use of paint, perhaps the cylindrical shaft wells of Level 2 (reminiscent of the rock-cut *bilegas* used until recently in Gonja), and above all the rectangular flat-roofed houses. The last seem unusual only in the flimsiness of their walls. The flat roof is at home in areas with considerably lower rainfall than Ntereso. Though it has in the last few centuries intruded into northwestern Ghana as far south as the latitude of Ntereso, the White Volta Valley today is within the zone of round mud huts with conical thatched roofs, better suited to withstanding violent rain.

Four radiocarbon dates have been received from Ntereso:

SR-61, 3,190 ± 120 B.P., from the packing in the undercut part of a pit of Level 1. The sample was sealed and must be assigned at the latest to the filling of the pit at the end of Level 1.

SR-81, 3,270 ± 100 B.P., from dark earth with patches suggestive of burning beneath the collapsed daub roof of the rectangular house of Level 2. It belongs, therefore, either to the occupation of the house or to its destruction.

SR-52, 3,580 ± 130 B.P., a large piece of charred wood beside and just above a lump of burnt daub two centimeters above the collapsed daub roof of the round house of Level 2. It was assigned to Level 3 but may be part of the destruction of Level 2.

SR-90, 1,890 ± 110 B.P., a single piece of charred wood in a much contaminated area. It seems to date the first intrusion and will be discussed below.

Of the first three dates, SR-61 and SR-81, though reversed chronologically, lie within a single statistical error and presumably date the Neolithic occupation, the end of Level 1 and Level 2. SR-52 belongs at the earliest to Level 2 and must have been an old piece of wood, either heartwood or a reused piece. I would therefore date the primary site at Ntereso to about 1300 B.C.

Careful analysis of the pottery revealed two groups which did not occur in Level 1 and seemed stylistically foreign to the Neolithic corpus. I therefore concluded that there had been two reoccupations of the site. In Level 1 there was no suspicion of contamination except on the extreme western edge of the site and in two pits which had been exposed by roadmen ten years before the excavation. One of these had been largely destroyed, and intrusive sherds were uncertain (probably Figure 8, *3*). The other had undoubtedly late sherds only at a deep level, and the contamination had probably been lateral and perhaps recent. In a few squares Level 2 showed signs of contamination. Level 3 was much disturbed; three burials and a cairn, possibly ritual, had been intruded into it.

In the black, sticky site earth it was normally impossible to detect intrusion even where it had obviously taken place, for instance, around

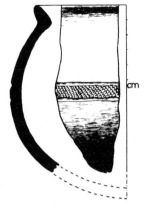

Figure 16.   Black-polished jar with narrow band of cord impressions framed by grooves
(T6E); first reoccupation

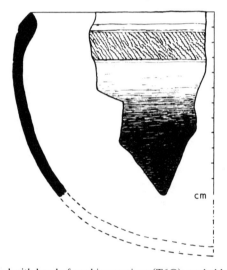

Figure 17.   Red bowl with band of cord impressions (T6G); probably first reoccupation

the burials. Contamination could have taken several forms: complete
overturning of the site earth, with widespread mixture of Neolithic and
later objects; the digging of pits of limited size; and tree-holes or burrows
down which small objects could slip.

The earlier intrusion created much disturbance on the extreme west of
the site near the old pool but was hardly noticed elsewhere. It was
characterized by small, neat, black-polished jars and bowls with
restrained decoration of a narrow band of cord impressions framed by
grooves (Figures 16, 17) and also probably by pointed rims, angular
junction of rim and neck (Figure 8, 3), and carinated shoulders (Figure

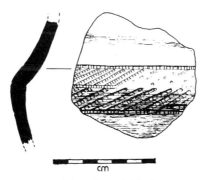

Figure 18.   Yellow carinated bowl (Q1B); probably first reoccupation

18). Pottery of this type has not been identified elsewhere in Gonja and did not occur in the long but interrupted sequence at New Buipe (York 1966b). It is therefore reasonable to assign it to the gap between New Buipe I (probably Kintampo Neolithic, I-2707, 2,865 ± 290 B.P.) and New Buipe II (I-2702, 1,170, ± 100 B.P.). It was abundant in the square and level whence came the charcoal sample SR-90, dated 1,890 ± 110 B.P. As this sample was taken from a single piece of charred wood and was not a mixture, the date must refer to this intrusion.

The second intrusion was more widespread and usually more superficial. It carried a rather hard ware, specializing in wide-lipped jars and colanders, sometimes with cob impressions (Figure 9, *1*). It was probably responsible for the burials and the cairn. Such pottery has often been found on surface sites in Gonja, sometimes in association with painted Deber ware. Though dates are not available, it is believed not to be older than the seventeenth century.

The occurrence of iron and slag at Ntereso has aroused controversy. We found twenty pieces of iron, one probable whetstone, and twelve scraps of slag probably the result of smithying, rather than smelting. By means of my rigid criteria for intrusive sherds, I have determined that all the metal and slag except one piece of iron came from squares and levels where there was independent evidence for intrusion — largely from Level 3, which was much disturbed. This creates an *a priori* presumption that all the iron except the one piece is post-Neolithic; it is no direct proof. Much of the intrusive pottery is typologically Gonja.

The one exception is a piece of iron from the base of Level 3, about fifteen centimeters below the level at which intrusion was proved in that square on other grounds. This creates a presumption that this piece belongs to the site, but it does not provide proof, because the piece could have slipped down a burrow or tree-hole without any post-Neolithic sherds. It is a curved strip with one end broken, the other bent back onto itself to form a loop (Davies 1966: Figure 9, *5*). Its purpose is uncertain; it could have been part of a small bracelet. There is a possibility that a personal ornament of metal could have reached Ntereso by trade long before the iron is otherwise attested in West Africa. Nevertheless, the knowledge of iron by the people of Ntereso must be considered doubtful in view of the amount of disturbance in Level 3.

REFERENCES

BALOUT, LIONEL
  1958 *Algérie préhistorique*. Paris: Arts et Métiers Graphiques.
CALVOCORESSI, D., R. N. YORK
  1971 The state of archaeological research in Ghana. *West African Journal of Archaeology* 1:87–103.
CARTER, P. L., C. FLIGHT
  1972 A report on the fauna from Ntereso and Kintampo rock shelter 6 in Ghana. *Man* 7:277–282.
DAVIES, OLIVER
  1962 "Neolithic cultures in Ghana." *Actes du Quatrième Congrès Panafricain de Préhistoire et de l'Etude du Quaternaire*, volume two. Edited by G. Mortelmans and H. Nenquin, 291–302. Tervuren: Musée Royal de l'Afrique Centrale.
  1964a Gonja painted pottery. *Transactions of the Ghana Historical Society* 7:4–11.
  1964b *The Quaternary in the coastlands of Guinea*. Glasgow: Jackson.
  1966 "Invasion of Ghana from the Sahara in the early Iron Age." *Actas del Quinto Congreso Panafricano de Prehistoria y del Estudio del Cuaternario*, volume two, 27–42.
  1967a *West Africa before the Europeans*. London: Methuen.
  1967b Timber-construction and wood-carving in West Africa in the second millennium B.C. *Man* 2:115–118.
  1968 Mesoneolithic excavations at Legon and New Todzi, Ghana. *Bulletin de l'Institut Fondamental de l'Afrique Noire* B30:1147–1194.
  1971 *Archaeology of the flooded Volta Basin*. Legon: University of Ghana.
DE HEINZELIN, J.
  1962 Ishango. *Scientific American* 206(6):105–116.
DELIBRIAS, G., M. T. GUILLIER, J. LABEYRIE
  1971 Gif natural radiocarbon measurements VI. *Radiocarbon* 13:213–254.
FLIGHT, C.
  1968 Kintampo 1967. *West African Archaeological Newsletter* 8:15–19.
  1970 Excavations at Kintampo. *West African Archaeological Newsletter* 12:71–72.
HUGOT, H. J.
  1957 Essai sur les armatures de pointes de flèches du Sahara. *Libyca Anthropologie Prehistoire Ethnologie* 5:89–236.
MATHEWSON, D.
  1968 Painted pottery sequence in the Volta Basin. *West African Archaeological Newsletter* 8:24–31.
VITA-FINZI, C., R. A. KENNEDY
  1965 Seven Saharan sites. *Journal of the Royal Anthropological Institute* 95:195–213.

WILLETT, FRANK
  1971   A survey of recent results in the radiocarbon chronology of western and northern Africa. *Journal of African History* 12:339–370.
YORK, R. N.
  1966a   Drawings of microliths from Bui. *West African Archaeological Newsletter* 4:42–43.
  1966b   The Volta Basin Research Project, Ghana. *West African Archaeological Newsletter* 5:27–29.
YORK, R. N., D. MATHEWSON, D. CALVOCORESSI, C. FLIGHT
  1967   *Archaeology in the Volta Basin*. Legon: University of Ghana.

The Emergence of Iron Technology in West Africa, with Special Emphasis on the Nok Culture of Nigeria

JOHN A. RUSTAD

The emergence of iron technology in West Africa has been explained in terms of diffusion from Anatolia. Students of the subject (Arkell 1962; Cline 1937; Davidson 1966, 1974; Davies 1967; Fage 1969; Mauny 1971; Oliver and Fagan 1975; Oliver and Fage 1962; Sassoon 1963; Shaw 1972; Shinnie 1967, 1971; Van der Merwe and Stuiver 1968b; Trigger 1969; Tylecote 1975; Willett 1971b) have focused their attention almost entirely upon the different possible routes of such diffusion. In the first portion of this paper, a critical survey is made of the bases of such theories. In the second portion there is a discussion of the role the Nok culture and iron technology played in West African cultural dynamics.

The question of the emergence of iron technology in Africa is a complex one. Because of the immense geographical distances, it is possible to ask it about three distinct areas: the Nile Valley, the Nok culture area, and western West Africa. What is true for one area in relation to diffusion or autochthony may not be true for the others. Also, the question is not simply one of establishing the presence or absence of iron objects which can be accounted for on the basis of trade, but rather one of accounting for a technology devoted to iron production. Here iron technology is defined as a sophisticated system of ideas and procedures, the material means to achieve the intended end of smelting iron ore, and the occurrence of these ideas, procedures, and means within the context of a dynamic and integrated culture.

Two areas, one in Ghana, the other in Nigeria, have yielded supposedly early manifestations of ironworking. This paper will concern itself with the Nok culture in Nigeria because this area has the earliest dates in the context of a reliable stratigraphy. One Ghana site, Ntereso, contains no furnaces, and there is considerable controversy about the reliability of its stratigraphy and dates (see Shaw 1969:228). A second Ghana site, Hani, which does have iron-smelting furnaces, has been dated to 180 ± 75 A.D. (Posnansky and MacIntosh 1976:165–166). The remains of the Nok culture have been identified in over thirty sites south and west of the Jos Plateau. Such sites as Nok, Kagura, Jemaa, and Katsina Ala extend over an area approximately 100 miles wide and 300 miles long. Most of the assemblages originate in alluvial deposits, a fact which has made the dating and associations subject to some uncertainty. Summary reports of two *in situ* sites have been published by Bernard Fagg (1969) and Angela Fagg (1972).

Bernard Fagg's résumé concerns material that may represent a specialized industrial function or the domestic debris of a permanent village. The site is Taruga, which lies in the well-watered, forested Taruga Valley near the village of Takushara, about thirty-four miles southeast of Abuja. Materials from Taruga include large quantities of domestic pottery, figurines, worn-out querns, terracotta figurines, and distinctive pottery graters, which are shallow, flat-bottomed dishes deeply scored inside with a diced pattern while the undersurface is generally much embellished (Fagg 1969:46). There are two principal types of domestic pottery: shallow basins with diameters ranging from twenty-six to thirty-six centimeters and globular pots having everted lips with diameters ranging from fourteen to twenty-two centimeters. The decorating techniques include comb-reeding, channeling, rouletting, curvilinear incisions, cross-hatching, and impressed circles. One interesting find is a fragment of a human figurine about eighty centimeters high. Iron technology is represented by wrought-iron objects, iron slag, quartz hammerstones, tuyeres, and the bases and walls of ten furnaces. At least one of the furnaces appears to be of the shaft type (Fagg 1969:146, 147 and Plate 10). Tylecote (1975) provides some analysis and comparison of Nok furnaces and the associated slag.

The second site is Samun Dukiya, located in the Nok Valley (Fagg 1972). The occupation horizons, which are thirty to eighty centimeters below the surface, have yielded an assemblage typical of those found in the alluvial deposits of the Nok culture. It includes fragmented domestic pottery, grinding stones, fragments of iron, beads, and figurines of stone. The most frequently occurring motif is a raised-dot roulette decoration. The manifestations of iron include fragments of knife blades, arrow and spearheads, hooks, bracelets, and one bead.

The dating of the Nok culture includes three dates from the Taruga site. The first is 280 ± 120 B.C. from Layer 3, which is forty centimeters in depth and is the densest occupation layer (Fagg 1969:46). A layer twenty-four centimeters below Layer 3 containing iron slag has yielded the second date of 440 ± 140 B.C. One of the furnaces has provided the third date of 300 ± 100 B.C. (Fagg 1969:49). The lower part of the occupation layer at Samun Dukiya gave a date of 210 ± 95 B.C. (Fagg

1972:76). A third Nok site has been dated at A.D. 200 ± 500 (Fagg 1965:22). Van der Merwe and Stuiver (1968b:55–56) have published dates of 925 ± 70 B.C. and 2110 ± 140 B.C. for two Nok sites which do not contain any iron objects. Shaw (1969:226–227) claims that a third date of 3265 ± 65 B.C. should have been published and that the dates reflect the unstratified nature of the site from which the samples were retrieved. He also thinks that the date of 925 ± 70 B.C. is not valid for the beginning of iron use. On the other hand, Fagg (1972:75) states that the Iron Age assemblage has been bracketed for Nok from 925±70 B.C. to A.D. 200± 50. A degree of uncertainty also attends the question of whether the Nok culture is transitional in relation to iron technology. The absence of polished stone axes at Taruga is suggestive of heavy reliance upon iron technology for tool production. At Samun Dukiya, on the other hand, polished stone axes are associated with Iron Age material (Fagg 1972:78). More site reports are needed to settle either issue.

The question of the emergence of iron technology within the Nok culture and in West Africa in general can be refined in two ways. First, it is important to consider the criteria for determining whether iron technology in West Africa and/or in the Nok culture was the result of convergence in historically unrelated societies or of a historical connection, genetic or diffusionary. Various methods for differentiating diffusion, convergence, and genetic connection have been outlined by Trigger (1968:29–39). Traits must be selected for analysis and then compared. (Such traits or trait complexes must not be too general; pottery, for example, is too broad a category to be useful for comparison.) The traits selected must be analyzed in terms of form and function, considered independently. The analysis of a trait's function must include its sociocultural as well as its technological role. Once the analysis of the traits in each culture has been done, a comparison can be made. If genuine resemblances can be observed, then it has to be established that genetic connection or convergence did not produce them. Convergence may occur because traits fulfill similar functional requirements, because of limitations in the human range of responses or channeling of choice by a preceding sequence of choices, or because a similar cultural process is operating in the two societies.

To overcome these problems, Trigger suggests, the element(s) of the trait to be compared should be ones that are more a product of human will than of natural laws. Focusing on features which are human-created makes it more likely that similarities will be due to a desire to resemble rather than to a functional requirement. The desire or intent to resemble, whatever other motivations there may be, is the means by which ideas and their manifestations spread from one unit of culture to another. Thus similarities in humanly defined features are more likely to be indicative of a diffusionary process. (I would add that the desire *not* to resemble may be as strong as the desire to resemble and that opposition may also follow a diffusionary process.) Once an appropriate nonfunctional and/or non-natural element, or group of elements, has been selected for comparison, the historical antecedents of the selected feature(s) in the specified societies must be determined. On the basis of such sequences, convergence in societies or genetic connections between societies can be observed or inferred. Just as the historical antecedents in each society must be empirically determined, there must also be a demonstration of the route along which the trait(s) passed. This entails establishing their exact position in archaeological sites and discovering dates compatible with the postulated direction of diffusion.

To refine the question of the emergence of iron technology further, one can break the technology down into its components. One major component revolves around ore. An ore is a cultural product; it results from some substance's having a humanly desired utility and from a specification of the substance which can be incorporated into the perceptual process of recognition. Recognition of ores has been going on for tens of thousands of years the world over. The next step after recognition is mining. Some insight into the relationship between mining and cultural dynamics is provided by evidence from western Swaziland, where there is a site at which iron ore mining has been practiced since 28,000 B.C. Dart and Beaumont (1969:127) report that of the fifty tons of material removed from the cave, thirty-four tons were removed during the Middle Stone Age. The stone mining tools present at the site include choppers, wedges, chisels, and hammerstones. Some important conclusions which can be drawn from this example have a direct bearing on the interpretation of the Nok culture. First, mining need not be done to supply ore for smelting. Second, mining need not be associated with a Neolithic technological base. Finally, mining does not presuppose knowledge of the metallurgical potential of a mineral. In the Nok culture area, there is no evidence that copper or bronze metallurgy occurred earlier than iron metallurgy, but the absence of such a technology is not an insurmountable barrier to the development of iron metallurgy. Thus, in looking for the antecedents of iron production in the Nok area, these considerations shift concern from searching for bronze or copper metallurgies to the focusing of attention on the discovery of locations of mines which supplied iron ores for purposes other than smelting.

The second major component of iron technology is smelting, which involves a knowledge of heat, of the properties of ore, and of the transformation of ores into metal, as well as the material prerequisites for realizing the transformation. Since the fuel used for iron smelting was, until the seventeenth century A.D., exclusively charcoal (Van der Merwe and Stuiver 1968a:48), Taruga was well situated from the point of view of fuel supply in an area of savanna woodland and heavier forest growth in the lower valley (Fagg 1969:46). Further information is needed about the nature of the tools used to fell the trees and the type of transportation used to haul the wood or charcoal.

Fuel and ore must be combined in a structure that can achieve a minimum temperature of 1,150° Centigrade. This temperature range does not produce a molten iron ore, but only reduces the ore. The design of the furnace must make it possible to control the interior atmospheric conditions and to provide enough oxygen to burn the charcoal at the highest temperature. The blast is increased by the presence of tuyeres, which have been found at Taruga. The tuyeres in turn can be augmented by bellows, no evidence of which has been found at any Nok site. The thirteen furnaces found at Taruga are all of the same type. They all consist of thin-walled mud shafts over shallow pits cut into the decomposed granite. The shafts are free-standing and range in height from one to two meters (Tylecote 1975:5). No information is available on the method of tapping slags and removing the bloom.

According to Coghlan (1956:46–48), in the evolution of the smelting type of kiln, the prototype was probably the pottery kiln. Since there is no evidence of the smelting of other metals prior to the time of iron metallurgy, an iron-smelting furnace would have had to develop directly from the pottery kiln. To determine if convergence was operating in this instance, it has to be determined whether or not there is in the Nok area a sequence of pottery kilns with increasing heat capabilities leading directly to iron-smelting furnaces. As for the tools used in smelting, Coghlan (1956:109–110) has shown that granite can be used as an anvil and hammer while wood can be used as tongs. The Nok culture used quartz hammerstones. If tongs were made of wood, there would be little chance of finding evidence of their presence. From these considerations it can be concluded that a prior knowledge of nonferrous metallurgical principles is unnecessary for the development of the mining and smelting of iron ore. It is entirely possible for iron technology to have developed directly from pottery firing techniques. Thus the fact that in the Nok area there is no evidence of metallurgical knowledge prior to a knowledge of iron metallurgy cannot be used as an argument against the autochthonous development of iron technology in the Nok culture.

Smelting can be accomplished in one of two ways. The indirect method was developed in China during the period from the sixth to the third century B.C. but was not used in southwestern Asia or Europe until the late fourteenth century A.D. (Van der Merwe and Stuiver 1968a:48). It employs a blast furnace and a crucible capable of handling temperatures of 1,530° Centigrade. The product is cast iron with a carbon content of 1.5 to 5.0 percent, which can be converted into steel by removing the carbon. In southwestern Asia, the Hittites used the direct method of smelting (Van der Merwe and Stuiver 1968a:48). This method employs a bloomery furnace, which has no crucible and in which the iron ores are reduced, leaving metallic iron. At temperatures around 1,150° Centigrade, iron particles begin to flow together, forming a pasty, semifused and somewhat porous mass called a bloom. If the bloom is reheated and hammered, a compact block is formed from which the slag and charcoal have been extruded. The result is a piece of wrought iron with a carbon content lower than 0.25 percent.

Wrought iron, however, is not particularly useful (Hawkes and Woolley 1963:562): it is not fusible; it cannot be annealed; it cannot be cast; it cannot be cold-hammered; and it is soft and quickly loses its edge. For these reasons, the technique which made iron production important in southwestern Asia was not the smelting technique but the hardening process. By adding carbon to the wrought iron in various ways, it is possible to produce a steel. Further, steel can be made much harder by heating it to red-hot and then quenching it. Since this makes the steel brittle, it can be reheated to a temperature below red-hot and quenched (Coghlan 1956:55) to temper it into a more usable product. The evidence in Anatolia does not indicate when or where the techniques of hardening and tempering developed.

It is clear that iron technology must be broken down into its components to permit valid comparisons. Since the components of iron technology have alternative realizations, the question "Did iron technology diffuse?" is too broad and vague. Many of the components could have diffused independently of the others. The appropriate line of thought is to begin with specific traits which are capable of comparison. With the exception of Tylecote's (1975) study, there are not sufficient comparative data on the traits of iron technology in the relevant cultures and time periods. In the absence of adequate analysis and comparison, establishing the occurrence of diffusion is on very uncertain ground. Other evidence, however, is capable of yielding information as to the possibility of diffusion, such as possible sources and routes.

Before proceeding to a discussion of such evidence, a review of the historical sequence of iron technology in the Nok culture is in order. The earliest date for manifestations of iron technology is 440 ± 140 B.C. No evidence is as yet available about the sequence of pottery kilns preceding 440 B.C. in the Nok culture area, although there is evidence of pottery as far back as 3000 B.C. at Iwo Eleru and Ukpa, in southwestern and southeastern Nigeria respectively (Willett 1971a:354).

In discussing potential centers of diffusion of iron technology to the Nok area, one must keep in mind that in southwestern Asia ironworking was originally a monopoly of the Hittite kings. By 1200 B.C., the knowledge had become fairly general throughout southwestern Asia (Hawkes and Woolley 1963:564), but it took considerably longer to diffuse to Egypt. "Prior to the 7th century B.C. iron appears to have been rare in

Egypt and was used mainly for magical and ornamental purposes" (Trigger 1969:34). It is only during the Saite period (665–525 B.C.) that there is evidence of iron smelting, and such knowledge probably came from Greeks or Assyrians. By the fifth century B.C., it would seem that iron was in general use in Egypt (Trigger 1969:36).

In the Nilotic Sudan, the beginning of ironworking seems to be marked by the reign of Harsiyotef, who ruled during the period 416–398 B.C. (Trigger 1969:43; Arkell 1966:452). From 750 B.C. to the fourth century A.D., there is a complete archaeological sequence for Meroe based mostly upon excavations of royal cemeteries. The iron objects that are dated ca. 750 B.C. to ca. 400 B.C. tend to be small and infrequent (Trigger 1969:39). Of 1,550 graves predating 400 B.C. at Napata, only 18 contain iron objects (Arkell 1966:452). Trigger (1969:42) thinks that the presence of iron objects at this time represents trade, since there is no positive evidence that iron was being produced. Also, the objects have a non-Meroitic style, and the frequency of iron objects declines after the period in which Kush was expelled from Egypt. In the foundation deposits of the royal tombs of Reigns 23 (ca. 416–398 B.C.), 24 (ca. 398–367 B.C.), and 26 (355–337 B.C.), there appear model iron tools. Also, there are finds of seven tanged spearheads from Reign 26 and of spearheads and twelve single-barbed arrowheads from Reign 27 (322–315 B.C.). The shapes of these weapons remain standard throughout the Meroitic period. After Reign 40 (116–99 B.C.), iron becomes increasingly common. The objects generally remain small and/or utilitarian, including arrowheads, spearheads, jewelry, tweezers, and knives (Trigger 1969:45). For this period Trigger (1969:46) draws the conclusion that ironworking knowledge did not fundamentally alter the economic basis of life, since the smaller cemeteries have iron objects much less frequently than the main centers and the iron objects in the latter are not of direct value for agriculture.

It is not until the end of Meroitic power in A.D. 350 that the nature of iron objects changes. Iron jewelry becomes scarce. Numerous heavy objects appear for the first time, while the number of types of utilitarian objects increases. The tool kit includes knives, swords, horse bits, chairs, frying pans, axes, hoes, saws, and hammers. Many of the iron objects have socketed attachments, unlike the tanged tools of the Meroite period. It would seem that only after the fall of Meroe did iron technology become oriented to tool manufacture and large-scale production and thereby increased productivity (Trigger 1969:49).

Trigger points out several reservations about this interpretation. The excavations are almost entirely of graves, not of habitation sites. The representativeness of the grave goods has yet to be determined; they may not reflect the normal tool kit (Trigger 1969:44). Another reservation is due to the incomplete knowledge concerning the use of iron, i.e., whether it was used for weaponry, industrial tools, or agricultural tools.

Phillipson (1970:5) has published a date of 514 ± 73 B.C. for a piece of charcoal found associated with fragments of iron, iron slag, and pottery at the very bottom of the largest slag heap, Birmingham 97. He thinks that it was at this time that the Meroites first started to produce iron. Tylecote (1975:5) states that the Early Iron Age phase at Meroe is represented by small bowl furnaces found at a level immediately above one dated to 280 ± 120 B.C. Even at a gross level of comparison one can observe that Meroite bowl furnaces are not at all similar to Taruga shaft furnaces. One can conclude, then, that early Meroitic iron-smelting furnaces did not diffuse from Meroe to Taruga. The conclusions of Trigger about the sequence of iron technology at Meroe, the dates for ironworking in the Nok culture and for Birmingham 97, and the dissimilarity of Taruga and early Meroitic furnaces for iron smelting make it a virtual impossibility for Meroe to have been a center for the diffusion of iron technology to West Africa. In fact, Shinnie (1967:44; 1971:99) considers the Meroite culture to have been exclusively oriented to the Nile River on the basis of the fact that no Meroite material has been found farther west than the banks of the Nile. Furthermore, according to Trigger (1969:26), the earliest evidence of contact between the Nilotic Sudan and Darfur dates to A.D. 550.

The route between the Middle Nile and the Jos Plateau contains a series of excavations around Lake Chad. Thirty miles south of Lake Chad is a large tell site 10.6 meters high called Daima. The site lies in the approach to the Lake Chad-Mandara Mountains corridor through which east-west contact in the Sudan area is likely to have occurred. The area was inundated yearly and was attractive for cattle and food crops. In the lowest layers of the tell there are the remains of a cattle-husbanding people who produced polished stone axes, polished bone harpoons, and "good" pottery (*Illustrated London News* 1967). Rather near the top, there is a pavement of potsherds laid on edge in a herringbone pattern (Fagg 1969:43). The tell has yielded the following sequence of dates with associated layers (Fagan 1967:518; see Shaw 1969): A.D. 980 ± 90 (2.4-3.2 meters), A.D. 810 ± 90, A.D. 480 ± 270 (6.0-6.8 meters), A.D. 450 ± 670, and 450 ± 95 B.C. (9.37-9.82 meters). The third and fourth are not considered accurate because they came from bone samples, which give late dates (Tamera and Pearson 1965). The prolific polished-stone assemblages in the earliest layers are indicative of a Neolithic pattern. Within this sequence, the earliest iron was found at a depth of 6.5 meters, suggesting a date of the fifth century A.D. Three more dates were later published by Fagan (1969:153): A.D. 1060 ± 90 (.38-.79 meters to end), A.D. 630 ± 190 (7.7-8.16 meters), and 570 ± 100 B.C. (9.82-10.25 meters to beginning). On the basis of the next to last date, which is from a bone sample, Graham Connah revised his estimate of the introduction of iron objects from the first to the fifth century A.D. (Fagan 1969:153). More recently, S. G. H. Daniels has examined statistically the entire sequence of dates from the site and has concluded that a fifth-to-sixth-century-A.D. date is indicated for the introduction of iron (Willett 1971a:355–356).

In addition to the Daima finds, sites of the Sao culture on the Republic of Chad side of Lake Chad have been excavated. The dates for these tells are as follows (Shaw 1969:228): Mdaga, 425 B.C., A.D. 690, A.D. 1040, A.D. 1620; Amkoundjo, 120 B.C., A.D. 30, A.D. 40; Messo, A.D. 940; Maguira, A.D. 1700. Shaw (1969:228) following J.-P. Lebeuf, who excavated the sites, considers the commencement date for the Sao culture to be 425 B.C. The use or smelting of iron has not yet been associated with a definite date.

No analysis of the iron objects at Daima has been made, and it is impossible to determine whether they resemble Nok culture materials or Meroe materials or both. Also, it has not been established whether they are trade items or locally produced. Their dates, however, coupled with the dates for Meroe, would indicate that neither iron objects nor iron technology diffused from Meroe to the Nok area.

The other proposed center of diffusion to the Nok culture is Carthage. Since no analysis of the manifestations of iron technology in Carthage has been made, it is impossible to determine if genuine resemblances exist between the two cultures. The argument for diffusion relies solely on the dates for the Phoenician and Carthaginian cultures in North Africa. No material from Carthage and Utica and, in fact, no site with Phoenician material has been found to be earlier than the eighth century B.C. (Warmington 1969:31). Although the Carthaginians were producing armour on a mass scale by the third century B.C. (Warmington 1969:136), the beginnings of iron-working extend back to the sixth century B.C. According to Mauny (1971:67), following Gsell, "it is only from the sixth century B.C. that iron appears in their tombs. From the third century on, it definitely replaces bronze as a material of ordinary use." The time interval of 100–200 years between the presence of iron technology at Carthage and its appearance in Nok makes it possible for diffusion to have occurred, but the interval's shortness makes it improbable.

There are two possible routes along which the knowledge of iron smelting could have crossed the Sahara. One route goes from the Gulf of Syrtis to the bend of the Niger at Gao, the other from southern Morocco through Mauritania, along the Oualata-Tichitt cliff to the Middle Niger. There are rock paintings along these routes which indicate that horse-drawn chariots traversed them before 1000 B.C. (see Mauny 1971:68–69; Davidson 1966:11–12). No sites containing iron objects dated prior to the fifth century B.C. have been found along these routes or in the area of the Upper and Middle Niger. Yet, even if iron objects and smelting furnaces of an appropriate date are discovered in the Middle Niger area, there is still a distance of 500 or more miles between Gao and the Nok culture area in which no sites containing iron objects have been discovered.

Although evidence relating to the diffusion of iron technology for the routes and their southern termini is nonexistent, there is some evidence about the northern termini. The history of northern Africa between 800 and 400 B.C. may be divided into two periods. In the first (eighth to seventh century B.C.), Phoenicia established colony-settlements; in the second (sixth to fifth century B.C.), Carthage achieved independence and began its expansion and conquest of North Africa and the western Mediterranean. The northern termini of the central Sahara route, Sabratha and Lepcis, are dated to the second period. Warmington (1969:62) believes that Carthage was interested in the Gulf of Syrtis area before 500 B.C. but made no permanent settlement until after that date. Discoveries at Sabratha indicate that there was seasonal occupation late in the fifth century, after which a small permanent settlement was built. No Phoenician or Carthaginian colony was located at the terminus of the western trans-Saharan route. However, the Phoenicians had an early interest in the Atlantic coast of Morocco and established the settlements of Lixus, Siga, and Mogador, for which the earliest archaeological evidence is from the seventh century (Warmington 1969:34). At these sites, the Carthaginians (and probably also the Phoenicians) obtained large quantities of gold in trade. Evidence concerning iron technology at these sites is not available. One can infer from the dates for the sites near or at the northern termini that there is no more than a slight probability of diffusion of iron technology from the Gulf of Syrtis. Upon observation of the dates for the Atlantic coast sites, a slightly greater probability can be inferred.

In addition to the time intervals, there are other factors affecting the possibility of diffusion. These are the patterns of relationship between the Phoenicians and the Carthaginians and the peoples of North Africa. The Phoenicians were involved in two patterns, trade and settlement-colonies. The Carthaginians added a third pattern, conquest. Warmington (1969:62) characterizes the colonies as follows: "Carthaginian colonies were numerous, but like those of the Phoenicians, were mostly small: . . . We must envisage small settlements of at most a few hundred people at places to which native tribes brought their goods to trade, which could serve as anchorages and watering places. . . ." Trade was the overarching principle within which the Phoenician and Carthaginian colonies fit (Warmington 1969:23). Later, the Carthaginians fit their colonies into a pattern of conquest. The basic premises upon which both the Phoenicians and Carthaginians built their trade have been succinctly stated by Strabo: "Formerly it was the Phoenicians [this includes Carthaginians] who had a monopoly of this commerce and kept the routes a secret" (quoted in Warmington 1969:77; brackets added by Warmington).

The general pattern in Phoenician trading was the exchange of manufactured goods of little value for precious metals, particularly silver, tin, and gold (Warmington 1969:24). The exchange of cheap manufactured goods for raw materials was also practiced by the Carthaginians (Warmington 1969:42, 63, 69, 77, 134, 135), who, in addition to precious metals, acquired foodstuffs, metal in an unworked state, textiles, skins, and slaves in trade. Warmington (1969:136) thinks it highly probable that metal objects, including iron, were exported to Libyan and Numidian tribes and that this trade became much more common in the fourth century B.C. Swanson (1975:594), however, asserts that "no substantial evidence, literary or archaeological, suggests caravans carrying West African gold or anything else — with the possible exception of carbuncles — to Carthaginian North Africa."

On the assumption that there was some trade with the indigenous North African peoples and/or a "trans-Saharan trade," we can infer from the basic premises of Carthaginian trade (and Phoenician trade) that traders would have used every means possible to maintain their monopoly over the trade in manufactured objects; this would have meant keeping the iron-smelting process secret. The fact that the Carthaginians were exporting iron objects would indicate that the peoples of North Africa did not possess such knowledge. Another factor which would have tended to make the Phoenicians and Carthaginians keep iron smelting a secret is a military one. Although the settlements were located among military weaker societies, they were effectively at the mercy of these societies because of their small size. The military consideration for secrecy would have held also when Carthage began its conquest of the North African hinterland. For trade and military considerations, a premium would have been placed upon keeping iron technology a secret from the peoples of North Africa. The reasons that affected Carthage would also have affected any other society that obtained knowledge of iron smelting. One can conclude that the short time interval between the presence of iron objects at both Nok and Carthage, in combination with trade and military factors inhibiting the speed of the dissemination of such knowledge, makes diffusion very unlikely.

As tentative conclusions to this portion of the paper, one can make the following statements: The emergence of iron technology in the Nok culture cannot be explained by diffusion from Meroe. Further, it is highly unlikely that Carthage was a source of knowledge about iron technology for the participants in Nok culture. Therefore, in the absence of evidence to the contrary, iron technology may be considered an autochthonous development in the Nok area and/or culture.[1]

---

[1] A question which has not yet been adequately dealt with by the proponents of diffusion is why only iron technology, and not copper or bronze technology, diffused from Carthage to the Nok area, even though knowledge about bronze occurs earlier at Carthage than

The question as to whether iron technology diffused to the Nok culture area and/or West Africa is inextricably tied to the more fundamental consideration of the role of the Nok culture in the cultural dynamics of West Africa. West Africa participated in the general trend, documented the world over, toward the independent emergence of stratified, politically organized societies. This trend, in West Africa, was represented by a series of transformations in which food-collecting bands became settled villages associated with food production and these villages in turn developed into urban centers. It is a plausible hypothesis that the Nok culture occurred at the juncture between Neolithic-type systems and urban, stratified state systems.

The key factor in the urban revolution, according to Adams (1966:12), was a transformation at the level of social organization rather than at the technological level. To understand what happened at that time, "[one] must describe a functionally related core of institutions as they interacted and evolved through time and not features defined in terms of presence or absence" (Adams 1966:11). In applying this framework to the Nok culture, one must analyze not only iron technology, but also the context within which it operated, including social stratification, urbanization, political differentiation, militarization, and craft specialization.

Preceding the Nok culture was the West African Neolithic, involving the domestication of plants and a shift to food production. In West Africa, indigenous grasses were domesticated into the tropical cereals of millet and sorghum. A rice grain and the yam were other indigenous species brought under domestication. It has been speculated that the practice of plant domestication came from the Fertile Crescent, but the argument is not persuasive. Although there is some indication that Egyptian influence of a Neolithic kind reached as far west as the Ahaggar (Shaw 1972:59), the influence is still several hundreds of miles removed from most of West Africa. The fact that the eastern and central Sahara had knowledge of pottery as early as southwestern Asia (Willett 1971a:345) precludes the diffusion of such knowledge between the two areas and indicates that Saharan Africa was acting autonomously in the sixth millennium B.C. Additionally, it must be considered that the domesticated plants in West Africa are indigenous, while barley and wheat, the cereals domesticated in the Fertile Crescent, cannot grow southwest of the Nile. In characterizing the beginning of plant domestication in the New and Old Worlds, Adams (1963:123) states: "The domestication of the crops [in the New World] reflects, in other words, the same kind of prolonged, independent

---

knowledge about iron. This question assumes further importance in that the prerequisites for bronze technology were available and it eventually did develop in southern Nigeria and in that copper technology probably did diffuse from northern Africa to northwestern Mauritania, where copper mining and smelting have been dated to 570–400 B.C. (Herbert 1973:180; Willett 1971b:359).

experimentation in many diverse centers as that which I have suggested earlier for the Old World cereals. Moreover, the same process of many divergent local derivations of food crops probably could be documented elsewhere in the New World." If it was the case that there were local but independent centers of domestication within the major areas of domestication, it is very probable, in the light of the geographical distance and ecological difference between the Fertile Crescent and West Africa, that West Africa was an independent locus of plant domestication. At a minimum, it can be concluded that West Africa was exhibiting its own dynamic processes and tendencies in the food-producing revolution. These independent tendencies were reinforced by increasing isolation due to the desiccation of the Sahara between 3000 and 2500 B.C.

At the heart of the transformation from food collection to food production is prolonged independent experimentation. The mental structures necessary for that experimental process to occur have been posited by Lévi-Strauss (1966:1–16). Drawing upon ethnography, he argues that the Neolithic revolution was based on classificatory schemes capable of reflecting objective species. Most of the qualities used in constructing classifications can be correlated with one another to produce generalizations based on perceptual knowledge. Also, the qualities can be observed for changes under different conditions, and this observation is the basis of the experimental method. In combination with observations, the experimental method includes risk-taking and exploration. By accumulating knowledge through observation, correlation, classification, generalization, and experimentation, humans were able to control the reproductive process of plants through seed selection, to create new environments for plants (see Adams 1966:41), and to process plants for consumption.

Commenting on plant domestication in West Africa, Davies (1968:481–482) states: "As the wild predecessors of millet and sorghum would not well lend themselves to food collecting or protoagriculture because of the limited yield per plant, their use may be presumed to be not earlier than the full agricultural state of the Neolithic." The implication is that experimentation with plant domestication continued for centuries and that the experimenters were not concerned with immediate practical use. Thus the mental prerequisites of experimentation provided the intellectual basis for the shift to food production in West Africa as they did in other areas of the world. Even if the idea of plant domestication diffused from southwestern Asia to West Africa — as certainly the plants did not — the situation in West Africa must have been ready for its acceptance. The mental set of domestication cannot have been practiced in a vacuum. There must, in addition to the mental structures, have been supportive material and social organizational structures.

The urban revolution also has deep roots in West Africa. Urban centers near the Nok culture area are located in southwestern Nigeria, only some

200 miles separating the Nok area and Ife, the oldest known urban site. The basic pattern in the area was one of independent city-states with economies based on a wide range of craft specialties. They exhibited considerable social differentiation and were ruled by kings with some relationship to the divine. How far back in time they go has not yet been determined, but some information is available. The urbanization process has been dated as far back as A.D. 560, along with some of the craft specialties (Willett 1971b:28). Social differentiation can be inferred from terracotta sculptures which have been dated to A.D. 960 (Willett 1971b:24, 25), and the institution of kingship seems to have been well-developed by the ninth or tenth centry A.D. (Willett 1971b:25). In the area to the east of the Ife culture area, the Neolithic revolution seems not to have led to urbanization. However, a find of a treasure house and grave at Igbo-Ukwu dated to A.D. 840–875 (but see Lawal 1973 and Shaw 1975 for reservations) indicates that at the time there was social differentiation and a considerable range of craft skills (Shaw 1965:182–184; Fagan 1969:153).

Not much is known about the Nok culture in these terms. It seems likely that it was based on food production in settled villages with some craft specialization and a high level of technological skill. At present, there is no evidence as to the extent of social or political differentiation. On the basis of the available evidence it seems very likely that the Nok culture occupied an intermediate position between the Neolithic-type systems and the urban, stratified systems of southwestern Nigeria. A tentative hypothesis is that the Nok culture was a protourban phase, bringing the Neolithic base to the point at which urban centers could develop. The characteristics of the Nok culture fit into a position that is intermediate in the developmental sequence in Nigeria. The Neolithic has been dated to as far back as 3000 B.C. (Fagan 1969:152), while Ife has been dated to possibly as early as A.D. 560; the Nok culture has been dated from 950 B.C. to A.D. 200. The only available comparative evidence concerns the terracotta figurines in the Nok and Ife cultures. They are similar in that they are naturalistic in style, are adorned with elaborate beadwork, and represent human beings at close to life-size (Willett 1971b:23–24). Although no comparison has been made of the respective iron technologies, it is very likely, in view of their geographic propinquity, that the Nok culture provided the basis of Ife's iron technology.

The Nok culture or its successor may have affected the whole area to the east, south, and west of the Jos Plateau. Iron objects have been dated to the fifth and sixth centuries A.D. at Daima and to A.D. 840 at Igbo-Ukwu, but no date has yet been given for iron at Ife. Bronze objects have been dated to the eighth century A.D. at Daima (Willett 1971b:10) and to A.D. 840 at Igbo-Ukwu, but, again, no date has been determined for the beginning of bronze work at Ife. Although the latter has been thought to have diffused to West Africa, it is equally plausible that it developed on the basis of existing knowledge of iron smelting. In addition to the spread of iron and bronze, either as objects or as technical skills, there is evidence in many places of potsherd pavements. Pavements in a herring-bone pattern occur at the 6.0-meter level at Daima (Willett 1971b:10), dated to the fifth century A.D., and at various sites along the Benue River (David 1968:24). The people of Ife used pavements of potsherds placed on edge, and similar pavements have been found at Benin and at Ketu in Dahomey. The classic period of Ife, with its pavements and terracottas, has been dated to the first half of the second millennium A.D.: A.D. 1160 ± 130 (Willett 1971b:24), A.D. 1110 ± 95, A.D. 1095 ± 95, and A.D. 1630 ± 95 (Posnansky and MacIntosh 1976:169, 189). To the immediate west of the Nok culture is the site of Yelwa, dated from A.D. 100 to A.D. 700, which contains terracotta figurines (Fagan 1969:153). Ife culture also contains terracotta figurines dated to the tenth century. It seems that by the tenth century A.D. the area from Ketu to Daima was becoming technologically homogeneous while displaying internal stylistic distinc-tions with respect to iron, bronze, potsherd pavements, and terracottas. It is postulated here that the initial impetus for the homogeneity came from the Nok culture.

Davidson (1966:16–17) has offered a theory as to the role iron tech-nology played within West Africa. He implies that technology is the primary factor in the transformation from Neolithic patterns to urban stratified societies. With better tools, it was possible to increase the production of food, and this allowed population to increase. The increase in population was offset by the increase in land brought under cultivation with iron axes and hoes. Further, those who mastered iron first were able to dominate and rule their neighbors. New ways of ensuring order became necessary, and more complex political organization led to the development of the state.

Davidson's theory does not yet have a firm basis. The following empiri-cal conditions have to be considered: (1) in West Africa, fire is the main way of clearing forested areas of brush, and (2) it has yet to be determined whether steel or wrought iron is more effective (and to what extent) than stone in chopping brush or digging holes (Willett 1971b:18, 19). Further, the possibilities of a technology do not have an automatic effect on productivity. Also, some societies are oriented to change while others resist innovation. Another consideration is the fact that it has not been determined for what purpose the Nok people manufactured iron objects — whether the orientation was toward ritual objects, utilitarian objects, jewelry, weapons, or tools. It may have been the case that iron was used primarily to manufacture weapons and that war techniques changed before productive ones, as happened with the use of copper in south-western Asia (Childe 1964:88).

The societal effects of iron technology are highly speculative. It certainly increased craft specialization, but it has yet to be ascertained to what extent it promoted a more complex division of labor or whether the ironworkers were autonomous, subservient, or directly administered by some type of central authority, either the state, a temple, or an estate. Not much can be concluded about iron technology's relationship to state formation in West Africa. In assessing that relationship, it should be noted that in southwestern Asia and East Asia iron played no role in either the food-producing revolution or the urban transformation. It was only after fully developed state systems had been in existence for more than 1,000 years that iron technology appeared in both areas. In fact, metallurgy played no part in the Neolithic revolution and seems to have played no significant part in the initial impetus toward the urban transformation (see Adams 1966:1–37). Within the context of established elites, metallurgy provided new modes for constructing, consolidating, and destroying state systems. Elites in southwestern Asia were built, in part, upon the control and redistribution of vegetable and animal products. The metals in use before iron were a monopoly of the elites. Since nonferrous metals were too expensive, the rural population used stone, bone, and wood. Once the Hittite monopoly over iron smelting was broken, and since iron was a common ore, iron smelting after 1300 B.C. was able to develop at the local or village level. This process democratized industry, agriculture, and warfare by undercutting the monopoly that the elite had over the other metals (Childe 1964:190–192). In West Africa, iron replaced stone, bone, and wood and not monopolistically controlled metals. Thus the impact of iron technology in West Africa would depend upon whether the distribution of iron ores was widespread or concentrated and whether the knowledge of smelting was secret or public. With this information it would be possible to determine whether iron technology was neutral, had a democratic influence, or increased the possibilities for the formation of elites and states. If the Nok culture represents a protourban phase, iron technology may have had an effect on the West African urban transformation much like the effect that copper and bronze had in southwestern Asia because of their similar positions in the processual sequences of the two areas.

The processes involved in the independent transformation of societies from food-collecting bands to settled villages and/or food-producing villages to stratified urban centers in various parts of the world also operated in West Africa. The emergence of iron technology in the Nok culture was not an isolated event, but part of a process in which cultural, institutional, and politico-economic as well as technological factors were operating. These factors were internal to West African societies and provided the conditions under which iron technology could either have developed internally or have been incorporated from the outside. The same factors that impelled the inheritors of the Neolithic revolution in southwestern Asia to develop metallurgy impelled the inheritors of the Neolithic in West Africa to develop metallurgy. Members of societies in these areas were simply developing in an experimental manner the potentialities unleashed by the Neolithic experience.

I have stressed the fact that the rational and cultural features found in the "science of the concrete" — objective knowledge, experimentation, and classificatory schemes — provided the basis of the Neolithic transformation around the world. I have also stressed the fact that the urban revolution involved urbanization, social stratification, craft specialization, and political centralization wherever it took place. Although the Nok culture must be placed within the context of these seeming universals, it was nevertheless a fully African culture. It was Africa which created the conditions and problems, and it was Africans who developed the adaptations and solutions.

REFERENCES

ADAMS, R. Mc C.
1963 "The origins of agriculture," in *Horizons of anthropology*. Edited by Sol Tax, 120–131. Chicago: Aldine.
1966 *The evolution of urban society*. Chicago: Aldine.
ARKELL, A.
1962 *A history of the Sudan*. London: University of London, Athlone Press.
1966 The Iron Age in the Sudan. *Current Anthropology* 7:451–452.
CHILDE, V.
1964 *What happened in history*. Harmondsworth: Penguin Books.
CLINE, W.
1937 *Mining and metallurgy in Negro Africa*. General Series in Anthropology 5. Menasha, Wis.: George Banta.
COGHLAN, A.
1956 *Notes on prehistoric and early iron in the Old World*. Occasional Papers on Technology 8. Oxford: Pitt-Rivers Museum.
DART, R., P. BEAUMONT
1969 Evidence of iron ore mining in southern Africa in the Middle Stone Age. *Current Anthropology* 10:127–128.
DAVID, N.
1968 Reconnaissance in Cameroun. *West African Archaeological Newsletter* 10:24–26.
DAVIDSON, B.
1966 *A history of West Africa*. Garden City: Doubleday.
1974 *Africa in history: themes and outlines*. New York: Macmillan.
DAVIES, O.
1967 *West Africa before the Europeans*. London: Methuen.
1968 The origins of agriculture in West Africa. *Current Anthropology* 9:479–482.
FAGAN, B.
1967 Radiocarbon dates for sub-Saharan Africa 5. *Journal of African History* 8:513–527.

1969 Radiocarbon dates for sub-Saharan Africa 6. *Journal of African History* 10:149–169.

FAGE, J.
1969 *A history of West Africa: an introductory survey* (fourth edition). London: Cambridge University Press.

FAGG, ANGELA
1972 Excavations of an occupation site in the Nok Valley, Nigeria. *West African Journal of Archaeology* 2:75–79.

FAGG, BERNARD
1965 Carbon dates for Nigeria. *Man* 65(8):22–23.
1969 Recent work in West Africa: New light on the Nok culture. *World Archaeology* 1:41–50.

HAWKES, J., L. WOOLLEY
1963 *Prehistory and the beginnings of civilization*. New York: Harper and Row.

HERBERT, E.
1973 Aspects of the use of copper in pre-colonial West Africa. *Journal of African History* 14:179–194.

Illustrated London News
1967 "'Classic' excavation in north-east Nigeria." *Illustrated London News*, section 2276, October 14.

LAWAL, B.
1973 Dating problems at Igbo-Ukwu. *Journal of African History* 14: 1–8.

LÉVI-STRAUSS, C.
1966 *The savage mind*. Chicago: University of Chicago Press.

MAUNY, R.
1971 "The Western Sudan," in *The African Iron Age*. Edited by P. L. Shinnie, 66–88. Oxford: Clarendon.

OLIVER, R., B. FAGAN
1975 *Africa in the Iron Age: c. 500 B.C. to A.D. 1400*. Cambridge: Cambridge University Press.

OLIVER, R., J. FAGE
1962 *A short history of Africa*. Baltimore: Penguin Books.

PHILLIPSON, D.
1970 Notes on the later prehistoric radiocarbon chronology of eastern and southern Africa. *Journal of African History* 11:1–15.

POSNANSKY, M., R. Mac INTOSH
1976 New radiocarbon dates for northern and western Africa. *Journal of African History* 17:161–195.

SASSOON, H.
1963 Early sources of iron in Africa. *South African Archaeological Bulletin* 18(72):176–180.

SHAW, T.
1965 Further excavations at Igbo-Ukwu. *Man* 65 (217):181–184.
1969 On radiocarbon chronology of the Iron Age in sub-Saharan Africa. *Current Anthropology* 10:226–231.
1972 "The prehistory of West Africa," in *History of West Africa*, volume one. Edited by J. F. A. Ajayi and Michael Crowder. New York: Columbia University Press.
1975 Those Igbo-Ukwu radiocarbon dates: Facts, fictions, and probabilities. *Journal of African History* 16:503–517.

SHINNIE, P.
1967   Meroe and West Africa. *West African Archaeological Newsletter* 6:12–16.
1971   "The Sudan," in *The African Iron Age*. Edited by P. L. Shinnie, 89–107. Oxford: Clarendon.
SWANSON, J.
1975   The myth of trans-Saharan trade during the Roman era. *International Journal of African Historical Studies* 8:582–600.
TAMERA, M., F. PEARSON
1965   Validity of radiocarbon dates on bone. *Nature* 5015:1053–1055.
TRIGGER, B.
1968   *Beyond prehistory: the methods of prehistory*. New York: Holt, Rinehart and Winston.
1969   The myth of Meroe and the African Iron Age. *African Historical Studies* 2:23–50.
TYLECOTE, R. F.
1975   The origin of iron smelting in Africa. *West African Journal of Archaeology* 5:1–10.
VAN DER MERWE, N., M. STUIVER
1968a Dating iron by the carbon-14 method. *Current Anthropology* 10:48–53.
1968b Radiocarbon chronology of the Iron Age in sub-Saharan Africa. *Current Anthropology* 9:53–59.
WARMINGTON, B.
1969   *Carthage*. New York: Praeger.
WILLETT, F.
1971a A survey of recent results in the radiocarbon chronology of western and northern Africa. *Journal of African History* 12:339–370.
1971b "Nigeria," in *The African Iron Age*. Edited by P. L. Shinnie, 1–15. Oxford: Clarendon.

The Geographic Distribution of Footed Bowls in the Upper and Middle Niger Region

R. M. A. BEDAUX

In the framework of the Tellem research project of the Institute of Human Biology, State University, Utrecht, excavations were carried out in caves near Sanga in the high cliff of Bandiagara, central Mali, in the region now inhabited by the Dogon.

The majority of the twenty-nine caves examined contain small buildings, human skeletal remains, and all kinds of remarkably well-preserved grave goods. It was possible to establish a sequence from the eleventh to the seventeenth century A.D. on the basis of carbon-14 dates, differences in architectural details of the buildings, and changes in burial ritual as expressed in grave goods.

The remains belong to an agrarian community that also practiced animal husbandry and numbered 1,500 to 1,600 persons in the eleventh and twelfth centuries A.D. (Bedaux 1972). Until the fifteenth century A.D., the material culture is homogeneous enough to be considered one culture (for which has been adopted the term Tellem, a word used by the Dogon to denote the people who lived in the region before them). Also, judging from the skeletal remains, this people seems to have belonged to a rather homogeneous group (Huizinga, Birnie-Tellier, and Glanville 1967; Huizinga 1968; Knip 1971). In the fifteenth century a marked change in material culture occurred, followed shortly by a change in population. Oral tradition (Griaule 1963 [1938]:28) and archaeological finds strongly suggest that this was the result of the arrival of the Dogon (Bedaux 1972).

The Tellem expeditions at Sanga were made possible by grants to J. Huizinga, Director of the Institute of Human Biology, State University, Utrecht, from the Netherlands Foundation for the Advancement of Tropical Research, The Hague (1965, 1967), The Wenner-Gren Foundation for Anthropological Research, New York (1966, 1967), the Boise Fund, Oxford (1966, 1967, 1971), and the National Geographic Society, Washington (1971).

This paper deals with the geographic distribution of a special kind of pottery, footed bowls, found by us at only two Tellem sites, Cave D and Plateau G, which yielded fragments of more than thirty specimens. Besides the footed bowls, the sites contained other kinds of pottery (Bazuin-Sira 1968; Bedaux 1971), as well as iron objects (bracelets, rings, voluted pins, arrowheads), carnelian beads, and quartz lip-plugs. Above each of these two sites was a large burial cave, and a relationship has been established between Cave D and its burial cave C (Plate 1) and between Plateau G and its burial cave J (Bedaux 1972). It is obvious that this relationship is a ritual one because several objects have been intentionally placed in spatial relation to one another. This conclusion is further substantiated by the absence of buildings and by the choice of material culture objects. Except for one piece, all the pottery was broken, as were most objects in the burial caves, perhaps as part of the burial ritual. Both sites belong to the eleventh and twelfth centuries A.D., Phase 1 of the Tellem culture, although Plateau G is slightly later than Cave D.

THE TELLEM FOOTED BOWLS

The pots in question are bowls with outstanding rims and three or four curved feet on a disk base (Plate 2 and Figure 1). The bowl walls may have horizontal ridges, plaited fiber cord impressions, grooves, and sometimes painting with red ocher.

H. J. Franken and J. Kalsbeek of the Institute of Palestinian Archaeology, Leiden University, have studied the techniques of manufacture of this pottery (Figure 2). First clay is smeared in a mold. A ridge is formed by rolling the clay over the edges of the mold. Up to two coils may be added. After a short drying period, the bowl is removed from the mold and turned upside down. Then a disk base supported by three or four feet (usually consisting of one or two coils of clay) is added.

GEOGRAPHIC DISTRIBUTION OF FOOTED BOWLS

Pots similar to these Tellem bowls have been found in a narrow area some 1,000 kilometers long, from Niani, Guinea, to beyond Timbuktu, Mali (Figure 3 and Table 1).[1]

---

[1]   Since this article was submitted for publication, additional footed bowls have been discovered at several sites. During the continuation of his excavations at Niani, Filipowiak found many fragments of footed bowls in 1973. One bowl was found in a burial at Site 32, probably to be dated to the thirteenth century A.D. (Filipowiak and Szerniewicz 1976: Plate 4). Excavations by Liesegang in the Dogo region, some 100 kilometers southeast of Bamako, have yielded three fragments of footed bowls associated with material comparable to the Niani 6IIID ware and dated by carbon-14 to the eleventh and twelfth centuries

Plate 1.   Tellem Cave D, bottom left, and the entrance to its burial cave C, above

Plate 2.   Tellem footed bowl, Cave D, National Museum, Bamako (No. D1)

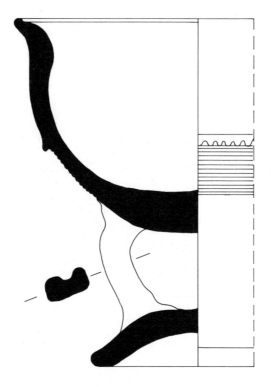

Figure 1.   Tellem footed bowl, Cave D, National Museum, Bamako (No. D1) (by courtesy of the Institute of Palestinian Archaeology, Leiden University)

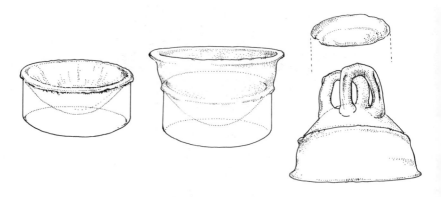

Figure 2.   Stages in the manufacture of a Tellem footed bowl (by courtesy of the Institute of Palestinian Archaeology, Leiden University)

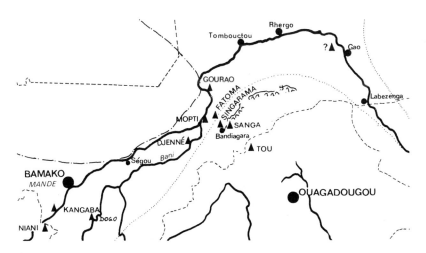

Figure 3.   Sites yielding footed bowls. The broken/dotted line indicates the extent of the Ghana Empire, eleventh century A.D., the dotted line the extent of the Mali Empire, fourteenth century A.D. (based on Mauny 1967)

Niani, the presumed capital of the Mali Empire (Meillassoux 1972; Mauny 1967 [1961]:122), is situated on the banks of the Sankarani, an affluent of the Niger. Trial excavations by a joint Guinean-Polish expedition have yielded a convincing stratigraphy and carbon-14 datings (Filipowiak, Janosz, and Wolagiewicz 1968). Footed pottery was found at all levels dated from the sixth to the seventeenth century A.D. (Filipowiak, Janosz, and Wolagiewicz 1968: Figures 21a–22, 5–34, 2–35, *1, 2, 3*, 5–37, *1, 2, 3*). These pots are of two basic types: very shallow ones used, according to Filipowiak, as oil lamps and actual bowls with thin walls and a horizontal ridge around the part of the bottom to which the feet were attached. Both types have two feet, each consisting of two coils of clay, connecting the bowl with a disk base. The shallow ones occur in all levels, the actual bowls only from Level IIa (Site 6D) onward. This level must be dated somewhere between the eleventh (upper part of Level V) and the sixteenth century A.D. and therefore is presumably later than Tellem Phase 1. This pottery has no association other than with domestic activities.

Kangaba, on the Niger bank, is the residence of the royal Keita clan of Mali. Every seven years members of thirty populations come together to

(Liesegang 1975:56 and Figure 45). During a survey carried out by the Institute of Human Biology in 1974, three fragments of footed bowls were found near Djenné on the surface of mounds (Bedaux and Huizinga 1975). Subsequent excavation in 1975 of one of these mounds, Toguéré Galia, yielded fragments of seven such bowls (Bedaux and van der Waals 1976). They were found together with, among other things, spindle whorls and tobacco pipes on the surface only, which may suggest a rather late date for this material. Samples have been submitted for carbon-14 analysis.

Table 1.   Distribution of footed bowls

Site	Date	Minimum number of pots	Association			Type			Number of feet
			Domestic	Burial	None	Niani oil-lamp	Niani thin-walled	Tellem	
Niani { 6th–17th cent. / 11th?–16th cent. }		7	x			x			2
Kangaba	?	1			x		x		2
Djenné	?	1			x		x		3
Mopti	?	1			x				4
Fatoma	?	2	x						3
Gourao	?	3	x					x	2/3
Rhergo-Labezenga	?	2			x				3
Singarama	?	1		x					3
Sanga	11th–12th cent.	30		x				x	3/4
Tou	?	2		?				x	3

hold a ceremony during which the dispersion of the Mande families is narrated (Dieterlen 1955). In 1971 a fairly complete bowl with two feet was found here by Cheick Oumar Mara of the National Museum, Bamako, who kindly provided a photograph. This bowl is of the same type as the thin-walled ones from Niani.

At Djenné, Mali, a footed bowl was found by Vieillard (1940: Figure 2E) on the surface of a mound near the Niger called Kaniana, together with fragments of figurines. This pot differs from the Niani specimen in that it has three feet, each consisting of one coil of clay, presumably not attached to a disk base.

We bought a bowl with four feet in Mopti in 1971 that was said to have been found on the caving-in Niger bank nearby. In comparison with the other specimens, this pot is rather crudely made. Around the part of the bottom to which the feet are attached is a heavy horizontal ridge. There is also a disk base.

Fragments of bowls with feet were found by Szumowski (1954) during trial excavations in Village Mound 2 at Fatoma, near Mopti. It was impossible to date this mound adequately (Davies 1967:262 and Figure 87). According to Szumowski's illustrations (1954: Plate III b, *1, 2, 3, 4, 5, 6, 7*), at least two disk bases of bowls with three feet, each foot consisting of one coil of clay, were found.

In habitation sites at Gourao, Mali, on the shores of Lake Debo, at least three bowls with two or three feet attached to a disk base were found by Desplagnes (1907:30 and Figure 29). The figures are not such as to permit a closer determination of the type of bowl.

Two footed bowls found by Desplagnes along the Niger bank between Rhergo and Labezenga, Mali, are published in the catalogue of the Desplagnes collection of the Musée de l'Homme, Paris, by Lebeuf and Pâques (1970:51 and Figure 47). The exact site could not be traced. Each bowl has three feet, and one has a rather heavy horizontal ridge around the part of the bottom to which the feet are attached.

Near the entrances of little buildings in caves at Singarama, Mali, some fifty kilometers from the Niger, Desplagnes (1907:52, 53, 88, 89 and Figures 60, 61) found several footed bowls. In an enclosure lined with a curved wall within the building were found human skeletal remains of about twenty-five to thirty individuals. According to the figures, the pots seem to have three feet attached to a disk base. As is clear from the observations just mentioned, this pottery is spatially associated with burial ritual.

A fragment of a bowl on three feet was found at Tou, Upper Volta, by Schweeger-Hefel (1965:61, 62, 63; 1969: Figures 5, 26) in a hillock mainly built of stone artifacts. According to Schweeger-Hefel (1969), this hillock may resemble the ritual places used for rain making by the Dogon. Nearby in a refuse heap was found a disk base with three feet attached to it (1969: Figure 37). It was not possible to date this material adequately.

DISTRIBUTIONAL ANALYSIS

The area under consideration has never been systematically investigated. The only reliable datings for footed bowls are those from Niani and Sanga. In the Sanga region, the bowls are good horizon markers of Phase 1 of the Tellem culture (eleventh and twelfth centuries A.D.). Although the "oil lamps" in Niani occur in all levels from the sixth to the seventeenth century A.D., the footed bowls cannot yet be precisely dated. They presumably appear after Tellem Phase 1, as there are two levels between the eleventh century (Level V) and the appearance of the first bowls (Level IIa).

Despite these limitations, a look at the distribution of the bowls reveals a rather coherent pattern. Most sites are situated along the Upper Niger; only Singarama, Sanga, and Tou are some distance east of the river. Along the Niger between Kangaba and Djenné, no footed bowls have been found. It may be that the distribution pattern is discontinuous here. Trial excavations undertaken by Szumowski near Bamako (1956; 1957a; 1958) and near Ségou (1957b) have yielded no footed bowls.

The illustrations of footed bowls in the published excavation reports do not allow rigorous comparative analysis. It is clear, however, that there are at least three major types: (1) the "oil lamps" from Niani, (2) the thin-walled footed bowls from Niani and Kangaba, and (3) the footed bowls from the Sanga region, Fatoma, and Tou. For the time being, these different types seem to correspond to different areas: the Niani-Kangaba region near the river and the interior Singarama-Sanga-Tou region.

The connection of the bowls with burial rites at the interior sites and the connection of the bowls along the Niger with domestic activities also suggest regional differences. Briefly:

1. The Niani-Kangaba area has yielded two types of footed pottery, the first datable from the sixth to the seventeenth century A.D. and the second somewhere between the eleventh and the sixteenth century A.D., both probably associated with domestic activities.

2. The northern Niger area has yielded footed bowls of somewhat different types, sometimes associated with domestic activities and not datable.

3. The interior area has yielded a different type of footed bowl associated with burial ritual. Bowls belonging to the Tellem culture must be dated in the eleventh and twelfth centuries A.D.

Of course, with the present insufficient knowledge of the age and actual distribution of footed bowls, a distribution pattern analysis faces real difficulties. Also, the cultural context of the finds is frequently unknown. The data collected may nevertheless furnish archaeological indications of links between human groups, links that are already known historically from Arab sources. The peculiar shape and the complex technique of manufacture of the bowls almost excludes independent invention. The fact that most of the sites are found along that part of the Niger which served as an important route in the trade between northern Africa and the Sudan points in the same direction (Mauny 1967 [1961]:406–409).

Since the oil-lamp-making tradition is present in Niani before the sixth century A.D., the place of origin of this tradition seems to be the Niani region. The tradition probably spread to the Sanga region before the eleventh century, for by that time a local tradition of making footed bowls had already been established. These bowls were used for burial ritual instead of for domestic purposes as in Niani. Trade cannot be responsible for this diffusion, as the bowls of the two sites are different. Population movements during the decline of the Ghana Empire could be mentioned as a possible cause of this diffusion. A population movement from the nuclear Mande area (southwest of present-day Bamako) to the Bandiagara cliff is supported by oral tradition (Dieterlen 1955; 1967:35). That this movement was not extensive is suggested by the cultural continuity at Niani, the virtual absence of finds of footed bowls in the region between Kangaba and Sanga, and the differences in utilization and shape of the pottery between the two regions. Migration of small groups of people caused by population pressure, e.g., the establishment of daughter communities, seems more likely. Using this model, the differences could be explained as resulting from cultural drift (Binford 1963).

A development of the footed bowls is apparent in the Sanga region from the eleventh to the twelfth centuries. In the earlier phase, the ridge in the middle of the bowl wall made by the edge of the mold is left in place. Later, this ridge is obscured by superimposing a decorative incised line or an applied ridge. After the twelfth century this pottery is no longer found in the burial sites studied.

It is not certain that the tradition of making footed bowls did not diffuse back from its new center near Sanga to the Niger region, as the Niani bowls are to be dated later than the Tellem ones. A more likely cause of the appearance of the bowls in Niani sometime after the eleventh century, however, seems to be a local development of the oil-lamp-making tradition. The differences between the Niani oil lamps and bowls are less pronounced than the differences between the Niani and Tellem bowls.

As no dates are available, the presence of footed bowls in the northern Niger area is difficult to explain. Here elements of both the Niani and the Tellem bowl-making traditions are present. The whole Niger area was politically controlled by the Mali Empire (see Figure 3). The rise of this empire strongly favored trade. The presence of a navigable river facilitates long-distance trade in pottery (Nicklin 1971). Ibn Battuta, visiting the area in 1352–1353, was surprised to find the country safe for traveling (Mauny 1959). Oral tradition attests to population movements of, among others, the Dogon from the Mande area to their present habitat before the fifteenth century (Griaule 1963 [1938]:28).

The Tellem area was not politically controlled by the Mali Empire. Because of the Tellem preference for strongly defensible habitations (Bedaux 1972), regular contacts with the outside world do not seem to have been encouraged. The disappearance of the footed bowls in burial sites at the end of the twelfth century coincides with the disappearance of certain iron objects such as voluted pins. As there is no major break in the Tellem culture or change in population as judged by skeletal remains, these minor cultural changes may be accounted for by the emigration, without disturbing the essential continuity of the culture, of the particular small groups of people responsible for the manufacture of iron objects and pottery. Blacksmiths generally form a kind of endogamous caste and remain virtually independent of the host culture (Dieterlen 1965–1966), and their wives frequently engage in pottery manufacture (Mauny 1967 [1961]:349). The presence of footed bowls in the northern Niger region after the twelfth century might be explained by influences from the Tellem area exercised by the emigration from this area of small groups such as blacksmiths and by trade contacts with the Niani area.

At our present stage of knowledge, the difficulties in analyzing the distribution pattern of footed bowls are apparent. The results should be viewed as hypotheses which are liable to be disproved by the next excavation.

REFERENCES

BAZUIN-SIRA, B. J.
  1968   Cultural remains from Tellem caves near Pégué (falaise de Bandiagara), Mali, West Africa. *West African Archaeological Newsletter* 10:14–15.
BEDAUX, R.
  1971   Pottery making techniques of the so-called "Tellem" (Mali). *Papers presented to the 4th Conference of West African Archaeologists, Jos, 1971*. Edited by Angela Fagg, 82–92.
  1972   Tellem; reconnaissance archéologique d'une culture de l'Ouest africain au moyen âge: recherches architectoniques. *Journal de la Société des Africanistes* 42:103–185.
BEDAUX, R., J. HUIZINGA
  1975   Rapport sur une prospection archéologique dans la région Bani-Niger (Mali) de sites d'intérêt anthropobiologique. *Etudes Maliennes* 15:1–10.
BEDAUX, R., J. D. VAN DER WAALS
  1976   Rapport préliminaire des fouilles archéologiques de Toguéré Doupwil

et Toguéré Galia dans la région Bani-Niger. *Etudes Maliennes* 18:44–50.

BINFORD, L. R.
1963 "Red ocher" caches from the Michigan area: a possible case of cultural drift. *Southwestern Journal of Anthropology* 19:89–108.

DAVIES, O.
1967 *West Africa before the Europeans.* London: Methuen.

DESPLAGNES, L.
1907 *Le plateau central nigérien.* Paris: Larose.

DIETERLEN, G.
1955 Mythe et organisation sociale au Soudan français. *Journal de la Société des Africanistes* 25:39–76.
1965–1966 Contribution à l'étude des forgerons en Afrique occidentale. *Annuaire de l'Ecole Pratique des Hautes Etudes, Paris Veme Section, Sciences Religieuses* 73:4–28.
1967 *Colloque sur les cultures voltaïques.* Recherches Voltaïques 8.

FILIPOWIAK, W., S. JANOSZ, R. WOLAGIEWICZ
1968 Les recherches archéologiques polono-guinéennes à Niani en 1968. *Materiały Zachodniopomorskie* 14:575–648.

FILIPOWIAK, W., B. SZERNIEWICZ
1976 *Afrikanische Plastik.* Rostock: Kunsthalle. Sczcecin: National Museum.

GRIAULE, M.
1963 [1938] *Masques dogons.* Paris: Institut d'Ethnologie.

HUIZINGA, J.
1968 New physical anthropological evidence bearing on the relationships between Dogon, Kurumba, and the extinct West African Tellem populations. *Proceedings van de Koninklijke Nederlandse Akademie van Wetenschappen* C71:16–30.

HUIZINGA, J., N. F. BIRNIE-TELLIER, E. V. GLANVILLE
1967 Description and carbon-14 dating of Tellem cave skulls from the Mali Republic: a comparison with other Negroid groups. I and II. *Proceedings van de Koninklijke Nederlandse Akademie van Wetenschappen* C70:338–367.

KNIP, A. S.
1971 The frequencies of non-metrical variants in Tellem and Nokara skulls from the Mali Republic. I and II. *Proceedings van de Koninklijke Nederlandse Akademie van Wetenschappen* C74:422–443.

LEBEUF, A. M. D., V. PÂQUES
1970 *Archéologie malienne: collections Desplagnes.* Catalogues du Musée de l'Homme, Série C, Afrique Noire 1.

LIESEGANG, G.
1975 "Eisenzeitliche Siedlungsplätze von Famanbougou." Unpublished manuscript, Frobenius-Institut, Frankfurt.

MAUNY, R.
1959 Evocation de l'empire du Mali. *Notes Africaines* 82:33–37.
1967 [1961] *Tableau géographique de l'Ouest africain au moyen âge d'après les sources écrites, la tradition et l'archéologie.* Amsterdam: Swets and Zeitlinger. (Dakar: I.F.A.N.)

MEILLASSOUX, C.
1972 L'itinéraire d'Ibn Battuta de Walata à Mali. *Journal of African History* 13:389–395.

NICKLIN, K.
1971   Stability and innovation in pottery manufacture. *World Archaeology* 3:13–48, 94–98.
SCHWEEGER-HEFEL, A.
1965   *Frühhistorische Bodenfunde im Raum von Mengao (Ober-Volta, Westafrika)*. Vienna: Hermann Böhlaus.
1969   Ein frühhistorischer Kultplatz bei dem Dogon-Dorf Tou und seine Bedeutung für die heutigen Bewohner des Dorfes. *Mitteilungen der Anthropologischen Gesellschaft in Wien* 99:111–125.
SZUMOWSKI, G.
1954   Fouilles à Fatoma, région de Mopti, Soudan. *Notes Africaines* 64:102–108.
1956   Fouilles de l'abri sous roche de Kourounkorokalé (Soudan français). *Bulletin de l'Institut Français d'Afrique Noire* B18:462–508.
1957a   Pseudotumulus des environs de Bamako. *Notes Africaines* 75:66–73.
1957b   Fouilles au nord du Macina et dans la région de Ségou. *Bulletin de l'Institut Français d'Afrique Noire* B19:224–258.
1958   Pseudotumulus des environs de Bamako (suite). *Notes Africaines* 77:1–11.
VIEILLARD, G.
1940   Sur quelques objets en terre cuite de Dienné. *Bulletin de l'Institut Français d'Afrique Noire* 11:347–349.

Speculations on Functions of Some Prehistoric Archaeological Materials from Sierra Leone

JOHN H. ATHERTON

At the beginning of the sixteenth century, Valentim Fernandes, in discussing observations made during some of the earliest European trips to the West African coast, noted that "in Serra Lyoa [Sierra Leone] the men are very clever and inventive, and make really marvellous objects out of ivory of anything you ask them to do, for instance they make spoons, or salt-cellars, or dagger-handles, or other subtle work" (Fyfe 1964:30). The pieces made for and collected by these early explorers can still be seen in several private and museum collections. Writing in 1616, Manuel Alvares praised the artistry of the people of Sierra Leone, describing their wooden ancestor images, stools, and ivory pieces, carved "with such perfection that when one has viewed them one has seen everything" (Rodney 1970:63; P. E. H. Hair, personal communication; see also Kimble 1937:98). The people about whom these early travelers were speaking were the Sapes, a generic term comprising the Bullom, Temne, Limba, and contiguous related groups. The sixteenth and seventeenth centuries spelt disaster for much of traditional Sape culture; the Sapes were burdened with slavers on the coast and invaders in the interior. Alvares commented: "it is the fault of these foreign kings that the country is so poor, because they have captured so many potters, and . . . have committed so many vexations on the indigenous people that these latter have become less and less concerned and have given up the exercise of their arts" (Rodney 1970:63). Remnants of Sape culture persist, especially in those areas in which the influences of the foreign invaders were least felt; secret societies, relations with the "supernatural," and some languages are still quite similar to pre-sixteenth-century varieties. Many

I thank J. D. Clark, V. R. Dorjahn, and A. B. Smith for their comments on an earlier draft of this paper.

similarities still persist in material culture and agricultural techniques, but the elaborate artistic techniques have disappeared in most areas. Since most manifestations of Sape art were in perishable materials, only a few examples remain. Alongside these few surviving examples and the descriptions left by early explorers, there are remains of works in stone which can be used in an attempt to broaden knowledge of early Sape culture. Toward this end, this paper investigates three classes of stone artifacts found in Sierra Leone: double-edged ground stone celts, carved soapstone figures, and bored stones.

THE PREHISTORIC BACKGROUND

Little is known of the prehistory of Upper Guinea, the area comprising Sierra Leone and the rest of the land drained by mostly westward-flowing rivers between Gambia and Cape Mount. Archaeological work in the area had its beginnings at the end of the last century, and many excavations have been carried out; few, however, have been adequately reported, and few have been done by trained archaeologists. Absolute dating has been possible only in the past few years, and there are still very few dates, especially in the south. Present data indicate a prehistoric separateness from the rest of West Africa, probably reflecting an areal variant of the ill-defined Guinea Neolithic. Upper Guinea is primarily characterized by celt forms thinner than elsewhere, some having two working ends instead of one. The area can be subdivided by noting other features not necessarily connected with the stone tools. Thus in some areas characteristic types of stone circles are found, in others soapstone figures, and so on. Only preliminary attempts have been made to correlate these features with what is known about Upper Guinea's ethnohistory and ethnography. Other than a few preliminary excavations, sites reported by the Sierra Leone Monuments and Relics Commission, and scattered finds during mining operations, investigations into Sierra Leone's prehistoric past have been undertaken only in the past dozen years. Of the three types of artifacts to be discussed in this paper, only one has been found so far in archaeological investigations — the celts.

DOUBLE-EDGED GROUND CELTS

Four types of dolerite celts can be distinguished among the artifacts from archaeological excavations: flaked with a single working edge, flaked with a double working edge, ground with a single working edge, and ground with a double working edge. Varieties other than those illustrated here have been found on surface sites. As can be seen from Figure 1, there

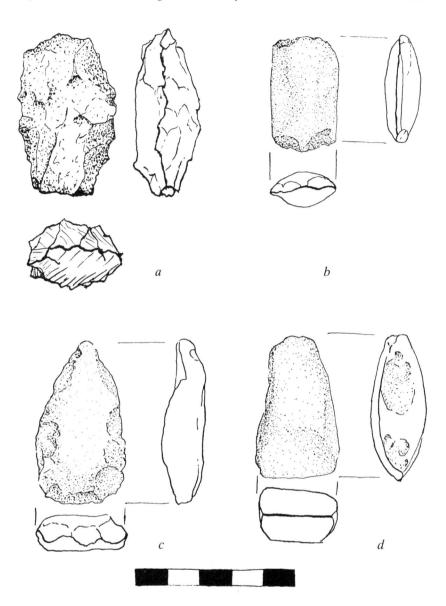

Figure 1.   Dolerite celts from Sierra Leone. *a*, flaked with double working edge; *b*, ground with double working edge; *c*, flaked with single working edge; *d*, ground with single working edge

are pronounced morphological differences and possible differences in function among them. Since the double-edged ground pieces seem to be characteristic of Upper Guinea assemblages, only they will be dealt with here.

Double-edged ground celts seem to be restricted in distribution to the forest-fringe areas of Upper Guinea and the Upper Niger drainage. They were first described by Hamy (1901) from excavations carried out at Kakimbon cave, about a dozen kilometers northeast of Conakry, the capital of the Republic of Guinea. He reports finding more than fifty axes or adzes made of labradorite, six or seven of which were double-ended. They ranged in length from 5 to 9.3 centimeters. Hamy also noted that "the two ends were essentially identical" and that "if used as adzes, the pieces could have been successively hafted by both ends" (1901:390, translation mine). This type of tool has been found in at least one other location (Friguiagbé) in Guinea (Joire 1952:331) and at a site (Nhampasseré) in Portuguese Guinea (Mateus 1952:382). It has also been found in the upper levels of the Kourounkorokalé rock shelter, near Bamako, Mali (Szumowski 1956:490), and in the Gouro area of the Ivory Coast (Tauxier 1924:Plate 3). In Sierra Leone, double-ended ground celts appear at Yagala and Kamabai rock shelters (Atherton 1972a) and, though much less numerous here, at Yengema cave (Coon 1968 and personal communication). The celts are generally smaller than any of the other West African types. Those from Kamabai rock shelter average 3.93 centimeters in length ($N = 11$, S.D. $= 0.8$). The two whole pieces from Yagala rock shelter are both smaller than the smallest celt from Kamabai: one measures 2.5 by 1.8 by 0.9 centimeters and the other 2.8 by 1.6 by 0.7 centimeters. A fragment from this site measures (1.2) by 2.0 by 1.0 centimeters.

Dolerite is fairly homogeneous and lends itself to flaking by direct percussion. None of the pieces examined gives any evidence of having required anything other than a hammerstone for its manufacture, though different means may have been employed for some of the associated microlithic quartz pieces. The initial shaping by flaking was almost certainly a prelude to the finishing work on the polished pieces. The latter could have been polished with the aid of some of the rough quartz pieces found with the celts at Kamabai rock shelter, but they could also have been worked simply by rubbing them against a stone of harder material, such as granite, which abounds in the region. No grooved sharpening stones were found in excavations, but one (probably used for iron tools) was found at a surface site, the mountain-top village of Yagala.

Other than their two working edges, two important features characterize these pieces: (1) they are always very flat and thin in comparison with other West African celts, and (2) most of them have a pronounced twist to them, so that their working edges are not directly parallel. As suggested by Hamy, they were almost certainly hafted as adzes; their size, shape, and twist would have made them very difficult to haft and use as axes. Their morphology also casts doubt on the possibility of their having been used for cutting motions parallel to the working edges; this is confirmed by the presence of the long, flat wear scars running perpendicular to the working edges and by the fact that the easily available quartz makes a much stronger and sharper edge for that type of cutting. That they were used as adzes is also suggested by the following evidence:

1. Axes of the sort that used a celtlike blade apparently were not used in the area. Even today, large-scale cutting is done with a machete-like instrument. This is very effective; in Liberia in 1968 I had the opportunity to witness a woman cutting through a large log in a time which would easily match that of an experienced logger using a Western-style axe. In some areas, the felling of trees appears to have been done with fire rather than tools (Arcin 1907:86), the splitting of logs is still done in many areas with the use of wedges (personal observations in 1967 and 1968).

2. During the first extensive contacts with the interior, in the latter part of the nineteenth century, iron was used for four types of tools: (*a*) machete-like tools used in the clearing of brush and the gathering of some types of vegetable materials, (*b*) iron arrow points, (*c*) agricultural tools, and (*d*) adzes. Only the last two have working edges approximating those of the celts under consideration. Most of the agricultural tools, however, have much wider blades and seem to be patterned after European picks (Fatu Kamara, personal communication). Iron agricultural instruments seem to have been a recent introduction and apparently had no analogues in earlier stone assemblages; instead, agricultural tools were probably made from wood. This assertion finds support in a statement made by Laing (1825:103–104) describing the agricultural tools of the Temne in 1822: "The hoe with which they turn up the ground, is made of hard wood; and the instrument for clearing the grain from the husk is merely a small hooked stick, like that used by boys in England at the game of hockey." In any case, the celts under consideration, because of their size, shape, and material, would have made inadequate tips for agricultural tools: they would have broken to pieces upon striking one of the granite stones which abound in the soils of the farmlands in the area. It is also doubtful that they were used for heavy work in clearing, since experiments have shown small stone adze blades to crack with hard use on wood (Howell 1966:120).

3. In their main location in Sierra Leone, Kamabai rock shelter, these celts are found with an impressive variety of other tools of both dolerite and quartz (Atherton 1972a). No living floors — concentrations of artifacts, often associated with changes in soil density and composition — were found. Moreover, at none of the caves or rock-shelters where these pieces have been found are there any traditions about the sites' having been used as habitations. Similar rock shelters in nearby areas were used as temporary living sites during the wars of the sixteenth through the nineteenth century (Atherton 1968, 1972b), but only in areas to the north, where caves and rock shelters were larger and more open, does evidence exist of

their having been used for permanent habitations. Caves similar to and near Kamabai rock shelter are still used in connection with secret-society activities. Kakimbon cave, in Guinea, was and is so used (Hamy 1901:394; Joire 1952:298). The celts found in open sites seem to have a considerably different character (e.g., Nos. 66.41–220 and 66.48 in the collections of the Institute of African Studies, Fourah Bay College, Freetown, Sierra Leone). It is therefore suggested that the cave sites may have been not living sites, but specialized activity centers connected with the manufacture of art works, artifacts which are today associated with secret societies.

4. Other than these artistic productions, there appears to have been little else that could not have been made with the simplest of tools — or even with no tools at all. The weapons of, for example, the Limba consisted of simple bows and arrows (the latter usually not even feathered). The only carving necessary here was in roughly shaping the bow, notching it on the top and the bottom, and notching the elephant-grass arrow shaft. A type of cord called *nkerepete* was used for the bowstring. Of interest also is that the Limba make more than twenty kinds of animal traps, each with a separate name. All of these traps are made of wood and *nkerepete*, and *all can be made without the use of any tools*. This simple non-art material culture seems to have characterized the other groups in the area also (Beatty 1915:96; Corry 1807:48; Laing 1825:103–104; Schlenker 1861:3).

That stone tools were used to manufacture articles for the secret societies is given some support by the fact that stone tools were used in secret societies in recent times (and possibly still are). According to Corry (1807:72), clitoridectomy was performed in the "bunda" initiation "by the rude application of two stones, fashioned and sharpened for the purpose. . ." (see also Butt-Thompson 1929:125).

5. The earliest visitors to the Sierra Leone coast noted the wide variety and large number of artistic works in wood and ivory. Fernandes mentioned that the Bullom and Temne made many different types of idols (Fyfe 1964:25–27). Cadamosto, in the fifteenth century, noted that at least some of the people near Sierra Leone had "statues of wood in the form of men" and that "they have no weapons, for iron is not to be found in their country" (Crone 1937:80). Certainly, they were using stone tools to make these figures, and, judging from the extremely high degree of skill they exhibited in carving, they must have been practicing this art for a considerable length of time. Specialized quartz pieces such as those found at Kamabai and Yagala rock shelters (Atherton 1972a) were undoubtedly used for these handicrafts. The dolerite celts were also almost certainly employed, since "the principal tool of the African wood sculptor is the adze (which combines the functions of the European mallet and chisel)" (Fagg and Plass 1966:33).

6. At Kamabai rock shelter, an iron tool fragment, probably part of an adze, was found in the upper levels along with a few other fragments of iron and slag. Although other types of stone tools and pottery continue after the introduction of iron, the celts under consideration do not (see Figure 2). A tentative conclusion would be that the iron replaced the dolerite celts for use as adze blades.

7. Finally, the manufacturing marks on an unfinished soapstone sculpture from Sierra Leone correspond to the size of the working edges of the stone celts (see below).

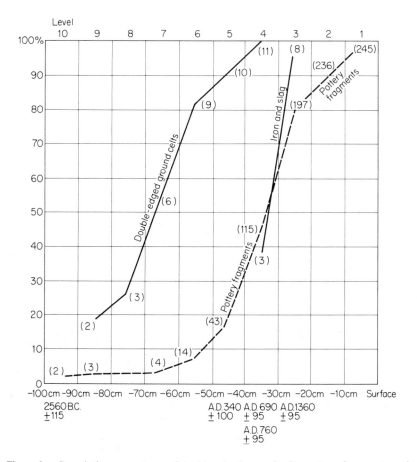

Figure 2. Cumulative percentages of double-edged ground celts, pottery fragments, and iron and slag, by ten-centimeter excavation units, Kamabai rock shelter, Sierra Leone (numbers in parentheses refer to raw count; percentages are total in each of the artifact classes)

BORED STONES

Bored stones or *kwes* are well-known from southern Africa as digging-stick weights. They have also sometimes been used by some Bantu-speaking peoples as weights on the heads of picks or hoes (J. Desmond Clark, personal communication, 1973). In other areas of the continent they have apparently been used in agricultural and hunting activities, but in West Africa most seem to be associated with mining (Davies 1964:197; 1967:203). In recent times, bored stones have been used for divination and in connection with ancestor cults among the Kissi (Paulme 1949:119). Many occurrences of *kwes* in West Africa appear to be associated with gold mining. Others, though, are associated with diamond workings. Davies (1964:197) does not attach any significance to this, arguing that "the diamond-placers in which these stones are found were probably formerly auriferous."

It seems fairly certain that early gold mining was conducted in highland southeastern Sierra Leone, where bored stones (Plates 1, 2, and 3) and other stone artifacts have been found. Many of the earliest Europeans on the coast, for example, Pacheco (Kimble 1937:108) and Gomes (Crone 1937:93), mention this region of West Africa specifically as a source of gold. Gold can still be found in many areas of the interior of Sierra Leone (Wilson and Marmo 1958:75ff.; Marmo 1962:112–115). The Baule in

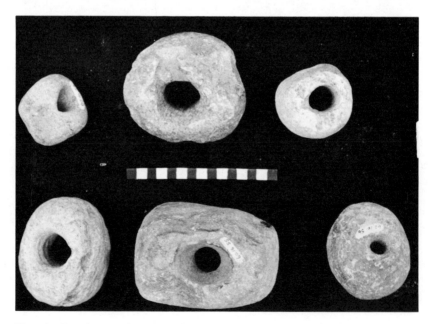

Plate 1.   Bored stones from southeastern Sierra Leone in the collections of the Sierra Leone Museum (scale in cm)

Plate 2. Bored stones from southeastern Sierra Leone in the collections of the Sierra Leone Museum (scale in cm)

Plate 3. Bored stones from southeastern Sierra Leone in the collections of the Sierra Leone Museum (scale in cm)

the Ivory Coast used picks and other tools to work geologically similar auriferous deposits (Borremans de Batist 1972:36). That the early inhabitants of Sierra Leone may have mined gold in this way is supported by the presence of what are apparently stone picks in the same areas as the bored stones (see Figure 3 and Plates 4 and 5).

It also seems possible that diamond mining was carried on before the great disturbances of the sixteenth through nineteenth centuries. Diamonds were not found by the British in Sierra Leone until 1930, and mining did not begin until 1933 (van der Laan 1965:45). Considering the number of prehistoric tools found during the modern mining of the diamondiferous regions of Sierra Leone and other places in West Africa (Davies 1964:197), however, it seems that the practice might also have been carried on in prehistoric times.

We know that gold was traded from Africa before the arrival of the Arabs (de La Roncière 1925:96; Law 1967:189) and possibly in classical times (Law 1967:188–189). One other item of trans-Saharan trade which is certainly of great antiquity is the carbuncle (Law 1967:187–188). Like the term for another trade item, the enigmatic "akori bead" (Kalous 1968), "carbuncle" undoubtedly has more than one referent. Laufer (1915:62) has suggested that the diamond might be one of these; it is possible that it might have been the original one. Classical authors are not very helpful on the subject of diamonds in the Mediterranean world, but "the copious and reliable accounts of the Chinese authors advance our knowledge of the subject to a considerable degree beyond the point

Figure 3.   Stone "picks" from southeastern Sierra Leone in the collections of the Sierra Leone Museum, one-quarter natural size

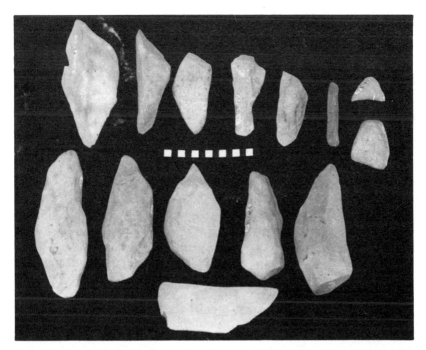

Plate 4. Stone "picks" and other artifacts from southeastern Sierra Leone in the collections of the Sierra Leone Museum (scale in cm)

Plate 5. Stone "picks" and other artifacts from Sierra Leone in the collections of the Sierra Leone Museum (scale in cm)

where the classical writers leave us" (Laufer 1915:6). Among the items relevant to the present discussion are mentions of diamonds' being found in the proximity of gold — 主金中 (Laufer 1915:35). Although the passage has been translated as referring to India, Ethiopia (Africa) and India are very often confused in early texts. Gold and diamonds are often found together in Sierra Leone as well as other parts of West Africa. Many Chinese contacts with the West were made, and in at least one (during the reign of Suan-wu, A.D. 500–515), at a time at which gold was probably being traded across the Sahara, diamonds — 金 剛 石 are mentioned (Hirth and Rockhill 1911:111).

The idea of early diamond mining in Sierra Leone is suggested by the intriguing tales told by early visitors to the coast (for example, Coelho 1953:216) about people in the interior who have stones that shine in the dark. Diamonds, in addition to reflecting light "in a way unequalled by other gemstones" (van der Laan 1965:41), do, under certain conditions, give out a light "plainly visible in a dark room" (Laufer 1915:63). In addition, the stories connected with the Sierra Leone stones are remarkably like those told about the diamond in the Mediterranean area in classical times (Laufer 1915).

SOAPSTONE FIGURES

In an area centered in southern Sierra Leone are found numerous carved soapstone figures, known as *nomoli* or *nomori* (Plate 6). Although many have been carved in recent times, many are certainly prehistoric. Of their age and origin, however, little is known. Stylistic, chronological, and other characteristics have been dealt with elsewhere (Atherton and Kalous 1970; Dittmer 1967; Person 1961); only some aspects of manufacture and use are discussed here.

Soapstone or steatite is a very soft stone which can be worked easily and which can be carved with woodworking tools (A. Maeson, personal communication). That the figures were carved with woodworking tools is suggested by manufacturing marks on unfinished pieces which closely resemble those found on unfinished wooden sculptures. Preliminary carving was probably done with an adze, while work on the head and nostril holes and other details must have been done with chisels (Plates 7 and 8). It is of interest that the marks made on the pieces correspond exactly to the size of the working edges of many of the dolerite celts and quartz "micro-chisels" (Atherton 1972a).

The figures were manufactured in a very interesting way. A steatite vein was uncovered and the carving done directly on the rock outcropping; not until the sculpture was completed was it detached from the matrix (Joyce 1909:67). An explanation of this curious technique can be

Plate 6.   *Nomoli* figure from Sierra Leone in the collection of the British Museum

Plate 7.   Close-up of manufacturing marks on an unfinished *nomoli* figure

Plate 8.   Close-up of manufacturing marks on an unfinished *nomoli* figure

found in noting certain cultural characteristics of local populations. The figures were meant to be representations of the dead and a residing spot for their "spirit." The dead were very closely connected — and in many cases identified — with the earth and with rock; it would be through these media that the "spirit" would travel. Thus, if the figure were carved to represent a particular ancestor, a particular spirit might be lured into the sculpture made for it, at which time the figure would be removed from the vein thus trapping the spirit in it. Such suppositions find support in ethnographic data from areas where the figures have been made recently (Atherton and Kalous 1970).

SUMMARY

Two main hypotheses emerge from this discussion: (1) A considerable proportion of the artifactual remains of the prehistoric populations of Upper Guinea (and probably other parts of West Africa) may reflect activities not directly involved with subsistence; instead, these artifacts may have been used to manufacture socioreligious and other artifacts from soapstone and organic materials. (2) Bored stones and associated artifacts found in diamondiferous deposits in Sierra Leone and other parts of West Africa may have been used in the mining of diamonds as well as gold; these diamonds may have been the mysterious "carbuncles" of the trans-Saharan trade in classical and later times.

REFERENCES

ARCIN, ANDRÉ
  1907 *La Guinée française*. Paris: Libraire Maritime et Coloniale.
ATHERTON, JOHN H.
  1968 Válečné jeskyně kmene Limba. *Nový Orient* 23:257–258.
  1972a Excavations at Kamabai and Yagala rock shelters, Sierra Leone. *West African Journal of Archaeology* 2:39–74.
  1972b Protohistoric habitation sites in northeastern Sierra Leone. *Bulletin de la Société Royale Belge d'Anthropologie et de Préhistoire* 83:5–17.
ATHERTON, JOHN H., MILAN KALOUS
  1970 Nomoli. *Journal of African History* 11:303–317.
BEATTY, K. J.
  1915 *Human leopards*. London: Hugh Rees.
BORREMANS DE BATIST, G.
  1972 Bijdrage tot een beter inzicht in de betekenis van het goud in de cultuur van de Baulé (Côte d'Ivoire). *Africa-Tervuren* 18:35–48.
BUTT-THOMPSON, F. W.
  1929 *West African secret societies*. London: H. F. and G. Witherby.
COELHO, FRANCISCO DE LEMOS
  1953 *Duas descricões seiscentistas da Guiné*. Lisbon: Academia Portuguesa da História.
COON, CARLETON S.
  1968 *Yengema cave report*. Philadelphia: University Museum.
CORRY, JOSEPH
  1807 *Observations upon the windward coast of Africa*. London: G. and W. Nicol.
CRONE, G. R., *translator and editor*
  1937 *The voyages of Cadamosto and other documents on western Africa in the second half of the fifteenth century*. London: Hakluyt Society.
DAVIES, OLIVER
  1964 *The Quaternary in the coastlands of Guinea*. Glasgow: Jackson.
  1967 *West Africa before the Europeans*. London: Methuen.
DE LA RONCIÈRE, CHARLES
  1925 *Le découverte de l'Afrique au moyen âge: cartographie et explorateurs*. Cairo: Société Royale de Géographie d'Egypte.
DITTMER, KUNZ
  1967 Bedeutung, Datierung und kulturhistorische Zusammenhänge der "prähistorischen" Steinfiguren aus Sierra Leone und Guinée. *Baessler Archiv* 15:183–223.
FAGG, WILLIAM, MARGARET PLASS
  1966 *African sculpture*. London: Dutton Vista.
FYFE, CHRISTOPHER
  1964 *Sierra Leone inheritance*. London: Oxford University Press.
HAMY, M. E. T.
  1901 La grotte du Kakimbon à Rotoma, près Konakry (Guinée française). *L'Anthropologie* 12:380–395.
HIRTH, FRIEDRICH, W. W. ROCKHILL, *translators and annotators*

1911   *Chau Ju-kua: his work on the Chinese and Arab trade in the twelfth and thirteenth centuries, entitled Chu-fan-ehi.* St. Petersburg: Imperial Academy of Sciences.

HOWELL, F. CLARK
1966   *Early man.* Amsterdam: Time-Life.

JOIRE, JEAN
1952   "La préhistoire de Guinée française: inventaire et mise au point de nos connaissances." *Comptes Rendus de la Conférence Internationale des Africanistes de l'Ouest, Bissau, 1947.* Lisbon.

JOYCE, T. A.
1909   Steatite figures from Sierra Leone. *Man* 40:65–68.

KALOUS, MILAN
1968   Akori beads. *Baessler Archiv* 16:89–97.

KIMBLE, GEORGE H. T., *translator and editor*
1937   *Esmeraldo de situ orbis, by Duarte Pacheco Pereira.* London: Hakluyt Society.

LAING, ALEXANDER GORDON
1825   *Travels in the Timanee, Kooranko and Soolima countries in western Africa.* London: John Murray.

LAUFER, BERTHOLD
1915   *The diamond: a study in Chinese and Hellenistic folk-lore.* Chicago: Field Museum of Natural History.

LAW, R. C. C.
1967   The Garamantes and trans-Saharan enterprise in classical times. *Journal of African History* 8:181–200.

MARMO, VLADI
1962   *Geology and mineral resources of the Kangari Hills schist belt.* Freetown: Government Bookshop.

MATEUS, AMILCAR DE MAGALHAES
1952   "Nota preliminar acerca da estacão prehistorica de Nhampassaré." *Comptes Rendus de la Conférence Internationale des Africanistes de l'Ouest, Bissau, 1947.* Lisbon.

PAULME, DENISE
1949   Utilisation moderne d'objets préhistoriques à des fins rituelles en pays Kissi. *Notes Africaines* 44:119.

PERSON, YVES
1961   Les Kissi et leurs statuettes de pierre dans la cadre de l'histoire ouest-africaine. *Bulletin de l'Institut Français d'Afrique Noire* B23:1–60.

RODNEY, WALTER
1970   *A history of the Upper Guinea coast 1545 to 1800.* London: Oxford University Press.

SCHLENKER, C. G.
1861   *A collection of Temne traditions, fables, and proverbs.* London: Church Missionary Society.

SZUMOWSKI, GEORGES
1956   Fouilles de l'abri sous roche de Kourounkorokalé (Soudan français). *Bulletin de l'Institut Français d'Afrique Noire* B18:462–508.

TAUXIER, L.
1924   *Nègres Gouro et Gagou.* Paris: Geuthner.

VAN DER LAAN, H. L.
1965   *The Sierra Leone diamonds.* London: Oxford University Press.

WILSON, N. W., V. MARMO
   1958   *Geology, geomorphology, and mineral resources of the Sula Mountains.*
       London: Crown Agents.

PART TWO

History

Introduction: Research Trends in West African History

RAYMOND E. DUMETT

The period 1955 to 1975 witnessed a revolution in historical writing and study about the continent of Africa which ran parallel to and was nourished by the rise of African nationalism and the establishment of independent African states in more than forty-five former colonial territories. From the status of nullity in most American university study programs of the early 1950's, African history by the early 1960's had become an important segment of full-fledged African-studies programs at some twelve American universities and was recognized in two- or three-semester course sequences in many other institutions. While British universities continued as major centers of graduate study, another trend was the development of important research and training institutes at African universities. The consequences of this awakening for historical scholarship were far-reaching. First, African history was freed from its previous subservience to European colonial history: there was a sustained effort to examine Africa's past from the inside. Second, pioneering research in the 1960's helped to establish a general chronological framework and pattern of causation and change for precolonial Africa, with a major emphasis on the centralized states and empires. A third consequence was to provide Africans with a usable past which reinforced a sense of pride and identity and could serve as a basis for nationalism and unity. Finally, African history matured through the adaptation of theories and methodologies derived from other disciplines in the social sciences, including archaeology, anthropology, linguistics, demography, epidemiology, economic theory, and statistics.

Contributors to this part were not asked to conform to a rigid format or confining definition of the main theme. The term "culture dynamics" was interpreted not in the older sense of mere culture history, but according to a broader notion of multidimensional analysis of politi-

cal, economic, and cultural change. If there is a single leitmotiv for many
of the papers it is that of the weight of economic and environmental forces
as determinants of political and sociocultural change. Research topics in
the essays range from the analysis of court rituals and precolonial state
formation to trading diasporas and the economics of migratory cattle
herding; from the impact of slave raiding to the origins of modern
nationalism. Societies of the forest zone and of the drier savanna and
Sahelian regions receive about equal attention. Ethnic groups and traditional states which come in for analysis include the Walo-Walo and Ayor
of Senegal, the Trarzas and Brakna of Mauritania, the Bagas and SuSu
people of Guinea, the Segu-Tukulor Empire, and the Manding jula.
From the original Congress session come two papers on the Igbo of
eastern Nigeria. Other groups included are the Kru and Grebo of Liberia,
the Baule of the Ivory Coast, the Akyem and Akwamu peoples of Gold
Coast/Ghana, the Idoma of Nigeria, and the Tuareg of the Central Sudan.

EARLY MIGRATIONS AND SETTLEMENT: HISTORY AND ARCHAEOLOGY

Whether one is speaking of the history of Africa or that of other
continents of the world, there is no clear-cut boundary between prehistory and history, and the division of papers in this part between those
which are historical and those which use archaeological tools is somewhat
arbitrary. Because of a dearth of written records for many periods and
regions, historians of Africa have had to look to such disciplines as
anthropology, linguistics, and folklore — as well as to paleontology,
botany, zooarchaeology, and metallurgy, for data on the earliest human
settlements and politics. Thus, the paper by J. O. Hunwick on ancient
Ghana makes extensive use of Arabic epigraphy, which has been of
no small importance in unveiling the early history of Islamic Africa.
Another topic on which there continues to be great interest and debate is
the origins and migration routes of major ethnic groups in West Africa
during the first millennium of the present era. Precisely when did Negro
ancestral groups begin to move into the Guinea forest zone in large
numbers? When did the major linguistic divisions and ethnicities that we
know today begin to take shape? One older, oversimplified view was that
the people of the Guinea forest are the descendants of Nilo-Saharan
pastoralists who moved south toward the moister regions after the desiccation of the Sahara, which many scholars consider to have taken place in
the second half of the third millennium B.C. (for example, see Ellis's paper
in Part One of this volume). This has to be reconciled, however, with
more recent conclusions that when the Saharan pastoralists moved south,
they encountered Later Stone Age hunters using rather "advanced"

microlithic tools (see Swartz's introduction to Part One), which suggests that the forest zone was already inhabited by people with cultures of a Later Stone Age type (Shaw 1972:56–57, citing Davies 1968:27–42). Most hypotheses on the dispersal of the Niger-Congo language family into various parts of the forest zone are, therefore, at best conjectural. Partly because of the dearth of trained archaeologists working in West Africa, little precise evidence has been retrieved concerning the stages in the migrations and settlements of peoples in the Guinea forest zone before about A.D. 1000, despite the existence of radiocarbon dating methods. Much of the speculative discussion, including that presented here, has been about the processes rather than the precise chronology by which conquest of the forest may have taken place.

Another methodological issue concerns the uses that can be made of oral data. Given the paucity of written evidence for many African societies prior to the period of Islamic expansion or (for the Guinea Coast) European exploration, oral tradition often comprises the historian's main data base. Some of the best studies of African kingdoms written during the 1960's and 1970's made sophisticated use of oral traditions, and comparative analysis showed that folktales, poetry, and song could also be examined for symbolic meanings which might have some basis in observed fact. Comparison of the oral traditions of small lineages has also proven useful for tracing the migrations and early economic histories of major groups, particularly in East Africa. Despite optimism in some quarters regarding the uses which might be made of oral tradition, there is now greater recognition of its limitations. Both the "fixed texts" associated with the royal lineages of centralized states and the "free texts" recited by the elders of stateless societies can be used by the historian, but both may telescope time and contain serious gaps and distortions. Etiological myths passed on from one generation to another can be useful, as Vansina has shown, for understanding the cosmological concepts of a people, but they tend to be unreliable as a base for recording actual historical events (Vansina 1961:158–159; also 1971:442–468). The most effective uses of oral evidence in this volume are by R. G. Armstrong, who uses explanations of royal customs, etiquette, and rituals to cast light on the nature of Idoma kingship, and Jan S. Hogendorn, who uses eyewitness testimony, together with contemporary travelers' accounts, to investigate warfare and slave raiding in the Zaria Emirate of northern Nigeria.

ORIGINS AND EXPANSION OF THE IGBO PEOPLE

It is appropriate that A. E. Afigbo's "Prolegomena to the study of the Igbo-speaking peoples of Nigeria" should lead off this section, since it deals at length with the historiographical problem of tracing the origins and early migrations of West African peoples from the standpoint of oral tradition and myths of origin. In general, Afigbo tends to be quite skeptical of the value of folklore for the reconstruction of Igbo history, partly because of the problem of verification and partly because some myths of Igbo origin have reinforced popular prejudices. Recent archaeological work in other parts of Guinea suggests, however, that even local traditions concerning the origins of ancestors from "a hole in the ground" should not be entirely discounted and may offer more important clues to a Stone Age past than appears at first glance (see the work of E. Effah-Gyamfi 1975, cited in Posnansky and McIntosh, 1976:166).

Owing to the somewhat random organization of the West African History session at the IXth ICAES, there was overlap in the subjects covered in several papers. The two essays on the Igbo people — one by Afigbo and the other by S. J. S. Cookey — complement rather than duplicate one another, however. They tend to take divergent lines of interpretation, organize major subtopics differently, and interpret data in varying ways. Thus the Cookey paper amplifies in historical detail the processes of institutional development (the organization of Igbo village democracies and the slave trade, for example) while Afigbo emphasizes more sweeping and cultural themes. From the two essays it is possible to obtain a good overview of the people who came to be called Igbo over an approximate 2,000-year time span.

The two papers set the tone for others that follow by emphasizing the environmental and demographic conditions which have shaped settlement patterns and the development of Igbo institutions. On the basis of the limited archaeological data for Igboland thus far retrieved, Cookey and Afigbo concur that the original Igbo stock lived along an axis from Orlu to Awka in the north-central plateau before dispersing to the south, west, east, and north-east. These earliest settlements, radiocarbon-dated at about 3000 B.C., lie on the perimeter of the forest zone in areas that could have been cultivated with stone tools. Still, Cookey doubts that the Igbo could have conquered the forest region proper before the coming of iron technology. Yet, as Shaw (1972:60) has pointed out, the discovery of iron tools on the Jos Plateau dating to about 500 B.C. tells us little about diffusion of iron technology among large masses of people or its spread into the forest zone. The final verdict on approximate dates of settlement is not yet in. Fage (1977:468–469) has recently argued that it is unlikely that Kwa-speaking subgroups moved into the dense forest and westwards either at so early a date or in the great numbers that some histories postulated. He doubts that there was large-scale settlement of forested areas until the introduction of new food crops of Southeast Asian or American origin, such as cocoyams, plantains, cassava, and maize and suggests that the conquest of the forest was probably not complete until the slave-trade era of the seventeenth century. In fact there is a good deal of indirect evidence which supports the speculations of Afigbo and Cookey on settlement of the Igbo forest zone at a much earlier period. There is a clear record of Igala slaving against the Igbo in the Onitsha-Enugu and Awka-Nsukka areas by the seventeenth century. By the eighteenth century there was a dense Igbo population behind the coast for slavers to tap. In addition, dialect differences were by then well defined in Igboland, a fact which indicates a long period of settlement. From this and recent unpublished archaeological data, the Afigbo-Cookey date of A.D. 1000 for early southward migration of Igbo and ethnic subgroups to the Niger delta does not seem unreasonable and may, in fact, be too conservative an estimate (see paper by Harlte, this volume; also John E. Flint, personal communication, 1979).

STATE FORMATION IN THE GUINEA FOREST ZONE: AKYEM AND THE AKWAMU EMPIRE

From the beginning of the breakthrough in African historical studies, collection of evidence on precolonial state formation has been one of the dominant pursuits. Most of the great kingdoms and empires and many of the smaller states have been subjected to detailed narrative histories. Some of these studies have theorized about the economic, military, and technological dynamics which brought stable administrative units into being, and, during the first decades of the new historiography, "trade and politics" was a popular theme (Dike 1957; Ryder 1969; Daaku 1970). Others have elaborated on the leadership principles and organizational hierarchies by which states were governed: for example, the offices of "the inside" and "the outside," core states and tributary states, or forces of equilibrium versus those for disequilibrium and change (see Argyle 1966; Lloyd 1968; Wilks 1975). In the process of these investigations, several antiquated notions — such as the diffusionist concept that "divine kingship" was transmitted into sub-Saharan Africa from Egypt via the Kushitic kingdom of Meroe or the idea of political centers automatically emerging from market towns astride arteries of trade — have been discarded or revised, while neo-Marxist attempts to correlate political systems in evolutionary schema according to underlying "modes of production" (kin-based, slave-based, or feudal) have gained favor.

Ronald R. Atkinson's paper on the state of Akyem (in Gold Coast/Ghana) sheds new light on the foundations of chiefdoms and states in the heartland of the Akan region. The approach is multidimensional in that it takes cognizance of environmental, technological, and economic as well as political factors. In line with the trend in both Marxist and non-Marxist studies, Atkinson places great emphasis on rudimentary labor organization in the early stages of pre-state development and, particularly, on the addition of "captive" (slave) labor to kin-based labor units. Implicit is an assumption that a full-fledged iron-based tool culture was required for the conquest of the forest and that this came about at a relatively late period. Utilizing recent work by Ivor Wilks on early Akan economic and social history, Atkinson argues that the transition from a hunting-and-gathering society based on the Akan matriclan to a predominantly agricultural one supporting first stools and then states probably took place on the northern forest fringes of what is today Ghana during the fourteenth and fifteenth centuries, because it was only then that the Akan were able to secure slave labor in sufficient quantities for the arduous task of forest clearance. This imported labor was also significant politically, since it added to the numerical size and power of the sociopolitical unit. Thus the matriclan system proved an effective device for absorbing new and diverse ethnic groups into a homogeneous Akan cultural entity. From here Atkinson traces the processes of state formation in the seventeenth and eighteenth centuries. One powerful stimulus in the early stages came from the desire of Akyem chiefs to gain control of gold supplies and the gold trade: it is noteworthy that the early stool organizations of Akyem Kotoku were nearly coterminous with the gold-mining sites of Old Akyem. Finally, military organization and new opportunities arising from warfare between the major rival kingdoms of Asante and Akwamu were also significant. Political subdivisions, as in other major Akan states, were based initially on the wing-chief system of the army. Ironically, the defeat of Akwamu by the combined forces of Asante and Akyem in 1730 led to the breakup of the unified polity of Old Akyem but at the same time paved the way for reconsolidation into two new states, Akyem Abuakwa and Akyem Kotoku, during the next generation.

Some of these themes are developed further in the paper by Raymond Kea on the centralized kingdom and empire of Akwamu. Kea's research is impressive for its use of Danish and Dutch, as well as English, archival sources. In a process which was later followed by other powerful trading states of the Guinea forest zone (Dahomey and Asante), Akwamu began as an inland state and gradually extended the perimeters of its control southward by absorbing as client states the smaller trading communities that had served as the prime intermediaries with European merchants on the coast. This expansion can be correlated with what has been called the "turnabout" in West African history — the quantitative shift in trade flows in Guinea from the north and east toward the south and west. As is well known, the consolidation of state structures in the forest zone can be correlated with the revolution in military technology and organization which was contingent upon the importation of European firearms in exchange for slaves. Gold was again important. As Wilks (1971:435-436) has shown, the core of the Akwamu kingdom was built up by the Abrade people at a place called Abonse, which became a leading mart for the flow of gold from the eastern interior to Europeans at Accra. Expansion from the original core area began with penetration into the Akwapim hills about 1646; Akyem was absorbed about 1673, but the final conquest of Accra did not come until 1681 and of the remainder of the eastern Adangbe area until about 1700. At the height of its imperial power, the total territory which Akwamu held under its sway ran for more than 250 miles along the coast from Agona in the west to Whydah on the "Slave Coast" in the east.

Many other issues, too numerous to summarize here, emerge from Kea's study. Among them are the influence of Akwamu political and administrative experience on later Akan states and the nature of the Akwamu economy. The answer to the first question seems fairly clear: Osei Tutu, the first great *asantahene*, acquired knowledge of the Akwamu political system during residence there, and the basic structure of the Asante kingdom was probably modeled after that of Akwamu. While at first reading there would seem to be some factual support in the Akwamu case for Polanyi's model (1957) of a "state-administered" economic system — monopolization of certain branches of foreign trade, control of foreign traders by government officials at designated "ports of trade," state control over the prices of certain goods, an economy of "redistribution" existing side by side with an economy of exchange — there are too many examples of untrammeled private trading and other discrepancies for the model to hold. Indeed, the validity of the Polanyi model even for the classic West African case of Dahomey has been opened to serious question (Law 1977:555-557). As a more accurate replication of reality, Kea puts forward the concept of a dual economy. This contained a centralized, state-controlled sector of commerce with large agricultural estates in the hinterland of the capital city, on the one hand, and a more loosely regulated outer perimeter, where there was opportunity for private trading and where government remained in the hands of traditional local rulers.

STATELESS SOCIETIES

Several papers examine the structure and histories of "middle-range" or stateless societies (the term "middle-range" is used in contradistinction to "small-scale," which generally denotes hunting bands or small autonomous farming or herding communities). By a very rough estimate, it has been suggested that there may be about 35,000,000 West Africans, out of a total population of about 100,000,000, living in stateless societies. We still know far too little about these groups, partly because of the paucity of written data and the difficulty of gathering oral evidence about them. Common elements are the absence of centralized leadership and elaborate administrative hierarchies coupled with emphasis on unilineal descent groups.

The complex "diffuse authority system" of the Igbo, in which there is no fixed focus of political power and the unit to which the individual gives obedience varies with circumstances, is examined in Cookey's paper. Igbo organization has been called one of the purest examples of a segmentary lineage system in West Africa (the other being the Tiv of Central Nigeria), and it has also been interpreted as village democracy. Traditionally, every Igbo village considered itself a self-contained corporate group governed by a council of elders and by a general assembly in which every male villager had the right to participate. Decisions were reached by consensus. At a higher level there could also be a clan or "village group." This unit could make certain decisions based on a consensus of representatives of the villages, but it met only for special ceremonial occasions or in time of emergency; it had no sustained powers and could not force obedience. As Cookey notes, the absence of a centralized political system does not mean the absence of government. It is difficult, however, to abstract the main features of Igbo government, because these were complex and varied as to region. Frequently the village political structure was superimposed on the kinship structure; in other instances, there was a connection between commercial wealth and political roles. Secret societies and other associations might also exercise considerable political and judicial power (Ottenberg 1965: 14–19). Contrary to stereotype, there were also some Igbo monarchies along the Niger, but these seem to have been an exogenous element derived from the neighboring kingdom of Benin.

The paper by R. G. Armstrong, "The Dynamics of Idoma Kingship," fills important gaps in our knowledge concerning those polities in West Africa which lie intermediate on the spectrum between true stateless societies (the Ibo, the Tiv) and the centralized bureaucratic kingdoms (Benin, Asante, Dahomey). Armstrong challenges the conventional wisdom on several important grounds. His conclusions reinforce the cautionary remarks of Horton (1971:78–79), who argues that the supposed dichotomy between acephalous or stateless societies and highly organized states fails to convey a complete picture of African polities in the pre-colonial period and after. By concentrating on the great kingdoms and empires, African historians since the late 1950's may have created the impression that centralized polities were the norm, whereas anthropologists in their early emphasis on segmentary lineage systems may have lent exaggerated importance to what was a comparatively rare phenomenon.

Armstrong's fieldwork among the Idoma suggests that the evolution of

African sociopolitical organization should be viewed more as a continuum between "tribes without rulers," on the one hand, and highly bureaucratized states and empires, on the other, in which there were varying stages of intermediate political organization. One of the unconventional points which Armstrong makes is that a society may possess the institution of "kingship" without necessarily qualifying as a "state." Second, he repudiates the notion that large armies and military conquest must invariably have played a fundamental role in the process of political consolidation in precolonial West Africa. Even though the oral traditions of many states often trace the origins of kingship to invasion by alien forces, he notes the equally strong possibility that kingship and the incorporation process may have proceeded by voluntary methods from purely autochthonous roots. In using linguistic evidence to search for the meaning of basic institutional and ritualistic elements in Idoma kingship, he also points up the importance of land as a fundamental integrating element in Idoma society and further clarifies the meaning of "divine kingship" in African religion and political theory. Finally, his study is valuable for its evidence of the enduring quality of traditional kingship as a source of strength in Idoma society, even in the face of the severe disruptions of the colonial and postindependence periods in modern Nigerian history. His remarks on the colonial impact should be compared with others (e.g. Weiskel and Baier) in this volume.

ISLAM IN WEST AFRICA

Yet another major development of the last two decades reflected in papers in this section is the growth of research on the history of Islam and Muslim societies in West Africa. Prior to the 1960's, there were only a few historians with research expertise in Islamic Africa (outside Egypt), and most of these were trained as linguists and associated with British universities. By the 1970's the research map for Islamic African studies had markedly changed (see Hunwick 1976; Willis 1972: 406, 411–418). Major topics now well covered in the literature include the diffusion of Islamic religious influence, interconnections between Islam and the consolidation of great empires, the organization of the trans-Saharan trade, and the histories of the West African Islamic religious brotherhoods and jihads of the late eighteen and nineteenth centuries. There have also been numerous biographical studies. At the same time, there are still relatively few trained Arabists in the field and there are numerous other topics which call for attention: the spread of Islamic law in Africa, specific sectors of the Sudanic trade, the impact of Islam on commercial organization (partnership agreements, etc.) and social institutions (stratification and slavery), and, finally, the histories of the great towns and trade centers, such as Bonduku, Bobo-Dyulasso, Ghadames, Jenne, Gao, and Timbuktu.

While there is a fair amount of evidence in Arabic for the later Sudanic empires of the "middle age" — Mali, Songhay, and Kanem-Bonu — much less is available for the period which preceded them (A.D. 800–1000). We still know very little about the political histories and administrative structures of the earliest Sudanic kingdoms of Ghana and Gao. Nor do we know very much about the southern wing of the militant Islamic brotherhood of the Almoravids ("the people of the hermitage"), whose invasion of the Sudan is said to have brought an end to the Ghanaian Empire. Hunwick's deductive work ("Gao and the Almoravids: A Hypothesis") in reexamining the epigraphic evidence of famous royal tombstones dating back to about A.D. 1100 is therefore valuable in illuminating a period of West African history for which there has been a dearth of scholarship. Who were the Almoravids? What was the basis for their movement? The bare facts are well known. Originating among the Lamtuna and Goddala Berber tribes of Mauritania, the Almoravid movement split into two wings: one launched a jihad to the north, conquering Morocco and Spain, while a second under Abu Bakr imposed its rule on the Western Sudan about 1076. Less certain are answers to other questions: How complete was the Almoravid conquest of Ghana? What was the extent of local conversions to Islam? Was there a great Almoravid Empire which ran from the Iberian peninsula all the way to the River Niger in the eleventh and twelfth centuries?

While the Almoravid movement was undoubtedly important for the Western Sudan, Hunwick's evidence leads to the conclusion that the conquest was more of an expiring flash than a radical turning point. Although he concedes that for a ten-year period the Almoravids exercised rule over Ghana, he reminds us that the death of their leader Abu Bakr b. Umar in 1087 led to the breakup of the southern Almoravid Empire. In fact, we know very little about the nature of Almoravid rule or the way in which the Sudanese were converted to Islam. Levtzion (1973:185) tends to dichotomize between a lack of Islamic influence in Ghana before the Almoravids (although he concedes that there were undoubtedly Muslims attached to the royal court) and Islamicization in the period following, but his conclusions have been disputed by other authorities (see Farias 1974: 483). In a difficult piece of synthesis, Hunwick draws together evidence on continuities and discontinuities in the political order, the expansion of Islam, and what happened to the trans-Saharan trade in gold.

Although it is likely that Ghana lost its monopolistic middleman's role in the gold trade, Hunwick refutes the supposition that the Almoravid invasion led to any marked decline of the trans-Saharan trade. Indeed, the Almoravids in Spain proved to be the greatest European minters of African gold since Roman times. Precisely where this gold came from is still not clear. Hunwick suggests that there was probably initially a diversion of the gold trade of Bambuhu (Wangara) down the River Senegal to the state of Takrur and thence to the north. A later and more lasting effect was the shift in sources of gold supply from Bambuhu to Bure on the Upper Niger and diversion of trade routes farther east to Gao and along the Fezzan route to Ghadames and the North African coast. While there was no long-lived Almoravid government in the Western Sudan, it seems likely from the author's findings that there remained an Almoravid presence at Gao until 1120 and probably after. In a complex piece of detective work, Hunwick concludes that the famous Arabic tombstones found near Gao — which bear the names of apparent royalty but cannot be reconciled with the names of any recognizable Gao kings — were Berbers of the Massufa group, a remnant of the southern Almoravids who drifted east to establish an independent government at Gao after the collapse of the main movement in 1087.

In contrast to Hunwick's study, the paper by Eugenia Herbert on Timbuktu presents little that is new for the specialist. It does, however, provide an interesting synthesis of known evidence which helps to integrate for the general reader a number of the broad themes — cities and towns in precolonial Africa, the spread of Islam, the trans-Saharan trade, the role of the Manding jula and European imperialism — basic in the historiography of West Africa and touched on elsewhere in this volume. Herbert's narrative scans the long history of Timbuktu mainly from the standpoint of foreign travelers — the Arabic chroniclers as well as Europeans. She is less concerned with the internal governance and social structures of the city. It is interesting that while Timbuktu is closely bound up in the popular imagination with the wealth and glory of the Empire of Mali, it was never the capital or administrative center of that empire. Indeed, as Hunwick has pointed out, the exact capital of Mali under Mansa Musa the Great (1312–1337) is uncertain in the sources, and its place on the map is still a subject for lively debate by scholars (Hunwick 1973: 195–197). In this Timbuktu was unlike the city of Gao, which was both a thriving commercial center and the capital of the Songhai Empire (ca. 1464–1591). Herbert gives appropriate weight not only to Timbuktu but to its adjunct city, Jenne, in linking, through Niger boat traffic and jula networks, the trans-Saharan trade with that of the savanna and forest lands to the south. The essentially agrarian nature of most African cities and the question of interconnections between Timbuktu and the local hinterland cattle and produce markets remains open for further study.

Herbert concludes the first half of her essay with the subjugation of the Songhay Empire by the army of al-Mansur of Morocco in 1591. While she concedes that the Songhay Empire collapsed, she follows Willis (1971:512-554) in arguing that the Moroccan invasion was probably less destructive of trade and Islamic civilization in the long run than some earlier writers had supposed. That this is still a topic for debate is seen in the recent work of Levtzion (1977:515-517), who, focusing specifically on the greatness of Timbuktu under Songhai, argues that the factionalism, unwarranted interventionism, and sheer oppressiveness of the Moroccan Arma hastened the drift toward long-term economic and cultural decline.

In recent years, study of the Manding peoples has become another expanding branch of West African Islamic studies. Research areas include linguistics, Manding kinship and social organization, their role as harbingers of Islam, and their military organization (especially in connection with the late nineteenth-century "moving empire" of Samori Touré). Among economic historians, particular attention has focused on the great Manding-jula commercial diaspora. The concept of diaspora is a useful one for explaining how a given ethnic group may achieve wide geographic dispersion and commercial success through organized networks of interconnected family trading communities. It has been applied to such varied groups as the Hausa, Parsees of India, Jews, Basques, overseas Chinese, and other groups (for West Africa, see Sanneh 1976; Perinbam 1974:679; Cohen 1971: 266–281; Curtin 1975:68–83; Lovejoy 1978). Extending in a broad arc of over 800 miles from the River Gambia in the west to the hinterland of the Ivory Coast in the east, this migration of Manding traders reached substantial proportions in the sixteenth but continued until the nineteenth century. The jula diaspora is a remarkable phenomenon because it involved the largely peaceful penetration of alien societies by Manding-speaking traders who managed to preserve their language, religion, and cultural identity while gaining considerable power and influence within those societies. In this, the ideology of Islam also provided a powerful cohesive force. Wagadugu, Bobo-Julasso, Kong, Bonduku, and Sansanne Mango are among the major market towns south of the Niger bend on which they left their mark.

The paper by B. Marie Perinbam is a broad synthesis of previously published materials on the Manding jula, which she has reinterpreted in terms of her hypothesis on the role of the julas as developers of economic resources. In addition she takes on the complex task of delineating jula subgroups. The julas were not simply traders, but mercantile entrepreneurs who entered into closely knit partnerships and contractual relationships, recruited local labor, and developed complex communications networks and transport systems. By widening markets they stimulated new production and entrance into long-distance export by previously self-sufficient village economies. Examples she cites are (1) direct entrance by Manding traders into cloth production in the Senegambia region; (2) early transmission of knowledge about gold production and methods of gold extraction from the earlier Bambuhu and Bure goldfields to the Lobi and Banda goldfields of the Akan hinterland;

(3) spread of textile weaving and trade into the Voltaic region; and (4) development of the kola nut trade of the Ivory Coast hinterland. The lubricants for the working of these disparate networks were the commercial credit and market information which the julas supplied to their clients and customers. Perinbam suggests that traditional Islamic partnership arrangements from the Mediterranean region may also have been utilized. Also interesting from the standpoint of culture dynamics are Perinbam's observations concerning the interrelationships between jula economic pursuits and lineage structures. It should be noted, however, that the problem of jula clan origins and patronymics is extremely difficult to handle and could not be dealt with in the space allotted here. Each of these topics can best be treated in the future through a series of detailed local studies. The history of West African Islam also figures in the papers of Hogendorn, Barrows, and Baier later in this volume.

SLAVE RAIDING, THE SLAVE TRADE, AND ABOLITION

Few aspects of West African history have been subjected to more intensive new research and drastic reinterpretation in recent years than slavery and the slave trade. Important pathbreaking studies were those of Curtin (1969), which made use of sophisticated statistical methods to revise downward previous impressionistic estimates on the total numbers of slaves shipped from Africa to the New World between 1600 and 1860, and Fisher and Fisher (1971), which opened up new lines of research on slavery in Islamic Africa. Miers and Kopytoff's *Slavery in Africa* (1977) is the first comprehensive and comparative study of internal slavery as it existed in many societies of Africa. While the full story is not yet in, each of these books has stimulated additional research and debate. Among the papers in this collection which touch obliquely on questions of African slavery and participation in the slave trade are those by Atkinson, Kea, Afigbo, Cookey, Perinbam, Mouser, and Weiskel. A striking example of the in-depth research now being published is found in the paper by Jan S. Hogendorn, which brings forward valuable new evidence on the nature of warfare and slave raiding in the savanna lands of West Africa. By what methods were slaves acquired? What was the relationship of traditional slavery and slave raiding to the economic and political systems of precolonial African kingdoms?

In a penetrating earlier comment, Goody (1971) argued that a key distinction between the kingdoms of the forest zone and the sprawling polyglot empires of the savanna was the ability of the latter to make effective use of cavalry in political conquest and in tribute collection, including slave capture. He argued, furthermore, that wealth and power in precolonial African political systems, in contrast to medieval Europe, tended to be based less on control over the land than on the capture of and control over people. Lacking the heavy cavalry of Europe, the armies of the Sudanic empires did possess mixed forces of infantry and light cavalry which could be very effective in rounding up slaves and booty. Frequent raiding, according to this interpretation, had at least three fundamental connections to the economy and to state power: (1) it could enforce effective political control over distant territories; (2) it could add to the numerical strength and, presumably, the productive capacity of the host society through influx of new captives; and (3) it could add directly to the revenues of the state through plunder and the collection of tribute. Goody has called this the ownership, not of the means of production, but of the "means of destruction." Hopkins (1973:104–105) and Hogendorn suggest that, even with the extreme cruelty and suffering which it inflicted, slave raiding was a highly profitable enterprise for the ruling groups who participated and that it can be subjected to economic analysis.

To understand the political background to Hogendorn's study, it is necessary to keep in mind that the nineteenth-century Zaria Emirate was one part of the sprawling Fulani Empire of Sokoto established over the formerly independent Hausa states by the great Islamic jihad of Usuman dan Fodio between 1804 and 1810. Under Islamic law slavery was accepted, and among the Muslim states of the Sudan slave capture and slave use was a fact of life. By the mid-nineteenth century, the separate emirates, such as Zaria, exercised considerable control over their own affairs, including the right to collect taxes, partly in slaves, from the fiefdoms that were subordinate to them (Last 1967: 96–108, 114–138). Each of the emirates possessed its own army and engaged in frequent wars. In contrast to the views of several other historians, Hogendorn denies that slave raiding was merely a side-effect of wars waged for essentially political purposes. Instead, he argues that slave collection was organized on a deliberate basis by the emirates as an economic enterprise and as a regular tax-gathering function of the state. He argues, further-more, that slave-taking expeditions involved out-and-out warfare, not merely minor skirmishes against weak and unsuspecting stateless societies. Organized armies were made up of a vanguard, a main force of infantry, bowmen, and cavalry, and an elite force of musketeers. The villages which were attacked for slaves were fortified, and the inhabitants learned to put up stout defenses. While he concedes that his emphasis on army operations may understate the numbers of slaves acquired through relatively peaceful methods, such as tribute collection, punishment for criminal offenses, etc., Hogendorn leaves little doubt that systematic military raids were the most common method of slave acquisition in Zaria and perhaps throughout the Western and Central Sudan.

Two other essays which touch on questions concerning the impact of the slave trade and the uses of slaves within African societies are those of

Cookey and Afigbo. Cookey argues that the Igbo were basically an agricultural people, but population pressures and soil exhaustion drove certain groups to take up occupations in skilled crafts and in long-distance trade, including the slave trade. One of the most prominent of the Igbo trading subgroups was the Aro of the Bende region, whose rise to prominence dates from the middle of the seventeenth century — about the time that the Atlantic slave trade reached its peak. Cookey is explicit in relating how the Aro Chukwu oracle became the basis for a powerful theocratic state in which fetish priests used religious gullibility to lure the unwary into slavery. It can be argued that the underlying dynamic for the perpetuation of this entity was the slave trade. Put another way, it shows how religious, economic, and political strategies could be combined to serve the ends of profit and power.

New information supplied by Kea on Akwamu helps cast additional light on the question of what was done with slaves who were not sold into the Atlantic commercial system. What were the functions of slaves within precolonial African economies? The conventional view is that African "domestic slavery" was a patriarchal sociopolitical institution which bore no resemblance to the plantation "chattel" slavery of the American New World and must, therefore, be judged by essentially different criteria (see Miers and Kopytoff 1977:3–69 and *passim*; Curtin 1975:34–35; also Dumett 1979). According to the accepted view, African internal slavery was an adjunct to the traditional "kin-based" mode of production and did not constitute a full-fledged "slave-based mode of production" in the Marxist sense of the term. On this argument, bondage in African societies was mediated by the facts that slaves were ordinarily attached to households in small numbers, that the work and life of slaves normally did not differ markedly from that of ordinary peasant farmers, that there was no differentiation between slave and "free" on the basis of color, and that slaves and their families were normally assimilated into host societies after one or more generations. These views have recently been challenged by Klein and Lovejoy (1979) and by Hogendorn (1977). Basing their argument on fieldwork in northern Nigeria and Senegambia, they argue that there were often heavy concentrations of slave populations in and around the capital cities and walled towns of the larger states and empires and that in these instances there were far greater differences between slave and free and much slower integration of slaves into host societies than is suggested in the assimilationist model. This view is also supported to some extent by the information Kea provides on the dual economy of Akwamu. He notes that the prevailing form of labor in the outlying parts of the Akwamu kingdom was that supplied by peasant households, but he adds that the "agricultural labor of the metropolitan district was to a large extent unfree." This slave labor was apparently housed on the large estates of the powerful chief officials or nobles of the realm. The surplus product from these estates was appropriated to support the ruling class. One would still like to know more about the size and number of these estates or "plantations," the numbers of slaves that were involved in each case, the conditions of labor in comparison with those for "free" peasants, and whether slaves possessed any rights at all. On the basis of present fragmented knowledge, it is still far too early to generalize about the underlying dynamics of labor for West Africa as a whole.

Bruce L. Mouser analyzes some of the commercial arrangements which established conduits for the flow of slaves into the Atlantic system in his paper "Accommodation and Assimilation in the Landlord–Stranger Relationship." The paper casts light on at least three important issues which have continued to intrigue historians and remain at the forefront of research interests in the 1970's: (1) the economic history of Upper Guinea, (2) the European commercial impact on Africa, and (3) the dynamics of British slave-trade "abolition" and the supposed transition to "legitimate trade" in the mid-nineteenth century. Here Mouser develops with detail and new interpretation on one region ideas originally put forward by Brooks (1970) and Rodney (1970). This essay points up for the general reader the need to set aside old stereotypes which simplify history by setting up dichotomies between chronological periods and conflicting groups.

Taking issue with the older conception which viewed the connection between European slave traders and coastal African peoples as primarily one of domination by the former over the latter, Mouser contends that the reality was far more complicated. African chiefs and middlemen as well as European merchants profited from arrangements that were geared to the export of slaves and other products of West Africa, including salt, gold, ivory, gum, and hides, in return for the importation of European merchandise. The European and Afro-European merchants who first traded from shipboard offshore and later built trading factories along the Nunez and the Pongo Rivers in Guinea-Conakry did so only through agreements with local rulers (see Kea, this volume). While in an important sense the advent of Europeans constituted a break with the past (the slave trade did not reach floodtide proportions until the eighteenth century, and the quantity of slaves exported from Upper Guinea did not compare with that of the Lower Guinea Coast), Mouser argues that the relationship between the Portuguese *lançados,* their Luso-African descendants and African rulers differed little in practice from earlier arrangements made by coastal chiefs with African traders from the interior. Rodney (1970) presents a contrasting (though not necessarily incompatible) interpretation of the trade of the Upper Guinea Coast with more detail than can be expected in Mouser's article on both the mechanics of the trade and the nature of the goods traded. While Rodney concedes that accommodation was reached between parties in the Atlantic trade, he does not let us forget that the basic impetus nonetheless came from Europe and that the economy of the Upper Guinea Coast "became geared to serve the capitalist system."

Mouser also clears up older misconceptions concerning British abolition of the slave trade and the subsequent period of so-called legitimate trade, which earlier historians assumed spanned the era 1807–1870. The conception of a sharp break now seems more artificial than real. Mouser's evidence supports that of other recent studies suggesting that the ships of the British navy's anti-slave-trade squadron were ineffective in stopping the surreptitious export of slaves by the vessels of Portugal, the United States, and other nations. He also suggests that the use of military and naval violence, even for the humanitarian purpose of crushing slavery, could often have a disruptive effect on local socioeconomic systems equal to or greater than that of the slave trade itself. Most ironic of all, he shows that successful peanut production — one of the most publicized features of the "era of legitimate trade" — was predicated on the continued use of captive labor on African plantations.

NEW PERSPECTIVES ON EUROPEAN IMPERIALISM, AFRICAN RESISTANCE AND ECONOMIC UNDERDEVELOPMENT

In turning to some of the dynamics of change in West Africa in modern times, three dominant themes are European imperialism and colonialism, African resistance and the rise of nationalist movements, and the contradictory trends of economic development and underdevelopment. The interactions among these forces are analyzed in different ways and with divergent foci of attention in the final papers by Barrows, Weiskel, Wilson, and Baier. Three of these essays deal with territories in Francophone Africa; the paper by Wilson focuses on the independent Republic of Liberia.

What were the origins of imperialism and nationalism in West Africa? What was the interface between European power, economic exploitation, and African wars of resistance? What were the connections and continuities — if any — between early forms of African opposition ("tribal rebellions" and ethnic nationalism) and modern movements for national unity and independence? Is it accurate or even useful to categorize Africans as either "resisters" or "collaborators"? Is it possible that historians and political scientists have exaggerated the "progress-oriented" or unifying aspects of these early resistance struggles while minimizing the separatist tendencies? Each of these issues is explored in the papers that follow. Instead of treating the age of imperialism and the age of nationalism as separate and distinct sequences in African history, there has been some attempt in recent scholarship to point out ways in which the two trends overlapped and may be viewed as opposite sides of the same general historical phenomenon. This phenomenon has been variously labeled as "Westernization" and the absorption of the 'Third World" into the "modern global system." Obviously a collection of this length can do no more than dent the surface of a vast congeries of political and economic issues. For fuller discussion readers should consult such larger works as Gann and Duignan (1969–1975), Fieldhouse (1973), Hopkins (1973), Arrighi and Saul (1973), and many others.

Recent Africa-centered currents of scholarship and a European colonial orientation are combined in the paper by Leland Barrows on the expansionist policies of Governor Louis Faidherbe of Senegal in the 1850's and 1860's. Barrows places rather less emphasis than earlier studies on Faidherbe's personal designs for a vast French Sudanic Empire which would extend to Timbuktu (Kanya-Forstner 1969:39–43) and more on the ferment and disequilibrium in Senegambia created by African interests and initiatives (see also Klein 1968). The dynamics of French hinterland penetration were complex, and the mix of motives — economic, political, and military — varied with the time and geographic location. The dynamic force of reformist and expansionist Islam as the main challenge to French hegemony is central to Barrows's analysis. The most explosive agent for change was the Tijjaniya, a militant Sufite order whose influence reached the Western Sudan via Mauritania in the late eighteenth century. To protect French commercial interests on the River Senegal, Faidherbe felt compelled to counter the growing influence of the powerful Trarza and Brakna Moors south of that boundary. Maba of Badibu/Rip, Lat Dior of Cayor, and al-Hajj 'Umar of the powerful Tukulor Empire were major Tijjani rulers whose growing territorial power appeared to threaten French interests.

Though it is not delineated explicitly, there is considerable support in the Barrows paper for two of the central ideas of Robinson and Gallagher (1953, 1961) on nineteenth-century European expansion in Africa. The first is the concept of informal "free trade" imperialism, motivated in this case by France's need to maintain the flow of trading profits and revenue to its trading settlements at Saint-Louis, Gorée and Dakar; the second is that direct forms of European military intervention were often set in train more by disturbances and breakdown of old balances at the periphery than by direct orders from the centers of empire in Europe (Robinson and Gallagher 1953:1–15; 1961:465–469). Barrows is at pains to argue that Faidherbe was not the great territorial conqueror and annexationist that he is sometimes made out to be. Against a formidable array of African opponents and with limited backing from Paris, the governor had to pursue varied strategies and tactics. In some instances the French tolerated the power of the Tijjani rulers because they preferred them to the *tyeddos*, the quasi-feudal military elite who attacked trade routes and pillaged interior villages. During Faidherbe's two administrations, only Walo, of all the Senegambian kingdoms, was annexed directly. Until the 1880's the French were content to rely on a complex set of indirect arrangements — treaties, bribes, support for preferred African leaders, and sporadic military expeditions — to maintain a rough balance of power and commercial prosperity in the region. From the Barrows paper a complex picture emerges not simply of European imperialism and African resistance, but of rival African forms of expansion.

Timothy Weiskel's paper adds a new dimension to the study of proto-nationalist resistance movements against colonial regimes by examining the record of a "middle-range" society with no centralized political institutions or military organizations. Having coalesced from a synthesis of pre-existent Manding and Voltaic stock with immigrant Akan peoples during the seventeenth and eighteenth centuries, the Baule are part of the Akan language subgroup and close relatives of the Asante of Ghana. Only limited work has been published on Baule history in English, and Weiskel has succeeded, through extensive research in Paris and in West African archives, in opening up fertile new ground. Several striking features of the Baule struggle against French imperialism are under-scored in this essay. The first is that loosely organized polities might wage as effective a military resistance against colonial rule as the better-known centralized West African states. Baule resistance began fairly early on (1893–1895) in retaliation against French conscription of Baule slave porters for northern military expeditions. The revolts exhibited consider-able continuity and were remarkably effective, occupying the full atten-tion of the French colonial authorities at several stages during the first decade of the twentieth century. Second, Weiskel suggests that there can be no easy categorization of African responses to colonial rule in terms of "resistance" as opposed to "collaboration." Some Baule leaders and villages undoubtedly cooperated with the French; others fought furiously against them. As in most regions of Africa, leaders frequently shifted their position with regard to imperialism, alternating their strategies with changing circumstances.

Equally illuminating is the original economic interpretation Weiskel brings to his material. Under a moderate Ivory Coast governor, Clozel, the Baule were gradually incorporated into the expanding export economy based on rubber collection through collaborative arrangements between the French and village groups. The harsher rule of Governor Angoulvant (head taxes, land tenure reform, and forced labor) coupled with a downturn in the trade cycle for tropical products produced open guerrilla warfare in 1908–1911 which proved very difficult for the French to put down. Interesting from a Marxist slant is the triggering effect for revolt which Weiskel attributes to French destruction of the Baule "slave mode of production" and its impact on the traditional village economy and social structure. Weiskel makes it clear that much of the inspiration for his provocative interpretation comes from the writings of Ranger (1969 and earlier) on the importance of African "primary resistance" against colonialism as a bridge to the independence struggles of the mid-twentieth century. The question remains, however, whether there is a fundamental or organic connection between these early acts of protest and resistance by particular ethnic groups (Baule, Agni, etc.) and modern nationalism. For an informative complementary view, following different lines of interpretation, readers should consult Asiwaju (1976).

The paper "Nation Building, Ethnicity, and the New Imperialism" by Henry S. Wilson casts new light on the complex synthesis of ideas, personalities, and political parties that injected new dynamism into the struggle for nationhood in Liberia at the turn of the century. In contrast to the rural orientation of the Weiskel study, Wilson directs his attention to the middle-class nationalism of President Arthur Barclay and the latter's efforts to move Liberia along the path of development in the face of the threatening imperial rivalries of the European and American super-powers. The paper is interesting for its analysis of several significant substreams of modern African nationalism, including the Pan-Africanist ideologies of West Indian intellectuals such as E. W. Blyden and H. Sylvester Williams, the ethnic nationalisms of rural protest groups, and the practical statesmanship of the Americo-Liberians led by Barclay. In spite of his emphasis on personalities and ideas, Wilson avoids the temptation to describe the evolution of African nationalism in a vacuum either as the heroic saga of great men or as mere intellectual history.

In fact, the causal interconnections between African nationalism as an elite ideology and the formidable realities of building a unified modern nation were extremely complex. Against numerous opponents, internal as well as external, the pioneers of West African nationhood frequently had to play a delaying game and steer a zigzag course. As Wilson puts it, "the problem which . . . confronted West African writers and politicians, nurtured on the nationalist ideas of the founding fathers, was how to adapt their notions of identity, autonomy, and nation building to changing constraints and opportunities." The paper points up very well the many contradictions and paradoxes in nineteenth-century Liberian history. Despite the early date of its independence (1847), Liberia continued to be heavily dependent on the protection and support of foreign powers. That this was a dangerous game is demonstrated by the fact that the self-styled protectors of Liberian independence — the United States, Great Britain, and France — also aimed at political and economic influence in the Negro Republic. Barclay, as a pragmatist, attempted to make use of the foreign imperial rivalries for the fulfillment of Liberian interests as he saw them.

Wilson's paper also underscores domestic sociopolitical problems that have continued to plague Liberia into the late twentieth century. Thus Barclay had to contend with a backlash against his use of European advisers in the government by leaders of his own True Whig party centered at Monrovia, while insurrections by the Luawa and Grebo reflected the deep cleavages between traditional ethnic groups of the hinterland and the ruling Americo-Liberians. Wilson's analysis provides a useful antidote to those simplistic histories of West African nationalism which have fostered a belief in a unilinear pattern of development from ethnic nationalism to a broader cultural nationalism to mass political parties and nationhood. Recent studies by political scientists also have tended to focus on the disintegrative problems of class conflict, uneven economic development, and cultural pluralism as the major sociopolitical themes of the late twentieth century (see, for example, Liebenow 1969; Lofchie 1971).

Rounding out the volume is Stephen Baier's essay on the history of the desert-edge economy of central Niger during the last 100 years. This exemplifies the trend toward regional studies in the economic history of West Africa and scholarly concern with the causes of current economic underdevelopment. The analysis is particularly pertinent to our understanding of the problems of drought, starvation, and severe cattle loss which afflicted practically the entire Sudanic belt of Africa during the late 1960's and early 1970's.

There are three major interlocking subsystems in the desert-edge economy: (1) a northern sector, in which nomadic pastoralism centered on the Tuareg is the dominant pursuit; (2) a southern or sedentary agricultural sector, in which the Hausa are the dominant ethnic group; and (3) the trans-Saharan trading sector, which connects the other two. The successful working of this interregional system depends on specialization and the complementarity of the commodities produced in different zones and by different ethnic groups. The dynamic factor in the desert-edge economy is transhumance — pastoral migration over a long distance according to a predictable annual cycle of rain and drought. In his fieldwork, Baier has concentrated primarily on the Tuareg confederations of the Aïr massif in central Niger. Over the centuries these groups have had the resiliency to withstand recurring drought provided that the desiccation was not too severe or protracted.

Baier is not content to write the ethnohistory of the Tuareg, but also correlates long-term economic change with the impact of French colonial administration. As elsewhere in West Africa, a policy of state-assisted economic development was adopted not so much to improve the standard of living of the people as to provide a tax base for stable colonial government and further imperial military conquests. As Baier points out, the various aspects of French economic strategy often ran at cross-purposes,

and in the end the entire policy, so far as the Central Sudan was concerned, proved self-destructive. Thus the commandeering of camels by
the French authorities undermined the Tuareg socioeconomic system.
Inevitable resentment sparked the Tuareg revolt of 1911–1914, which
brought the French no end of trouble and devastated the countryside.
Heavy Tuareg emigration resulting from this episode, coupled with the
effects of recurring droughts, the decline of the trans-Saharan trade, and
other factors, has led to the increased economic isolation of the central
Niger and a shift in economic activity south to Nigeria in the mid-
twentieth century.

REFERENCES

ARGYLE, W. J.
  1966   *The Fon of Dahomey.* London: Oxford University Press.
ARRIGHI, G., J. SAUL
  1973   *Essays on the political economy of Africa.* New York: Monthly Review.
ASIWAJU, A. I.
  1976   Migrations as revolt: the example of the Ivory Coast and the Upper
         Volta before 1945. *Journal of African History* 17:577–594.
BROOKS, GEORGE E.
  1970   *Yankee traders, old coasters, and African middlemen.* Boston: Boston
         University Press.
COHEN, ABNER
  1971   "Cultural strategies in the organization of trading diasporas," in *The
         development of indigenous trade and markets in West Africa.* Edited by
         Claude Meillassoux. London: Oxford University Press.
CURTIN, P. D.
  1969   *The Atlantic slave trade: a census.* Madison: University of Wisconsin
         Press.
  1975   *Economic change in precolonial Africa: Senegambia in the era of the
         slave trade.* Madison: University of Wisconsin Press.
DAAKU, KWAME Y.
  1970   *Trade and politics on the Gold Coast, 1600–1720.* London: Oxford
         University Press.
DIKE, K. O.
  1957   *Trade and politics in the Niger delta.* London: Oxford University Press.
DUMETT, R. E.
  1979   "Precolonial goldmining and the state in the Akan region," in *Research
         in economic anthropology*, volume two. Edited by G. Dalton, 37–68.
         Greenwich, Con.: JAI Press.
FAGE, J. D.
  1977   "Upper and Lower Guinea," in *The Cambridge history of Africa*,
         volume three. Edited by R. Oliver, 463–518. Cambridge: Cambridge
         University Press.
FARIAS, P. F. DE MORAIS
  1974   Great states revisited. *Journal of African History* 15:479–488.
FIELDHOUSE, D. K.
  1973   *Economics and empire, 1831–1914.* Edited by Charles Wilson. Ithaca:
         Cornell University Press.

FISHER, A. G., H. J. FISHER
  1971 *Slavery and Muslim society in Africa*. New York: Doubleday.
GANN, L. H., P. DUIGNAN, *editors*
  1969–1975 *Colonialism in Africa, 1870–1960*, four volumes. Cambridge: Cambridge University Press.
GOODY, J.
  1971 *Technology, tradition, and the state in Africa*. London: Oxford University Press.
HOGENDORN, J. S.
  1977 The economics of slave use on two "plantations," Biye and Hanwa, in the Zaria Emirate of the Sokoto Caliphate. *African Historical Studies* 10:369–383.
HOPKINS, A. G.
  1973 *An economic history of West Africa*. New York and London: Columbia University Press.
HORTON, ROBIN
  1971 "Stateless societies in the history of West Africa," in *History of West Africa*, volume one. Edited by J. F. A. Ajayi and Michael Crowder, 72–113. New York: Columbia University Press.
HUNWICK, J. O.
  1973 The mid-fourteenth-century capital of Mali. *Journal of African History* 14:195–208.
  1976 "The study of Muslim Africa: retrospect and prospect," in *African studies since 1945*. Edited by C. Fyfe. London and New York: Oxford University Press.
KANYA-FORSTNER, A. S.
  1969 *The conquest of the Western Sudan*. Cambridge: Cambridge University Press.
KLEIN, MARTIN
  1968 *Islam and imperialism in Senegal*. Stanford: University Press.
KLEIN, MARTIN, P. LOVEJOY
  1979 "Domestic slavery in West Africa," in *The uncommon market: the economics of the trans-Atlantic slave trade*. Edited by H. Gemery and J. S. Hogendorn. New York: Academic Press.
LAST, MURRAY
  1967 *The Sokoto Caliphate*. New York: Humanities Press.
LAW, ROBIN
  1977 Royal monopoly and private enterprise in the Atlantic trade: the case of Dahomey. *Journal of African History* 18:555–577.
LEVTZION, N.
  1973 *Ancient Ghana and Mali*. London: Methuen.
  1977 "The western Maghrib and Sudan," in *The Cambridge history of Africa*, volume three. Edited by R. Oliver, 331–462. Cambridge: Cambridge University Press.
LIEBENOW, J. GUS
  1969 *Liberia: the evolution of privilege*. Ithaca: Cornell University Press.
LLOYD, P. C.
  1968 The political development of West African kingdoms. *Journal of African History* 9:319–329.
LOFCHIE, M., *editor*
  1971 *The state of the nations: constraints on development in independent Africa*. Berkeley: University of California Press.

LOVEJOY, P., S. BAIER
1978   The role of the Wangara in the economic transformation of the Central Sudan in the fifteenth and sixteenth centuries. *Journal of African History* 19:173–193.
MIERS, S., I. KOPYTOFF, *editors*
1977   *Slavery in Africa: historical and anthropological perspectives.* Madison: University of Wisconsin Press.
OTTENBERG, P.
1965   "The Afikpo Ibo of eastern Nigeria," in *Peoples of Africa.* Edited by James L. Gibbs, Jr., 1–39. New York: Holt, Rinehart and Winston.
PERINBAM, B. MARIE
1974   Notes on dyula origins and nomenclature. *Bulletin de l'Institut Fondamental d'Afrique Noire* B36:676–690.
POLANYI, KARL
1957   "The economy as instituted process," in *Trade and markets in the early empires.* Edited by K. Polanyi, C. Arensberg, and H. Pearson, 243–269. Glencoe: Free Press.
POSNANSKY, M., R. Mc INTOSH
1976   New radiocarbon dates for northern and western Africa. *Journal of African History* 17:161–195.
RANGER, T. O.
1969   "African reactions to the imposition of colonial rule in East and Central Africa," in *Colonialism in Africa, 1870–1960,* volume one, *History and politics of colonialism, 1870–1914.* Edited by L. H. Gann and P. Duignan, 293–324. Cambridge: Cambridge University Press.
ROBINSON, R., J. GALLAGHER
1953   The imperialism of free trade. *Economic History Review* 4:1–15.
1961   *Africa and the Victorians.* London.
RODNEY, WALTER
1970   *A history of the Upper Guinea Coast, 1545–1800.* Oxford: Clarendon.
RYDER, A. F. C.
1969   *Benin and the Europeans, 1485–1897.* New York: Humanities Press.
SANNEH, LAMINE
1976   The origins of clericalism in West African Islam. *Journal of African History* 17:49–72.
SHAW, THURSTAN
1972   "The prehistory of West Africa," in *History of West Africa,* volume one. Edited by J. F. A. Ajayi and Michael Crowder, 33–77. New York: Columbia University Press.
VANSINA, J.
1961   *Oral tradition: a study in historical methodology.* Translated by H. M. Wright. London.
1971   Once upon a time: oral traditions as history in Africa. *Daedalus* 100:442–468.
WILKS, IVOR
1972   "The Mossi and Akan states, 1500–1800," in *History of West Africa,* volume one. Edited by J. F. A. Ajayi and Michael Crowder, 344–386. New York: Columbia University Press.
1975   *Asante in the nineteenth century.* Cambridge: Cambridge University Press.

WILLIS, J. R.
    1971   "The historiography of Islam in Africa: the last decade (1960–1970)."
               African Studies Review 14:403–424.
    1972   "The Western Sudan from the Moroccan invasion (1591) to the death
               of al-Mukhtar al-Kunti (1811)," in *History of West Africa*, volume one.
               Edited by J. F. A. Ajayi and Michael Crowder, 441–484. New York:
               Columbia University Press.

Prolegomena to the Study of the Culture History of the Igbo-speaking Peoples of Nigeria

A. E. AFIGBO

EARLY TRENDS IN THE STUDY OF IGBO CULTURE HISTORY

Speculation on the culture history of the Igbo-speaking peoples of Nigeria goes back at least to the last decades of the eighteenth century (Equiano 1794:25–28). It has at different times engaged the attention of both the Igbo themselves and some members of the British colonial service who served in Igboland. The Igbo are interested in the matter partly because, like any other group of people, they are anxious to discover their origin and reconstruct how they came to be what they are. More important, however, their experiences under colonialism and since Nigeria's independence have emphasized for them the reality of their group identity, and they want to anchor it in authenticated history. The increasing number of Igbo historians who have turned their attention to Igbo historical studies since the Biafran episode says something of the possible connection between this Igbo interest in their culture history and their crisis in modern times. Indeed, Olaudah Equiano, the first to show interest in Igbo culture history, probably did so because of the cultural crisis he faced first as a slave and then as an ex-slave in the West Indies and in Britain. On their side, British colonial officials became interested in Igbo culture history partly for scientific reasons, partly to provide explanations for certain mental, psychological, linguistic, and other traits which they considered peculiar to the Igbo, and partly to understand the Igbo and their society as a first step toward evolving suitable institutions for governing them.

Until about the middle of the 1940's, the two groups of theorists were agreed on their methods and conclusions if not always on their aims. As to method, they depended on "culture-trait chasing" — isolating those

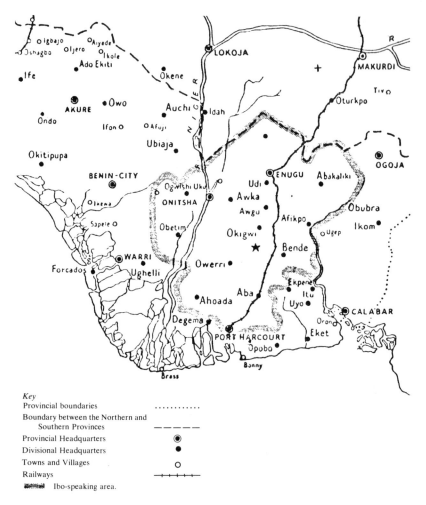

Key
Provincial boundaries ....
Boundary between the Northern and
    Southern Provinces ------
Provincial Headquarters ◉
Divisional Headquarters ●
Towns and Villages ○
Railways ++++++
▥▥ Ibo-speaking area.

Figure 1.   Map of Igboland and the Niger delta region. *Source*: M. M. Green (1947),
Igbo village affairs. London: Sidgwick and Jackson. *Scale*: 1 inch to 47.35 miles

aspects of Igbo culture which they believed gave some indication of the
origin either of the people or of their culture or both. In this exercise such
traits as circumcision, the manner of naming children, sentence structure
and similarity in word sounds, dual organization, religion in general and
sun worship in particular, ritual symbolism, and so on have been frequently used. Generally both groups have come to the conclusion either
that the Igbo came from the Near East or that their culture evolved under
the influence of a small elite of culture carriers from there. Two places
were usually favored — Egypt and the Holy Land.

Basing his argument on the fact that the Igbo practice circumcision, name their children after some special event or experience, and insist on the seclusion and purification of women after childbirth, Equiano (1794:25–28) concluded that the Igbo were most likely one of the lost tribes of Israel. Basden (1912), pointing to certain constructions found in the Igbo language and what he considered the deep religious feeling of the people, propagated the view that Igbo culture probably evolved under the impact of the Levitical Code. Impressed by what he considered the superior intelligence of the Aro Igbo and by their religious system and rituals, Palmer (1921, 1928) contended that they carried Hamitic blood in their veins and that it was under their leadership that the "higher" aspects of Igbo culture had evolved. Similarly, impressed by Igbo sunworship and by the feature of dual organization in their social structure, Jeffreys (1946, 1951, 1954, 1956) held that the Igbo at some stage in the past had come under Egyptian influence, the carriers of this influence probably being the Nri of Awka in Northern Igboland.

With regard to aims, both the Igbo and the British colonial elite hoped, through the use of this "Oriental hypothesis," to unravel the mystery of the Igbo past, but beyond this the two groups were not in agreement. Thus, while the Igbo would assert that they were originally Hebrews or Egyptians (Ike 1951:1–4; Mathews 1927), their British counterparts went no farther than to assert that the Igbo had come under the influence of either the ancient Egyptians or the Jews. This was no mere verbal quibble. Equiano, the first Igbo to claim an Eastern origin for his people, was primarily concerned with the problem of the dismal lot of the black man *vis-à-vis* the white man, his utter impotence in the face of Europe, his enslavement and exploitation, his humiliation in slavery, his misery and poverty. Had this always been, and would it always be, the case? In short, had Equiano's kinsmen, the Igbo, the inborn ability to rise to the level of Europe? It was partly in affirmative answer to this question that Equiano claimed for his people a Jewish ancestry. The Igbo, Equiano would seem to say, were originally a branch of the Jews, whose culture gave rise to the Christianity which later civilized "barbarous" Europe.

The pseudo-scientific racial theories prominent in the colonial period made their impact on the Igbo in two ways. In the first place, colonialism was a severe humiliation for the Igbo. It also gave them Western education, which made them capable of accepting the myths about the cultural similarities between them and the peoples of the Near East. To show that they had not always been as "despicable" as the colonialists found them, they started laying claim to an Eastern origin on the basis of such cultural similarities. Since at this time history taught that the East was the civilizer of mankind, the Igbo, through the claim to Eastern origin, came to assign themselves a higher place in the history of the world than they would assign to their British masters.

Nor was that all, for the Oriental hypothesis has continued to wax

308   A. E. AFIGBO

strong among the Igbo. Under colonial rule, the Igbo came to see all the
world as a fair field for business and spread out in large numbers as
traders, mission agents, government officials, migrant farmers, and so on.
The allegedly "aggressive" Igbo approach to business soon won them the
deep-seated distrust and hatred of their more easygoing Nigerian neighbors. Consequently, they became the victims of communal riots, or
threats of them, wherever they went in Nigeria. Publicists and others soon
started drawing parallels between Igbo business acumen and their suffer-
ings at the hands of other Nigerian ethnic nationalities, on the one hand,
and the Jewish experience throughout history, on the other. Between
1967 and 1970, embattled Biafra provided the perfect parallel to the
state of Israel surrounded by hostile Arab nations. The Igbo not only
made this comparison themselves, but also believed in it. They came to
hope that they would weather the storm. Thus there have been many
enlightened Igbo to whom the claim to Eastern origin is no mere history
or the "Oriental mirage" of S. Reinach, but an ideology for group survival.

In the same manner, the application of the Oriental hypothesis to Igbo
cultural history by colonial officials had a propagandistic side to it. These
men refused to concede that the Igbo cultural traits which they traced to
the East could indicate that the Igbo came from there. To do so would, in
the intellectual climate of the time, have been to assign this despised
colonial people a higher place on the world tree of culture than the
colonial masters would have found convenient. Instead, the colonial
theorists claimed that these traits showed that the Igbo had once been
under Egyptian or Jewish cultural dominance. Implicit in this claim was
the idea, not hitherto emphasized by anyone, that British colonialism was
not a radical departure from the past, but in some sense a continuation of
the cultural education of the Igbo which had been started long ago by the
Egyptians. In this regard it is revealing that the Oriental hypothesis was
imported as an explanation of Igbo history in the 1920's, when the
colonial government was experiencing great difficulty in the administration of the Igbo. It was in this situation that it came to be argued first that
Igboland had once been under Egyptian influence, second that the spread
of Egyptian culture in Igboland was the work of a small elite who, after
interbreeding with the people, became the Nri and the Aro of today, and
third that if the British really wanted to rule the Igbo "indirectly," then
they had to do so through the Nri and the Aro (Afigbo 1965).

By the late 1930's, the Oriental hypothesis had been argued out *ad
nauseam* and abandoned, since no amount of research, not even
Mathews's at Arochukwu and Jeffreys's at Awka, could uncover solid
historical or anthropological evidence in its support. C. K. Meek, the
government anthropologist who had coordinated the research into this
and related issues in Igboland, closed the debate as far as the government
was concerned when he warned (1937:5) that

no purpose would be served by engaging in speculations about ancient cultural contacts, such as that the prevalence of sun-worship, of forms of mummification, and of dual organization points to some distant connection with Ancient Egypt. As far back as we can see within historic times the bulk of the Igbo peoples appear to have lived an isolated existence.

This warning was all the more significant in that Meek's work among the Jukun had been largely responsible for the extension of the Oriental hypothesis to Igbo culture history. Unofficially and privately, though, Jeffreys continued to push the hypothesis through his publications on Igbo ethnography.

By 1940, then, the Oriental hypothesis was to all intents and purposes dead as a serious explanation of Igbo culture history. In fact, one could go so far as to say that because of the futility of the speculations and researchers of the 1920's and 1930's on this matter, the ideologues and theorists of the colonial government lost interest in the matter of charting the course of Igbo culture history. Scholars such as G. I. Jones, who have continued to write in depth on the Igbo and who constitute links with the earlier period, have given up attempts to find a solution to the problem of origins. Instead, they have focused their energies upon the ethnographic description of the Igbo people. Jones's reticence, in particular, may be due not so much to the failure of the earlier efforts as to his functional approach, which emphasizes understanding societies as they are without worrying overmuch about how they came to be.

THE NEED FOR A NEW BEGINNING

Since 1940, therefore, we have been without a general explanation of Igbo culture history. It may be that what befell the efforts of those who were ambitious enough to seek such an explanation in the past should constitute a warning against any such efforts now, but then, as the Igbo say, *anagh ekworo mgbagbu ghara ogu* [you do not stop waging necessary wars because men get shot]. In any case, we now know a little more than the men of the 1920's and 1930's did about the evolution of West African societies in general, and archaeological, anthropological, and historical researches in Igboland have unearthed a few more facts then were known in those days. As Armstrong (1966:11) has cogently observed, "West African studies have come quite some distance since Frobenius and Meek wrote their principal works, and if newer materials now available seem still too patchy to support wide-ranging speculation, still we may hope that our thinking today stands on a more solid foundation than it did formerly." Furthermore, we can proudly claim that we are free of many of the prejudices which made it difficult for the theorists of those days to be guided mainly by the facts before them.

In place of the Oriental hypothesis, I shall try to put forward here an explanation of how Igbo culture evolved based largely on the study of the interaction between the Igbo and their environment. This approach derives from a number of established assumptions. The first is that all human societies have undergone continuous changes. Some of this change is perceptible, while some can only be recognized after it has occurred; some is induced by external forces and some by processes internal to the social organism in question. The second assumption is the fact that most West African societies are very ancient indeed, infinitely more ancient than the theorists of the colonial period ever thought (Armstrong 1960). One implication of this is that even if external influences impinged on these parts as is suggested, they did not impinge on a cultural vacuum. Therefore, a simple explanation of Igbo cultural evolution in terms of Egyptian or European influence alone would miss the point.

The part which interaction between a people and its environment plays in cultural evolution has long been recognized. Some scholars have even used it, to the exclusion of diffusion, to explain the rise of civilizations. Applying this theory to the study of Yoruba culture, Ojo (1966:269–273) came to the conclusion that recognition of the role of environment in Yoruba culture urges one "to look more towards the country rather than to the outside world for the causes and sources of its high cultural development." In his view, it was because the Yoruba were able to come to terms with their environment that "they produced enough food to maintain large urban centers [and] a pattern of settlements . . . on which the prohibitive and permissive influences of the environment are boldly written." Earlier scholars, he maintained, "sought outside influence [as an explanation for Yoruba culture] to a large extent because they overlooked, or could not appreciate, the relationships between the environment and the culture of the people."

Few of those who have considered the issue of the evolution of Igbo culture have fully taken into account this interaction. Among those few is Jones (1945, 1961), who has sought to explain Igbo village planning, at least with respect to the social structure of the Central and Northeastern Igbo, in terms of ecology. As already mentioned, however, Jones has not yet built up a general theory of Igbo culture history through elaborating on this concept. While it will be argued here that the interaction between the Igbo and their environment holds the key to an understanding of Igbo cultural development, this must not be seen as a surrender to geographic determinism. In any case, appropriate emphasis will be laid on the part which external influences have played in this process.

RECENT ARCHAEOLOGICAL AND LINGUISTIC RESEARCH

Once we set aside the claims to an Eastern origin discussed above, we discover that Igbo oral traditions offer little help to the serious scholar investigating Igbo culture history. The research problem here centers on the distillation of fact from myth. When these traditions are not pre-occupied with describing those long-distance migrations which led to the Igbo settlement of the area they now inhabit, they are content to assert either that the ancestors of the Igbo were sent down from heaven by Chukwu (the Igbo supreme god) or that they sprang from the ground. In these circumstances we have to base any opinions we express on the matter of origins on the findings of other disciplines. Interpreting the views of certain scholars, one would place the Igbo homeland somewhere farther north, probably in the region of the Niger–Benue confluence (Henderson 1972:39). According to linguists, it seems likely that speakers of the member languages of the Kwa subfamily, of which Igbo is one, separated from their ancestral stock in that region and moved out to occupy their present locations. Many members of the subfamily are found in Nigeria. A study of their artistic traditions has led art historians to draw attention to the likely primacy of the general area of the Niger–Benue confluence in the early history of these peoples (Rubin 1971). For now, therefore, one can at least subscribe to the conclusion of Karmon (1966:28–29) that the Igbo probably originated somewhere farther north than their present habitat, in the sub-Guinean zone of the Middle Belt region of Nigeria, where they multiplied rather rapidly before invading the forest region in which they then made their home.

Another issue is when did the Igbo begin to emerge as a distinct people. Here again one is reduced to sophisticated guesswork until archaeological research among these people makes sufficient progress to be called to our aid. Armstrong (1962:284; 1964:22–23), using glottochronological evidence, has suggested that the members of the Kwa subfamily started separating from their ancestral stock between 5,000 and 6,000 years ago. This estimate has been greeted with skepticism in a few quarters (Henderson 1972:39), but by and large scholars are becoming more and more impressed with the antiquity of the societies concerned and with their stability over the centuries. In the light of other cultural data, Armstrong's estimate may not be far off the mark. On the strength of what evidence we now have, one can say with reasonable confidence that the upper limit for the emergence of the Igbo as a distinct people with a characteristic language is about 6,000 years ago. This conclusion would appear to be reinforced by the findings of preliminary archaeological research in Igboland. Hartle's (1967) work there has shown that Igboland was occupied by the early Neolithic. Whether occupation has been continuous or not remains to be established. The results of some test excavations at Nsukka (Northern Igboland) would seem to reveal, however, a degree of ethnographic continuity in the area such as could suggest that the ancestors of the Igbo were already living in parts of present-day Igboland at least by the third millennium B.C. (Hartle 1967). Other data — the character of Igbo traditions of origin, the extent to which the Igbo succeeded in transforming their environment using only simple tools, deductions that might be made from the age and maturity of the Igbo-Ukwu culture — lend support to the conclusion that Igbo origins probably goes back 6,000 years.

THE PRIMACY OF THE NORTHERN IGBO PLATEAU

Apart from looking toward the general area of the Niger–Benue confluence for the origin of the Igbo and seeing Igbo culture history as spanning at least 6,000 years, the historian of Igbo culture has reason to suspect that the Northern Igbo area occupies a position of the first importance in the story of the emergence of Igbo culture. From all the available data it seems to have been the first place to be settled by the Igbo after they came into the forest; it was apparently there that they evolved a distinct culture and moved out to occupy the other areas they now inhabit.

What, one may ask, are the grounds for these suggestions? First, there is the fact that among Northern Igbo communities the investigator rarely comes across traditions of movement from any area outside this plateau region. In fact, most of the communities claim to have moved in from only a short distance away. This feature of the Northern Igbo traditions cannot be explained entirely by the lack of centralized institutions around which such traditions could be preserved. The priest-kingship of Nri was in fact one such institution, and the Nri, like many other Northern Igbo communities, have retained many other traditions about their past. Thus, one is led to suspect that Igbo settlement of this region was very ancient, in any case more ancient than that of any other part of Igboland. In this connection it is relevant that most other Igbo groups claim that their ancestors originally lived on the Northern Igbo plateau before moving out in search of unoccupied land. As will be shown later, most of the movements would appear to have originated from the Nri-Awka and Orlu areas. This, in any case, is the Igbo explanation, uncovered within a few years of British penetration of the Igbo heartland, for the eminence of Nri and Amaigbo (Orlu) amongst them (Leonard 1906:11–47). Starting from this and analyzing the claims of descent from the Awka-Orlu axis, Jones (1963:30) has produced a pattern of Igbo dispersal within the area they now occupy.

Another reason for suggesting the primacy of the Northern Igbo plateau in the history of Igbo culture is ecological. Most of the authorities who have considered this matter, including Karmon (1966:28–29), Buchanan and Pugh (1969:35), Jones and Mulhall (1949:11), Allison (1962), and many others are in general agreement that what is now Igboland originally supported tropical rain-forest vegetation. As a consequence of intensive and extended human use, this primordial vegetal cover has been reduced to "derived savanna" and palm bush. In explaining this deterioration, which has been accompanied by soil exhaustion, a number of writers have emphasized the density of population, which has been compared to that of the Nile Valley (Karmon 1966:5; Flint 1966:63), the poor means of soil conservation, and so on. We must also take into account, however, the length of time during which the Igbo have lived in and exploited this environment. The importance of this appears all the more obvious when it is remembered that the technology at the disposal of the Igbo remained until very recently at a relatively primitive stage. Since of all parts of Igboland the Northern Igbo area has been the most denuded of its vegetal cover, it would seem to follow that it has been under continuous Igbo occupation for a longer period than the other parts.

One can also draw some supporting evidence from the pattern of Igbo settlement. After an exhaustive study of this topic, Karmon came to the conclusion that the Igbo in general have tended to avoid watercourses, the eroded surfaces of slopes, and clayey soils, which tend to become waterlogged. This settlement habit is induced not by the search for fertile soils, but by considerations of ease of communication with parent communities and of easy farming. The soil in watercourses and in low-lying areas tends to be difficult to farm. Not only is it heavy, but the forest undergrowth does not burn easily after the bush has been cleared for planting. One may also add health considerations to the reasons for avoiding such sites; the Igbo tend to abandon homesteads which have become "cold" by being overgrown with trees.

The Northern Igbo area is the most elevated region of Igboland. Around it are relatively low-lying plains and river valleys which still support rather dense forests and 6,000 years ago would have supported even denser ones. The population density on these plains is still far below what obtains on the plateau. The Cross River plains are seriously underpopulated, and traditions indicate that they are an area of late Igbo settlement. If the Igbo until lately have resisted the settlement in large numbers of these low-lying areas, it becomes easy to see why they would have settled first on the Northern Igbo plateau; it was likely to have been drier and less densely covered by forest than the surrounding regions.

THE SEQUENCE OF IGBO DISPERSAL

The plateau lands now occupied by the Northern Igbo would thus appear to have been the first part of Igboland to be settled. An analysis of the oral traditions of most of the other Igbo groups reveals that after some time this region came under severe population pressure. One result of this was that hard-pressed groups left in search of unoccupied lands to the south, west, and southeast. The movement to the south of the ancestors of some of the present-day Southern Igbo (the Uratta, Ikwerre, Etche, Asa, and Ndoki) would appear to have been the earliest of these movements. It may be that these peoples were in the vanguard of the Igbo migration into the forest and, moving along the northern plateau, had been pushed into the southern plains by those behind them. In any case, like their Northern brothers, they no longer have any traditions of movement from anywhere outside their immediate area.

We would appear, however, to be on surer ground when we come to consider the settlement of the Western, Isuama, and Northeastern Igbo areas, for their movements still survive in the traditions of these peoples. An analysis of these would indicate that the Western Igbo left the Nri-Awka area and crossed the humid and waterlogged Anambara-Niger floodplain to occupy the uplands stretching from Asaba to Agbor. On running into the Edo to the west, the tip of this migration would appear to have been blunted. One result of this was the settlement of the Southern Ika and the Riverain Igbo area around Aboh. Another result was that some of the groups which had gone farthest west retraced their steps eastward, some of them, in fact, recrossing the Niger to settle at Onitsha. Among those involved in this recoil were the Umuezechima, and it is their recoil from Edo pressure and the subsequent arrival of some non-Igbo refugees from the *oba* of Benin's rule that survive in the traditions of some Western Igbo communities in the form of origin legends deriving them from Benin or, in any case, from the domain of the *oba*.

Meanwhile, another group of migrants had moved eastward from the Orlu area — their traditions in fact say from Amaigbo [the "street" or ritual "square" of the Igbo] — to give rise to the Isuama (a term sometimes used to include the Eastern Igbo and the Ngwa as well as those designated Isuama by Forde and Jones [1950:35]). *Isuama* means "the Isu who had gone abroad" (that is, "taken to the streets") and was applied to these Igbo because they had left their home, Isu (in Orlu), in search of unoccupied lands. According to the traditions also, it would appear that this people later ran into the Ibibio and other Cross River peoples and curved north to settle the region now occupied by the Northeastern Igbo or Ogu-Ukwu.

A question which arises is how one is to date these movements. At present there is no direct evidence to make it possible to suggest a precise chronology. It may be that archaeology will come to our aid in the future, but meanwhile it is necessary to consider the following points. First, the movements out of the Awka and Orlu uplands probably took place in about the same period and in response to the crisis of population pressure induced by increased mastery of the environment through agriculture and iron technology. Secondly, the westward expansion must have taken place before the emergence of the aggressive and expansionist Bini empire to the west; otherwise it is difficult to imagine how the fragmented Igbo could have moved as far west of the Niger as they did. In fact, it is probable that the western border of Igboland was farther west than it has been in recent times. Thirdly, it was more than likely the same population pressure which inspired the social consolidation which made possible the rise of the priest-kingship of Nri with which the Igbo-Ukwu culture has been associated.

The Bini monarchy is dated to about the thirteenth century. One can thus suggest that Igbo expansion westward had by and large been completed by approximately that date. This in turn suggests that the movement must have commenced several centuries earlier. Furthermore, the migration most likely did not take place in a single wave. The Igbo-Ukwu culture has been dated to the ninth century A.D. and must have taken centuries to attain the level of sophistication and wealth associated with it. Also, it was an Iron Age culture, and the Iron Age in West Africa has been dated to not earlier than 500 B.C. This would mean, on present reckoning, that the Igbo-Ukwu culture arose from about 500 B.C. If we are correct in asserting that it was probably the same population pressure that stimulated the Igbo-Ukwu culture and led to the migrations, then we can place the migrations between 500 B.C. and A.D. 500.

It is of course possible that archaeological research could push the Iron Age farther back, especially if it could be established that Negro Africa did not borrow the secret of working iron from the Hamites as Hambly (1935:405–407) has suggested. If this were to happen, it would lead to a revision of the date at which this population pressure would have become sufficient to precipitate the rise of Igbo-Ukwu and the migrations. Jones and Mulhall (1949:13) have suggested, without giving any reasons, that the Northeastern Igbo area, probably the last region of Igbo settlement, was not settled until about the sixteenth century. Working from the dates suggested above, I am inclined to the view that this last area to be settled by the Igbo was occupied much earlier than this.

AGRICULTURE AND IGBO SOCIETY

The origin and spread of agriculture in West Africa is as yet an unresolved problem. Thus, assuming that the Igbo were already in Igboland by the third millennium B.C., it is impossible to say whether they were by that time practicing agriculture or were still hunter-gatherers. From the study of Northern Igbo traditions, however, especially those of the Nri, there is little doubt about the fact that it was cultivation and then the working of iron that enabled the Igbo to master their environment and evolve advanced social and cultural patterns. Thus it is with the coming of cultivation that Igbo tradition associates the priest-kingship of Nri, the Igbo staff of office and symbol of right conduct (*ofo*), Igbo facial marks (*ichi*), the four-day week (*izu*), the institution of slavery, and the rise of trade. The role of agriculture in the development of Igbo culture is a very large issue which has not yet received the attention it deserves. We can do little more than scratch the surface of the problem here.

Largely because of agriculture, land (*ala*) more or less became the center of Igbo existence. It was for them not only the most important economic asset, but also the most vital and the most active spirit force in their lives. As an economic factor it influenced Igbo sociopolitical evolution. Those communities which were able to work out some arrangement for the exploitation of the land on which they lived became "brothers," and each group of "brothers," by functioning as a landowning, land-defending, and land-seizing federation, became a political unit. Since it was as much as the Igbo could do to work out such arrangements at the level of the village-group, the village-group became the largest political unit. Any grouping, such as the clan (Jones's "tribe"), which did not have land-administering functions failed to become a political unit in the normal sense. Neighboring communities which failed to work out an agreement for the exploitation of land never became "brothers" and therefore never became members of the same polity.

Land not only influenced the evolution of Igbo sociopolitical units, but also helped to determine their settlement patterns. Here two considerations were paramount. The first was to ensure that the land-using activities of the members of a political federation did not clash. The second was to ensure that each member had a definite portion of land to exploit and to defend against alien encroachment. The result was that among most Igbo the member villages of a village-group settled in a circle around their common market or ritual square, with their faces to the group center and their backs to the farmlands. Each village had usufructuary rights to the lands around its homestead and to the stretch of uninhabited land lying directly beyond the homestead (Jones 1961:125). In this way all the land under exploitation by a village was within easy reach, and the occasions for clashes between "brothers" were drastically reduced.

Beyond that, because it was the key factor in agriculture, the premier Igbo occupation, land came to occupy a very prominent place in Igbo religion and cosmology. It was worshipped, and it was a hard taskmistress which, on provocation, could cause the harvests to fail and men to die prematurely — for the Igbo two of the worst disasters imaginable. It imposed innumerable laws and taboos to guide conduct between man and man and between man and itself. The transgression of any of these rules, known as *omenala* [conduct sanctioned by the land], was promptly punished. In this way *omenala* came to be the highest law. It was distinguished from, and superior to, *iwu*, rules made by man, the transgression of which involved no offense to *ala* and the ancestors and implied no moral lapse. *Ala* was thus the guardian of Igbo morality.

The Nri of the Northern Igbo achieved ascendancy in most of Igboland by representing themselves as a people that enjoyed a special relationship with *ala*. Not only could they reveal and declare the wishes of *ala*, but also they could intercede between it and any person or community that broke its injunctions and remove the pollution (*nso*) arising from such transgression (Thomas 1914:11; Leonard 1906:34–39; Talbot 1926:592–298). This privileged position of the Nri with regard to *ala*, the premier active deity of the Igbo, serves to strengthen the suggestion that Igbo culture originated in the Northern Igbo area. Onwuejeogwu (1972), who has carried out extensive researches into this matter, has even expressed the opinion that it was the Nri who originated the concept of *ala* as a spirit force and propogated it in the rest of Igboland. If this is so, then it could indeed be argued that they synthesized Igbo culture.

This matter of the role of agriculture in determining Igbo culture could be pursued further to show how agriculture determined Igbo technology and calendar, how the food crops determined Igbo dietary habits and beliefs, or how the veneration of agricultural spirits like Njoku or Ifejioku (the yam spirit) conditioned aspects of the life and world view of the Igbo. What should be pointed out here, however, is that, considering our argument that Northern Igboland was the first part of Igboland to be settled and that the rest was colonized from there, it can be concluded that this agricultural civilization first penetrated the Northern Igbo plateau. Thus Igbo civilization, would appear to have been nurtured on the Northern Igbo plateau, most likely in the Awka-Orlu axis.

THE RISE OF THE COMMERCIAL SIDE OF IGBO CULTURE

We may never know for certain how trade and marketing developed in Igbo culture. Hodder and Ukwu (1969:126–159) have expressed the view that they probably developed out of the institution of the Igbo rest day, but one suspects that here we are entering a circle as vicious as that formed by the question of the chicken and the egg. I am inclined to the view that trade and marketing in Igbo culture arose out of the tradition of reciprocal gift exchanges, through which individuals and groups got rid of what they had in excess and obtained commodities that they lacked. From here it would have been but a short step to trade by barter and from the latter to full-fledged commercial exchange based on some currency such as salt or pieces of iron.

Northern Igbo traditions, however, are quite definite on the point that trade, markets, and marketing were institutionalized by the Igbo high god, Chukwu. He sent four heavenly fishmongers who gave their names — Eke, Orie, Afo, and Nkwo — to the four days of the Igbo week, established markets, and sold fish. The Northern Igbo area lacks rivers and ponds. Thus from earliest times fish was a delicacy, as it could only be obtained from the Niger and Anambara Rivers to the west, from the Cross River to the east, or, more distant still from the Ijo of the delta. The Northern Igbo legend regarding the origin of markets would thus seem to emphasize the point made above, that trade in Igbo culture originated in the exchange of surplus goods for goods in short supply. This point is further emphasized in another legend regarding the origin of cultivated crops. According to this story, after Nri had obtained yams, cocoyams, the oil palm, and the breadfruit from Chukwu, the neighboring peoples brought him livestock and other forms of wealth in exchange for food crops. This, in other words, was barter.

There are deductions to be drawn from ecological data to support this theory. Heavy exploitation of the Northern Igbo area led to destruction of its vegetation and deterioration of the quality of its soil. In this situation, agriculture was incapable of meeting all the food needs of the people, and they responded by taking up other professions — trade, smithery, medicine, the running of oracles, and so on. In other words, they developed specialties which they peddled among the other Igbo groups whose soils could still support profitable agriculture. In this regard it is noteworthy that most of the traders and other specialists of Igboland, such as the Awka, Aro, Nkwerre, Abiriba, and Nri, live on the Northern Igbo plateau and its southeasterly extension through Bende to Arochukwu (Harris 1942; Henderson 1972:36–37). This is precisely that part of Igboland in which agriculture started failing early in the people's history. Thus regional trade in Igboland developed in part out of the growing ecological differentiation between the Northern Igbo area and the plains and uplands surrounding it.

Another factor was the differential distribution of essential mineral deposits in Igboland. The Northern Igbo plateau and its extension to Bende are rich in iron ore deposits, and it was here that smelting and ironworking in Igboland were most highly developed. The iron tools and implements produced on the plateau were in great demand all over Igboland and beyond. On the other hand, in the northeastern Igbo area there are brine springs and lead deposits which would appear to have been exploited from very early times (Talbot 1926). There seems to have been a demand for lead among the smiths of the Northern Igbo area (Onwuejeogwu 1972), while salt was in demand throughout Igboland.

Though Igbo needs for salt could not have been met entirely from the Northeastern Igbo springs, most of it was probably met from there until lately. The movement of these minerals must have helped to stimulate the further development of an exchange economy among the Igbo. Thus such development did not have to wait for the contact with Europe in the sixteenth century.

In fact, a study of the Igbo-Ukwu finds by Shaw (1970) would seem to reveal that by the ninth century A.D. Igboland was already engaged in long- and short-range exchange. Long-range exchange brought in such items as the horse, bronze, and carnelian beads from markets in the Sudan and beyond. Short-range or regional exchange helped to assemble the slaves and ivory which paid for these luxury goods, as well as to collect the worked bronze. According to Shaw, it is unlikely that all the bronze was cast at Igbo-Ukwu, though its distinctive style indicates that it was cast east of the Niger and south of the Benue. The assembling of all those masterpieces from the master craftsmen of the period would suggest a well-developed network of regional trade. The further development of this trading network in subsequent centuries has been studied in some detail and with success by Northrup (1972) and need not be recounted here.

THE CONTRIBUTION OF NEIGHBORING PEOPLES

Though it must be emphasized that Igbo culture resulted from the working of the Igbo spirit or genius on its environment, it must not be forgotten that the Igbo did not live in isolation from their neighbors. On the contrary, the available evidence shows that the Igbo were closely linked to other ethnic groups whom they influenced and who influenced them in turn. Even though the influence of these neighbors, especially that of the Bini and Igala, has been overemphasized by Meek (1937:4–5), Jeffreys (1956), Shelton (1921), and others, it is still to be studied in detail with a view to ascertaining its proper role in Igbo culture history. Even before that is done, however, the following observations based on a reinterpretation of the existing evidence are worthy of note.

Of all the neighbors of the Igbo, the Edo kingdom of Benin and the Igala state of Idah would appear to have had the most far-reaching impact on the evolution of Igbo culture. The influence of Benin was most felt in the Western Igbo area — the riverain region around Aboh and Onitsha. Benin influence was largely political and can be seen in the village monarchies which exist all through this area. It is also seen in the character of the title systems and in the names of some of the titles. Idah influence was mainly limited to the Nsukka and Anambara areas, though some of it penetrated to the southern Riverain Igbo. Though it would appear to have been pushed at the point of the sword like that of Benin, it did not leave as obvious an impact on the political systems of the Nsukka and Anambara Igbo. It would appear, however, to have influenced their speech and their material culture.

The impact of the Ibibio, Ijo, and Cross River peoples on the Igbo would appear to have been less dramatic; certainly it has not been proclaimed as loudly. Here the Igbo found themselves in contact with peoples who were as politically fragmented as they were and who therefore could not subject them to military terrorism. Consequently, whatever influence they had on Igbo development would appear to have come about more by the informal processes of acculturation than by enforced imposition. Their impact on the Igbo may be best seen in the secret societies and age-grade organizations of the Eastern and Ngwa Igbo, among whom these institutions are more highly evolved than among their brothers farther west and north. The Eastern and Ngwa Igbo also borrowed from their non-Igbo neighbors the practice of headhunting.

Apart from the character and extent of this influence, it was with a more or less mature Igbo culture that each of these neighboring peoples came into contact. Thus Igbo-Ukwu flourished at a time when, in the words of Willett (1967:175), Idah "probably had nothing whatever to do with" it. In any case, the influence of Idah and Benin was asserted after the fourteenth century, by which time Igbo dispersal from the Northern Igbo area was probably already completed. Furthermore, as already observed, it is likely that when the migrants left the Awka-Orlu axis they carried with them the basic ingredients of Igbo culture. Thus the impact of neighboring peoples is most accurately seen as leading to minor adjustments in the basically Igbo way of life, rather than as stimulating the development of that culture in the first instance.

THE RESULTS OF EUROPEAN IMPACT

Igboland must have felt, though faintly at first, the impact of Europe from about the sixteenth century. In time, the contact with Europe, which remained indirect until the nineteenth century, boiled down to a commercial relationship in which the Igbo exported some of their population in return for certain European goods. What contribution this commerce made to the evolution of Igbo culture is still a matter for argument and conjecture, although several scholars have recently undertaken this study.

For much of the colonial period and after, it was fashionable to claim that the European impact — the slave trade in particular — retarded the political and social evolution of the Igbo. The argument was that as a densely populated area which was also politically and militarily weak,

Igboland was devastated by slave raiders from the coast, Benin, and Idah in the attempt to supply the European slavers. This was said to have left the people socially and politically fragmented and morally debased. According to Basden (1938:xiv–xx), these devastations were so thoroughgoing that, by the time European rule was imposed, in at least the southern parts of Igboland there was no indigenous culture to speak of.

At the same time, however, it was maintained, rather illogically, that the European impact encouraged the closer integration of Igbo society in the sense that it instigated the rise of the Aro oligarchy, believed to have monopolized the trade and oracle business in Igboland and sometimes beyond (Mathews 1926). So much was it believed that Aro activities knit Igboland together that some people started talking about an Aro empire and suggesting that the "difficult" Igbo be ruled through the Aro (Grier 1923; Ormsby-Gore 1926). More recently it has been suggested by Ottenberg (1961:222) that the European impact brought about a dramatic expansion of Igbo population, thus making it possible for them to absorb many of their neighbors:

One might hypothesize, for example, that before the European slave trade Ibo society was small in geographic area and that numerous cultural groups speaking different languages lived side by side with Ibo much as there is a diversity of peoples in the Obubra area today. The European slave trade led to a rapid rise in population in the area. . . . The Ibo spread and absorbed surrounding groups. . . .

The truth, however, is that it is not likely that European contact in this period had the momentous impact, good or ill, on the evolution of Igbo culture that is so often attributed to it. I would argue that it was neither a retarding nor an accelerating factor. I suggest that by the sixteenth century Igbo society was already too ancient and too mature to be either easily fractured or easily galvanized into revolutionary developmental effort by a contact so indirect and so diffused as that with the European slavers along the coast. The activities associated with such oligarchies as the Aro, Awka, Abiriba, Nkwerre, Nri, and so on, were such as were already being pursued in Igboland before the European onslaught. The rise of these oligarchies, therefore, could not have been instigated by the European trade, however much it might have broadened their business horizon. Furthermore, the thesis that the introduction of New World crops led to a spectacular expansion of Igbo population (Ottenberg 1961:222) must have arisen from an underestimation of the efficiency of pre-European Igbo agriculture as well as from unfamiliarity with the fact that many of these crops did not establish themselves firmly in Igboland before the nineteenth century.

The question of the impact of the slave trade on Igbo society will long be debated. Investigations into the matter by Talbot (Talbot and Mulhall 1962:1–9), Jones (Jones and Mulhall 1949:11), and the present writer suggest that socially destructive raiding played a relatively small part in the slave-recruiting business in Igboland. One point not strongly emphasized in the past is that density of population remained the great shield of the Igbo against some of the worst effects of the slave trade. For one thing, it meant that Igboland was too resilient for the tiny Ijo communities to overrun. The Ijo were powerful on the creeks, where their war canoes could operate, but the Igbo lived beyond the creeks. For another, the density of Igbo population meant that without unduly stretching themselves the Igbo could supply nearly as many slaves as the city-states and the European slavers wanted. In fact it would appear they tended to supply many more, for there is evidence that the Igbo slave populations of these city-states in time became so large as to threaten the identity of the Ijo. This made it necessary for the latter to design special institutions and usages for absorbing the slaves (Horton 1966).

For the rest, European impact has to be seen largely in terms of flimsy and perishable wares (consumer goods) which carried no dynamics for social change and left no permanent structures, even in the form of industries. The guns and gunpowder which could have been used to revolutionize warfare and politics were not put to that use in Igboland. Why this is so no one yet knows. One can, however, suggest that by the time quantities of European firearms penetrated the Igbo area, the alignments of the various village-groups had long since been worked out and boundaries demarcated. This would mean that the gun came too late to be of use to the Igbo in the vital process of boundary definition. This comes back to the suggestion made earlier that Igbo culture had already attained maturity by the time the Europeans established a foothold in Nigeria. Guns were used in Igbo wars, but much less frequently than matchets and cudgels. The major social significance of the gun was perhaps as a symbol of manhood and material success. In most districts anybody who attained adulthood felt that he must – in addition to doing such things as entering a secret society and marrying — purchase a gun and a hunting knife (*obejili*) with which to adorn himself on ceremonial occasions.

SUMMARY

The Oriental hypothesis, which was once used to explain the evolution of Igbo culture, tells us nothing about actual history, though it may be an attractive ideology to satisfy nonhistorical needs. On the other hand, a study of the interaction between the Igbo and their environment and between them and their neighbors throws much welcome light on Igbo cultural history. It suggests that after separation from their Kwa brothers somewhere around the Niger-Benue confluence, the Igbo settled first on the Northern Igbo plateau, where, under the impact of the agricultural and iron revolutions, they evolved their characteristic culture. Under pressure of population, some of them left the plateau for the plains and uplands, where they developed along their own lines while retaining the basic Igbo speech and culture. This dispersal brought the Igbo into contact with the Edo, Ijo, Ibibio, and other peoples, from whom they borrowed certain social and political institutions, items of material culture, and ideas. Regional trade developed early in Igbo culture, partly because of the failure of agriculture on the northern plateau and partly because of the differential distribution of mineral resources. When indirect contact was established with Europeans in the sixteenth century or so, Igbo society was mature enough to meet the demands arising from this contact without departing radically from its established ways. As a result, the Igbo culture which the British encountered in the nineteenth century was, to a greater extent than has hitherto been thought possible, the result of the working of Igbo genius on its native environment.

REFERENCES

AFIGBO, A. E.
  1965 Herbert Richmond Palmer and indirect rule in eastern Nigeria. *Journal of the Historical Society of Nigeria* 3:295–312.
ALLISON, P. A.
  1962 Historical inferences to be drawn from the effect of human settlement on the vegetation of Africa. *Journal of African History* 3:241–249.
ARMSTRONG, R. G.
  1960 The development of kingdoms in Negro Africa. *Journal of the Historical Society of Nigeria* 2:27–39.
  1962 Glottochronology and African languages. *Journal of African History* 2:283–290.
  1964 *The study of West African languages.* Ibadan: Ibadan University Press for the Institute of African Studies.
  1966 Prolegomena to the study of the Idoma concept of God. *African Notes* 4:11–17.
BASDEN, G. T.
  1912 Notes on the Ibo country. *Geographical Journal* 39:246–247.
  1938 *Niger Ibos.* London.
BUCHANAN, K. M., J. C. PUGH
  1969 *Land and people in Nigeria.* London: University of London Press.
EQUIANO, OLAUDAH
  1794 *The interesting narrative of the life of Olaudah Equiano or Gustavus Vassa the African.* Norwich.
FLINT, J. E.
  1966 *Nigeria and Ghana.* Englewood Clifs: Prentice-Hall.

FORDE, D., G. I. JONES
1950   *The Ibo and Ibibo-speaking peoples of south-eastern Nigeria.* Ethnographic Survey of Africa, Western Africa, part three. London: International African Institute.

GRIER, S. M.
1923   *Report on a tour in the eastern provinces by the Secretary for Native Affairs.* Lagos

HAMBLY, W. D.
1935   *Culture areas of Nigeria.* Field Museum of Natural History Publication 346, Anthropological Series 21 (3).

HARRIS, JACK
1942   Human relationships to land in southern Nigeria. *Rural Sociology* 7:89–92.

HARTLE, D. D.
1967   Archaeology in eastern Nigeria. *Nigeria Magazine* 93:134–143.

HENDERSON, RICHARD N.
1972   *The king in every man: evolutionary trends in Ibo society and culture.* New Haven and London: Yale University Press.

HODDER, B. W., U. I. UKWU
1969   *Markets in West Africa: studies of markets and trade among the Yoruba and Ibo.* Ibadan: Ibadan University Press.

HORTON, R.
1966   Igbo: an ordeal for aristocrats. *Nigeria Magazine* 90:169–183.

IKE, AKWAELUMO
1951   *The origin of the Ibos.* Aba.

JEFFREYS, M. D. W.
1946   Dual organisation in Africa. *African Studies* 5:82–105, 155–176.
1951   The winged solar disk. *Africa* 21:93–111.
1954   Ikenga: the Ibo ram-headed god. *African Studies* 13:25–40.
1956   The Umundri tradition of origin. *African Studies* 15:119–131.

JONES, G. I.
1945   Agriculture and Ibo village planning. *Farm and Forest* 6:9–15.
1961   Ecology and social structure among the North-Eastern Ibo. *Africa* 31:117–134.

JONES, G. I., H. MULHALL
1949   An examination of the physical type of certain peoples of south-eastern Nigeria. *Journal of the Royal Anthropological Institute* 79:11–18.

KARMON, YEHUDA
1966   *A geography of settlement in eastern Nigeria.* Jerusalem: Magnes Press, Hebrew University.

LEONARD, A. G.
1906   *The Lower Niger and its tribes.* London: Macmillan.

MATHEWS, H. F.
1927   Aro subtribes. Manuscript, A.D. 635, National Archives, Enugu, Nigeria.

MEEK, C. K.
1937   *Law and authority in a Nigerian tribe.* London: Oxford University Press.

NORTHRUP, DAVID
1972   The growth of trade among the Igbo before 1800. *Journal of African History* 8:217–236.

OJO, G. J. A.
1966   *Yoruba culture.* London: University of London Press.

ONWUEJEOGWU, M. A.
1972   The dawn of Igbo civilization. *Odinani* 1:15–56.
ORMSBY-GORE, W. A. G.
1926   *Report on a visit to West Africa (cmd 2744).* London: H.M.S.O.
OTTENBERG, S.
1961   The present state of Ibo studies. *Journal of the Historical Society of Nigeria* 2:211–230.
PALMER, H. R.
1921   Tribes of Nigeria. Lokoprof 159/1921, Kaduna Archives, Kaduna, Nigeria.
1928   Memorandum on the Eastern Provinces. 15911, vol. 1, attached to 8014/1921/90 of 19.6.28, Kaduna Archives, Kaduna, Nigeria.
RUBIN, ARNOLD
1971   Review of: *African stone sculpture*, by Philip Allison (New York: Praeger, 1968) and *Ife in the history of West African art*, by Frank Willett (London: Thames and Hudson, 1967). *African Notes* 6:113–123.
SHAW, T.
1970   *Igbo-Ukwu: an account of archaeological discoveries in eastern Nigeria.* London: Faber and Faber for the Institute of African Studies, University of Ibadan.
SHELTON, A. J.
1921   *The Igbo-Igala border land.* Albany: State University of New York Press.
TALBOT, P. A.
1926   *The peoples of southern Nigeria.* London: Oxford University Press.
TALBOT, P. A., H. MULHALL
1962   *The physical anthropology of southern Nigeria.* Cambridge: Cambridge University Press.
THOMAS, N. W.
1914   *Anthropological report on the Ibo-speaking peoples of Nigeria,* part one. London: Harrison.
WILLETT, F.
1967   *Ife in the history of West African art.* London: Thames and Hudson.

An Ethnohistorical Reconstruction of Traditional Igbo Society

S. J. S. COOKEY

The Igbo-speaking people constitute the bulk of the population inhabiting the East Central State of Nigeria. Some of them are also to be found in the Rivers State to the south, and a substantial number, designated as Ika Ibo, live on the west bank of the Lower Niger. The total population of the Igbo is unknown but may well exceed 10,000,000, making them one of the largest ethnic groups in Africa south of the Sahara. Writing nearly four decades ago, a scholar declared that "the Ibo have no tribal history" (Meek 1950 [1937]:4). Judging by the recent *History of West Africa* (Ajayi and Crowder 1972), which embodies the latest historiography, it would appear that this view of the Igbo still prevails. While the early histories of the Oyo, Dahomey, Akan, and Mossi are discussed *in extenso*, the Igbo are mentioned only in relation to studies on statelessness and the external contacts of the eastern delta city-states. This attitude toward the Igbo is understandable, for the historian is usually fascinated by the evolution and dynamics of polities with centralized political institutions such as empires, kingdoms, and republics. Nevertheless, it is erroneous and misleading, since it ignores the past of a sizable African population. What is called for is more research and new methods of historical investigation. The following discussion is an attempt to present a brief overview of the results of current research in the evolution of Igbo society from the earliest times to the eve of direct contact with the external world and to highlight gaps in our knowledge that remain to be filled.

IGBO STONE AGE

Archaeological studies in Igboland are still in their infancy. Excavations begun only in the 1960's which had started to yield exciting results were interrupted by the Nigerian civil war and are just being resumed. Consequently, very little is yet known about the culture of the region in prehistoric times. Nevertheless, the scanty data available provide interesting insights on the subject and enable us to proceed beyond the realm of pure conjecture.

By the period of the later Stone Age, modern man seems to have been firmly settled in the tropical forest. This is suggested by the finds at Iwo Eleru, to the west of Igboland, which have yielded dates of 9250 ± 200 B.C. and 7200 ± 150 B.C. The culture of this man was evidently preagricultural (Shaw 1972:57). His shelter was in caves, and he lived largely on raw tubers, which were fairly abundant in the forest. If this type of man did exist in the Igbo tropical forest, no evidence of him has so far come to light. Yet it is possible that the evidence might become available with further archaeological investigation, for the Iwo Eleru habitat had Igbo counterparts and the distance between the two regions was relatively small. The earliest signs so far of human presence in the area inhabited by the Igbo have rather been found at the Ezi-Ukwu Ukpa rock shelter in Afikpo, an area of wooded grassland. The dates associated with the site range from 2935 B.C. to A.D. 15 (Hartle 1969:35–38). A second site, in the same ecological environment, is at Nsukka and has yielded the date 2555 ± 130 B.C. (Hartle 1967). Both sites were associated with, *inter alia*, fired and unfired pottery sherds and crude stone tools. It has been accepted that these were early Neolithic cultures, although other evidence for this, such as polished stone axes or adzes, bifacially flaked arrowheads, and signs of agriculture, was not confirmed.

If the conclusion is accepted that the skeleton found at Iwo Eleru is Negroid, it might also be assumed that men with similar physical characteristics had begun to settle in the habitat where they are now found by the tenth millennium B.C. Was this also the period in which the Kwa branch of Niger-Congo, the linguistic family to which Igbo belongs, began to diverge from the other branches as a result of the diffusion of peoples in the savanna and tropical forest? The evidence is conjectural, but the variations within the language group would lead to that assumption (Armstrong 1964:22–23; Williamson 1968). It is now generally accepted that the final desiccation of the Sahara was well under way during the second millennium. The result, it is presumed, was the dispersal of the Neolithic peoples of the central Sahara, some of them shifting southward and probably causing population pressure which forced the peoples at the periphery to move into the forest. Through the influence of the Saharan immigrants, who were predominantly hunters and pastoralists, domesticated animals such as sheep, goats, and cattle might have reached the tropical forest, leading to the development of a strain which was resistant to the tsetse fly. Precisely when all this happened is yet to be determined. Within the tropical belt, few data such as rock paintings or osteological evidence are as yet available for dating. The Igbo, who, according to some scholars (Karmon 1966: 28–29; Henderson 1972:39), might earlier have inhabited the general area of the Niger-Benue confluence, would be among the peripheral groups affected by the developments farther north.

If the Neolithic forest dweller lived on wild tubers, the process by which agriculture could develop must be envisaged. It is now known that a species of yam, *Dioscorea cayenensis*, was indigenous to the West African forest. Having dug up the tubers and probably taken some to his shelter, Neolithic man might have thrown away the tops, only to find them sprouting up after some weeks (Shaw 1972:66). This might have led to a conscious planting of the crop in cleared patches of the forest or woodland and an increasing reliance on the harvest. Thus farming would have taken the place of food gathering, leading to a more settled life by the later Neolithic.

THE IRON AGE

Nevertheless, little advance could have been made toward the settlement of such an environment until metal tools became available. The process of taming the forest by cutting trees and clearing undergrowth could not intensively be undertaken until metal had replaced stone as the chief agricultural implement. Such a development was apparently slow in taking place in Igboland.

The reason for this relates to a larger question of the late use of metal in sub-Saharan Africa. The Bronze Age had begun to flourish in Egypt by the third millennium and had spread as far as the central Sahara. It was precisely at this time that the Sahara began to dry up, thereby separating West Africa from technological developments taking place to the north and northwest. This geographical obstacle, which was not to be overcome until the introduction of the camel at the dawn of the Christian era, ensured that sub-Saharan Africa did not experience the Bronze Age, for when communication was reestablished that Age had vanished and the Iron Age had supervened. Consequently, sub-Saharan Africa was to move directly from the Neolithic to the Iron Age.

For the purpose of this paper, the most significant evidence for the beginning of the Iron Age comes from the cultural complex which has been given the name Nok. It is marked by an abundance of such artifacts as terracotta figurines of human beings and animals, stone implements, pottery, quartz ornaments, and iron-smelting implements and structures. It used to be thought that this culture was transitional between the Stone Age and the Iron Age, but subsequent analysis has concluded that it was fully iron-using (Shaw 1963:455). It has been ascribed to between 500

B.C. and A.D. 200, which makes it, so far, with the exception of the suspect dating of the Ntereso (Ghana) site (Davies 1966:470–471), the earliest known iron-using culture in sub-Saharan Africa.

The Nok culture covered an oval area extending from the Jos Plateau southeastward across the Benue River. From this latter end it is believed that the proto-Bantu-speakers dispersed ultimately into Central, East, and South Africa. Whatever might have been the cause of the movement, which has been described as one of the greatest in the history of the world, it must be presumed to have also influenced the proximate lands to the south. Thus some resemblance has been noted between the Nok terracotta figurines and those of Ife. The precise nature of this impact is controversial, however, and remains to be thoroughly investigated.

One impact that might be taken as fairly obvious would have been the introduction of metal technology into Igboland. When this occurred is uncertain. Archaeological excavations at Nwankwor in Bende have revealed a culture clearly associated with iron and yielding a date of 805 ±95 B.C. This date is suspect, since a lower level yielded less than 145 B.P. (Hartle 1966:15). Nevertheless, assuming that the earlier is correct and that the dates could be explained by the disturbance of the site as a result of digging, it would indicate the existence of an iron-culture in the area during the second half of the first millennium.

More significant and intriguing are the finds at Igbo-Ukwu. The name covers three sites excavated in 1959–1960 and 1964 by Shaw (1970). The sites revealed large quantities of pottery decorated with considerable artistic detail, ivory tusks, forged iron objects, large quantities of bead ornaments, and, finally, copper and bronze objects, some produced by the lost-wax process and adorned with intricate designs. The last has attracted considerable attention as much for its artistry as for the fact that it differs from the tradition of the Benin and Ife bronzes found to the west of the Niger. Curiosity has been heightened by the carbon-14 dates obtained, which indicate that the culture was probably not later than the tenth century A.D.[1] As might be expected, the existence of an advanced Iron Age culture at such an early period in Igboland has raised many problems about the reconstruction of the history of southern Nigeria. Although radiocarbon dating for the magnificent Ife bronzes is not available, oral tradition and stylistic evidence led to the conclusion that this was the earliest culture to use the lost-wax process in the region and that the period could be the eleventh century A.D. or earlier (Dark 1957:206). From this conclusion it was deduced that the Ife source influenced artistic developments elsewhere. The Igbo-Ukwu dates, coupled with its artistic style, which differs markedly from that of Ife, would either change the

[1] The following dates were obtained from two of the sites: I-2008, Igbo Richard, A.D. 850 ± 120; Hv–1514, Igbo Jonah, A.D. 875 ± 130; Hv–1515, Igbo Jonah, A.D. 840 ± 110; Hv–1516, Igbo Jonah, A.D. 1445 ±70; I–1784, Igbo Jonah, A.D. 840 ± 145; (Shaw 1968).

inspirational source of bronze casting in southern Nigeria or indicate the probability of independent sources. One scholar, however, has gone on to question the date of the Igbo-Ukwu complex and to hint that the single fifteenth-century date obtained from the site, instead of being the odd man out, is the most probable (Lawal 1973).

The problem of dating the Igbo-Ukwu complex may not be resolved until more evidence becomes available through further archaeological work. In the meantime, the finds do lead to certain speculations and conclusions which link Igboland to the neighboring region in the north. The first, as already noted, is that Igboland was the heir of the iron technology developed by the Nok culture. This culture and its artists seem to have vanished by A.D. 200. It is not inconceivable that some of them, or the knowledge they possessed, became available to the areas in the south. Once this knowledge had been mastered over several centuries, its pos-sessors would have been ready to experiment with new ideas and metals when these became available. As regards the source of the new ideas and metal, it is known that the lost-wax process had been used in Egypt from about the second millennium on and from there diffused to the North African littoral. Just as the technology of ironworking penetrated West Africa from either North Africa, ancient Meroe, or both, so undoubtedly did the lost-wax process. Curiously enough, however, there is no evidence so far of its having been practiced at Nok. It might be inferred that the knowledge of the technique arrived after the decay of Nok and that those who subsequently profited from it were the "Sao" (south of Lake Chad), Adamawa, Bamenda, Igala, Ife, and Igbo. As regards the metal itself, spectographic tests on the Igbo-Ukwu bronzes indicate varying percen-tages in the mixture of copper, lead, tin, and zinc. Shaw (1970:279) has suggested that the earliest source of the metals used in the bronzes might lie in North Africa, where bronze had already been alloyed. A resolution of the problem must await further work, but, as he has also noted, lead and zinc as well as ferrous metal are found in northern Igboland in isolated forms, and the deposits were worked in ancient times. It required only the addition of copper for bronze to be produced efficiently locally, and such copper was evidently available from external sources in the north.

Associated with the bronze objects were beads of various makes and colors. Shaw (1970:280) suggests that while "some of the carnelian beads and perhaps a small number of the glass beads may be of local, or at any rate of West African origin, by far the majority must be regarded as imports from outside the area." The source of the imports is said to be Venice and India, from where they were traded across the Sahara. Finally, the textiles, which show evidence of raffia fiber, are assumed to have been produced locally. The use of fiber from the palm species *Raphia textilis* for cloth weaving was noted in the kingdom of the Kongo as early as the sixteenth century, and the technical quality of the cloth would indicate decades of development (Balandier 1968:114–116). Similar palms are found in Igboland, and the evidence suggests that their uses there were a repitition of the Kongo example.

Apart from the question of dating, the most important issue raised by the Igbo-Ukwu finds is the type of society that sustained such a sophisticated culture. The imported copper and beads are evidence that the region, far from being isolated, was in contact, even if tenuously, with the external world and that its trading connections ran over a very long distance. In exchange for the imports the Igbo probably offered ivory, kola, iron ware, and eventually slaves, but the organization of the trade and its control remain obscure. What the Igbo-Ukwu finds do contribute is the illumination, although shadowy, of the social and political life of the period. The Igbo Richard site represents the burial of a notable person who might have possessed considerable authority and wealth. The fact that other human beings were inhumed with him denotes not only the existence of slavery, but also belief in an afterlife and hence ancestor worship. Both were still observed in historic times, and this evidence would suggest that their origins could probably be traced to the dawn of the Iron Age, at which time differentiation in status might have become significant for cultures that had not experienced the Bronze Age.

What kind of authority did the individual at Igbo Richard possess? Attention has been drawn in the past (Jeffreys 1935) to the priestly office of *eze nri,* still in existence during the 1930's in Aguku and Oreri, two clans close to Igbo-Ukwu. The office was nonpolitical, but it was widely recognized in Igboland that its occupant had the power to sanctify titles, settle disputes, solicit for fertility from the deities, and cleanse individuals guilty of a crime against the deeply revered earth deity, *ala.* As a result, the office enjoyed great prestige and received tribute from supplicants which generated considerable wealth. The regalia of the officeholder, which included copper and bronze ornaments, beads, and a cowhide crown adorned with *ugo* (fish eagle) feathers, bear some resemblance to the objects recovered from Igbo Richard. On the basis of these, Shaw (1970:270) has cautiously concluded that there has been a "basic continuity of underlying ideas," though the details have been modified over centuries, and that the vessels and regalia excavated from Igbo Isaiah are connected with the *eze nri* office. The political implication is not very clear, but there is no reason to suppose that the powers of the *eze nri* were much different in the earlier period than later. The firmly held belief among the core Igbo that they have no kings seems to have prevailed from earliest times and firmly implanted itself in the Igbo mode of life. There was certainly among them a differentiation in social status, and their religious beliefs produced a priesthood, but no individual emerged whose full-time function was to wield political power over the rest.

THE ERA OF MIGRATIONS

The use of iron obviously intensified man's activity in the struggle to survive and dominate his environment. In the tropical-forest areas it became possible to lead a settled life and to cultivate the land or expand the acreage under cultivation. It must also be supposed that increased agricultural production led to an increase in population and consequently the gradual expansion of the inhabited territory. It was probably for this reason and in this way that the Igbo began to spread.

From data now available, it would appear that the Igbo dispersed from a core area which lies in the modern Awka and Orlu divisions, for the people in this area, unlike their neighbors, have no traditions of migration. The direction of the movement would appear to have been eastward to the Nsukka-Udi highlands, westward across the Niger, and southward toward the edge of the eastern Niger delta (Jones 1963:30). It must have been a gradual process involving small lineages and generally lacking a predetermined direction. As each group disappeared into the forest, it retained only tenuous links with its ancestral home, which sometimes became severed with the passage of time. Clearly, during this process, dialectal variations in the Igbo language began to emerge. Another possible consequence of the dispersal would have been its effect on non-Igbo groups within the area, which was to force them either to be absorbed by the Igbo or to disperse from the direction of the Igbo advance. Thus, traditions of the Ijo-speaking Bonny and Kalabari people indicate that their original migration was from the central delta to the eastern edge of the delta, south of the Igbo, and that they settled there for some length of time before moving directly south into the inhospitable delta itself. Some Ibibio traditions also reveal a dispersal from an ancestral homeland located to the southeast of the Igbo into regions south and east, probably culminating in the movement of the section now known as Efik into the area which became famous as Calabar. Similar migrations across the Upper Cross River probably occurred. These movements cannot now be dated with any kind of precision, but linguistic data and the examination of oral traditions of the delta city-states would indicate a period around the opening centuries of the present millennium (cf. Alagoa 1966:6–10).

It was about the same time, from what can now be conjectured, that the Benin kingdom emerged to the west of Igboland. The origins of this kingdom lie outside the scope of the present work. However, its consolidation under a ruler titled *oba*, its hierarchical organization, and its military might enabled it to expand its influence in all directions, so that by the middle of the sixteenth century it had become the dominant power within the territory extending from the Lagos lagoon to the west bank of the Niger. Benin imperialism gradually brought the Igbo of the west bank under the influence of Benin culture, and although the details remain unclear, the emergence among these Igbo of the office of *obi* or *ovie* [king], which is not common among other Igbo east of the Niger, might well date to this period.

If the traditions of some Western and Riverain (Ogbaru) Igbo are accepted, it was during this period, also, that the founders of these Benin-type institutions migrated from Benin, for a number of reasons which are not relevant to this discussion. One of the most important of these migrations, apparently, was led by a rebel Bini element, Chima, whose followers or sons (hence called Umuezechima) are said to have founded the chiefdoms of Onicha-Ugbo, Onicha-Ukwu, Onicha Olona, Obamkpa, Isele, Obio, and Ezi.[2] The remaining sons of Chima, according to the traditions of modern Onitsha, proceeded to the Niger, crossed it, and settled at the present site of that town after defeating the original Igbo inhabitants. The people of Abo also assert that their ancestors were part of the Chima migration and, indeed, that the founder of their town, Esumai, was the brother of Chima who had separated from them at Agbor. A third significant migration which is believed to have occurred contemporaneously with the preceding two is that of Ekenyi, Ugwunta, and Inyi, who settled first among the Igala and whose descendants eventually founded the town of Oguta.

Although the Benin origin is commonly acknowledged, details of these migrations vary and must be accepted with great caution: the numbers involved here were probably quite small, the whole journey took far longer than the accounts indicate, and there were several areas settled before the final destination was reached. Indeed, the traditions might perhaps represent no more than the ability of a few Igbo who had come in contact with Benin power at its height to use its influence to impose themselves on their less "sophisticated" countrymen. Its only permanent consequence, as already pointed out, was the introduction of Benin-type government; for the rest, Igbo language and culture retained their dominance.

Another source of change in political institutions among the Igbo, apart from Benin, seems to have been Igala. The Oguta claim of sojourn among the Igala has already been noted. At an indeterminate period in the past, perhaps about the time that the Oguta also departed, the people of Osomari and related villages such as Ika, Iteku, Inyamam, Inoma, Uje Odekpe, and Oko claim to have left Idah and moved to their present location on the banks of the Niger. A third claim of Igala connection was that of the Umunri. Whether this claim was influenced by the rise of Igala power, probably after the seventeenth century, and the desire of the

---

[2]   For brief summaries of oral traditions relating to the Riverain Igbo, see Nzimiro (1972:6–19).

Umunri to identify with it in order to reinforce their influence over the neighboring Igbo is a matter for conjecture. Thus, for example, the Umunri, unlike the Osomari, do not exhibit clear evidence of Igala influence in their political institutions and language. The people of Nsukka, on the other hand, because of their close proximity to the Igala, have been deeply influenced and in turn influenced the latter (Shelton 1971). This process might have reached its height in the eighteenth and early nineteenth centuries when Igala suffered from the pressure of the Fulani jihad. According to Shelton, the Igala eventually conquered a number of Nsukka villages and appointed chiefs as well as shrine priests with the Igala title of *attama*.

For most Igbo, perhaps the most important migrations, because of the impact on their economic and social life from the mid-seventeenth century onward, were those of the people who founded Arochukwu. From a collation of their traditions (Ekejiuba 1972), it would appear that Igbo farming communities such as Iwerri, Losi, Nkalaku, and Ohadu fell out with their Ibibio-speaking neighbors over a piece of land and intermittent fighting ensued. A third element known as Akpa (also called Ibom) appeared on the scene and, because of their superior military might, subdued both parties in the conflict and incorporated them into what became the Aro community. Who were the Akpa, and why did they intervene in the conflict? The details remain obscure. However, it seems that they originally lived to the south, either along the Cross River or toward its mouth. Alternatively, they might have lived at the place still called Ibom in the Oban forest (Talbot 1969:182–183). In either case, this would place them close to the Efik and Ibibio, probably accounting for their peculiar cultural complexity.

The occupation of the Aro was hunting and trading. They bought from the coastal people fish and salt and sold smoked meat and foodstuffs which had been obtained from their neighbors. After the discovery of the Calabar Coast by Sequeira in 1472, the Akpa also began trading with the Europeans through the Efik and soon realized the potentialities of this connection. Their chief item of trade became slaves, in return for which they received firearms as well as other foreign commodities. It was perhaps in their desire to increase the supply of slaves that they relocated northward, their possession of firearms affording them a decisive advantage over the warring parties at Arochukwu. Did they also bring with them a few of the European adventurers who wished to explore the Cross River? The answer is unknown, but the traditions of the area around Arochukwu recall that the Akpa invasion comprised "a group of red people armed with blunderbusses (*utaoku*)" (Jones 1963:31). Having consolidated their position, the Aro began to establish a trading network which ultimately spread throughout eastern Nigeria, with consequences that will be discussed later.

IGBO SOCIETY AND POLITICS

Following the above movements of the Igbo, it might be assumed that by the beginning of the seventeenth century the major Igbo groups occupied the territories where they are now found. According to the division outlined by Forde and Jones (1967:10), there were five main regional groups: the Western Igbo; the Northern or Onitsha Igbo; the Southern or Owerri Igbo; the Eastern or Cross River Igbo; and the Northeastern Igbo. These groups had distinctive features peculiar to each which were characterized by a dialect, social organization, and, in the case of the Western Igbo, political institutions. Nevertheless, they also shared a great many characteristics which have given them, in addition to their language, an identity as a national group.

The smallest unit of the social organization of the Igbo was the extended family, sometimes called *omonna* or *umunna* (cf. Uchendu 1965:39–41), which thus represented a minimal lineage. It was made up of a man, his wife (or wives), his unmarried daughters and sons, and his married sons, their wives, and their children. It was the ambition of the Igbo man to ensure that this family, which was largely dependent on his resources, continued to grow and even to absorb his agnates, since his status within the community often depended on it. If he was successful, he could then constitute a "compound" family (*ezi* or *obi*), or minor lineage, comprising an aggregate of extended families which formed its segments. Within this unit, the head was responsible for sharing the family land at the planting season, resolving conflict, and disciplining its members in their internal relationships as well as representing their external interests. In addition, he exercised such ritual functions as ministering at the family shrines.

With the death of the head of a large compound, tensions were likely to arise over the inheritance or the distribution of the estate among siblings or half-brothers, and the segmentary character of the unit might become manifest, as the malcontents could then establish autonomous compounds or affiliate with other agnates. Most Igbo were patrilineal. However, as a result of contact with Cross River cultures, some Eastern Igbo adopted a double-descent system, both patrilineal and matrilineal (Ottenberg 1968). In either system, the practice of polygyny enhanced the potential for friction and conflict.

A group of minor lineages or compounds made up the major lineages, and these in turn formed the village (*ogbe*). This was the maximal lineage. It was usually an exogamous group because of the real or putative consanguineal ties that bound the members.[3] However, some large maximal lineages might become endogamous, in which case exogamy was

---

[3]   Among them the dictum is that "we worship together, therefore we cannot marry." I owe this to Ikenna Nzimiro.

observed within the segments, that is, the major lineages. In many instances, the residential pattern of the village settlement was organized on a dual basis, with senior and junior or upper and lower sections. Authority within the village as a whole rested with the head of the senior section (*okpara* or *opara*), who was usually its oldest member. His ritual authority was symbolized by the ancestral staff called *ofo* which he had inherited and the control of the communal or *ofo* land. As the head of his own personal compound, he wielded considerable authority over its members, as did other heads of households. Beyond this, his authority was severely limited. He would offer at intervals sacrifices to the ancestors for the welfare of the village, but he could not act in important matters affecting the whole lineage without consulting other household heads. Defiance of his authority could only be punished by his *ofo*. As in the case of the sublineages, the village might segment as a result of chronic conflict.

Finally, an aggregate of villages made up the clan or the village-group, the highest political organization among the Igbo (Forde and Jones 1967:16). The clan or village-group derived its corporate identity from a founding ancestor who might be real or putative. It often bore his name, to which might be attached a prefix such as *umu* [children of], *ndi* [people or descendants of], or *ama* [place of]. The settlement pattern of the clans has been affected by demographic variations over the years. Where the population was relatively small and the land abundant, there was a tendency for the clan to be dispersed over a wide area, with lineage lines clearly drawn. Where the population was large and land scarce, the settlement of the clan was invariably compact, and in extreme cases the lineages tended to overlap as farmlands shrank. Again, in the case of the Eastern Igbo, a distinction deserves notice. Two types of clans emerged: the patriclan, which tended to be localized, and the matriclan, which was scattered, although its members still recognized a common head. Whatever the nature of the clan, most Igbo settlement patterns differed fundamentally from those of the Yoruba and Hausa, for example, by remaining rural and not developing into real or nascent urban centers. In addition, they failed to evolve large-scale political organizations and for this reason are regarded as stateless societies.

According to Horton (1972:78), stateless societies are defined by the fact that (*a*) "there is little concentration of authority;" (*b*) "such authority roles as exist affect a rather limited sector of the lives of those subject to them;" (*c*) the "wielding of authority as a specialized, full-time occupation is virtually unknown;" and (*d*) the "unit within which people feel an obligation to settle their disputes according to agreed rules and without resort to force tends to be relatively small." These characteristics were applicable to the Igbo village. Authority within the village was rather diffuse. The *okpara* provided leadership in matters involving the entire village, but he had no right of independent action. He had to summon all the male adults and present major issues for their exhaustive deliberation, from which he took the sense of the discussion. If a new law was agreed upon, this was ratified by him and all the lineage heads, invoking the sanction of the ancestors with their *ofo* by striking them on the ground. The execution of a decision was assigned on an ad hoc basis to one or more of the age-grade or title organizations. On the other hand, the *okpara* could not interfere in matters which did not concern the entire village and for the most part confined his attention to the affairs of his own lineage.

The segmentary nature of intravillage relationships manifested itself in times of conflict. As each lineage was equivalent structurally and functionally to its counterpart, so was the senior to the junior village. Thus within the village the allegiance of the individual was relative to the situation (see Horton 1972:89–93). A man in one lineage segment might be in conflict with a rival in another segment but would act in concert with him if the entire lineage was threatened, resuming his independence of action once the external threat disappeared. Similarly, two sections of a village could coalesce to face a common foe but revert to their autonomous status after the danger had been dealt with. The unwillingness of the individual to accept permanently a higher authority was characteristic of Igbo political organization and prevented the rise of state systems. Nevertheless, it cannot be overemphasized that statelessness in no way implies the absence of government. At the various levels of Igbo society already outlined, there were institutionalized methods, perhaps informal to the outsider, which ensured that legislation was enacted, legal cases adjudicated, and decisions implemented.

Particularly in the riverain areas of the Niger and among the Ika Ibo, state systems did emerge as a result of the influence of intrusive elements and ideas. Although significant differences as regards the degree of centralization and the mode of recruitment to political office existed, there were common underlying principles of organization which lent uniformity to this group of Igbo polities. Each had a king (*obi*) who was the focus of unity and whose authority over the community was reinforced by divine sanction. He was appointed from a royal lineage and underwent an installation ceremony which was supposed to raise him above the level of mortals. Thereafter, he presided over a council of state and the highest judicial court and assumed responsibility for the conduct of external relations. Below the king were titled chiefs who were appointed by him according to well-defined principles and organized in a hierarchical order. The chiefs acted as a check upon the exercise of arbitrary or despotic power by the king, and the most powerful among them also exercised judicial functions. The executive functions of the state were entrusted, according to the nature of the task, to title associations, age-grades, and women's organizations. The various statewide associations, to which the leadership and many adults of the lineages belonged, helped to minimize local particularism and strengthen intergrative ties. In matters of crucial importance to the lives of the people, a general assembly of the state was convened, and every adult male could attend and express an opinion. However, such meetings were rare. Each of the states was made up of administrative units (*ebo* or *egbo*) organized according to a patrilineal descent system. These acted as units of local government and regulated their internal affairs without interference from the center.

ECONOMIC TRENDS

While little change took place in the political and social organization of the Igbo until after the imposition of colonial rule, their economic activity responded to strong external stimuli connected primarily with the rise of the trans-Atlantic trade in the Niger delta. The result was a weakening of Igbo trade with the north and an intensification of trading relations with the south.

Before discussing the role of trade, it should be noted that the Igbo community remained essentially rural. It survived largely by subsistence agriculture, for the tropical forest and the high incidence of the tsetse fly precluded a pastoral life. Thus, although livestock such as sheep, goats, fowls, and dwarf cattle might be kept, these played only a supplementary role in the domestic economy. As the pressure of population on land increased in the core Igbo areas, some groups were induced to specialize in other occupations. The Aro, as will soon be seen, organized a long-distance trading system which integrated Igbo trade through the delta middlemen with the trans-Atlantic trading system. The people of Nkwerre and Abiriba became specialists in smithing and practiced their craft throughout southern Igboland and the eastern delta. Awka people became famous as smiths and medicine men. Nevertheless, despite the specialization, each Igbo retained a piece of patrimonial land, small or large according to the environment and social structure, which his household cultivated even if he himself pursued another calling. Thus farming remained the dominant occupation of the Igbo, while Igbo life was organized around a farming calendar.

The produce of the land and the wares of the artisans were exchanged in a highly developed market-oriented economy (Hodder and Ukwu 1969). The markets were held in a specific village on one of the four days which made up the Igbo week (these days were called Nkwo, Eke, Orie or Oye, and Afo; where an eight-day week was recognized, each was differentiated by having "big" or "small" suffixed to it) and attracted a large concourse of people from neighboring villages. These people came to buy and sell, but the market also served other vital social functions. It provided an opportunity to exchange news concerning births, deaths, weddings, etc., to settle disputes, to celebrate happy events, and to meet relatives who would not be seen in the normal course of the week. Indeed, so closely were market and social activities identified that most festivals had their dates on particular market days.

Not all these markets were of equal importance. Some catered for the needs of the village-group as well as of a whole clan; others attracted a clientele beyond the clan and amounted to fairs where people from rather long distances converged to trade in scarce commodities. These would subsequently be conveyed in bulk to the lesser markets and through them diffuse to the village level. One of these fairs seems by the nineteenth century to have become the dominant trading capital of Igboland, for it was legendary among the Igbo and its reputation universal. This fair was at Bende, midway between the Imo and Cross Rivers. From Bende radiated trading routes that led northward through Uzuakoli, Uburu, and Nike to Idah; southward through Oloko and Aba to the city-states of the Niger delta; westward through Aro-Ndizuogu to Aboh, Oguta, and Awka; and eastward to Arochukwu and Calabar. In addition, an important trading route ran along the Lower Niger and was based on the maritime activities of the Igala, Igbo and Ijaw who occupied its banks. As became known from European accounts of the nineteenth century, the most important of these riverain markets were held on sand bars which appeared in the Niger when the river was low or, otherwise, in canoes. One of these was situated opposite Asaba and attracted traders from Benin and Ika Ibo in the west, Igala in the north, the Niger Igbo states in the east, and the delta states in the south. A similar trading location north of Idah attracted the same type of clientele but also drew traders from Nupe and Igbirra farther north.

The long-distance network which had its center at Bende was firmly under the control of a single Igbo group, the Aro. It is yet to be ascertained by historians when the Aro organized their trading network. Available evidence (Ekejiuba 1972) suggests that it began gradually, probably in the middle of the seventeenth century, but took about a century to reach its fullest ramifications. During this period the Aro established settlements or colonies at strategic places throughout eastern Nigeria, and these became focal points for the spread of Aro influence and relay centers for Aro entrepreneurs. Aro expansionism was stimulated by the internal demand for domestic slaves in the region and by the rise of the trans-Atlantic slave trade. The slaves supplied to meet the latter demand were sold to the Niger delta traders by the Aro, who in turn bought from their customers clothes, hardware, ornaments, tobacco, spirits, and firearms, the control of which further enhanced Aro importance in the hinterland economy.

The Aro were able to achieve their dominating position through the exploitation of traditional religious beliefs and a genius for organizing military alliances. It is generally accepted that when the Aro settled in their present location they came into contact with an Ibibio deity known as Ibinukpabi. Realizing the potential of the deity, they adopted it, and through their military prowess and proselytizing ability encouraged the surrounding clans to recognize the shrine of Ibinukpabi as the earthly residence of the high god. The Igbo, who called their high god Chukwu, began to regard the Aro as Umuchukwu [children of God] and, therefore, to accord them great respect. Even the Ibibio, who called the Aro Inokun, and the Ijo did the same. As a result, the Aro enjoyed virtual immunity wherever they sojourned and could therefore travel and settle in any place they chose. As far away as Aboh, on the banks of the Niger, Schön (Schön and Crowther 1970 [1842]:51–52) who accompanied the Niger Expedition of 1841, reported,

> it is their common belief that there is a certain place or town in the Ibo country in which "Tshuku" dwells, and where he delivers his oracles and answers inquiries. Any matter of importance is left to his decision, and people travel to the place from every part of the country. . . . Tshuku cannot be seen by any human eye: his voice is heard from the ground. He speaks every language on earth; makes known thieves; and if there is fraud in the heart of the inquirer, he is sure to find it out. . . .

Thus the shrine of Chukwu became an oracle and the Aro homeland a local Delphi which attracted disputants and supplicants from eastern Nigeria under the encouragement and guidance of the itinerant Aro. As one historian (Dike 1956:38) has said, "Acting as mediators between God and the clans and assuming themselves to be the spokesmen of the Almighty, they held a privileged position throughout the land, erecting what amounted to a theocratic state over Eastern Nigeria." In the absence of a centralized political system among the Igbo, the Aro oracle provided a forum for the adjudication of intractable disputes. On some occasions, an Igbo village might prove defiant or recalcitrant, ignoring the awful prestige of the Aro. The latter, however, were not without more tangible means of supplementing and bolstering their spiritual powers. Close to the Aro homeland were the Abam and Ada, two unique Igbo subgroups that encouraged military prowess among their people as a means of proving their manhood. The interest of these people in warfare coincided with the Aros need for armed support to maintain their influence; hence an alliance was formed between the two whereby the former provided the warriors against Aro foes and in return were assured of weapons and loot. Thus Aro power could be said to have been founded on a spiritual aura backed by the military might of their mercenaries.

The Aro exploited their advantage to further the slave trade on which their economic prosperity came to depend. The system which they perfected was described as follows by Baikie (1966 [1856]:313):

> When a man goes to Aro to consult *Tshúku*, he is received by some of the priests outside of the town, near a small stream. Here he makes an offering, after which a fowl is killed, and, if it appears unpropitious, a quantity of red dye, probably camwood, is spilt into the water, which the priests tell the people is blood, and on this the votary is hurried off by the priests and is seen no more, it being given out that *Tshúku* has been displeased, and has taken him. The result of this preliminary ceremony is determined in general by the amount of the present given to the priests, and those reported to have been carried off by *Tshúku* are usually sold as slaves.

Some of these slaves were traded at the fairs of Bende and others led southward to the Niger delta ports of Calabar, Bonny, Kalabari, and Brass for sale to the middlemen chiefs who were in contact with the European slave traders. As Aro colonies spread and consolidated their influence, they came to dominate other regional oracles of the same type, such as the Igwekala of Ummunneoha, the Kamalu of Ozuzu, and the Ojukwu of Diobu.

By the middle of the nineteenth century, the trans-Atlantic slave trade of the delta had virtually come to a close following the withdrawal of the British, who had been its leading sponsors. At the same time, the industrialists of England had discovered that palm oil, which had been available in the delta from the earliest times, was essential for lubricating machinery as well as for making candles and soap. Hence, following the increased demand, the Southern Igbo began to concentrate on supplying palm produce rather than human cargos. However, for a time the changeover did not entail the suppression of the slave traffic. Statistics are impossible to come by, but there is some indication that the increase in palm-oil production, by necessitating a larger personnel in the delta states to handle the transactions at various stages, actually sustained the internal slave trade at a very high level and contributed to an increasing influx of the Igbo into the trading city-states of the eastern delta and the dilution of Ijo with Igbo culture.

Although the Aro influence pervaded the trade of the region throughout the nineteenth century, other Igbo groups seem to have also participated, especially after palm oil and palm kernel displaced slaves as the chief items of the delta trade. The most active in this trade, no doubt because of their proximity to the delta and the abundance of oil palms in their area, were the Southern Igbo, made up of the Isuama, Oratta-Ikwerre, Ohuhu-Ngwa, and Isu-Item groups. An important element in this trade was the Igbo middleman, who purchased palm products from local markets and transported them in bulk to the riverbanks where his delta customers awaited delivery.

The Igbo middlemen could not have recourse to the spiritual aura that surrounded the Aro traders and adopted other modes of action to safeguard their enterprise. One mode was to organize small caravans protected by armed parties to deter potential assailants. This was only a precautionary action. More important was for the entrepreneur to marry into one or more families along the route that his caravans would have to follow. The Igbo practice of exogamy, by linking lineages of the bride and groom, helped in widening the contacts of both (Green 1964:151). It only required the ingenuity of the enterprising trader to extend the practice for the purpose of establishing long-distance trade. Alternatively, or in addition, the trader might enter into blood covenants (*ogbugbandu*) with influential men on the proposed route, which secured his trade and personnel against harm. Whichever method he adopted, the route thus established became available to others who might be related to him through family ties or the bonds of marriage.

Unless there were strong countervailing reasons, such as deep-seated or long-existing hostility between one clan and another, the Southern Igbo generally welcomed the flow of trade in palm produce because of its great advantages. The villages on the route had the opportunity of disposing of their own produce and food to the caravans and in turn secured goods that were not locally available. Furthermore, tolls were paid by the caravans and were collected by the Okonko, a secret society exclusive to local influential men, which acted as a village executive committee in southern Igboland. Such tolls contributed to the resources of the community, assisted in financing its traditional rituals' and encouraged the maintenance of the village approach roads. It was in this way that the thousands of tons of palm produce which gave the name Oil Rivers to the eastern delta were supplied by entrepreneurs of the hinterland.

Whether the trade was conducted at the local markets or at distant ones, the transactions were undertaken, not by barter, as is often supposed, but by a well-developed currency system which pre-dated the advent of Europeans. The earlier principal currencies of Igboland included *umumu* and cowries. The former, peculiar to the area between Auka and Enugu, was described by Basden (1966 [1938]:339) as "tiny pieces of thin flat iron, with one end barked, resembling a miniature arrow-head." This currency was probably produced by Awka and Ohafia blacksmiths, craftsmen well known throughout eastern Nigeria. The second currency, the cowrie, was of two varieties: the larger, *Cypraea annulus*, was used mainly at Onitsha and on the west bank of the Niger, and the smaller, *Cypraea moneta*, was commonly used throughout Igboland. Following the opening of the trans-Atlantic trade, new currencies were introduced, among them the manilla and bars of iron, copper, and brass, which were supplied to Igboland through trade with the delta city-states.

CONCLUSION

It is intriguing to speculate what would ultimately have happened to Igbo society without the imposition of colonial rule toward the end of the nineteenth century. Political Darwinists are inclined to see the emergence of the state as the logical development of human societies. Would the Igbo have eventually been subsumed within larger political groupings? The answer is by no means certain. On the eve of colonial rule, most of the ingredients that have resulted in the emergence of states elsewhere seem to have been present, such as the existence of long-distance trade, pressure of population on land, and the notion of kingship in western Igbo-land and the delta city-states. These elements had also been present, however, at least throughout the preceding century, and there seems no reason to assume that there would have been a change in the next. It might be argued that if the Igbo had been faced with a common foe a leader might have emerged to unify them and create permanent administrative institutions. However, the British conquest of Igboland in the early twentieth century did not produce such a leader; rather, each Igbo village or village-group defended itself as best it could without much assistance from its neighbors. The permanence of statelessness among the Igbo is attributable to the fact that their society had evolved a number of co-equivalent units capable of performing the maximum functions necessary for the welfare of the community. In the circumstances, it was unnecessary for them to improvise or introduce new political arrangements. Even when such an attempt was made by restructuring the society administratively during the colonial period, it led to violent reactions from the Igbo which were overcome by superior force. The Igbo case would support the opinion that under certain circumstances there is no logical progression from statelessness to statehood.

REFERENCES

AJAYI, J. F. A., MICHAEL CROWDER, *editors*
  1972   *History of West Africa,* volume one. New York: Columbia University Press.
ALAGOA, E. J.
  1966   The development of institutions in the states of the eastern Niger delta. *Journal of African History* 12:269–278.
ARMSTRONG, R. G.
  1964   *The study of West African languages.* Ibadan: Ibadan University Press for the Institute of African Studies.
BAIKIE, W. B.
  1966[1856]   *Narratives of an exploring voyage up the rivers Kwora and Binue.* London: Frank Cass.

BALANDIER, GEORGES
1968   *Daily life in the kingdom of the Kongo.* London: George Allen and Unwin.

BASDEN, G. T.
1966 [1938]   *Niger Ibos.* London: Frank Cass.

DARK, P.
1957   Benin: West African kingdom. *Discovery* 18:206.

DAVIES, O.
1966   Comment on: The Iron Age in sub-Saharan Africa, by A. J. Arkell, Brian Fagan, and Roger Summers. *Current Anthropology* 7:470–471.

DIKE, K. O.
1956   *Trade and politics in the Niger delta.* London: Oxford University Press.

EKEJIUBA, F. IFEOMA
1972   The Aro system of trade in the nineteenth century. *Ikenga* 1:11–26.

FORDE, DARYLL, G. I. JONES
1967   *The Ibo and Ibibio-speaking peoples of south-eastern Nigeria.* Ethnographic Survey of Africa, Western Africa, part three. London: International African Institute. (Reprint of 1950 edition.)

GREEN, M. M.
1964   *Igbo village affairs* (second edition). London: Frank Cass.

HARTLE, DONALD, D.
1966   Archaeology in eastern Nigeria. *West African Archaeological Newsletter* 5:13–17.
1967   Archaeology in eastern Nigeria. *Nigeria Magazine* 93:134–143.
1969   An archaeological survey in West Cameroon. *West African Archaeological Newsletter* 11:35–38.

HENDERSON, R. N.
1972   *The king in every man: evolutionary trends in Ibo society and culture.* New Haven and London: Yale University Press.

HODDER, B. W., U. I. UKWU
1969   *Markets in West Africa.* Ibadan: Ibadan University Press.

HORTON, ROBIN
1972   "Stateless societies in the history of West Africa," in *History of West Africa,* volume one. Edited by J. F. A. Ajayi and Michael Crowder, 78–119. New York: Columbia University Press.

JEFFREYS, M. D. W.
1935   The divine Umundri king. *Africa* 8:346–354.

JONES, G. I.
1963   *The trading states of the Oil Rivers.* London: Oxford University Press.

KARMON, YEHUDA
1966   *A geography of settlement in eastern Nigeria.* Jerusalem: Magnes Press, Hebrew University.

LAWAL, BABATUNDE
1973   Dating problems at Igbo-Ukwu. *Journal of African History* 14:1–8.

MEEK, C. K.
1950 [1937]   *Law and authority in a Nigerian tribe.* London: Oxford University Press.

NZIMIRO, IKENNA
1972   *Studies in Ibo political systems.* Berkeley and Los Angeles: University of California Press.

OTTENBERG, SIMON
1968   *Double descent in an African society: the Afikpo village-group.* Seattle: University of Washington Press.

SCHÖN, JAMES FREDERICK, SAMUEL CROWTHER
   1970 [1842]   *Journals of the Rev. James Frederick Schön and Mr. Samuel Crowther.* London: Frank Cass.
SHAW, THURSTAN
   1963   Field research in Nigerian archaeology. *Journal of the Historical Society of Nigeria* 2:455.
   1968   Radiocarbon dating in Nigeria. *Journal of the Historical Society of Nigeria* 4:453–465.
   1970   *Igbo-Ukwu: an account of archaeological discoveries in eastern Nigeria,* volume one. London: Faber and Faber for the Institute of African Studies, University of Ibadan.
   1972   "The prehistory of West Africa," in *History of West Africa,* volume one. Edited by J. F. A. Ajayi and Michael Crowder, 33–77. New York: Columbia University Press.
SHELTON, A. J.
   1971   *The Igbo-Igala borderland.* Albany: State University of New York Press.
TALBOT, P. A.
   1969   *The peoples of southern Nigeria,* volume one. London: Frank Cass.
UCHENDU, VICTOR C.
   1965   *The Igbo of southeast Nigeria.* New York: Holt, Rinehart and Winston.
WILLIAMSON, KAY
   1968   Languages of the Niger delta. *Nigeria Magazine* 97:124–130.

COMMENT by S. J. S. Cookey

A great deal has been written on West African cultures. Most of these writings, of course, have dealt with West African kingdoms and states because these states or kingdoms have been able to preserve their history. This has enabled modern scholars to investigate the way in which their cultures have evolved in the past. The problem, however, has been to determine how to examine those African communities that did not evolve large-scale political organizations. Such communities constitute the vast majority of Africans. One might, in fact, say that states and kingdoms are mere islands in a sea of statelessness in Africa. We recognize that every human community has a culture, that the cultures are not static, that they are constantly evolving and have a history. The problem with which we are faced is how to deal with those areas of the African continent that do not have standardized works of their history. Oral traditions are important, but they do not help us much in tackling the history of stateless communities because most of the Africans concerned do not remember everything and their oral traditions lack historical depth.

   This is a problem to which I refer in examining the culture history of the Igbo. My paper really attempts to see whether a compilation of Igbo history is feasible. What I have done is to identify various stages which, perhaps, could be employed to study other stateless communities in West Africa. First I have looked at the Stone Age and the Iron Age in Igboland. Then, as records and memories become clearer, I have looked at what I call the era of migrations and intermingling of peoples which led to new institutions and new ideas as well as new means of communication. I conclude by pointing out that we must not see statelessness as simply a stage in the development of states. Although the Igbo, throughout their culture history, did have some, or most, of the attributes of the culture that created the kingdoms and states, they did not evolve states themselves and, indeed, they might never have evolved them.

COMMENT *by Simon Ottenberg*

I wonder whether we haven't played down oral history. Having worked with the Igbo myself, I have had some experience with this situation. I admit that there are many difficulties. For example, the founder of Afikpo, when it was time to die, lit a fire, threw a rope into the sky (above it), climbed up it, and then pulled the rope up after him and was gone. I do not think that this contributes much to history, but there are other elements in oral history that do. An example is the behavior patterns involved in movements of people. The movements are small, but they involve the breaking off of patrilineal groups — a younger brother staying at one place, an older brother going on to another. The movements are usually of younger brothers in relation to the place of origin, and they are outward from the Central Igbo area. So we can, at least for the last 400 or 500 years, skillfully use oral history, tying it in with cultural differences and other data.

REPLY *by S. J. S. Cookey*

I agree with you that more can be done with oral traditions; indeed, I did indicate that in my paper. I mentioned the dispersal of the Igbos when I discussed what I call the era of migration and the way the dispersal took place. One can draw lines criss-crossing many parts of Igboland showing how patrilineal groups broke up and how descendants segmented from their original homeland. I think considerable detail could be added to work of this nature, but I am concerned with the period prior to the last 500 years; that is the period where we have considerable difficulty in filling the gaps. Of course, as I suggested, we could also use archaeological, linguistic, and some anthropological data to help us to reconstruct Igbo culture history.

Old Akyem and the Origins of Akyems Abuakwa and Kotoku 1675–1775

RONALD R. ATKINSON

The Akyem are Akan-speaking forest peoples located in southeastern Ghana. Most attempts to reconstruct early southern Akan history have focused on the polities of Akwamu, Denkyira, and, eventually most powerful of all, Asante. As will become clear, however, Akyem played a crucial role in the far-reaching economic, social, and political changes which marked the late seventeenth- and eighteenth-century history of the old Gold Coast and its interior and was significantly involved with the better-researched and better-known Akan states noted above. In short, Akyem in this early period deserves more attention than it has received, and this paper is a brief and introductory attempt to grant that attention.

Once Akyem, rather than one or another of its neighbors, becomes the focus of historical inquiry, one basic question (among many less imposing ones) quickly comes to the fore: that of the relationship between Old Akyem and its offspring Akyem Abuakwa and Akyem Kotoku. Nearly all historians of the early Gold Coast have written as if Akyem Abuakwa and Akyem Kotoku were distinct polities, or at least distinct segments of Old Akyem, from at least the beginning of the eighteenth century. Given the concentration either on nearby polities or on a general history of the region, this is more often inferred or assumed than discussed or analyzed. Ward (1958) is an early case in point; Fynn (1971: esp. 19–20) and the introductory sections on the eighteenth century in Wilks (1975) are more recent ones. These inferences and assumptions are generally supported by Abuakwa and Kotoku traditions, which tend, because of the two polities' long dissociation from one another and frequently unfriendly

I thank Ivor Wilks, R. A. Kea, Larry Yarak, and Jeffrey Rice for their assistance in the preparation of this paper. The format and nature of this volume have led me to keep references to a minimum and to emphasize wherever possible the more readily available sources.

relations throughout the late eighteenth and nineteenth centuries, to deprecate or gloss over their common history.

This usual interpretation of the relationship between Old Akyem and Akyems Abuakwa and Kotoku needs drastic revision, for it fails to explain much of the evidence available on the Akyem past. The evidence instead suggests strongly that old Akyem divided into Akyems Abuakwa and Kotoku only in the second half of the eighteenth century. This evidence, and arguments derived from it, will be presented in the format of an investigation over time of four basic areas of Akyem's life: (1) movements of people into and out of Akyem; (2) economic factors and policies; (3) aspects of internal politics and government; and (4) interpolity relations. While a brief section will be devoted to an outline of events up to ca. 1675, the crucial period under consideration is ca. 1675 to ca. 1775. As we shall see, Akyem was not a highly unified polity during any of this period, but its basic structure until the middle of the eighteenth century was essentially different from that which, in about the third quarter of the century, produced Akyems Abuakwa and Kotoku. I hope to show that embryonic Abuakwas or Kotokus simply did not exist before that time.

AKYEM UP TO 1675

Akyem before 1675 has received little attention and is still little understood.[1] A brief outline of events up to ca. 1675 will suffice to set the stage for the more intensive investigation of the succeeding period.

The area in which Old Akyem developed included both sides (especially the west) of that section of the Pra River which today separates Asante and the northern part of Akyem Kotoku. It was significant for developments both before and after 1675 that this is one of the auriferous areas which made up the rich southern Akan goldfields. The earliest settlements thus far identified in the Akyem area date to the late fifteenth and early sixteenth centuries,[2] and nearby fortified entrenchments scattered throughout the area have been dated to the sixteenth century as well (see Davies 1967:287–290; also Kea 1974:160–161). While there are traditions of "aboriginal" settlements in the Akyem area (see Field

---

[1] The collected papers on early Akan history in Fynn (1966) and Wilks (1971) provide some basic information and an indication of the range and complexity of the problems involved. The work of Kea (1974) and Wilks (1978), in particular, has begun to make crucial aspects of this early period more understandable, and the results of David Kyagga-Mulindwa's combined archaeological and historical research into the early history of the Birim Valley should provide an even clearer and more comprehensive picture.

[2] David Kyagga-Mulindwa has generously provided me two radiocarbon dates for such early villages: A.D. 1510 ± 80 and A.D. 1465 ± 65.

1948:1–5, 199), many of Akyem's earliest settlers, including those associated with the early management and organization of the Akyem-area mines and the group which provided the Asona clan paramount of later Akyem Abuakwa, were matrilineally organized groups from the old Adanse area, now southern Asante (see, e.g., Field 1948:2–3; Ward 1958:109; Institute of African Studies 1963a:1; 1963b:1–2). This is precisely what southern Akan traditions in general, which claim the Adanse area as the "homeland" of the southern Akan (see Boaten 1971), and the more inclusive reconstruction of early developments among the southern Akan by Wilks (1978) would lead one to expect.

In Wilks's reconstruction (and in subsequent comments on that reconstruction), from a beginning in the old Adanse area, the fifteenth and especially the sixteenth century are seen as the height of the extensive clearing of the southern Akan forest region and the creation there of an agrarian order. This great socioeconomic transformation was based on the utilization of massive inputs of unfree labor made available by trade, both to the north and to the coast, of southern Akan gold. It was structured through the creation of the Akan matriclan system, which provided the means to organize the necessary manpower for the tasks of forest clearance and subsequent agricultural production and to permit the integration of the immigrants with the Akan already established in the forest zone. As this transformation led to the replacement of hunting and gathering by food crop production as the dominant mode of production, people were redistributed, including the unfree immigrants, into agricultural work units each organized under the aegis and control of a putatively matrilineal lineage (*abusua*). Membership in an *abusua*, however, was regulated by complex rules which referred not only to kinship, but to adoption as well, and in both cases was based primarily upon an individual's contribution to the productive unit.

Traditions are clear in associating the beginnings of this agricultural order organized on matrilineal principles with the beginnings of offices (stools) vested in *abusua*. For example, in one recension of tradition concerning the beginnings of the new order made by *asantehene* Nana Agyeman Prempeh I while in exile in 1907, a hunter's encounter with the new order involved his meeting first a herald and then a woman bearing a stool (Wilks 1978). With the founding of each new settlement by an *abusua* came the founding of a stool vested in that *abusua* and located, at least in the beginning, in the founding settlement. Frequently the boundaries initially established for such a settlement included an area large enough for additional settlements, each with its own stool, eventually to be established within the area by off-shoot (or other related) *abusua* (for an Akyem Kotoku example of a process such as this, see Field 1948:58). It seems that through at least the first half of the sixteenth century either individual communal agricultural groups or related and contiguous groups such as those just described formed the highest political authority in Akyem and elsewhere in the forest interior (see Field 1948:2; Kea 1974: 160–162, Wilks 1978).

Only very gradually, over the sixteenth and early seventeenth centuries, did the inhabitants of Akyem and elsewhere in the forest interior seem to develop a general territorial consciousness transcending individual (or a small number of closely related and contiguous) settlements and *abusua* and in some instances begin to organize into political units which transcended these local boundaries. The impetus toward this expansion of consciousness and organization seems to have derived from two related concerns over the control of basic economic resources. One of these concerns was to gain more local control of the production and marketing of gold. (Prior to this, such control lay primarily in an elaborate and extensive organization based essentially on extraterritorial or "linear" principles; this organization was pioneered by Malian julas or Wangara and then gradually taken over and expanded during the sixteenth and seventeenth centuries by forest traders centered initially in the Adanse area and known as Akani — see Kea 1974:9–19, 88–147.) A second and growing concern was with the management of land and the structuring of land rights as the number and proximity of settlements headed by *abusua* of different matriclans increased. (For a brief discussion of these concerns and their relationship to the rise of small polities in Asante, see Wilks 1978.)

It is not yet clear whether during this period small polities developed in Akyem as they did, for example, in Asante and Adanse.[3] The existence of some consciousness of a general Akyem territory by the early seventeenth century is attested to by the identification of "Akim or Great Acanij" to the northwest of Akwamu in the famous Dutch map of the Gold Coast of 1629 (translated and reproduced as the end map to *Ghana Notes and Queries* in Fynn 1966). Some local control (including trading) of the area's main exportable resources — gold and slaves — also seems implied in this and other early seventeenth-century sources (e.g., Brun

---

[3]   The list of the predecessors of Ofori Panin, one of the principal Akyem leaders of the early eighteenth century and in the remembered line of Akyem Abuakwa paramounts — Oduro, Boakye, Agyekum Aduware, Boakye Mesah, and Aninkwatia — as recorded in Djan (1936:104) reads, however, suspiciously as if these were the alternating patrilineal *ntoro* names Boakye and Agye (cf. n. 14 below and also the lists in Reindorf n.d. [1895]:348–349 and Danquah 1928:242–243). If the stool occupied by Ofori Panin had passed in a patrilineal line for some three to five generations before settling into a matrilineal succession pattern with him and his successors, it might have been the focus of a small early polity (or polity-like structure) similar to that described in Adanse during roughly this same period by Berberich (i.p.): "Traditionally independent . . . the Adanse towns recognized a leader in the holder of the *Afenakwa,* a state sword. Although originally passed patrilineally, and held by different towns, the *Afenakwa* was kept in the royal family of Fomena and passed matrilineally after the mid-seventeenth century. Thus a state, built around a common tradition and loyalty to the *Afenakwa,* had probably begun to develop in Adanse. It was composed of about seven towns."

1969 [1624]:28 identifies traders in Accra in 1614 who almost surely were from the Akyem area).

THE RISE OF OLD AKYEM AND RELATIONS WITH ASANTE, DENKYIRA, AND AKWAMU

While the Akyem had been evolving throughout most of the seventeenth century as an increasingly distinct identity and began in the second half of that century to develop structures which led to the creation of an Akyem state, the final consolidation of that state and its rise as a significant political power occurred in the period from ca. 1675 to 1730. It is notable that these developments in Akyem were contemporary with the even more striking rise of two of its neighbors: Asante, on Akyem's northwestern border, and Akwamu to the immediate southeast. Under the fabled Osei Tutu during the last quarter of the seventeenth century, an Asante kingdom emerged which over the course of the eighteenth century became the largest and most centralized polity in the Gold Coast region and beyond (on the rise of Asante see, e.g., Wilks 1971:372–381; Fynn 1966, 1971). Preceding, while not eventually matching, the emergence of Asante as a great power was the rise to eminence of Akwamu. With the seizure of power in 1677 from its patron, the king of Accra, Akwamu began a period of territorial expansion and governmental centralization on a scale without precedent in the Gold Coast region. By the early eighteenth century, Akwamu was the most powerful and centralized state the region had ever seen (see Kea, this volume; also Kea 1974:169–275; Wilks 1957, 1958, 1971:367–369). As we shall see, Akyem was able, at least through 1730, to maintain itself *vis-à-vis* Asante while at the same time strengthening its position in the face of Akwamu power to such an extent that by 1730 Akyem forces helped destroy the Akwamu empire.

Significant movements of people did not end with the establishment of early settlers from Adanse in the area of Old Akyem. Rather, throughout the seventeenth and eighteenth centuries people continued to move into and beyond Akyem. In the 1675-1730 period, two movements of people deserve special mention. The first was the migration to Akyem of the occupant and supporters of the stool which eventually became the paramount stool of Akyem Kotoku. The second was the gradual movement of various Akyem into the northwestern Akwamu hinterland.

Akyem Kotoku traditions are clear in their assertion that the state of Denkyira, farther west, was the original home of their paramount stool, the Denkyira-Mmerayam stool (Institute of African Studies 1966:1–2; also 1963c:1; Ward 1958:109; Field 1948:3). The occupant of the stool when it came to Akyem was Ofosu Apenten (d. 1717) of the Agona clan; he led his followers from their Denkyira homeland to, eventually, the

Bomfa area on the western bank of the Anum River, then part of or bordering Akyem territory and now well within Asante. Kotoku traditions continue by claiming that trouble between Apenten and his relative, the *denkyirahene*, caused the former to leave Denkyira with his supporters. The timing of this move is not quite clear, but it appears that it was shortly before the 1699–1701 war between Denkyira and Asante (Institute of African Studies 1966:1–2). Apenten's decision to settle fewer than thirty miles from Kumase, the center of Asante power, and moreover on the Kumase side of the Anum, implies that he may have taken, at least indirectly, Asante's side in the Denkyira-Asante conflict. Such a position would certainly match up with the tradition of the quarrel between Apenten and the *denkyirahene*, whether this quarrel occurred before or after the Denkyira defeat.

The gradual movement of Akyem into the northwestern Akwamu hinterland before 1730 is treated somewhat less directly in tradition. Akwamu traditions claim that Ofori Panin requested and received from the *akwamuhene* a grant of land in Akwamu. This land was reportedly located at and around Banso, some eight miles from the present-day Akyem Abuakwa capital of Kibi (traditions of the old Akwamu towns Akwatia and Asamankese report the transaction and the specific location — Institute of African Studies 1963a:1; 1963b:1–2; the transaction is also noted in Wilks 1958:115; Field 1948:3; and Ward 1958:108).[4]

TRADE AND STATE FINANCES, 1675–1730

Gold and slaves, the major Akyem resources in the pre-1675 period, remained the major sources of wealth after 1675. The Danish, Dutch, and English merchants around 1700 all recognized Akyem as one of the major sources of gold (as reported respectively by Norregard 1966:63; Bosman 1967 [1705]:78; Kea 1974:224). The rising power of Akwamu, its frequent enmity toward Akyem, and its even more frequent attempts to control and limit Akyem's trade to the coast caused continual economic problems for Akyem. Danish, Dutch, and English traders at

---

[4]   While this seems rather near Akwamu centers, the location of Banso to the west of the Atewa Range (while Kibi, established by Akyem Abuakwa much later, lies on its eastern slope) tends to strengthen traditional claims that Akyem settlers moved into this area prior to 1730. The natural geographical break provided by the Atewa Range could have served as a *de facto* geopolitical marker, with the most significant Akwamu population limited to east of the range (settlements to the west may have been unsafe during the frequent periods when Akyem and Akwamu were at odds during the late seventeenth and early eighteenth centuries). Of all the important old Akwamu towns remembered, only one, Kwabeng, lay in the northwest, beyond the Atewa Range (Institute of African Studies 1963a:1–2; Johnson 1964:9). Conversely, of the five divisional seats — the most important towns — of later Abuakwa, all lie in the northwest of former old Akwamu or beyond and only one, Kwabeng, is remembered as being also an important Akwamu town.

Cape Coast all commented upon Akwamu hindrance of Akyem trade to the coast (Kwamena-Poh 1973:35). Rømer (1965[1760]:7), on the Gold Coast from about 1735 to 1750, even claimed that the Akyem could not trade southward at all: "the Aqvamboes [Akwamu] practiced the policy of never letting the Akims come down to the coast, not even to Aqvamboe; the Aqvamboes black traders, however, brought their goods to Akim. They painted us Europeans as horrid; that we were sea monsters. . . ." This is clearly an exaggeration and a simplification of a complex issue. Kea (1974:226–228) argues that the "Akwamu government maintained an ambivalent attitude towards the [traders] from inland kingdoms such as Akyem and Kwahu." The numerous Dutch, Danish, and English sources he cites from the late seventeenth and early eighteenth century indicate both periods of Akwamu limitation and control of Akyem trade and periods (e.g., when Akwamu was engaged in a major military campaign elsewhere) in which Akyem merchants were not prevented from traveling to the coast to trade. He summarizes: "Akyem access to the ports on the Akwamu coast was contingent upon the vagaries of the Akwamu governments' commercial and political policies."

Akwamu governmental interference with Akyem trade had its roots in the pre-1675 period. For example, Wilks (1957:104–105) notes that the Dutch fiscal Caarloff paid several visits in 1646–1647 "in person to the King of Akwamu in an attempt to persuade him to open the paths to Kwamana and Akim merchants." Fynn (1971:23) points out that Akwamu's alliance with Agona between 1659 and 1680 was not only to secure Akwamu's western frontier, but to prevent Akyem and other inland traders from bypassing Accra and Akwamu control by trading to the coast through Agona (see also Rømer 1965 [1760]:8; Reindorf n.d. [1895]:62). Moreover, this Akwamu interference seems at least as politically as economically motivated. For example, it was a capital offense for an Akwamu to sell firearms or powder to Akyem (Rømer 1965 [1760]:8; see also Fynn 1971:40, 46–47). Akwamu institutional control of Akyem trade to the south operated primarily in times of peace. As noted above, when Akwamu was at war elsewhere, Akyem traders were allowed to come to the coast. Conversely, when war between Akwamu and Akyem threatened or actually took place, Akyem trade through Akwamu-controlled territory was not limited or controlled, but halted as completely as the Akwamu government could manage.

Akyem was thus not in an enviable economic or political position. The gold and slaves which represented the main sources of prestige and wealth for both individuals and the state and which made possible the purchase of European goods could often be traded only on Akwamu sufferance and subject to Akwamu restrictions. Potentially the most damaging of these restrictions for Akyem was the Akwamu government's attempts to limit Akyem's access to the European commodity becoming crucial for the building or maintenance of a strong state: firearms and their accessories.

Recognized as important both on the coast and in the interior by the 1660's, firearms had become the dominant weapon of warfare in the Gold Coast region by the end of the seventeenth century (Kea 1971; 1974: ch. 4). Almost from the beginning, rulers and their governmental functionaries used the wealth and trading organization available to them to make firearms and their accessories essentially state monopolies. By 1700, for example, Akwamu's large and powerful army was composed almost entirely of musketeers whose weapons, gunpowder, and ammunition were supplied primarily by the state (Kea 1974:322–337). Such major expenditures were made possible by the development of state treasuries, a development Wilks has emphasized and demonstrated as important both for the rise of Akwamu (1957:104; 1958:6–8) and later for the growth and maintenance of Asante (1975: esp. 418–445). There can be no doubt, then, that any limitations imposed by Akwamu on both one of the primary means (trade) and one of the most important ends (firearms and accessories) of building up the Akyem treasury would have had negative effects on Akyem. That Akwamu restrictions on Akyem trade in general and Akyem access to firearms in particular were not ultimately effective, however, is made clear by the Akyem success in the 1730 conflict with Akwamu and the fact that significant armed Akyem contingents fought against Asante in 1699–1702 and 1717.

When we turn from the economics of trade to the economics of production, we find that information concerning the organization of the extractive gold industry in Akyem is meager. We can only assume that some kind of organization and control by the Akyem state did exist, as government control of the extractive industry was common practice among Akan polities (see, e.g., Wilks 1975:435–436).

A reference to gold extraction in Akyem is found in Akyem Oda (Kotoku) tradition (Institute of African Studies 1966:5–6), where it is asserted that the Kotoku were the only Akyem who "owned" gold mines or, more importantly, knew how to mine gold. This assertion deserves careful consideration. A connection with the mines would have tended to make certain Akyem relatively immobile. It would follow, then, that because the Akyem Kotoku state developed in the territory most nearly coterminous with Old Akyem (which included most of the Old Akyem gold mines), those Akyem who were associated with the mines should have become Kotoku. Association with the mines was not based on allegiance to some embryonic Kotoku which existed in the Old Akyem polity. Rather, it was ties to the mines and the economic activities associated with them that linked certain Kotoku to specific locations. When a distinct Kotoku polity gradually emerged which incorporated the area of the mines, those associated with the mines tended to become a part of it.

It was this economic "allegiance," as it were, rather than a political allegiance to a segment of Old Akyem destined to become Kotoku, that accounted for these persons' becoming Kotoku.

ASPECTS OF AKYEM GOVERNMENT, 1675–1730

Writing of the 1680's, Barbot (1746 [1732]:189) describes Akyem government in the following terms: "This country was formerly a monarchy, and now a commonwealth, after several changes and revolutions in the government, which renders it the less formidable to its neighbours, because of the factions and divisions the republican government is subject to; ... and therefore this country, for want of unity and a good understanding among the natives, is not so powerful as formerly." This passage and other detailed references by Bosman (1967 [1705]:69, 78) underscore the following points: (1) Europeans on the coast believed that Akyem had formerly been a monarchy; (2) the late seventeenth century saw "several changes and revolutions in the government" of Akyem; (3) the result of these changes was "a sort of Commonwealth," with "the Governing Men of the Kingdom" taking a part of the administration into their hands; (4) this decentralized leadership was seen as making Akyem weaker than it otherwise might have been; and (5) the shared Akyem leadership was exploited by Akwamu, which sowed "Dissensions betwixt the Governing Men of *Akim.*"[5]

By 1729, on the eve of the fall of Akwamu, additional information is available on Akyem government which confirms and adds detail to the earlier descriptions. Akyem in 1729 was governed by three rulers, the "three great Caboceers" Frempong Manso (who succeeded Apenten in 1717), Bakwante (who succeeded Ofori Panin in 1727), and Owusu. Wilks (1958:95–96) admits that the relationship among the three is vague, but we may conjecture that this threefold division of Akyem royal power had its origins in three fundamental historical processes: first, the traditional division of the Akan military into three main wings; second, the incorporation into Akyem of the Denkyira-Mmerayam stool, which later became the paramount stool of Akyem Kotoku; and third, the early development of shared authority in Akyem.[6] While no specific informa-

---

[5] While Barbot wrote in the 1680's, his observations were not published until 1732 (by a surviving brother), and certain passages read as if they might have been taken from the earlier-published Bosman. For example, while the quotations above on Akyem are not especially similar, the nearby Barbot passages on Denkyira and Akani (pp. 188–189) are very close paraphrases of the corresponding Bosman (pp. 73, 77).

[6] An Akyem Kotoku tradition inadvertently supports this proposition. The tradition, which has as its purpose the attempt to demonstrate that the Abuakwa were at one time "subjects" of the Kotoku, states that in the campaign against Asante which can be dated to 1717 the Abuakwa formed, supposedly under the Kotoku, the *adonten* or center division of

tion on Akyem army organization for the late seventeenth and early eighteenth centuries has yet been discovered, recent studies of predecessor states (Akwamu and Denkyira) leave little doubt that the same basic pattern of wings — the center (*adonten*), left wing (*benkum*), and right wing (*nifa*), in which early political divisions or provinces replicated military organization — was also adopted in Akyem. Second, as already noted, Ofosu Apenten came from Denkyira to settle on the borders of Akyem in about 1699–1701. It would have been advantageous both for the immigrants and for Akyem for the former to be integrated into the Akyem state as rapidly as possible.[7] Once integrated, a stool of such age and previous importance as the Denkyira-Mmerayam stool would surely have held a position of considerable rank. The tradition of shared authority may also have derived from a situation resembling a regency, in which the elder "governing men of the kingdom" exercised control during the reign of a young and weak king. This situation could have persisted in later stages of development, so that the paramount ruler was considered only *primus inter pares* (see, for example, Kea 1974:185 on Akwamu). A possible parallel can be found in a description of political leadership in the western Akan state of Assini (Loyer 1714:260–261): "There are three generals in the kingdom, who are nearly equal in the authority they have." One of these "generals" was also titled king, one was the king's "nephew," and the other was the king's "brother."[8] The likelihood that the "nephew" was a sister's son and that the "brother" was of a different matriclan (having the same father as the king, but a different mother, from a different clan) means that authority in Assini in the early eighteenth century may have been shared among two matrilineally related leaders and one from a different clan, just as in Akyem. Even if this last detailed similarity did not obtain, however, the sharing of power among three military leaders possessing "nearly equal authority" makes Assini leadership sound very like Akyem's. What has to be emphasized is that the ongoing (and from all appearances successful) effort to keep the major divisions of Akyem roughly equal in numbers and strength through

---

the Akyem forces. What this tradition seems to indicate is not some past Kotoku dominance of Abuakwa, but rather that the holder of the stool that later became the Abuakwa paramount was in 1717 the *adontenhene* in Old Akyem.

[7]   While the general turmoil of the period surrounding the Asante-Denkyira war would seem to provide support for this view, circumstances following the war may have led Akyem to perceive special benefits in the incorporation of Apenten and his followers. Not only would they have added numbers to Akyem (surely seen as a benefit, and a not insignificant one in light of Akyem's reputed battle losses in the war — see below), but, if Apenten had, as suggested above, somehow taken Asante's side in the conflict between Asante and Denkyira, he would have offered the prospect of a more secure flank and more positive ties to Asante in a period when Akyem could hardly have desired further confrontation.

[8]   I thank R. A. Kea for providing me with this source; the translation used in the text is also his.

constant reshuffling (Field 1948:6) does not imply disunity. Assertions by Fynn (1971:20), Daaku (1970:173), and others that Akyem leadership was split between the rulers of Akyem Abuakwa and Akyem Kotoku from an early period seem to be straightforward examples of reading back into the early eighteenth century the later situation.

AKYEM CONFLICT WITH AKWAMU AND ASANTE

Akyem's interstate relations were dominated by the basic problem of having to deal simultaneously with great — and expanding — powers on both its southeastern and its northwestern border. These two powers, Akwamu and Asante, not only were often hostile to Akyem individually, but frequently acted in concert to isolate and weaken it (Daaku 1970:180–181; Fynn 1971:30). In its dealings with these two neighbors, the results for Akyem were mixed: with Akwamu, Akyem was ultimately more than able to hold its own; Asante, however, eventually proved too strong, though Asante supremacy was not clearly established until after 1730.

   In 1675, problems seemed to lie almost entirely with Akwamu. As noted above, Akwamu was about to enter its period of greatest expansion and centralization, and it must have been clear by the last quarter of the seventeenth century that its economic policies (that is, control of trade to the coast) were becoming more and more detrimental to the development of the Akyem treasury and army. Akyem's responses to the rising — and, from Akyem's perspective, frequently oppressive or hostile — power of Akwamu were many, including such tactics as outflanking Akwamu to reach the coast westward of Akwamu control (see, e.g., Kea 1974:201, 228) and taking advantage of the periodic lapses in Akwamu control noted above. Even more drastic and irritating to Akwamu were Akyem's frequent raids on it, carried out either independently or in league with other anti-Akwamu forces. Raids and skirmishes or the threat of them were almost constant between 1675 and 1730.[9] The seriousness of the Akyem threat to Akwamu is attested to by the continual movement of the latter's capital south and east, apparently motivated not only by shifting trade activities and patterns, but by the fear of Akyem harassment. There even grew up a saying, reported by the Dane Tilleman in 1697 and quoted by Fynn (1971:23): "when the Akwamu, on their oath and fetish, say

---

[9]   For example, between 1677 and 1681 there were frequent Akyem raids into northwestern Akwamu while Akwamu forces were busy conquering Accra; during the 1680's, Akwamu threats and eventual intervention prevented an Akyem alliance with Agona which would have provided Akyem access to such coastal settlements as Winneba and Apam; meanwhile, in 1688 there were several Akyem-Akwamu skirmishes; 1715 and 1716 were marked by many threats and a few skirmishes; in 1723 Akyem attacked Akwamu; and from 1724 on events were building toward the decisive 1730 conflict.

they are going to make war in the east, it is then that they will generally turn to the west." Even Akwamu's general policy of expansion primarily to the south and east was at least partially determined by the formidability of Akyem on its northwestern border (Wilks 1958:5–6, 21–23). All in all, despite Akwamu's favorable position for controlling trade and coastal access, Akyem was not overwhelmed by its powerful neighbor to the south. Bosman (1967[1705]:65) seems to sum up the situation well: "Aquamboe power is also very terrible to their neighbouring countries, except Akim." Finally, when internal dissensions within the royal Abrade group had sufficiently weakened Akwamu in 1730, Akyem took advantage of the situation and joined Akwamu homeland and provincial rebels in the overthrow of Akwamu.[10]

To the northwest, Akyem was not so successful. Akyem's first clash with Asante came in the 1699–1701 war between Asante and Denkyira. At least two reasons suggest themselves as to why Akyem chose to ally itself with Denkyira in this conflict. The first was Akyem's apparently long-standing differences with Akani (Adanse-Assin), which was allied with Asante against Denkyira. One basis for conflict between Akyem and Akani was suggested above: that Akyem had had to gain control over the mining and trading of gold in their area from Akani traders. Also, Dapper (1966[1670]:16–17) indicates differences between Akyem and Akani in the 1660's, and Daaku (1970:168–169) offers evidence of differences between the two during the late seventeenth and early eighteenth centuries. A second and even more important reason for Akyem to oppose Asante at this time was Akyem's realization that its neighbor was growing extremely powerful and that it was in Akyem's interest to help Denkyira check that power if it could (Dupuis 1824:230). It could not. The loss of Akyem men was great (as indicated by Bosman 1967[1705]:76, though his figure of 30,000 casualties should not be taken literally).

A surprise Denkyira-Akyem victory over Asante in 1702 was only a temporary reversal of Asante ascendancy (Daaku 1970: 173–174; Fynn 1971:24), and by opposing Asante in this period Akyem helped determine that Asante's rising power would be directed against it in the future. By 1715 the two were building up arms to face one another, and in 1717 they went to war again. The Akyem, evidently utilizing what would become familiar tactics with the later Kotoku and Abuakwa, melted into the forest and fought primarily from ambush. While Apenten, one of the three Akyem leaders, was killed in the fighting, one surprise Akyem attack resulted not only in the death of the Asante king, but the capturing

[10]   The most comprehensive and analytical treatment of the complex internal and external factors that led to the fall of Akwamu remains that of Wilks (1958:80–110), though he incorrectly affixes the names Kotoku and Abuakwa to the Akyem forces. See also Wilks (1971:368–369), Daaku (1970:171–181), and Kwamena-Poh (1973:6, 22, 30–39), this last providing a reconstruction primarily from an Akwapim perspective.

of his skull — the most serious defeat and humiliation that could befall an Akan state (a narrative of this 1717 war and the events surrounding it is included in nearly all accounts of early Gold Coast history; see especially Priestly and Wilks 1960; Kwamena-Poh 1973:35–36).

In the early 1720's, Opoku Ware, the new Asante king, not only carried out a successful retaliatory expedition against Akyem, but then helped forge an uneasy and limited rapprochement between Asante and Akyem that held until 1742 (Kwamena-Poh 1973:36). The existence of some form of peaceful relationship between Asante and Akyem by the late 1720's (and the deterioration of Asante-Akwamu relations) is evident from Asante inactivity as Akyem made preparations for and then carried out its attack on Akwamu in 1730. Asante may have tacitly agreed to the Akyem attack, as Rømer (1965[1760]:18) indicates; at any rate, as Fynn (1971:69–70) points out, Asante did not help its alleged ally Akwamu even as it fell.

THE PASSING OF OLD AKYEM, 1730–1775

The success of Akyem in the 1730 war with Akwamu was, paradoxically, the beginning of the end of Old Akyem as a political entity. The governmental structure of Akyem before 1730, with its tripartite sharing of leadership, was not highly unified, but the divisive tendencies present in this structure did not represent in any way embryonic Kotoku or Abuakwa polities. Only when large numbers of Akyem became spatially separated from the Old Akyem homeland, after flooding into the former territory of defeated and dispersed Akwamu, did divisive forces within the Old Akyem polity begin to follow lines that eventually differentiated Akyem Abuakwa from Akyem Kotoku. Divisions along these new lines were made sharper by the 1742 Asante defeat of Old Akyem and a series of events greatly influenced by Asante power and interference in internal Akyem affairs. I hope to show that the divisions in Akyem represented by such characteristics as relative geographical mobility versus immobility and pro-Asante versus anti-Asante positions had as one of their most important *results* the creation of Abuakwa and Kotoku polities from the parent Old Akyem. This is in contradistinction to the commonly held view that such divisions were determined by or reflected already existing political differentiation between Kotoku and Abuakwa (as put forth, e.g., by Wilks 1957, 1958, 1975; Johnson 1964; Fynn 1971; and Kwamena-Poh 1973).

There is no question that Akyem settlers moved into the old Akwamu homeland after 1730, and on a large scale: "after the collapse of Akwamu in the west, Abuakwa settlers, eager for *lebensraum*, poured into the conquered territories and established new towns side by side with the surviving Akwamu towns" (Wilks 1958:116). Though the reference here is to *Abuakwa* settlers, there is no evidence that a distinct Abuakwa polity was being relocated in the old Akwamu homeland. The Akyem who migrated southward appear not have been accompanied by any of their major leaders. In fact, when the Akyem were faced with the problem of administering old Akwamu, they chose to govern it, despite the large influx of Akyem settlers, through a defeated Akwamu general, not an Akyem. It retained this indirectly ruled, subordinate status for over forty years (Wilks 1958:114, 129–135).

The movement of Akyem settlers to, and subsequent residence in, old Akwamu was a geographical phenomenon that only later took on political significance. Once they had moved, these Akyem were physically separated from the Akyem who remained in the Old Akyem territory. This could not have helped but create differences and rigidify whatever differences were already present. It was only with the banishment by Asante of one of the two Akyem rulers to the old Akwamu homeland in 1773, however, that political divisions developing over the previous thirty years or more were firmly aligned with geographical divisions and Old Akyem was finally replaced by Akyems Abuakwa and Kotoku.

The economic ramifications for Akyem of the fall of Akwamu were not confined to the old Akwamu lands now available to Akyem settlers. First, the notes specifying the ground rent owed by each of the three European forts in Accra passed from vanquished to victor. Fynn (1971:71) writes that Frempong Manso "became the political overlord of the Osu district in which stood Danish Christiansborg Castle," while Bakwante "had charge of the Accra townships in which stood Dutch Crèvecoeur [Ussher Fort] and British James Fort. Thus, the Akyem chiefs, like the Akwamu kings before them, received ground rents from three European settlements and thereby secured a permanent, regular means of purchasing muskets and powder which were essential for their political and economic expansion."[11] There was also general control of and free access to the coast at Accra, with all the trade benefits this brought, not least importantly the direct access to firearms and their accessories. In addition, the fall of Akwamu brought numerous captives under Akyem control. Akyem policy toward these slaves seemed designed to assimilate them rapidly, thus increasing Akyem's numbers and strength (Rømer 1965[1760]:21);[12] Fynn (1971:72) reports that it was believed on the coast that Akyem feared an Asante attack from the end of 1730 on and hoped to use the captured Akwamu against such an attack. Finally,

[11]   Owusu was the recipient of regular ground rent payments from the later 1730's on the Danish fort Fredensborg at Great Ningo on the coast opposite Akwapim (Kwamena-Poh 1973:75–76; Norregard 1966:97).
[12]   Reindorf's passage (n.d. [1895]:78–79) on this topic reads suspiciously like Rømer's; this is one of many instances in which it appears as if Reindorf had access to Rømer's work.

territory beyond the old Akwamu area, most importantly the Akwapim hills, passed from Akwamu to Akyem control. The Akyem leader who took jurisdiction over much of this area was Owusu (Kwamena-Poh 1973:74–75; see also n. 11). Directly or indirectly, all these sources provided new wealth for both the Akyem treasury and many individual Akyem. Europeans at the Accra forts had mixed reactions to Akyem's good fortunes and increased presence. The Akyem were preferred over-all to either the Akwamu before or Asante after; the gold brought to the coast during the brief period of Akyem dominance was of higher quality, but the trade was less regular and there were far fewer slaves to comple-ment the gold (Rømer, 1965[1760]:20–25; Norregard 1966:80–83, 97).

The manner in which individuals or groups attempted to take advan-tage of the new opportunities made available by the 1730 victory, espe-cially the opening up of old Akwamu land for settlement, surely played a role in the determination of which Akyem became Kotoku and which Abuakwa. Those Akyem who were areally tied, such as those tied to the gold mines of Old Akyem, or preferentially tied, such as the "owners" of land on which important towns or mines were located, or those with positive ties or relations with Asante would have been less likely to leave the Old Akyem homeland. It was factors such as these, I would argue, and not ties to embryonic or actual Abuakwa and Kotoku segments, that were the primary determinants influencing which Akyem moved or did not move.

The three leaders — Frempong Manso, Bakwante, and Owusu — who had ruled in Akyem before 1730 and led the Akyem to victory against Akwamu seem to have shared almost equally the new power and adminis-trative responsibilities that came with their victory, including the admini-stration, usually by indirect means, of conquered areas (Rømer 1965[1760]:23–24; Wilks 1958:112–124). This tripartite division of sup-reme authority continued until Asante interference in Akyem succession after 1742, which led to the loss of legitimacy and then to the elimination of one of the three Akyem stools. It was the elimination of this stool that aligned the patterns of division in Akyem in a way which led eventually to the disintegration of the Old Akyem polity into two components — Abuakwa and Kotoku.

In the 1742 war, all three Akyem rulers met their death. Apau, who had succeeded Frempong Manso in 1741, and Owusu were killed; Bak-wante was captured and committed suicide. In the course of the fighting Asante also captured possible heirs to both Apau and Bakwante (Rømer 1965[1760]:31–32).[13] Following the war the Asante "offered" these

[13] Rømer specifically notes that it was heirs of these two lines that were captured, and Norregard (1966:108) identifies Owusu's successor as Pobi, i.e., *not* one of the two heirs captured by Asante. In light of this evidence, Fynn's assertions (n.d.:4; 1971:75) that Pobi succeeded Bakwante seem very strange.

royals as successors to their respective stools. The power of Asante caused their "offer" to be accepted, even though the candidates did not conform to Akyem succession preferences and had besides been captives of the *asantehene* and could be called his "slaves." Both Rømer (1965[1760]:32) and Kotoku tradition (Institute of African Studies 1966:8) claim that there were "older and consequently closer heirs" to the respective stools.

While it seems there was no alternative, in the face of Asante power, to seeing the two Asante-backed candidates enstooled, the two Akyem ruling lines which were affected ultimately responded to their respective imposed rulers in very different ways. The Denkyira-Mmerayam line includes Broni, the Asante-imposed successor to Apau, in its stool list, though significantly he is remembered not as a fully legitimate ruler, but as a regent (Institute of African Studies 1966:38). The man identified by Rømer (1965[1760]:31) as the Asante-imposed candidate to succeed Bakwante, "Ascharry" or Asare, was apparently even less acceptable to the Asona clan his stool represented, for with Asare's death, sometime after 1746 (Rømer 1965[1760]:45 refers to Asare as late as this), the Asona clan either did not fill the vacancy or did not recognize the legitimacy of the successor. This was possible without disinheriting the Asona line represented by the disfavored stool because the third Akyem stool was filled by a member of that line. After Asare's death, the Asona were represented at the highest level in Akyem by only one stool, filled at this time by Pobi, the successor to Owusu (see n. 13). It was this stool which became the paramount stool of Abuakwa.[14]

Two of the three major structural factors that produced distinct Akyems Abuakwa and Kotoku from the parent Old Akyem were now present. The first was a real separation and differentiation between the Old Akyem homeland and the area of old Akwamu opened up to large-scale Akyem settlement after the 1730 war. The second was dual paramounts rather than the older situation of sharing authority among three rulers. The tendency to fission is much greater with bipolar sharing of power than in a tripartite or other multiple-rule system. What was needed now was for the geographical tendencies toward fission (between the Old Akyem and old Akwamu homelands) to coincide with the new politico-administrative division between only two ruling stools (representing the Agona Denkyira-Mmerayam and Asona Owusu-Pobi lines).

Asante political power was the catalytic agent for that coincidence.

---

[14] It is not surprising that Abuakwa king lists (provided by Djan 1936:104; Danquah 1928:242–243; and Reindorf n.d.[1895]:348–349) do not include Asare or indicate that Pobi and his successors represented a different Asona stool than did Ofori Panin and Bakwante; one of the purposes of such lists is to show an unbroken line of "Abuakwa" rulers stretching as far back in time as possible. For Fynn to have missed all of this (see also n. 13), however, is not so understandable.

During the period from the late 1740's to the early 1770's, the area of new Akyem settlements, at least partly because it was simply farther away from Asante than the Old Akyem homeland, became firmly identified as anti-Asante. Meanwhile, the area of Old Akyem seems to have been at least not as hostile to, and in limited ways even aligned with, Asante interests. This is not to say that pro- and anti-Asante factions did not exist in both areas or that the problem ever lent itself to clear-cut or permanent solutions (as the internal politics and shifting allegiances of later Abuakwa and Kotoku clearly reveal). In the main, however, and for most of the period under consideration, anti-Asante activities tended to be centered in the new Akyem settlements rather than in the Old Akyem homeland.[15]

Anti-Asante activities in Akyem surfaced less than five years after the 1742 war, when according to Danish reports Akyem repudiated Asante overlordship, left their country to take refuge in Fante, Kwahu, and Little Popo, and entered into an alliance with the Fante, Wassa, and others to fight Asante (Fynn 1971:80). There was no immediate war, but over the next several years the anti-Asante alliance added new members, and Asante access to the coast through the allied states was frequently blocked — a policy designed, as Tenkorang (1968) points out, primarily to restrict Asante access to firearms. While it is not clear from available 1740's sources whether or in what fashion Akyem was divided over the course of these events, sources from the 1750's and 1760's do provide such information.

Beginning in the mid-1750's, references appear which distinguish, for the first time, territorial divisions in Akyem which can be matched to one or the other of the two Akyem leaders. One such reference appears in a 1758 report submitted by two Dutch chief brokers who had visited both the anti-Asante allies and the Asante, between 1754 and 1758, in an attempt to settle the differences between the two. The *asantehene* Kusi Obodom proposed to them eight conditions for peace with the allies, one of which read as follows (National Archives, The Hague 1758):[16] "Second, that he had taken under his protection together half of the countries of Akjim and Aowinie, that is the caboceers and peoples, who had come out of these countries to him, and now render his obedience, [and they] would for that reason remain unmolested by all of them [i.e., the four "allied Districts, namely Wassa, Dinkira, Tjuffer (Twifo), and Akjim"].'

It is evident that Akyem at this time was clearly divided, with one portion

---

[15] This basic north-south division in Akyem with respect to being essentially pro- or anti-Asante is matched by developments all around Asante's southern periphery — e.g., it is traced in Assin by Berberich (i.p.), and Larry Yarak of Northwestern University, working on eighteenth- and nineteenth-century Wassaw history, has discovered not only a north-south division, but other basic similarities between Wassa and Akyem as well.

[16] I thank Larry Yarak for the translation from the Dutch (cf. Fynn's summation and use of this document [1971:89–91]).

enmeshed in an anti-Asante alliance and the other — Kusi Obodom claimed "half" seemingly aligned with Asante. There is little room for doubt that the "half" to which Kusi Obodom referred to as rendering him obedience was Old Akyem or portions of Old Akyem (essentially those portions lying between the Pra and Anum Rivers) that were surrounded by lands that were part of metropolitan Asante. While these portions of Old Akyem were not actually incorporated into Asante until the nineteenth century (Wilks 1975:51–52), already by the mid-eighteenth century their vulnerable location made them unsuitable as a base for anti-Asante activities. Moreover, they seem to have been ruled at this time by the man the Asante imposed on the Denkyira-Mmerayam stool after the 1742 war, the "slave" of Asante, Broni.

This last is implied by the fact that the anti-Asante portion of Akyem was then led by Pobi Asomanin, who had succeeded Owusu in 1742. It must have been Pobi who led the Akyem opposed to Asante into the anti-Asante alliance with the Wassaw and others and who kept the paths through Akyem and Akwapim closed from the late 1740's on, but Pobi was killed following the Asante defeat of Akyem forces in 1765. His successor, Obirikoran, was chosen and enstooled by the Asante. It was not long, however, before Obirikoran was leading a "Residue of the Akim nation" in various anti-Asante activities.[17] In 1767, Obirikoran irritated Asante with his aggressive policies to the east of the old Akwamu homeland, and from 1767 to 1772 he led his "Residue" of Akyem in several clashes with Asante. Finally, in 1772, the Asante sent a large army into Akyem once again. Obirikoran's "lands [presumably to the west of the Atewa Range — see n. 4] were occupied and Obirikane retreated to Old Akwamu [presumably to the east] and submitted to Asantehene Osei Kojo" (Wilks 1958:134; Kwamena-Poh 1973:81).

The next year Obirikoran invited the Dutch to attempt reconciliation with Asante so that he could return to his lands. Despite this attempt, he was deposed by the Asante (he continued to fight Asante from exile into the 1780's). The Asante enstooled in his place another candidate of their choosing, Twum Ampoforo. Even though Ampoforo affirmed allegiance to Asante (and maintained this allegiance until he was deposed by his people ca. 1794), he was not allowed to return to Old Akyem. This was presumably to prevent him from becoming a focus for any anti-Asante activities in that "half" of Akyem. Instead, he "was obliged to remain with his people in Old Akwamu, where a new Abuakwa capital was established at Kibi" (Wilks 1958:134).

Thus, Wilks states (p. 135), came the final disappearance of old Akwamu as a political entity: "the Akwamu chiefs swore allegiance to Mpoforo, recognizing him as their paramount, and were integrated into

---

[17]   The phrase "Residue of the Akim nation" is from English documents dated to the later 1760's (Public Records Office, London, T70/31) quoted in Wilks (1975:28).

the Akim Abuakwa state." Thence, also, though Wilks apparently does not recognize it, came the final stage in the emergence of the polities of Akyem Abuakwa and Akyem Kotoku. The two geographical and the two political divisions that had been present in Akyem and in the process of aligning themselves for almost a quarter-century were now firmly congruent. Akyems Abuakwa and Kotoku were the results.

REFERENCES

BARBOT, J.
   1746 [1732]   *A description of the coasts of North and South Guinea.* Churchill's Collection of Voyages and Travels 5. London. (Originally published in Paris.)
BERBERICH, CHARLES
   i.p.   "Loyalty, revolt, and emigration: Assin in eighteenth- and early nineteenth century Akan power politics," in *Kwame Daaku memorial volume.* Legon: Longman.
BOATEN, K.
   1971   The Asante before 1700. *Research Review* (Institute of African Studies, Legon) 8(1):50–65.
BOSMAN, WILLIAM
   1967 [1705]   *A new and accurate description of the coast of Guinea* (Fourth edition). London: Frank Cass.
BRUN [BRAUN], SAMUEL
   1969 [1624]   *Schiffarten in etliche neue Länder und Insulen.* Graz.
DAAKU, K. Y.
   1970   *Trade and politics on the Gold Coast 1600–1720.* Oxford: Clarendon.
DANQUAH, J. B.
   1928   *Akan laws and customs and the Akim Abuakwa constitution.* London: G. Routledge.
DAPPER, O.
   1966 [1670]   *Beschreiburg von Afrika.* Amsterdam. (Translated in part in *Ghana Notes and Queries,* no. 9, 15–17.)
DAVIES, OLIVER
   1967   *West Africa before the Europeans.* London: Methuen.
DJAN, S.
   1936   *The Sunlight reference almanac of the Gold Coast Colony and its dependencies.* Aburi, Gold Coast.
DUPUIS, J.
   1824   *Journal of a residence in Ashanti.* London.
FIELD, M. J.
   1948   *Akim Kotoku: an oman of the Gold Coast.* Accra: Crown Agents.
FYNN, J. K.
   1966   The rise of Ashanti. *Ghana Notes and Queries,* no. 9, 24–30.
   1971   *Asante and its neighbours 1700–1807.* London: Longman.
   n.d.   "Akim Abuakwa kings of the eighteenth century: a chronology." Unpublished manuscript.

GOODY, JACK
1963   "Introduction," in *Succession to high office*. Edited by Jack Goody. Cambridge: Published for the Department of Archaeology and Anthropology at the University Press.
INSTITUTE OF AFRICAN STUDIES, LEGON
1963a Tradition of Akwatia. KAG 2, recorded by Kwabena Ameyaw.
1963b Tradition of Asamankese. KAG 4, recorded by Kwabena Ameyaw.
1963c Tradition of Akroso. AM 15, recorded by Kwabena Ameyaw.
1966   Akim Oda (Kotoku) tradition. KAG 7, recorded by Kwabena Ameyaw.
JOHNSON, MARION
1964   Migrants' progress, part one. *Bulletin of the Ghana Geographical Association* 9(2):4–27.
KEA, R. A.
1971   Firearms and warfare on the Gold and Slave coasts from the sixteenth to the nineteenth centuries. *Journal of African History* 12:185–213.
1974   "Trade, state formation, and warfare on the Gold Coast, 1600–1826." Unpublished Ph.D. dissertation, University of London.
KWAMENA-POH, M. A.
1973   *Government and politics in the Akuapem state 1730–1850*. London: Longman.
LOYER, R. PÈRE GODEFROY
1714   *Relation du voyage du Royaume d'Issyny, Côte d'Or, Païs de Guinée, en Afrique*. Paris.
NATIONAL ARCHIVES, THE HAGUE
1758   Director-General Ulzen to Assembly of X dd. November 20, 1758. WIC 114.
NORREGARD, G.
1966   *Danish settlements in West Africa, 1658–1850*. New York: Holmes and Meier. (Originally published in Danish in Copenhagen, 1954.)
PRIESTLY, MARGARET, IVOR WILKS
1960   The Ashanti kings in the eighteenth century: a revised chronology. *Journal of African History* 1(1).
REINDORF, C. C.
n.d. [1895]   *The history of the Gold Coast and Asante* (second edition). Basel.
RØMER, L. F.
1965 [1760]   *Tilforladelig efterretning om negotien paa Kysten Guinea*. (Translated in part by K. Bertelsen for the Institute of African Studies, Legon. Originally published in Copenhagen.)
TENKORANG, S.
1968   The importance of firearms in the struggle between the Ashanti and the coastal states, 1708–1807. *Transactions of the Historical Society of Ghana* 9:1–16.
WARD, W. E. F.
1958   *A history of Ghana* (revised second edition). London: Allen and Unwin.
WILKS, IVOR
1957   The rise of the Akwamu empire, 1650–1710. *Transactions of the Historical Society of Ghana* 3:99–136.
1958   "Akwamu 1650–1750: a study of the rise and fall of a West African empire." Unpublished M.A. thesis, University of Wales.

1964   "The growth of the Akwapim state," in *The historian in tropical Africa*.
        Edited by J. Vansina, R. Mauny, and L. V. Thomas, 390–411. London:
        Oxford University Press for the International African Institute.
1971   "The Mossi and Akan states 1500–1800," in *History of West Africa*,
        volume one. Edited by J. F. A. Ajayi and Michael Crowder, 344–386.
        London: Longman.
1975   *Asante in the nineteenth century: the structure and evolution of a political
        order*. London: Cambridge University Press.
1978   "Land, labour, capital, and the forest kingdom of Asante: a model of
        early change," in *The evolution of social systems*. Edited by J. Friedman
        and M. J. Rowlands, 487–534. Pittsburgh: University of Pittsburgh
        Press.

Administration and Trade in the
Akwamu Empire, 1681–1730

RAY A. KEA

The small inland kingdom of Akwamu, with its capital at Nyanaoase, had become, by the beginning of the eighteenth century, the dominant politi- cal and military power on the eastern Gold Coast and the western Slave Coast. The authority of the Nyanaoase government extended along the coast for a distance of over 200 miles — from the Agona state in the west to the borders of the Whydah kingdom in the east (see Figure 1). In the interior, Nyanaoase rule was manifest over a broad area stretching 100 or more miles behind the seaboard. The military and political power of the state was broken in 1730. In that year, following a series of internal revolts, a coalition of invading armies from the northwest and west destroyed Nyanaoase and occupied all of the western part of the empire. A reconstituted, but smaller, state, with its capital at Akwamufie, was founded on the eastern bank of the Volta in the early 1730's. The new Akwamu kingdom was unable, however, to recreate the old imperial order (Wilks 1957).

This study will focus on the period between 1681 and 1730 and will be concerned with two aspects of imperial administration: first, the control and management of the state's external trade, the commercial order, and second, the control and management of the dependent territories, the imperial or tribute order. I hope to show the complexity of the Akwamu social formation and to demonstrate that its social-historical evolution cannot be reduced to a "response" to the European "impact" or to the guns-slaves-guns syndrome. Since the founding of Nyanaoase in the late

This study is based largely on research in the records of the Danish West Indies-Guinea Company, the Dutch West Indies Company, and the Royal African Company conducted at the National Archives, Copenhagen, in the summer of 1975. I wish to thank the American Philosophical Society for a grant from the Penrose Fund and the Department of History, The Johns Hopkins University, for travel expenses. I am also grateful for the helpful suggestions of Irene Odotei of the Institute of African Studies, University of Ghana, Legon.

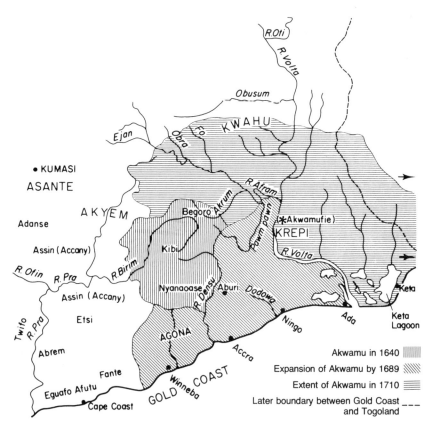

Figure 1.   The empire of Akwamu

sixteenth century, long-distance trade had been a vital sector of the
Akwamu economy and a major source of revenue for the rulers of the
state. An Akwamu tradition current in the early eighteenth century may
be interpreted to show that the commercial and military organization and
resources of the founders of the state provided sufficient conditions for
the kingdom's later territorial expansion (Rask 1754:151–152). Other
evidence suggests that the Akwamu kingdom of the late sixteenth and
early seventeenth centuries may be termed a trade state within which a
single ruling class (consolidated out of principally two social groups,
professional merchants and soldiers) derived the greater proportion of its
revenues from commerce: the regulation of the Abonse market, the
control of commodity circulation, the taxation of trade, and price fixing
(Wilks 1971:365–369; also Djan 1936:131–132; Kea 1974:156–172).

The early Akwamu kingdom was centered on Nyanaoase and its environs. This was the place where the "proper Akwamu" lived; its size was
such that the king "could have summoned his nobles with a cannon shot
whenever he wanted to hold counsel with them" (Rømer 1760:120). The

small inland trade state had developed into a different type of political system by 1670. D'Elbée (1671:381, translation mine) gives a brief account of what I assume to be the Akwamu state and its political influence east of the Volta:

The King of these countries [between the Volta and Little Popo] has a lot of land and *grand politique*; he devotes himself to nothing but the settling of disputes and lawsuits among his people, since his neighbors dare not wage war against him because of his strength. He is said to field an army of 500,000, and the town where he lives is more populous and larger than Paris.

While part of D'Elbée's account is clearly exaggerated, it nevertheless draws attention to the scale of Akwamu political development since the late sixteenth century.

Between 1681 and 1702, the Nyanaoase government gained undisputed control of the ports on the eastern Gold and western Slave Coasts. Among the residents of these ports were the agents of the Danish, Dutch, and English trading companies, each of which maintained several mercantile establishments along the Akwamu-dominated coast. Through its coastal marts, the Akwamu state was linked to the overseas markets of western Europe and the Americas. The ports served as major import-export centers for the commodities distributed by the Akwamu commercial network, and, in consequence, the Nyanaoase government imposed on them, particularly the Accra ports, stringent controls.

The European overseas trade represented one aspect of the commodity relations of the Akwamu state.[1] The latter was also an integral part of a land-based commercial network, a geographically extensive exchange system that embraced the gold-producing districts to the northwest (e.g., those of Akyem), the social-economic formations of the Ardra and Whydah kingdoms to the east, and those of the Guinea savanna states of Dagbon (Dagomba) and Gonja to the north. Merchandise imported through the Akwamu ports was redistributed to the market centers of these places, and they, in turn, channelled their commodity exports through the Akwamu ports. The Nyanaoase government supervised commodity relations between Akwamu and its neighbors.

Wealth distribution within the Akwamu state was articulated in two distinct forms. Commodity circulation, in which the movement of merchandise was determined by commercial transactions, constituted one form. The second entailed the appropriation of the surplus product (labor) as corvée, tax, tribute, fines, etc., to support the ruling class and the central government administration. This mode of wealth distribution was determined by the administrative-political structure of the state, not by commercial operations. Thus, in the later seventeenth century and the

---

[1]   For a careful theoretical discussion of the concepts used in this study — surplus product, social formation, commodity relations, etc. — see Hindess and Hirst (1975).

early eighteenth century, there existed wealth distribution based on commercial determinants and wealth distribution based on political determinants. While structurally distinct, the two forms were not wholly independent of one another. The development of the state's external trade was directly related to the level of surplus appropriation within the empire and the extent to which the ruling class utilized this surplus as merchant capital. If the Akwamu state of the late sixteenth century was a trade state in which internal wealth distribution was based in large measure on commercial determinants, the Akwamu polity of the late seventeenth century was a tribute state in which political conditions regulated this distribution. The first section of this study will examine certain aspects of these political conditions; the second section will consider commerce and its management within the state.

AKWAMU POLITICAL ORGANIZATION

Until its destruction in 1730, Nyanaoase was the imperial seat of government, the king's town. It was the largest urban center in the Akwamu state. The earliest description of the city is a brief account of 1688 (Du Casse 1935[1688]:14, translation mine):

The king [Ansa Sasraku (d. 1689)] lives twelve leagues from the sea; he is one of the greatest rulers of Guinea. The place where he lives is well-policed, and the Frenchmen whom I sent there assured me that they had never seen a place of greater beauty: the streets of the town, which are thirty feet wide, are lined for a distance of three leagues with trees. He has 600 officers at his court and numerous soldiers and much gold.

About 1695 a Dane, Erik Tilleman, visited the *akwamuhene* [king] Basua (1689–1699) at the capital. The city, he reported, was two (Danish) miles long (nearly nine statute miles), but only 160 feet wide. It had one well-aligned main street with houses on both sides. Basua's residence was in the center of the city. Prince Ado, the heir-apparent and co-ruler of the state, lived half a Danish mile (about two statute miles) to the northwest "with many . . . free blacks and their slaves; both the king's and the prince's dwellings stand in the middle of the [main] street and on either side of their residences were the *rade huuse*" (Tilleman 1697:102, 105–106, translation mine). The latter were state buildings: council buildings, courts, stool houses, the treasury, and the shrines of the state deities. The section of the city in which the *rade huuse* were located constituted the government quarter or *abanmu* (Meyerowitz 1951:188; Wilks 1959:43). It formed the nucleus around which the residential structure — the various quarters and suburban settlements — of the capital was organized.

Nyanaoase was the focal point or central place of a populous, urban-ized metropolitan district. Within the district, whose exact geographical dimensions are not known, were twenty-two large and small towns (Reindorf 1895:60; Johnson 1964:9–11). Together with Nyanaoase, they could mobilize 7,000 men (Tilleman 1697:106). Around the capital, large royal or state plantations worked by unfree laborers were main-tained (Kea 1974:210–212, 218–219). The latter were, for the most part, prisoners of war who, during the course of the seventeenth century, had been resettled in the rural hinterland of the capital. Like Nyanaoase, the other metropolitan towns appear to have had plantations worked by servile labor. These plantations were not royal property, but were held by the "great caboceers' or *abirempon* of Akwamu.[2] By the early eighteenth century, the evidence suggests, a sizable proportion of the labor em-ployed in agriculture in the metropolitan district was unfree (cf. Tilleman 1697:114; Rask 1754:80).[3] This phenomenon is related to the growth of the Nyanaoase political-military establishment after 1650.

The Nyanaoase plantations provisioned the court and probably many of the townspeople as well. They also furnished produce which "was exported to the towns on the coast and was bartered in great quantity for salt and fish; in addition, some foodstuffs were sold for money [cowries and gold] to anyone who cared to buy some" (Tilleman 1697:111, translation mine). The plantations of Nyanaoase and the other metropolitan towns were among the major suppliers of foodstuffs to the European trading establishments and to the ships that traded on the Akwamu coast. Until 1730 Nyanaoase was undoubtedly the main center of commercial-ized agricultural production within the state.

Nyanaoase was also an important market center. Livestock — cattle, sheep, goats, swine, horses, and fowl — was brought from the states of Little Popo, Whydah, and Ardra (Tilleman 1697:141). Rural farming peoples of the Akwapim scarp took foodstuffs to the capital and pur-chased tools produced by metropolitan-based blacksmiths. Traders from the coastal towns carried fish, salt, and imported trade goods and bought produce, tools, etc. Craftsmen, cultivators, livestock breeders, fishermen, and salt makers were engaged in commodity production for the metro-politan market. Krobo oral traditions assert that buyers and sellers in the Nyanaoase market did not carry out face-to-face transactions, but engaged in "silent trade" (Huber 1963:57, 62). The implication is that the Nyanaoase market authorities, combining the functions of broker and toll collector, served as intermediaries between them.[4]

[2] In Rask's time, the Akwamu Akan term *abirempon* (sing. *obirempon*), or *abringpung*, was defined as "hero," "a distinguished or great man," "King," "noble," or "lord" (Rask 1754:90, 171).
[3] Around Nyanaoase there were apparently extensive palm-oil and sugarcane plantations (see Kea 1974:210–211).
[4] For a recent analysis of the myth of the silent trade, see Farias (1974).

The development of commodity production and commodity circulation within the metropolitan district was contingent on the demand for
livestock, imported wares, gold ornaments, etc.; the demand was directly
related to the level of wealth accumulation within the metropolitan
district. The forms and level of wealth accumulation were corollaries of
the military and political hegemony the Nyanaoase government exercised
over its dependencies, on the one hand, and the needs and consumption
habits of the Akwamu ruling class, on the other.

The coastal towns and villages belonged to the *akwamuhene* by right of
conquest and, from the point of view of the Nyanaoase government, were
state property. The king, therefore, had at his disposal an extensive
domain which constituted, with respect to the metropolitan district, a
dependent "hinterland." The coastal tributaries were divided into fiscal-
administrative units or districts. The king distributed them among the
abirempon, a class of officials which consisted, essentially, of two social
groups: the princes and the king's men (Kea 1974:242–251).

The records of the European trading companies (see Kea
1974:428–430 for full references) and various oral histories (e.g., Reindorf 1895, Saxton 1925, Field 1940) contain scattered references to
abirempon as overlords of the different coastal towns. Between 1703 and
1730 there were from ten to fifteen coastal fiscal-administrative districts.
A Danish report of January 1, 1727 (National Archives 1727a, translation mine) has an interesting reference to the appointment by
akwamuhene Ansa Kwao (1725–1730) of an Akwamu *obirempon,* "the
king's most distinguished caboceer," over Osu (Danish Accra):

Since caboceer Kwaku Kansiang has for a long time been very serviceable toward
the fort [i.e., Christiansborg], and continues to be faithful and helpful toward the
Company [the Danish West Indies-Guinea company] both with his own person
and with his people, whether in disputes or other matters with which he is capable
of dealing, and as the king of Akwamu, Ansa Kwao, has ceded to him this town
Osu and enfeoffed him as protector over it, Kwaku Kansiang is resolved to take
over as the protector of the town.

Kansiang (d. 1729) had been associated with the Danish fort of Christiansborg since at least 1703. Until about 1709 he seems to have been a
middle-level official in the Nyanaoase government, a subordinate to a
dignitary described as the "king's great caboceer." In that year the
akwamuhene Akonno (1702–1725) appointed him government broker
of Christiansborg (see below), and by 1720 Kansiang occupied the post of
the "king's great caboceer." As a reward for his many years of service, he
was granted the governorship of the town of Osu. As governor, or
protector, he received from the Danes a monthly fee of eight rigsdalers
(or half an ounce of gold) and from the town a (?) monthly tribute of

sixteen rigsdalers (or half a *benda*).[5] These payments were made in the form of imported merchandise, salt, and cowries. In addition, both the Danes and the *mantsei* [members of the town council] of Osu regularly presented gifts to him. At an unknown date, but probably during the reign of Akonno, Kansiang was assigned the inland district of Osudoku. His annual income from this district is unknown. In view of his important political position, it is likely that he had jurisdiction over other districts. His duties as protector were commerical, judicial, political, and military.

Other examples of appointments to governorships are known. About 1703 Ansa Kwao, then a prince, was granted the coastal town of Labadi. Around the same period "Bobbi" or "Abobi," perhaps a son of the *akwamuhene* Ansa Sasraku (d. 1689), was assigned the towns of Kpone, Prampram, and "Chabra" (or "Siabra") and the inland district of Shai. Akonno's predecessor Ado (1699–1702) granted Ashabra (or Captain James, as he was known to the Europeans) jurisdiction over the littoral towns of Tema and Great Ningo in 1701 or 1702.[6] A certain "caboceer Hotiaffu" appears to have been the overlord of the town of Teshie in the 1720's. The "great captain" Amo (d. 1731) was responsible for the towns of Dutch (or Little) Accra and Lay and the Lower Volta town of Malfy. "Odday Amonie" (d. 1729), one of the "king's men," had jurisdiction over the twelve to twenty towns on the Akwapim scarp. This system of governorships was the dominant form of imperial administration within the state.

With the exceptions of Amo, who lived in Dutch Accra, and Ashabra, who had houses in Tema and Great Ningo, the *abirempon* resided in the metropolitan district, either in Nyanaoase or in one of the other metropolitan towns. They were an urban aristocracy, and their power and authority were based in the towns in which they lived. Their plantations were located in the metropolitan area, and the large corps of armed retainers which they maintained were also found there. The retainers were the means by which the *abirempon* exercised economic and political control over their respective tributary districts and also formed the military forces that were sent on expeditions and raids into lands beyond Akwamu. A single *obirempon* might have hundreds of retainers at his disposal (Tilleman 1697:113–114; Rask 1754:89, 90). He also had a great number of other dependents: relatives, clients, servants of all kinds, and slaves (cf. Rask, 1754:128, 249–250).

[5] Cowrie shells and gold were the currencies used in the Akwamu state; Danish accounts were kept in rigsdalers. One *benda* = two ounces of gold or thirty-two rigsdalers (see Johnson 1970).
[6] Shai oral history refers to the appointment of "Bobbi" as ruler of the Shai people (Saxton 1925:139–140). According to Tema tradition, Adzeite Ashabra was an early king of Tema (Field 1940:116; see also Reindorf 1895:10, 367).

TAXATION AND FISCAL ADMINISTRATION

Abirempon power was based in part on the fiscal and military authority this class exercised in the various dependent political units and in part on the positions its members held in the central government. The *abirempon* appear, in certain respects, to have been a kind of government aristocracy. Their revenues depended on their connection with the state. As a class they coincided with the military-political structure of the state. From their ranks came the chief army commanders, the principal advisors of the king, the heads of the various departments of government, and the members of the state council, which administered the daily affairs of the empire. With respect to the *abirempon,* the *akwamuhene* was first among equals. Bosman (1967[1705]:64) recognized what appears to have been an institutionalized relationship between the "house" of the king and the "houses" of the "great caboceers": "[The king's] arbitrary despotic power occasions the proverbial saying that there are only two sorts of men in Akwamu, of which the King and his friends are one, and their slaves the other so that he wants no other attendants than those of his own house."[7]

The *abirempon* adhered to the view that one of the main purposes of government was the maintenance of a regular flow of taxes, tribute, fines, etc., from the dependent territories to the metropolitan district. The Nyanaose system of imperial administration led to the accumulation and concentration of vast quantities of material wealth in the metropolitan district (Bosman 1967[1705]:64): "The King and his nobles, or rather favorites, are so very rich in gold and slaves, that I am of the opinion that this country singly possesses greater treasures than all those [Gold Coast countries] we have hitherto described taken together." "The King and his nobles" devoted their revenues, to a great extent, to the maintenance and reproduction of the legal and political conditions which permitted their continued appropriation of the surplus product from the subordinate districts. Commodity circulation, commodity production, and the market commodities depended primarily on the consumption habits of the *abirempon,* their agents, and other dependents, on the one hand, and administrative and other state expenditures, on the other. To a limited extent these conditions generated investment in production, for example, the purchase of slaves, who were employed in agriculture, and of instruments of production. Funds were expended on the upkeep of the roads that linked Nyanaoase and the seaboard towns and to pay the soldiers who policed them. For the most part, however, individual expenditures among the *abirempon* were in great measure directed at the maintenance

---

[7] For a discussion of the use of the term "house," see Field (1940:1ff.); see also Wilks (1975:329 and n. 7) on the use of the term in an Asante context.

or improvement of their political and social positions within the society.[8]
Towns and villages throughout the empire paid a regular tax or tribute
to the Nyanaoase government. Tilleman (1697:107, translation mine),
who visited the capital about 1695, reported that the king "receives every
year after harvest some of the land's produce from all of those who live in
the kingdom, not so much for the value of the produce, but as proof of the
submission they owe him." The tax or tribute structure defined the
legal-political relation between the rural agrarian communities and the
central government. The structure was based upon the cooperative labor
of peasant households, the prevailing form of labor organization within
the state. However, as we have seen, the agricultural labor of the metropolitan district was to a large extent unfree. There were, thus, two distinct
forms of social organization of labor within the agricultural sector of the
Akwamu economy, but only one form was incorporated within the
tribute structure described by Tilleman.

Unlike the rural communities, the coastal urban centers were required
to pay their imposts in the form of merchandise and money (gold and/or
cowries) and in some instances in livestock, salt, fish, and locally produced craft goods. Each town, like each village, paid as a corporate unit.
The tribute assessment was based on the size of the community concerned. Unfortunately, the available data do not indicate the precise
amount paid by each town or the frequency of payment. Danish trading
company records suggest that Osu may have paid in the 1720's a (?)
monthly tribute in merchandise and cowries equivalent to forty-eight
rigsdalers (or one and a half *benda*); Labadi may have paid sixty-four
rigsdalers (or two *benda*) a (?) month. In addition to the tribute paid to
the officers of the king, each town was obligated to pay tribute to its
governor. As we have seen, Osu paid its governor Kwaku Kansiang
sixteen rigsdalers (or half a *benda*) a (?) month.

The littoral towns were subject to the imposition of fines and extraordinary levies of diverse kinds and were also required periodically to
present gifts to the king, his principal wives, and the leading *abirempon*.
In 1709, for instance, the Nyanaoase government imposed fines amounting to more than 15,000 rigsdalers (over 1,000 *benda*) on the towns from
Great Ningo to Soko (English Accra) for offenses *contra pacem regis*
(National Archives 1711).[9] In 1716 the Accra towns were fined a total of
200 *benda* for failing to send forces to join the Akwamu army in an
expedition against the Akyem state. Three years later Ama Kuma, an
abirempon and rich broker-merchant of Dutch Accra, was accused of
having committed adultery with one of the king's wives and fined a sum of

[8] See Hindess and Hirst (1975:79–108) for a theoretical exposition of this point within the
conceptual framework of the "ancient mode of production."
[9] For the use of the term *contra pacem regis* in the Akwamu context, see Wilks
(1959:66–67).

1,500 *benda* (Wilks 1959:66–68). In February 1728 Osu borrowed goods worth thirty-two rigsdalers (or one *benda*) from the Danes "in order to mourn for the deceased [Akwamu prince] Otting" (National Archives n.d.a).

The metropolitan-based military contingents ensured that the various imposts were paid. Describing the situation at the beginning of the eighteenth century, Bosman (1967[1705]:65) commented that the seaboard towns were "miserably tormented with daily plunderings, or rather robbing visits the Akwamu soldiers make them, they not daring to oppose them in the least for fear the King, who never fails severely to revenge his soldiers' quarrels should hear of it."

A second tax or tribute structure may be said to have existed within the Akwamu state: one based upon the commodity relations which the coastal towns had with the Europeans. The relationship between this structure and commerce is clearly exemplified by the fact that the coastal towns paid their various imposts in the form of imported trade goods and cash. The Danes of Christiansborg frequently lent merchandise and cowries to Labadi and Osu and to the community of "free fishermen" in Osu; occasionally, loans were made to Teshie, Nungwa (Little Ningo), Tubreku (Togbloku), Lay, and Kpone. Many of these loans were used by the towns concerned to pay their tributes, fines, etc., to the Nyanaoase government. The loans were repaid in slaves, firewood, seashells (used to manufacture lime), and cowries.

In July 1719, Odoi Kpoti (d. 1757), ruler of Labadi, borrowed forty-six rigsdalers in spirits and textiles in order to pay a war tax the *akwamuhene* had imposed on all of the tributary districts (National Archives 1719, n.d.b) The debt was to be repaid in seashells. The ruler of Tubreku, "Aichu," borrowed, in October 1723, trade goods to the value of 522 rigsdalers (a little over sixteen *benda*) from the chief merchant of Christiansborg in order to meet his tribute obligations; the loan was to be repaid with seven good male slaves (National Archives n.d.c) In September 1727, Osu and the "free fishermen" of the town borrowed a total of 212 rigsdalers in goods and cowries from the Danes "in order to make a present to the king." At the beginning of the following month Labadi obtained a loan of thirty-four rigsdalers in wares and cowries for the same purpose. Osu was to repay its debt in firewood, the town's fishermen in cowries, and Labadi in seashells (National Archives 1727b). Further examples could be cited for these and other towns. Through different methods of surplus appropriation, the Nyanaoase government was able to dominate and in large measure control the economies of these towns.

The coastal centers, especially those in which European trading establishments were located, were, by virtue of their extensive commercial operations, important centers of wealth accumulation and concentration. Much of this wealth, as we have seen, was appropriated through the tribute structure. In December 1728, the leading dignitaries of the towns of Accra and Labadi held a meeting at which they expressed their grievances against the heavy exactions of the Nyanaoase administration (National Archives 1728, translation mine).

Formerly the servants of the Akwamu caboceers imposed great demands on them for no reason. It was resolved that whenever Akwamu caboceers and the king's servants come to any of their towns to demand the payment of a debt, the debtor should without delay, pay immediately. Should an Accra man damage the goods of a king's servant or break his tobacco pipe in half or if any of the Accra man's cattle should damage the royal servant's property, then the Accra man should, for damage amounting to one cloth, pay one cloth, and, for damage amounting to one pipe, one pipe, but for damage caused by his cattle he should pay nothing, and the Akwamu [royal] servant should not be accorded more than this. Other excesses committed among the Accras [and] Labadis either by themselves or by strangers should hereafter be punished as formerly according to the laws of the land. Formerly, whenever an Accra man spoiled an Akwamu [royal] servant's cloths or broke his pipe or cattle damaged his property, he had to pay considerable sums in compensation, and when the Accras went to the king to complain, they did not receive justice. Thus they, together with the mountain peoples [i.e., those living on the Akwapim scarp], have agreed that if the Akwamu king, his servants and caboceers do not accept these conditions, then the Accras and the others will unite to defend themselves. They are willing to serve the king and caboceers as their conquerors, but they are not willing to be treated like their bought slaves.

Control over the circulation of a large proportion of local surplus was clearly in the hands of the *abirempon* and the king.

The European merchant-administrators, soldiers, etc., who resided in the Akwamu ports were also numbered among the tributaries of the state. As a stranger group specializing in trade they had, however, a special status: they were classified as the *akwamuhene*'s "wives." This social classification or definition seems to have meant that the Europeans enjoyed a semiautonomous, but subordinate, position *vis-à-vis* the Nyanaoase government. Their special status did not exempt them from the many financial obligations which tributary peoples were compelled to meet.

Each of the three Accra forts paid one *benda* a month to the *akwamuhene*, a payment often referred to in the documents as "ground rent." It was paid in the form of imported merchandise, cowries, and, occasionally, gold. The Europeans also paid monthly "ground rents" for their lodges. Permission to erect a lodge, several of which were built in various ports along the Akwamu coast between 1699 and 1730, had to be obtained from the *akwamuhene*. The king usually "farmed out" the ground rent for a lodge to the ruler of the town where the lodge was located or to the *obirempon* protector of the town. Between 1702 and 1712 the Dutch paid half an ounce of gold per month to the *obirempon* "Bobbi" for their lodge at Kpone. The Dutch closed it about 1712, but in

382   RAY A. KEA

the early 1720's the Danes established one there. They paid a monthly ground rent of about a quarter-ounce of gold to Apim, the resident Akwamu ruler of the town, and his son. Apim was not an *obirempon*, but one of several lower-level Akwamu *ahene* (sing. *ohene*) who resided in and ruled over a number of coastal communities (Wilks 1959:63–71; Kea 1974:220–222).

The Europeans were obliged to present, on a regular basis, gifts to the *akwamuhene*, his wives, and some of the leading *abirempon*. These gifts were given for several reasons: to promote trade, to obtain a commercial or political advantage over a rival, and to keep the goodwill of the *akwamuhene* and his administration. The Europeans were also liable for any fines imposed on them by the king. In 1709, for example, the Danes were fined over twenty *benda* in trade goods because they supported the 1708 revolt of Labadi, Osu, Teshie, Nungwa, and other coastal towns. In 1712 the English of James Fort were fined fifteen *benda* in merchandise for failing to pay their ground rent when it was due. In 1726 the Danes paid over fifty *benda* in goods and cowries on the grounds that they had sold, without permission, a gold pawn which the *akwamuhene* Akonno had deposited at Christiansborg. The following year the English were fined a sum of ninety *benda* for having brought a "false palaver" against the Dutch and for having "disturbed the peace of the realm and the state of trade" (Wilks 1959:69, 70–71). The same year the Dutch and the people of Dutch Accra were fined the extraordinary sum of 10,000 *benda* (or 2,000, according to other sources) because of their alleged complicity in the murder of an Akwamu prince (Wilks 1959:71–72).

In addition to rents, fines, gifts, the Europeans were required to make other contributions to the central government. In 1699 the Akwamu ruler Ado sent 300 *benda* (or 3,000, according to another source) in gold, slaves, and imported wares to the Akyem government in order to effect a cessation of hostilities between the two states. The tributary districts were taxed in order to replenish the state treasury from which the sum was drawn. Each of the European forts paid six *benda* in merchandise (National Archives 1700).

The fragmentary nature of the evidence makes it difficult to ascertain the annual value of the merchandise appropriated from the Europeans as rents, fines, etc.; however, it probably ranged from several hundred to a few thousand *benda*. Together with the wealth extracted from the subject towns and villages throughout the state, the yearly revenue of the government must have been very large indeed.

The surplus was channelled into Nyanaoase and the other metropolitan urban centers. It constituted one of the main sources of revenue for the *abirempon*. It has been mentioned above that the *abirempon* used their incomes to maintain and improve their political and social positions; however, their incomes also served another purpose. As officeholders

within the state's political structure, they possessed the means of administration and, in consequence, were obliged to bear the costs of administration out of the tribute, fines, etc., which they received. Each *obirempon* had his own functionaries (or caboceers) and servants who had to be
maintained. Part of the appropriated wealth accrued to the king, who
utilized it to meet various court, household, and state expenditures. The
tributary dependencies were thus the main supporters of the Akwamu
imperial or tribute order.

The wealth drawn from the dependent districts represented extensive
physical movements of produce, imported trade goods, gold, livestock,
craft goods, etc., within the state. These movements did not take the form
of commodity circulation; they did not involve commodity relations or
commercial transactions. The appropriation and distribution of the surplus occurred through the intervention of politics, that is, through the
mechanisms of the political-administrative machinery of the tribute
order. This represented one of the two distinct forms of geographical
circulation of wealth within the state.

The second form of wealth circulation was commerce. Within the
Akwamu context, its expansion was directly related to that of the first.
The wealth acumulated in Nyanaoase and the other metropolitan towns
was converted to merchant capital when it was used to promote commodity relations with the Europeans and the market centers of neighboring
states, or when it was used to develop commodity production within the
metropolitan district, or when it was invested in credit transactions. For
the king and the *abirempon*, trade was an important "instrument" of
state.

PRODUCTION, DISTRIBUTION, AND PORTS OF TRADE

The main sectors of the coastal economy included farming, livestock
breeding, fishing, salt making, hunting, and crafts. These infrastructural
activities supported the international and interregional trade in which the
ports, the main coastal urban centers, were engaged.

The principal port complex of the state was Accra. It consisted of three
distinct towns, each of which had a fort: English Accra (or Soko) and
James Fort, Dutch (or Little or Small) Accra and Crèvecoeur Fort, and
Danish Accra (or Osu) and Christiansborg Fort. These ports handled the
bulk of the overseas trade. At the beginning of the eighteenth century, an
estimated fifty to sixty ships visited the Accra towns annually. They
provided the forts, a 1727 observer remarked, with "an extraordinary
good trade from the inland countries, especially for slaves" (Smith
1744:135). The towns were prosperous and possessed "many cornfields,
salt-pans, and other marks of industry" (Atkins 1737:107). The Accra

trading complex had a well-developed (relative to the dominant mode of production) "business structure": capital resources as represented by the many "marks of industry," a sizable and wealthy merchant-broker class, and extensive commercial and shipping contacts.

None of the other Akwamu ports could compete with the Accra towns as commercial centers. Nevertheless, many of them had small European trading posts at various times between 1699 and 1730. They included Shidoe, Labadi, Nungwa, Tema, Great Ningo, Kpone, Lay, Tubreku, Keta, and Aflahu. The coastal towns were the economic and political centers of districts which, on average, extended five to ten miles inland and contained villages, farms, pasture, and the like. The towns were supported in part by the production of their rural hinterlands and in part by the trade in which they were involved. Each of them was ruled by one or more leading "houses," some of which were of Akwamu origin, others of Ga, Adangme, or Ewe origin.

The coastal towns were specialized economic formations. Their internal organization provided the framework necessary for the importation and exportation of commodities. The total value of the trade that passed through the Akwamu ports each year amounted to several thousand *benda.* Textiles of all kinds, metal ware, leather goods, pottery, firearms, gunpowder, spirits, beads, and cowries were among the many imports. The main overseas exports were gold, ivory, and slaves, the latter assuming greater importance as an export after 1700.

The ports were also engaged in an important coastal maritime trade. That of the Accra towns, for example, extended from Axim in the west to Whydah in the east. Textiles and other craft products, agricultural produce, salt, and livestock were the main staples of this trade. It was in the hands of local African merchants and included Europeans among its participants. There existed, too, an overland trade route which ran along the seaboard from Whydah to Axim. The main staples of this trade were gold, livestock, and slaves.

The coastal trade centers maintained close connections with the towns and villages in the interior. In spite of the existence of farms in their immediate hinterlands, nearly all of the Akwamu ports were dependent for their provisions on the agricultural production of inland farms. Reference has already been made to the exportation of produce from the Nyanaoase plantations to the coastal towns. The agrarian communities on the Akwapim scarp also served as food farms for the seaboard populations. Their produce was exchanged for fish, salt, and imported merchandise.

The salt making and fishing industries were also linked to the overseas trade. The Danish priest Rask, who lived in Osu from 1709 to 1714, reported that between December and February forty to fifty Akwamu traders visited the Accra towns daily in order to buy (with cowries or gold) dried fish and salt. The latter were carried over 100 miles into the interior, where they were exchanged at inland markets for slaves and textiles. Most of the slaves were sold to the Europeans; the textiles were disposed of in the different trading centers of Akwamu (Rask 1754:124–126; cf. Tilleman 1697:110–111).

The commodity relations of the Accra and other coastal towns involved commercial operations that represented distinct yet interconnected trade structures. On the one hand, there was the overseas trade structure of mercantile capitalism, which was represented on the shores of Akwamu by the agents of the European trading companies. On the other hand, the trade structures that linked the Akwamu ports with other Gold and Slave Coast ports and with the inland markets of Akwamu and its neighbors functioned within the framework of "feudal/tributary" and slave modes of production.[10] The merchant representatives of this trade structure were the *abirempon* and those merchants whom the Danes called "wholesale traders."

The Accra forts were wholly dependent on the *abirempon* and the "wholesale traders." In 1730 a Danish factor remarked that the forts had no exports apart from those provided by Akwamu merchants, "for the Accras furnish not the least trade [i.e., for the overseas markets] but live solely on their brokerage [fees] which they can secure from the Akwamu merchants" (National Archives 1730, translation mine). Three years earlier the brokers and town council members of Dutch Accra expressed the extent of their dependence on Akwamu trade: "If the trade routes were closed and the waterhole . . . was occupied by the Akwamu, and all the traders stopped coming down, then they could expect nothing but the complete ruination of their [town], themselves, and their wives and children" (quoted in Wilks 1959:71). In 1707 the chief merchant of Christiansborg, Erik Lygaard, expressed a similar view in one of his reports to Copenhagen. If he failed to send the Akwamu sovereign his customary gift, he wrote, then the king would keep "the peasants or buyers from coming to the fort to purchase their goods; the buyers, who are Akwamu and their subjects, can go to whichever fort they desire in order to obtain whatever they need, but [the king] can close the roads, which imposes the greatest restrictions on trade" (quoted in Kea 1974:207). Akonno closed the trade routes leading to the Accra forts in March 1725. This action meant not only an interdiction on the sale of gold, ivory, and slaves, but also a prohibition on the sale of produce, livestock, salt, etc., to the forts' personnel. The Dutch and English each paid two and a half *benda* in merchandise to have the trade ban lifted; the Danes paid four *benda*. The nine *benda* were distributed among the

---

[10] For a discussion of these modes of production, see Amin (1973:9–48) and Hindess and Hirst (1975).

soldiers of Amega, a prince and Ashabra's successor, who had closed the routes (National Archives 1725a, 1725b). When the trade routes were closed, the European forts and lodges were not the only victims. The brokers resident in the different ports could also expect, as the Dutch Accra brokers pointed out, "their complete ruination."

The brokerage system of the Accra towns was organized by the Nyana-oase government soon after the destruction of the Accra kingdom in 1681. The government decreed that the Accra caboceers were not allowed to settle more than four miles from the coast, "but they should live under the forts as brokers for the trade which the Akwamu merchants brought to the Europeans" (Rømer 1760:122–123; see also Tilleman 1697:98, 112–113). They were to serve as interpreters and inter-mediaries between the European factors and the Akwamu and other inland traders, and they were also expected to provide lodgings and storage facilities. Following the completion of each sale the broker received a standard commission of twelve rigsdalers from the factor and the same fee from the local trader (National Archives 1727c). Every broker was also paid a monthly salary or fee by the Europeans in his port. The Accra brokerage system was fully operational by 1687 (National Archives 1687–1689). As a substantial portion of the brokers' incomes derived from the services they rendered, any interdictions on trade could prove financially disastrous to many of them.

The Accra brokers formed one level of what might be termed a broker-age hierarchy. By the late 1680's they had been joined by Akwamu brokers (originally from the metropolitan district) who, like their Accra counterparts, served as commission agents for buyers visiting the Euro-pean forts. In some of the coastal towns they were resident rulers, local representatives of the Nyanaoase government. In other towns they did not hold political offices. The three Accra forts employed Accra and Akwamu brokers on a full-time basis by the beginning of the eighteenth century. They received monthly salaries and were frequently sent to inland markets as trading agents of the Europeans.

In his capacity as overlord, Ashabra commanded the several hundred Akwamu soldiers garrisoned around Tema and Great Ningo. They repre-sented the military presence of the Nyanaoase government in the area. They policed the local trade routes and, on orders from the capital, closed them. They could thus prevent merchants from east of the Volta (from Keta, Little Popo, etc.) and those traveling down the Volta (e.g., from Kwahu) from bringing slaves, livestock, etc., to the Accra ports. The garrison was also employed to enforce tribute levies and other payments from the towns and villages between Tema and Keta.

The brokerage system of the Akwamu ports was a superstructural institution organized to promote and facilitate the external trade of the state. All of those involved in this trade utilized it. A 1727 Danish account gives a brief description of one aspect of the external trade structure (National Archives 1727d, translation mine):

Those who are wholesale traders sell slaves to the Europeans for cowries and other goods, and with these buy slaves far in the interior; the rest of the people and the caboceers gladly buy what they need with cowries and sometimes gold; they purchase spirits, gunpowder, flintlock muskets, tallow, iron, knives, flintstones, *slaplagen*, [etc.].

Generally the "company brokers" served as intermediaries between the Europeans and the wholesale traders, while the brokers in the ports acted as agents for "the rest of the people and the caboceers." Credit transactions formed the basis of the trade between the "wholesale traders" and the European factors. The company or government brokers often stood as surety for the former. They deposited gold ornaments, aggry beads, slaves, etc., in the forts as pawns or security.

On occasion the Nyanaoase government prevented the "wholesale traders" from visiting the Accra forts. A Dutch report of 1706 relates that Akyem traders brought gold and slaves to inland Akwamu markets where the king arranged for his officials to carry them to the forts and lodges on the coast. The king's officers, who negotiated their sales through the agency of the coastal brokerage system, returned to the markets with trade goods and handed them over to the Akyem merchants. The king imposed a duty of 50 percent *ad valorem* or even more on the merchandise (Wilks 1959:74). To avoid restrictions of this sort, the Akyem ruler in 1715, for example, paid the *akwamuhene* 200 *benda* in gold in order to secure a free passage through Akwamu territory for Akyem traders (Kea 1974:227–228). Akyem access to the Akwamu ports was contingent upon the policies and political acts of the Nyanaoase government.

Fante merchants from the port of Anomabu were not subject to any restraints when they traded in Akwamu. A Danish report of 1727 relates that these traders

have the freedom to go inland into Akwamu and there exchange goods for slaves which they sell to English ships at Anomabu, by which they have caused the price of slaves to be higher than formerly. . . . When the peasants do not have slaves to sell, they can buy various goods from the Fante with cowries which the Fante take to other peasants who have slaves and exchange them for cowries (quoted in Kea 1974:229).

The Fante traders of Anomabu were granted the right of free-trade in Akwamu as a result of the 1715 commercial-political treaty between the governments of Nyanaoase and Anomabu (Kea 1974:229–230, 255).

Akyem, Fante, and other merchants (e.g., Ewe and Kwahu) were active participants in the commercial order of the Akwamu state. Their operations contributed to the expansion of commodity circulation within the empire and connected Akwamu trading centers with those of neighboring and distant polities. It was within this context — the Akwamu "zone of commerce" — that the trade of the European factors existed as a viable enterprise, but, as has been suggested above, the expansion of the external and internal trade of Akwamu was largely dependent on political determinants within the state.

The mercantile growth of Nyanoase and the other metropolitan towns in the later seventeenth and early eighteenth centuries was due in large measure to the intense involvement of the *akwamuhene* and *abirempon* in commerce. A considerable portion of the surplus obtained through the tribute order was converted to merchant capital through the establishment of commodity relations with the European factors and Akyem, Anomabu, and other merchants. The king and the *abirempon* accumulated debts with some of these traders and extended credit to others; at the same time, they sold and bought a wide range of commodities. Notwithstanding the scale of their commercial transactions, the king and the *abirempon* were not professional merchants. Trade, or perhaps more correctly the commercial order, was merely one "instrument" that ensured the political hegemony of the Nyanaoase government.

The brokers of the highest class were those whom the Europeans called "company brokers" or "company caboceers." Each fort had its "company broker." He was invariably an *obirempon* whom the *akwamuhene* assigned to a fort. From the point of view of the Nyanaoase administration, he was the official government broker of the fort. The company or government broker was not necessarily the protector or overlord of the town in which the fort was located. The trading company documents contain numerous references to the "company brokers." Otu Ahiakwa (d. ca. 1711) and his son Amo Nakawa served successively as company brokers of Crèvecoeur and as overlords of Dutch Accra (Wilks 1959). From around 1720 to 1730 the broker of James Fort was the "great caboceer" Kwesi Biri (or Bibiri); however, he does not appear to have been the overlord of Soko. His immediate predecessor might have been "Cobree" or "Cobra" (fl. 1714). In the 1680's and 1690's Asamoni (d. 1703) served as the company broker of Christiansborg. He was succeeded, probably at the beginning of the eighteenth century, by "Dede" or "Dedie." "Dede" held the position until about 1709, when he was replaced by Kwaku Kansiang. (The latter's career we have considered earlier.) All of the company brokers received from their forts regular payments in the form of imported trade goods. With the exceptions of Otu and Amo, all of them lived in the metropolitan district (see Kea 1974:265–274).

The duties of the company brokers were essentially commercial in character. They served as intermediaries between their forts and the "wholesale traders," and they negotiated sales on behalf of the *akwamuhene* and the *abirempon* of the metropolitan district. They settled conflicts that arose within the broker communities of the Accra towns, and they helped resolve disputes between the king and the Europeans. Within this context, a Danish report of 1702 is of interest for the information it provides on one of the duties of the company broker, in this case the broker of Christiansborg (National Archives 1702, translation mine).

The Akwamu king summoned to his court the caboceer [probably "Dede"], who is always employed in the king's most important business here at the fort, and admonished him to keep a good watch at this fort [to ensure] that no wrongs or other injustices are committed by any Akwamu, otherwise he will be removed from the position entrusted to him.

The main responsibility of the company or government brokers was to ensure the unimpeded movement of commodities through the Accra ports, in particular those associated with the overseas trade.

In the Akwamu ports east of the Accra towns, there were no forts, only lodges. All ships that traded at the Accra ports did so through the forts and the ports' brokers. Those that traded in the leeward ports did so under the authority of the rulers and brokers of these ports. Between ca. 1702 and ca. 1722, the most powerful ruler on the leeward coast was the *obirempon* Ashabra (Captain James). A publication of 1728 (*Atlas maritimus & commercialis* 1728:90) described how he supervised the ships that traded in his area of jurisdiction:

[At] a Negro town called Trimine [Tema] lives the famous Negro merchant Captain James; [he] manages all the trade and directs all the ships; he is factor, broker and merchant for all nations; and if the ships act without him they may as well steer without a helm or ride without an anchor; so that they call the Road Capt. James's Bay.
    There are many small places places between [Great Ningo and Lay or "Baya"] where the ships go a'slaving . . . and ride generally in the open sea, sending their shallops in to wait the orders of the great Negro James who directs where they shall ride.

Ashabra was the overlord of the towns of Tema and Great Ningo, but not of the intervening towns of Kpone, Prampram, and "Chabra." He served, however, as the government broker for all of the ports between Tema and Lay. The brokers resident in these different places were under his jurisdiction. From each ship he received what was known as "custom," a payment for the right to purchase water, wood, livestock, and produce and to conduct trade in ivory, slaves, and gold. From the English lodge at Tema he received, at regular intervals, gifts. He was the arbiter in all disputes involving Europeans and local brokers and traders, and he was also responsible for directing the inland merchants to the ports where the ships were anchored.

CONCLUSION

A salient feature of the political development of the Akwamu state apparatus during the period under study was the elaboration of a fiscal-administrative system. New political posts, such as the governorships, were created and new forms of taxation were introduced. Political development enabled the state to exercise increased control over external (and internal) trade — the commercial order — and over revenue-paying dependencies — the tribute order. The social basis of this process was rooted in the needs and demands of the Akwamu ruling class, the *abirempon*. Increased control over trade and tributary territories enabled the *abirempon* to appropriate and accumulate greater stores of wealth. Greater wealth meant expanded incomes, and hence an opportunity to trade at the European mercantile establishments on an increasing scale. Larger incomes also provided the *abirempon* with the resources needed to support the state apparatus. The ruling class held a monopoly over the economic means of central administration. However, the political hegemony of this class was destroyed following the revolt of the tributary districts and provinces in 1729 and 1730. The mass uprising of the tribute-paying territories inevitably led to the collapse of the state structure and to the end of *abirempon* rule.

REFERENCES

AMIN, S.
  1973   *Le développement inégal*. Paris: Editions de Minuit.
ATKINS, J.
  1737   *A voyage to Guinea, Brazil and the West Indies* (second edition). London.
Atlas maritimus & commercialis
  1728   *Atlas maritimus & commercialis, or A general view of the world so far as related to trade and navigation*. London.
BOSMAN, W.
  1967 [1705]   *A new and accurate description of the coast of Guinea* (fourth edition). London: Frank Cass.
D'ELBÉE
  1671   "Journal du voyage du Sr. d'Elbée, aux isles dans la coste de Guinée," in *Relation de ce qui s'est passé dans les isles et terreforme de l'Amérique*, volume two. Edited by J. Clodore. Paris.
DJAN, O. S.
  1936   *The Sunlight reference almanac of the Gold Coast Colony and its dependencies*. Aburi, Gold Coast.
DU CASSE
  1935 [1688]   "Mémoire ou relation du Sr. Du Casse sur son voyage de Guynée avec 'la Tempeste' en 1687 et 1688," in *L'établissement d'Issiny 1687–1702*. Edited by P. Roussier. Paris.

FARIAS, P. F. DE M.
1974   Silent trade: myth and historical evidence. *History in Africa* 1:9–24.
FIELD, M. J.
1940   *Social organization of the Ga people.* Accra and London: Crown Agents.
HINDESS, B., P. Q. HIRST
1975   *Pre-capitalist modes of production.* London and Boston: Routledge and Kegan Paul.
HUBER, H.
1963   *The Krobo.* St. Augustin near Bonn: Anthropos Institute.
JOHNSON, M.
1964   Migrants' progress, part one. *Bulletin of the Ghana Geographical Association* 9(2):4–27.
1970   The cowrie currencies of West Africa. *Journal of African History* 11:17–49, 331–353.
KEA, R. A.
1974   "Trade, state formation, and warfare on the gold Coast, 1600–1826." Unpublished Ph.D. dissertation, University of London.
MEYEROWITZ, E. L. R.
1951   *The sacred state of the Akan.* London: Faber and Faber.
NATIONAL ARCHIVES, COPENHAGEN, ARCHIVES OF THE DANISH WEST INDIES -GUINEA COMPANY
1687–1689   Breve og dokumenter fra Guinea 1683, 1684, 1689, 1698–1705. [Accounts book 1687–1689].
1700   Dag-Journaler fört paa Christiansborg 1698–1705. Entries from May 17 to June 19, 1700.
1702   Copie af Dag-Journaler fra 23 Dec. 1698 till 1 Sept. 1703. Entry for November 30, 1702.
1711   Dokumenter vedk. diverse Köbenhavnske Retssager II. 1720–1728. F. Boye, Christiansborg, August 1711.
1719   Breve og dokumenter fra Guinea 1705–1722. K. Rost, Christiansborg, December 10, 1719.
1725a Sekretprotokoller, fört paa Christiansborg. H. Suhm et al., Christiansborg, March 22–24, 1725.
1725b Breve og dokumenter fra Guinea 1722–1731. H. Suhm, Christiansborg, April 10, 1725.
1727a Sekretprotokoller, fört paa Christiansborg i Guinea 1723–1754. Suhm et al., Christiansborg, January 1, 1727.
1727b Negotie-Journaler fra Guinea 1698–1721, 1723–1754. Entries for September 24, 25, and 27 and October 3, 1727.
1727c Negotie-Journaler fra Guinea 1698–1721, 1723–1754. Entry for December 31, 1727.
1727d Breve og dokumenter fra Guinea 1722–1731. H. Suhm et al., Christiansborg, March 5, 1727.
1728   Sekretprotokoller, fört paa Christiansborg i Guinea 1728–1730. A. Wellemsen et al., Christiansborg, December 12, 1728.
1730   Breve og dokumenter fra Guinea 1722–1731. A. P. Waeröe, Christiansborg, December 24, 1730.
n.d.a   Gaeldböger fra Guinea 1723–1738. Cabuseer Teete her udj Orsue Negerie.
n.d.b   Gaeldböger fra Guinea 1723–1733. Putty udj Labedeye.
n.d.c   Gaeldböger fra Guinea 1723–1733. Aichu udj Tuberkue.

RASK, J.
1754   *En Kort og sanferdig reise beskrivelse til og fra Guinea.* Trondheim.
REINDORF, C. C.
n.d [1895]   *The history of the Gold Coast and Asante* (second edition). Basel.
RØMER, L. F.
1760   *Tilforladelig efterretning om negotien paa Kysten Guinea.* Copenhagen.
SAXTON, S. W.
1925   Historical survey of the Shai people. *Gold Coast Review* 1.
SMITH, W.
1744   *A new voyage to Guinea.* London.
TILLEMAN, E.
1697   *En liden enfoldige beretning om det landskab Guinea og dets beskaffenhed langs ved sö-kanten.* Copenhagen.
WILKS, I.
1957   The rise of the Akwamu empire, 1650–1710. *Transactions of the Historical Society of Ghana* 3:99–136.
1959   "Akwamu 1650–1750: a study of the rise and fall of a West African empire." Unpublished M.A. thesis, University of Wales.
1971   "The Mossi and Akan states 1500–1800," in *History of West Africa,* volume one. Edited by J. F. A. Ajayi and Michael Crowder, 344–386. London: Longman.
1975   *Asante in the nineteenth century: the structure and evolution of a political order.* London: Cambridge University Press.

The Dynamics and Symbolism of
Idoma Kingship

ROBERT G. ARMSTRONG

This study seeks to give a brief inside view of the kingly office in one Idoma land, Otukpó, with some consideration of similar institutions in other parts of Idoma and Nigeria.[1] Most other treatments of kingship in West Africa have dealt with the phenomenon from so remote, abstract, and "administrative" a point of view that the meaning of African kingship is missed and replaced with an essentially trivial European concept, which the colorful African costumes, regalia, and ceremonies are implicitly supposed to express. Some writers have been so eager to prove that the king is "divine" that they have neglected to discover what the people really think about their king and how they relate him to their religion and cosmology. For example, Irstam (1944, quoted in Boston 1968:189–192) argued that "the king was the living expression of a permanently divine principle, which was considered to have begun with the primeval Father and to continue to all eternity." As we shall see, many of the kings of the Benue and Lower Niger areas, far from being a "living expression," are regarded as symbolically dead.

THEORETICAL INTERPRETATIONS OF KINGSHIP IN WEST AFRICA

Some writers have been so ready to prove some point about military

---

[1] Most of the Idoma live in Benue State, south of the Benue River, in Nigeria. The materials which I shall present here were largely collected during my visits to Idoma from late 1950 up till the present. I supplement written documents with my own observations. In my monograph on this area (Armstrong 1955), I have listed and discussed government documents on Idoma and neighboring areas to give a conspectus of the constitutions of all these lands into which the much deeper materials on Otukpó may be fitted.

force[2] that they have not noticed that the kingdoms of the Benue and Lower Niger Valleys were almost without armies that could play a political role. Their numerous wars were essentially fought with citizens' militias organized ad hoc for the occasion. The very powerful Nri kingdom, to the east of Onitsha, lacked even an armed militia, depending instead on the moral force of its highly organized priesthood. Militias can be readily mobilized against an external foe, but armed combat in an internal quarrel over succession was very rare in the small kingdoms with which we are mainly concerned here. In the Igala kingdom, which was another order of size larger, one does hear of wars over the kingship (see Boston 1968:54, 60 *et passim*). Even in Igala, however, quarrels over succession were far more likely to involve lineage or clan politics than military action. Historians are usually attracted to wars, armies, and great generals. They have not shown themselves to be very interested in the Benue and Lower Niger areas, about which the authors of the papers in Ajayi and Crowder (1971–1974), for example, say almost nothing. Very likely the discovery of oil in the Benue Valley will make the area more interesting in the decades to come. Military-minded historians might also note that the warrior peoples of the Benue Valley stopped the jihad in the nineteenth century, and federal soldiers from the Benue played a very important role in stopping the Biafran secession in the twentieth.

Most of the small Idoma states were earlier a part of the Jukun Empire and have traditions of flight and migration following its breakup. The large and politically "acephalous" Tiv nation lies to the east and is a classic example of a bifurcating, segmentary society (Bohannan and Bohannan 1953:19–37). To the west is the large, centralized Igala kingdom, with which many Idoma groups have traditional ties.

The constitutional and symbolic arrangements of these small states are of great theoretical interest in the study of the evolution of human society from one based on the relationships of kin-based associations or corporations to the establishment of territorial states, in which citizenship comes from residence, not from descent or kinship. West Africa has a great variety of models of intermediate states — territorial states whose constituent units are kin-based lineage corporations rather than townships, wards, and precincts. The study of these societies is a matter of practical interest as well, since in countries like Nigeria they have come to play a rapidly increasing role in state and national governments, in the military, and in the national market. It may be that the traditional state systems will "wither away," but it has not happened yet, and who is to say that they

---

[2]   E.g., Goody (1966:5, 18): "An examination of the concomitants of different modes of transferring high office raises the general question of the 'power' of the office and its relation to the structure of the dynasty, the character of the whole governmental system and the organization of the armed force on which it finally depends. . . . Whatever the system of succession, force is the final arbiter."

may not find ways to adapt and survive in the so-called modern world? In developing the theoretical framework implicit in this study (see Armstrong 1950: esp. 295–300), I have found Maine's dictum especially helpful: "The most nearly universal fact concerning the origin of known states" is that they "were formed by the coalescence of groups" (Maine 1875:386, quoted in Nadel 1942:69). Nadel uses this, wrongly in my view, as the basis of his own version of the conquest theory of state formation:

(1) The state is a political unit based on territorial sovereignty. . . . The state is thus inter-tribal or inter-racial. . . . (2) A centralized machinery of government assumes the maintenance of law and order, to the exclusion of all independent action. (3) The state involves the existence of a specialized, privileged, ruling group or class separated in training, status and organization from the main body of the population. This group monopolizes, corporately, the machinery of political control. . . . These three factors of state structure . . . can be reduced to the basic principle of territorial sovereignty maintained over groups of different cultural or ethnic extraction.

It is not hard to find examples of states that fit this pattern, such as the Nupe kingdom, with its Fulani overlords; but I have found that Nadel's "basic principle" does not stand up. It cannot be shown that such well-known states as Benin, Dahomey, and Asante are governed by ruling groups which are ethnically distinct from their subjects. Nadel's theory is partially derived from the work of his older Austrian compatriot, Ludwig Gumplowicz, who expanded Maine's statement. According to Gumplowicz (1892:41–42, 54–55; original emphasis), the sociological idea of the state "regards as the constituent elements of the state not the free and equal individuals, but those social *groups* whose reciprocal relationship makes up the constitution of the state. . . . [It derives] . . . from the battle of the component parts which form the state." The attempt of both Nadel and Gumplowicz to prove from the above arguments that all states were formed by conquest, in "an *historical event* brought about by superior power of a military organized human group over an unmilitary one" (Gumplowicz 1892:55; original emphasis), is in my view a non sequitur. Maine stopped short of saying any such thing.

Fortes and Evans-Pritchard (1940:9) argue from Maine's position:

The evidence at our disposal in this book suggests that cultural and economic heterogeneity is associated with a state-like political structure. Centralized authority and an administrative organization seem to be necessary to accommodate culturally diverse groups within a single political system, especially if they have different modes of livelihood. A class or caste system may result if there are great cultural and, especially, great economic divergencies. But centralized forms of government are found also with peoples of homogeneous culture and little economic differentiation, like the Zulu.

It is their last sentence that is crucial for our present study.

THE STRUCTURAL BASE FOR IDOMA KINGSHIP

The groups which make up the Idoma states are corporate lineages. There is a considerable anthropological literature on the concept of corporation, but lack of space prevents my considering it here. Suffice it to say that the Idoma lineage ("ipɔ́ɔpu") is a landholding association of anything up to 5,000 people, that it is administered by a council of elders, and that it can be mobilized for such purposes as legal and judicial action (Armstrong 1956) and the choice of a king, in association with the other lineages that make up the land (ajɛ). The kingship rotates among the lineages and inside these among their sublineages, but the process is not automatic and is subject to months or years of negotiation. The final agreement can best be described as a contract, and a very complex contract at that. The rotational feature implies that the king will more often than not be chosen from one of the less senior lineages. In the end, the new king-elect visits every sublineage (ɔkwu) of the three lineages and makes a substantial money payment to each. This kind of procedure, which is customary in a whole series of highly traditional Nigerian kingdoms, may be compared with Maine's well-known "law of progress": that the course of cultural evolution in such societies is from status to contract (Maine 1950 [1861]: 141). Quite emphatically it must be said that in the typical southern Nigerian kingdom — including the Yoruba — there is no one who by his ascribed, inherited status is the sole and legitimate heir of the king. Kingship is a conferred status from the point of view of the lineage elders or "king makers" and an achieved status from the point of view of the candidate. It must be sanctified and made permanent by a series of dramatic, public rituals and also by spiritual means, many of which are expressed in secret rituals.

The Nuer lineage, according to Evans-Pritchard (1940a:203; 1940b:286), is not a corporation; it exists only relative to its rivalries with and antagonisms toward other lineages. For him, the West African unilateral descent groups are not lineages at all — in this sense at least (personal communication, about 1959). African lineage sociology has never been easy for Americans and Europeans to understand, and I have never been quite sure what Evans-Pritchard meant by his statement. It makes most sense to me to say that the principal point of contrast between Idoma and Nuer unilineal descent groups is precisely that the former are landholding corporations and the latter are not. A great deal of research remains to be done on this matter.

In any case, however, the Idoma lineages live in a high state of rivalry with each other, despite the fact that they think of themselves as arranged in a genealogical relationship. From the point of view of land ownership, they are *separate* corporations, united politically in the land around the institution of the kingship. As in the Zulu case, the groups which make up the state are ethnically almost identical and much intermarried, but the intergroup rivalries ensure their distinctness and require a central political institution to prevent fission and to maintain the moral climate that prevents feuds from developing inside these quite warlike societies.

It is in this context that we must understand that Idoma kingdoms are based on lineage systems in such a way that a group of corporate lineages constitutes the state. Such a state may also include stranger lineages, which are not regarded as constituent lineages in this sense, although they may live in an elaborately defined and ancient relationship to the state. The Ákpací lineage of Otukpó Land, for example, has a function of arbitration of disputes that goes back to the days of the Apá (Jukun) Empire, but it is still regarded as a stranger lineage.

The problem then arises as to how a king who is himself a member of one of the lineages can achieve — at least plausibly — the necessary generality of interest to function as the chief officer of the whole, at once ruler and servant of all. One solution to this problem that is seen in many states is the establishment of a specialized royal lineage or clan whose function it is to provide kings successively, according to some well understood procedure of selection and installation. This is usually the kind of system found in the larger and wealthier states, such as Igala, west of Idoma (cf. Boston 1968:3, esp. 56–57; see also Meek 1931:336 on the Jukun royal house). In a great many smaller states, however, there is no royal lineage, and, as we have seen, the kingship rotates among the constituent lineages. This is surely an ancient pattern and one theoretically very relevant to the problem of the evolution of society from a kinship to a territorial base. It is found in nearly pure form in several lands (or districts) of Idoma (roughly the former Idoma Division, now the Otukpó and Okpokwu Divisions of Benue State, Nigeria). They provide a useful model of one kind of solution to the question of legitimacy in an asymmetrical system: given a ranked system of four corporate lineages, A, B, C, and D, in descending order of seniority, how can a king from Lineage A plausibly and legitimately embody and represent the interests of Lineages B, C, and D? Or a king from Lineage C? In the Idoma case, as we shall see below, he does it by dying symbolically.

In ancient times and up till today, Idoma has consisted of twenty-five or thirty lands (*ajɛ*). These are county-size units, roughly speaking, and until about 1920 they were independent of each other. They regard themselves as being related to each other genealogically. Each is typically constituted by two, three, or four corporate lineages ("ipɔ́ɔpu"), which are the effective landowning units and which hold the kingship of the land in rotation. A land usually also has one or more stranger lineages, also subject to the king. It is therefore apparent that a land differs from a clan, whose head might be expected to be the head of the most senior lineage. (In saying this, I disagree explicitly with Magid [1972:291]. I see no reason for preferring the terminology of the old colonial officers to that of the Idoma themselves. There is nothing ambiguous about the word *ajɛ*. It means "soil," "earth," "dirt," "downward direction," "land," "political unit," "geographical territory," and "area served by a particular land shrine" (*ikpáajɛ*). *Ajɛ* is arguably the most senior of all concepts, since even *Owɔicō* [God] calls Earth "senior" in Idoma prayer.) The system of rotation ensures that the king will more often than not come from a lineage which is not senior and that he himself will not usually be the most senior elder of his own lineage. Since he is chosen by the lineage elders, he is controlled by them. When he acts, he acts in their name; when he speaks, he enunciates their decisions. It should not be thought, however, that the choice of a successor is easy and automatic. There are likely to be protracted debates lasting many months or even years. As I have suggested, the whole procedure may be regarded as the negotiation of a contract, under an elaborate set of preconditions which function to counteract the strong tendencies toward fission which are always present in these societies.

The office of kingship (*ɔcɛ́*) shows every sign of being ancient in Idoma. The word is found in this meaning in every Idoma dialect. Even in the southernmost, that of Yala (Ikom), in Ogoja Province, where there is no chief or king in the political and ceremonial sense to which this discussion refers, we find its cognate reflex *ɔsɛ́* [hereditary head of the family]. At the extreme northern end of Idoma country, the king of the land in Lafia Emirate which bears the name Idōma Nōkwū ("Doma" on the official maps) bears the title *Osɛ́ gídōma* [king of Idoma]. (In Central Idoma, this land is also referred to as Idɔma Nɔkwū [Great Idoma].) Throughout Idoma, the king is referred to as *ɔcáajɛ* [king of the land]. This has a meaning which goes far beyond that of political control of a territory. It should be noted that a similar title and office is found among the Igbira, including the Igbira Tao, in and around the modern city of Okene, in Kabba Province.

As has been noted above, the king is not a clan head, nor is he usually even a lineage head. Although he is chosen by lineages, he stands between them, and his responsibility is general and to the whole land. He assumes office by an act of symbolic death, beginning with the sacking of his compound. He dies to his family and lineage attachments. His wives become widows and his children become orphans. He lies in state, after which his 'ɔwɔ'-tree is cut and he is hidden for fourteen days. This allows his children to give gifts to citizens of the land who have come to "mourn" for him. During this time many ceremonies are performed on his behalf. He loses all his personal belongings to the society as a whole. An ancestral mask performs the "Opening of the Path to the Grave" ceremony for him. He loses his personal identity, and he loses all the obligations that he owes to individuals and to his own family. He becomes the general son of the land. He becomes king owning no property of his own, but as king he owns the whole land and its citizens.[3] On formal occasions he will be reminded by the most senior elders that he is king because it is they who have made him king.[4] Acting as judge, he will hear many personal disputes and land disputes; but homicide, in the old days, was a matter for the lineages meeting as a court. Furthermore, the full court-of-lineages could hear a constitutional case between the king and a commoner (Armstrong 1956). The position of the king may be thought of as in some way like that of a microphone which is suspended by springs or rubber bands from a rigid frame, to which it is equally but flexibly connected in all directions.

THE RITUALS AND REGALIA OF IDOMA KINGSHIP

The king's status is marked by certain traditional regalia, of which a bracelet of coral beads is the most essential. He is surrounded by a special etiquette and is addressed by a traditional title that differs in the various lands and that may be translated as "Your Majesty." In ancient times one prostrated oneself before him and threw dirt on one's shoulders. Today this custom is in most places preserved only in a common idiom of speech

---

[3]   There is almost nothing about all this in the published literature on the Idoma. My information is from many oral sources, including a long, tape-recorded interview with the now deceased king of Otukpó and his advisory council.
   I have not found it easy to elicit the meaning of this symbolic funeral. The king himself is debarred from discussing it. The anthropologist will probably have a working hypothesis — indeed, that is what prompts him to conduct the interview — but he must never suggest it to his informants or in any sense put words in their mouths, on pain of spoiling the whole interview situation. In the Ǫcheíbí interview, it was only at the very end that the now deceased elder Aduma (the father of Mr. Aduma of the Federal Ministry of External Affairs) finally spoke to the heart of the matter:

562.   ǪGƐBƐ: Do you hear? After they have all spoken like that , as he is now, nevertheless if he sings those taboo songs, nevertheless nothing happens [i.e., the symbolically dead king is not subject to the ordinary taboos].
563.   ĀDŪMĀ: See here now.
564.   ǪGƐBƐ: If you sing in his house here, it is not forbidden.
565.   ĀDŪMĀ: It is the finish of it that we shall conclude. Look here, look at all the reasons why they do things like this here . . . look at him as he is lying here like this: he does not belong to his brothers any more. He has become king of all of us. Look at the beads which he is wearing here, it is the beads of all of us which he is wearing so.
566.   ǪGƐBƐ: Yes.
567.   ĀDŪMĀ: He is no longer king for his children, he is no longer king for his father's people; we who are the children of Okō [i.e., the whole of the Otukpó people], who made him king, he is foi every last one of us.
568.   ǪGƐBƐ: Yes.
569.   ĀDŪMĀ: We agree . . . in this bush which is here, we have to agree before we carry him all together; it is no longer done by his children. That is its meaning there.
570.   ǪTÉÍKWŪ: Thank you.
571.   ĀDŪMĀ: Yes.

[4]   E.g., at the annual sacrifice at the land shrine (tape-recorded by me, transcribed, and translated).

meaning "I beg you" ('η háajɛ gāɔ' [I cut earth for you].[5] In one or two isolated lands, the symbolic gesture of throwing dirt on one's shoulders may still be seen. Only the king has the right to the 'ɔkaŋgā' (the two-membrane bass drum) and to the special royal music in which 'ɔkpancílé' flutes and the drum play together. He receives a royal tribute, known as ēgbā,' consisting of the trophies of fierce game animals and other symbols of war and brave exploits: elephant tusks, lion and leopard skins, python skins, feathers of the Senegal coucal (*uloko*), and captured slaves. In some places, such as Agila, he receives the first meats of the hunting season. On his death, and subject to certain limiting rules, the king should be "resurrected" in the form of an ancestral mask (*alekwū*). The *alekwū* of the ancient kings are among the most sacred relics in the land. The king is also the owner of the principal cults and shrines of the land, such as Achukwu, Alekwū, and Idu.

The king's most basic religious function is as chief priest of the earth cult. He performs the annual ceremony at the land shrine early in the dry season. The basic symbolism of the earth cult, the senior of all the cults, relates to the hunt and in particular to the preservation or restoration of the moral climate that will ensure a successful and, above all, peaceful hunt. If the land has been "spoiled" by homicide or other crimes, it must be "repaired" at the land shrine to prevent hunting accidents and quarrels in the bush. Like the king of Igala, the various kings of the Idoma lands are therefore related to the hunt by the symbolism of their office (Boston 1968:18–20, 95, 227–231). The kings do not themselves go hunting, nor do they go to war. They are usually very old men. When the king travels, his drums and flutes must follow along with him and play, and his youngest child must precede him. A king must never see a corpse; nor must he see the western rainbow ('ɔŋájī'), which marks the death of some great doctor (*obócí*). The king is also a farmer, insofar as his strength allows him to be. When he goes to his farm, he divests himself of his kingly robes and regalia and hangs them on an impromptu frame. Then he may do what work he likes. He is not dependent on his own farming, however, and the main work of farming is done for him by other people (Onche Amali and Ijauka, personal communication, reported by Odumu Amali). When I visited the king of Otukpó, the late Oglĭ, in 1952, he was called in from his farm to receive me, and he had obviously been working despite having a heavy cold and despite his great age. Symbolically, it may be said that it is the king who owns the land and that it is the lineage elders who own the king.

The following accounts of the death of a king and the installation of a new king were dictated to me in Idoma in 1953 by an elder, the late

---

[5]   ['hɛ́' *cut* + 'ajɛ' *earth*]. If, alternatively, 'hɛ́' has the same meaning as in 'hérɲkpɔ' *draw water*, the phrase might mean "I take up earth for you."

Qwɔichō of Ákpégēdē. They may help to give some feeling of the nature of the office:

When a king has died, his son sends messages to the different elders that the king has gone to bush. People hasten to bush to prepare his hunting-hut in bush at the royal burial-place, *ikpámllī*. All the elders go to meet at the burial-place, the place where the corpse is lying. The elders send a message to his eldest daughter that she should come to prepare gruel for her father to drink in bush. His eldest daughter goes to sit beside his corpse. If she weeps even once, she must give a goat to the elders. Nobody else may cry either. The elders send a messenger to see the eldest daughter of the king, who is sitting beside him. That person asks her what has happened to her that her eyes have become so very red there. His eldest daughter says that it is smoke that has affected her. That man goes back to tell the elders what she has said. The elders send him again to tell his eldest daughter that her father has died away, just see! A man-of-female-attachment [to the lineage] comes to tell his [the king's] eldest daughter that they [the elders] have thrown him out to rot away so that the vultures might eat his corpse. They begin to pull his child. The elders tell her that she should bring a goat to them before she can watch over her father's body. She goes to bring them a goat; then they give her the chance to watch over her father's corpse.

The elders send a messenger to his eldest son saying that they have had no news from the bush to which his father has gone. Whether he has died or not they do not know. The eldest son says, "Please, if he has died, dig some earth to put on him for me." They tell him to bring a goat to them. He goes to bring them a goat. The elders tell those-of-female-attachment that they should go and dig some earth to cover him. The latter refuse, saying that they will never bury that slave here. His eldest son brings ten shillings to them; then they dig a hole, drive his son out of the bush, and bury the corpse. All of them go back home to be in the elders' enclosure of his compound. In the evening, they call his children and say that, regarding the bush to which their father has gone, "If he has killed a big animal, we do not know it. Although we waited for him long in the bush-hut, as we have not seen him any more, therefore we have come away. The animal which he has killed must be a big one."

The elders remain there in the enclosure for seven days. Then his children take a cow to them. They slaughter it there in the enclosure. At that time they take the man who is to be [the next] king [the *alápā*] and mark his arm with camwood. Then that man slaughters the cow.

Then the elders stay again for fourteen days. The children of the king still bring a cow to the elders. They [the elders] also slaughter the cow in the enclosure and tell his children that the bush to which their father has gone is the bush-of-not-coming-home-soon. They are in one place, and none of them may go anywhere. His children stay a while; then the man who is going to be the king brings a cow to them so they may break his [the late king's] bed. Then they kill the cow. The elders skin it and eat it.

When they are going to make his mask, the person who is going to be king also brings another cow. It is only then that they will take his wives as widows. It is only at that time that they will say to his children that their father has died. Then they begin to cry.

Another very senior elder commented that the grave of a king is the same shape as an ordinary grave, but bigger. (Traditional Idoma graves consist of a vertical shaft more than six feet deep with a chamber off to one side at the bottom ['ọlọlókwū'] in which the corpse lies flat.) The vertical shaft must be so deep that when a man standing at the bottom raises his hands over his head, nobody can see them. The chamber at the bottom must be high enough so that a man standing with his hands on his knees will not touch the ceiling with his back.

It seems obvious that the seclusion of the elders described enables them to begin the delicate negotiations around the choice or confirmation of the *alápā* [the man who is going to be king]. There will later be a public debate on the matter, followed by the sacking of his compound.

The custom of concealment of the death of the king was also rigorously followed among the Jukun (Meek 1931:166ff.; *Sunday Standard* 1976) and among the Igala (Boston 1968:93ff.) Irstam (1944, quoted in Boston 1968:189–190) regarded the concealment of the Igala king's death as one of the diagnostic features of his divine status. Qwọicō continues:

While the [body of] the king is [lying] at the royal burial place, the people-of-female-attachment [to the lineage] cut his beads from his arm and take them and hide them. The man who is to be the [next] king brings five pounds to the eldest son of the king who has died; then they take the beads and place them on his arm. At that time he will become a real king. Then they take him on their shoulders and go to sack his compound: the property which they will see in the house they take, and they own it, and goats and everything which they will see in his house.

They play the 'ọkaŋgā'-drum in the inner enclosure of his compound continuously until the seventh day. They take him to the land shrine to wash his face [with honour; *eōgwóōna*]. On the fourteenth day they again wash his face at the land shrine. He has become a complete king. After a time he makes beer which the council drinks; then the council gives him power.

What, then, do we mean when we say that the contractual office of 'ọcé' is equivalent to such European offices as king,[6] *roi, könig, rex, basileus,* or *korol,* succession to which was a matter of ascribed status? He is the highest officer in the land; the lineage elders are higher than he is collectively, in council, but not individually. He is the most general officer, and the generality of his responsibility is stated dramatically by his public and symbolic death on his installation in office. Tribute is paid to him. He is chief priest of the most senior cult, the earth cult. He is chief judge, although the court-of-lineages outranks him. He is surrounded by an etiquette unique to him and is addressed by a unique title. He wears and carries certain unique symbols, and he has the sole right to an orchestra of bass drums and flutes which play a very fine, special music. He is surrounded by special taboos unique to him. When he dies, there is

[6]   I have earlier spoken of "king" as "an official whom I define minimally as the chief executive of a state who is selected by some systematic process from a small group of persons eligible to the office by birth, whose term of office is not specified, and who combines within himself at least one of the following roles: law maker, chief judge, chief priest, unifying sacred symbol, commander-in-chief of the armed forces. A really strong king may play all these roles" (Armstrong 1950:43).

an elaborate, special procedure involving the concealment of his decease for weeks or even months. He is buried in a special place with a special and unique name (*ikpámĺlī*), and his tomb is much larger than the tombs of other people. He has a strong sense of *noblesse oblige*. (In 1967, when the southeastern Idoma district of Ijigbam was attacked and both the Idoma and Izi Igbo populations fled, the 'ɔcɛ́' sat proudly in the reception-house of his compound and was duly murdered by the incoming Biafran soldiers.) The 'ɔcɛ́' is the center and key figure of any official or social gathering he attends.

It remains to be said that the executive function was not much developed in the modern sense. There was no taxation, as distinct from the symbolic tribute already mentioned. The partly secret men's societies, or dance guilds, served as constabularies on special occasions, for example, guarding the markets. Roads would be made or repaired by announcing that everybody must come on a particular day and fining any absentees. The men's societies were responsible to the council of elders and the king. The organization for war was by still another system, and the commander-in-chief (*ogbēñjūā*) was responsible to the council of elders.

It is clear that according to my definition the Idoma 'ɔcɛ́' easily qualifies as king or *rex* despite the fact that he is chosen by a contractual procedure from a set of perhaps a dozen eligible candidates. From this point of view, the heir-apparent to the throne in Europe is a set of one, of which he is the sole member from the moment of his birth.

The idea that the reigning king is "dead," and therefore a spirit or an ancestor, is widespread in southern Nigeria. That the ceremonial death of the new king is intended to confirm him in the generality of his office and the symmetry of his responsibility to all the groups in the land is explicit in the statement of an elder which closes the long interview referred to above (n. 3). This meaning is less clear in the literature on other kingdoms. Boston (1968:94–95) says that the Igala king-to-be spends nine days in the royal burial ground and is then "ritually reborn by the Onẹde, an Igala Mela chief" (see also Clifford 1936:422).

At Nri in Igboland (Onwuejeogwu 1974:ch. 5; see also Afigbo and Cookey in this volume), the new *Eze Nri* was

buried in a shallow grave. His wives began to do the real mortuary rites, which lasted for 21 days. He "rose" from the "dead" clothed with white cloth and decorated with white chalk, *nzu*. He was now a spirit (*mmụọ*) and a living *alụsị*. He announced his new name, and the people greeted him as *igwe*, the sky, the most high. He was now the Eze Nri.

(Onwuejeogwu defines *mmụọ* as "the invisible spirits of the dead"; the *alụsị* are "invisible supernatural beings and/or forces" [p. 79]; cf. Henderson 1972: 372 n. 12.)

Similarly, at Onitsha, according to Henderson (1972),

> ... the candidate for kingship must submit to the authority of the hidden King of the Ọbiọ clan, who escorts him inside an enclosure made of burial mats at the mouth of the sacred grave. While the young men of the community stand in waiting outside, the hidden king performs a number of rituals within this coffin-like seclusion. ... [p. 304]

> ... the king, as cult-slave of Udo, is defined as free from charges of abomination. He is regarded as "dead" and therefore free from the requirements of funerary performance. ... [p. 305]

> Since the king is a ghost who remains in the world contrary to the normal order of events, and since the collective incarnate dead are ghosts incarnate who have followed this normal order, he must never encounter these masked beings. Should the most feared of the incarnate dead, the tall ghost, ever pass beneath the archway guarding the entrance to the palace, and thence enter the king's square, the king would have to step down from his throne, and he would be deposed. For although the king is above ordinary laws, he is not above the dead and in fact must answer to them ... [p. 308]
> ... the king approximates god. [p. 275]

He is addressed as *igwe* (sky), etc. — an "emergent" notion, since Henderson regards it as consonant with the royal sun-moon-sky symbolism. Further,

> Onitsha kingship and 'ọzọ' title are clearly related historically to the Nri kingship complex. [p. 364]

> Accession to both kingship and 'ọzọ' requires the establishment of a relationship to *nze* [tabooed sacred objects-symbols of patrilineal exogamy], and in both cases the candidate "dies" and becomes ghost-like. ... [p. 370]

> ... [the] 'ọzọ' title is a kind of partial kingship, a metaphor of kingship attainable by every man. The 'ọzọ' man dies and re-emerges as a whitened ancestor; the king's installation takes this process further, with his funeral ceremonies actually performed during his lifetime. ... [p. 372 and n. 12]

At Ọyọ, in Western Nigeria, the *aláàfin*-to-be goes to Bàrà, the royal burial place, and the women begin the mourning rites. Only after this symbolic death does he go to the palace (*ààfin*) to become king (S. Babayẹmi, personal communication). The *oba* of Benin seems also to fit into this pattern (see Bradbury 1967:32–33).

Clearly the symbolism of the "dead" king on the throne is widespread in Nigeria. Its meaning may vary somewhat from one kingdom to another, but the task of eliciting the full complexity and subtlety of the meaning from oral sources still lies ahead of us. Perhaps Frazer's golden words about "kings as incarnate life spirits" have dazzled us and made it hard to perceive kings as incarnate ghosts.

TRADITIONAL LEADERSHIP AND BRITISH COLONIAL RULE

The general treatments of traditional leadership in West African and Nigerian history are on the whole too remote and abstract to be of much use to the present discussion. Afigbo (1974:428–429), for example, has only ten lines on his own people, the Igbo. He ignores the Idoma, Igala, and Tiv almost completely. Crowder (1962) likewise has almost nothing to say about the Benue Valley and of its peoples and mentions only the Jukun. The symposium published by Crowder and Ikime (1970) was concerned with colonial local administrative policy. The editors are not even wholly agreed on what officers are to be called "chief." Ikime, reacting to the constitutionally distorting effects of the eighty-eight-year interregnum in Itsẹkiriland (Warri), calls the *olu* "king" and says that the chiefs are the titleholders (*ojoye*). He nevertheless has much to say about the office of *olu*, which became functional again in 1936. There are few points of comparison between the development of the Idoma kingship and so specialized a history as that of Warri. In any case, the research procedure that Crowder and Ikime adopt (p. x) would make it very difficult for a student who used it to perceive or discover the kind of data with which this study is concerned.

Of the kingdoms discussed in Forde and Kaberry (1967), only Benin and Ọyọ seem culturally close enough to be comparable to the Idoma kingship. Benin and Ọyọ were imperial capitals, however, and the whole structure of power and administration reflected that fact. From that point of view they are scarcely comparable with the very much smaller Idoma polities. There are points of ideological similarity, however, as we have seen above with the case of the installation of the *aláàfìn* of Ọyọ. Bradbury (1967:32) says of the *oba* of Benin, "By [the] act of succession he ceased to be a mere man. Once installed, dogma had it, the king needed neither food nor sleep, nor would he ever die." We are not given an account of the details of his installation, but the above characterization is at least not in contradiction with the notion of a symbolically dead king reigning.

Gann and Duignan (1970) are concerned with the politics of colonialism. Consequently, the papers in their book have little relevance to the problems and developments discussed in this article, which tries to look at Idoma kingship from the inside.

Serious colonial administration of most of Idoma began about 1920, with the preparations for the construction of the railroad from Jos to Port Harcourt. The policy of the colonial government was to find or create chiefs who would become a part of the governmental system (see Bohannan and Bohannan 1953:37; Jones 1970). In Idoma they naturally chose the 'ɔcɛ́' for this role and called him "chief." He was given a salary, made president of the Native Authority court, and made responsible for the collection of taxes from the heads of the sublineages (not from the lineage heads, because they were senior to him). It was not easy to get such a system established and operative in Idoma. If one can trust the district and divisional records in this matter, nearly every stool was vacant at the time that administration started, and there had been interregna as long as fifty years. It is possible that the kings were being concealed from the government, but I have no conclusive evidence to prove or disprove this. What is clear is that the government had to exert strong and persistent pressure in many districts in order to get the lineage elders to agree on a chief and further strong, persistent pressure to get the Native Authority courts operative (Armstrong 1955:106–107, 109, *passim*; Captain Money, a divisional officer at various times in the 1930's, personal communication, 1951).

It is not hard to see that the requirements of agency in a system of indirect rule did considerable violence to the authority of the kingly office. For one thing, it is never easy to get modern taxation started in a large area in which people have never paid taxes, and the persons responsible for collecting it quite naturally become the object of a lot of resentment. For another thing, it is clear from the archives and from my own observation that the decisions of the chiefs were subject to being suddenly reversed, altered or "quashed" by the divisional officer or by some assistant divisional officer who was often less than half his age. This was probably necessary on many occasions, but it was often done in at least partial ignorance of what was really involved; and kings do not like to be told they have judged badly. For another thing, court records were kept by more or less literate court clerks, who lived at the local Native Authority court. Between the visits of the political officers, these court clerks were the authorities on law and procedure, and they often became — and are still — persons of quite undue local importance, in my own observation. (The problem is widespread in Nigeria, as one can see in the Western State, where the judge must write out the court record himself while the trial is proceeding in order to ensure that control of the courts remains in the hands of the judiciary.)

On the other hand, the chiefs did have a regular money income and many other signs of favor and status. A meeting of the council of chiefs was a colorful and dramatic occasion. There were Native Authority police attached to the courts, and behind their authority stood the ultimate sanction of the Nigeria Regiment. Although in many places in Africa this structure enabled the king to become a local autocrat, it cannot be said that the Idoma kings went very far in that direction.

RECENT DEVELOPMENTS

In 1948, the colonial government set up an office of paramount chief, king of Idoma ('ǫchídɔ̄ma') elected by the Council of Idoma, which was made up of all the kings recognized by the government as district heads. At about the same time, a similar office, *tor Tiv,* was created in Tiv Division, immediately to the east. There was no real model of kingship in Tiv, and for this and other reasons the office of *tor Tiv* has produced mixed results. The role of 'ǫchídɔ̄ma,' however, was built on a set of widely accepted traditional concepts and on the whole was successful in establishing itself. In the first place, the Council of Idoma was quickly accepted as a legitimate body, and this fact made much easier the acceptance of its choice of the 'ǫchídɔ̄ma,' as legitimate. In the second place, the office of 'ǫchídɔ̄ma,' has facilitated the collection of taxes in Idoma Division. In the third place, it helped in the establishment of a centralized court system in the 1950's, although the official court system has now been entirely separated from kingship both on the district and on the divisional level. In 1976, Otukpó Division was divided into three divisions: Otukpó Division, from Otukpó District north, Okpokwu Division, the western and southern districts, and Oju Division made up of the Ígēdē-speaking districts. This leaves the office of 'ǫchídɔ̄ma,' rather ill-defined, and some adjustment will surely be made.

The first 'ǫchídɔ̄ma,' Oglíí Okō, of Adoka died in early 1960, and when the Council of Idoma met it chose the king of Itóō, Ajɛnɛ Ǫkpabi, as his successor. Itóō is an Igēdē-speaking land, although a great many people there also speak very good Idoma. This established the principle that the 'ǫchídɔ̄ma,' need not necessarily be an Idoma. Since at least a third of the population of (old) Idoma Division speaks some other language than Idoma, this was an interesting precedent. In 1966 came the Igbo-led military coup and from 1967 to 1970 the painful Nigerian-Biafran civil war.

The first military government dismissed the Native Authority council and appointed the 'ǫchídɔ̄ma,' as Sole Native Authority. Idoma found the coup of January 15, 1966, very disturbing and by May tension had risen quite high in the Division. The 'ǫchídɔ̄ma,' and the divisional officer together toured every district and managed to keep Idoma peaceful.

After the July 1966 coup, the Igbo deserted Idoma, leaving just two Idoma traders sitting in an otherwise empty Otukpó market. The 'ǫchídɔ̄ma,' helped to get trade started again and encouraged Idoma to get into trade. Apart from troubles on the southeastern border, which had their roots deep in the past and which were almost inevitable once tension and disorganization in the country had risen past a certain point, there was only one really serious incident involving the Idoma during the troubled period of September–October 1966. The bad weekend of

October 1 passed with only some troubles caused by mutinous soldiers, but a few days later a refugee train came north from Enugu loaded with wounded northerners, including some Idoma. This sparked an attack on a southbound train on October 8, in which between thirty and forty people died. In the state of feeling at the time, there was nothing that the 'ọchĬdɔma,' or the 'ọchÓtukpó' could have done to prevent the attack on the train. The army unit stationed in Otukpó kept the incident from getting far worse, as it could easily have done. The 'ọchĬdɔma,' and the kings of the lands did work hard to limit the troubles, and it should be emphasized that on the night of the attack on the train there were many dozens of Igbo in hiding in the very villages from which the rioters came, between two and five miles away. During the weeks that preceded and followed this time, tens of thousands of Igbo passed through Idoma Division, and many thousands of them traveled by bush paths with local help. In those terrible times, it was the traditional kings and the 'ọchĬdɔma,' who maintained substantial law and order in Idoma.

In November and December 1966, when rail and road transport of gasoline had broken down almost completely, it was the 'ọchĬdɔma,' who went to Lagos and arranged directly with the oil companies for tank trucks to come to Idoma via the Lokoja ferry.

Earlier, in September he had been part of the Northern delegation to the Ad Hoc Constitutional Conference in Lagos and participated actively in the decision of that delegation in favor of a federal solution for Nigeria. He was active in urging the creation of states.

The first half of 1966 saw the intensive exploration of Idoma Division for oil. This was carried out by a French oil-exploration company, Safrap, which worked out of Enugu and Nsukka and did not trouble to inform the Military governor of the North that Idoma was being prospected. For that matter, it did not bother to inform the 'ọchĬdɔma,' either or the kings of the lands where it was working, and it appeared to regard the Idoma people as merely an obstruction. The 'ọchĬdɔma,' quietly kept track of everything the Safrap engineers did, noting which holes they sheathed with iron and capped with cement and where they made their large strikes. This work became strategically important in May 1967, when Ojukwu demanded that federal soldiers be pulled away from the southern Idoma border as a gesture of good will. The 'ọchĬdɔma,' went to Kaduna and to Lagos and was able to show with maps that the French oil company had quietly made a whole series of paths and motor traces that left Idoma wide open to invasion. His action may well have spared Idoma an attack like the one launched against the Midwest State a few weeks later.[7]

---

[7]   It goes without saying that I take grave exception to Magid's comments about H. H. Ajene Ọkpabi, the 'ọchĬdɔma,' and about the Igede people. There can be no question of the legitimacy of his election by the Council of Idoma. There can be no traditional pattern of

From the point of view of the functioning of government as a whole, it is the kings who are in direct touch with the ordinary people of Idoma. Better than any other part of the government, they know what is actually going on in the districts. In a time which has seen the emergence of a new literate, trading class, the kings represent and express the human dignity of the great majority of the people, who still have no hope of achieving real literacy or of participating in the world market and in national or international cultural institutions. On their success in helping their subjects to expand their field of activity depends the long-term future of the kings. They will necessarily move slowly because they are moving a great mass, and they may look conservative or backward to urbanized "elite" groups who are not encumbered by such responsibilities; still the kings are moving, and move they must. A great many of the soldiers of the Nigerian Army come from the country districts where kingship is largely intact. With the end of the Civil war, the problems of the returning veterans presented the kings with a great test of their adaptability and a great opportunity to assist in the reintegration of strong, tough men into civilian life. Traditional Idoma society has a body of sophisticated tradition that deals with such problems, and the kings may well prove once again that they can serve the nation. At least one district had a literate ex-soldier as its king before the war began, and it seems possible that this pattern may be repeated in other places.

It seems likely, too, that the pattern of election of kings by rotation has been a helpful schooling in elections of a more democratic type. The king, by the generality of his office, represents even those sections of the community who may have opposed his election. This is surely a useful model for democracy generally, since there can be no democracy if the parties feel they cannot afford to lose an election and would rather start shooting than risk extirpation at the hands of the winners. Traditional Idoma kingship has many constitutionally democratic features. The (physiological) death of the aged king of Otukpó in December 1975 produced a great outpouring of public feeling. His inquest (cf. Armstrong 1955, 1960) was attended by people from all sections of society, from the town bourgeoisie to the most traditional villagers.

I should like to conclude this paper, the latter half of which is based more on personal experience during many visits to Idoma than on sys-

---

rotation of kingship among twenty-three districts, but the first 'o̩chíd3ma,' was king of Adoka Land, and the present incumbent was king of Ito Land. The first was a very traditionally minded man and had many wives and children. Like African kings all over the continent, he used marriages as a technique for building and strengthening his political following. Nor is this practice strange among European royalty. Magid's comments about the Igede people (p. 299) are simply unacceptable. The truth is that there is no substitute for anthropology, and a degree in political science is not in itself a sufficient preparation for fieldwork in so complex a place as West Africa.

tematic study, by saying that the kings of the various lands of Idoma Division have played a basic role in the development of Idoma and Nigeria. The son of one of these kings, J. C. Obande, was a minister in the federal government of the First Republic. Edwin Ogbu, the Nigerian Permanent Representative to the United Nations (retired), is the son of the late king of Utonkon, in Otukpó Division. There is every reason to think that despite — or perhaps because of — its removal from the judiciary and from politics, kingship will continue to play an important role in the future.

REFERENCES

AFIGBO, A. E.
  1974 "The establishment of colonial rule, 1900–1918," in *History of West Africa*, volume two. Edited by J. F. A. Ajayi and Michael Crowder, 424–483, London: Longman.
AJAYI, J. F. A., MICHAEL CROWDER, editors
  1971–1974 *History of West Africa,* two volumes. London: Longman.
ARMSTRONG, R. G.
  1950 "State formation in Negro Africa." Unpublished Ph.D. dissertation, University of Chicago.
  1955 "The Igala" and "The Idoma-speaking peoples," in *Peoples of the Niger-Benue confluence.* Ethnographic Survey of Africa, Western Africa, part ten. Edited by D. Forde, P. Brown and R. G. Armstrong. London: International African Institute.
  1956 "The Idoma court-of-lineages in law and political structure." *Selected papers of the Fifth International Congress of Anthropological and Ethnological Sciences, Philadelphia, September 1–9, 1956,* 390–395. Philadelphia: University of Pennsylvania Press.
  1960 The development of kingdoms in Negro Africa. *Journal of the Historical Society of Nigeria* 2:27–39.
BOHANNAN, PAUL, LAURA BOHANNAN
  1953 *The Tiv of central Nigeria.* Ethnographic Survey of Africa, Western Africa, part eight. London: International African Institute.
BOSTON, JOHN S.
  1968 *The Igala kingdom.* Ibadan: Oxford University Press for the Nigerian Institute of Social and Economic Research.
BRADBURY, R. E.
  1967 "The kingdom of Benin," in *West African kingdoms in the nineteenth century.* Edited by Daryll Forde and P. M. Kaberry, 1–35. London: Oxford University Press for the International African Institute.
CLIFFORD, MILES
  1936 A Nigerian chiefdom. *Journal of the Royal Anthropological Institute* 66:393–436.
CROWDER, MICHAEL
  1962 *The story of Nigeria.* London: Faber and Faber.
CROWDER, MICHAEL, OBARO IKIME, editors
  1970 *West African chiefs: their changing status under colonial rule and independence.* Ile-Ife: University of Ife Press.

EVANS-PRITCHARD, EDWARD EVAN
1940a *The Nuer.* Oxford: Clarendon.
1940b "The Nuer of the southern Sudan," in *African political systems.* Edited by M. Fortes and E. E. Evans-Pritchard, 272–296. London: Oxford University Press for the International African Institute.
FORDE, DARYLL, P. M. KABERRY, *editors*
1967 *West African kingdoms in the nineteenth century.* London: Oxford University Press for the International African Institute.
FORTES, M., E. E. EVANS-PRITCHARD, *editors*
1940 *African political systems.* London: Oxford University Press for the International African Institute.
GANN, L. H., PETER DUIGNAN, *editors*
1970 *Colonialism in Africa 1870–1962,* volume two: *The history and politics of colonialism 1924–1960.* Cambridge: Cambridge University Press.
GOODY, JACK, *editor*
1966 *Succession to high office.* Cambridge Papers in Social Anthropology. Cambridge: Published for the Department of Archaeology and Anthropology at the University Press.
GUMPLOWICZ, LUDWIG
1892 *Die soziologische Staatsidee.* Graz: Leuschner and Lubensky.
HENDERSON, RICHARD N.
1972 *The king in every man: evolutionary trends in Ibo society and culture.* New Haven and London: Yale University Press.
IKIME, OBARO
1970 "The changing status of chiefs among the Itsekiri," in *West African chiefs.* Edited by Michael Crowder and Obaro Ikime, 289–311. Ile-Ife: University of Ife Press.
IRSTAM, TOR
1944 *The king of Ganda.* Stockholm.
JONES, G. I.
1970 "Chieftaincy in the former Eastern Region of Nigeria," in *West African chiefs.* Edited by Michael Crowder and Obaro Ikime, 312–325. Ile-Ife: University of Ife Press.
MAGID, ALVIN
1972 Political traditionalism in Nigeria: a case-study of secret societies and dance groups in local government. *Africa* 47:289–304.
MAINE, SIR HENRY SUMNER
1950 [1861] *Ancient law.* London: Oxford University Press.
MEEK, C. K.
1931 *A Sudanese kingdom: an ethnographical study of the Jukun-speaking peoples of Nigeria.* London: Kegan Paul, Trench, Trubner.
NADEL, S. F.
1942 *A black Byzantium: the kingdom of Nupe in Nigeria.* London: Oxford University Press for the International African Institute.
ONWUEJEOGWU, MICHAEL ANGULU
1974 "The political organization of Nri, south-eastern Nigeria." Unpublished M.A. thesis, University of London.
Sunday Standard (Jos, Nigeria)
1976 *Sunday Standard.* August 15.

Gao and the Almoravids:
A Hypothesis

J. O. HUNWICK

One of the most intriguing problems in the history of the medieval Western Sudan has been that of the nature and effects of the intervention of the nomadic Almoravid warriors of the Western Sahara, inspired by a fervent Islamic ideology, on the highly developed centralized state of ancient Ghana in the Sahel lands to the south. In particular, the question has been asked whether Ghana was overrun and devastated or whether the Almoravid intervention was just an episode, albeit traumatic, in the history of that state. A similar mystery hangs over the fate of the southern wing of Almoravid movement after its intervention in Ghana. Our sources virtually dry up at this point and only reemerge in any richness during the high period of the Mali Empire in the fourteenth century.

This paper attempts, by picking up a number of slender threads of evidence in the existing sources, to throw some light on this obscure period. In so doing it also attempts to offer a solution to the mystery of the twelfth-century royal tombstones found near Gao on the Middle Niger, which we have hitherto been unable to reconcile with anything else we know about the area at this period. The paper, in fact, takes these tombstones as its point of departure and builds on the suggestions already made by other scholars that the Andalusian style of their inscriptions points to links between Gao and the Almoravids of Spain. The hypothesis presented seeks to show that such links did exist, the way in which they came to be established, and the possible role of the southern Almoravids in forging them.

I am most grateful to H. T. Norris, N. Levtzion, and P. F. de Morais Farias for the valuable comments they made on the first draft of this paper. I am grateful, too, to Lamine Sanneh for reading and commenting on the second draft.

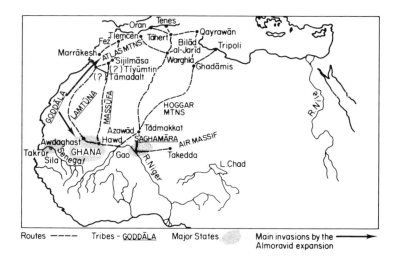

Routes — — — —   Tribes - GODDĀLA   Major States   Main invasions by the ——————▶
Almoravid expansion

Figure 1.   Map of the western Sudan showing empire of Ghana, trade routes and routes of Almoravid invasions. (Location of tribes and towns based on al-Bakri, 1068)

EPIGRAPHIC EVIDENCE FROM ROYAL TOMBSTONES

In 1949 the French Orientalist Jean Sauvaget published the text and translation of ten Arabic inscriptions (some complete and some fragmentary) recording the deaths of Muslim men and women between the years 1100 and 1133.[1] The tombstones from which they were taken had been discovered ten years earlier at an ancient cemetery site just north of a large mound at Sané, some ten kilometers northeast of Gao, which was covered with material remains — potsherds, beads, copper fragments, etc.[2] Quite apart from the fact that these inscriptions represent the earliest epigraphic evidence of Islam in the Middle Niger area, their overriding interest lies in the fact that three of them record the deaths of "kings" (sing. *malik*) and two others the deaths of "queens" (*malika*). No

[1]   "Les épitaphes royales de Gao," *Al-Andalus* 14, no. 1 (1949): 123–141; republished in *Bulletin de l'Institut Français d'Afrique Noire* 12(1950):418–440, to which publication citations in this article refer.
[2]   For a map of the area and a brief résumé of archaeological work undertaken there, see R. Mauny, *Tableau géographique de l'ouest africain au moyen âge,* Mémoires de l'Institut Français d'Afrique Noire, no. 61 (Dakar, 1961), pp. 112–114. Apart from a small sounding by Mauny, no work has yet been done on the habitation mound. I have visited it several times and estimate it to be about one kilometer long by half a kilometer wide at its greatest extent, with an average height of about twelve metres along the top of the ridge. Over the past five years, Colin Flight of the Centre of West African Studies, University of Birmingham, has conducted excavations at the cemetery (see *West African Journal of Archaeology* 5 [1975] for a preliminary report), and he hopes to work on the mound.

less interesting, and indeed mystifying, is the question of their prove-
nance or inspiration. Sauvaget was able to point out from the evidence of
their script and epigraphic conventions, the pious formulae employed,
the Qur'ānic citations, the honorific of the kings (*al-nāṣir li dīn Allāh* [he
who gives victory to God's religion]), and certain linguistic traits that the
inscriptions are closely related to those of Muslim Spain (Andalusia) at a
similar period.³ More specifically, their closest resemblance is to the
funerary inscriptions of Almeria, on the southwestern coast of Andalusia.

The five royal inscriptions under consideration in this article record the
deaths of the following persons: King Muḥammad b. 'Abdullāh b.
Rā'ī/Zāghī⁴ (d. 1100), Queen Suwā/Sawā/Siwā (d. 1108), King Abū Bakr
b. Abī Quḥāfa (d. 1110), Queen M-s-n/M-s-r (d. 1119), and King Māmā
b. K(a)mā b. Ā'ī (sc. Rā'ī/Zāghī), known as 'Umar b. al-Khaṭṭāb (d.
1120). On another tombstone occurs the name of the *malik* K-w-rī
(Kūrī/Kore/Gore?), whose daughter 'Ā'isha died in 1117. His own tombstone has not been discovered, and we therefore do not know his full
names (including any Muslim names) or his relationship to the other
rulers.⁵

The identity of these rulers has so far remained a mystery. They do not
figure among the rulers named in the king lists of the Zā dynasty of
Kukiya-Gao as recorded in the mid-seventeenth-century chronicles, the
Ta'rīkh al-Sūdān and the *Ta'rīkh al-Fattāsh*.⁶ None of the rulers in these
lists bears a clearly Muslim name, although they are alleged to have been
Muslims from the fifteenth ruler to the thirty-first and last (late thirteenth
century), nor yet is there any name among them which might be satisfactorily correlated with any of the non-Muslim names recorded on the
tombstones. Nevertheless, Sauvaget felt that a correspondence could be
established if one could find the right "key." He pointed out that the

³ The epithet *al-nāṣir li dīn Allāh* was used by the Umayyad caliphs of Cordova.
⁴ The two possible readings of this name and the transcription of the other non-Arab
names will be given below.
⁵ There are two other Sané tombstones on which the word *malik* occurs, both recording
deaths in the thirteenth century. See P. F. de Morais Farias, "Du nouveau sur les stèles de
Gao: les épitaphes du prince Yāmā Kūrī et du roi F. n. dā (xiii siècle)," *Bulletin de l'Institut
Fondamental d'Afrique Noire* 36 (1974):511–524. The grandfather of King F.n.dā is
inscribed fairly clearly as Zāghī. This cannot possibly be the same man as the grandfather of
kings Muḥammad and Māmā, who died in 1100 and 1120 respectively, but the recurrence of
the name suggests that they might belong to the same stock. The names of Yāmā Kūrī's
father and grandfather suggest that he was a Songhay and possibly of the Zā dynasty. He
died in 1264–1265.
⁶ 'Abd al-Raḥmān al-Sa'dī, *Ta'rīkh al-Sūdan*, ed. and trans. O. Houdas (Paris,
1898–1900), pp. 2–4 (text) = 4–5 (trans.); Maḥmūd Ka'ti-Ibn al-Mukhtār, *Ta'rīkh al-
Fattāsh*, ed. and trans. O. Houdas and M. Delafosse (Paris, 1913–1914), Fragment (in
translation only) at end of main text, pp. 332–333. This anonymous Fragment is thought to
have constituted the original first chapter before its expurgation by Shaykh Aḥmad Lobbo
of Masina in the early nineteenth century. These rulers will be reexamined in the context of a
number of other steles recently photographed at Sané and those already published in a full
corpus of the Sané material being prepared by Farias and myself.

names of three kings who might be assumed to have succeeded one
another are respectively Muḥammad b. 'Abdullāh, his first successor Abū
Bakr b. Abī Quḥāfa, and the second caliph 'Umar b. al-Khaṭṭāb.[7] He
postulated that these rulers must have been new converts to Islam who
chose such names as a good omen, even adopting paternal names, while
also making use of their traditional names (as is evidenced by the tombstone of Māmā b. K[a]mā). While this explanation is plausible, too much
should not be made out of the coincidence of names and the supposed
order of succession. In the first place, there is nothing to show that these
rulers were the first three of a new dynasty. There may have been others
before King Muḥammad, for example. Again, the name Muḥammad b.
'Abdullāh is probably the commonest of all combinations of Muslim
names. The names Abū Bakr and 'Umar are likewise extremely popular.
If, in fact these two kings succeeded King Muḥammad, their adoption of the
paternal names Ibn Abī Quḥāfa and Ibn al-Khaṭṭāb respectively would
have been to maintain the parallelism with the early caliphate, thus
reinforcing their authority in the popular mind. This does not compel us
to assume that they were recent converts, nor is there any sound reason
for supposing that the names "conceal" names of Zā rulers mentioned in
the ta'rīkhs.

There are, in fact, serious objections to this last proposition. Even
allowing for a long period of oral transmission of the lists recorded in the
ta'rīkhs and subsequent corruptions by copyists, there is no name in the
lists which might correspond to any of the non-Muslim names on the
tombstones such as Rā'ī/Zāghī, Māmā, or K(a)mā. K-w-rī, the father of
'Ā'isha, could be correlated with Yama Karawī, but in the Zā lists he
appears as the fifth ruler before Kosei, the first to be acknowledged as a
Muslim, and he is supposed to have been converted in 400/1009–1010.[8]
This latter date, however, should be taken as only indicative of a general
period — it is a suspiciously round figure. A date not later than the middle
of the tenth century for the conversion of a local (Zā?) ruler at Gao is
indicated by the evidence of al-Muhallabī, who wrote between 975 and
996. According to him, the ruler of Kawkaw (Gao) "makes an external
profession of Islam before his subjects and most of them imitate him in
this." He goes on to tell us that this ruler lived in a town on the west bank
of the "Nile" (i.e., Niger) — fact supported by the Fragment of the
Ta'rīkh al-fattāsh[9] — while on the east bank was a town called Sarnāh
(Sané?) inhabited by merchants "to which caravans come continuously
from all directions."[10] Al-Bakrī, writing in 1068, confirms this and states:

---

[7]   pp. 428–429.
[8]   'Abd al-Raḥmān al-Sa'dī. p. 3 (text) = 5 (trans.).
[9]   p. 329.
[10]   Al-Muhallabī wrote a geographical treatise, now lost, for the Fāṭimid caliph al-'Azīz
(reg. 975–996). His passage on Gao is preserved in Yāqūt al-Ḥamawī, Mu'jam al-buldān
(Beirut, 1957), entry KAWKAW.

"Their ruler is a Muslim, for none but a Muslim may rule."[11] All of this evidence indicates that the local rulers at Gao had adopted Islam long before the advent of King Muḥammad. Thus, even if he were himself a neophyte (and this is questionable), he and his successors could not have been members of the Zā dynasty. Who, then, were these rulers, and how were they able to establish such close contacts with Almeria that they could have tombstones made in Almerian style and perhaps, as in the cases of King Muḥammad, King Abū Bakr, and Queen Suwā, have actually had the stones carved to order and sent across the Sahara as Sauvaget suggests?

The obvious historical factor linking Gao with distant Almeria at this period was, as Sauvaget points out, the Almoravid movement: "Relations could thus readily be established, *throughout their empire,* between the region of Almeria, where the steles were carved, and the town of Gao, where they were erected."[12] He does not, however, devote any space in his exposition to showing how it came about that the Almoravids had brought their influence to bear on Gao to the point where (if his logic about the identity of the kings and queens is followed through) they might have had the Zā rulers as their lieutenants in the eastern Middle Niger. Study of the Arabic sources relating to both the Almoravids and the town of Gao have hitherto failed to yield any indication of such a state of affairs.

The point is taken up again, however, by Bivar,[13] who considers the historical context of the earliest of these tombstones and concludes: "It is difficult to escape the conclusion that the tombstone was sent to order from one end of the Almoravid Empire to the other. The ruler whose death it records was not it seems himself one of the Almoravid princes but a federated or vassal local ruler."[14] He thus implies some sort of Almoravid intervention at Gao while leaving open the question as to whether or not this dynasty of rulers had anything to do with the Zās. More recently, Triaud has taken the argument a stage farther and, while apparently endorsing the notion of an "Almoravid empire" stretching from Spain to the Niger, rejects any attempt to connect the rulers whose names are inscribed on the tombstones with the Zās. Like Sauvaget, he concludes that they were neophytes but is vague on their origins and the motives and means which brought them to power.[15]

---

[11] Abū 'Ubayd al-Bakrī, *Kitāb al masālik wa' l-mamālik*, ed. M. De Slane (Alger, 1857), p. 181.

[12] "Des rapports pouvaient ainsi commodément s'établir, *à travers leur empire*, entre la région d'Alméria, où auraient été sculpté les stèles, et la ville de Gao où elles furent érigées" (pp. 429–430, translation mine; emphasis added).

[13] A. D. H. Bivar, "The Arabic calligraphy of West Africa," *African Language Review* 7 (1968):3–15.

[14] Ibid, pp. 6–7.

[15] J.-L. Triaud, *Islam et sociétés soudanaises au moyen-âge*, Recherches Voltaïques 16 (Paris-Ouagadougou, 1973), p. 141.

We are left, then, with an apparently short-lived dynasty of rulers at Gao, of unknown antecedents, closely in touch with Almoravid Andalusia from shortly before 1100 to 1120 and probably after. How long after we do not know, since no other tombstones clearly related to this group have been discovered,[16] and there may have been no more. In the total range of tombstones so far discovered at Sané there are none recording deaths in the second half of the twelfth century, and all those between 1120 and ca. 1150 appear to belong to nonroyal females.[17] While the notion of a vast Almoravid empire stretching from Andalusia to the Niger may be overstating the case, the remainder of this paper will be devoted to putting forward a hypothesis which could explain an Almoravid "presence" at Gao at this period and at the same time suggest solutions to a number of knotty problems arising from our sources. The evidence is largely circumstantial, but taken all together it adds up to a theory which has strong probability. Our sources are difficult to interpret, and their accuracy is sometimes questionable, but I hope that this attempt to unravel their complexities may stimulate further debate on this fascinating but still understudied area of African history. Further research (particularly archaeological) will serve no doubt to modify, and possibly to disprove, my hypothesis, but in the meantime a start may be made with the evidence at our disposal.

THE ALMORAVID MOVEMENT AND GHANA

Little is known about the activites of the Saharan wing of the Almoravid movement after Abū Bakr b. 'Umar gave his cousin Yūsuf b. Tāshfīn control of the Almoravid state in North Africa and retired into the Sahara in late 1072 or early 1073.[18] He appears to have continued campaigns against various populations in the southern Sahara, during the course of one of which he was killed in 1087.[19] What happened to the movement after his death is uncertain, but it is generally thought that as a concerted

---

[16]   But see fn. 5 above.

[17]   They are all clearly of local manufacture but stylistically related to the Almerian tradition. One, very difficult to decipher, may belong to a daughter of King Māmā. There are also a number of thirteenth-century stones, and I believe some of them belong to members of the Zā dynasty. The point will be taken up again in the corpus mentioned in fn. 6.

[18]   Here I am following the chronology of Ibn 'Idhārī, al-Bayān al-mughrib fī akhbār al-Andalus wa 'l-Maghrib, ed. Iḥsān 'Abbās (Beirut, 1967), 4:24–26. See also P. Semonin, "The Almoravid movement in the Western Sudan," Transactions of the Historical Society of Ghana 7 (1964):42–59.

[19]   This is the generally accepted date, though Ibn 'Idhārī (4:26) gives 468/1075–1076. Even after the division of responsibilities with Ibn Tāshfīn, Abū Bakr remained titular head of the Almoravid movement, and gold coins were issued in North Africa bearing his name up to 1087. As far as we can tell, however, the two leaders acted in their respective areas in virtual independence of one another.

force the southern Almoravid movement broke up following intergroup disputes and that its component tribes and clans dispersed over a wide area.[20] One of the more vexed questions of this latter period of Almoravid activity in the south is that of its intervention in Ghana. Ibn Khaldūn, writing in the late thirteenth century, talks of their pillaging the land of Ghana and imposing tax and tribute on the people and causing many of them to embrace Islam.[21] He then passes straight on to the period of Soso domination, though this probably occurred a century and a half later. The actual dating of the Almoravid intervention in Ghana comes from al-Zuhrī, who wrote in Andalusia ca. 1150. The picture he presents is a much milder one and indicates that a Ghana state continued to exist long after the Almoravid episode:[22]

[Ghana] is the capital of Gināwa [i.e., the western *bilād al-Sūdān*] and to it come caravans from Sūs al-aqṣā and the Maghreb. Formerly the people of this land were holding fast to "unbelief" until the year 469/1076–1077. That was at the time when Yaḥyā b. Abī Bakr, the amīr of Massūfa came forth. They converted to Islam in the days of the Lamtūna [i.e., the Almoravids] and became sound Muslims. Today they are still Muslims and among them are scholars, jurists and reciters of the Qur'ān in which they have become preeminent.

He goes on to state that some of the Muslims of Ghana went to Andalusia (which suggests a source for his information) and took part in jihads there (presumably in Almoravid campaigns against the Christian states), performed the pilgrimage, and, after returning to their own land, spent much of their wealth in pursuing jihad. In another passage al-Zuhrī says that the town of Ghana is the capital (*ḥāḍira*) of the Almoravids and the seat of their sovereignty (*dār mamlakatihim*).[23] Elsewhere, however, and

---

[20] See H. T. Norris, *Saharan myth and saga* (Oxford, 1972), p. 110. He also points out (pp. 219–220) that in North Africa feuds between the Massūfa and the Lamtūna hastened the demise of the Almoravid movement. The source for this view would appear to be Ibn Khaldūn, *Kitāb al-'Ibar* (Būlāq, 1284/1867–1868), 6:230 = trans. M. De Slane (*Histoire des Berbères*, new ed., Paris, 1925), 2:175.

[21] 6:200 (text) = 2:110 (trans.).

[22] See *Kitāb al-Dja'rāfiyya: Mappemonde du calife al-Ma'mūn reproduite par Fazārī (IIIe/IXe s.) réeditée et commentée par Zuhrī (VIe/XIIe s.)*, ed. Maḥammad Hadj-Sadok (Damas: Institut Français de Damas, 1968), par. 336.

[23] Par. 340. The paragraph as a whole is very difficult to interpret. It may therefore be useful to put forward a tentative translation:
"To the east of Ghāna at about twenty parasangs [= 160 kilometers; var. "days" = approx. 640 kilometers] is the town of Qarāfūn [var. Zāfūn/Rāfūn], which is the nearest of the Saharan towns to Wārqalān [Warghla] and Sijilmāsa. Between these two towns [Ghāna and Qarāfūn?] live the Almoravids. These people became Muslims at the same time as the people of Wārqalān in the days of Hishām b. 'Abd al-Malik ['Abbāsid caliph 724–743], but they were following a doctrine (*madhhab*) which put them outside the pale of the holy law (*kharajū bihi 'an al-shar'*, var. *'an madhhab ahl al-sunna* [outside the pale of Sunnī doctrine]). Then their Islam became sound when the people of Ghāna, Tādmakkat, and Qarāfūn became Muslims. They are centered on (*yanḍāfūna ilā*) the town of Ghāna, since it is their capital and the seat of their sovereignty."

perhaps with greater accuracy, he calls Āzuggī their "capital."²⁴ Al-Zuhrī's contemporary, al-Idrīsī, writing in Sicily, has nothing to say of the Almoravids in the south but gives a fairly elaborate account of Ghana, whose ruler he describes as an independent Muslim sovereign who recognized the authority of the 'Abbāsid caliph in Baghdad (as the Almoravids had done).²⁵

Before the Almoravid intervention Ghana was, as we know from al-Bakrī's description, a non-Muslim state, though the court was coming under Islamic influence and some of the king's ministers were Muslims.²⁶ What happened to the ruling house of Ghana following the Almoravid intervention is not clear. It is hard to imagine that after a four-year struggle against the Almoravids it ended up by accepting Islam and Almoravid dominance. If it was not annihilated, it probably fled in the face of defeat and took refuge elsewhere.²⁷ On the other hand, the Muslim faction in Ghana, which may perhaps have included a branch of the ruling house,²⁸ may have collaborated with the Almoravids to overthrow the pagan ruler in order to assume power itself under the tutelage of the Almoravids. Thus in the period 1076–ca. 1087 the Almoravids may have exercised a sort of indirect rule over at least the northern territories of ancient Ghana, using Muslim members of the royal lineage (or others) as their lieutenants. In this connection it is not without interest that al-Zuhrī makes mention of a joint campaign by Ghana and the Almoravids against Tādmakkat in 1083 which resulted in the "conversion" of the people of that town.²⁹ After the death of Abū Bakr b. 'Umar in 1087 and the breakup of the Almoravid movement, a Muslim Ghana state may have continued to exist independently in the twelfth century, as seems to be indicated by our sources.

A possible inference to be drawn from this passage is that the Sanhaja were originally converted to Islam of the Khārijite school, which had begun to become active in North Africa in the period concerned. If so, Ibn Yāsīn's missionary activities among them would have had the primary objective of reconverting them to Sunnism. This would be an added reason for Almoravid ferocity toward Khārijites.

The town of Qarāfūn cannot be identified, but if the area of Almoravid activity extended twenty *days* (not parasangs) to the *east* of Ghana, this would take them into the area of the Middle Niger (see the other arguments on this point below). T. Lewicki, "Un état médiéval inconnu: le royaume de Zāfūn(u)," *Cahiers d'Etudes Africaines* 11, no. 44 (1971):501–525, identifies al-Zuhrī's Qarāfūn/Zāfūn with Diafunu (the evidently miscopied Zāfuqū of al-Bakrī, p. 173), but this lay to the *west* of Ghana.

²⁴ Par. 315.

²⁵ *Opus geographicum siver liber ad eorum delectationem qui terras peregrare studeant* (*Nuzhat al-mushtāq fī ikhtirāq al-āfāq*), ed. A. Bombaci, U. Rizitano et al. (Napoli-Roma, 1970–), 1:23.

²⁶ pp. 174–175. These ministers were doubtless converted Soninke and not North Africans as has often been thought.

²⁷ See N. Levtzion, *Ancient Ghana and Mali* (London, 1973), pp. 46–51.

²⁸ See N. Levtzion, "Was royal succession in Ghana matrilineal?"*African Historical Studies* (Boston) 5 (1972), pp. 91–93.

²⁹ Par. 338. Certain difficulties in this account are examined below.

Before 1076 Ghana's authority had extended down to the towns of the Upper Senegal River, where the gold originally derived from the Bambuk (Bambuhu) area was obtained.[30] The ruler of Ghana evidently exercised a very tight control over the gold trade and was able to ensure that the vast bulk of the gold obtained passed through his territory and was taxed by him. It was for this reason that Ghana, itself a nonproducer of gold, had since the late eighth century been known as *bilād al-dhahab* or *bilād al-tibr* [the land of gold].[31] The gold of Bambuk was brought to the capital of Ghana by Muslim (Soninke) merchants and thence passed into North Africa, either by way of Awdaghast and the western Saharan routes or through the Middle Niger and the central Sahara. The latter route was probably the one first used, with Gao as its focal point. From Gao, in the ninth century, one route crossed the Sahara diagonally to Egypt,[32] while another went northward through Tādmakkat to Ibāḍī-controlled areas such as Tāhert in central Algeria and the Bilād al-Jarīd in southern Tunisia.[33] The western Saharan routes led up to the Darʿa Valley in southern Morocco and to Sijilmāsa in Tāfilalt.[34] That this route was a very important one by the early tenth century is evidenced by the successive struggles of the Fāṭimids of Tunisia and the Umayyads of Andalusia to control the oasis of Sijilmāsa.[35] Both western and central Saharan routes were evidently well known and used in the eleventh century. Al-Bakrī mentions several different routes in either sector, drawing his information from merchants who had traveled along them.[36]

What effect may we suppose Almoravid intervention in Ghana to have had upon the flow of gold obtained on its southern borders and over the trade its ruler controlled? In 1054 the Almoravids had conquered the important northern trading terminus of Sijilmāsa and had followed this up with the capture of the southern terminus, Awdaghast. The latter town, which was at the time under the suzerainty of Ghana, was dealt with very severely, but its conquest did not represent a direct threat to the state

[30] Al-Bakrī, pp. 176–177. The gold dust was brought up from these towns by non-Arab black merchants. Their name is given in De Slane's text as Nūnghamārata, which is almost certainly a corruption of Banū Wangharāta (i.e., Wangara).

[31] First mentioned by al-Fazārī (ca. 788) in his *Kitāb al-Zīj* (now lost), quoted by al-Masʿūdī in his *Murūj al-dhahab*.

[32] See Ibn Ḥawqal, *Ṣūrat al-arḍ*, ed. J. Kramers (Leiden, 1938), p. 61, who tells us that the route ceased to be used in the reign of Aḥmad b. Ṭūlūn (868–884).

[33] T. Lewicki has published a great deal of information on the early use of this route by Ibāḍī traders. The evidence is conveniently brought together in his study "The Ibádites in Arabia and Africa," *Cahiers d'Histoire Mondiale* (UNESCO) 13, no. 1 (1971):51–130, esp. 113–129.

[34] See J. Devisse, La question d'Audaġust," in D. Robert, S. Robert, and J. Devisse, *Tegdaoust I: recherches sur Aoudaghast* (Paris, 1970), pp. 141–153.

[35] Cf. the evidence of Ibn Hawqal, p. 99. On medieval trade routes across the Sahara, see also J. Devisse, "Routes de commerce et échange en Afrique occidentale en relation avec la Méditerranée: un essai sur le commerce africain médiévale du XIe au XVIe siècle," *Revue d'Histoire Economique et Sociale* 50 (1972):42–73, 357–397.

[36] pp. 172–183.

of Ghana as a whole.[37] For the next eighteen years the main arena of
Almoravid activity was the Maghreb, and without any direct pressure on
Ghana the old pattern of trade no doubt continued, though the composition of the merchant community at Awdaghast would have changed. Such
trading would not, however, have been possible in the period of
Almoravid military campaigns against Ghana in the period 1072–1076,
and it seems reasonable to suppose that the bulk of the gold trade in this
period may have been rechanneled along the other well-trodden route
through the Middle Niger and the central Sahara.

The eruption of militant Sanhaja nomads into the settled lands of
Ghana in 1076 must have had disruptive effects both on the inhabitants of
the area and on the trade routes passing through it, and the general
insecurity must have increased after the breakup of the Almoravid
movement. Under these circumstances the merchants, now freed of any
royal control over their activities, would have sought new routes for
bringing their gold to points where they could conduct trade with merchants from North Africa.

One of the routes along which the gold of Bambuk apparently traveled
was down the Senegal River to the state of Takrūr. It seems that in the
period following the Almoravid intervention in Ghana, Takrūr was able
to extend its authority farther up the Senegal and as far as Yaresnā
(Iresnā?), which was an important center of the gold trade.[38] Al-Idrīsī
makes it clear that Takrūr was directly involved in the gold trade (and the
slave trade) in the twelfth century, trading directly with Sijilmāsa, from
which it received woolen cloth, copper, and beads.[39] Other evidence of
al-Idrīsī also suggests that the central Saharan route came into prominence in the first half of the twelfth century as a channel for the exportation of Bambuk gold.[40] Writing of Warghla, to which the trade route from
Tādmakkat, Gao, and the Middle Niger led, he says: "It is a town in which
there are prosperous tribes and rich merchants who travel around in the
bilād al-Sūdān to the land of Ghana and the land of Wangara and bring
forth from these lands gold-dust which they make into coins in their own

---

[37]   Al-Bakrī, p. 168, says that Awdaghast was "the *manzil* ["residence" or perhaps "staging
post"] of the king of Ghana before the Arabs [sic] entered Ghana." He also attributes
Almoravid harshness toward the inhabitants of the town to their being under the authority
of Ghana. On the other hand, many of the groups represented there, such as the Barqajāna,
Nafūsa, and Nafzāwa, were traditionally Khārijite, while another important element was
the Zenāta, a group which the Almoravids had just been fighting in Sijilmāsa (cf. Devisse,
"La question d'Audaġust," pp. 129–130).
[38]   Al-Idrīsī, 1:19. He spells it Barīsā, another possible reading of the consonantal skeleton.
[39]   1:18. Cf. Levtzion, *Ancient Ghana and Mali*, p. 44.
[40]   Cf. M. Brett, "Ifrīqiya as a market for Saharan trade from the tenth to the twelfth
century A.D.," *Journal of African History* 10(1969):361–362, who suggests that Almoravid
activity in the southwestern Sahara may have enabled merchants using the Tādmakkat-
Warghla route to increase their share of the gold trade. Levtzion, *Ancient Ghana and Mali*,
pp. 41–42, appears to take a contrary view.

lands in the name of their town."[41] The minting of coins in Warghla is also mentioned in the anonymous *Kitāb al-Istibṣār,* written ca. 1200; it states that coins were made there in the style of Almoravid dinars, which seems curious because Warghla was an Ibāḍī center and was never, so far as we know, subjected to the Almoravids.[42] The importance of Warghla as a gateway to *bilād al-Sūdan* is also stressed by al-Zuhrī, who mentions the caravan traffic between there and Gao.[43]

One may wonder why Warghla was minting its own coins and indeed why, if the account of the *K. al-Istibṣār* is accurate, it was minting them in Almoravid style. They are not likely to have been needed for internal trading within the oasis; rather, they may have served as a more solid form of exchange for the trading activities of the Warghla merchants in the Mediterranean lands, for Warghla was linked by trade routes to many important towns from Qayrawān in the east to Tlemçen and Oran in the west. Trade with Qayrawān and the eastern Maghreb would certainly have fallen off in the second half of the eleventh century following the dislocation of economic life in the area brought about by the activities of the Banū Hilāl. Whether or not as a direct result of this, the Zīrids issued no gold coinage after 1067. Warghla's trade is more likely to have been with the two prosperous empires at either end of the Mediterranean, the Fāṭimids in Egypt and the Almoravids in Morocco and Andalusia. It is the latter connection which especially concerns us.

By 1085 the Almoravids had extended their state eastward as far as Algiers. Tlemçen seems to have become their major stronghold in this eastern sector and Oran, two days' journey away and one of the finest harbors on the coast, their main port and naval base. Directly opposite Oran on the Andalusian coast was the great city of Almeria, which submitted to the Almoravids in 1091, and between the two ports there was a lively commerce.[44] Although no firm evidence can be put forward on this point, it seems not unreasonable to suppose that an important part of Warghla's trade with Almoravid domains would have been conducted with Tlemçen, their major center in the east. Tlemçen itself had easy access to the trade of Almoravid Spain through Oran, and thus, it would appear, trading links existed all the way from Gao to Almeria. Some hint of this is to be found in the passage of al-Zuhrī dealing with Gao's external trade, for he mentions that goods were brought there from Andalusia, including the cloths of Murcia.[45] The gold which the merchants of

41 al-Idrīsī, 3:296.
42 See ed. of Saʿd Zaghlūl ʿAbd al-Ḥamīd (Alexandria, 1958), p. 224. Even more curious is the anonymous author's statement that these dinars are "of low value and much adulterated" (*wa hiya nāzila fīhā taḥmīl kathīr*). A possible emendation would give the rendering "they are rare, being highly embellished" (*hiya nādira fīhā tajmīl kathīr*). No coin of this type seems to have survived, so the mystery remains.
43 Pars. 318 and 333.
44 Al-Idrīsī, 3:252.
45 al-Zuhrī, Par. 333.

Warghla obtained in the *bilād al-Sūdān* (and largely, I would suggest, in the last quarter of the eleventh and the first quarter of the twelfth centuries, at Gao) and which was then turned into coin provided the means to purchase the goods of the Maghreb and Andalusia for the Sudan trade and provided an important source of gold for the Almoravid state.

ALMORAVID COINS, SUDANESE GOLD, AND ETHNIC MIGRATIONS

In this connection it is instructive to examine the known features of the minting of gold coins in the Almoravid period as may be deduced from the surviving specimens. Though these specimens may not, of course, tell the full story, we have a body of 423 Almoravid gold coins produced between 1054 and 1148 from nine major mints in Spain and eight in Morocco to go on.[46] Even on the basis of survivals, an examination of the production of the various mints and at various periods within the century of Almoravid power is likely to give some reflection of the greater picture. From such an examination it emerges that while Sijilmāsa, the only mint in operation over the entire period, is represented by the largest number of coins (77), its nearest rival is Almeria (58), which even surpasses Aghmāt (49) and Fez (36). The Almeria series covers the period 1098–1145, the number of survivals gradually increasing by decade throughout the period. Other towns of the southwestern Andalusian coast (including Malaga slightly inland) produce a total of 46 survivals in the overall period 1098–1127, and these, together with the coins of Almeria, account for 104 out of 173 survivals for the whole of Almoravid Spain. During the period in which the Almeria mint was actually in production there are more survivals than there are for Sijil-māsa (58 as against 44). Hazard, from whose work these figures are derived, underlines the importance of the Almeria mint, which produced "a rich series of dīnārs *with several varieties per year at a time.*"[47]

This does not, of course, prove that Almeria's apparently abundant supply of gold was obtained through the Warghla-Gao axis, or even that it was all from the Western Sudan.[48] Considering, however, the clear evidence that a lot of Sudanese gold was reaching Warghla in the early twelfth century, the great likelihood that much of Warghla's trade was with the Almoravid state, the evidence that Andalusian products reached

[46]   See the table in Devisse, "Routes de commerce et échange," p. 68, derived from information in H. Hazard, *The numismatic history of late medieval North Africa* (New York, 1952).

[47]   p. 15; emphasis added.

[48]   It was evidently not. See R. A. Messier, "The Almoravids: West African gold and the gold currency of the Mediterranean basin," *Journal of the Economic and Social History of the Orient* 17, no. 1 (1974):31–47.

Gao, and finally the evidence of the Sané tombstones, which show a clear link between Gao and Almeria, the hypothesis that the prosperity of Almeria was partly due to its trading links with Gao may not be thought implausible.[49]

There is also evidence that Gao, in the early part of the twelfth century, was enjoying a period of exceptional prosperity. Al-Zuhrī describes it as the chief town of al-Ḥabasha (by which he meant the central *bilād al-Sūdān*), a town to which come caravans from Egypt and Warghla and a few from Sijilmāsa and whose inhabitants are the richest and the best-dressed in al-Ḥabasha.[50] Al-Idrīsī portrays it as an independent and prosperous state whose rulers participated in an evidently lucrative trade:[51]

The ruler of Kawkaw is an independent sovereign who has prayer said in his own name. He has an extensive retinue, a large revenue, commanders, armies, full ceremonial dress and fine regalia. They ride horses and camels and are courageous, dominating the peoples who border their land. The dress of the common people is skins with which they cover their nakedness. Their merchants wear long tunics, woolen cloaks and turbans and gold ornaments. Their nobles and notables wear mantles (*uzur*) and collaborate with the merchants, supplying them with goods on credit against a share in the profits.

The kind of ruler described here by al-Idrīsī does, in fact, sound very much like the sort of person we might expect King Māmā (d. 1120) to have been if we are to judge from his epitaph: "The most noble sovereign of exalted status, he who gives victory to God's religion, the one dependent on God, who executes His orders and who carries out *jihād* in the Path of God."[52]

The evidence so far presented suggests that in the latter part of the eleventh century and the first part of the twelfth a significant part of the gold produced in Bambuk was passing along a route which led through the Middle Niger, with Gao as its main commercial center, and across the central Sahara to Warghla and thence into Almoravid-ruled North Africa and eastern Andalusia. We turn again now to the problem with which we

[49] It is not without interest that Almeria, of all Andalusian towns in the twelfth century, produced the most developed and most prolific series of epitaphs, a sure sign of its prosperity. See E. Lévi-Provençal, *Les inscriptions arabes d'Espagne* (Paris, 1931), XXI–XXII.
[50] Par. 333.
[51] 1:28. S. J. Trimingham, *History of Islam in West Africa* (Oxford, 1962), p. 88, casts some doubt on whether this description really refers to Gao, and he is skeptical about the passages in al-Muhallabī and al-Bakrī, since he finds them difficult to interpret. Admittedly, al-Idrīsī's attempts to describe the location of Gao are confusing. His knowledge of the physical features of the interior of Africa was often based on Ptolemy, however, and he does not seem to have been acquainted with the work of al-Bakrī, the most accurate and detailed of all the medieval Arabic accounts. This does not invalidate his information about the town.
[52] Sauvaget, pp. 452–453.

426 J. O. HUNWICK

started — the identity of the rulers recorded on the Sané tombstones, who appear to have formed a short-lived dynasty during the period when this trade appears to have been at its height. Is there any evidence that they might have arisen as the result of Almoravid intervention in the area?

First of all, in a general sense, there is evidence of an eastward movement of Sanhaja along the Sahelian corridor to as far east as Aïr which may be roughly dated to the twelfth and thirteenth centuries. Of the three major tribes of the Sanhaja, the Massūfa, whose territory was the most easterly in the Sahara, appear to have taken the lead in this migration. The evidence of Ibn Baṭṭūṭa, relating to the years 1352–1353, is illuminating in this respect. He described both Walāta and Timbuktu as towns chiefly inhabited by Massūfa;[53] in Takedda, just to the west of Aïr, he was entertained by a Massūfa resident.[54] The Ta'rīkh al-Sūdān indicates that Timbuktu was in fact originally a settlement of Massūfa nomads, who began to camp there around 1100.[55] In the passage concerned, al-Sa'dī calls them Tuareg, but in a separate section devoted to the Tuareg he equates the Tuareg with the Massūfa and goes on to quote a passage on Sanhaja genealogy taken from al-Ḥulal al-mawshiya.[56] The Tuareg-Massūfa confusion is probably explicable by the fact that when al-Sa'dī wrote in the mid-seventeenth century the Tuareg, who had earlier inhabited the Ahaggar and Adrar-n-Ifoghas, had moved into the Azawād area of the Middle Niger. The dispersed Sanhaja would have been absorbed by them in this area, while farther west the Sanhaja were being swallowed up by the advancing Banū Ḥassān Arabs.

Ibn Khaldūn also indicated that in his day (late fourteenth century) the Sanhaja tribes were dispersed along the Sahelian corridor of the southern Sahara. In the far west were the Goddāla, living in an area opposite to the Sūs al-aqṣā (i.e., near the Atlantic coast, their pre-Almoravid habitat); after them came the Lamtūna, opposite to the Far Maghreb (i.e., in the Ḥawd-Bāghena area), then the Massūfa, opposite to the Central Maghreb (i.e., in the Middle Niger area), then the Lamṭa, opposite to the Zāb (i.e., between Gao and Aïr), and finally the Tārika (Targa-Tuareg?), opposite to Ifriqiyya (i.e., in Aïr).[57] Even allowing for some possible inexactitude in the locations of these tribes, the general distribution pattern is clear. Further evidence from al-Sa'dī also points to Sanhaja activity as far east as the borders of Aïr. He states that the town of Takedda itself was founded by Sanhaja[58] and that one of its best-known

[53] Ibn Baṭṭūṭa, Tuḥfat al-nuzzār ("Voyages"), ed. and trans. C. Defréméry and B. Sanguinetti (Paris, 1854), 4:387, 430.
[54] Ibid., p. 438.
[55] p. 20 (text) = 35 (trans.).
[56] p. 25 (text) = 42 (trans.).
[57] 6:197–198 (text) = 2:104–105 (trans.).
[58] p. 41 (text) = 67 (trans.), quoting from Aḥmad Bābā, the printed text of whose Nayl al-Ibtihāj (Cairo, 1351/1932–1933), pp. 217–218, has "Agades" instead of Takedda at this point.

scholars in the late fifteenth century, al-ʿĀqib al-Anuṣamanī, bore the *nisba* al-Massūfī.[59] This scholar's contemporary, Muḥammad al-Lamtūnī, whose correspondence with al-Suyūṭī I have discussed elsewhere, also probably came from this area.[60] Finally, we may note that the names of several of the Sanhaja tribes listed by Ibn Ḥawqal bear a striking resemblance to those of Tuareg now living in Aïr.[61] Of these we may particularly note the Inusoufen (cf. Massūfa) of Takedda. All Aïr traditions speak of Massūfa moving west-east and east-west, coming and going, from earliest times.[62]

The next question which faces us is whether or not this eastward movement of Massūfa might have its origins in an initial push into the Middle Niger in the latter days of the existence of the Saharan Almoravids. Mention has already been made of the alleged Ghana expedition against Tādmakkat supported by the Almoravids in 1083 and the supposed "conversion" of the people of Tādmakkat at this time. Alongside this we may also consider the statement attributed to Maḥmūd Kaʿti in the Fragment of the *Taʾrīkh al-Fattāsh* that the people of Gao became Muslims between 471/1078 and 475/1083.[63] I have already shown that the rulers, at least, of west-bank Gao had formally been Muslims since sometime in the second half of the tenth century, while east-bank Gao (Sané) had its origin as a settlement of North African Muslim merchants. As for Tādmakkat, Ibn Ḥawqal (referring to about the mid-tenth century) makes it clear (though he does not state it expressly) that the Berber rulers of the town were Muslims; he describes them as having learning (*ʿilm*), knowledge of the law (*fiqh*), and acquaintance with the life of the Prophet (*sīra*).[64] The very name of the town marks it as a Muslim settlement; *tād Makkat* means in Berber "this is Mecca," alluding to the similar geographical settings of the two towns. Al-Bakrī confirms that the people of Tādmakkat are "Muslim Berbers who veil themselves like the Saharan Berbers."[65]

Since the early ninth century the town had been visited by North African merchants, who made it a base for their journeys into *bilād al-Sūdān*, just as they did with Awdaghast farther west and probably the Kawār oasis in the east. These merchants who visited Tādmakkat and Gao were mostly, so far as our evidence indicates, of the Ibāḍī school of the Khārijite sect,[66] and it was presumably to the doctrines of this school

---

[59]   Ibid.
[60]   "Notes on a late fifteenth-century document concerning 'al-Takrūr,' " in *African perspectives,* ed. C. Allen and R. W. Johnson (Cambridge, 1970), pp. 7–33.
[61]   Norris, p. 58, fn. 3.
[62]   I owe these two latter pieces of information to the kindness of H. T. Norris (personal communication, 1975).
[63]   pp. 332–333.
[64]   p. 105.
[65]   p. 181.
[66]   See fn. 33 above.

428 J. O. HUNWICK

that the Berbers of Tādmakkat and the rulers of west-bank Gao were originally converted. If, then, there was a case of "conversion" of the people of these two towns in the period 1078–1083, this might be interpreted as a conversion from the "deviant" school of Khārijism to Sunnī Mālikī Islam. This could well have been the work of Sanhaja imbued with an Almoravid ideology, which was strongly Sunnī and Mālikī and very intolerant toward all other expressions of Islam.[67] We have the indication of al-Zuhrī that there was Almoravid intervention in Tādmakkat — and it is more probable that Ghana supported the Sanhaja than vice versa — and it is thus not difficult to imagine that there should also have been Sanhaja intervention at Gao in the same period.

The reasons for such intervention are not altogether clear, but two suggestions may be made. In the first place, after the Almoravids had asserted their authority over the powerful kingdom of Ghana, the way lay open for further movement eastward along the Sahelian belt, which was ideally suited to their pastoral way of life. Other groups of Sanhaja or Berberophone nomads, such as the Banū Maddāsa around Goundam, the Issekomaren (Saghamāra of al-Bakrī) near Gao, and the Banū Tānmāk of Tādmakkat,[68] lay in that direction, and there may have been some desire to impose the strong Sunnī ideology of the Almoravid movement on such related people.

Secondly, if we are correct in assuming that Almoravid intervention in Ghana caused some dislocation of trading patterns, resulting in the diversion of an important part of the gold traffic to the Gao-Warghla route, then it would seem natural for the Sanhaja to seek either to close up this outlet in favor of others they controlled or to control this outlet itself. If, in fact, they did the latter, as I am postulating, then after the breakup of the Almoravid movement in the south the group which went to Gao may have established itself quite independently there and endeavored to ensure that a steady supply of gold passed through its hands rather than into the hands of rival Sanhaja groups farther west. If, as the later evidence suggests, the major group which went east was composed of Massūfa, this may help to explain why such special links were maintained with eastern Andalusia, since this was, at any rate latterly, an area in which the Massūfa were more influential in the Almoravid empire.[69]

---

[67] The more so if the Sanhaja themselves had earlier been tainted with Khārijism; see fn. 23 above.
[68] See al-Bakrī, pp. 180–181, for the Maddāsa and Saghamāra, Ibn Ḥawqal, p. 105, for the Banū Tānmāk.
[69] For example, in 1126 Muḥammad b. Ghāniya al-Massūfī was made governor of Denia and the Balearic Islands, and in 1131–1132 Abū Bakr b. Ibrāhīm al-Massūfī was made governor of eastern Andalusia, with his seat at Valencia; see Ibn Khaldūn, 6:188–190 (text) = 2:83–87 (trans.). Tlemçen, too, was governed for a time by a Massūfī, Yahyā b. Isḥāq, who defected to the Almohads in 1142; Ibid., 6:230 (text) = 2:175 (trans.).

OTHER TENTATIVE CONCLUSIONS

Finally, in examining the hypothesis that the royal tombstones of Sané belong to Massūfa Sanhaja who were an offshoot of the southern Almoravid movement, we must look at the meager clues on the tombstones themselves. First of all, one is struck by the fact that two of the six inscriptions under consideration record the deaths of queens and another that of a king's daughter. While it is not unusual for epitaphs to be inscribed on Muslim women's graves, it is very unusual for a woman to bear the title *malika*. This suggests that women among the group that ruled at Gao enjoyed a very high status in society, and this inevitably reminds one of the remarks of Ibn Baṭṭūṭa about the Massūfa women of Walāta.[70] It is also clear that during the period of Almoravid ascendancy Sanhaja women were accorded a similarly elevated status.[71] Sanhaja society was, in fact, matrilineal, and succession to power may have passed in the female line, as it did among the more easterly Berberophones of Takedda in Ibn Baṭṭūṭa's day.[72]

The other point from which one might hope to derive some evidence of the identity of these rulers is from the non-Arab names found in the inscriptions, but here only the most tentative suggestions can be made. The Kufic script used on the inscriptions lacks diacritical points, and short vowels are not marked. Thus the name Rā'ī may as well be read as Zāghī and S-wā as Siwā, Sawā, Suwā/Shiwā, Shawā, or Shuwā, while for M-s-n/M-s-r there around thirty possible readings. The name K-mā may be read Kimā, Kumā, Kamā/Gimā, Gumā, Gamā. In all these readings only the standard Arabic short vowels have been taken into consideration, but since these are non-Arab names the putative vowel "u" in the transcriptions may stand for a sound closer to "o" and "i" for a sound closer to "e."

For only one of these names have we any evidence of its currency in medieval times in the Saharan area. Bivar[73] draws attention to a ruler called Zāghī b. Zāghī, who is mentioned in the *Kitāb al-masālik wa 'l-mamālik* of Ibn Khurradādhbih, a geographer of Persian origin writing in the last quarter of the ninth century. In this work the author informs us that the kingdom of the Idrīsids, with its capital at Fez, was bordered on the south by the lands of Zāghī b. Zāghī. Although the location of this ruler's lands is vague, it would seem to indicate somewhere beyond the Atlas mountains, in or toward the Sahara. In such a case it is not improb-

---

[70] Tuḥfat al-ruẓẓār, 4:387–389.
[71] See Norris p. 109.
[72] Ibn Baṭṭūṭa, 4:443.
[73] p. 7, fn. 11. He also draws attention to a passage in the anonymous Persian geography *Ḥudūd al-'ālam* (written in 982) in which Rā'ī b. Rā'ī [*sic*] is described as a king in a gold-bearing region in the *bilad al-Sūdān*. The relationship between this work and the geography of Ibn Khurradādhbih is not clear.

able that this Zāghī b. Zāghī was a Sanhaja chief.[74] Another of the names has a parallel in modern Tuareg nomenclature: Gomā, which is a possible reading to be derived from the name inscribed as K-mā.[75] Mamma (cf. Māmā) is also used by the Tuareg, but this seems likely to be a corruption of Muḥammad.

In sum, the evidence presented above, circumstantial though it is, leads to the conclusion that the short-lived dynasty at Sané was of Sanhaja origin, probably Massūfa. They established their authority over Gao-Sané in the 1080's and, after the Almoravid conquest of Almeria in the next decade, were able to maintain close commercial and cultural relations with that city at least until the 1120's and perhaps (though inscriptional evidence is lacking) until the end of Almoravid rule in the central Maghreb in the early 1140's. What happened thereafter is conjectural. For all we know, a Sanhaja presence may have been maintained at Sané after this date, though its loss of contact with its kinsmen in the north may have reduced it to insignificance. Other evidence (which cannot be examined in this paper) suggests that later in the twelfth century the Zās of the west bank moved over the east bank, probably remaining at the waterside rather than living at the remoter Sané, though the cemetery there continued to be used until the late thirteenth century. The new Almohad dynasty in North Africa seems to have established its own trading links with Ghana or one of its successor states.[76] The Sanhaja of Gao-Sané may have dispersed, either moving back westward to Timbuktu or the caravan towns of the Ḥawḍ or continuing the eastward movement which eventually led to Sanhaja settlement in the region of Aïr and the founding of a trading settlement at Takedda.

[74]   Bivar, p. 7, suggests that the name may have something to do with the title Zā. T. Lewicki, Arabic external sources for the history of Africa to the south of the Sahara (Warsaw, 1969), pp. 17–18, tries to connect the name with the term Zaghāy, which one of Ibn Khaldūn's informants told him was applied to the people of Takrūr. The information about Zāghī b. Zāghī presumably originated from a Fez source, since his territory is defined in relation to the territory of the Idrīsids and it seems perhaps a little unlikely that such distant localities as Takrūr or Kukiya (where the Zās probably were in the period to which Ibn Khurradādhbih's information refers, 798–828) might have been thought to be on the peripheries of the somewhat circumscribed state of the Idrīsids.
[75]   Information from H. T. Norris (personal communication, 1975).
[76]   See Shihāb al-Dīn Aḥmad al-Maqqarī, Nafḥ al-ṭīb, ed. R. Dozy et al. (Leiden, 1855–1861), 2:72–74.

Timbuktu: A Case Study of the Role of Legend in History

EUGENIA HERBERT

> Wide Afric, doth thy sun
> Lighten, thy hills enfold a city as fair
> As those which starr'd the night o' the elder
> world?
> Or is the rumour of thy Timbuctoo
> A dream as frail as those of ancient time?
> TENNYSON, "Timbuctoo" (1829)

Certain cities have long captured the popular, poetic, and even scholarly imagination. Ophir, Golconda, El Dorado, Samarkand, and the Seven Cities of Cibola conjure visions of untold if elusive wealth. Timbuktu was once part of this legendary company: for centuries it was the symbol of Africa's splendor and "golden joys," but it is now merely a byword for remoteness.

Timbuktu was important not only as an entrepôt and terminus for the caravan trade of the Sahara. It was a focal point for many of the major cross-currents of Sudanese history: the march of Islam, ethnic migrations, the rise and fall of the great Sudanic political systems, early European explorations, the gold trade, and imperialism. This paper surveys what is known of the historical Timbuktu, emphasizing its mediating position between the economic and cultural systems of North and West Africa. It then explores the phenomenon of its continuing fame, a fame that refused to die even in the centuries of relative eclipse following the Moroccan invasion in 1591. The final sections of the paper reveal how the myth of Timbuktu served as a major catalyst for the European exploration and conquest of the Sudan in the nineteenth century.

THE HISTORICAL TIMBUKTU, 1100–1590

Timbuktu was founded about A.D. 1100 by Tuareg nomads from Arawan, who brought their flocks south to graze along the Niger in the summer. According to one tradition, "Timbuktu" was the name of an old female slave to whom they confided their belongings when they returned home. A few huts were added for slaves, and the camp was shifted several times until it came to rest on the present site, behind a protective wall of dunes which hold back the flooding Niger on all but rare occasions. Soon the settlement became a crossroads for travelers, "coming by land and water:" first Soninke merchants from Wagadu, later Arabs and Berbers from the Sahara and the Maghreb (al-Saʻdi 1964:35–36).

Along this part of its course the Niger is fringed on both banks by desert. The summer rains bring a season of lush pasturage, but no farming is possible in the region of Timbuktu itself. This is not a true oasis or the center of a fertile floodplain; rather, it is a city surrounded perpetually by sand, located far enough from the river to be accessible at all seasons to camel caravans but close enough to be the port of the desert on the great waterway of the Sudan at its most northerly thrust.

The harbor is at Kabara, about five miles away, with secondary ports to accommodate to the rising and falling of the Niger. Like other great trading cities, Timbuktu was an entrepôt, not a center of primary production; it was a junction where different ethnic groups, different religions, different modes of transportation, and the produce of different ecological systems converged.

From the north by camel caravan came salt from the salines of the desert, dates from the oases of its northern belt, textiles from North Africa and Europe, metal ware, arms, beads, horses, and books. This portion of the trade was largely an Arab-Berber monopoly with some Jewish participation, although the Saharan salt deposits belonged to Sudanese rather than Maghrebian states until the later sixteenth century. North African merchants themselves went as far as the Sahel or maintained representatives in Sahelian cities which traditionally had quarters reserved for foreign traders. Few ventured farther south, and all remained remarkably ignorant about the West African interior and the sources of their own wealth (Mauny 1961). Antonio Malfante's informant in Tuat in 1447 claimed to have spent thirty years in Timbuktu and half that number in lands farther south, but when he was asked about the origins of Sudanese gold, he insisted that in all that time "I have never heard nor seen anyone who could reply from definite knowledge. . . . What appears plain is that it comes from a distant land, and, as I believe, from a definite place" (Crone 1937:90).

Perhaps the informant was feigning ignorance to the Italian interloper; what is more likely is that he himself was the victim of a policy of secrecy, not an uncommon practice in medieval or modern commerce. African traders were determined to keep foreigners out of the interior any way they could — hence the fanciful stories of cannibals and monsters working the goldfields, well calculated to play on the credulity of the North Africans and on their attitudes of cultural superiority. The climate, too, insalubrious as it was for whites and their horses and camels, conspired to keep outsiders from a knowledge of the interior and its wealth.

From about the fourteenth century onward, the trade of the interior was dominated by Manding (Mandingo) julas, professional and semi-professional itinerant traders who developed the far-reaching network of routes and markets that gradually opened up the West African hinterland and channeled its goods into the world market. Their adherence to Islam gave them an internal cohesion and provided a bridge with the North African commercial community but reinforced their alien, supranational status among the animist and agricultural peoples with whom they traded and among whom they settled (see Perinbam, this volume). Responding to the steadily increasing demand for gold from the Christian and Muslim lands during the later Middle Ages, juulas pushed their search for new sources of supply south from the Niger basin to the goldfields of Lobi (Upper Black Volta) and ultimately to the Akan forest. The route from Jenne to Bighu on the northern fringe of the forest was opened up by juulas in the late fourteenth and early fifteenth centuries and must have been a crucial factor in the subsequent rise of Jenne and Timbuktu, particularly since this rise was achieved at the expense of cities oriented toward older sources of supply (Wilks 1962:337–341; Perinbam 1974:676–689).

Jenne was probably founded between the eleventh and thirteenth centuries by Nono (Soninke) settlers and traders. Writing in the nineteenth century, both René Caillié and Felix Dubois saw Jenne as the prosperous city Timbuktu once had been. Where Timbuktu drew heavily on the desert for its population and culture, Jenne was essentially Sudan-ese, despite a veneer of Islam. Situated on a branch of the Bani River not far from its confluence with the Niger, Jenne had the priceless security of an island location — a security lacking in Timbuktu, which was without natural defenses of any kind. It also enjoyed a rich agricultural hinter-land. The result was an intimate symbiosis between Jenne and Timbuktu, cities of opposites: Jenne provisioned its northern neighbor with food and cotton and with the gold, ivory, slaves, kola nuts, dried skins, and spices that were its chief exports, while Timbuktu channeled to Jenne the products of the northern caravan trade, above all the salt whose value increased geometrically as it moved south from the desert. "It is because of this blessed city," al-Sa'di (1964:23) readily conceded, "that caravans flock to Timbuktu from all points of the horizon."

The interdependence of these two cities reflects not only a high degree of commercial specialization, but also a significant volume of river trans-port, since they lie some 300 miles apart. There is curiously little concrete information in the sources, however, about the commercial exploitation of the Niger. Potentially it offered over a thousand miles of navigable waterway in the heart of the Sudan, yet much of the river seems to have remained little utilized for other than fishing and local communication. Curtin (1975:280–281) has shown, for example, that during the nineteenth century traders between Timbuktu and the Senegal Valley found it cheaper to follow a northerly route into the desert than to combine water and land transport. During much of the region's history it would appear that only the central axis of the river system — Jenne-Timbuktu-Gao — was extensively employed for trade.

To what extent even this exploitation was limited by the shortage of ship timber is difficult to say, nor do we know for certain the capacity of boats in service at earlier periods (cf. Bovill 1925; Tymowski 1967). Both Ibn Battuta, who sailed from Timbuktu to Gao in 1353 (after traveling from the capital of Mali *overland*), and Leo Africanus, who claims to have gone from Timbuktu to Jenne about 1510 (since he misrepresents the direction of the Niger's flow, there is some doubt about his journey), describe their vessels as small pirogues, hollowed out of a single tree trunk. The *ta'rikhs* of the late sixteenth and seventeenth centuries, on the other hand, speak of multitudes of royal barks transporting the entire retinue of the *askia* [emperor] and of various flotillas assembled for other purposes (e.g., Kati 1964:270). The references to hundreds of boats gathered at one time may of course be poetic license and in any case are confined to the later Songhai Empire. In 1828, Caillié found transport canoes of sixty to eighty tons, made of planks held together with cords of hemp, plying the Bani and Niger between Jenne and Timbuktu (1830: vol. 2, p. 9). These may well have had a long history, but we cannot be certain without contemporary evidence.[1]

The fortunes of Timbuktu were linked not only to Jenne but also to the Songhay Empire (see Figure 1). Though the city had begun its rise under Tuareg and Malian suzerainty, it did not rival Walata to the northwest as the chief southern terminus of the trans-Saharan trade until the power of Mali was on the wane in the fifteenth century. With the expansion of Songhay and the consequent shift of political and economic centers of gravity eastward to the Niger bend, the preeminence of Timbuktu was assured (al-Sa'di 1964:36–38; Levtzion 1973: 157–158).

ISLAM AND TIMBUKTU

Indeed, Timbuktu inherited the intellectual as well as the commercial mantle of Walata. As the caravans deserted to Timbuktu, "the pick of

[1]   In a footnote Caillié comments that the planks used have been cut by saw, a tool he believes was introduced by the Moors.

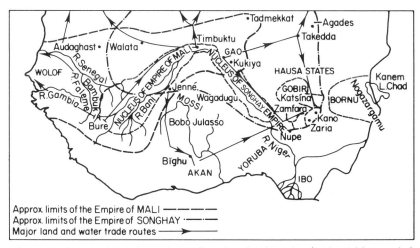

Figure 1.   Timbuktu in relation to the empires of Mali and Songhay (14th to 16th centuries)

scholars, pious and rich men from every tribe and country," also migrated hither (al-Saʿdi 1964:37). They settled in the quarter of the Sankore mosque and became the nucleus of what in later times was referred to as the "university" of Timbuktu, in reality an assemblage of scholars teaching the Qurʾan and major works of the Islamic canon without an institutional framework. Among the earliest to make the move from Walata was Muhammad Aqit, the scion of the Massūfa Tuareg clan that furnished most of the city's qadis for more than a century. His great-great-grandson was Ahmad Baba (1556–1627), the most renowned of many distinguished scholars of Timbuktu. Forty-seven of his works have been identified, including a treatise categorizing the various peoples of the Sudan as Muslim or pagan which later became the authority for Usuman dan Fodio. Several of his works are still studied in the Sudan (Hunwick 1962:311–313; 1964:568–570; 1966a:20).

Al-Saʿdi, the seventeenth-century chronicler of Timbuktu, boasted that its civilization "came uniquely from the Maghreb, as much in affairs of religion as in those of commerce" (1964:36, translation mine), but Hunwick (1966a) has shown that this was no longer true by the sixteenth century, though it may have been earlier (Levtzion 1973:201–204); analyzing the "chains of authority" that licensed a scholar to teach each work, he has found that Ahmad Baba and his contemporaries drew their learning from Egypt and Mecca, then the brightest spots in the Muslim intellectual firmament, not from the Maghreb, which had fallen into decadence. Since pilgrims from the Sudan commonly followed the route from Murzuq to Cairo, contacts with Egypt and the east were constantly being renewed.

Unlike the Hausa states to the east, Timbuktu was never politically independent and had to submit to periodic Tuareg exactions and to less frequent but more destructive sacking by the Mossi and by the Songhay ruler Sunni Ali. Nevertheless, even under Songhay hegemony the city enjoyed a high degree of autonomy and became virtually a second capital of the empire after Gao.[2] According to the *Ta'rikh al-Fattash*, it had no governor other than its own qadi (Kati 1964:314; but see below). The qadis themselves felt authorized to remind the rulers of their duty and to point out their failings. The great-uncle of Ahmad Baba, for example, who was qadi for most of the half-century 1498–1548, was influential enough to persuade *askia* Muhammad I to call off the persecution of the Jews of Gao even though it had been urged by the North African scholar al-Maghili (Hunwick 1966b:311–313). Songhay rulers, seeking a necessarily delicate balance between animism and Islam to maintain their authority over a heterogeneous population, found it expedient to honor Muslim scholars and pilgrims and thereby partake of their *baraka* [spiritual power] (Hunwick 1966b:307–309). Sunni Ali himself, after looting the city and terrorizing its clerics, later showered them with slave girls and other presents.

Even in Timbuktu, however, Islam was never applied as rigidly as in the lands to the north, and there was always an undercurrent of paganism, much as this might be denied by Muslim apologists (cf. al-Sa'di 1964:36). Ibn Battuta was shocked by the easy relations between the sexes and the nudity of young women in the Sahel and the Sudan. Leo Africanus seems to have been relieved to find the women of Timbuktu veiling their faces but remarked on the dancing and music to which the people of the city gave themselves over late every night. After rigors of the desert crossing, the less censorious traveler found in Timbuktu a mixture of the reassuringly familiar and the pleasingly exotic, a point that Dubois and others were quick to appreciate in later times.

I have already mentioned Leo Africanus (al-Hasan ibn Muhammad al-Wazzan al-Zayyati), who accompanied two diplomatic missions from the court of Fez to *askia* Muhammad I of Songhai early in the sixteenth century. As a firsthand picture of Timbuktu in its golden age, his *Description of Africa* (1525–1526) complements the sixteenth- and seventeenth-century chronicles, the *Ta'rikh al-Fattash* and the *Ta'rikh al-Sudan*.

Except for its mosque and royal residence, Leo found nothing very remarkable about the physical appearance of this city of thatched-roofed mud-brick houses, but its economic life made a deep impression on him. Salt from Taghaza sold for eighty ducats a load, Barbary horses and European textiles enjoyed a brisk demand; the many weavers and other artisans offered goods in abundance. "The inhabitants of the city are very

---

[2]   The relative autonomy continued in the period following the Moroccan invasion with the *pashalik* of Timbuktu and even under the Masina Caliphate (Qloruntimẹhin 1972:22–23).

rich," he declared (Jean-Léon l'Africain 1956:467–468, translation mine), "especially foreigners who have settled in the country, so much so that the present king has given two of his daughters to two merchant brothers because of their fortunes." Such an inducement would seem to have been superfluous: the king himself possessed "a great treasure in minted coin and in ingots of gold. One of these ingots weighs 1,300 pounds." This piece of gold was, in fact, part of Sudanese folklore, retailed over the centuries by al-Bakri, al-Idrisi, and Ibn Khaldun before reaching Leo. It became heavier with each telling but no less credible to North Africans.

Leo found the court and royal entourage magnificent and noted that the king (whose identity is not clear, since Timbuktu was an appanage of Songhay at this time)[3] could field a well-organized army of cavalry and infantry to exact tribute and capture slaves. The king was also liberal in his gifts to the many jurists, scholars, and clerics of the city. "Many books in manuscripts from Barbary are sold here," Leo observed. "There is more profit from their sale than from all the rest of the goods." Beyond these few islands of literati in the cities of the Sudan, however, he saw only abysmal ignorance and degradation, the confirmation of all his prejudices about the Land of the Blacks (1956:467–469, 472).

Until the nineteenth century, the *Description* of Leo Africanus, written for a Christian pope, remained Europe's primary source for Timbuktu and the Sudan; with his account, the legend of Timbuktu crystallized and time seemed to stand still.

THE LURE OF GOLD AND EARLY PORTUGUESE INTEREST IN TIMBUKTU

"Timbuktu was the magnet which drew Europe into the heart of West Africa" (Kanya-Forstner 1969:23), but Europe's knowledge of Timbuktu was largely mediated by North Africa. Ever since the Middle Ages, traders from the maritime cities of France and Italy had carried on commercial relations with the states of the North African littoral, gradually winning rights and privileges from Safi to Tunis. A few made their way inland to Sijilmasa and Tlemcen (Bovill 1958:111–112; Mauny 1961:463; Crone 1937:xi; Jean-Léon l'Africain 1956:170–171). Curiously enough, Marrakech became for several centuries an episcopal see, so great were the numbers of European mercenaries employed in the service of the sultan. From their contacts with North Africa, the medieval Iberians had long heard of the "golden trade" of the Moors with the Sudan. In the period of gold shortage in western Europe and silver famine

---

[3] Leo's misleading reference to the "Kingdom of Timbuktu" recurs persistently on subsequent maps of Africa.

in the East, both Christians and Muslims became vitally concerned about enlarging the flow of precious metal from West Africa, their primary supplier (Lombard 1947; Braudel 1946).

The first European source to make explicit the close association of Timbuktu with the "lands of gold" was the Catalan Map of Abraham Cresques, presented to Philip III of Aragon in 1375 and given to the king of France a few years later. A Jewish cartographer from the island of Mallorca, Cresques had intimate ties with Jewish trading communities in North Africa. He depicts "Musa Mali . . . the richest and most noble king" of the blacks, as flanked by the cities of "tenbuch," "geugeu" (Gao), and "melli" (Bovill 1958: frontispiece and 91, 112–114). Thus, in the course of the fourteenth century, Europeans became aware of the Western Sudan as the land of gold and of Timbuktu as one of its major emporia. They were soon to act on this knowledge.

The opening wedge, in 1415, was the Portuguese conquest of Ceuta, where the youthful Prince Henry, later surnamed "the Navigator," won his spurs. Henry remained in Africa for some months, and if he and his compatriots had not already known about the flow of gold and other valuables from across the desert, they must surely have learned of it during their sojourn in Ceuta. At this time, however, the export trade from North African ports was largely a monopoly of the maritime cities of northern Italy. Portugal had only just achieved the consolidation of power at home after a long struggle against the Moors and neighboring Castilians; a poor and underpopulated country, it was a latecomer to the scene. If it wanted a share in the golden trade, it would have to win it by force (Blake 1937:5ff).

There is good evidence that Portugal first considered conquering Morocco itself in order to break the Muslim and Italian monopoly of the gold trade and to obtain Moroccan grain, sorely needed at home (Godinho 1962:211–212). The Portuguese, in fact, returned periodically to this scheme. It was initially rejected in favor of outflanking Islam by diverting the gold of sub-Saharan West Africa to the coast, bypassing the Maghreb and the Mediterranean altogether. This, not the discovery of a sea route to India (which was dubious, given the geographical conceptions of the times), was the object of Portuguese exploration at its outset and possibly even until Prince Henry's death in 1460. Gold and the desire to continue the crusade against the Moors were the driving forces of Portuguese policy (Pacheco Pereira 1937:62; Fernandes 1938:44; Blake 1937:4–5).

In 1434 Portuguese seamen doubled Cape Bojador in southern Morocco, since classical times the *nec plus ultra* because of its fogs and contrary winds. A decade later the first permanent European factory and fort in West Africa were built on Arguin Island, off the Mauritanian coast. Here the Portuguese hoped to cut into the caravan trade of the

Mauritanian route controlled by Arab and Berber merchants. Soon, however, the disadvantage of so peripheral a location made itself felt, and the Iberians sent agents inland to Waddan, an entrepôt of the western-most route across the Sahara. Because of Moorish hostility, the rigors of the desert climate, and the poor competitive position of the Portuguese, the venture was a commercial failure, but it did add information about the Sudano-Saharan system (Herbert 1974:412–413). In Waddan a Vene-tian captain in the service of Prince Henry, Cadamosto, learned of the three main routes by which gold reached Morocco, Tunis, and Egypt and particularly of the crucial role played by the salt of Taghaza (Crone 1937:21):

Every year large caravans of camels . . . carry it to Tanbutu [Timbuktu]; thence they go to Melli, the empire of the Blacks, where, so rapidly is it sold, within eight days of its arrival all is disposed of at a price of 2 to 3 hundred mitigalli, according to the quantity. . . . Then with the gold they return to their homes.

The salt was then carried by human porters a great distance "until they reach certain waters," and there it was traded for gold. Unlike many who followed, Cadamosto realized that Timbuktu was a central entrepôt in the north-south trade, not the source of gold.

About the same time as the Portuguese experiment at Waddan, Italian mercantile interests, not to be outflanked themselves, were exploring the possibilities of a direct connection with Timbuktu. Thus the Genoese Antonio Malfante reached the oasis of Tuat in the northwestern Sahara in 1447, presumably to trade Italian textiles for gold. The appearance of a Christian so far inland created a sensation, but he was well treated. His efforts to learn more about the sources of gold were fruitless, however; he lost money on his goods, and his journey had no known sequel (Crone 1937:85–90). Yet several decades later, the *Chronicle* of Benedetto Dei, a representative of the Florentine banking family of Portinari, contains the following cryptic entry (de la Roncière 1924:163): "I have been to Timbuktu, a place situated below the kingdoms of Barbary in a very arid land; and [there] they do a great business in coarse stuffs, in serges and ribbed materials made in Lombardy." This is the sum total of Dei's comments about Timbuktu and the Sudan in the catalog of his travels. His visit would have occurred in 1470, and the traffic in Lombard textiles was confirmed early in the sixteenth century by Leo Africanus (Jean-Léon l'Africain 1956:471). Though Dei's mention of the whole affair is so casual as to suggest he did not consider it unusual, the more likely explanation is that all such ventures were kept highly secret because of the fierce commercial rivalries of the period.

If the Saharan approaches to Timbuktu were dead ends, the Por-tuguese soon found gold aplenty along the Guinea Coast. The fort at São

Jorge da Mina, built in 1482, became the fulcrum of Portuguese activity on the West African coast for 150 years. By 1500 they were obtaining some 170,000 dobras of gold annually from Mina (Pacheco Pereira 1937:120) and lesser amounts from the Gambia (Rodney 1970:81). Paradoxically, this golden harvest made them more eager than ever to reach Timbuktu in order to dominate the trade at what they believed was its center — ending their dependence on African middlemen while triumphing over European interlopers on the coast.

The main stumbling block was that the Portuguese never learned just where Timbuktu was. They and other Europeans after them generally underestimated the distance from Timbuktu to the coast — indeed, underestimated the north-south and east-west dimensions of West Africa — as well as believing that the river systems were interconnected.[4] So convinced was King John II ("the Perfect") of Portugal that the Senegal penetrated far into the interior, to the very gates of "Tambucutu and Mombare where are the richest traders and markets of gold in the world, from which all Berberia from east and west up to Jerusalem is supplied and provided," that he conceived an audacious plan of attack. A Wolof prince named Bemoym had been taken to Portugal earlier, converted to Christianity, and brought back to Africa. With Bemoym as a puppet king on the Wolof throne, John II counted on opening up a direct route to Timbuktu in order to divert the gold trade to the mouth of the Senegal. He also hoped to make contact with the king of Mossi, who seemed to him to answer the description of Prester John, the Christian king of the Indies. Before the geographical and ethnological fallacies of the scheme became evident, Bemoym was murdered by the Portuguese leader of the expedition (Crone 1937:128–141). The Portuguese made at least two more attempts to reach Timbuktu in the next century — both failures, it seems, although they did make contact with the king of Mali much closer to the coast (Crone 1937:143; Blake 1942:34–35).

If the Portuguese did not reach Timbuktu and take control of the African trade at its reputed source, the larger question remains: Did their grand strategy nevertheless succeed? Did they outflank the Moor and divert the golden trade of Timbuktu to their coastal factories? The general verdict of recent scholarship (in contrast to earlier work) would appear to be negative. Hopkins (1973:80) finds "little evidence . . . that the arrival of the Europeans on the West Coast had a dramatic or even an immediate impact on the economy of the interior." He argues (p. 131) that the trans-Saharan trade not only survived, but increased in value during the nineteenth century, declining only in its last quarter. Newbury

---

[4] There were two widely held but conflicting views of the Niger: one, dating from Herodotus and Pliny and followed by most Arabs, insisted that the river flowed from west to east and eventually joined the Nile; the other, deriving from Leo Africanus, held that it flowed west, emptying into the Atlantic by its branches, the Senegal and Gambia.

(1966:233–234), too, has contended that the desert and coastal trades were "two unrelated activities," and Curtin's (1975:281) research on Senegambian trade would seem to confirm this view.[5]

THE MOROCCAN INVASION OF THE WESTERN SUDAN

The next important turning point in the history of Timbuktu came with the invasion of the Songhay Empire by al-Mansur of Morocco in 1591. The purposes of the invasion were threefold: (1) to establish a universal caliphate in response to the expansionism of the Ottoman Turks in North Africa, (2) to counter the Christian Portuguese, lest the latter divert the trans-Saharan trade to the Atlantic, and (3) to control the wealth of the Sudan itself. The army of 3,000 which conquered Songhay was made up largely of enslaved mercenaries from Spain and Morocco led by Jawdhar Basha, and the resulting administration was primarily a military one relying on Moroccan divisional leaders (*qa'ids*) ruling through traditional Sudanese officials. There are a number of myths connected with the Moroccan invasion, including the seizure of great wealth by the sultan and the breakup of the trans-Saharan trade to the extent that the economy and the intellectual life of the Western Sudan was thrown into chaos and stagnation for centuries. Each of these myths can be challenged. Certainly the Moroccans expected the sack of the Songhay capital at Gao to yield untold riches, but not a single object of gold was found. The longer the army stayed encamped at the Songhay capital, the greater the toll from disease, and it was to escape this that the invaders moved their headquarters to Timbuktu. Using the resistance of local merchants and ulama as a pretext, the Moroccans then sacked the proud city and sent the notables, deprived of their books and wealth, into exile. The treasure obtained must have been considerable; yet the sultan's share — 100,000 mithqals of gold — was considered by all to be shamefully meager (al-Sa'di 1964:261).

Looting cannot provide a steady source of riches, nor can rulers control the cupidity of soldiers hundreds of miles away beyond the desert; for all the propaganda put out by Sultan Mawlay Ahmad, now surnamed al-Dhahabi, "the Golden," it seems highly probable that his expectations were bitterly disappointed. Even the reports of European agents in Marrakech must be viewed with caution: in some cases they claim to have seen trains of pack animals laden with gold dust; in others they only relate

---

[5] There may have been points of interaction between the two systems, however, at least at certain periods. For example, the great fluctuations in the amounts of gold reaching the Gold Coast — indeed, the virtual cessation in the later eighteenth century, when Europeans had to pay for slaves with gold — suggests a flexibility in the trade; thus, depending on conditions, gold from the Akan fields probably could have been directed either north or south.

that such shipments are "expected" (de Castries 1905–1936:83–84; cf. al-Ufrani 1889:16–19; Bovill 1958:179–181).

Ironically, more gold may have flowed into the sherifian treasury from the ransom of Christian captives after the battle of al-Ksar al-Kabir (the "Battle of the Three Kings") than from the Sudan in the years following the conquest (Julien 1966:215–216).

The Moroccans had made the same mistake as the Portuguese, confusing trading entrepôts with centers of production; they assumed that the conquest of the Songhay Empire would automatically lead to direct control over the lands of gold. There is no evidence that they ever reached the goldfields or that their power extended beyond the cities of the Middle Niger. While some tribute was forthcoming, the only steady supply of gold came indirectly, as it had long done, by way of the trade in salt and other goods.

Like the Portuguese bid for empire, too, the Moroccan invasions and occupation of the Western Sudan proved in the end a greater drain of manpower than the country could survive. Regular communication could not be maintained with Marrakech and Fez over such vast distances. Civil strife broke out even in Mawlay Ahmad's lifetime, and affairs were left to drift in Timbuktu, so that it was abandoned altogether in the next century: "When the Moroccan army arrived in the Sudan, it found one of the lands most favored by God in its richness and fertility. Peace and stability reigned everywhere. . . . All that changed in this moment" (al-Sa'di 1964:222–223). The Middle Niger became an intermittent battle zone for Fulani, Bambara, Tuareg, and Arma (the descendants of the Moroccan soldiery). Pashas came and went, scarcely able to control their own garrisons, much less to protect the few cities they professed to govern. A generation of scholars had been deported, their libraries scattered to the winds; without them "Timbuktu became a body without a soul" (Kati 1964:308; *Tedzkiret en Nisian* 1964: *passim*).

With the fervor of the moralist, al-Sa'di exaggerates both the perfection of life in Timbuktu before the Moroccan conquest and the ruin that followed. Willis (1971) is surely right in asserting that the picture of anarchy, famine, pestilence, and darkness for the period 1591–1750 is overdrawn. The Moroccan rulers wanted to maintain political stability and the flow of trade. Thus, merchants were protected rather than dominated and exploited. Nor was Timbuktu extinguished as a center of learning. Both *ta'rikhs* and undoubtedly other books now lost were completed in the seventeenth century. Animism may have experienced a resurgence in the Niger bend, but Timbuktu continued to be visited by peripatetic scholars and holy men and to send her own teachers to found schools in the central Sudan. The city had always been vulnerable to the depredations of the Tuareg and Mossi; insecurity was nothing new, even if it now became more the rule than the exception.

In the Sudan itself there is testimony to the continuation of trade implicit even in the reports of brigandage. The *Tadhkirat al-Nisyan*, a biographical dictionary of the pashas of Timbuktu, mentions, for example, that in about 1694 a commander of the Moroccan garrison confiscated thirty-seven boats, seventeen of them loaded with salt and seventeen bearing goods from Jenne, including 37,000 mithqals of gold dust (*Tedzkiret en Nisian* 1964:149–150).

BRITISH AND FRENCH PROBES — "TIMBUKTU THE MYSTERIOUS"

Whatever the vicissitudes that followed the downfall of Songhay, it is evident that Timbuktu (and to a lesser extent Gao) continued to incarnate the riches of the Sudan in European eyes and to act as a powerful lure to the more adventurous among their traders. In the opening decades of the seventeenth century, English merchants descended on the River Gambia, rivals to the Afro-Portuguese *lançados*, who had evolved into an indigenous trading caste (see Mouser, this volume). Like the Portuguese crown in its more energetic days, the English identified Timbuktu with their dreams of gold and hoped "to discover some way to those rich mines of Gago or Timbatu, from whence is supposed the Moores of Barbary have their gold" (Jobson 1904 [1623]:4).

An English company was formed in 1618 expressly to penetrate to the gold country and to reach Timbuktu, still believed to lie in the heart of the goldfields. Since the Gambia was assumed to be one of the mouths of the Niger, this seemed the obvious route, but the first expedition ended in disaster. Undaunted, the company sent out a second, commanded by Richard Jobson, in 1620. Jobson succeeded in finding Buckar Sano, the leading merchant on the river, and in trading with him. At Tenda he heard of two cities, Tomba-konda and Jaye, which he assumed to be the Timbuktu and Gao of Leo Africanus, subscribing as he did to the prevailing view that these cities were not distant from the coast. Since his informant "tolde us of houses covered with gold," his confusion was only natural (Jobson 1904[1623]:129). A factory was established on the Gambia and gold of good quality obtained in the form of bars, but his countrymen made no sustained effort to reach its source and, owing to the secrecy of their African suppliers, never learned where it was coming from.

French enterprise on the Senegal followed a parallel course. Gold was the lure, and Delcourt (1952:170) argues that it was the detailed information gained through their consuls in the Maghreb and through French slaves that provided the impetus to French attempts to reach Timbuktu and the gold country via the Senegal. An overenthusiastic champion of empire claims that Colbert was the father of the scheme (Gatelet

1901:11), but the honor belongs more properly to André Brue, the energetic governor of Senegal 1697–1702 and again 1714–1720.

Even before Brue's first administration, the French had reached Galam, near the confluence of the River Faleme and close to the frontiers of Bambuk. Little gold was obtained, nevertheless, and Brue was determined to send out explorers to press the trade more vigorously and to find out more about the country beyond, specifically to "learn about the route to Timbuktu and its riches which are said to be immense and which is thought to be about 600 leagues east of Galam." Like so many others, Brue believed Timbuktu to be the "pays de l'or," although he seems to have been aware that it was not identical with Bambuk (Delcourt 1952:170–175; cf. Labat, quoted in Moore 1738:303; Pruneau de Pommegorge 1789:77; cf. Curtin 1973:623–624). He also underestimated the hostility of Mandingo and Moorish traders and the indigenous population of the region, few of whom were eager to see an extension of French commerce into the interior. After several more attempts to open up Bambuk, Brue's successors fell back to the Senegal and the safer trade in slaves and gum.

Though Timbuktu seemed destined to remain a will-o'-the-wisp, a "mirage soudanais," English and French trade with West Africa increased dramatically during the eighteenth century and with it the clash of their interests in Senegambia. Mercantile and political rivalries of themselves provoked a certain curiosity, but it was also a time of great interest in travel, universal history, the natural sciences, and geographical discovery. In an age of enlightenment, it was a sobering thought that the best source on Africa, the *Description* of Leo Africanus, was several centuries old, that Europeans still had not set eyes on the sources of Sudanese gold (at Timbuktu or elsewhere), and that none of the great river systems of the continent was understood.

All that changed in a few decades at the turn of the century. The catalyst was provided by the African Association, founded in 1788 by a private group of well-to-do Englishmen, many of them amateurs of botany, interested in promoting the cause of African exploration in the broadest sense and willing to support it at their own expense. In due time its efforts were joined by the British government, the Paris Société de Géographie, the administration of Senegal, and a handful of intrepid private travelers. The paramount object was to discover the course of the Niger and to reach Timbuktu. The sequence of expeditions, the great majority of them tragic failures, is too well known to need repeating (see e.g., Hallett 1964; Bovill 1968; Miège 1961–1962: vol. 2, pp. 148–149; Bodichon 1849). What is not always brought out is that the legend of Timbuktu created by the publication and republication of Leo Africanus in Europe since the sixteenth century could not have persisted with such power had it not been constantly corroborated, indeed magnified, by reports out of Barbary. These convinced the African Association not only that Timbuktu was "one of the principal marts for the supply of the Interior of Africa" (Hallett 1964:74), but that the area it drained was rich and vast, as tempting a plum for European enterprise as it had ever been.

The most glowing and detailed report came in 1790 from a Moor called Shabeeny (al-Shabbani), who claimed to have lived for seven years in Timbuktu. "Some of its inhabitants," he declared, "are amazingly rich. The dress of common women has been often worth 1000 dollars." Shabeeny also dwelt on the tradition of learning still very much alive in Timbuktu, as well as on the security, toleration, and stability of government there and in the neighboring and even more prosperous city of Houssa (Awsa) (Hallett 1964:103f.; cf. Wilks and Ferguson 1970:48–51; see Jackson 1820). So excited was one Association member by these disclosures that he wrote a friend: "We have heard of a city called Tombouctou, gold is so plentiful there as to adorn even the slaves. . . . If we could get our manufactures into that country, we should soon have gold enough" (Hallett 1964:108 n.), and the secretary of the Association speculated that these cities might be the heirs to ancient Carthage, with "those arts and sciences and that commercial knowledge, for which the inhabitants of Carthage were once so eminently famous" (Hallet 1964:117). Mungo Park's (1799:215) data seemed to confirm this picture of the wealth of Timbuktu, although it was based only on hearsay:

> The present King of Timbouctou is named Abu Abrahima; he is reported to possess immense riches. His wives and concubines are said to be clothed in silk, and the chief officers of state live in considerable splendour. The whole expense of his government is defrayed, as I was told, by a tax upon merchandize which is collected at the gates of the city.

With the end of the Napoleonic Wars, interest in West African discovery was rekindled. There was little talk for the moment of conquest but a great deal about the "civilizing mission" — and profitability — of trade. The most indefatigable publicist was the former English consul in Mogador, James Grey Jackson. In a burst of enthusiasm, he wrote that "the immense quantity of gold dust and gold bars that would be brought from Timbuctoo, Wangara and Gana, in exchange for our merchandize, would be incalculable, and perhaps has never yet been contemplated by Europeans" (Jackson 1819; cf. 1810, 1814, 1820). The governor of Sierra Leone, General Charles Turner, proposed that patrol boats and military units be sent to the Windward Coast to insure British control of trade with the interior and that the British resident at Timbo spearhead peaceful commercial penetration to Segu and Timbuktu (Curtin 1964: 171). The British government balked at the commitment demanded by the Turner plan, but it did favor subsidizing exploration with the aim of opening up the continent to British manufactures — as long as it did not cost too much.

The lure of commercial gain and British-French rivalries are inadequate to explain the veritable *ruée sur Tombouctou* of the 1820's. As Baron Rousseau, French consul-general in Tripoli, expressed it, "Timbuctoo . . . has become for us what the enchanted city of Irem-Zatilemad was to the ancient Arabs or the fountain of youth to oriental mythology" (Rousseau 1827:176). A footnote explained that Irem-Zatilemad (Iram Dhát al-'Imād) was a splendid pleasure-city built by a sultan of the Hadramawt to rival the deity. While the English painted the city in tones of gold, it was the French, apparently beginning with Rousseau, who added the adjective "mysterious." With more perception than many of his contemporaries, however, Rousseau wondered if the glory of Timbuktu might after all be only a "chimera that will evaporate as soon as the many obstacles that block its access have been surmounted."

No such doubts assailed explorers such as Major Alexander Gordon Laing. Making his painful and almost fatal journey across the Sahara to the fabled city, he wrote:

I have not travelled to Timbuctoo for the sake of any other reward than that which I shall derive from the consciousness of having achieved an enterprise which will rescue my name from oblivion —

> Tis that which bids my bosom glow
> To climb the stiff ascent of fame
> To share the praise the just bestow
> And give myself a deathless name.

Laing's obsession grew almost to megalomania as the city appeared almost within his grasp: he was willing to give everything he had to get there "because I am well aware that if I do not visit it, the World will ever remain in ignorance of the place" (Bovill 1964:286–303).

In 1825 the Paris Société de Géographie had offered a prize of 10,000 francs and a gold medal to the first man to reach Timbuktu by way of Senegambia and produce a description of the city. A half-dozen explorers were rumored to be in the field or about to set out, in spite of the many who had already lost their lives in the attempt. British magazines parodied the craze for Timbuktu and the credulity of savants in accepting the claims of shipwrecked sailors such as Adams (1816) and Riley (1817) that they had been to that metropolis in their wanderings (H. 1824; R.S.T. 1826).

Of the twenty-odd adventurers who had set their sights on Timbuktu since 1788, the first to make it was indeed Laing, who reached the city in August 1826. In the single extant letter written from Timbuktu, he deliberately avoided any description save that "in every respect except in size (which does not exceed four miles in circumference) it has completely met my expectations" (Bovill 1964:312). A few days later he was murdered in the desert and his journals were lost forever.

Not quite two years after that, René Caillié entered the city disguised as an Arab and lived to return to France and claim the gold medal. There is no need to repeat the arrogant incredulity with which the news was received in Britain, the bitter charges made against Jomard, his champion and the president of the Société de Géographie, or the insinuations in some quarters that the entire story was a fabrication drawn from the papers of the murdered Laing (e.g., Barrow 1830:450–475). The sad truth was that Laing had been cast in a heroic mold befitting the conqueror of Timbuktu and Caillié was uneducated, a provincial, a man obsessed, acting entirely on his own. Not until Barth (1965 [1865]) verified the essentials twenty years later was Caillié grudgingly given his due in England.

To compound the insult of Caillié's success, he had found Timbuktu wanting. The city, he declared simply but unforgivably (Caillié 1830: vol. 2, p. 49),

did not answer my expectations. I had formed a totally different idea of the grandeur and wealth of Timbuktu. The city presented, at first view, nothing but a mass of ill-looking houses, built of earth. Nothing was to be seen in all directions but immense plains of quicksand of a yellowish white color. The sky was a pale red as far as the horizon: all nature wore a dreary aspect, and the most profound silence prevailed; not even the warbling of a bird was to be heard. . . . Still, there was something imposing in the aspect of a great city, raised in the midst of sands, and the difficulties surmounted by the founders cannot fail to excite admiration.

The contrast with Jenne was particularly striking. Though Jenne, like Timbuktu, had been caught up in the turmoil of Fulani expansion under Seku Ahmadu, it was "full of bustle and animation; every day numerous caravans of merchants are arriving and departing with all kinds of useful products" (Caillié 1830: vol. 1, p. 460). It was an important market town as well as an entrepôt, even if the bulk of the traffic in gold had shifted to Sansanding and Bamako. In Timbuktu the sole trade of importance was the long-distance trade, and this went on behind closed doors: only a glimmer of it could be seen in the ornaments worn by female slaves of rich masters.

THE FINAL ACT: FRENCH CONQUEST, 1894

Timbuktu had been unveiled, but it had not been "opened up" by the European powers. British interest shifted increasingly to the Central Sudan and, above all, to the Lower Niger, which held out greater promise

of return. Across the Channel, however, interest in the Western Sudan
was still very much alive. Two points of view tended to dominate French
imperialist thinking with respect to Africa, the one emphasizing Algeria,
the other Senegal.

The long-drawn out French conquest of Algeria was proving to be a
commercial disappointment. Surveys showed that the caravan trade was
still immensely lucrative but was bypassing Algeria for Morocco, Tunis,
or Tripoli. The government therefore addressed itself to reversing this
tide and finding the means to exploit the Sudan as the natural and integral
hinterland of Algeria (Emerit 1941; Miège 1961–1962: vol. 2, p. 154;
vol. 3, pp. 74–79; Newbury 1966:233–246). Initially they thought of
accomplishing this by creating a series of oases across the desert to
Timbuktu; later there was the much more ambitious project of a trans-
Saharan railroad.

For Louis Faidherbe, governor of Senegal (1854–1861, 1863–1865),
the Sahara was irrelevant (see Barrows, this volume). What was far more
practicable and would bring rich rewards to France would be to join the
Senegal and Niger Valleys in order to gain complete control over the
commerce and production of the Sudan (see Quintin 1881:514; Kanya-
Forstner 1969:28f.). Though the economy of the Sudan was in serious
decline because of the devastation of the Fulani and Tukulor jihads, he
did not doubt that, once the area was joined to the coast and exposed to
the civilizing influence of France, trade and agriculture would regain their
former levels (Faidherbe 1889:8, esp. 349; cf. Bodichon's [1849:9]
reference to the Sudan as "une Californie africaine" as well as Tautain
1885:633). Timbuktu was the linchpin of the design.

Faidherbe's ideas were to triumph, but not immediately. They were
only taken up by influential members of the government and public in the
later 1870's and 1880's, given a greater urgency by the perennially
revived fears of British — and then German — schemes for the Sudan
(Hopkins 1973:157–166). Even so, the Chamber was reluctant to vote
the credits necessary for expansion. The result was that commanders in
the field were in the habit of taking the initiative, then calling on the
government to accept *faits accomplis* and assume the expenses involved.
To put an end to this practice, the government of Senegal and the Sudan
was reorganized in 1893 and placed under civilian control. "The period of
conquest and territorial expansion must be considered . . . at an end," the
Minister of the Colonies wrote emphatically to the new civil governor,
Grodet (Kanya-Forstner 1969:211). Ironically, it was this intended
reform that set the stage for an act of the purest insubordination — of vain-
glorious mutiny: the capture of Timbuktu.

The military commander of the Sudan, Lieutenant Colonel Etienne
Bonnier, was determined to fulfill his lifelong ambition to conquer Timbuktu, civilian governor or no. On December 25, 1893, before Grodet

had had time to interfere, Bonnier set off with transport barges down the Niger. Grodet quickly guessed what was being planned and ordered Bonnier back to Segu. Bonnier ignored the order but was faced with a problem of disobedience of his own: his subordinate, Lieutenant Boiteux, had defied his orders and taken a flotilla from Mopti to Timbuktu ahead of him and was now calling for help. This provided a useful pretext for Bonnier, who telegraphed Grodet that he was on his way to Timbuktu, "whose submission has been seriously offered," to rescue Boiteux.

Boiteux occupied Timbuktu on December 15. His contingent of nineteen had taken the city without firing a shot, but though the inhabitants of the city were resigned to their fate, the Tuareg in its environs were intensely hostile and for a time were able to cut the lifeline to Kabara; only the arrival of Bonnier with his troops on January 10, 1894, secured the occupation.

Almost immediately Bonnier set out again with most of his men to meet Colonel Joffre, who was approaching by land, although it is not clear why this was necessary. Not far from Goundam, an early morning attack by Tuareg from whom the French had been raiding cattle virtually wiped out the French force: Bonnier, twelve of his European officers and N.C.O.s, and sixty-eight native *tirailleurs* were killed. It was the worst disaster of the Sudanese campaign (Kanya-Forstner 1969:216–221).

News of the capture of "la ville sainte et mystérieuse" (*Le Temps*, January 26, 1894) brought a thrill even to those Frenchmen opposed to unchecked military expansion. It quickly turned to horror at the news of the massacre at Dongoï (referred to as a "glorieuse catastrophe"). The English spitefully suggested it might be wise to withdraw, but the French flag had been raised over Timbuktu, and there it would remain for sixty-seven years.

CONCLUSION

The image of Timbuktu that gained currency in North Africa and Europe and that exerted such a powerful attraction on individuals and nations was a composite of fact, distortion, and contradiction, fed by ignorance, credulity, and above all the *aurae sacra fames*, the consuming passion for gold that obsessed Muslim and Christian alike. "The extraordinary city . . . created solely by the wants of commerce and destitute of every resource except what its accidental position as a place of exchange affords" (Caillié 1830: vol. 2, p. 71) became confused with the sources of wealth themselves, with the mines of gold that were the lodestone for discovery and conquest. It was a case of historical metonymy, where the part came to stand for the whole, an entrepôt for a center of production. It was also, to borrow another term from rhetoric, a case of hyperbole. Just as the genuine wealth that passed through Timbuktu was exaggerated beyond all reason, so the real and solid tradition of Islamic scholarship of the city was magnified; it became Carthage and Alexandria rolled into one, a repository of lost knowledge of the ancients as well as of gold.

The question remains: why Timbuktu? Why not Jenne, or even Gao or Kano? All were trading cities of great importance as well as centers of learning, but none could match the fame of Timbuktu outside the Sudan. One need only look at the index for the *Bulletin de la Société de Géographie* 1822–1861, where there are only two references to Jenne, one to Kano, none to Gao, and some sixty-four to Timbuktu. The reasons for this singular preeminence are certainly many. Is it frivolous to suggest that there is something in the name itself that catches the ear and conveys images of wonder? On a more concrete level, Timbuktu was ideally oriented geographically for the caravan trade of the western Sahara and hence best known to the Arabs and Berbers from Barbary, who in turn were the major source of Europe's knowledge into the nineteenth century.

Perhaps the most important reason is the most revealing about the nature of cultural contact. Timbuktu was sought out by travelers, traders, and settlers from North Africa not only because of its geographical position and commercial advantages, but also because it was the *least* African of the cities of the Sudan. It was a city where one could live surrounded by North Africans or at least fellow Muslims, largely insulated from the alien culture that prevailed to the south. Intermarriage of course took place, but the sources give an impression of almost total lack of genuine interest on the part of North Africans in the more profound reality of Sudanese culture; integration of the Saharan and Sudanese economic systems does not seem to have brought in its wake integration of cultural systems. Like the proverbial "ugly American," Arabs and Berbers came with preconceived notions which they sought to verify, often unaware of the contradictions these implied. Is not Leo Africanus, who could declare at one moment that all Africans lived like beasts, without laws or governments or customs, and then proceed, in fact, to describe a perfectly orderly society, the prime example of this type of traveler?

Legend is by nature oversimplification. Timbuktu provided the stuff of legend because it could be simplified into basic elements of the most universal appeal, material and spiritual.

REFERENCES

ADAMS, ROBT.
   1816   *The narrative of Robert Adams.* . . . London: Murray.

AL-SAʿDI, ABDERRAHMAN
1964   *Ta'rikh al-Sudan.* Translated by O. Houdas. Paris: Maisonneuve.
AL-UFRANI, MUHAMMAD AL-SAGHIR
1889   *Histoire de la dynastie saadienne au Maroc (1511–1670).* Translated by O. Houdas. Paris: Leroux.
[BARROW, JOHN]
1830   M. Caillié, Central Africa. *Quarterly Review* 42:450–475.
BARTH, HEINRICH
1965 [1865]   *Travels and discoveries in north and central Africa, 1849–55,* three volumes (centenary edition). London: Frank Cass.
BLAKE, J. W.
1937   *European beginnings in West Africa, 1454–1578.* London: Longmans Green.
1942   *Europeans in West Africa, 1450–1560,* volume one. London: Hakluyt Society.
BODICHON, DR.
1849   Projet d'une exploration politique, commerciale et scientifique. . . . *Bulletin de la Société de Géographie* 12:5–56.
BOVILL, E. W.
1925   The Niger and the Songhai Empire. *Journal of the African Society* 25:138–146.
1958   *The golden trade of the Moors.* London: Oxford University Press.
1968   *The Niger explored.* London: Oxford University Press.
BOVILL, E. W., *editor*
1964   *Missions to the Niger,* volume one. Cambridge: Cambridge University Press for the Hakluyt Society.
BRAUDEL, F.
1946   Monnaies et civilisation: de l'or du Soudan à l'argent d'Amérique. *Annales: Economies, Sociétés, Civilisations* 1:9–22.
CAILLIÉ, R.
1830   *Travels through Central Africa to Timbuctoo,* two volumes.
CRONE, G. R., *translator and editor*
1937   *The voyages of Cadamosto and other documents on western Africa in the second half of the fifteenth century.* London: Hakluyt Society.
CURTIN, P. D.
1964   *The image of Africa.* Madison: University of Wisconsin Press.
1973   The lure of Bambuk gold. *Journal of African History* 14:623–631.
1975   *Economic change in precolonial Africa: Senegambia in the era of the slave trade.* Madison: University of Wisconsin Press.
DE CASTRIES, H.
1905–1936   *Les sources inédites de l'histoire du Maroc,* volume two. Paris: Guethner.
DE LA RONCIÈRE, C.
1924   *La dévouverte de l'Afrique au moyen âge,* volume one. Cairo: Institut Français d'Archéologie Orientale. (Translated from the French.) London: Colburn and Bentley.
DELCOURT, A.
1952   *La France et les établissements français au Sénégal entre 1713 et 1763.* Dakar: Institut Français d'Afrique Noire.
DUBOIS, F.
1897   *Tombouctou la mystérieuse.* Paris.
EMERIT, M.
1941   *Les Saint-Simoniens en Algérie.* Paris: Les Belles Lettres.

FAIDHERBE, L. L. C.
1889   *Le Sénégal: la France dans l'Afrique occidentale.* Paris: Hachette.
FERNANDES, VALENTIM
1938   *Description de la côte d'Afrique de Ceuta au Sénégal.* Edited by P. de Cenival and Th. Monod. Paris: Larose.
GATELET, LT.
1901   *Histoire de la conquête du Soudan français (1878–1889).* Paris: Berger-Levrault.
GODINHO, V. MAGALHAES
1962   *A economia dos descobrimentos henriquinos.* Lisbon: Da Costa.
1824   Specimens of a Timbuctoo anthology. *New Monthly Magazine* 11 (July), 22–28.
HALLETT, R.
1964   *Records of the African Association, 1788–1831.* London: Nelson.
HERBERT, E.
1974   Portuguese adaptation to trade patterns: Guinea to Angola. *African Studies Review* 17:411–424.
HOPKINS, A. G.
1973   *An economic history of West Africa.* London: Longman.
HUNWICK, J. O.
1962   A new source for the biography of Aḥmad Bābā al-Tinbuktī. *Bulletin of the School of Oriental and African Studies* 27:568–570.
1966a   Further light on Ahmad Baba. *Research Bulletin* (Ibadan) 2:19–31.
1966b   "Religion and state in the Songhay Empire, 1464–1591," in *Islam in tropical Africa.* Edited by I. M. Lewis and Daryll Forde. London: Oxford University Press.
JACKSON, J. G.
1810   *An account of the empire of Marocco and the districts of Sus and Tafilet ... and an interesting account of Timbuctoo, the great emporium of central Africa.* London: Bulmer.
1814   *An account of Timbuctoo and Haussa ... by el haje Abd Salam Shabeeny* (third edition). London: Bulmer.
1819   Hints concerning the colonization of Africa. *Blackwood's Magazine* 4:652–653.
1820   *An account of Timbuctoo and Haussa ... by el haje Abd Salam Shabeeny.* London: Bulmer.
JEAN-LÉON L'AFRICAIN [LEO AFRICANUS]
1956   *Description de l'Afrique,* volume two. Translated and annotated by A. Epaulard, Th. Monod, H. Lhote, and R. Mauny. Paris: Maisonneuve.
JOBSON, R.
1904 [1623]   *The golden trade.* Teignmouth: Speight and Walpole.
JULIEN, C. A.
1966   *Histoire de l'Afrique du Nord,* volume two (second edition). Paris: Payot.
KANYA-FORSTNER, A. S.
1969   *The conquest of the Western Sudan.* London: Cambridge University Press.
KATI, MAHMOUD [IBN AL-MUKHTAR?]
1964   *Ta'rikh al-Fattash.* Translated by O. Houdas. Paris: Maisonneuve.

LEVTZION, N.
1973   *Ancient Ghana and Mali.* London: Methuen.
LOMBARD, M.
1947   L'or musulman du septième au seizième siècle. *Annales: Economies, Sociétés, Civilisations* 2:143–160.
MAUNY, R.
1961   *Tableau géographique de l'Ouest africain au moyen âge d'après les sources écrites, la tradition et l'archéologie.* Mémoires de l'Institut Français d'Afrique Noire 61. Dakar.
MOORE, FRANCIS
1738   *Travels to the inland parts of Africa.* London.
MIÈGE, J. L.
1961–1962   *Le Maroc et l'Europe (1830–94),* four volumes. Paris: Presses Universitaires de France.
NEWBURY, C. W.
1966   North Africa and Western Sudan trade in the nineteenth century: a reevaluation. *Journal of African History* 7:233–246.
OLORUNTIMEHIN, B. O.
1972   *The Segu Tukolor Empire.* New York: Humanities Press.
PACHECO PEREIRA, D.
1937   *Esmeraldo de situ orbis.* Translated and edited by H. T. Kimble. London: Hakluyt Society.
PARK, M
1799   *Travels in the interior districts of Africa.* London: Bulmer.
PERINBAM, B. M.
1974   Notes on dyula origins and nomenclature. *Bulletin de l'Institut Fondamental d'Afrique Noir* B 36:676–690.
PRUNEAU DE POMMEGORGE, A.
1789   *Description de la Nigritie.* Paris.
QUINTIN, L.
1881   Souvenirs d'un voyage du Sénégal au Niger (1863–1866). *Bulletin de la Société de Géographie,* 7ᵉ série, 1:514–551.
R. S. T.
1826   Memorabilia of Jerry . . . under-sub-scribe to the Tombouctou Review. *Blackwood's Magazine* 20:188–191.
RILEY, JAMES
1817   *Loss of the American brig* Commerce. . . . London: Murray.
RODNEY, W.
1970   *A history of the Upper Guinea Coast, 1545–1800.* London: Oxford University Press.
ROUSSEAU, BARON
1827   [Letter.] *Bulletin de la Société de Géographie* 8:176–177.
TAUTAIN, DR.
1885   Tombouctou. *Nouvelle Revue* 1:631–633.
Tedzkiret en Nisian [Tadhkirat al-Nisyan]
1964   *Tedzkiret en Nisian.* Translated by O. Houdas. Paris: Maisonneuve.
TYMOWSKI, M.
1967   Le Niger, voie de communication des grand états du Soudan occidentale jusqu'à la fin du seizième siècle. *Africana Bulletin* 6:73–95.
WILKS, IVOR
1962   A medieval trade route from the Niger to the gulf of Guinea. *Journal of African History* 3:337–341.

WILKS, IVOR, P. FERGUSON
1970   "In vindication of Sīdi al-Hājj 'Abd al-Salām Shabayni," in *African perspectives*. Edited by C. Allen and R. W. Johnson. Cambridge: Cambridge University Press.
WILLIS, J. R.
1971   "The Western Sudan from the Moroccan invasion (1591) to the death of al-Mukhtar al-Kunti (1811)," in *History of West Africa*, volume one. Edited by J. F. A. Ajayi and Michael Crowder, 441–484. London: Longman.

The Julas in Western Sudanese History: Long-Distance Traders and Developers of Resources

B. MARIE PERINBAM

> Julietto ... signifies a Merchant
> that goes from place to place.
> RICHARD JOBSON, *The golden trade* (1623)

The term *jula* (*dyula* or *dyoula* in French) refers to a professional or semiprofessional, market-oriented, organized group of long-distance traders or distributors, who are Islamicized and mainly Manding-speaking.[1] Julas developed and organized trading networks and commercial partnerships and indirectly contributed to the exploitation of other Western Sudanese resources, such as gold and kola nuts. They also participated directly in the production of textiles. Their commercial enterprises neither conformed to formalist market concepts, which focus on the price-regulating market and on supply-demand ratios, including those of the factors of production, nor were regulated by the formalist market principle, which quantifies and allocates factor resources among alternative outputs. As market-oriented (as opposed to market-dominated) groups, however, julas invested and reinvested capital. Divi-

---

[1] The julas must not be confused with the similar group of long-distance traders who speak Dyula, a Manding dialect, and generally espouse Islam. These market-oriented distributors of the Ivory Coast, Upper Volta, southern Mali, northern Ghana, and Guinea have been assimilated linguistically and culturally into the Manding core from other quite separate ethnic groups, such as Senufo, Kulango, Abron, and Mossi. They do not as a rule trace their origins to the early Manding trading clans of the Upper Niger. Moreover, as recently assimilated groups which have now come to share a language, function, sense of community, and identity they tend to identify with those regions to which their lineages migrated during or after the nineteenth century. Gingiss (1972) discusses the Dyula dialect, arguing that it is not a pidgin (although it has acquired an inferior status among Manding-speakers). Other studies of the Dyula are Person (1968: ch. 1–3) and Lewis (1971). Nor should the julas be confused with the Diola, a non-Mande ethnic group of the Lower Casamance (see Thomas 1956). For a brief discussion of *jula* origins and nomenclature, see Perinbam (1974).

sion of labor, market exchange through currency, and notions of competition and profit were part of their operations. At the same time, market prices were seldom self-regulating, and market-related production decisions were irregular. Moreover, among some jula communities, social rather than market factors frequently prevailed, to the extent that privately owned capital was managed and controlled almost exclusively through social institutions such as the clan or family. Property, means of production, and labor were infrequently integrated, and there was invariably a fusion in the use, exchange, and accumulation of particular products. Furthermore, whereas in market-dominated societies production and distributive organization are subject to market phenomena, jula relations of production (the linkages between the structure of the society's productive forces and the social forms that are an expression of those forces) and of distribution (the cognitive and affective linkages through which the distributors of resources are organized) were rooted in family, lineage, and clan, sometimes reinforced by religious ties.

Methodological problems limit our understanding of jula origins. Because so little is known, a discussion of some of their distinguishing characteristics, acquired during the course of their migrations, seems more appropriate. Faced with a somewhat different interpretive problem in his study of Hausa traders, Cohen (1969, 1971) has used the concept of diaspora as the theoretical framework for an inquiry into the cultural strategies of trading relationships away from the traders' homeland. In his study of a select group of nineteenth-century Hausa kola traders, Lovejoy (1971, 1973) approaches a similar problem by separating "the dispersed settlements of the diaspora" from "the homeland, where most of the professional traders of a commercial network maintained their residency." Finally, in his inquiries into jula trading networks in the Black Volta region and into Hausa communities in Yoruba towns, Wilks (1968) has stressed adherence to the Islamic faith, learning, institutions, and communities as the *modus operandi* for developing and maintaining an autonomous diaspora culture.

A discussion of the homeland and original societies of the julas seems inadvisable given the state of present knowledge. The methodological problems are compounded by the fact that, unlike Hausa traders, who lived in or near Hausa cities (Lovejoy 1973:634), the julas have been divorced from their original societies. Moreover, neither linguistic data nor oral traditions throw adequate light on these societies, although the general area of the Upper Niger has been suggested as a possible homeland and the Soninke and early Manding trading clans as likely societies of origin. Similarly, linguistics provides no certain indication of when jula trading groups acquired their distinguishing characteristics, although sometime during or after the late fourteenth and early fifteenth centuries has been suggested.

Accordingly, no schema parallel to Lovejoy's distinction between the Hausa homeland and the diaspora network can yet be developed for the julas. Rather, the focus is on those features that distinguish the julas from other related and similar groups and on their cultural strategies. Our time period is from the late fourteenth through the nineteenth century, when numbers of Manding traders migrated from their original societies and developed the structure and diaspora culture of their trading networks. Problems stem from generalizing across centuries, and data may be inadequately treated; for a compressed study of complex social, economic, and political phenomena, however, this approach seems viable, pending further archival and field investigation.

Fundamental among jula distinguishing characteristics are the dialects most commonly spoken. The jula dialects — Bambara (Bamana), Maninka, Manya, Dyula, Khasonke, Wangara, Marka, Dafing, etc., referred to collectively as "Manding dialects" — form part of the northern subgroup of languages which unfortunately has come be known by the similar name "Mande" (Bird 1970; Dalby 1972). The latter trace their origin to "Mandekan" or "Mande" on the Upper Niger, and Greenberg (1966) has classified them as Niger-Congo.[2] Today, Manding-speakers (first and second language) occupy an area extending from north of the Gambia in the west to the Volta River in the east and from the Mali-Mauritania border in the north to Liberia, Sierra Leone, and Guinea in the south, as well as parts of northern Ghana. Where they occur, Soninke *jamu* [patronyms] form a second distinguishing characteristic of jula communities. Although a member of the Mande language group, Soninke is not a Manding dialect. It probably separated from the parent group sometime before the Christian era.[3] In contrast, Manding dialect differentiation is believed to have occurred during the fourteenth century (Wilks 1962:337–341). Linguistic differences apart, early jula associations with Soninke-speaking people somehow seem likely, at least in those instances where Soninke patronyms have prevailed. Some of these Soninke were associated with the Niger town of Jenne, which the julas subsequently incorporated into their trading networks, probably sometime during or after the thirteenth century, when the town's commercial activities were expanding (Monteil 1932:29–36). Status and commercial function, reinforced by Islam, represent a third distinguishing characteristic of jula communities as opposed to the sedentary agricultural, animist Manding-speaking (Malinke) clans into which they sometimes married.

---

[2] Welmers (1958:19) argues that "Mande had long been an independent entity before any of the other branches of Niger-Congo began their separate existence. Indeed the position of Mande in Niger-Congo is somewhat parallel to the position of Hittite in Indo-European."
[3] Curtin (1975:72) indicates that oral traditions trace all Soninke to Wagadu in western Mali (not to be confused with Wagadugu in Upper Volta).

JULA MIGRATIONS

It is likely that the júlas' characteristics evolved during the course of their migrations. These may be traced to the late fourteenth and early fifteenth centuries, when Manding trading clans moved southward into the Upper Niger region and then toward the Black Volta and the Akan goldfields (Goody 1964; Wilks 1971:354).

Moreover, probably in the late fourteenth century, similar Islamicized trading clans migrated along with animist warrior (Malinke) and *numu* [blacksmith] groups into Upper Guinea, where they settled in such *kafu* [administrative units] as Kono and Kuranko.[4] By the late fifteenth century, trading groups with Soninke and Upper Niger associations had migrated to Diakhaba, a clerical town on the Bafing in Senegambia, where they established an exchange center for nearby Bambuhu (Bambuk) gold and merchandise shipped overland from the north. Some settled at Gadiaga on the Senegal, another clerical and trading town in competition with Diakhaba.[5] Other such trading clans migrated eastward to Hausaland during the last two decades of the fifteenth century, where they contributed to the spread of Islam at the Kano court (al-Hajj 1968:8–16).

In the sixteenth century (during the reign of Na Yedega), Manding trading clans migrated into Mossi settlements in Yatenga, where they developed centers such as Gourcey. During the seventeenth century, migrations also occurred into other Mossi areas, such as the Kaya and Mane districts of Wagadugu and Dagomba (Izard 1965:72–75). Finally, between the sixteenth and eighteenth centuries, trading clans migrated into parts of the Ivory Coast (such as Kong), Sierra Leone, Liberia, and Guinea. By the eighteenth century, therefore, Manding traders had extended their enterprises from Senegambia to northern Nigeria and from the Niger to just north of the forest zone. In the west, Manding trading clans had established centers in areas which previously had been settled mainly by Malinke. In the east, at Yatenga and Wagadugu, in the Black Volta and Akan regions, and in northern Nigeria, they settled among mixed communities.

Although it was Islamicized trading clans (which Tauxier [1921] called

[4] Wilks (1961:337–338) suggests the fourteenth-century date. Both Person (1967) and Goody (1964), however, use a later one, something closer to the middle of the fifteenth century.
[5] Sanneh (1976) points out that while traders were associated with Diakhaba, it was founded as a clerical town. To this extent he is in disagreement with Curtin (1971, 1975), who attributes a clerical origin only to Gadiaga. Moreover, according to Sanneh (p. 60), resident merchants at Diakhaba "were not a collective commercial guild, and they never undertook trade as professional carriers nor as resident agents with monopoly control." On the founding of Diakhaba, Sanneh's evidence suggests some time around the mid-twelfth to thirteenth century. The late fifteenth-century date in the text is Curtin's.

"proto-dyula") that initially migrated from the Upper Niger, it was the julas who emerged. Unfortunately, we cannot be sure of the changes wrought by these migrations, nor can we trace the course of jula development. For example, we know little about the Nono, a Soninke subgroup associated with Jenne sometime between the eleventh and thirteenth centuries. We need more information on how and why the julas claim early association with the Soninke. Moreover, it is not clear when or how julas acquired regional nomenclature; they are called Marka in the Niger bend, Yarse in Voltaic states, and Dafing in the Black Volta region. Nor have their early trading activities in Jenne and the Niger towns and their links with the trans-Saharan commerce been clarified. We can, however, indicate at least three developments:

First, some julas appear to have changed their dialect, for although many early trading clans had Soninke associations, today most are Manding-speaking. Even the current Soninke word for "itinerant trader" (*jūla*) is a Manding loanword (Dalby 1972:7). It seems likely, therefore, that as the trading clans migrated, dialect differentiation was accelerated. Second, dialect differentiation seems to have coincided approximately with the "Mandingization" of the trading clans. During the later years of the Mali Empire, when long-distance trade networks were being organized, administrators extended their patronage especially to the gold trade,[6] which was a jula enterprise. This recognition may have contributed to the Mandingization of the clans at the expense of the Soninke. We can only speculate on the extent of this development by the nineteenth century. It may have been considerable in Upper Guinea, around Kono and Kuranko, and in the Senegambian waterways approaching Diakhaba and Gadiaga. Even so, Mandingization was not complete. As late as the 1860's, Mage (1866) remarked that Soninke julas were in evidence in the Western Sudan and were "slightly less reduced in importance" than in the days of the Ghana Empire.[7] Third, those trading clans which migrated to Hausaland completely changed their language, as according to Barth (1865:111) they had "entirely forgotten" their mother tongue and were speaking Fulfulde and "even Hausa." Trading clans which settled east of the Black Volta, in the Mossi region of Dagomba, Wa, and Gonja, also abandoned their dialects and adopted the languages of their host communities. Consequently, while the western Mandingization laid the groundwork for the emergence of

---

[6] Both the Ghanian and Malian administrations controlled the circulation of gold (el-Bakri 1956:331; al-'Umari 1972:72, 79). Leo Africanus (Jean-Léon l'Africain 1956:466) indicated the Malian administration's interest in long-distance trade when he reported that "foreign" merchants were held in higher esteem than their local counterparts.

[7] Curtin (1975:69) indicates that by the seventeenth century the Soninke who remained Soninke in speech and culture were principally based in Gadiaga in Senegambia, while "Mandingized" Soninke (Diakhanke) were principally based at Diakhaba on the Bafing "but gradually pushing their sphere to the west and south."

jula culture, the eastern assimilation, wherever it occurred, created the preconditions for the emergence of other long-distance traders who still claim Soninke-Manding associations but are now known by other names.

As the julas migrated, they developed Western Sudanese resources by organizing trading networks and commercial partnerships and by applying their organizational, managerial, and financial skills to production and distribution. They also contributed to the spread of gold-mining techniques, kola-nut culture, and the textile industry.

JULA TRADING NETWORKS: GOLD

Sometime between the eleventh and fifteenth centuries, when the gold trade was in progress and the Manding migrations were just beginning, julas began to develop trade networks. Some of the earliest networks extended from Senegal, Upper Niger, and Wangara towns such as Gyaru, Kuga, Yarsna (al-Idrisi's Iresni), Sila, Barisa, and Takrur to Jenne and Timbuktu. As the yield of the Black Volta mines increased, networks were developed from towns such as Jorga (origin ca. 1000–1200), Bighu (Be'o, Bitu),[8] and Bona north to the Niger bend and, in the fifteenth century, into Mossi country. More westerly networks developed between the fifteenth and seventeenth centuries in the Upper Senegal and Gambian regions, all linked to the Bambuhu gold trade. After the seventeenth century, they extended south to the Futa Jalon. Westerly networks locked into the Niger Valley network at Segu and Sikasso, into the more westerly structures at points such as Joal and Portugal and at Gadiaga on the Senegal, and, after the seventeenth and nineteenth centuries, into the southern Kankan and Tuba trade routes respectively. There was also a southern network through which gold was shipped to Elmina and Axim, and, during the nineteenth century, even after production had declined, Black Volta gold was still circulating between Bonduku, Assini, Cape Coast, and Grand-Bassam.

Towns were focal points of trade and politics, and it is likely that they were essential to the development of jula diaspora culture. Very little is known of these early urban developments. Scattered descriptive references to julas in towns have survived in the works of Arab authors such as al-Bakri (1067), al-Idrisi (1154), and Ibn Battuta (1352–1353), as well as in those of early European voyagers such as Duarte Pacheco Pereira (ca. 1505), Richard Jobson (1623), and Mungo Park (1795–1797). Yet beyond general references to town planning, town life, commercial transactions, and central administrations, which oral accounts hardly clarify, little is known of these early towns which julas either founded or

[8]   Bighu was known as Bitu in the Western Sudan and may be the "Bitu" referred to in the Timbuktu ta'rikhs; see Tauxier (1921: ch. 3), Wilks (1971), and Hunwick (1973:204–205).

developed. Caution in attributing towns and urban expansion to the julas, and especially to specific Manding trading clans, is therefore advisable — although in some instances probable associations can be identified. For example, it is possible that some jula clans were long associated with specialized interests. In the case of the gold trade, we can identify gold merchants with Manding and/or Soninke patronyms from the Bamba, Kamaghate, Jabaghate, Timite, Kurubari, and Gbani clans, who developed Jenne and Bighu while organizing the gold route.[9] Members of these clans also may have been among those which opened the Volta mines. Presumably, as Voltaic interests expanded, probably during the seventeenth and eighteenth centuries, the Bamba extended their trade northeast from Bighu to Bole and Banda, thereby expanding the commercial scope of these towns, while the Kamaghate and the Jabaghate opened a commercial center at Yagbum. Between the seventeenth and mid-nineteenth centuries, the Kurubari, Jabaghate, Kambara, Kombila, and Bamba extended their commercial networks from Bighu to Bono-Manso. Similarly, the Timite may have expanded their enterprises, in the first part of the sixteenth century to Bono, which also may have been an earlier site for gold extraction (Levtzion 1968:7–9). Finally, jula clans from Bighu developed the commercial sectors of Bonduku, probably during the eighteenth century.[10] Thus, between the fifteenth and nineteenth centuries, the Voltaic gold networks probably were controlled by a group of Manding trading clans that can tentatively be associated with urban development. Some clan names are suggested in the northeast, where traders, ancestors of the Yarse, developed Gourcey and Wagadugu. On the eve of the eighteenth century, the Tarawiri (Troare) and Baro had clan representatives in Kong and in Bobo-Julasso. The Tarawiri were also in Wa and Nasa on the east bank of the Black Volta, where they were joined by the Konate, who also extended their interests to the settlement at Visi. On the Upper Niger, Sansanding was developed by the Komo, Berete, Jabi, Kone, and Cisse.

KOLA TRADING NETWORKS

Like gold networks, kola networks focused upon urban centers which Manding trading clans had established. Earlier towns were close to production centers, and what Bighu was to the Volta gold mines Man. in the western Ivory Coast was to the kola forests. Eventually all roads led to Kankan and Jenne. It should come as no surprise, therefore, that some clans which had interests in the gold trade were also associated with the

[9] For clan names, see Wilks (1971:355 and *passim*). The founding dates for Bighu are uncertain; the date cited here comes from Wilks (1971:356). Person (1972), who bases his calculations on evidence of migrations, suggests the fourteenth century.
[10] Person (1972) suggests the seventeenth century for the development of Bonduku.

kola business. Apparently these julas worked in conjunction with Malinke in the development of the southern kola routes and towns — a warrior-merchant combination which somehow anticipated Samori Touré in the latter part of the nineteenth century. Warriors assisted in the partial pacification of neighboring hostile rural populations which interrupted trade (Wilks 1971:382).

Accordingly, in combination with the pagan warrior Jomande, Dosso, and Sumahoro Malinke, the Bakayoko and Bamba were among the first to establish trading centers in the Man region, immediately north of the forest in the western Ivory Coast. By the late sixteenth century, Islamicized Watara horsemen and Dosso assisted julas in the founding of Old Soron, south of what became Mankono. Like Bighu in the east and Diakhaba in the west, Old Soron became a center for further dispersals. As networks extended north to Jenne, the jula-Watara combination founded Kong and Bobo-Julasso, probably in the eighteenth century. Shehu 'Umar Watara (d. 1745–1746) and his brother Fa Maghan Watara (d. 1750–1751) have been associated with these endeavors (Wilks 1971:382). Similarly, as the demand for kola increased, the Jomande and the trading Binate founded Seguela (Stryker 1969:17, 25) just south of Mankono in the Ivory Coast, where they were later joined by the Timite and Bakayoko trading clans. About the same time, the Jomande achieved dominance over the Tuba region in the west, where by the nineteenth century the Fadiga trading clan had settled in the town of Tuba. Meanwhile (ca. 1780), the Dosso authorized the Muslim Karamoko to settle Mankono as a rival center to Seguela, to which the Cisse and the Bamba later migrated (Stryker 1969:25).

By the nineteenth century, kola networks focused upon Kong, Odienne, and Kankan, on which most major western routes converged. From these centers, networks fanned north to Middle Niger towns: from Kong to Bobo-Dioulasso to San and Sefara, both in Mali, or from Odienne north to Tengrela (northwest Ivory Coast), Sikasso (Mali), and Sarro (Mali). Others ran south from Odienne to Kani and Zuenula in Guru country. Farther west, kola networks extended northeast from the Rivers to centers such as Kono, Kisi, Knoya in Sierra Leone, and Guinea and north from Kankan to Sansanding (Mali) and Sarro. Finally, from Kankan in Guinea, they extended south to Kissi Beyla (Guinea) in Toma country and Danane (western Ivory Coast), Tuleplu (northeast Ivory Coast), and Tappi (eastern Liberia) in Guerze country (Gallais 1967:476–478).

In effect, by the nineteenth century, the kola networks were linked with the gold networks of the Upper Senegal, Upper Niger, and Black Volta towns.[11] Jula enterprise had extended throughout large areas of West

---

[11]   Binger (1892:315) reported that the julas of Kong were combining the diminishing gold trade with the expanding kola commerce and the coastal trade.

Africa. The evidence above suggests at least two observations: First, jula trade routes and migrations overlapped in every instance. Migrating julas extended the range of long-distance markets in West Africa from Senegambia in the west to northern Nigeria and from the western savanna to the forest and beyond. Second, the extent of jula culture corresponded with their market range: a supportive culture, which included language, religion, and social relations, developed wherever jula enterprises were established. In order to increase business opportunities, julas forged alliances with those who might aid their cause, whether coreligionists or animists. The kola trade was probably more challenging than the gold trade. Long-distance trade in a rather perishable commodity called for advance planning, reliable partnerships, quick decisions, and a fairly rapid means of transport. A few days' delay could make a difference in profits. Furthermore, raids by hostile populations on towns and caravans threatened the jula's livelihood, in some instances even his life, and winning the trust of the kola producers in the forest was no mean feat for the Muslim jula, who was suspect by virtue of his "stranger" status. Yet the supportive diaspora culture made these business exchanges possible, even in kola country on the fringes of jula networks.

THE POLITICS OF JULA CULTURE

This identification of julas with trade routes, towns, alliances, and partnerships is central to an understanding of the structure of their culture. Once divorced from their homeland, major jula clans became pillars of an autonomous culture which gave the appearance of being permanently in diaspora. Unlike itinerant Hausa traders, who traveled to distant lands, julas tended to identify more with the regions and host communities into which they had migrated. Accordingly, the cultural strategies which evolved over a long period of time were designed not only to enhance their commercial endeavors, but to mitigate their *dunan* [stranger] status. A range of relationships, customs, symbols, and ideologies came into existence which enabled julas to operate within the wide geographical, social, and political range just described. Commercial transactions involved members of the principal resident or urban jula clans as partners, patrons, protectors, hosts, and intermediaries between the itinerant julas and the host community. Invariably these arrangements invoked the cultural constant of kinship conceptualization. The politics of jula culture also included managerial and financial skills, know-how in labor recruitment and security provisions for the journey, and criteria for decision making and action: when to abandon one market for another, how to verify news of good prices in distant markets. Finally, the politics of jula culture revolved around shared ethnic and religous affinities, common patronyms, language, myths of a homeland, contracts and social connections, the seeking and granting of favors, honesty, trust, and a host of intangibles which bound rooted hierarchical societies, on the one hand, to an extremely mobile trading group, on the other. (For a discussion of these customs and institutions, see Launay 1972.)

Jula cultural strategies required the peripatetic traders to demonstrate their identity and to establish partnerships by association either with a sedentary urban lineage or with coreligionists. The *jatigi* [patron, protector, partner — the Manding word might be translated "soul lord"] represented the stable side of the partnership. Frequently a jula who had abandoned the traveling life, tended to be the main source of capital, labor, organizational skills, and advice on market conditions. On the other side of the partnership, the mobile jula contributed his time, labor, and situational market skills.

While the literature provides insights into the functions of the peripatetic jula, there are few satisfactory accounts of the *jatigi*'s role in precolonial days. Most Arab and European authors either failed to recognize his function or were barred from observing jula-*jatigi* transactions. The two best accounts come from Binger (1892; 1903:92–93) and Dubois (1897:298–299), who as "strangers" were apparently assigned to *jatigis* and whose descriptions, incidentally, are similar to those contained in Meillassoux's (1963) account of the Niare traditions of Bamako. (Accounts of the *jatigi*'s function are also found in *Gazette Géographique* 1886 and *Bulletin de la Société de Géographie Commerciale de Paris* 1889–1890.) According to these observers, the *jatigi* provided accommodations, informed the jula of market conditions, offered the use of his house for commercial transactions, initiated negotiations with prospective buyers, and guaranteed the integrity of buyer and seller to their mutual satisfaction — an important service if credit transactions were involved. He gave advice on local matters from trade routes to trinkets, from kolas to cowries, and, where necessary, acted as a local guide. The *jatigi*, moreover, was a liaison between the jula and the local authorities, to whom he guaranteed the trader's integrity. Furthermore, the *jatigi* stored the jula's merchandise during the latter's absence and made sales on market demand, reporting the profits, minus his commission (where it was customary for him to take one), to the jula on his return. Where slaves were brought into a local market, the *jatigi* might arrange for slave lodgings; he might assist in the purchase of more slaves by acting as intermediary with his approximate counterpart in the slave trade. It was probably also he who requested the armed slave guard for caravans en route from the *jagotigi* [trade master]. Moreover, he advanced credit, and some of the largest creditors were Arab and Berber dealers from Timbuktu commercial houses. If Valentim Fernandes is correct, credit was sometimes given for a year, without collateral, witnesses, or any written statement (Fernandes 1938:87). Dubois (1897:301–302) reports that the period could sometimes be extended to two or three years, and if the jula never returned "it [was] . . . less by dishonesty than by wars and insecurity of routes." If he died before meeting his debts, his relatives would honor them.

THE INFLUENCE OF ISLAM: TRADING PARTNERSHIPS

The politics of jula culture seemingly required, moreover, that partnerships be structured, presumably according to Islamic principles. We are largely ignorant of the specific ways in which Islam performed this function in jula communities, although we know that partnerships for long-distance trade were widespread throughout medieval Europe (Postan 1927) as well as in Arabic and Islamic trading communities (Caiani 1953; Goitein 1964). Cohen (1971:276) has referred to Islam as the "blueprint" for commercial organization among Hausa traders in Yorubaland. Similarly, Wilks (1968:162–197) has explained the Islamic educational and social links between dispersed communities, while Lovejoy (1971:540) has shown that Islam performed an important function among other itinerant groups, such as the Yarse and Dendi.

Important as these contributions may be, they give few technical insights into the character of partnerships. Islamic law offers precise models for various types of commercial partnerships and agreements (Udovitch 1970:170–248): proprietary partnership (*sharikat al-milk*), Hanafi *mūfawaḍa* partnership, Hanafi limited investment partnership (*'inān*), Malikī partnership, and *commenda* (*muḍāraba, qirāḍ, muqāraḍa*). The *commenda* was the principal formula by which long-distance trade was undertaken in Islamic communities. It enabled an investor or group of investors to entrust capital or merchandise to an agent-manager, who traded with it and returned the principal and previously agreed-upon share of profits to the investor. The agent received the remaining share of the profits as a reward for his time and labor. He was considered trustworthy with respect to the capital he handled and could not be held liable for any loss occurring in the normal course of business.

The simplest form of *commenda* was a unilateral arrangement in which the investor was the sole source of capital. Such an arrangement might be restricted by geographical area, market location, or commodity specialization. On the completion of business, the previously agreed-upon profits were shared proportionately by investor and agent. While Islamic law made no provision for a standard division, custom determined divisions of one third to two thirds, one quarter to three quarters, two fifths to three fifths, and sometimes even half and half. In the bilateral *commenda*, which in every other respect resembled the unilateral one, part of the capital was furnished by the agent. Here according to Maliki law — the sole law in West Africa — profit sharing was not proportional, but limited to the sum contributed by each partner to the total capital. Neither investor nor agent could claim profits on capital invested by the other. The *commenda,* which combined the advantages of a loan with those of partnership, was a contract which regulated the use of capital, trading skills, and labor for mutual profit. Similar to the *commenda* was the *ijāra* or hire contract. Here the employer or investor supplied the capital while the agent or employee offered his time, labor, and skills. All profits accrued to the employer-investor, and all losses were borne by him. The agent or employee was entitled to an equitable remuneration (*air mithluhu*) in addition to specified expenses.

Amselle (1971) has described *jūla-ba/jūla-den* relationships among the Kooroko of Bamako (and formerly of Wasulu). In one kind of contract, the junior partner begins by receiving his keep as "wages" and turning over all profits to the senior; after a certain period of time, however, he is entitled to request a lump sum with which to trade on his own behalf. Refusal to honor this request on the part of the *jūla-ba* would break the contract, and so would irresponsible use of the sum granted on the part of the *jūla-den*. Success in this endeavor results in a continuing partnership in which profits and losses are shared two thirds to one third or sometimes even half and half between senior and junior. Amselle's description comes from the postcolonial era; his data suggest that the relationship may be considerably older, but extrapolation requires extreme caution. These observations on the technical aspects of precolonial trading relationships are therefore tentative pending further investigation.

GOLD AND KOLA PRODUCTION

If julas developed resources such as trade networks, markets, capital, partnerships, as well as managerial and organizational skills, they also contributed indirectly to the expansion of gold production. Arab accounts contain references to gold merchants, whom they called Wangara, and to their valuable commodity. While al-Mas'udi, the tenth-century Baghdad geographer, was the first to report on silent gold exchanges (Kamal 1926–1938:623–639, 651), el-Bakri's account contains what may be the earliest reference to black "Noughmarta" (*wangharata*: Wangara) who were selling "Ghiarou gold . . . the best in the country" at Iresni (el-Bakri 1956:331, 31). Moreover, Yaqut, who wrote in the thirteenth century, was probably the earliest to mention the brokerage (*samāsira* [broker, middleman, agent]) system of partnerships to which I have referred above (Farias 1974:11).

While julas aided gold production indirectly by marketing gold, tradi-

tions suggest that they also played a part in the spread of mining techniques from the older Bambuhu mines to the Akan and Black Volta
mines, more specifically in the areas of Banda and Bono-Manso. Evidently a relationship of trust developed between producers and distributors, as, according to Fernandes, the julas had a monopoly on the
gold trade, if only because no other outsiders were permitted (Mauny
1961:239–244). Unfortunately, tradition tells us no more. We do not
know when mining was first introduced — although the fifteenth century,
which corresponds with the Manding migrations, does not sound
unreasonable. Furthermore, there are virtually no data on whether julas
introduced new mining techniques or modified existing ones. According
to evidence gathered by Meyerowitz (1958:115, 117, 120), several of the
kings of the early Akan state of Bono-Manso (ca. 1450–1550) imported
Wangara mining specialists from the Upper Niger region to assist in the
development of the gold fields of Nsoko.

It seems reasonable to suggest that julas also contributed to the expansion of kola production. Attempts to discuss the early kola trade unfortunately are restricted by scarcity of data. Dazzled by the glamorous gold
trade, Arab writers were sparing in their references to the seemingly
humble fruit, and, like the gold producers, kola producers veiled their
activities in secrecy. Pending further investigation, we may only sketch
general outlines.

While kola trees may have grown wild in the forest, kola culture was
probably an early development. The kola nut, resembling the chestnut,
was highly valued in West Africa as a symbol of vigor and power. Used
sometimes as a mild stimulant among Muslims, whose religion forbade
the use of alchohol, kola nuts also were part of the ritual associated with
marriage and other contracts among both animists and Muslims. Kolas
may have been traded within the Western Sudan from as early as the
eighth century. Julas began developing the kola (*Stercullia macrocarpa*)[12]
trade sometime in the fourteenth century. Kola nuts probably were used,
along with *sompe* [iron bars], in salt exchanges in forest areas where there
was no gold. Apart from two early references (al-'Umari and al-
Maqqari)[13] to kolas on sale in North Africa, however, Arabs seem to have
been slow to recognize their properties. Kola nuts were not included in
the Arab pharmacopoeia until the eighteenth century, and Europeans did
not recognize their value until the nineteenth.

---

[12]   *Sterculia acuminata*, or red kola nut, which was not traded along the Kong-Bobo-
Dioulasso route until the twentieth century, came from the Asante region and was marketed
mainly in Salaga.
[13]   According to Person (1968) and Mauny (1961:248–250), both al-'Umari (fourteenth
century) and al-Maqqari (seventeenth century, reporting on thirteenth-century trading
practices) referred to the trade, the latter reporting that kola nuts were for sale in Tlemcen.
The first description of the trade comes from Leo Africanus; Cadamosto, Pacheco Pereira,
and Fernandes also refer to it. See also Lewicki (1974:122–123).

Julas aided kola production by expanding existing markets. Moreover, special relationships of trust, including partnerships and brokerage, with kola producers in the forest seem to have developed, because the latter kept their techniques secret (Binger 1892:141–144; Meillassoux 1964: ch. 11; also 1962–1963). Indeed, some market locations were known only to the most trusted dealers. Once more, we are ignorant of the precise ways in which the julas may have utilized these trust relationships and the extent to which they influenced production directly. It seems reasonably clear, however, that between the fifteenth and eighteenth centuries they expanded markets by establishing trading centers on the forest fringe in Worodugu (*woro* 'kola', *dugu* 'country') in the Ivory Coast. Within this zone, the centers were Kono, Kisi, Toma, and Guerze country in the west and, to a lesser extent, Guru country. In the east they established contact with the Ano kola producers, and, as early as the sixteenth century, animist and Muslim Manding had developed kola production and trade in the regions of Gonja. Apart from the observation that julas were forbidden to enter the forest, we know little about these early kola production and trading interactions. In most instances, merchandise was brought out of the forests to prearranged contact zones by autochthonous middlemen with whom the julas had trading agreements. Equally little is known about early production and trade volumes in markets such as Grumania and Mango in the Komoe Valley (Ivory Coast).

TEXTILE TRADE AND INDUSTRY

Julas also made important contributions to the textile industry. Increased demand for textiles frequently followed conversion, as Muslims wore long, flowing garments, and in a number of instances trade and industry followed the Qur'an. Moreover, in parts of the Western Sudan, especially in Senegambia, cloth was used as currency from as early as the fourteenth century. Jula market exchanges and need for currencies therefore stimulated the cloth industry.

Julas' contributions to the textile industry were, however, more fundamental than providing increased market demands for currency and clothing. In this case they actually organized and controlled production. Long-distance trading and weaving occupations frequently were found in the same lineages, especially that of the Jawara. Hence julas, more probably those with Soninke patronyms, were in a position to spread weaving techniques throughout the Western Sudan, even as far east as Asante, where the latter's strip weaving is known today as "Kente cloth." Moreover, frequent overlap of weaving and trading lineages enabled them to control and organize textile production as well as distribution.

Apart from a few Arab and early European travelers' accounts, few written sources throw light on the production and distribution aspects of the trade. According to Mauny (1961:343–345), who relies on these Arabic and European sources, textile weaving developed about the beginning of the eleventh century, probably in the region of the Senegal River. By the sixteenth century, the industry had grown considerably in response to domestic market demands, which Mauny estimates as small, together with those of the Sahara and the Maghreb. Most textile industries were urban-based, and textile centers were found extending from the Senegal region in the west to Kanem and Bornu in the east and from Guinea to the Gambia. Cotton clothing evidently was worn by the well-to-do urban inhabitants. Arabic and European accounts also suggest that Gao cloth, when sold to Saharan Berbers, competed in desert markets with leather and wool fabrics. Available knowledge about Manding social structure may also offer insights as to how innovations in cloth production may have spread. It is generally agreed that migrating Manding groups often reproduced the social structures of their parent communities: each ideally contained the main patrilineage (*jgmu*), *felaton* [age-groups], each with its *tontigi* [chief], *jo* [secret societies], *jali* [griots], *numu* [blacksmiths], and *jon* and *woroso* [slaves] (Hopkins 1971).

Because it was common for members of the same or related specialized lineages to work collectively, we may assume that julas had direct access to the means of textile production. For example, in the eighteenth century, the Ture lineage, which claimed Soninke associations, had traders and weavers within its ranks. Organizing and controlling a large labor force drawn from the lineage and from captives, they engaged in village-based textile production throughout the western part of Worodugu. Similarly, in Gbaralo and Maafele in the Wasulu region and at Samatigila, the Ture organized and controlled large groups engaged in textile production and marketed finished products along with kola nuts (Person 1968:120).

In Senegambia, where cloth currencies were in use, the Manding traders of Bondu also controlled cotton culture and production. It is not clear whether labor from the lineage was utilized, although slaves and Fulbe free laborers seem to have been employed. In the east, the spread of the textile industry to Voltaic towns coincided with the development of the gold trade, which suggests that weavers and traders may have migrated together. A similar phenomenon is suggested farther north, where the Yarse (the regional name for julas among the Mossi-Dagbane of Wagadugu and farther east from Buna to Salaga) were combining weaving and dyeing with the marketing of cloth. Others were functioning as middlemen for small producers, whose produce they sold in bulk (Izard 1965:219). The most interesting example of Manding industrial enterprise comes from Caillié's, (1830:113) celebrated account of the Manding female "industrialist" from Segu who bought cotton in bulk from Tengre in the northern Ivory Coast and farmed it out to slave labor, which she apparently controlled.

CONCLUSION

While their role in long-distance trade is beyond dispute, julas are not as a rule associated with production. For the most part, the literature portrays them as market-oriented distributors who accumulated mercantile capital. Yet this brief inquiry into the textile industry has identified their role in those production sectors to which their lineages had access. Kinship and migration were apparently the crucial factors. We know that in the region of Jenne, where many jula lineages resided, they developed and organized farms that provided Timbuktu with most of its food supply. The evidence suggests, therefore, that where location and lineage ties permitted, julas were capable of entering into the production sector.

This hypothesis is reinforced by other evidence that suggests the absence of jula involvement in production activities in sectors from which their lineages were excluded — gold and kola production. Here julas were "strangers" even among Manding people, with whom they shared a cultural and linguistic heritage. In the forest areas where kola was produced, julas were not only "strangers," but, as Binger (1892:141–144) observed, were forbidden direct access to the area. In fact, they seem to have been the only "strangers" the forest-dwellers of the Ivory Coast hinterland would permit anywhere near the kola areas. Meillassoux's (1964:79) data suggest a similar separation from the kola-production sector. Apparently, during the colonial era, the northern patrilineal Guru of the Ivory Coast, who harvest kola nuts, sold them to the Vaa (regional name for julas) at a higher price than the regional exchange rate because they were "strangers." Restricted by social distance, it is unlikely that julas could have participated directly in kola production.

While jula endeavors had but slight impact on the methods of production of West African economies, they expanded existing markets, incorporating large sections of West Africa into a long-distance market economy. Even areas on the periphery of the forest zone, which hitherto had had but marginal associations with long-distance exchanges, were brought into the wider market nexus. This expansion affected regional and social production-consumption ratios. For example, on the production side, Malinke blacksmiths in the region of Tuba, Seguela, and Mankono (Worodugu) responded to expanded market demands by increasing production of the iron bars which were used as currency (Stryker 1969:18). On the consumption side, the increased wealth which julas brought to Worodugu communities (in the form of either gifts, trade, revenues, or immigrants) was sometimes redistributed to the community through existing political processes. Moreover, as some Malinke chiefs of Worodugu accumulated wealth in the form of slaves, cloth, kola nuts, and edible provisions, their potential for control over other resources, including people, increased (Stryker 1969:29).

It is difficult to generalize about the degree of involvement of julas in the politics of the communities in which they resided, partly because this varied greatly over time and with the region in which they settled. The political role of julas is a complex topic open to much further research. With the notable exception of Samori Touré, the julas were not great state or empire builders. In general, they avoided struggles for political power in their host communities and preferred the right to trade to the power to rule. This is not to say that they shunned participation in government or lacked political influence. As semipermanent traders, they obviously controlled their own quarters of the towns in which they settled, and they frequently served as advisers and officials of the kings and chiefs of states. More than this, a number of writers have suggested that early Muslim traders from Mali may have brought the first knowledge of political organization and bureaucracy to the early kingdoms of the northern Akan and Middle Black Volta regions. This influence was probably even stronger where the indigenous rulers became Muslims. Thus Wilks (1971:432, 450–453) has shown that julas from Bighu who later settled in Gonja were awarded the *imamates* of the divisional capitals of the Muslim kingdom. Here their roles as literate Muslims in interpreting the Qur'anic law and presiding over religious functions could be extremely important. In other parts of this region, pluralistic states (e.g., Gyaman, Wa, and Chakosi) were established in which the political offices were sometimes divided between the julas and other ethnic groups. In a majority of instances in more recent times it is probably accurate to say that julas have preferred to maintain a "background" or low-profile political role. This and their ability to assimilate to local customs while maintaining their identity may have been in part a strategy which ensured their survival for approximately 500 years as protected "strangers" in non-jula and non-Manding communities. Wending their way through a maze of commercial, lineage, marital, and religious encounters, they effectively used their political acumen to maintain the support of rulers who had the power to frustrate or destroy them.

As part of their strategy, on the one hand, julas offered gifts and paid tariffs to local rulers in return for settlement rights, including usufruct rights to agricultural lands. On the other hand, they kept their distance by maintaining their autonomy, especially in urban areas, through the establishment of imams and mosques, religious observances, and in some instance Qur'anic schools which attracted marabouts and *talibé* from far afield. As Islamic and Manding subgroups within a larger community, they retained in-group cohesiveness by tending to identify more with internal cultural norms than with out-group or external criteria. Conceivably, had julas adopted a militant religious-commercial policy their development in diaspora would have been different. Maintaining social, cultural, and political distance from their host communities made possible the jula imprint on West African cultural pluralities.

REFERENCES

AL-HAJJ, MUHAMMAD
  1968   A seventeenth-century chronicle on the origins and missionary activities of the "Wangara." *Kano Studies* 1(4):1–16.
AL-'UMARI, IBN FADL ALLAH
  1972   *L'Afrique moins l'Egypte*. Translated from the Arabic by Maurice Gaudfroy-Demombymes. Paris.
AMSELLE, JEAN-LOUP
  1971   "Parenté et commerce chez les Kooroko," in *The development of indigenous trade and markets in West Africa*. Edited by Claude Meillassoux. London: Oxford University Press.
BARTH, HEINRICH
  1865   *Travels and discoveries in North and Central Africa, 1849–85*, volume three. New York.
BERNUS, E.
  1960   Kong et sa région. *Etudes Eburnéennes* 8:245–251.
BINGER, LOUIS
  1892   *Du Niger au Golfe du Guinée*, volume one. Paris.
  1903   Le péril de l'Islam. *Bulletin du Comité de l'Afrique Française, Renseignement Coloniaux* 11:92–93.
BIRD, CHARLES B.
  1970   "The development of Mandekan (Manding): a study of the role of extra-linguistic factors in linguistic change," in *Language and history in Africa*. Edited by D. Dalby. London: Frank Cass.
Bulletin de la Société de Géographie Commerciale de Paris
  1889–1890   Transactions, objet de commerce, monnaie des contrées d'entre le Niger et la Côte d'Ivoire. *Bulletin de la Société de Géographie Commerciale de Paris* 12:77–90.
CAIANI, ALBERTO
  1953   The juridical nature of the Moslem *qirād* partnership. *East and West* 4(2):81–86.
CAILLIÉ, RENÉ
  1830   *Travels through Central Africa to Timbuctoo*, volume two. Translated from the French. London: Colburn and Bentley.
COHEN, ABNER
  1969   *Custom and politics in urban Africa*. Berkeley: University of California Press.
  1971   "Cultural strategies in the organization of trading diasporas," in *The development of indigenous trade and markets in West Africa*. Edited by Claude Meillassoux. London: Oxford University Press.

CURTIN, PHILIP D.
1971   "Precolonial trading networks and traders: the Diakhanke," in *The development of indigenous trade and markets in West Africa*. Edited by Claude Meillassoux. London: Oxford University Press.
1975   *Economic change in precolonial Africa: Senegambia in the era of the slave trade*. Madison: University of Wisconsin Press.
DALBY, DAVID
1972   "The people and their language," in *Manding: focus on an African civilisation*. Edited by Guy Atkins. London: School of Oriental and African Studies, Centre for African Studies.
DUBOIS, FÉLIX
1897   *Tombouctou la mystérieuse*. Paris.
EL-BAKRI, ABOU-OBEID
1956   *Description de l'Afrique septentrionale*. Translated from the Arabic by M. de Slane. Paris.
FARIAS, P. F. DE MORAIS
1974   Silent trade: myth and historical evidence. *History in Africa* 1:9–24.
FERNANDES, VALENTIM
1938   *Description de la côte d'Afrique de Ceuta au Sénégal*. Edited by P. de Cernival and Th. Monod. Paris: Larose.
GALLAIS, JEAN
1967   *Le delta intérieur du Niger*, volume one. Mémoires de l'Institut Fondamental d'Afrique Noire 79.
Gazette Géographique
1886   Les routes commerciales du Soudan occidental. *Gazette Géographique* 12:342–356.
GINGISS, PETER
1972   "Dyula: a sociological perspective," in *Manding: focus on an African civilisation*. Edited by Guy Atkins. London: School of Oriental and African Studies, Centre for African Studies.
GOITEIN, S. D.
1964   Commercial and family partnerships in the countries of medieval Islam. *Islamic Studies* 3:315–337.
GOODY, JACK R.
1964   "The Mande and the Akan hinterland," in *The historian in tropical Africa*. Edited by Jan Vansina, R. Mauny, and L. V. Thomas, 193–213. London: Oxford University Press for the International African Institute.
GREENBERG, JOSEPH
1966   *The languages of Africa*. The Hague: Mouton.
HOPKINS, NICHOLAS
1971   "Mandinka social organization," in *Papers on the Manding*. Edited by Carleton T. Hodge. Bloomington: Indiana University Press.
HUNWICK, J. O.
1973   The mid-fourteenth century capital of Mali. *Journal of African History* 14:195–208.
IZARD, MICHAEL
1965   Traditions historiques des villages du Yatenga: cercle de Gouroy. *Recherches Voltaïques* 1:72–75.
1971   "Les Yarse et le commerce dans le Yatenga précolonial," in *The development of indigenous trade and markets in West Africa*. Edited by Claude Meillassoux. London: Oxford University Press.

JEAN-LEON L'AFRICAIN
1956   *Description de l'Afrique*, volume two. Translated and annotated by A. Epaulard, Th. Monod, H. Lhote, and R. Mauny. Paris: Maisonneuve.

KAMAL, YUSUF
1926–1938   *Monumenta cartographica Africae et Aegypti*, volume three. Cairo.

LAUNAY, ROBERT
1972   "Social organization," in *Manding: focus on an African civilisation.* Edited by Guy Atkins. London: School of Oriental and African Studies, Centre for African Studies.

LEVTZION, NEHEMIAH
1968   *Muslims and chiefs in West Africa.* London: Oxford University Press.

LEWICKI, T.
1974   *West African food in the Middle Ages.* Cambridge: Cambridge University Press.

LEWIS, BARBARA
1971   "The Dioula in the Ivory Coast," in *Papers on the Manding.* Edited by Carleton T. Hodge, 273–307. Bloomington: Indiana University Press.

LOVEJOY, PAUL E.
1971   Long-distance trade and Islam: the case of the nineteenth-century Hausa kola trade. *Journal of the Historical Society of Nigeria* 5:537–547.
1973   The Kambarin Beriberi: the formation of a specialized group of Hausa kola traders in the nineteenth century." *Journal of African History* 14:633–651.

MAGE, EUGENE
1866   Note sur le voyage de MM. Mage et Quintin au pays de Ségou. *Bulletin de la Société de Géographie de Paris* 7:306.

MAUNY, RAYMOND
1961   *Tableau géographique de l'Ouest africain au moyen âge d'après les sources écrites, la tradition et l'archéologie.* Mémoires de l'Institut Française d'Afrique Noire 61.

MEILLASSOUX, CLAUDE
1962–1963   L'économie de échanges pré-coloniaux en pays Gourou. *Cahiers d'Etudes Africaines* 3:551–576.
1963   Histoire et institutions du Kafo de Bamako. *Cahiers d'Etudes Africaines* 4:187–227.
1964   *Anthropologie économique des Gourou de Côte d'Ivoire.* Paris.

MEYEROWITZ, E.
1958   *The Akan of Ghana.* London: Faber and Faber.

MONTEIL, CHARLES
1932   *Une cité soudanaise: Djenné, métropolis du delta du Niger.* Paris.

PERINBAM, B. MARIE
1974   Notes on Dyula origins and nomenclature. *Bulletin de l'Institut Fondamental de l'Afrique Noire* 26:676–690.

PERSON, YVES
1964   "Enquête d'une chronologie ivorienne," in *The historian in tropical Africa.* Edited by Jan Vansina, R. Mauny, and L. V. Thomas, 322–338. London: Oxford University Press for the International African Institute.
1967   Samori et la Sierra Leone. *Cahiers d'Etudes Africaines* 7:25.
1968   *Samori: une révolution dyula*, volume one. Mémoires de l'Institut Fondamental d'Afrique Noire 80.

1972 "The Dyula in the Manding world," in *Manding: focus on an African civilisation*. Edited by Guy Atkins. London: School of Oriental and African Studies, Centre for African Studies.

POSTAN, M.
1927 "Partnership in English medieval commerce," in *Studi in onore de A. Sapori*, volume one, 521–549. Milan.

SANNEH, LAMINE
1976 The origins of clericalism in West African Islam. *Journal of African History* 17:49–72.

STRYKER, R.
1969 "The Mande of the northern Ivory Coast." Unpublished manuscript, Stanford University.

TAUXIER, LOUIS
1921 *Le Noir de Bondouku*. Paris.

THOMAS, LOUIS-VINCENT
1956 *Les Diola: essai d'analyse fonctionelle sur une population de Basse-Casamance*, two volumes. Mémoires de l'Institut Français de l'Afrique Noire 55.

UDOVITCH, ABRAHAM L.
1970 *Partnership and profit in medieval Islam*. Princeton: Princeton University Press.

WELMERS, W. E.
1958 *The Mande languages*. Georgetown University Monograph Series 11.

WILKS, IVOR
1961 *The northern factor in Ashanti history*. Legon: Institute of African Studies, University of Ghana.
1962 "A medieval trade route from the Niger to the Gulf of Guinea. *Journal of African History* 3:337–341.
1965 A note on the early spread of Islam to Dagomba. *Transactions of the Historical Society of Ghana* 8:87–98.
1968 "The transmission of Islamic learning in the Western Sudan," in *Literacy in the traditional societies*. Edited by Jack Goody, 162–197. Cambridge: Cambridge University Press.
1971 "The Mossi and Akan states 1500–1800," in *History of West Africa*, volume one. Edited by J. F. A. Ajayi and Michael Crowder, 344–386. London: Longman.

Slave Acquisition and Delivery in Precolonial Hausaland

JAN S. HOGENDORN

Research on slavery and the slave trade in the precolonial Sokoto Caliphate is now a thriving industry. Oral data collection has already filled many gaps in information left in the travelers' accounts of the nineteenth century (see Figure 1 for map of this area at that time). Such collections of data were largely begun by M G. Smith and Mary Smith in the late 1940's and 1950's (M. G. Smith 1954, 1955, 1960, 1965a, 1965b, 1967; Mary Smith 1954). The studies now extend to slave management, employment, living conditions, legal and social position, plantation operation, and prices (Hill 1972, 1975, 1976; Lovejoy 1976; Tambo 1976; Meillassoux 1975; Ayandele 1967; Klein and Lovejoy 1979). Very little of this research has, however, touched on the original acquisition of slaves and their initial delivery. Most authors include a section on how slaves were acquired, drawing largely on the nineteenth-century travelers, and most also make reference to the inquiries into slave origins made in Sierra Leone by S. W. Koelle, thirty-six of whose informants came from the caliphate (Hair 1965). The purpose of this paper is to examine slave acquisition and delivery with special reference to the Zaria Emirate of Hausaland, using oral data collected during 1975 to extend and emendate our knowledge of this relatively obscure aspect of the caliphate slave system. Its temporal frame of reference is largely the latter years of the nineteenth century.

Thanks are due to Henry Gemery of Colby College, Paul Lovejoy of York University, David Tambo of the University of Wisconsin, and Mahdi Adamu of Ahmadu Bello University for advice and encouragement. The main research assistants in collecting the oral data discussed in the paper were Muhammed Lawal, Yau Haruna, Yusufu Yunusa, and Ahmed Maccido. Funding for the project was generously provided through a Penrose Grant of the American Philosophical Society, a Cole Grant of the Council for Research in Economic History, a joint grant of the Social Science Research Council and the American Council for Learned Studies, and a grant from the Colby College Social Science Division's research funds.

Figure 1.   The Fulani empires of Sokoto and Gwandu (Nigeria and Central Sudan) in the mid-nineteenth century. *Source*: H. A. S. Johnston (1967)

RAIDING AND ACQUISITION

It has been a commonplace to state that original slave acquisition was due to wars and raids, tribute, kidnapping, and judicial process (Tambo 1976:199; Adamu 1979:166–199; Kopytoff and Miers 1977). The Zaria Emirate is presumably an excellent area in which to examine this contention, since Zaria was famous as a taker of slaves. The "slave raider *par excellence*," it had easy access to pagan populations of the plateau and in the area near the Benue River (Colvin 1971:124). Its speciality as a slaver-state seems to have been long-lasting. One myth of Zaria's origin refers to an eponymous ancestor who was a slave dealer (Fisher and Fisher 1970:5), and, most southerly of the Hausa Bokwoi (seven states), there was a long tradition which ascribed to it the role of slaver (Klein 1971:8; Mortimore 1970:102). Finally, the presence of numerous knowledgeable informants in Zaria and its vicinity, several of them former slaves themselves, made oral data collection there a feasible proposition.[1]

The first question on which some light may be shed is "What was slave raiding?" There is a distinct looseness of definition surrounding the use of the term "raid" or its synonym, "razzia." What is meant, for example, by Koelle when he says that twenty-one of his sample of thirty-six caliphate slaves were taken in war, while eight were kidnapped (Tambo 1976:199)? For Hausaland in general, this question is as little studied as it had been in Nupe, where Mason (1969:553) argues that "the term 'slave raiding', although widely used, is nowhere clearly defined."

Slave raiding might be a side effect of full-scale warfare, such as accompanied the growth and expansion of new savanna states like those of Ahmed of Hamdullahi, al-Hajj'Umar, Samori, Rabeh, and others (Lovejoy and Hogendorn 1979:221). This would presumably accord with the "political model," with slave acquisition as a by-product, discussed by Curtin (1975:156). At the other end of the spectrum might be the "free entry" into slave acquisition suggested by Thomas and Bean (1975), who argue that, as in an ocean fishery, any entrepreneur with the desire to do so might tap the available sources of supply. Organizing a raid, in this view, is a simple matter of "casting the nets" and bringing home the "catch."

For Zaria neither the war model nor the fisheries model appears to correspond very closely to reality, at least for the latter years of the nineteenth century, when good oral evidence is available. Meyers (1971:178) has already suggested for Hausaland as a whole that the warfare case would run afoul of the reluctance to enslave free Muslims (admittedly a reluctance often overcome) and the strategic difficulties of capturing and evacuating slaves in the midst of a full-scale war. From the documentary sources, Meyers argues that raids "organized with the express object of slave capture" were the much more likely source. Certainly this appears true for Zaria, as will be seen below. The fisheries analogy seems even less appropriate. Only the emir had the authority to authorize slaving expeditions, and violation was a penal offense (M. G.

---

[1] The main informants were, at Zaria, Mallam Shehu, about seventy-five years old, Mallam Muhammadu, about ninety, Mallam Sule, perhaps seventy-five, Mallam Adamu, about eighty, and, at Hanwa a few miles from Zaria, Mallam Bawa. Mallam Bawa (the name means "slave" in Hausa, but that is a naming coincidence having to do with his being a son following several daughters) was the son of a slave of Kwarama descent. His mother was also a slave. His father had become the Qur'anic teacher in Hanwa, and Mallam Bawa inherited from him a taste for history. His most patient assistance is gratefully acknowledged, as is the help of Bernard Buntjer of the Institute of Agricultural Research, Samaru, who introduced me to him. The complete tape recordings and Hausa transcripts of the interview referred to here will be deposited with the Department of History, Ahmadu Bello University, under the title "Hogendorn Collection." Each tape and transcript is marked with the interview number, and these numbers are used in the references below. The interviews were conducted between January and June of 1975.

Smith 1960:99; and oral evidence). Further, we will see that the taking of slaves was an expensive proposition undertaken against people who knew how to defend themselves. It was as if the fish could fight back.

What, then, was the usual method of slave acquisition in the Zaria Emirate, if not general warfare or a model of open fisheries? The evidence indicates that acquisition was ordinarily a product of well-organized raiding by government military units, either by the Zaria army, to enforce the payment of slaves by tributary states, or by these same tributary states on acephalous, nontributary neighbors far out on the emirate's periphery. The view is one of acquisition through design and not accident and of large enterprises involving substantial economies of scale.

The structure of tributary relations seems to have been of some antiquity. Johnston (1967:69) notes that by the end of the eighteenth century and antedating the Fulani conquest, five petty chiefs on the southern borders of Zaria (Zazzau) ruled a conglomerate of Gwari, Bassa, and others, all owing allegiance to the emir and paying tribute in slaves. Peoples not having made submission were fair game for slave raiding, either by the Zazzau army or by the tributaries themselves, with the result that the emirate supported itself economically and provided large numbers of slaves for the rest of Hausaland. With the establishment of the Sokoto Caliphate, Zaria commenced tribute payments of its own in the form of annual large-scale shipments to the sultan of Sokoto.[2] The payment of this tribute made constant, efficient collection a necessity and was apparently the main motivation for developing the collection system (M. G. Smith 1960:87). Overdue payments were collected in force, either by the emir himself or by the chief military official. Smith notes (p. 99) that Muslim Hausa-Fulani fiefdoms never invited such treatment by refusing payment; only the non-Muslim states had regularly to be chastised.

The geographical extent of the tributary relations was several hundred miles.[3] Information collected by Temple and Temple (1922:10, 122–125, 194, 375) describes raids to collect payment from the Angas, the Gwari, the Kaje, the Yeskwa (who figured largely in the early accounts of slave raiding to the south of Zaria), and others. M. G. Smith notes that one name used for "slave settlement" in Zaria was *keffi*, after the southern vassal state of that name, which was regarded as a slave reserve (M. G. Smith 1960:81). (*Rinji* is the more familiar word.) *Bauta*, the Hausa word for slavery, is

---

[2]   There is a pressing need for a full study of the structure of tribute payments from the emirates to Sokoto (see Adamu 1979). Meyers (1971:181) suggests that as many as 10,000 slaves per year were shipped to Sokoto. It is not clear how many of these came from Zaria, though the number was several hundred annually at the least and probably over a thousand (see, for example, Hogendorn Collection, Interview 19 with Mallam Bawa). There is a discussion of tribute in Clapperton (1966[1829]:216).

[3]   See, for example, the map and accompanying text in M. G. Smith (1970: 87, 90) and the comment that the tributary relationships may well have extended even farther than shown.

said to be the derivation of Bauchi, the plateau region where many raided peoples lived (M. G. Smith 1960:81). Mallam Bawa, whose vivid description of a slaving attack by the Zaria army is given below, relates that his father was captured in a Zaria raid on a tributary Kwarama town (Hogendorn Collection, Interview 19). The tributary states conducted their own slaving expeditions, and although I did not conduct fieldwork in the border areas (fieldwork which is much needed, incidentally) the situation seems to accord with the general picture painted recently by van Dantzig (1975:267), who speaks of mutual slave raiding by peoples on the periphery of stronger states. A very similar situation of raiding to enforce tribute payment has been described by Mason (1969:544) for Nupe.[4]

Frequently it has been asserted that the capture of slaves on raids of this sort was politically, not economically, motivated. For example, Ayandele (1967:334) writes:

> It would appear that slave catching should be regarded more as an effect than a cause of warfare in Northern Nigeria. The wars fought by the stronger and bigger Emirates against the smaller and weaker "pagan" peoples had the characteristics of many wars in contemporary indigenous Africa. They were primarily political wars undertaken by the stronger states to extend their boundaries and sovereignty.

Again Adamu (1979:167) asserts that "in nearly all cases politics was the cause" of military campaigns in the region. This contention seems doubtful for Zaria. By the late nineteenth century, as we have seen, a structure of tribute relations had been in place for nearly a century. Raids to enforce the collection of slaves had a political side to them, no doubt, but the offensive posture of the Zaria army, the scarcity of horses among the raided peoples, the virtual absence of firearms among them, and their own defensive posture do not validate the claim that Zaria was simply searching for peaceful frontiers. As Temple stated (1968 [1918]:226), the argument that slaves were merely a by-product of wars for political purposes is refuted because the expeditions into pagan country would have been most unprofitable had captured goats, sheep, and grain been the only booty.

One way to settle this difference of opinion is to draw on the available evidence, much of it oral, for a view of the Zaria army on campaign. Was that army a balanced force for both offense and defense, or was it designed for slave catching? The first realization is that the military levies

---

[4] Says Mason, "In both enforcing their demands on the non-Muslims and upholding them, the Nupe armies acquired captives. . . . A dependable supply of slaves was essential. This supply was obviously better ensured if it were forwarded as a regular tribute rather than collected by irregular raiding." In fact, the most regular supply came from areas with which treaties were in force.

of the emirate were distinctly not marching out to raid defenseless and unsuspecting settlements. Contrary to a popular view, the defenses were often rather impressive. Often the subjects of the raid had established their farming in areas where hills aided in defense — at the cost, incidentally, of greater difficulty in grain production (Meek 1971 [1922]:290; see also Gemery and Hogendorn 1979:152–153). Descriptions of "defensive geography" round about the Zaria periphery and elsewhere are frequent (Morgan and Pugh 1969:19, 27, 37, 41, 242). Two inselberg forts immediately to the south of Zaria, at Dumbi and Turunku, are excellent examples of the use of a natural citadel. Though these forts date from a much earlier period than the nineteenth century, their catchment water supply, steep access paths blocked by stone walls, and storage areas all show a form of military architecture which was well developed throughout the Zaria hinterland (Mortimore 1970:103, 106). Travelers were impressed at the extent of village fortifications (Robinson 1969[1900]:16). The Angas had a system of entrenchments integrated with riverbanks which, when stormed, had to be broken through with pickaxes (Temple and Temple 1922:10). To the south in Tiv country, Orr (1965[1911]:55) described villages surrounded by ditches, the earth thrown up into ramparts, the ramparts topped with stockades. The Gwari erected stone ramparts as part of their defense works, and tradition has it that of the thirteen raids on one town (Kushaka) only seven were successful (Temple and Temple 1922:122–124).[5] Sometimes defensive works in the border country involved "not less than three concentric walls and moats" (van Dantzig 1975:261). The cotton-quilt armor worn by the heavy cavalry is said to have been primarily a defense against the "justly dreaded poisoned arrows" fired from behind these fortifications (Schultze 1968[1910]:193).[6] Regular patrols seem also to have been employed by peoples subject to raid, as was noted especially by Clapperton (1966[1829]:146) on his journey from Bussa to Kano.

Thus it is not at all surprising that successful slave raiding involved large forces and expensive equipment. The Zaria army was organized as an offensive force designed to overcome the defenses just described. The best description of that army's structure is provided by the oral evidence collected by M. G. Smith (1960:96–98). Campaigning was conducted in the dry season, with slave gathering the main tactical goal. Mobilization was a slow process involving levies raised by the fief holders, and the slowness iself is evidence that the army was intended to play an offensive role. Zaria thus bore no burden of a standing army, and the costs and benefits of a campaign were widely distributed among the nobles.

On the march the army's organizational plan clearly reflected an offen-

---

[5]   The traditions are unclear, and some of Temple's informants remembered sixteen raids.
[6]   Though the quotation is for Bornu, poisoned arrows seem to have been an important weapon for almost all the peoples raided by Zaria.

sive slant. In advance of the main forces were the pathfinders under a nomad Fulani (*kato*) followed by scouts (*gonau*) commanded by officers with such revealing titles as *sata* [theft] and *baraya* [robber]. Then came the main force of infantry, bowmen, and heavy cavalry under the *madaki*, the military leader. The elite force of musketeers marched with this division. The flanks of the main force were protected by mounted light cavalry. Should the emir be with the army, he would ride just behind with the very heavy cavalry, armored with leather helmets, chain mail, and quilted cotton, and followed by the heavy infantry reserve. Two nobles, *wombai*, with the reserve horses, and *rubu*, with the medical supplies and the barber-doctors for the wounded, plus the camp builders, were the last units. Far to the rear, a slave official, *madauci*, was responsible for organizing and forwarding supplies to the army in the field. On the march a crude arrowhead formation was adopted. The main force weapons were muskets, swords, lances, and axes, the bow and arrow, and incendiaries (*sango*) which the archers could launch against thatched roofs. Only the emir had the authority to put this force in motion or to levy troops in the first place, although noble fief holders vied eagerly for permission to lead smaller expeditions because of the larger share of booty which might thereby be attained (M. G. Smith 1960:99).[7]

The plan of attack, according to oral data, seems to have corresponded with what Bovill (1968b:67) has called the "procedure for capturing slaves . . . generally practiced in the Western Sudan right up to the European occupation early in the present century." This "general practice" is well-described by Lyon (1821:255):

They rest for the night, two or three hours ride from the village intended to be attacked; and after midnight, leaving their camp with a small guard, they advance, so as to arrive by daylight; they then surround the place, and, closing in, generally succeed in taking all the inhabitants. . . . At a convenient distance is placed a standard, round which are stationed men prepared to receive and bind the captives. . . .

Lyon's account may be compared with the story of the attack by the Zaria army which resulted, about 1890, in the capture and enslavement of Mallam Bawa's father (Hogendorn Collection, Interviews 19 and 20). The father, Mallam Abdullahi, was, as already recounted, a Kwarama. He lived at Lere, a town near Jos, where he and his mother were taken in a raid to enforce tribute payment. Lere's home defense units were ready within the walls of the town and were not surprised by the appearance of the emir with the Zaria army, which had camped nearby for the night. The emir's representatives demanded immediate capitulation and payment of

[7] Compare Mason's (1969:553) statement for Nupe that "a close look at the Nupe armies in the field, in spite of European assumptions to the contrary, reveals the complex and varied nature of their military undertakings."

the slave tribute, but the Lere forces sallied forth and an engagement was joined outside the walls. By bow and arrow and by individual "commando" units climbing the walls, the Zaria forces soon had the town set afire.[8] As resistance began to crumble, many townspeople attempted flight. Horsemen patrolling the walls yelled at the fugitives to stand and surrender; if the flight continued the horsemen ran them right down with the horses, knocking them to the ground. Each horseman carried perhaps five to ten pieces of rope, with one of which he tied the new slave and then ran him or her ahead of the horse.[9] Foot soldiers stationed around the town were then given charge of the slave, who was escorted with others newly captured in a small group to the army's camp. Meanwhile, back in the town foot soldiers searched the smoldering huts and combed the hill over the town for additional refugees.

Several technical details stand out. Smaldone (1972:594) has already noted that firearms were a decided advantage to slave raiding in the savanna, and this appears to have been true of Zaria. The volley at dawn, the flashes and loud reports, had an effect on morale surpassing the actual worth of the muskets themselves. Expensive and requiring a supply system covering thousands of miles (for gunpowder), they represented technological superiority and were largely unavailable to the smaller, poorer tributary states (see Gemery and Hogendorn 1977, where attention is directed to the need for imported "corned" gunpowder and to the efficacy of the musket in slaving). Guns could be loaded with bits of stone rather than the more lethal ball and fired with a reduced charge if desired. For reaching across distance in the initial capture and in policing slaves on the march, they were far superior to other available weapons. They were also very expensive, one slave sometimes exchanging for one musket; on the coast, the gun:slave ratio was as much as six or eight to one (Gemery and Hogendorn 1977).

A further substantial technical advantage was embodied in the horse (Gemery and Hogendorn 1977:251; Fisher 1972–1973:364). Mares were often used rather than stallions because they neighed less (Bovill 1968a:247). They too were exceedingly expensive items of "capital equipment." In Kano in 1824, Clapperton reported that good horses sold for $100–$120, while Nachtigal reported that a sick, doctored horse still sold for $50 (Fisher 1972–1973:384, 387). (At Segu, a horse was exchanged for between two and twelve slaves [Bazin 1975].) Says Ayandele (1967:332), "invariably a horse was more expensive than a slave." Gemery and Hogendorn (1979:152) off the calculation, computed from Barth (1965 [1865]), that a subsistence ration of grain (one kilogram per day)

---

[8] A Maradi attack described by M. G. Smith (1967:120) involved the shooting of incendiaries over the walls to set the huts on fire, by volleying archers to clear the walls, and the cutting of foot rests into the walls so that they could be scaled by infantry.
[9] At Segu it was rare for a soldier to capture more than one slave in an attack (Bazin 1975).

cost *annually* only about £0.30 in Bornu, £0.46 in Kano, and £0.60 in Katsina. In Kano, therefore, a $100 horse would exchange for enough food to feed a single slave for a lifetime.

The oral data accumulated at Zaria reveal one very substantial difference between the actions taken by the Zaria army and policies followed in many other areas. There are many reports of wholesale slaughter perpetrated by slave raiders elsewhere. Fisher and Fisher (1970:62, 76–82), quoting Nachtigal, dwell on the grim conditions when a town was captured by raiders. Bovill (1968a:247) says that the aged and the infirm were usually killed. Schultze (1968 [1910]:26, 203) notes many atrocities in Bornu and says that anything the slave raiders had no use for was destroyed on the spot. Orr (1965[1911]):100), writing of Adamawa, called it a particularly brutal slaving ground, where those useless as slaves were killed in large numbers; "nor are they even provident of their hunting-ground." Barth's description (1965[1865]:369) of a raid in Bornu tells, chillingly, of the slaughter of 170 males by the amputation of a leg. In a recent essay on slavery in Hausaland, Piault (1975:32–35) gives a similar harsh view, and Robinson (1969[1900]:205) has an excellent description of ravaged territory following the passage of slavers. These and other accounts contrast strangely with the evidence for Zaria, where I found no tradition of large-scale killings. The implication is that Zaria's slave gathering was too businesslike to require or permit indiscriminate killing. Women and girls, men and boys — all would bring a price. Wiping out a town or region would indeed be "improvident of the hunting-ground." In the heat of battle, to teach a lesson, deaths did occur, but apparently not nearly on the scale reported from other areas.

What of the newly acquired slaves? Orr (1965[1911]:157) has given us a view of an emir's war-camp "on the borders of the pagan districts," filled with "all the riff-raff and adventurers of the countryside," the neighborhood denuded of supplies. The Zaria war camp to which the new slaves were taken was recognizably similar, although oral testimony adds additional detail. The camp had no stockade. To prevent escape, horsemen kept up constant patrols on the perimeter (Hogendorn Collection, Interview 20 with Mallam Bawa). The army's slave cooks and slave water-bearers were employed in feeding the new acquisitions (Hogendorn Collection, Interview 19). Any village captured was despoiled of its food and pots, and the new slaves with an escort were detailed to collect firewood. They might also bring water from village wells. Others were detailed to help with the cooking (Hogendorn Collection, Interview 6, with Mallam Sule). Muslim law for the treatment of slaves was in abeyance, not to take effect until the army returned to Muslim territory (Fisher and Fisher 1970:77). Conditions do not seem to have been as unduly harsh as this might imply, however.

The division of the booty (*humusi*) seems to have taken place immediately. M. G. Smith reports that the conventions were quite formal. The
makama babba [big weapon] represented the *madaki*, the military leader,
and thus the *hakimai*, or fief holders, not in the emir's immediate entourage. The *sarkin yaki* represented the emir. The *fagaci*, another title
holder, presided to ensure fair play. The emir's share was 50 percent, the
madaki receiving the rest. Each rewarded his followers from his shares
(M. G. Smith 1960:98–99; Terray 1975).[10] Tambo (1976:199) states that
Maliki law entitled the emir to only a 20 percent share, with the remainder going to the individual warriors (cf. Adamu 1979), but he notes that
warriors seldom actually got more than half and this certainly appears
true for Zaria.

For the march to Zaria, the slaves were tied one hand to the neck, but
were not connected to each other. (The convoy of tribute slaves which
traveled from Zaria to Sokoto was ordinarily connected by rope from
neck to neck.) Many carried full loads of food, water, and other booty.
Unlike the army's own slaves, who wore a *riga* [gown], they went naked
(Hogendorn Collection, Interviews 6, 19, 20).[11] The trip to Zaria seems
to have been usually wholly uneventful, especially by contrast to slave
evacuation during raids in Bornu. There Nachtigal estimated that
perhaps three or four died or escaped for every one delivered. Other
estimates, by Lippert and Hourst, are even worse, six to one and ten to
one being mentioned (Fisher and Fisher 1970:76). The oral testimony for
Zaria makes it appear that the policing there was strict, the supply
organization competent, and the delivery system effective. It is unlikely
that more than a small fraction of the slaves captured died or escaped on
the march.

The informants who spoke of slave acquisition by Zaria concentrated
their attention very largely on military campaigns of the Zaria army. In
my opinion, this is partly because of the great attention and fanfare which
surrounded the annual expedition. The same glitter probably biased the
observations of travelers. Though more fieldwork will be necessary to
prove the point, the focus on army activities probably serves to underestimate the role of slave acquisition through peaceful (or relatively peaceful) tribute. Time and again, throughout the Temples' voluminous collection of northern Nigerian traditions, reference is found to enslavement as

[10]   Terray (1975) says that soldiers would try to hide children in sacks so as to escape the
sharing out. Piault (1975) gives a slightly different ratio: one part for the emir, one part for
the soldiers, and one part to the home villages in proportion to the number of men
participating in the raid.
[11]   In Bornu, when the supply of rope or chain was exhausted rawhide bindings were
substituted (Fisher and Fisher 1970:76). Clapperton's servant Richard Lander met thirty
slaves on the way to Zaria bound neck to neck with twisted bullock hide (Clapperton 1966
[1829]:79; a collection of foot irons and manacles is pictured on p. 88 of Clapperton's
work).

a punishment (Temple and Temple 1922). Murder, adultery, repeated theft, and a variety of other crimes and peccadillos could result in slavery. Such enslavement must have played a major role in the tribute system. Meyers (1971:179) has made much the same point. It is true that Koelle's sample in Sierra Leone included only one product of judicial enslavement (Tambo 1976:198–199), but this may be explained by market conditions. A steady annual flow of tribute slaves could easily have been absorbed in the domestic economies of the caliphate emirates. They might thus seldom appear in long-distance trade. It is possible that only the surplus slaves, such as might appear after a very successful punitive raid, would be sold south to the Atlantic markets. If this logic is reasonable, it will reconcile the frequency of judicial enslavement as a punishment reported by the Temples and others with its rarity in the Koelle sample.

Another unusual feature in the oral data is the low importance given to kidnapping. Meyers (1971:179) has written that "often individuals or small bands" carried out kidnapping, and Tambo (1976:198–199) argues that such seizures probably increased in importance during the nineteenth century (22 percent of the Caliphate slaves in Koelle's sample had been kidnapped [Hair 1965:199]). Certainly kidnapping did occur, even near Zaria during wartime. As a general rule, however, my informants reported it as infrequent. Adamu (1979) has concluded, from the oral evidence of Tape 3 of my collection, that *samame* [kidnapping for enslavement] was probably rarer than hitherto believed and that "the majority of the kidnapping incidents took place in the border zones where armed merchants occasionally raided small unprotected settlements and captured some able-bodied people to use as porter slaves." I am inclined to agree. The defensive preparations, plus the patrols and guards already mentioned, would seem to make kidnapping a difficult proposition. Ten or twelve kidnappers, deep in hostile territory, having to feed their horses, their musket volley weak in firepower, must have been in constant jeopardy. They could hardly have hoped to overcome a village or to move a large number of slaves even if they had caught them. On a per-man basis, their muskets, powder, and horses were just as expensive as if they had been part of a large army. Further, their activity was illegal. It seems reasonable to suggest that kidnapping by small groups probably has been overemphasized in the literature on slaving and that, as Lyon (1821:255) suggested, two or three hundred raiders at least were necessary for optimal effect. As Terray (1975) says for another area of the savanna, the purchase of arms, gunpowder, ball, and horses for a force of sufficient size severely restricted the potential for organizing such raids (cf. Lovejoy and Hogendorn 1979:234).[12]

---

[12] The credit advanced in kind for such raids was most likely to go to state officials rather than to private entrepreneurs.

THE DELIVERY AND SALE OF SLAVES

We have already witnessed the sharing out of slave booty on the battlefield. Once home in Zaria, there was a further sharing (Hogendorn Collection, Interviews 6, 18, and 19). The slaves were initially quartered in the "slave house" managed by the *sarkin yaki*, already mentioned as the official taking possession of the emir's share of slaves on the battlefield. After the big war-drum was beaten, crowds gathered to witness the selection of the slaves destined to fill the yearly quota for Sokoto. The selection appears to have been made out of the total "catch." Another, much smaller selection was made at this time (or soon thereafter) for the old *mallams*.[13] The emir and nobles then took their shares to their town houses in Zaria, where those intended for *rinji* or house employment stayed for some weeks or even months, engaged in domestic tasks under the watchful eyes of those in charge of the house slaves. There was danger of escape at this time, and although the slaves were not tied they were closely watched. After some time for observation and "seasoning," a division was made. Most of the slaves were sent to a *rinji* in the countryside owned by their new master, there set to work in agricultural labor (see Lovejoy 1976, Hogendorn 1977). The remainder were added to the ranks of the household slaves in town. Meanwhile, those slaves not to be retained for the master's own use had very quickly been taken to market. As intimated earlier, these marketed slaves appear to have been surplus to local requirements.

Interestingly, in the interviews the information came to light that the slaves destined for Sokoto's tribute were held for some time in the *sarkin yaki's* compound. Nobles could come there to exchange a slave they did not like for another until the annual caravan left for Sokoto. This winnowing must have meant that Sokoto received the "hard cases."

The slaves who went to market were sold in two ways. Those with special skills (smiths, for example) and beautiful women were ordinarily marketed from the houses of local slave dealers. Prices in this "house trade" were of course usually higher than for slaves exhibited openly in the market (cf. Tambo 1976:190 and n. 6; Adamu 1979:171). Few further oral data were obtainable on this sort of trade, although one informant noted that house sales were often negotiated as a repayment for a credit advance (Hogendorn Collection, Interview 2 with Mallam Shehu).

The majority of the slaves marketed ended up exposed for public examination (Hogendorn Collection, Interviews 2, 4, 6, 8, 11, 19: cf. Robinson 1969[1900]:160–164; Colvin 1971:130–131; Tambo 1976:190). They were confined at night in large rooms guarded by

---

[13]   Bernus and Bernus (1975) call attention to shares for the priests and even the blacksmiths, for their work in arms production.

warders, then chained and brought to market during the day. A prospective seller ordinarily deposited his slave with the *sarkin dillalan bayi* [chief slave broker] an appointee of the emir. (Alternatively, the slave could be kept by the owner offering him for sale and brought daily to the market by him.) Slave dealers (*dillalan bayi*) operated under the general supervision of the chief broker, and some were linked commercially with him. Sales were ordinarily on a commission basis (*la'ada*) the cowrie commission being split between the broker and the *sarkin dillalan bayi*. One informant said the usual split was one fifth to the chief broker, four-fifths to the broker handling the transaction. Estimates of the size of the commission as a proportion of the total sale price were all quite low. It was possible to sell directly to a broker (at a below-market price, of course), the broker financing the transaction until a final buyer was found. Witness fees were included in the sale price.

At the market, the slaves were lined up, shackled with leg-irons (*mari*), the males naked in one line, females partly clothed and with shaved heads in another, a path between them. (Robinson [1969(1900):130] saw 200 slaves exposed in the market when he passed through Zaria.) Just before the British occupation, two large brokers handled the largest number of transactions, each operating with five or six assistants, though there were other brokers as well. Depending on the arrangements, food for slaves awaiting sale was provided either by the seller or by the broker. The broker also provided a pawning service (*jingina*) wherein he would personally accept a slave for a period of time ranging from seven days to a year or more, putting him to work during the pawning period. Slaves on sale, however, were not required to work.

Some question has arisen as to the racial background of slave dealers in Hausaland (Colvin 1971:114). In Zaria the dealers appear to have been untitled commoners of the merchant class, largely of Hausa origin, not infrequently related to one another. This accords with Adamu's (1979) description of dealer origins elsewhere in Hausaland.

There is a well-known tradition, reported not only by many European travelers but also by most of my informants, that a slave could refuse to be sold to a particular buyer. No investigator has yet asked, as far as I know, what happened to a slave who repeatedly refused sale. The answer is that the rooms where the slaves were kept at night were filled with a layer of wood ashes. The slaves were smeared with this same ash every day before being taken to market, as — so it was said — a mark of their servile condition. Then they were kept immobile in their chains while at the market. Informants thought it not a very pleasant life, and hence refusing to be sold was not frequent.

Sale eventually took place, although sometimes it took a month or more when trade was slow. The buyer had been most careful to examine the feet, fingers, eyes, and genitals of his purchase. Many of those sold were purchased for local use in *rinji* plantation agriculture. (Perhaps 40 percent of the slaves at Hanwa, a *rinji* I studied in 1975, came from the Zaria market [Hogendorn 1977].) Another portion was sold to brokers coming down from Kano, whence they ended up in the Kano economy or sold away into the northern export trade. Kano buyers visited the Zaria market several times a year. A final portion was sold to Hausa merchants, who took them south for sale to the coastal palm-oil producers or, at an earlier period, into the Atlantic trade.[14] As a general rule, proportionately more women than men went north, because demand in the Saharan trade was skewed toward the female sex, while men predominated in the Atlantic trade (Colvin 1971:114; Gemery and Hogendorn 1979:154). Unfortunately, the oral data do not illuminate the interesting questions of how many slaves went through the Zaria market in an average year or what fraction was retained in the local economy and what fraction was exported. A great deal of work remains to be done if the patterns of trade beyond the Zaria market are to be clarified. That, however, is beyond the scope of this paper, the purpose of which has been to add to our knowledge of the precolonial mechanism for the original acquisition of slaves and their initial delivery.

REFERENCES

ADAMU, MAHDI
1979   "Aspects of the economics of the export of slaves from the Central Sudan to the Bight of Benin in the eighteenth and nineteenth centuries," in *The uncommon market: essays in the economic history of the Atlantic slave trade.* Edited by Henry Gemery and Jan S. Hogendorn. New York: Academic Press.
AYANDELE, E. A.
1967   Observations on some social and economic aspects of slavery in precolonial northern Nigeria. *Nigerian Journal of Economic and Social Studies* 9:329–338.
BARTH, HEINRICH
1965 [1865]   *Travels and discoveries in north and central Africa 1849–55,* three volumes (centenary edition). London: Frank Cass.
BAZIN, JEAN
1975   "Guerre et servitude à Ségou," in *L'esclavage en Afrique précoloniale.* Edited by Claude Meillassoux, 27–48. Paris: François Maspero.
BERNUS, EDMOND, SUZANNE BERNUS
1975   "L'évolution de la condition servile chez les touregs saheliens," in *L'esclavage en Afrique précoloniale.* Edited by Claude Meillassoux. Paris: François Maspero.

---

[14]   Adamu (1979), in the first direct study of this southerly delivery system in operation, emphasizes the use of slaves as porters, their supervision by armed guards, their sale and resale en route, and the use of *zango* rest stops by the slave caravans. The main route used Oyo as an entrepôt for the north-south exchange of goods (see Colvin 1971:122–123; Adamu 1979:173–176).

BOVILL, E. W.
1968a *The golden trade of the Moors* (second edition). London: Oxford University Press.
1968b *The Niger explored.* London: Oxford University Press.

CLAPPERTON, HUGH
1966 [1829] *Journal of a second expedition into the interior of Africa.* London: Frank Cass.

COLVIN, LUCIE G.
1971 "The commerce of Hausaland, 1780–1833," in *Aspects of West African Islam.* Edited by Daniel F. McCall and Norman R. Bennett, 101–135. Boston: Boston University African Studies Center.

CURTIN, PHILIP D.
1975 *Economic change in precolonial Africa: Senegambia in the era of the slave trade.* Madison: University of Wisconsin Press.

FISHER, ALLAN, H. J. FISHER
1970 *Slavery and Muslim society in Africa: the institution in Saharan and Sudanic Africa and the trans-Saharan trade.* London: Hurst.

FISHER, HUMPHREY J.
1972–1973 He swalloweth the ground with fierceness and rage: the horse in the Central Sudan. *Journal of African History* 13:369–388, 14:355–379.

GEMERY, HENRY, JAN S. HOGENDORN
1977 "Technological change, slavery, and the slave trade," in *The imperial impact: studies in the economic history of India and Africa.* Edited by C. J. Dewey and A. G. Hopkins. London: Athlone.
1979 "Economic costs of West African participation in the Atlantic slave trade: a preliminary sampling for the eighteenth century," in *The uncommon market: essays in the economic history of the Atlantic slave trade.* Edited by Henry Gemery and Jan S. Hogendorn. New York: Academic Press.

HAIR, P. E. H.
1965 The enslavement of Koelle's informants. *Journal of African History* 6:193–203.

HILL, POLLY
1972 *Rural Hausa: a village and a setting.* Cambridge: Cambridge University Press.
1975 From slavery to freedom: the case of farm-slavery in Nigerian Hausaland. *Comparative Studies in Society and History* 18:395–426.
1976 From slavery to freedom: the case of farm-slavery in the Kano Emirate. Paper presented at the Kano Seminar on the Economic History of the Central Savanna, Kano, Nigeria, January.

HOGENDORN, JAN S.
1977 The economics of slave use on two "plantations" in the Zaria Emirate of the Sokoto Caliphate. *African Historical Studies* 10:369–383.

JOHNSTON, H A. S.
1967 *The Fulani empire of Sokoto.* London: Oxford University Press.

KLEIN, MARTIN A.
1971 Slavery, the slave trade, and legitimate commerce in late nineteenth-century Africa. *Etudes d'Histoire Africaine* 2:5–28.

KLEIN, MARTIN A., PAUL LOVEJOY
1979 "Slavery in West Africa," in *The uncommon market: essays in the economic history of the Atlantic slave trade.* Edited by Henry Gemery and Jan S. Hogendorn. New York: Academic Press.

492   JAN S. HOGENDORN

KOPYTOFF, IGOR, SUZANNE MIERS
1977   "African 'slavery' as an institution of marginality," in *Slavery in Africa: historical and anthropological perspectives.* Edited by Suzanne Miers and Igor Kopytoff. Madison: University of Wisconsin Press.
LOVEJOY, PAUL
1976   "The plantation economy of the Sokoto Caliphate." Paper presented at the annual meeting of the American Historical Association, Washington, D.C., December.
LOVEJOY, PAUL, JAN S. HOGENDORN
1979   "Slave marketing in West Africa," in *The uncommon market: essays in the economic history of the Atlantic slave trade.* Edited by Henry Gemery and Jan S. Hogendorn. New York: Academic Press.
LYON, G. F.
1821   *A narrative of travels in northern Africa.* London.
MASON, MICHAEL
1969   Population density and "slave raiding": the case of the middle belt of Nigeria. *Journal of African History* 10:551–564.
MEEK, C. K.
1971 [1922]   *The northern tribes of Nigeria.* London: Frank Cass.
MEILLASSOUX, CLAUDE, editor
1975   *L'esclavage en Afrique précoloniale.* Paris: François Maspero.
MEYERS, ALLAN
1971   "Slavery in the Hausa-Fulani emirates," in *Aspects of West African Islam.* Edited by Daniel F. McCall and Norman R. Bennett, 173–184. Boston: Boston University African Studies Center.
MORGAN, W. B., J. C. PUGH
1969   *West Africa.* London: Methuen.
MORTIMORE, M. J.
1970   "Settlement evolution and land use," in *Zaria and its region.* Edited by M. J. Mortimore, 102–122. Samaru: Ahmadu Bello University Press.
ORR, CHARLES
1965 [1911]   *The making of northern Nigeria.* London: Frank Cass.
PIAULT, MARC-HENRI
1975   "Captifs du pouvoir et pouvoir des captifs," in *L'esclavage en Afrique précoloniale.* Edited by Claude Meillassoux, 321–350. Paris: François Maspero.
ROBINSON, CHARLES HENRY
1969 [1900]   *Nigeria, our latest protectorate.* London: Horace Marshall.
SCHULTZE, A.
1968 [1910]   *The sultanate of Bornu.* Translated by P. A. Benton. London: Frank Cass.
SMALDONE, JOSEPH P.
1972   Firearms in the Central Sudan: a revaluation. *Journal of African History* 13:591–607.
SMITH, M. G.
1954   Slavery and emancipation in two societies. *Social and Economic Studies* 3:239–290.
1955   *The economy of Hausa communities of Zaria.* London: H.M.S.O.
1960   *Government in Zazzau.* London: Oxford University Press.
1965a   "Hausa inheritance and succession," in *Studies in the laws of succession in Nigeria.* Edited by J. D. M. Derrett, 230–281. London: Oxford University Press.

1965b "The Hausa of northern Nigeria," in *Peoples of Africa*. Edited by James L. Gibbs, Jr., 119–155. New York: Holt, Rinehart and Winston.

1967 "A Hausa kingdom: Maradi under Dan Baskore, 1854–75," in *West African kingdoms in the nineteenth century*. Edited by Daryll Forde and P. M. Kaberry, 93–122. London: Oxford University Press for the International African Institute.

1970 "Notes on the history of Zazzau under the Hausa kings," in *Zaria and its region*. Edited by M. J. Mortimore. Samaru: Ahmadu Bello University Press.

SMITH, MARY
1954 *Baba of Karo: a woman of the Muslim Hausa*. London: Faber and Faber.

TAMBO, DAVID
1976 The Sokoto Caliphate slave trade in the nineteenth century. *African Historical Studies* 9:187–217.

TEMPLE, C. L.
1968 [1918] *Native races and their rulers* (second edition). London: Frank Cass.

TEMPLE, O., C. L. TEMPLE
1922 *Notes on the tribes, provinces, emirates, and states of the northern provinces of Nigeria* (second edition). New York: Barnes and Noble.

TERRAY, EMMANUEL
1975 "La captivité dans le royaume abron du Gyaman," in *L'esclavage en Afrique précoloniale*. Edited by Claude Meillassoux, 389–453. Paris: François Maspero.

THOMAS, R. P., R. N. BEAN
1975 The fishers of men: the profits of the slave trade. *Journal of Economic History* 34:885–914.

VAN DANTZIG, ALBERT
1975 "Effects of the Atlantic slave trade on some West African societies," in *La traite des noirs par l'Atlantique: nouvelle approches*, 252–269. Revue Française d'Histoire d'Outre-Mer 62.

Accommodation and Assimilation in the Landlord-Stranger Relationship

BRUCE L. MOUSER

The landlord-stranger relationship, as it applied to arrangements between Africans as owners of the land and Europeans seeking to settle or trade upon Africa's west coast during the eighteenth and nineteenth centuries, was all things to all parties. Africans saw these agreements as tending to contain Europeans within specified zones and forcing them to abide by African contractual regulations and proscriptions. By controlling foreigners, landlords could regulate the introduction of change and technology and maintain for themselves those by-products beneficial for continuance of local power. Naturally, landlords profited from increased trade and new markets for local products. Restricted from local politics by these agreements, Europeans often saw this relationship as little more than rents, anchorage duties, taxes, licenses, or African attempts to take advantage of European enterprise. Still, they remained on the coast, married Africans, had large families, and often sent sons abroad where they could receive a finishing education. This paper traces the evolution of the landlord-stranger relationship in the trading communities of two rivers on the Windward Coast, the Rio Nunez and the Rio Pongo (Figure 1), from approximately 1790 to 1860. Here the relationship was an agency of change and a process through which local societies allowed foreign ideas to influence local institutions. Both parties to these arrangements initially sought the security of rigid contractual tenancy guarantees. With time, however, accommodation to some European ideas and assimilation of Europeans in local institutions were the rule on both rivers.[1]

A somewhat different version of this paper appeared in *International Journal of African Historical Studies* 8:425–440.
[1] Dorjahn and Fyfe (1962:391–397) define "stranger" as tenant, traveler, and foreign resident. Curtin's (1975:298–299) discussion of landlord-brokership suggests a direct role

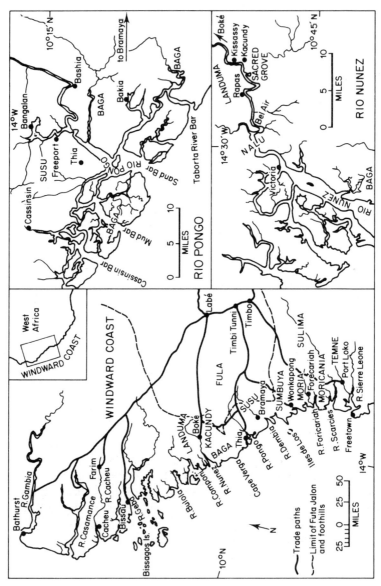

Figure 1.   Maps showing the Rio Pongo and Rio Nunez rivers on the Windward Coast

MAJOR ETHNIC GROUPS AND SOCIOPOLITICAL ORGANIZATION

The areas of the rivers and the peoples who lived there had long been subject to foreign influences from both the African interior and the sea. Sea salt and, according to tradition, elephants migrating toward the setting sun had first drawn Baga peoples from the Futa Jalon highlands to the inhospitable coast (Saint-Père 1930). Related as Mel-speakers to the Temne and Loko of the Sierra Leone-Guinea borderland, the newcomers absorbed or displaced earlier coastal inhabitants. The Nunez Baga played an important role in trade between the coast and the interior. They grew wet rice and extracted salt on the lowlands and sold surpluses to both African long-distance traders and Europeans visiting the rivers (Rivière 1968:733–735; Rodney 1968:274–276). They lived in small villages with chiefs descending in clans of the founders. Villages seldom contained more than two clans. Social relations and political interactions between villages were regulated by a secret society, the Simo, to which all males belonged. A bush spirit, also called the Simo, possessed power over life and death and, in the form of a mask, delivered swift justice for violation of accepted practice. The leader of the society was elected by a council of elders represented by heads of the major clans (Paulme 1956:101–104; 1958).

Once lines of long-distance trade were established, existing commerce attracted new migrants from the interior. Some were Muslims who moved coastward to control the supply of salt and rice and later firearms, and most of these lived under the auspices of local chiefs (Levtzion 1975:218). Others were Landuma and Nalu who moved into the Rio Nunez region, intermarried with the Baga in the littoral grasslands (the Baga of the mangroves were left relatively untouched by the later arrivals), and established their own primacy in the salt exchange (Arcin 1907:129–134). Traditions record that the Nalu migrated from the Upper Gambia during the sixteenth century, as a vanguard of Mandingo commercial hegemony along the Atlantic coastline (Méo 1919:282–283). The Nalu split the Baga and Landuma homelands, first seizing the northern bank of the Nunez and then occupying sections of the southern bank up to the Sacred Grove. The Nalu failed to adopt the institution of kingship or powerful chieftains until the mid-nineteenth century. The Landuma, related linguistically to the Baga, were the last "Mel"-speakers to leave the Futa Jalon, moving coastward during the fifteenth and sixteenth centuries. Of the same tradition as the Baga, the

---

for landlords in trade, a circumstance that seldom obtained in these rivers until the 1830's and then not to the extent noted by Curtin in Gambia. Sundström's (1974:8–15) discussion of customs, tolls, fees, and duties applies to European as well as African strangers.

Landuma also possessed the Simo, which regulated intervillage disputes and cooperation (Monheim 1931:7–8). Increasingly the Nunez became divided into ethnic zones, with Baga at the mouth of the river, Nalu in the middle river, and Landuma dominant above the Sacred Grove.

As in the Rio Nunez, long-distance trade also brought new migrants into the Rio Pongo. Various writers describe a gradual infiltration of Susu trading families into Baga communities on the Pongo, where they inter-married with ruling elites and Baga traders and over a long period modified Baga institutions (Saint-Père 1930). Susu adopted the Simo from the Baga as an institution of political and social control. The Susu ruled only two chieftaincies: Bangalan and Dominguia-Thia. On their part, the Pongo Baga asserted authority over local areas and recognized Susu predominance in regional polity. Accommodation and assimilation were the rule rather than the exception in the Pongo area. The diffusion of new political institutions along both rivers and the expansion of new markets for sea salt up-country led to an imposition of a general Mandingo hegemony in the areas, with *farim* [governors] appointed to maintain proper contacts with the interior trading systems (Rodney 1970:25–26).

While the extent or duration of the relationship between coastal peoples and the Mandingo is unclear in the sources, it would appear that both rivers were free of Mandingo *farim* control by 1700, when signifi-cant structural changes occurred. In Nunez area, shrinking Mandingo influence accompanied the emergence among the Landuma of a single royal family, with kingship alternating between branches. Mandiale Cumbassa, the first ruler, established his capital at Kacundy; Modiere, his brother, succeeded him and moved the capital to Boke, a few miles farther upstream. These traditions laid the foundation for a century-long struggle for control of commerce in the upper river (Berenger-Ferand 1879:335; Arcin 1911:168). No Landuma king list dates the develop-ment of a separate kingship earlier than 1700. The Simo played a signifi-cant role in the selection of candidates and in the election of rulers among the Landuma (Caillié 1930:153–160; Monheim 1931:7–8).

The Nalu, positioned between the larger entrepôts on the Upper Nunez and the sources of salt and rice in the mangroves, first arrived from the north as traders among the Baga and Landuma and as middlemen in the profitable salt trade. Gradually they carved for themselves a home-land in the middle river, especially after Nalu traders became involved in the competition between the Kacundy- and Boke-based branches of the Landuma royal family (Méo 1919:282–283). The position of the Nalu in the middle river was a disadvantage to them as long as interior trade could be regulated through the Landuma centers. This changed once the Atlan-tic trade became a focus for slaves in return for European products.

On the Pongo, a prominent shift from Baga to Susu political predomi-nance occurred at about the same time. Several writers have suggested that this was a result of a military coup (Arcin 1911:128–143). Rodney (1975:292–294) specifically points to Susu in the Sumbuya, Moria, and Foricariah districts as support for a conquest theory. On the other hand, the Susu of the Rio Pongo were earlier non-Muslim migrant traders who had adopted many Baga customs, including the Simo. These Susu may have merely filled the vacuum accompanying shrinking Mandingo control. Susu kingship descended through two branches during the nineteenth century; the Domin Kante branch descended from the founder and the Uli Kati Damba branch from a usurper of the early nineteenth century (Arcin 1907:141–142). Despite the emergence of apparent Susu dominance, many of the Pongo Baga remained in control of former chieftaincies. Interspersed Susu and Baga villages remained bases of political influence, with regional cooperation practices through conferences called to resolve intervillage disputes. Although the two groups were markedly different in language, in the organization of their secret societies and in their political structures the Baga and Susu communities were fundamentally indistinguishable.

Against the emergence of new political awareness and institutions on the coast, the demands for sea salt by Fula herdsmen in the Futa Jalon continued as before and perhaps expanded. To guarantee continued outlets for their products and a secure source of salt for their herds, the Fula extended their hegemony coastward in the mid-eighteenth century, subjecting the peoples of the Nunez and Pongo to a tributary alliance with the Fula empire of the Futa Jalon (Laing 1825:403–404). Each year the chiefs of Labe and Timbi Tunni, the principal *diwals* [administrative districts] responsible for maintaining proper relationships with chiefs on the Pongo and Nunez, sent representatives accompanied by armed caravans to collect the annual *sagale* [tribute] from their charges (Hopewell 1958:69; Suret-Canale 1970:81). This generally occurred once the paths dried and the grasses were cut, some time between October and January, the peak of the trading season (Méo 1919:286). At the beginning of the rains the Fula withdrew to the interior, leaving their subjects free from up-country supervision until the rains ended and a new trading season commenced. The Fula intervened in coastal politics only when events interfered with the free flow of European manufactures or of slaves, rice, salt, and other African products. They also reserved the right to overrule the selection of chiefs by local societies, especially when the choice of candidate endangered commerce (Mouser 1971: ch. 5).

EUROPEAN COMMERCIAL PENETRATION: THE SLAVE TRADE

The first to exert influence from the sea were Portuguese traders from the

Cape Verde Islands and from Bissau. Initial contact came through the auspices of company-sponsored merchants, some establishing factories or trading centers above the mangroves and in the upper reaches of the coastal rivers. Afro-Europeans of Portuguese descent, called *lançados* along this coast and usually outside the strictures of charter companies, soon became active throughout the area, and by 1600 several had established residences on the Rio Nunez and Rio Pongo (Rodney 1970: ch. 4). Rice, gold, dyes, cloth, ivory, raw hides, hippopotamus teeth, salt, and eventually slaves became the commercial fare of these traders, who gradually acquired important positions in the river trade and transformed commerce from one based on salt to one oriented toward the Atlantic (Golberry 1803:163–172). In the process, the *lançado* provided new markets for African products and brought in firearms, tobacco, knives, and beads and other trinkets. As a Portuguese or an Afro-Portuguese with a knowledge of European languages and techniques, the *lançado* received trade goods on credit (later called advances) to exchange for various products and thereby acquired status as trusted middleman between European ship captains and long-distance traders who carried products from the interior (Rodney 1970:125).

No recent research of a detailed nature on the dimensions of the slave trade in the regions of the Rio Pongo and Rio Nunez has yet been completed. The quantity of slaves shipped from the rivers is uncertain in the available records, and the task is made still more complicated by the shifting geographic terminologies used by most contemporary observers. Both rivers were included in the designations of Rivères du Sud, Portuguese Guinea, Northern Rivers, and Windward Coast. Curtin's (1969) study of the Atlantic slave trade uses the label "Sierra Leone" to cover the broad region from the Casamance in the north to Cape Mount in the south, but he points out the difficulties of estimating the flows of slaves from specific interior regions and specific ports. He also suggests that the exports of slaves from this general area were far more dependent on local supply conditions than on the demands of European traders. The lure of the rivers region for European slavers can probably be correlated with the ready supply of captives resulting from the wars between the Fula peoples and their neighbors, for example, in 1762–1763 (Hopewell 1958:68–70).

European foreigners resident on the coast accepted their relationship with the Africans they lived among as one between landlords and strangers. In fact, the process of accommodation was probably little different from that which had characterized previous associations between African coastal elites and interior traders. The European or Afro-European seeking to establish a factory on the rivers first presented himself to a host chief, who called a conference of his district paramount, the heads of surrounding villages, and the newcomer to formalize a contract among them. While the technicalities of such arrangements differed from chief to chief and from river to river, the patron generally agreed to protect the life and property of his client and to guarantee his client's debts. The composition of the conference symbolized the boundaries within which the trader might be active. In return for this hospitality, the stranger paid an annual custom, or rent, and a head tax on every slave exported from the territory. He also provided his landlord with guns and supplies in time of war (Mouser 1973a:46). Although theoretically strangers were restricted from politics, the success of the African trade inevitably improved the foreigner's leverage in river commerce. In addition, the activities of chiefs tended to confuse the relationship. Some were themselves traders and attempted to tie their prosperity to their clients' by marrying their daughters to them (Mayer 1854:110–117). Whatever the initial motive for such alliances, the relationship became even more complex in succeeding generations, when descendants of *lançados* claimed political privileges as descendants of chiefs (Saint-Père 1930:35–36; Rodney 1975:294–296). This was the case on the Pongo, where in the 1780's the Fernandez and Gomez families acquired power in the Bramaya and Bakia chieftaincies (Arcin 1911:141).

From the mid-eighteenth century, British and American traders joined the *lançados* on the Nunez and Pongo and established bulking centers from which they supplied local and distant marts with European and American products (Newbury 1971:94–96). More than twenty such men are identifiable on the Pongo by the turn of the century, with eight more on the Nunez. Few of the new Europeans dealt solely in slaves. Most purchased slaves and the ivory, gold, rice, and other products which slaves carried to the coast. Most initially sought to avoid the marriage alliances which would eventually entangle them in local politics (Mouser 1973a:51).

The structure of the commerce practiced at the end of the eighteenth century followed similar patterns in both rivers. European and Afro-European traders who had arrangements with local landlords built or purchased factories where they conducted their business. Factories took various forms, but most were located along the riverbank with a store and adjoining quarters, a barracoon for marketable slaves, a courtyard for protecting caravans in the process of bargaining, and a wharf for European visitors (Stock 1899:134). Coastal strangers generally remained near their factories, but some were known to venture as far as Timbo for the purpose of advertising their wares. Others sent African employees into the interior as hawkers, announcing prices and varieties of goods which particular traders had available on the coast (Public Record Office n.d.a). Resident traders purchased both slaves and other products and tried to supply a wide range of goods in exchange. Exportable slaves necessarily came from the interior and not from among the people of the area, since local labor was required to provision slave vessels for the

Middle Passage. Local chiefs therefore supported the traders as the source of markets for salt, foodstuffs, and local manufactures and for the customs, rents, and taxes which traditionally had brought income.

Caravans formed in the interior once the rains ended, between October and May, at the capitals of various Fula provinces. Custom required all traders having business with the coast to place themselves under the protection of a caravan leader, who guaranteed a safe journey, conducted the bargaining session at the factory, and in return received a percentage of the sale (Mayer 1854:179–180). Slaves carried ivory and hides coastward and returned to the interior with rice, salt, and European manufactures, excess porters remaining at coastal factories as merchandise (Watt 1794:74). The reputation of a caravan leader depended in part upon his contacts with Europeans, but also important was his ability to bargain for the group. This was complicated by the fact that the European traders provided the caravan with hospitality for the duration of the bargaining process, a circumstance which tended to insure that the caravan received a fair exchange even if it became necessary to remain a little longer on the coast.

The third partner in this triangle of commerce was the European ship captain, who generally sought specific African products and tended to return time after time to the same entrepôts. Most arranged for future cargos and attempted to minimize the time necessary for acquiring a full complement. Each day on the rivers increased the dangers of fevers and malaria (Bennett and Brooks 1965:283–294). The large number of Europeans on the Rio Pongo and Rio Nunez meant, moreover, that a full cargo could perhaps be collected from among the traders within a short time. One described a celebration which concluded one such sale in 1795 (Hawkins 1797:1550):

They [the traders] come to the table nearly intoxicated, and before dinner is completed, they become downright drunk. . . . The coarse jocularity of destroying their apparrel or wasting the food, is their amusement; while the most exquisite viands are wasted without utility, and the appetite being palled by superabundance, loses all its value but that which gratifies the vanity of the provider, by indulging the waste and absurdity of his guests. After the wine has circulated freely, the meats are even occasionally dashed about at the heads of the best humored, or most patient of the company, and the empty dishes, plates, and tables are demolished to shew the spirit of the party, and the lengths to which they could carry a joke.

SLAVE TRADE ABOLITION AND PROMOTION OF LEGITIMATE TRADE

The sequence of outside events and influences which modified the relationship between landlords and strangers and the structure of commerce between 1790 and 1860 is long and complicated. While it is difficult to pinpoint the direct causes of sociocultural change during this period, a brief historical catalog of events helps to put the changes into proper time perspective. First came the Sierra Leone Company settlement at the mouth of the Sierra Leone River (1791–1808), which increasingly sought to tap into the interior trade patterns which supplied goods for the Nunez and Pongo traders (Coupland 1964:64–65). Company officials attacked the rivers' trade from two directions. They relied initially on direct negotiations with Fula in the Futa Jalon to establish a new path that would divert commerce from the Nunez and Pongo (as well as from the rivers of Moria, Sumbuya, and Moricania) to the British settlement at Freetown (Public Record Office 1802; Robinson 1966: vii–viii).[2] James Watt's trip to the Fula capital of Timbo in 1794 and his unsuccessful attempts to establish a company factory there were the result of this policy. A second plan called for setting up trading settlements at the known terminals of caravans to seize control of legitimate commerce through monopolistic price manipulation and to end slave trading by providing improved markets for legitimate African products (Knutsford 1900:49). To this end the company built two factories on the Pongo and arranged with merchants on the Nunez for others. A combination of trader animosity, an Anglo-French war, rebellion in Freetown, and violations of accepted trading practices by company agents on the spot doomed the enterprise, and the company abandoned the rivers in 1802 (Brooks 1970:55; Peterson 1969:31; Afzelius 1967:13, 15, 20, 31). Traders and officials in Sierra Leone (among them Alexander Gordon Laing, Brian O'Beirne, and William Tuft) refused to forsake the dream of diverting trade from the rivers to Freetown directly through Port Loko, however, and periodically made new attempts into the 1820's. Their efforts were thwarted by frequent wars between the Fula and the Susu of Sulima and by the jealousy with which the chief of Foricariah guarded and guaranteed the trade terminals in Moria country (Laing 1825:413).[3]

While plans to divert the commerce to Sierra Leone had little influence on the peoples on the rivers, the company's presence on the Pongo opened the way for other agents of change. The first missionaries, from the Edinburgh Missionary Society, landed on the Pongo in 1798, but within a year that effort had collapsed (*Missionary Records* 1836:68–72). In 1807 missionaries from the Church Missionary Society moved into the area, where they remained for a decade, establishing two schools which they supported through tuition, gifts, and government subsidies

[2]   Howard (1972:54–60) places the Moria terminals within the Futa-Scarcies corridor of long-distance trade between the Niger and the coast. In chapter 3, he distinguishes between types of African strangers who used and often settled along this corridor.
[3]   See Mouser (1973b: 805–812) for more detailed treatment of Freetown-Moria relations to 1814 and Howard (1972: ch. 4) for the evolution of Mandingo authority in Moria.

(Butscher 1806–1809; Church Missionary Society Archives 1814a). Enrollment jumped from thirty-five in 1808 to nearly a hundred in 1814. Approximately half the students were the sons and daughters of chiefs. The remainder were offspring of traders on the Nunez, Pongo, and Dembia Rivers, and after 1814 liberated Africans were sent to the Pongo schools from Sierra Leone (*Missionary Records* 1836:93–94, Church Missionary Society Archives 1814b). Instruction was conducted in English, and at the insistence of the trading community the curriculum included commercial skills such as mathematics and bookkeeping (Butscher 1806–1809). The influence of the Church Missionary Society mission peaked in early 1816, when the council of chiefs granted them permission to proselytize freely throughout the area (*Missionary Register* 1817; Church Missionary Society Archives 1816). Yet in May 1817, after a year of war and turmoil in the region, the missionaries abandoned their schools and retreated to Freetown (Walker 1845:515).

The collapse of the mission was less the result of the missionaries actions (although some of them were not blameless) than of policy decisions, innovations, and changes occurring in Europe and in the Futa Jalon (Church Missionary Society Archives 1812a, 1814b). At the turn of the century, one European country after another outlawed slaving by its nationals, but Great Britain was the first to interfere with commerce on the Windward Coast, specifically along the Nunez and Pongo Rivers. The first recorded military action against slave merchants there took place in 1811, when Governor Charles Maxwell sent an expedition into the Pongo to seize British subjects equipping slavers for the Middle Passage (Fyfe 1962:120). The introduction of military violence as a means of transforming commercial patterns severely weakened the basis of support for the mission schools, and chiefs increasingly were forced to reconsider the benefits of continued patronage (Church Missionary Society Archives 1813, 1814b). When the missionaries were asked for gunpowder to fight British warships, they refused, and as a result their presence in the country became one of the casualties in the conflict (Church Missionary Society Archives 1817, n.d.).

The exit of the missionaries gave but small respite to those who sought a return to more profitable days. After 1818, the newly organized British antislavery squadron made the Iles de Los, only fifty miles south of the Pongo, a principal station for their surveillance activity on the coast (Lloyd 1968:45). With squadron vessels plying the shoreline at will, the physical characteristics of the rivers themselves became increasingly important. The Nunez was especially disadvantageous for continued slave trading. Only one of its exits was capable of handling large vessels, and a single warship could easily block the estuary and send longboats upstream to search for slavers (*Royal Gazette and Sierra Leone Advertizer* 1821; *Parliamentary Papers* 1821:45–46). To avoid entrapment, slavers increasingly bypassed the Nunez factories in favor of those of the Pongo, where multiple entrances, meandering inlets and lagoons, and friendly traders improved their chances of escaping an unannounced warship.[4] The result was a depressed Nunez economy and an at least temporarily improved one on the Pongo.

Moreover, these apparent transformations of market practices were affected by policy decisions in the Futa Jalon. Occasional contacts between the Freetown merchants and the Fula had led the Fula regime to consider designating specific products for specific routes. In 1794 and 1795 they had suggested that a company factory be established on the Pongo to serve as the official contact point between Freetown and Timbo for legitimate products (Public Record Office 1794). Post-1815 antislavery activities and the disruption of riverine commerce forced the Fula to take a direct role in resolving local disputes and in guaranteeing continued outlets for their products. They intervened in the Nunez in 1823 to insure a free flow of trade, for the first time stationing a governor and garrison there during each trading season from December to April (Public Record Office 1823). Under the altered system, the Pongo became the principal outlet for Fula slaves, and the Nunez was designated a terminal for legitimate trade.[5]

From the late 1820's coffee and from the late 1830's peanuts became new and important cash crops in the rivers' economies. These changes first occurred on the Pongo, where coffee and later peanut plantations provided old coasters with an opportune cover for continued slaving. British warships were forced to view slaves in factory barracoons as part of a plantation work force and therefore not liable to seizure. On the plantation, slaves worked during the rainy season; once it turned dry, both laborers and produce became marketable (*Parliamentary Papers* 1823:23). The symbiotic relationship between slave and legitimate trade which characterized the Pongo's commerce from the turn of the century would continue into the early 1850's.

The transformation to predominantly legitimate goods accelerated faster in the Nunez than in the Pongo once new markets for African products began to appear in Europe and in the Americas. Without long-entrenched slave-trading families to oppose their entry, a group of new Europeans — British subjects with commercial ties to Freetown markets — easily established a foothold on the upper river. While small, this group was encouraged by an apparent Fula design to transform the river's commerce and by a series of new treaties which permitted British warships to seize vessels equipped to carry slaves. At the same time, a

---

[4] Vessels could enter and leave the Pongo River over the Cassinsin Bar, Mud Bar, Sand Bar, or Taborta River Bar entrances.
[5] This was especially true after a successful raid upon property belonging to William Skelton, Jr., and John Serjeant in 1832 (Public Record Office 1832).

number of shallow-draft paddle steamers which could more easily surprise the slavers that occasionally visited the river were introduced into the antislavery squadron (Newbury 1965:133; Ward 1969:128–141; Pearsall 1959:213). A second group of newcomers entering the Nunez trade were French subjects with commercial ties on Gorée and in Saint-Louis, Senegal.[6] Coffee first attracted the French to the Nunez, but with rising demands for peanut oil by French soap manufacturers in the mid-1840's they rapidly shifted to peanuts (Vené 1837). Land was cleared along the middle river for peanut cultivation, ending dependence upon the uncertain and often interrupted trade with the interior. Cooperative naval officers further advanced French interests by interceding on their behalf. Moreover, the tariff reform bill of 1845 reversed earlier French policy on Nunez coffee. After 1845 Nunez coffee received a preferential tariff if its origin was attested by a French agent resident on the river. In addition, by increasing the duty on sesame, the regulation stimulated the use of peanut oil as a substitute cooking oil, and cultivation on the Nunez increased as French demands for peanuts rose sharply. In January 1846 the first French agent was appointed to certify produce from the Nunez area (Demougeot 1938:206–207).

These Europeans symbolized more than the infusion of so-called legitimate trade, for most represented, or soon would represent, the interests of large trading firms along the Windward Coast. Until 1835 factories had received the majority of their trade goods from American or other ships visiting the coast, exchanging them for whatever products were available in return. Some would continue this practice into the 1840's, but the arrival of companies that sought particular commodities ultimately transformed commerce.[7] Trading firms provided goods from their larger entrepôts on the coast, and the importance of the occasional visitor diminished. Companies advertised their interest in specific items and stimulated trade and the cultivation of produce along definite lines. At first coffee, hides, and wax dominated trade,but after 1840 they were dwarfed by the insatiable French demand for peanuts. In addition, firms were able to pressure colonial officials for increased protection of their investments, thereby prompting colonial intervention in the commercial system and the treaty-making process (Schnapper 1961:221–232).

TRADITIONAL ARRANGEMENTS AND THE TREATY SYSTEM

Given the radical transition from slaves to legitimate products occurring

[6]   These included René and Durand Valentine, Antoine and Pierre d'Erneville, Charles Boucaline, M. LaPorte, Auguste Santon, A. E. Carvallis, and subfactors who accompanied them to the river.
[7]   This was particularly true among traders who had established commercial relationships with Americans before 1840.

during this half-century on the Windward Coast, that the landlord-stranger relationship survived at all is remarkable. The traditional contract between the two parties had been an individual one, with obligations, restrictions, and lines of redress clearly defined. Once a trader had established a position in the commercial network, however, new options became available to him.

Between 1790 and 1808 only four trader families can be identified outside the system of obligations required by the traditional arrangement. All had established residences on the rivers by the mid-1700's. These included the Fernandez family of Bramaya, the Gomezes of Bakia, the Ormonds of the Bangalan branch of the Pongo, and Dr. Walker of Kacundy on the Nunez. Although free of the customary responsibilities, all had acquired positions as chiefs and had been absorbed into the rivers' political systems, which carried with them new sets of obligations. William Fernandez and Immanuel Gomez were paramount chiefs under the nominal control of the Susu rulers (Saint-Père 1930:35–36; Arcin 1911:141; Rivière 1968:742). John Ormond, Jr., who returned to the river around 1805 to inherit property belonging to his father, was chief of Bangalan town and subservient to the paramount of Bangalan district, also a tributary to the Susu (Mayer 1854:77). Walker was chief of Kacundy, where he played an additional important role as principal supporter and adviser to the Landuma king Calinguie.[8]

Traders who had arrived in the area at the turn of the century and who for the most part sought to avoid entangling alliances with the local elites found that the obligations of the landlord-stranger relationship did not preclude regional cooperation among themselves when established commercial patterns were challenged by outside influences. In 1794, Walker and David Lawrence of the Nunez drastically reduced prices for Fula products as a warning to Fula authorities against allowing James Watt to establish a factory at Timbo and a new path to Freetown (Watt 1794:70, 90). A year later in Pongo country, George Irving, Benjamin Curtis, William Skelton, Sr., and Mr. Ferrie, all bound by the traditional contract, agreed to share the cost of discouraging the Sierra Leone Company (Public Record Office 1795a). By lowering prices for interior products and boycotting caravans which traded with the company store at Freeport, they dealt the company factory a severe financial setback (Public Record Office 1796a, 1796b). While such activities were extra-legal and outside the customary agreements, other attempts to expel the company from the rivers' commerce clearly were directed through the landlord-stranger communication lines. Irving, Curtis, Skelton, Ferrie, and others warned their patrons that the company would "ruin the river."

[8] According to James Watt, Calinguie ruled at Walkaria, Walker's town. Later sources identify Kacundy as the residence of the Mandiale ruling branch. Consequently I use "Kacundy" to designate the town that Walker founded.

In reply, their chiefs met in a closed conference which ignored the traders' protests — perhaps to reemphasize the foreigners' subservience — and renewed their earlier pledge to protect company property (Public Record Office 1795b). By stimulating cooperation among traders, the challenge of company monopoly from 1794 to 1802 brought changes to the indigenous-foreigner relationship. Extralegal activity came to be tolerated, but the chiefs firmly resisted direct political interference in their privilege to grant protection, no matter how much it might upset the trader community.

The appearance of missionaries between 1807 and 1817 and the introduction of military force as part of the transformation from slave to legitimate trade after 1811 brought significant changes in their wake. While the decision to admit missionaries and their schools fundamentally belonged to the chiefs, some traders discreetly but successfully lobbied for the schools because of the commercial training they would provide. Most successful in this attempt was Benjamin Curtis, whose brother Thomas had married the daughter of King Uli Kati of Thia, the capital of the Pongo region (Church Missionary Society Archives 1811). Curtis donated the site and the buildings for the first school at Bashia (Butscher 1806–1809).

Unfortunately for the missionaries, their appearance there coincided with the emergence of a new slaver coalition which not only opposed their presence but was convinced that the missionaries reported their every move to authorities in Freetown. This extralegal consortium of commercial interests included William Cunningham Wilson, Paul and Mary Faber, Stiles and Bailey Lightburn, and John Ormond, Jr., of the Upper Pongo, who joined in 1809 with Samuel Samo of the lower river and Charles Hickson and William H. Leigh of the Iles de Los. The group hoped to minimize trader conflict by establishing a quota arrangement for provisioning slave ships, thus gaining monopolistic control of the Pongo trade through collective effort (*Trials of the slave traders* 1813; *Edinburgh Review* 1813). The immediate effect upon the landlord-stranger relationship was to elevate Ormond to a new level in the political system and to link the traders, his partners, more closely to the local political process. This became abundantly clear in September 1811, when King Kati created a crisis by seizing the colonial sloop *George* at the advice of his son-in-law, Thomas Curtis. Kati called a conference of all chiefs, traders, and missionaries to resolve his difficulties with the Sierra Leone colony (Church Missionary Society Archives 1811). For the first time traders took part in the decision-making process, but a pattern was established which would be repeated in coming years. Chiefs invited them to participate in disputes with Sierra Leone officials or with the captains of British men-of-war, although they continued to be excluded from conferences on the missionary problem. Invariably the English sought to deal with one chief rather than many, and as a result increasingly recognized Uli Kati as the representative of the Pongo chiefs (Church Missionary Society Archives 1814b). As a result, Kati was forced to defend not only his own strangers, but also those under contract with other paramounts. In return, he demanded and obtained military supplies and assistance against his English adversaries (Church Missionary Society Archives 1812b).

Many fewer traders had established factories in the Nunez area during the early 1800's, and most had allied with Mr. Fortune at Boke or with Chief John Pearce at Kacundy, who in 1796 had inherited Walker's position (Public Record Office 1797a, 1797b, n.d.; Watt 1794:6–8, 11, 40, 70). Sources for the nineteenth century reveal little about the technicalities of the landlord-stranger relationship among these people, but we can assume that they differed little from those in the Pongo. Pearce and Fortune also provided substantial support for opposing branches of the Landuma ruling family and for two competing entrepôts on the river (Watt 1794:5, 7; Public Record Office 1816). Pearce kept the political capital at Kacundy until his death in 1818. Although his son inherited his commercial estate, he was unable to maintain its former influence against the challenge of John Bateman of Boke, a protégé of Fortune who championed the opposing ruling family and commercial center (Public Record Office 1816). In the resulting war, which lasted from 1818 to 1822, Nunez chiefs used the resources and rivalry of traders to change the political system (*Royal Gazette and Sierra Leone Advertizer* 1819; Public Record Office 1823), while traders exploited family rivalries to assist commercial change.

Under the new Landuma ruler, Macande of Boke, the landlord-stranger relationship remained the same into the 1830's. Macande established stable duties for anchorage charges and customs, and partially as a result of this stability new traders moved into the river during the 1830's, among them a dozen from French possessions to the north (see fn. 6; Public Record Office 1839). Macande's death in 1838 was followed by a chieftaincy dispute which continued intermittently until 1852, bringing significant modification to traditional commercial relations. Contenders in the struggle demanded double and triple duties from new traders. Stores were destroyed in the fighting and trade was disrupted, and in self-defense French and British nationals applied to Gorée or Freetown for assistance (Public Record Office 1839).[9] By March 1839 traders were beginning to negotiate with opposing factions for collective rights and property protection (Public Record Office 1839). In January 1842 and April 1843, the captains of French and British men-of-war signed the first

[9]   The evolution of contractual arrangements between foreigners and the local rulers which accompanied the arrival of French traders and the development of a specialized cash-crop economy in the Nunez region is treated in more detail in Mouser (1973–1974).

treaties identifying special communities of foreigners and establishing specific obligations and restrictions between them and their African hosts (Archives Afrique Occidentale Français n.d.; Public Record Office 1843).[10] These treaties, renewed and modified as the outcome of war shifted from one side to the other after 1843, increasingly released traders from obligations to specific chiefs and instead guaranteed privileges for all Europeans trading on the coast. By the late 1850's, the landlord-stranger relationship on the Nunez River had given way to a treaty system.

Such changes were slower to come to Pongo country. In 1838 a war along the upper river forced Benjamin Campbell and William Emerson, the sole merchants tied to the traditional contract, out of the area (Ward 1969:216). Not until the 1860's did new Europeans enter the Pongo trade. A British attempt to impose a series of treaties in mid-1851 was opposed by trader chiefs on the Upper Pongo, and the paramount, Bala Bangu, rejected the overture (Public Record Office 1852a). A year later, however, he signed a treaty with Britain without consulting his subordinates (Public Record Office 1852b). The result was a protracted war which lasted until 1855, during which private armies destroyed peanut and coffee plantations and temporarily crippled the river's economy (Arcin 1911:142–143). Rather than risk involvement in the conflict, new legitimate traders avoided the region; France did not bother to sign a treaty with the Africans until 1866 (Archives Afrique Occidentale Française 1866).[11]

Before these changes ushered in a new era, the agreement between landlords and strangers was the accepted method of dealing with foreigners resident within a local political unit. The relationship stipulated the obligations between individuals, listing the rents and duties that made the arrangement operative. These responsibilities were never meant to be static, however. Outside influences and innovations and the passage of time brought a fusion of interests. Gradually strangers became advisors to the political elite and sometimes chiefs themselves, and after 1838 the process of accommodation and assimilation was modified by a treaty system. Yet such changes were not without precedent on either river. Rather, they were accepted with relative ease into a system designed to facilitate the influx of new ideas and institutions into a flexible society.

---

[10]   I am indebted to George E. Brooks, Jr., who supplied me with a microfilm of selected manuscripts from the Archives Afrique Occidentale Français. Deveneaux (1973:96) notes that this process of "gradual erosion of the traditional authority of chiefs over settlers and Europeans" began more than a decade earlier in the Port Loko area.
[11]   The relationship between the chiefs and a new missionary group which entered the Pongo in 1855 is described in Vassady (1972: ch. 5).

REFERENCES

AFZELIUS, ADAM
1967 *Sierra Leone journal, 1795–1796.* Edited by Alexander P. Kup. Uppsala: Almqvist and Wikells.
ARCHIVES AFRIQUE OCCIDENTALE FRANÇAISE, DAKAR
n.d. Folio 13–G–4.
1866 Treaty, February 15, 1866. Folio 13–G–4.
ARCIN, ANDRÉ
1907 *La Guinée française.* Paris: Challamel.
1911 *Histoire de la Guinée française.* Paris: Challamel
BENNETT, NORMAN R., GEORGE E. BROOKS, JR.
1965 *New England merchants in Africa: a history through documents, 1802 to 1865.* Boston: Boston University Press.
BERENGER-FERAND, LAURENT JEAN B.
1879 *Les peuples de la Sénégambie.* Paris: Leroux.
BROOKS, GEORGE E., JR.
1970 *Yankee traders, old coasters and African middlemen: a history of American legitimate trade with West Africa in the nineteenth century.* Boston: Boston University Press.
BUTSCHER, LEOPOLD
1806–1809 Extracts from the journal. *Proceeding of the Church Missionary Society* 2:493–496.
CAILLIÉ, RENE
1830 *Travels through Central Africa to Timbuctoo,* volume one. (Translated from the French.) London: Colburn and Bentley.
CHURCH MISSIONARY SOCIETY ARCHIVES, LONDON
1811 Renner to Secretary, October 30, 1811. CAI/E2/105.
1812a Renner to Secretary, June 8, 1812. CAI/E3/8.
1812b Renner to Secretary, July 29, 1812. CAI/E3/13.
1813 Renner to Secretary, November 5, 1813. CAI/E3/99.
1814a Wilhelm journal, entry dated December 6, 1814. CAI/E4/60.
1814b Renner to Secretary, June 24, 1814. CAI/E4/19.
1816 Bickersteth to Secretary, April 20, 1816. CAI/E5/116.
1817 Wilhelm to Secretary, April 21, 1817. CAI/E5A/91.
n.d. Renner journal. CAI/E6/63.
COUPLAND, REGINALD
1964 *The British anti-slavery movement* (second edition). London: Frank Cass.
CURTIN, PHILIP D.
1969 *The Atlantic slave trade.* Madison: University of Wisconsin Press.
1975 *Economic change in precolonial Africa: Senegambia in the era of the slave trade.* Madison: University of Wisconsin Press.
DALBY, DAVID
1967 The Mel languages: a reclassification of Southern "West Atlantic." *African Languages Studies* 4:1–17.
DEMOUGEOT, ANTOINE MARIE JEAN
1938 Histoire du Nunez. *Bulletin du Comité d'Etudes Historiques et Scientifiques de l'Afrique Occidentale Française* 21:177–289.
DEVENEAUX, GUSTAV KASHOPE
1973 "The political and social impact of the colony in northern Sierra Leone, 1821–1896." Unpublished Ph.D. dissertation, Boston University.

DORJAHN, V. R., CHRISTOPHER FYFE
  1962   Landlord and stranger: change in tenancy relations in Sierra Leone. *Journal of African History* 3:391–397.
Edinburgh Review
  1813   Review by "A Gentleman . . . at Sierra Leone" of: *Trials of the slave traders* (London, 1813). *Edinburgh Review* 21:78.
FYFE, CHIRISTOPHER
  1962   *A history of Sierra Leone*. London: Oxford University Press.
GOLBERRY, SILVESTER MEINRAD XAVIER
  1803   *Travels in Africa . . . 1785, 1786, and 1787*. Translated by William Mudford. London: M. Jones.
HAWKINS, JOSEPH
  1797   *A history of a voyage to the coast of Africa*. Troy: Luther Pratt.
HOPEWELL, JAMES FRANKLIN
  1958   "Muslim penetration into French Guinea, Sierra Leone and Liberia before 1850," Unpublished Ph.D. dissertation, Columbia University.
HOWARD, ALLEN M.
  1972   "Big men, traders, and chiefs: power, commerce, and spatial change in the Sierra Leone-Guinea plain, 1865–1895." Unpublished Ph.D. dissertation, University of Wisconsin.
KNUTSFORD, VISCOUNT
  1900   *Life and letters of Zachary MaCaulay*. London: Edward Arnold.
LAING, ALEXANDER GORDON
  1825   *Travels in the Timannee, Kooranko, and Soolima countries of Western Africa*. London: John Murray.
LEVTZION, NEHEMIA
  1975   "North-West Africa: from the Maghrib to the fringes of the forest," in *The Cambridge history of Africa*, volume four. Edited by R. Gray, 142–222. Cambridge: Cambridge University Press.
LLOYD, CHRISTOPHER
  1968   *The navy and the slave trade*. London: Frank Cass.
MAYER, BRANTZ
  1854   *Captain Canot, or Twenty years of an African slaver*. New York: D. Appleton.
MÉO, DOCTEUR
  1919   Etudes sur le Rio-Nunez. *Bulletin du Comité d'Etudes Historiques et Scientifiques de l'Afrique Occidentale Française* 2:281–317.
Missionary Records
  1836   *Missionary Records: West Africa*. London: The Religious Tract Society.
Missionary Register
  1817   *Missionary Register* 5:391–393.
MONHEIM, CHARLES
  1931   *L'affaire du Rio Nunez*. Louvain: Editions de l'Aucam.
MOUSER, BRUCE L.
  1971   "Trade and politics in the Nunez and Pongo Rivers, 1790 to 1865." Unpublished Ph.D. dissertation, Indiana University.
  1973a Trade, coasters, and conflict in the Rio Pongo from 1790 to 1808. *Journal of African History* 14:45–64.
  1973b Moira politics in 1814: Amara to Maxwell, March 2. *Bulletin de l'Institut Fondamental d'Afrique Noire* B35:805–812.
  1973–1974 The Nunez affair. *Bulletin des Séances, Académie Royale des Sciences d'Outre-Mer* (Bruxelles) 1973–1974:697–742.

NEWBURY, COLIN W.
1965   *British policy toward West Africa.* Oxford: Clarendon.
1971   "Prices and profitability in early nineteenth-century West African trade," in *The development of indigenous trade and markets in West Africa.* Edited by Claude Meillassoux, 91–106. London: Oxford University Press.
Parliamentary Papers (Commons)
1821   Further papers relating to the suppression of the slave trade. *Parliamentary Papers (Commons)* 355(23).
1823   Correspondence with British Commissioners. *Parliamentary Papers (Commons)* 19.
PAULME, DENISE
1956   Structures sociales en pays Baga. *Bulletin de l'Institut Français d'Afrique Noire* B18:98–116.
1958   La notion de sorcier chez les Baga. *Bulletin de l'Institut Français d'Afrique Noire* B20:406–416.
PEARSALL, S. W. H.
1959   Sierra Leone and the suppression of the slave trade. *Sierra Leone Studies* 1959:211–229.
PETERSON, JOHN
1969   *Province of freedom.* Evanston: Northwestern University Press.
PUBLIC RECORD OFFICE, LONDON
1793–1794   Council, October 29, 1793, and January 1, 1794. CO 267/2.
1794   Council, May 5, 1794. CO 270/2.
1795a   Cooper to Council, August 24, 1795, enclosed in Council, September 1, 1795. CO 270/3.
1795b   Buckle to Governor, May 29, 1795. CO 270/3.
1796a   Cooper to Council, enclosed in Council, February 3, 1796. CO 270/3.
1796b   Council, April 26, 1796. CO 270/4.
1797a   Macaulay to Cooper, July 18, 1797. CO 268/5.
1797b   Council, September 13, 1797. CO 270/4.
1802   On the means of establishing a commercial intercourse, enclosed in Macaulay to Sullivan, September 4, 1802. CO 2/1.
1816   Journal book of Campbell, entries dated December 23–28, 1816. CO/5.
1823   Commissions general report 4, April 29, 1823. FO 84/21.
1832   Findlay to Hay, March 20, 1832, and enclosure, David Wilson to Serjeant, October 25, 1832. CO 267/114.
1839   John Hill to Admiral, April 5, 1839, enclosed in Foreign Office to Colonial Office, November 18, 1839. CO 267/155/Offices.
1843   Admiralty to Colonial Office, August 5, 1843. CO 267/182/Offices.
1852a   Macdonald to Grey, February 17, 1852. CO 267/227/32.
1852b   Treaty, January 17, 1852, enclosed in Macdonald to Grey, February 17, 1852, CO 267/227/32.
n.d.a.   Macaulay to Cooper, enclosed in Council, April 26, 1796. CO 270/4.
n.d.b   Cambell memo 7. CO 2/5.
RIVIÈRE, CLAUDE
1968   Le long des côtes de Guinée avant la phase coloniale. *Bulletin de l'Institut Fondamental d'Afrique Noire* 30B:727–750.
ROBINSON, ROBERT
1966   "British colonial policy and trade on the Windward Coast of Africa, 1812–1832." Unpublished Ph.D. dissertation, Duke University.

RODNEY, WALTER A.
1968   Jihad and social revolution in Futa Djalon in the eighteenth century. *Journal of the Historical Society of Nigeria* 4:269–284.
1970   *A history of the Upper Guinea Coast, 1545–1800.* London: Oxford University Press.
1975   "The Guinea Coast," in *The Cambridge history of Africa* volume four. Edited by R. Gray, 234–324. Cambridge: Cambridge University Press.
Royal Gazette and Sierra Leone Advertizer
1819   *Royal Gazette and Sierra Leone Advertizer,* June 26, July 3.
1821   *Royal Gazette and Sierra Leone Advertizer,* December 29.
SAINT-PÈRE, JULES HUBURT
1930   Petit historique des Sossos du Rio Pongo. *Bulletin du Comité d'Etudes Historiques et Scientifiques de l'Afrique Occidentale Française* 13:26–47.
SCHNAPPER, BERNARD
1961   *La politique et le commerce français dans le Golfe de Guinée de 1838 à 1871.* Paris: Mouton.
STOCK, EUGENE
1899   *History of the Church Missionary Society,* volume one. London: Church Missionary Society.
SUNDSTRÖM, LARS
1974   *The exchange economy of pre-colonial tropical Africa.* New York: St. Martin's Press.
SURET-CANALE, JEAN
1970   "The Fouta-Djalon chieftaincy," in *West African chiefs.* Edited by Michael Crowder and Obaro Ikime, 79–97. New York: Africana.
Trials of the slave traders
1813   *Trials of the slave traders.* London.
VASSADY, BELA, JR.
1972   "The role of the Black missionary in West Africa, 1840–1890." Unpublished Ph.D. dissertation, Temple University.
VENÉ, A.
1837   Rapport sur les établissements anglais de la Gambie et les comptoirs française d'Albreda et de Casamance. *Annales Maritimes et Coloniales* 64:1163–1182.
WALKER, SAMUEL ABRAHAM
1845   *Missions in western Africa among the Soosoos, Bulloms, etc.* Dublin: William Curry.
WARD, W. E. F.
1969   *The Royal Navy and the slavers.* New York: Random House.
WATT, JAMES
1794   Journal of Mr. James Watt, in his Expedition to and from Teembo in the Year 1794. Rhodes House Library, Oxford University, Mss. African s.22.

Some Paradoxes of Pacification:
Senegal and France in the
1850's and 1860's

LELAND C. BARROWS

This study of the reaction of African rulers to European encroachment will focus on the rulers of those societies which line both banks of the navigable or seminavigable portion of the Senegal River west of the Felu Falls during the two governorships (1854–1861 and 1863–1865) of the French engineer officer Louis Léon César Faidherbe.

Faidherbe, of course, is generally considered to have been the founder of French West Africa and the proconsul who totally conquered Senegal for France a generation before the scramble. He himself helped to further this image of power through his writings.[1] However, his contemporaries believed that he had simply fulfilled a plan which had called for the pacification or intimidation of Senegalese polities and rulers to discourage them from interfering with colonial trade based, as far as Senegal was concerned, on gum and increasingly on peanuts (Maurel and Prom Papers 1863; Archives Nationales de France 1864a, n.d.a). Despite his having taken part in the *occupation totale* of Algeria in the 1840's, Faidherbe never conquered or annexed the whole of Senegal. Instead, his policy was one of military pacification followed in most cases by French-supervised nonrule.[2]

I would like to express my appreciation both to the committee in charge of administering the Andrew W. Mellon Faculty Fellowships in the Humanities at Harvard University and to the President of Voorhees College. That the former awarded me a fellowship for the 1976–1977 academic year and the latter a leave of absence from my normally heavy teaching schedule permitted me to complete this article on very short notice. Secondly, I would like to acknowledge that I have borrowed substantially from two articles I wrote earlier on Faidherbe and Senegal (Barrows 1976, 1978).

[1] See, in particular, Faidherbe (1881–1885, 1889). A third book (Ministère de la Marine 1885), unsigned by Faidherbe, was published by order of the Ministry of the Navy to rekindle public interest in the progress of French rule in Senegal and recapitulates portions of the 1881–1885 work, and it in turn is almost completely recapitulated in Faidherbe's 1889 volume.

[2] It seems remarkable that at the start of the governorship of the expansionist Brière de

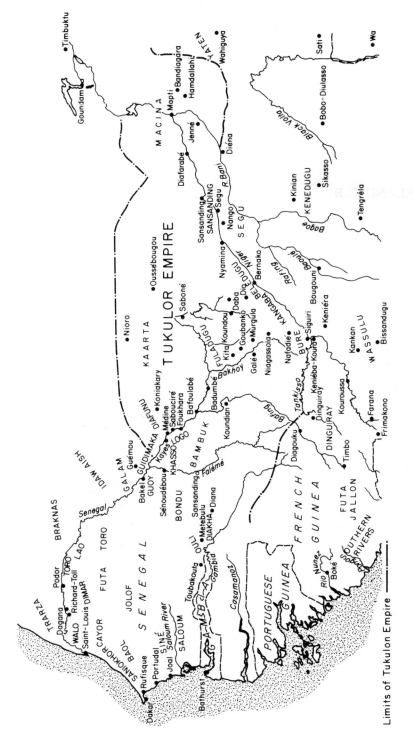

Limits of Tukulor Empire ▬▬▬▬

Figure 1. The Senegambia and Upper Niger regions in the mid-nineteenth century

Faidherbe began his first administration in December 1854 by attempting to put into effect a plan which had evolved since the 1830's. It had been the design both of naval officers who had served in Saint-Louis and Gorée and of several of the Bordeaux-based French merchants who bought Senegalese produce and transported it to market in France. This plan was given final form in ministerial instructions given in 1853 and 1854 to Captain Auguste Protet, Faidherbe's predecessor as governor (Archives Nationales de France 1853–1854) as well as to Faidherbe himself and in two petitions written by Marc Maurel of the Maurel and Prom Company and signed by major Saint-Louis wholesalers, one dated December 8, 1851 (Archives Nationales de France 1851a) and the other dated February 11, 1854, that were endorsed by the Ministry of the Navy in Paris.

The plan called for the Saint-Louis authorities (1) to suppress the three Mauritanian-controlled seasonal gum-trading *escales*[3] of the Lower Senegal River and to replace them with several fortified French-controlled trading posts; (2) to allow French-controlled African villages to form around these posts where wholesalers could open trading branches to buy and sell any products all year long; (3) to reduce and eventually end all *coutumes* [trade and land occupancy taxes paid by the colonial authorities or by private parties to African rulers and notables]; (4) to suppress all navigation tolls (also called *coutumes*) paid to various African rulers and officials along the Senegal River, particularly the major one at Salde (near Dirmbodya), in the Futa Toro *almamate*[4]; (5) to require that all Senegalese rulers recognize that the French were the proprietors of the Senegal River as far up as the Felu Falls in Khasso (about 1,000 kilometers); (6) to institute what the French called free trade — that is, trade freed of all African-imposed taxes and other regulations and restrictions; and (7) to free the left bank of the Senegal River, by force if necessary, from all Mauritanian political control and to end the practice of some Mauritanian clans of raiding the sedentary left-bank Negro

---

l'Isle in 1877 the minister of the navy, at that time Admiral Fourichon, could refer to Senegal as an "aggrégat de comptoirs commerciaux" (N'diaye 1968:465), echoing his predecessor of 1830, who had considered Senegal to be no more than "un simple comptoir" (Hardy 1921:247). Ricard (1865:235, 270–284) had written at the close of Faidherbe's second term that most of the polities of Senegal were still independent.

[3] In Senegalese French the term *escale* denoted a recognized trading point, usually one in which the French colonial authorities had not claimed sovereignty or built permanent warehousing facilities or fortifications. When they had seized and garrisoned an *escale*, it was usually called a *poste* or occasionally an *escale fortifié*.

[4] The term *almamy* is the Pular rendition of *al-imam*, the Arabic term designating the person who presides at public prayer. As a ruler's title it was first taken by Malik Sy, the founder of the theocratic regime in Bondu at the end of the seventeenth century, and came to designate a theocratic ruler. The same title was adopted by the theocratic rulers of Futa Jalon and then those of Futa Toro and Bondu.

populations.[5] Another, if less openly articulated, part of this plan called for the colonial government to end the special commercial privileges that had been accorded to the *habitants*.[6] In particular, they were to lose their guaranteed positions as middlemen in the gum trade. Realizing this part of the plan would be delicate because of the close links, in some cases family ties, which the *habitants* had established with the rulers of the surrounding African polities.

In short, Faidherbe was to be guided by a blueprint which called for French political and economic control of a major West African inland waterway from which the European treaty system excluded other Europeans. This waterway pointed to the upper reaches of a yet larger river which led to the far-off and mysterious Timbuktu, a French objective since the seventeenth century; and it was the only dry-season source of fresh water for many of the peoples who lived along its banks. Many of the delta channels of the Senegal River were navigable most of the time for the smaller French steam gunboats. The principal channel was navigable all the time to a point just beyond Podor in western Futa Toro. Farther upstream the French boats could pass only during the rainy season, from late July to late October. Light-draft boats could enter Lake Panieful east of Walo through the Tauey Creek. Upstream, French boats had seasonal access to about 150 kilometers of the Falémé River, now the boundary between Senegal and Mali.

The Senegal River between Saint-Louis and its mouth (it was separated from the sea at Saint-Louis only by a long sand spit called the Langue de Barbarie) fronted on a small part of Cayor, the major Wolof kingdom, which linked Saint-Louis to Cape Verde and Gorée. Between Saint-Louis and Bakel, some 800 kilometers inland, the river served as the southern boundary of the Mauritanian Trarza, Brakna, and Idaw 'Aish emirates.[7] It served also as the northern border of the Wolof kingdom of Walo, the Tukulor[8] Futa Toro *almamate,* and part of the Soninke kingdom of

[5]   For a detailed description of how the basic instructions given to Protet and then to Faidherbe were formulated, see Barrows (1974:238–246, 249–250).
[6]   During the period under study, the term *habitant* referred to the Negro or racially mixed permanent residents of the French enclaves, particularly Saint-Louis and Gorée.
[7]   By the end of the nineteenth century, the French colonial authorities, following French practice in Algeria, commonly referred to independent political units in Mauritania by this term and their secular rulers as *emirs* or *amirs*. Both terms suggest that the rulers in question had far more centralized religious and political authority than was the case in their nomadic and segmented societies. In the mid-nineteenth century, the Hassani rulers of the Trarza and the Brakna were referred to as shaykhs (*cheikhs*) or sultans by members of their own societies and as kings in the French correspondence (Stewart 1973:55, 56 n. 1, 2).
[8]   The question of terminology is very complex. The term Tukulor is derived from Tekrur or Takrur, the name Arab geographers gave to a ninth-century polity in the Middle Senegal Valley, the first in West Africa to convert on a wide scale to Islam. It can be used to designate all the inhabitants of what became Futa Toro, including emigrants like those who joined al-Hajj 'Umar's state-building activities in the east. It can also be used to designate those residents of Futa Toro who follow sedentary occupations, usually farming, who are Muslim, and who, by coincidence, are darker-skinned than the Fulbe, who are nomadic pastoralists

Guoye, in which was located Bakel, the principal upriver French post. Beyond the Falémé confluent, Guoye gave way to Kamera. Both Guoye and Kamera once formed part of the united kingdom of Gadiaga or Galam, the name by which the French knew it. Facing Gadiaga on the right bank was a fringe of independent Soninke city-states known collectively as Guidimakha. The region along the left bank as well as part of the right between the eastern boundary of Kamera and the Felu Falls was known as Khasso. Once a powerful kingdom, by the mid-nineteenth century it was breaking up. Both banks of the navigable portions of the Falémé River were dominated by the *almamate* of Bondu, with which the French traditionally had had good relations. East of it lay several Mande-speaking chieftaincies called collectively Bambuk and known for their gold mines. A long-term French objective had been, if not to seize Bambuk, at least to capture its gold trade. For the latter purpose, the French had founded the post of Senudebu along the Faleme in Bondu in 1844.

The French plan as given to Faidherbe called primarily for domination of the French-oriented trading system along the navigable Senegal and its affluents. Because at the start of its realization gum arabic was the principal trade staple, having fetched a little over 2,000,000 francs a year between 1841 and 1851,[9] and because the French believed that its nomadic Mauritanian producers were inaccessible in their desert homelands, the plan made no provision for direct control over them (Archives Nationale de France 1851b; Archives Nationales de la République du Sénégal n.d.). However, it was assumed that the Mauritanians' need for French goods would compel them to trade on French terms.[10]

---

of laxer religious practice and of a lighter color which suggests a distant and partial Berber origin. Both groups speak the same Pular language, and both when native to Futa Toro are referred to as Futankobe (singular Futanke) (Curtin 1975:18–22; Robinson 1975:1–18).
[9] During the period under consideration, the colonial economy of the Senegal River continued to derive most of its export wealth from gum. The value of peanuts exported from Saint-Louis was valued in 1860 at 1,876,261.60 francs in comparison to 444,828.50 francs for peanuts, and these were results of trade during a relatively peaceful year. In 1861, the value of gum went up to 1,883,500 francs and that of peanuts to 614,920.50 francs, despite the war which had broken out in Cayor. In 1864, the value of gum must have increased on the French market, because the *Courrier du Havre* estimated that the 1,600,000 kilograms of gum exported from Saint-Louis would fetch 4,000,000 francs in France. It did not guess at the value of the 1,550,000 kilograms of peanuts, but it was probably less than that of the gum. Despite exceptionally good years like 1864, the total value of the trade fell steadily in the 1840's, 1850's, and 1860's. The total value of peanuts exported from other parts of Senegambia claimed by the French, including the Southern Rivers of Guinea, did indeed surpass the value of gum from the Senegal River. This fact will explain why the French colonial authorities began turning away from the Senegal River itself after 1860, focusing on the coastal peanut areas (see Suret-Canale 1968:332; Archives Nationales de France 1861b, 1864–1865).
[10] Until 1857 the Trarza had the option of trading directly with the British at Portendick, near Nouakchott, on the Atlantic Coast. However, in 1857, they gave up this right, in return for which the French relinquished their small trading enclave at Albreda, opposite Bathurst, on the north bank of the Gambia.

Old hopes that plantations or some form of cash-cropping could be introduced into parts of Senegal left open the door to greater French involvement in some of the Senegalese sedentary societies. The growing importance of peanuts caused a broadening of the plan to include French intervention against those elements in traditional Wolof society that interfered with this new culture. The *tyeddos*, crown soldiers of servile origin — a military elite who were the mainstays of the Walo and Cayor monarchies — became a particular object of French hostility. Faidherbe's attempt to suppress the *tyeddos* in Cayor led him into a land war and complications which he had not expected.

The sedentary Negro societies of the Senegal Valley were segregated, unequal, plural societies with communal representation. The Wolof in particular had servile bureaucracies and armies. All of them were subdivided territorially into provinces or what the French called cantons, which were bound to their centers by ties that to the French observer appeared relatively loose. In addition, they included what might be called autonomous transnational groupings: clans of Fulbe pastoralists and, in the Wolof societies, Muslim clerical communities. The chiefs of state were chosen, for the most part, through systems of restricted election by which groups of title holders, including representatives of the regions and of the various servile and occupational groups, chose heads of state from among various eligible contenders belonging to certain set royal or otherwise eligible families or clans.

The Futa Toro *almamate* became more decentralized following the death of its founder, Abdul Kader, in 1806. Effective power was seized by a council of five hereditary electors, the heads of major aristocratic families who, themselves not eligible for the *almamy*ship, chose *almamies* from distinguished members of major eligible clerical families. The large number of eligible candidates available at any one time and the fact that the electors replaced the *almamy* on an average of once every one and a half to two years weakened the institutions of legitimate central government and gave the French an impression of instability. They referred to the *almamate* as a confederation or "theocratic republic" (Carrère and Holle 1855:127) rather than as a kingdom.

The Mauritanian emirates on the right bank were decentralized "segmentary monarchies" (Stewart 1973:1–16) which in some ways also fit the Senegalese pattern that has been presented. The Trarza and Brakna were ruled by warrior clans of Arabic origin called Hassaniyya, each headed by a ruling clan. The Idaw 'Aish, on the other hand, unconquered by the Arabs, were still ruled by Berber warrior clans. In the three emirates, gum was harvested by slaves and marketed by members of the Mauritanian maraboutic[11] clans.

---

[11]   The term "marabout," from which "maraboutic" is derived, is the Gallicized form of the Portuguese transliteration of the Arabic term *murabit*. In French-speaking Africa it denotes

All of the south-bank sedentary societies were characterized to a greater or lesser extent by a decline in the authority of "legitimate" chiefs of state, or of those chosen in the "legitimate" ways, in favor of members of the electoral lineages, territorial governors, and palace officials, who gradually usurped more than their legitimate shares of power. Also, Muslim clerics increasingly challenged the bases of traditional authority and proposed their own systems of reformed government. The state-building activities of al-Hajj 'Umar and Maba Diakhu are stellar examples of the latter process. However, the *almamate* of Futa Toro itself had grown out of such a theocratic revolution — one that after 1806 had turned sour. Muslim communities in Ndiambur province of Cayor increasingly threatened the authority of the *damel* of Cayor. The two forms of usurpation were linked in the cases of aspiring strongmen whose legitimate claims to rule were weak but who adopted reforming Islam as a means of gaining, holding, and strengthening their political power.

The French were aware of the gradual weakening of the traditional governments of the African polities surrounding them. It was the inability of these governments to keep order as well as the fall in the price of gum on the French market that stimulated the formulation of the instructions given to Protet and then to Faidherbe.[12] These instructions also reflected the reluctance of the French government to become overly involved in West African colonial ventures as well as the common European view that West African societies could be made to reform themselves by economic inducements combined with a minimum of European intervention. "Helping" some of the Senegalese riverine societies to eliminate sources of disorder and restrictions on trade would, it was conceded, increase the profits of French wholesalers; but, so it was rationalized, the African producers would also benefit — only the "parasites" in both camps would suffer, and they deservedly.

---

a Muslim holy man and teacher, one trained in Islamic sciences. In some cases it denoted the ruling members of Muslim clerical communities. In the Mauritanian context, the marabou-tic clans were the predominantly Berber aristocracy who lost secular power to the Arabic Hassani ruling clans as a result of the War of Char-Bubba in 1674. In the reallocation of privileges which followed, they retained control of religious activities and commercial affairs in the Trarza and Brakna societies.
[12] Few Frenchmen in the 1850's, not even the very observant Faidherbe, realized to what an extent this weakening of traditional Senegalese governments had occurred as a result of the French presence and the Atlantic trade. In the case of Walo, for instance, which in the eighteenth century extended well north of the Senegal River, the Trarza of Mauritania had begun making encroachments at its expense in order to obtain slaves to sell to the French. Later, when the rulers of both Walo and Cayor had begun to participate in the slave trade, they encouraged their *tyeddos* to raid the peasantry for slaves, which they then sold to the French for trinkets and *eau-de-vie*. Patterns of exploitation and devastation begun during the era of the Atlantic slave trade survived well into the era of legitimate trade. Indeed, by their recruitment for contract labor and *engagés* for the African companies attached to the colonial armed forces, the French colonial authorities themselves kept alive in the nineteenth century an important vestige of the Atlantic slave trade (Barry 1972: 111–131; Curtin 1975:194–196).

THE FRENCH ADVANCE INTO WALO

Because Faidherbe was a veteran of the French *occupation totale* of Algeria, he believed it essential that the most powerful Senegalese polities be defeated at least once by French forces to force them to adopt a "proper attitude" of respect. He also came to the Senegalese governorship with some understanding of the world of Islam, some knowledge of arabic, and strong ambivalence *vis-à-vis* Islamic state-builders. These attitudes and qualities would naturally influence his impending confrontation with the riverine Senegalese societies.

Within three months of his accession to the governorship, Faidherbe had drifted into war with the Trarza Emirate of Mauritania, several clans or lineages of the Brakna Walo, Futa Toro, and the partisans of al-Hajj 'Umar both in Futa Toro and in the upper river. His forces conquered only Walo. With the others he and his director of exterior affairs negotiated compromise peaces. Walo reacted to Faidherbe's attempt to liberate it in a way he had not expected. This small kingdom had been increasingly weakened by its more powerful neighbors — the Trarza in particular, but also Saint-Louis. Quarrels among the royal matrilineages (the Tediek, the Djeuss, and the Logar) and rivalry between the *brak*ship and the council of electors, supported by certain powerful territorial chiefs, had also taken their toll.

In 1831, the marriage of the Trarza emir Mohammed el Habib to the *linguère* [queen-mother] of Walo, Ndyombotte, a Tediek, had seemed to the French colonial authorities of the time to be the prelude to a Trarza annexation of Walo. Consequently French forces fought a small, inconclusive war in Walo against the Trarza and their Walo allies in an effort to break this Trarza-Tediek link. As a result, in 1835 Mohammed el Habib agreed as part of a compromise peace to respect the independence of Walo and to renounce the rights of possible accession to the *brak*ship of Walo of his young son, Eli, by Ndyombotte. However, in later years the colonial authorities did little more than make feeble protests as Mohammed el Habib strengthened his hold on Walo and groomed Eli for the eventual succession. Faidherbe justified his invasion of Walo and his expulsion of the Trarza by citing their violations of the 1835 treaty and others (Archives Nationales de la République du Sénégal 1855).

An article of faith as far as the French were concerned was that Walo would welcome a French deliverance from Trarza domination. Consequently, Faidherbe was unpleasantly surprised when his invasion in February 1855 met with resistance, not only from the Trarza, but also from the *brak* Mbodje Malik, the *linguere* (since 1846, Ndatte Yalla, Ndyombotte's sister), the *tyeddos* of Walo, and much of the population. French troops drove most of the 20,000 inhabitants of Walo into exile in Cayor and Futa Toro, gutting their settlements and sparing only a handful of

Djeuss villages. Neither the *brak* nor the *linguère* would agree to peace on Faidherbe's terms, which called on them to aid the French in expelling the Mauritanians from the left bank, particularly Walo, to end all officially recognized *coutumes*, and to end all pillaging by the *tyeddos*. The latter two conditions would have destroyed a major source of revenue and hence power for the monarchy. Eli led both Trarza bands and *tyeddos* in a struggle against the French that lasted until May 1858, by which time his effort was neutralized by the peace which Faidherbe was making with the Trarza Emirate.

The question which now posed itself for Faidherbe was what to do with conquered and nearly uninhabited Walo. For years many members of the Saint-Louis business community had been urging its annexation to the colony (Maurel and Prom Papers 1855a). A plan to this effect had been formulated by the aggressive governor Bouët-Willaumez in 1844. So annexed, it would be broken into four cantons corresponding to four major existing indigenous territorial divisions and be ruled by chiefs appointed (or confirmed) by the colonial government. Walo would then become a refuge for subjects mistreated by their chiefs, who would be encouraged to become farmers and to grow useful crops for the colonial market.

This plan is indeed the one which Faidherbe had adopted by December 1855 after failing in an attempt to provide Walo with local leadership. Possibly Faidherbe contrived this failure. He did not offer the *brak* ship to Diadie Cumba, the claimant of the relatively pro-French Djeuss clan. The unwillingness of Ndatte Yalla to cooperate prevented his working through her and her current husband, the *maroso tase*, an Ayor noble who had himself prior to the invasion been trying to build an anti-Mauritanian coalition. Of course, he had not been an ally of the French either, which made him unacceptable to Faidherbe (Barry 1972:298–299). Faidherbe turned to Yoro Diao, son of a powerful and sometimes pro-French elector and prime minister, inviting him to assume the *brak* ship, but he refused, suggesting instead another aristocrat, Fara Penda Aram Guey (Barry 1969:419). Fara Penda, however, failed to display leadership qualities, had not the slightest claim to the *brak* ship, and was tainted in the eyes of other Walo-Walo[13] by his willingness to collaborate with the French.

Of the four cantons into which Walo was divided, two went immediately to cooperating preconquest incumbents. However, few Walo-Walo returned home immediately to repopulate these cantons — because of Trarza and Tediek intimidation, explained Faidherbe (Archives Nationales de France 1855a). Until 1859, when Faidherbe appointed a

---

[13] The plural form designating persons native to several of the western Senegalese societies is the name of the society repeated once: hence, Walo-Walo, Sine-Sine, Salum-Salum. An exception is Cayor, whose people are called Ayor.

French *chef supérieur* for all of Walo, he claimed the title of *brak* himself by right of conquest and ordered all title holders, subjects, and servile groupings to perform for him many of the obligations which they owed to the *brak*[14] (Barry 1972:309). He ordered the crown slaves, particularly the *tyeddos,* to return to Walo and become farmers — in return for which he would give them their freedom. He had few takers. At that time he had not realized that in traditional Wolof society crown slaves generally had more power and a higher standard of living than common freemen — this a result of their links to the monarchy. Also, as a group, the *tyeddos* had great contempt for agriculturalists (Monteil 1966:85–88).

In 1859 Faidherbe granted Walo a constitution written in Wolof and French. It allowed the cantons a degree of local autonomy and the Walo-Walo a degree of cultural freedom. However, the colonial governor would still name the cantonal chiefs — albeit taking into account traditional claims to territorial commands. Chiefs so chosen were to be supervised by a French *chef supérieur* resident at Richard Toll.

Faidherbe seems to have pinned his hopes on the adolescent Sidia, son of Ndatte Yalla by her first husband, the *bethio* (hereditary ruler of Ross) Sakura M'Barcka Diop (Ba 1976:71 n.), wishing to use him to create a solid link with the traditional aristocracy of Walo. In April 1861, Sidia's circumcision ceremony became an occasion for some of the Tediek aristocracy to pledge an oath to reestablish the monarchy with Sidia as *brak*. Fara Penda attended, although it seems that he did not take part in the oath. Faidherbe ordered the arrest of all influential persons who had attended, exiling most of them, including Fara Penda, to Assini or to Gabon (Archives Nationales de France 1861a).

When Faidherbe left the governorship of Senegal in 1861, eventually to assume command of the subdivision of Sidi-Bel-Abbès in Algeria, he took Sidia with him and placed him in the Lycée Impérial of Algiers. At some point in the next two years Sidia became a Roman Catholic, adopting the name Léon (one of Faidherbe's middle names) as his Christian name. On his return to Senegal he took command of the canton of Nder. Influenced by his dissatisfied Tediek relatives, he converted back to Islam and then earned a reputation as a troublemaker by espousing the grievances of his people He remained chief of Nder, however, into the governorship of Valière (1869–1876). Given the threats posed by more powerful leaders such as Maba Diakhu, Lat Dior, and Ahmadu Cheikhu, Sidia, with his French education, seemed to be more the sort of African leader to be wooed. He fell afoul of a new and more aggressive governor, Brière de l'Isle (1876–1881), who accused him of plotting against the

[14]   This instance seems to have marked the only occasion when Faidherbe would attempt to rule a defeated African society by claiming for himself the title and the prerogatives of the defeated ruler.

French, dethroned him, and exiled him to Gabon. Here Sidia committed suicide in 1878 (Ba 1976:35 n.).[15]

Except in the immediate environs of Saint-Louis, Walo never attracted many non-Walo-Walo settlers, despite the high hopes of Faidherbe and several of his backers. Part of the reason was that Walo was not particularly fertile. The best lands were occupied by Walo-Walo, who had no desire to give them up. To have introduced plantation agriculture on the unoccupied lands of Walo would have required prohibitively expensive irrigation works and desalination of the soil. Moreover, the Walo-Walo did not welcome African settlers on their lands, except for certain transhumant pastoral Fulbe and Mauritanian clans with which they had traditionally had symbiotic relations. Although supposedly "a French province" (Archives Nationales de France 1859), Walo in fact remained opposed to the status quo, resisting it by "inertia and protestations" (Archives Nationales de France 1871).

MAURITANIAN POLITIES AND FRENCH INFLUENCE

If Faidherbe's treatment of Walo represents one extreme in his dealings with the independent Senegalese and Mauritanian polities, his dealings with the specifically Mauritanian Trarza, Brakna, and Idaw 'Aish emirates represent the other.

The principal Mauritanian threat to the French plan of 1854 was the ambition of the Trarza emir Mohammed el-Habib. Since his accession to the paramountcy in 1829 he had been using a combination of force, diplomacy, and marriage to bring Walo, northern Cayor, the Brakna Emirate, and Dimar province of Futa Toro under his control. By taking advantage of the death in 1841 of the powerful and popular Brakna emir Ahmadu, whose only direct heir, Sidi Eli, was an infant, Mohammed el-Habib had attempted to bring the Brakna under his control and to claim their gum-trade revenues.

Since 1841, various French governors and their political officers had vacillated between opposing Mohammed el-Habib's aims and favoring them. Because none of the French choices for the Brakna emirship was

---

[15] About Sidia, Barry (1972:313) writes, "trained in the French school, he was thus the first nationalist to understand the stakes of colonization and to preach the union of Kadyoor, Waalo, Djolof, and Fuuta — in a word, the raising of a veritable shield to put an end to colonial conquest" (formé à l'école française, [il] fut ainsi le premier nationaliste à comprendre l'enjeu de la colonisation, et à prêcher l'union du Kadyoor, du Waalo, du Djolof et du Fuuta, en un mot la levée d'un véritable bouclier pour mettre fin à la conquête coloniale"). If Sidia's uniqueness stemmed from his French education and his links to Faidherbe, then Barry is probably correct. However, Sidia was not the first to attempt a pan-Senegambian anticolonial alliance. The idea had been contemplated and even attempted to some extent by Maba Diakhu and Lat Dior, neither of whom had received formal Western education (Witherell 1964:76; Klein 1968:92).

particularly able or well qualified to rule, and because the French were in no position to oppose Mohammed el-Habib by force, they came to adopt a policy of grudging cooperation with him as the best way to maintain peace in the lower river and to protect the gum trade (Archives Nationales de France 1852). Yet this policy strengthened an already powerful African ruler who could be counted upon to oppose any attempt on the part of the Saint-Louis authorities to strengthen their own position.

As for the Idaw ʿAish, they traded with the French at Bakel; their home territory, extending from north of Bakel to the Tagant, was remote from the area of the French thrust in 1854–1855. Without too much difficulty, Brossard de Corbigny, the director of exterior affairs in 1853, had obtained a new commercial treaty from Emir Bakar and his chief minister Samba Tiguidi which made most of the *coutumes* paid to the Idaw ʿAish proportional to the value of trade. When war broke out between the French and Mohammed el-Habib, the Idaw ʿAish remained neutral. Indeed, they allied themselves with the French in their struggle in the upper river against al-Hajj ʿUmar and his partisans. Faidherbe cleverly exploited the religious (Qadiri and traditional versus Tijjani and ʿUmarian) and the racial ("White" versus "Black") cleavages separating Mauritanian and Tukulor. Rather than attempting to confine the Idaw ʿAish warriors to the right bank, Faidherbe encouraged them to raid anti-French settlements in Galam. Bondu, and eastern Futa Toro on the left bank (Archives Nationales de France 1857a, 1857b; Maurel and Prom Papers 1855b). By November 1857, Faidherbe had prevailed upon Bakar to sign a new treaty eliminating all *coutumes* but the duty on gum, which was now set at approximately 3 percent of the value of yearly trade. Of course, the colonial authorities continued to pay the emir and possibly other Idaw ʿAish officials most in contact with the French regular bribes for services rendered — a practice followed by Faidherbe's successors. These payments, Bakar's fear of al-Hajj ʿUmar, and the specific advantages which the new system gave to the emirs are no doubt what induced Bakar to sign this treaty and then to use his influence to help bring Mohammed el-Habib to terms.

The settlement which Faidherbe made in May 1858 with the Trarza and the one which he made several weeks later with the two contenders for the Brakna emirship resembled the one which he had concluded with the Idaw ʿAish. The Mauritanians recognized that the left bank was under at least nominal French protection. No armed bands of Mauritanians were to cross the Senegal River without French permission. However, the French agreed to recognize the complete independence of the Mauritanians north of the Senegal River. Each emir would receive an annual *coutume* of approximately 3 percent of the annual value of the gum exported from his emirate. Although the total value of the *coutumes* which the Mauritanians as a whole would receive from this new system would be less than that which they had received before, the emirs themselves, since they would now receive everything, would in fact receive more. As a consequence, the new system strengthened the hold of the emirs upon their subjects and was an aid to centralization.

The new system also forbade traders or wholesalers to give gifts directly to Mauritanian merchants or officials, but Faidherbe permitted the practice to reestablish itself by indirect means. Recognizing that the permanence of the settlement depended upon the regular payment of the *coutumes*, he refused to subtract any outstanding debts owed by the emirs or their subjects to French traders (Archives Nationales de France 1864c). Hence, a new system of *coutumes* had its inception in a systematic defaulting on debts. By 1879, new treaties, recognizing that the continuing fall in the price paid for gum by the French wholesalers and a reduction in the volume of the trade had reduced the 3 percent *coutume* to an unsatisfactory level, had restored a system of fixed *coutumes* (Saint-Martin 1966:91).

In dealing with the Brakna, Faidherbe first attempted to bribe the pro-Trarza emir Mohammed Sidi to break with Mohammed el-Habib (Maurel and Prom Papers 1855c; Archives Nationales de France 1856a). This failing, he switched his support to Sidi Eli, Ahmadu's heir, by now come of age. However, the latter seems not, at least initially, to have been a strong ruler. He failed to win the support of several important clans, which remained loyal to Mohammed Sidi, and to win immediate endorsement of the powerful Qadiri cleric, *cheikh* Sidia of Boutilimit. Faidherbe therefore made treaties both with Sidi Eli and with Mohammed Sidi, agreeing to pay the *coutume* to the one who could control the northern approaches to Podor, where the bulk of the Brakna gum was traded.

About six months after both Brakna contenders had signed their treaties, Sidi Eli murdered Mohammed Sidi and gradually took control over the latter's following. However, Sidi Eli fell into dispute after 1863 with Sidi, the son and heir of Mohammed el-Habib. The latter had been murdered in 1860 by members of the Uled-Dahman clan. Sidi wished to replace Sidi Eli with one of his own relatives. This plan reawakened French fears of Trarza domination of the gum trade in the Lower Senegal Valley. After threatening Sidi with French intervention, Faidherbe suggested a compromise by which the Trarza emir would guarantee the independence of the Brakna and the continued rule of Sidi Eli in return for half of the Brakna annual *coutume*. Both Sidi and Sidi Eli agreed to this arrangement, which lasted until the former's death in 1871 (Archives Nationales de France 1864b).

Generally speaking, these settlements with the three Mauritanian emirates can be counted as successes mainly because they were limited, because the French colonial authorities stayed out of Mauritania until the 1890's, and did not fail to pay the agreed-upon *coutume*, and because the arrangements seemed genuinely to satisfy both sides. Faidherbe's decision to back Sidi Eli for the Brakna emirship also proved to have been a good one; he retained his throne until his death in 1893. It is worth mentioning that after the short reign of one of Sidi's brothers, Ahmed Salum (1871–1873), Eli, the son of Ndyombotte of Walo, inherited the Trarza emirship. He ruled until his death in 1886 and maintained good relations with the French authorities.

FAIDHERBE AND THE TUKULOR EMPIRE OF AL-HAJJ 'UMAR

The degree of French intervention in the other polities of the Senegal Valley during the 1850's and 1860's fell somewhere between the extremes demonstrated by the cases of Walo, on one hand, and the Mauritanian emirates, on the other. Faidherbe's basic objective as far as the left-bank societies were concerned was to end all African controls over French navigation along the Senegal River — particularly the *coutumes* which the Futa Toro *almamate* collected at Salde but also those charged at Tuabo and Makhana in Gadiaga and at Medine in Khasso. His efforts in this regard embroiled him with the traditional leaders of the polities concerned and also with al-Hajj 'Umar.

Inheriting poor relations with the *almamate* as well as with al-Hajj 'Umar's partisans in the upper river when he acceded to the governorship in December 1854, Faidherbe reacted first by taking the military initiative against western Futa Toro. He hoped to drive a wedge between the Futankobe governing elite and 'Umar's movement, to expel the latter from the Senegal Valley west of Bafulabe (the point where the Bafing and the Bakhoy Rivers come together to form the Senegal proper), and to force the *almamate* and the polities of the upper river to agree to the new French conditions of trade and predominance in the Senegal Valley. He pursued these three aims simultaneously.

Al-Hajj 'Umar's movement was initially quite successful in the upper river, particularly among the common folk, who found the egalitarianism of his Tijjani Islam appealing (Suret-Canale 1968:218; Archives Nationales de France 1855b). But Faidherbe, reacting in a typical French-Algerian style, saw the movement as affecting his sphere of action and opposed it by direct force and by supporting the efforts of anti-'Umarian African allies to seize power in their societies.

In September and October 1855, during his first visit to the upper river as governor, Faidherbe enlisted the support of two leaders, Sambala of Khasso and Bokar Saada of Bondu, who were to be of great value to him.

Sambala, the chief of Medine, claimed the paramountcy of Khasso, which had once been a fairly substantial kingdom on both sides of the Upper Senegal. In 1854, however, he controlled only Medine. The other regions of Khasso had rejected centralized rule. The Bambara kingdom of Kaarta had claimed a degree of suzerainty over all of Khasso. Many Khassonke, led by Khartum Sambala, Sambala's brother, had rallied to al-Hajj 'Umar. Some of these latter had raided French properties at Medine just before the beginning of the high-water season of 1855.

When Faidherbe arrived at Medine with gunboats and a column to build a small fort there alongside Sambala's *tata* [fortified enclosure], the ruler offered him the land free of charge (Archives Nationales de France 1855b; Faidherbe 1889:172). Faidherbe offered to pay Sambala 5,000 francs outright for the land and an annual *coutume* of 1,200 francs, and the latter accepted. The new French fort was completed by November 1855.

Diuka Sambala, a legitimate, if little recognized, ruler with genuine claims to paramountcy in Khasso, took advantage of the French presence to build his authority in the surrounding Khassonke settlements. Yet with the approach of 'Umar's main army from the east in 1857, most of the Khassonke, led by Khartum Sambala, rallied to 'Umar (Faidherbe 1889:181–182). The French fort and Sambala's *tata* withstood a three-month siege that was only relieved at the last moment by the governor himself at the head of 500 men. Sambala did not really become a power in his own right until after the French destruction of the last 'Umarian stronghold in the French sphere, Guemu, north of Bakel, in 1859. By that time 'Umar had decided to abandon any attempt at political control west of Bafulabe and to concentrate on building his empire in the interior at the expense of Segu and Masina as well as Kaarta.

Bokar Saada of Bondu was a son of the powerful *almamy* Saada. He had been an 'Umarian *talibe*.[16] He had in fact taken part in the conquest of Kaarta but had fallen out with al-Hajj 'Umar over the latter's execution of some of his relatives in the Kaartan royal family (Robinson 1975:42). He returned to Bondu to head a faction opposed to al-Hajj 'Umar and to 'Umar's choice for the *almamy*ship of Bondu, 'Umar Sane.

At first Bokar Saada won few followers. Until 1859 he too hardly had definite control over more than a village or two near the French fort of Senudebu. His cause was aided by the French success at Medine. In August 1857, Bokar Saada joined forces with a French column of over 2,000 French and African troops and volunteers which marched, under Faidherbe's personal command, against the major 'Umarian stronghold

---

[16] In general, the term *talibe* (from the Arabic *talib*) designates a disciple of a prominent Muslim holy man. As far as al-Hajj 'Umar's movement is concerned it referred to 'Umar's original Tukulor followers, who constituted his military leadership and the growing aristocracy in the new empire built in the east.

at Somsom in the interior of Bondu. Here 'Umar's governor, Malik, was holding prisoner one Ala Khassun, a relative of Bokar Saada's. Although the French artillery destroyed the fort, Malik and most of his men escaped, taking care beforehand to kill Ala Khassun (Faidherbe 1889:204).

Bokar Saada, like Sambala, was to come into his own as a strong ruler after 'Umar's withdrawal to the east. Both rulers, of course, were to benefit from the French decision after 1860 to concentrate more on western Senegal, where peanuts were becoming increasingly important as a major export. No longer challenged by the 'Umarian movement, Bokar Saada would also avoid having his wings clipped by the French — the all too usual fate of French allies who were too successful. In 1864, when the French authorities deactivated the fort, Bokar Saada made it his castle. Both Bokar Saada and Sambala survived as rulers until the 1880's; indeed, the former became the dominant power in the upper Senegal-Gambia region. While maintaining close relations with Saint-Louis, Bondu also continued to trade with the Gambia. Bokar Saada indeed received small subsidies from Bathurst to encourage that trade. Abdul Bokar Kane, the strongman of Futa Toro in the period between 1860 and 1890 and a man with impeccable anticolonial credentials, found it politically wise to marry daughters of both Bokar Saada and Sambala.

Faidherbe also took advantage of the anti-'Umarian sentiments of the inhabitants of the gold-bearing area of Bambuk to win for the colonial government the right to search for and to exploit any profitable gold workings. In 1858 he signed a treaty with Bugul, the chief of one of the principal polities of Bambuk, in which the latter awarded the French the unrestricted right to prospect for gold, to mine, and to build as necessary all over Bambuk. Bugul, however, did not have the authority to speak for the other Bambuk chieftaincies, a fact which would have led to complications had this treaty ever been seriously put to the test. As it turned out, the French did not attempt any serious mining except at Kenieba, a settlement which was actually under Bondu control. The attempt, begun in the summer of 1858, had failed by 1860. The French then withdrew completely from Kenieba.

With the remaining polities of the upper river, Guoye and Kamera on the left bank and the Guidimakha chieftaincies on the right, Faidherbe was less successful in stimulating anti-'Umarian sentiments. Most of the polities here and their Bathily ruling clans had been won over to 'Umar's cause. During the rainy season of 1855, French gunboats destroyed a number of villages on both sides of the river between Dembacane, the eastern limit of Futa Toro, and Khasso, both to punish those who had pillaged or tolerated the pillaging of French traders and to frighten the others into breaking with the 'Umarian movement. Eventually members of the elites in the principal settlements made treaties with the French

agreeing to forgo the old *coutumes* and to reject "'Umarism." Much of
Guoye fronting the Senegal River was annexed to the colony but not
systematically organized. In 1855, the African town of Bakel, clustered
around the French fort, seemed so threatening because of its 'Umarian
sympathies that the commandant at that time, Bargone, had most of it
leveled.

Not only were many of the inhabitants of this region attracted by
'Umar's ideology, but the region itself served as the logical link between
Futa Toro and the 'Umarian empire to the east. Groups of Tukulor
emigrants passing through Gadiaga or Guidimakha on their way to Nioro
helped to keep alive the 'Umarian ardor of the inhabitants and attracted
French reprisals for "collaboration with the enemy."

Five years of war devasted the upper river. It took almost a generation
for it to recover. It is this situation which explains its peacefulness after
'Umar's withdrawal. Even the French head tax collected in the environs
of Bakel after January 1, 1862, was not openly resisted. No really effective local anticolonial leaders emerged here until the 1880's. Then, to the
surprise of the French, who by now took the loyalty of Gadiaga for
granted, the returned *hājj* Mahmadu Lamine put together in a matter of
months a massive coalition of Soninke. He drifted into war with the
French and almost succeeded in capturing Bakel in 1885. French forces
defeated him within a year.

With Futa Toro, the primary French objective in the 1850's and 1860's
was to secure unrestricted transit rights along the Senegal River. Related
objectives called for them to stimulate the breakup of the *almamate* and
above all to discourage any powerful indigenous leader from strengthening it. A few persons in Saint-Louis also hoped that the Futankobe might
be induced to grow cash crops on their rich alluvial lands for the French
market once sources of "instability" had been removed. Strong French-
backed regional leaders, they believed, would maintain stability and
security in the area.

In 1854, the Tukulor were the Senegalese grouping which the average
Saint-Louis colonial most disliked after the Trarza. They appeared
xenophobic, a trait attributed to their fervent practice of the Muslim faith.
Their central government appeared unstable and incapable of maintaining order (Archives Nationales de France 1856b). *Almamies* were shifted
on an average of every year and a half.[17] The fact that al-Hajj 'Umar was a
Tukulor born at Aloar in Toro province in 1797 and that so many other
Islamic reformers were either Tukulor or educated by Tukulor clerics
only confirmed the negative French view of Futa Toro.

---

[17]   To African observers of the period, French power must have seemed just as unstable.
Counting interims and divided assignments, there had been thirty-seven shifts in guber-
natorial assignments between 1817 and Faidherbe's accession in 1854. Only Roger
(1821–1827) and Protet (1850–1854) served longer than three years.

The forcible French occupation and fortification of Podor in March, followed by a raid on the stronghold of Dialmath in Dimar province, had led Governor Protet into hostilities with the *almamate*. Faidherbe continued these hostilities with the January 1855 burning of Bokol. During the next several years he regularly dispatched his flotilla of steam gunboats each rainy season to strafe and burn offending villages. He also pursued diplomatic objectives. He encouraged the secession of the western two provinces of Dimar, clearly more or less a Trarza vassal (Carrère and Holle 1855:133), and Toro, the center of Islamic orthodoxy, the separate existence of which had pre-dated the creation of the *almamate* by almost two centuries. He also sought to break off the less well-organized eastern regions of Ngenar and Damga. At the same time, he encouraged anti-'Umar sentiments and manifestations among the ruling elite throughout Futa Toro.

Dimar, accessible to the French at all times by river as well as by land, was the first of the Futa Toro provinces to come to terms. As a result of the bombardment of Bokol in January 1855, *eliman*[18] Seydu of Dimar sued for peace, agreeing to end the *coutumes* which he collected from the French post of Dagana, to separate from the *almamate*, and to sever his province's links with Mohammed el-Habib's Trarza. As a result of French pressure, the electors of Dimar revoked Seydu for the more compliant Abdul Boly. With the latter Faidherbe confirmed these arrangements by treaty in June 1858. In 1860, the French declared Dimar annexed to the colony, without, however, organizing it along the lines of Walo and without allowing the selection of a paramount ruler to replace Abdul Boly.

Feelings of powerlessness combined with a sense of superiority fueled autonomist sentiment in Toro. The founders of the *almamate*, Suleiman Bal and Abdul Kader, were Muslim clerics from Toro, and Toro had given its name to the whole *almamate*; yet the electoral system established after Abdul Kader's death in 1806 had excluded Toro from any real power in the affairs of the *almamate*. Toro provided neither electors nor eligibles but was heavily enfeoffed by central Futa Toro families (Robinson 1975:22–23). It continued to be ruled by a *lam* chosen by a council of electors alternately from the Dethie and the Hamady Ngaye branches of the Sall clan and then confirmed by the *almamy* of Futa Toro. As early as 1830, Governor Brou had attempted to stimulate autonomist sentiment in Toro by negotiating a treaty with the *lam* by which France agreed to pay separate *coutumes* to Toro and to treat it as neutral in case of war with the *almamate* (Saint-Martin 1967:58). The fact that al-Hajj 'Umar was from Toro, however, and that his message to the *alma-*

---

[18] This title, like *almamy*, is derived from the Arabic *al-imam*. In the Tukulor context it connotes political and territorial rulership at the village or provincial level. It was borne by several territorial and electoral chiefs.

mate reflected the traditional Toro grievances won him many adherents there.

After the attack on Bokol, the *lam toro* Hamat Ali made overtures of peace to the French, who refrained in the next few months from attacking Toro settlements. He was soon dethroned by pro-'Umarian elements in the Toro electoral council for being too pro-French. Reinstated by the end of that year, he appeared to agree tacitly to the independence of Toro and to favor Sidi Eli of the Brakna over Mohammed Sidi. When in 1857 he switched his support back to Mohammed Sidi, partly because of the support given the latter by *cheikh* Sidia of Boutilimit, the French commandant of Podor burned down Guédé, the capital of Toro. In 1859, heeding al-Hajj 'Umar's latest call for immigrants for his new empire, Hamat Ali left for Nioro. The next *lam toro*, Hamady Bokar, was considerably more pro-French. He signed a treaty accepting French protection, agreeing to independence from the *almamate*, and renouncing all rights to French *coutumes*. The French guaranteed Toro its traditional institutions; the *lam* would continue to be chosen in the traditional manner, subject only to French confirmation. Moreover, the treaty placed under the direct authority of the *lam* areas in eastern Toro and Lao province of central Futa that had never been ruled by the *lam* before. The arrangement included a secret French promise that a cooperating *lam* would receive secret French presents — *coutumes*. Two immediate consequences of these new arrangements were that Hamady Bokar and his successor, Sire Galadio, ruled Toro and the newly attached territories far more despotically than they had been ruled before and that French commandants at Podor developed the habit of meddling in the internal affairs of Toro (Robinson 1975:54–56).

The new situation in Toro could not help but create discontent, which was fanned by the presence of many of 'Umar's sympathizers and by a French decision to begin collecting a small head tax in parts of Toro as of January 1862. Between April 1862 and February 1863, Jean Jauréguiberry, Faidherbe's replacement between 1861 and 1863, sent four major and several minor military expeditions into the *almamate*, including Toro province, to "restore order," to little avail. The electors raised the pro-'Umar eligible, Ahmadu Thierno Demba Ly, to the *almamy*ship sometime between January and February 1862. He defied the French, reasserting the claims of the central *almamate* to Toro, much to the satisfaction of most of its population. In February 1863, he ordered the dethronement of Sire Galadio and his replacement by the pro-'Umar Samba Umane, of the Dethie branch of the Sall clan.

During their final intervention into Futa Toro that spring, Jauréguiberry's forces drove out Samba Umane and restored Sire Galadio. No sooner had the French forces withdrawn, however, than Samba Umane returned and ordered the execution of Sire Galadio. By now Jauréguiberry was under attack by the Saint-Louis wholesalers for his bellicose policies and coming to realize that Futa Toro had never been as much under French control as Faidherbe's reports had led the Paris authorities to believe. He therefore made peace with both Toro and the central *almamate* on a nonreprisal basis.

It is significant that a discussion in the executive council of Senegal at its meeting of March 20, 1863, revealed that some persons in the colonial bureaucracy believed that Toro had been annexed to the colony in 1860. Yet there was apparently no written proof of this annexation to be found anywhere in Saint-Louis but a footnote on page 278 of the 1861 edition of the *Annuaire du Sénégal*. Moreover, none of the members of the executive council, who would normally have been informed of such a matter, could remember ever having discussed it (Archives Nationales de France 1863a). Therefore the treaty which Governor Jauréguiberry offered to Samba Umane reaffirmed the agreement of 1859 without mentioning any question of annexation.

Although less well-organized than Dimar and Toro, eastern Futa Toro was also distinct from the central provinces of Futa Toro. Its population was a disparate mixture of nomadic Fulbe and elite clerical communities. It provided *almamies* but not electors. Many of its lands and people were enfeoffed to central Futa Toro families like that of the elector Ali Dundu and his grandson and heir Abdul Bokar.

Faidherbe began his attempt at detaching eastern Futa from the *almamate* by ordering the construction of a new French fort at Matam in 1857, using as his pretext the nonreimbursement of recent pillages. In 1859 he recognized as chief of the eastern region one Mahmadu Any, head of the elite family of *elfekis*.[19] He had a very tenuous claim to paramountcy in this area. A treaty signed by Mahmadu Any and Faidherbe himself in 1859 recognized the independence of eastern Futa Toro (or Damga, as the French called it).

As Mahmadu Any's rule became increasingly despotic and violated custom, he lost support to the elector Abdul Bokar, who took advantage of the *elfeki*'s growing unpopularity to build up a sphere of his own in eastern Futa Toro. By 1861, Mahmadu Any's authority was confined to the immediate vicinity of the Matam fort.

While Faidherbe was working to break off the peripheral regions from the *almamate* and to expel the 'Umarian movement, members of the ruling elite in the central provinces did what they could to defend the independence and the unity of the *almamate* from both French and 'Umarian threats and to further their own family interests. Many members of this elite favored supporting al-Hajj 'Umar's eastern ventures while refusing him any political authority in the *almamate* itself. Hence

---

[19]   According to Robinson (1972:60 n.), this title came from the Arabic *al-faqih*, designating one skilled in jurisprudence.

the course followed by the *almamate* in the following years often appeared confusing and contradictory.

A good example of a Futanke ruler who tried with some success to play both sides against the middle, sometimes for the good of the *almamate* but often only for his own good, was Mohammadu Birane Wane. Elected in May 1854 to his fourth term as a result of the inability of his predecessor, Racine, either to prevent the French from building the fort at Podor or to obtain payment for the land taken (Robinson 1975:39), Mohammadu sought to negotiate an end to the sporadic hostilities which broke out in the next three years between the French and parts of Futa Toro. At the same time, he lost the support of some of the electors by permitting al-Hajj 'Umar to name him his *alfa* [deputy] for Futa Toro in December 1854, and shortly thereafter he was deposed in favor of candidates of a less 'Umarian stance. The French shelled certain riverine areas from their boats during the rainy seasons of 1855, 1856, and 1857, and in the latter year a more pro-French faction brought Mohammadu back to power. Yet the French, who welcomed his accession to the *almamy*ship, compromised him by seizing and fortifying Matam without offering compensation. A year later Mohammadu was confronted with 'Umar's decision to come to Futa Toro to recruit for his venture in the east and to "settle" the outstanding problems of Futa Toro. At this point he organized the construction of a wood-and-stone barrier across the Senegal at Garly to prevent the French fleet from ascending. The dam did not hold, but the gesture impressed Faidherbe, who blamed it on al-Hajj 'Umar's machinations. While supervising the dam's construction, Mohammadu wrote letters to Faidherbe protesting his devotion; as 'Umar approached, he sent his slaves to Saint-Louis and Podor for safekeeping (Robinson 1975:45; Archives Nationales de France 1858). The electors deposed him in favor of Mustafa Ba in early 1859, and it was the latter who then signed a peace treaty with Faidherbe designating boundaries for the *almamate* which excluded Dimar, Toro, Ngenar, and Damga. Thus it was he who was blamed for the loss of these territories. The electors had revoked him and restored Mohammadu by September 1859.

With the final departure of al-Hajj 'Umar to the east, taking with him some of his most militant local partisans, Mohammadu settled down to rule Futa Toro. As in the cases of the rulers of Toro and Damga, however, French backing tended to make him despotic, which was particularly unappreciated in his case because of the prevailing view that an *almamy* should reign rather than rule and in a sense serve as the arbiter of the common good. Also, he failed to deal satisfactorily with the secession of the western and eastern regions and with the increasing insecurity due to raids by Mauritanian nomads (which the French victories over the Mauritanians had supposedly ended) from the north and Fulbe nomads from the Ferlo Desert to the south. Mohammadu was deposed once again in 1861 in favor of his half-brother, Ahmadu, whom he would have murdered by his son Ibra.

After Jauréguiberry left Saint-Louis in May 1863, and possibly because of rumors of Faidherbe's impending return to the governorship, the electors of Futa Toro again raised the now openly pro-French Mohammadu to the *almamy*ship. He in turn agreed, in response to Faidherbe's threats, to sign a new treaty (superseding one signed earlier by Ahmadu Thierno Demba Ly with Jauréguiberry's representative), this time specifically recognizing the separation of Dimar, Toro, and Damga. The much reduced *elfeki* of Damga, Mahmadu Any, also agreed to sign a new treaty reaffirming his dependence on the French and the separation of Damga from the *almamate*.

With Toro, the scenario was different. Faidherbe demanded that Samba Umane come aboard a French ship to sign a similar treaty with Toro and to pledge loyalty to France. The latter declined, citing the French practice of kidnapping riverine rulers and other notables with whom they were unhappy. Faidherbe therefore declared Samba Umane deposed and asked the Toro electors to select a new *lam*. They politely refused but agreed to accept whomever Faidherbe would choose for them. He chose one Mulay Pate of the Hamady Ngaye clan, a relative of the late Sire Galadio, "a peaceful man without initiative, who will act only according to our instructions" (Archives Nationales de France 1863b, n.d.b). In fact, Mulay Pate would carry little weight in Toro, the *de facto* ruler continuing to be Samba Umane except during a two-year period from the end of 1863 to early 1866, when he served with distinction in the armies of the 'Umarian empire. In 1869, by which time the French had greatly reduced their profile in the Senegal River valley, Samba 'Umane again became the titular *lam*, ruling until 1878 and remaining on good terms with the French authorities. Indeed, he allied himself with them to oppose the aims of Ahmadu Cheikhu, a militant Islamic reformer, and to thwart attempts on the part of the *almamate* to bring Toro back under its control.

In the case of eastern Futa Toro, Faidherbe recognized that Mahmadu Any had failed to rule in a satisfactory way, but rather than allowing this region to resume its old pattern of relationships with the *almamate* he attempted to create a second client ruler for it. While the commandant of Matam kidnapped Mahmadu Any and his son, Baidy, bringing them both to Saint-Louis for confinement, Faidherbe recognized al-Hajj Hamady Kane, the son of Abdul Kader, as "*almamy* of Damga," hoping that as a ruler he would derive political authority from his very real religious prestige (Robinson 1975:68). The new ruler's tenure was short; the *de facto* ruler of eastern Futa, the elector Abdul Bokar, shamed al-Hajj Hamady into retiring in early 1865. From this point until 1890, the French authorities tacitly recognized Abdul Bokar as the real ruler of eastern Futa as well as of increasing portions of the central *almamate*.

In the case of the *almamate* itself, Mohammadu was deposed for the last time in October 1864 and replaced by Ahmadu Thierno Demba Ly. The latter, who served only until August 1865, kept a low profile as far as the French were concerned. In this he was aided by their partial disengagement from the immediate Senegal River Valley.

Although battered and suffering the results of war, plague, famine, and emigration, Futa Toro had survived the Faidherbe epoch. Disunited from an institutional point of view, it remained for the most part independent. The institutions of centralized rule had suffered most, but they did continue to function. Yet their weakening at the expense of regional leaders and electors followed a pattern which had been in the making since the death of Abdul Kader in 1806. Al-Hajj 'Umar and Faidherbe had simply intensified it.

A new threat to the integrity of the *almamate* which would emerge in the 1860's and 1870's was that posed by local Islamic state-builders like Thierno Brahim and Ahmadu Cheikhu, who would attempt radical restructurings of society and political systems in northwestern Senegal, including not only Futa Toro but Cayor and Jolof as well. Abdul Bokar was able to overcome or neutralize these new threats and to counteract more limited threats posed by "legitimate" Futankobe strongmen like Ibra. The *almamate* continued to be headed by *almamies* chosen in the usual ways, but the real ruler until 1890 was Abdul Bokar Kane, whose personal sphere grew to include most of eastern and central Futa Toro.

THE WOLOF KINGDOM OF CAYOR

After 1859, Faidherbe directed his attention to the Wolof kingdom of Cayor. It too bordered on the Senegal River from Saint-Louis to the river's mouth, some 25 kilometers to the south. However, it was far more than a riverine state, for it linked Saint-Louis and the mouth of the Senegal to Cape Verde, down almost 200 kilometers of coastline, and extended nearly 100 kilometers inland to its boundary with Jolof. To many observers Cayor seemed to be the future peanut basket and economic salvation of Senegal. It would require a land campaign to subdue it, for which Faidherbe turned out to be less than adequately prepared.[20]

---

[20]   Faidherbe attempted a few amphibious operations in his Cayor campaigns. However, the Cayor coast did not easily lend itself to the sort of debarcation maneuvers which were so important in subduing the riverine polities. The shoreline is unbroken, and currents and surf are usually treacherous. In addition, it is paralleled by a sparsely inhabited strip of land

Faidherbe initially planned to intervene in Cayor only sufficiently, as suggested in the petition of February 11, 1854, to prevent *tyeddo* interference in the cultivation and marketing of peanuts by the Ayor peasantry. But he also wished to open a trail to be protected by three small forts to run along the coast and to connect Saint-Louis to Gorée. He seems to have believed at first that these aims might be accomplished peacefully. Having been refused permission by *Damel* Biraima to proceed, however, he turned in 1860 to the use of force, with the permission of the minister Chasseloup-Laubat (Archives Nationales de France 1859–1860). Faidherbe continued to believe that no permanent peace on French terms could be made with African powers until they had been militarily defeated at least once.

First Faidherbe led a filibustering expedition from Dakar into Sine and Salum, Serer kingdoms south of Cayor, in May 1859, ostensibly to avenge the outrages committed against French subjects at Rufisque but primarily to obtain agreements, similar to those being made with the Senegal River polities, with the rulers of Sine, Salum, and Bakel. As Faidherbe admitted later, he also had wished to convey to Biraima, who was the half-brother of the ruler of Salum, the unambiguous hint that Cayor would be raided next if he did not cooperate with the French colonial authorities (Archives Nationales de France 1860a). Following this expedition, Faidherbe began to take steps to persuade — and, when that failed, to intimidate — Biraima more directly into granting the telegraph right-of-way, the trail, and the three posts. Biraima, although reputed to be weak and alcoholic, refused to give in to any of Faidherbe's bullying. He died in January 1860, before Faidherbe was in a position to launch an invasion.

After Biraima's death, Faidherbe claimed in an executive council meeting of January 26, 1860 (Archives Nationales de France 1860b) that Biraima had agreed on his deathbed to a treaty with the required stipulations, even producing a draft of such a treaty to prove his point. Significantly, not only does no original copy of this treaty exist, but it is quoted *in extenso* only in the minutes of this meeting. No originals or copies of it can be found in the archives of either Paris or Dakar. Faidherbe, however, made it the basis for his claim against Macodu, Biraima's successor.

Faidherbe's next step was to attempt to influence the succession; but of the three candidates, Macodu, the least favorable to the French, was the one chosen. He refused to acknowledge the existence of any treaty or agreement which bound him to allow French installations on the soil of Cayor. Having received requested reinforcements from Algeria and France, Faidherbe launched a first invasion of Cayor in January 1863, which was followed by three others in the next five months. Unable to

nearly seven miles deep, covered with steep and difficult-to-traverse sand dunes. The heartland of precolonial Cayor lay well to the east of these dunes.

achieve any kind of satisfactory agreement with Macodu after the third expedition, Faidherbe declared the throne empty and offered it to Madiodio, a claimant from the rival Madior branch of the Fall patrilineage, on the condition that he agree to the French annexation of Gandiole and its salt pans as well as some border territories on the northern and southern fringes of Cayor. Madiodio, accepted Faidherbe's offer, but because few Ayor were prepared to accept a French-protected *damel* he received little support. He alienated the few who rallied to him by agreeing to this cession of territory and by being in general a very weak ruler.

Macodu, who had fled with some partisans into Baol, led periodic raids into southern Cayor. More importantly, Lat Dior, the youngest of the three candidates at the recent election (and the one whose sponsor, the *linguere*, Debo Suka, had been the most pro-French)[21] also led raids against Madiodio's supporters and rapidly built up a power base of his own. He would eventually utilize reforming Islam as a vehicle for cementing his movement and his political power.

When Jauréguiberry became governor, he allowed Lat Dior to expel Madiodio and to replace him as *damel*, believing that at least for the short term Cayor would be more peaceful and prosperous if ruled by a popular and powerful *damel*. Although suspicious of each other, the new governor and the new *damel* developed an effective *modus vivendi*. However, when Faidherbe returned to Senegal in 1863 he took steps to depose Lat Dior, virtually without reason, and to reinstall Madiodio, who was no more effective as a ruler now than he had been before. Moreover, Faidherbe required him to cede more territory to the French: the large province of Ndiambur and Mbauar in the north and Andal and Saniokhor in the south. This arrangement did not, however, bring order to Cayor, so just before he left Senegal for good in 1865 Faidherbe retired Madiodio and annexed what remained of independent Cayor. It was to be ruled through its provincial chiefs, who would be confirmed if not selected outright by the French authorities. Yet even this arrangement did not

---

[21] Although Lat Dior is best remembered for his tenacious struggle against French imperialism, it seems reasonable to believe that in his youth, influenced by his aunt, the powerful *linguère*, he looked to the French for support. At the time of the succession in 1860, Lat Dior was still a minor. Had he been elected, his ambitious aunt would probably have served as regent. More importantly, Lat Dior did not have any real claim to the throne. Although he was of the proper matrilineage, the Guedje, his father was not of the mandatory Fall lineage. He was a Diop, therefore a noble (*tagne*) but not really a prince of the blood (*garmi*). A little foreign influence in such a situation might prove very useful. During the struggle of the next ten years, Lat Dior and his growing numbers of partisans fought their Ayor foes, Macodu and then Madiodio and their partisans, then unpopular cantonal chiefs, more than they did the French. It even seems possible to believe that Lat Dior and the *linguère* really did not object to the kind of peripheral penetration of Cayor which Faidherbe wanted in 1859 and were for this reason willing to reach a compromise with Jauréguiberry, who wanted little more of Cayor in 1862. What triggered Lat Dior's anti-French stance was that Faidherbe expelled him from the *damel*ship.

bring peace to the area. Lat Dior joined forces with the Islamic state-builder Maba Diakhu, underwent a conversion to reforming Islam himself (Monteil 1967:91–92), and became one of Maba's successful generals. He played an important role in Maba's invasion of Jolof and his campaigns against the French during the governorship of Pinet-Laprade, Faidherbe's successor. After Maba's death in 1867, Lat Dior attempted to regain his throne. Governor Valière recognized him as *damel* in 1871. He remained *damel* until 1882, when another imperialistically minded French governor ousted him because of his opposition to the construction of the Dakar-Saint-Louis railway.

CONCLUSION

Generally speaking, most of the polities of the Senegal Valley survived this period of Second Empire French imperial activity which reached a climax during Faidherbe's administration. Only Walo was completely conquered and organized along the model, partly borrowed from Algeria, which would later characterize full-blown French colonial rule in West Africa. Other territories, like Cayor in 1865, even if annexed, were not very systematically organized by the colonial administration for direct rule. Lat Dior reestablished a system of independent rule in Cayor in 1871 which resembled what had prevailed before Faidherbe's disruptions.

This interval of colonial aggressiveness obviously did make its impact felt. Parts of the Senegal Valley and Cayor experienced total war and all its accompanying horrors for the first time. The export trade of many areas was brought under greater French control. By the time of Faidherbe's departure, peanut culture dominated parts of Cayor. French and 'Umarian pressures between them had stimulated the rise of new types of indigenous leadership. In some cases they sped up that process, the inception of which pre-dated both Faidherbe's and al-Hajj 'Umar's arrival on the scene, by which regional and electoral notables eclipsed the legitimate paramount rulers. Those legitimate rulers who survived and built up wide power bases owed their successes to their effectiveness in reacting to the challenges posed by the French and by 'Umar and to personal charisma rather than completely to their ascribed statuses.

The cases of Abdul Bokar Kane and Lat Dior illustrate some of the ways in which talented leaders could react to unsettled conditions and rise to the new challenges posed by the French and by reforming Islam. Many of the rulers of the riverine polities were aided by the limited nature of the plan which Faidherbe was fulfilling, particularly as it concerned the immediate Senegal River valley, and by French retrenchment, which began in this area after 1859.

A category of rulers that fared quite poorly, even though they often had backgrounds similar to those who succeeded, consisted for the most part of those chosen and backed directly by the French. These rulers increased their unpopularity by becoming despotic and by furthering French policies that were at variance with the wishes of their subjects. Then, too, the French often passed over the most talented potential collaborators for less talented but seemingly more reliable ones. From the French point of view, the question of who among the successful rulers was "good" or "bad" could also depend upon the degree of French imperial activity being directed at that ruler's sphere. Their "best" allies always seemed to rule in areas peripheral to their main thrusts. For this reason the French generally left them alone. An allied ruler's position *vis-à-vis* the French could change. Although Faidherbe had considered Lat Dior an enemy of French interests and had opposed him as such, Valière and even Brière de l'Isle, more oriented toward the upper river and the Niger basin than toward Cayor, treated Lat Dior as an ally and sometimes as a friend of France. Both Valière and Brière, of course, recognized that Lat Dior would resist any serious French advances into Cayor (Saint-Martin 1966:62–72).

Bokar Saada, who began as a puppet in 1855 when Faidherbe recognized him, and Sambala of Khasso, who had been more or less reduced to puppet status, both became quite strong and successful local rulers after 'Umar's final withdrawal to the east in 1859 and the French decision in 1860 to abandon their attempt at gold mining in Bambuk. For the next twenty years these rulers would dominate the local politics of this border zone between two rival imperialisms. Their successes lead one to suppose that other French client rulers nearer to Saint-Louis might have done as well had Faidherbe and his immediate successor been willing to trust them and to leave them alone. Certainly Faidherbe's Mauritanian settlement was successful, at least from the point of view of the colonial authorities. It left the three emirates independent, guaranteed a regular French subsidy to their rulers, and permitted a return to many of the old ways *vis-à-vis* the French and some of the south-bank societies.

As for Faidherbe himself, his theory of imperial domination was a unique combination of old-regime mercantilism, mid-nineteenth-century economic liberalism, informal empire, and savage military repression based on the Algerian model. He therefore may be said to have rung in the finale of the seventeenth- and eighteenth-century variety of limited French domination in Senegambia (minus the slave trade). He confirmed the economic control of the colonial economy of Senegal by Bordeaux. For the future, he strengthened an existing French orientation toward the Middle Niger from the Upper Senegal. He introduced the tradition of large-scale Algerian-style military campaigns into the nucleus of what became French West Africa but as a means of accomplishing aims different from those of the French army in Algeria — both his admirers and his detractors were quick to lose sight of this distinction. It was this tradition of militarism which was Faidherbe's chief contribution to the eventual creation of French West Africa.

REFERENCES

ARCHIVES NATIONALES DE FRANCE, SECTION OUTRE-MER, PARIS
1851a Sénégal XIII la, Marc Maurel to Minister of the Navy and Colonies, December 8, 1851.
1851b Sénégal II 37b, Protet to Minister of the Navy and Colonies, February 1, 1851.
1852 Sénégal I 37b, Protet to Minister of the Navy and Colonies, June 8 and August 7, 1852.
1853–1854 Sénégal I 37–40, Minister of the Navy and Colonies to Protet, January 4, January 5, November 13, and December 14, 1853; January 21, May 18, and July 27, 1854.
1855a Sénégal I 41b, Faidherbe to Minister of the Navy and Colonies, December 30, 1855.
1855b Sénégal I 41b, Faidherbe to Minister of the Navy and Colonies, October 1, 1855.
1856a Sénégal I 41b, Faidherbe to Minister of the Navy and Colonies, January 28, 1856.
1856b Sénégal I 43a, Mémoire by Faidherbe, August 5, 1856.
1857a Sénégal VII 26bis, September 15, 1857.
1857b Sénégal I 43a, Faidherbe to Minister of the Navy and Colonies, October 17, 1857.
1858 Sénégal I 43a, Faidherbe to Minister of the Navy and Colonies, August 30, 1858.
1859 Sénégal I 46a, October 13, 1859.
1859–1860 Sénégal I 46b, Minister of Algeria and the Colonies to Faidherbe, December 21, 1859 and March 22, 1860.
1860a Sénégal I 46b, Faidherbe to Minister of the Navy and Colonies, January 6, 1860.
1860b Sénégal VII 26bis, January 26, 1860.
1861a Sénégal VII 26bis, April 13, 1861.
1861b Sénégal I 46c, clipping from the *Journal du Hâvre,* February 15, 1861.
1863a Sénégal VII 26bis, March 20, 1863.
1863b Sénégal I 50b, Faidherbe to Minister of the Navy and Colonies, September 11, 1863.
1864a Sénégal VII 26bis, May 21, 1864.
1864b Sénégal VII 26bis, June 30, 1864.
1864c Sénégal I 50c, Minister of the Navy and Colonies to Faidherbe, December 7, 1864.
1864–1865 Sénégal I 50, clippings from the *Courrier du Hâvre,* October 14, 1864, and February 11, 1865.
1871 Sénégal VII 26bis, February 25, 1871.
n.d.a Sénégal I 41d, Banquet offert par le commerce. . . .
n.d.b Sénégal I 50c, Faidherbe to the inhabitants of Toro.

ARCHIVES NATIONALES DE LA RÉPUBLIQUE DU SÉNÉGAL, DAKAR
1855   3B93, Faidherbe to Mohammed el-Habib, April 3 and April 25, 1855.
n.d.   13G33, Valantin petition.
BA, O.
1976   *La pénétration française au Cayor du règne de Birimi N'Goné Latyr á
       l'intronisation de Madiodo Déguène Codou,* volume one. Abbeville:
       F. Paillart.
BARROWS, L. C.
1974   The merchants and General Faidherbe: aspects of French expansion in
       Senegal in the 1850's. *Revue Française d'Histoire d'Outre-Mer*
       61:236–283.
1976   Faidherbe and Senegal: a critical discussion. *African Studies Review*
       19:95–117.
1978   "Louis Léon César Faidherbe (1818–1889)," in *African proconsuls:
       European governers in Africa.* Edited by L. H. Gann and Peter Duignan,
       51–79. Stanford: Hoover Institution on War, Revolution, and Peace.
BARRY, B.
1969   Le royaume du Wâlo du traité de Ngio en 1819 à la conquête en 1855.
       Bulletin de l'Institut Fondamental d'Afrique Noire B31:339–444.
1972   *Le royaume du Waalo: le Sénégal avant la conquête.* Paris: François
       Maspero.
CARRÈRE, F., P. HOLLE
1855   *De la Sénégambie française.* Paris: Firmin and Didot.
CURTIN, P. D.
1975   *Economic change in precolonial Africa: Senegambia in the era of the
       slave trade.* Madison: University of Wisconsin Press.
FAIDHERBE, L. L. C.
1881–1885 *Le Soudan français: chemin-de-fer de Médine au Niger.* Lille:
       L. Danel.
1889   *Le Sénégal: la France dans l'Afrique occidentale.* Paris: Hachette.
HARDY, G.
1921   *La mise en valeur du Sénégal de 1817 à 1854.* Paris: Emile Larose.
KLEIN, M.
1968   *Islam and imperialism in Senegal: Sine-Saloum, 1847–1914.* Stanford:
       Hoover Institution on War, Revolution, and Peace.
MAUREL AND PROM PAPERS
1855a Marc Maurel to "Mon oncle," February 28 and February 29, 1855.
1855b Marc Maurel to "Mon oncle," May 9 and May 11, 1855.
1855c Marc Maurel to "Mon cher oncle," April 3, 1855.
1863   Marc Maurel to "Mes bons amis," April 22, 1863.
MINISTÈRE DE LA MARINE ET DES COLONIES
1885   *Annales sénégalaises de 1854 à 1855 suivies des traités passés avec les
       indigènes.* Paris: Maisonneuve.
MONTEIL, V.
1966   *Esquisses sénégalaises.* Dakar: Institut Fondamental d'Afrique Noire.
N'DIAYE, F.
1968   La colonie du Sénégal au temps de Brière de L'Isle, 1876–1881. *Bulle-
       tin de l'Institut Fondamental d'Afrique Noire* 30B:463–512.
RICARD, F.
1865   *Le Sénégal: étude intime.* Paris: Chalamel.
ROBINSON, D. W.
1972   "Abdul Bokar Kan and the history of Futa Toro, 1853–1891." Unpub-
       lished Ph.D. dissertation, Columbia University.

1975   *Chiefs and clerics: Abdul Bokar Kan and Futa Toro 1853–1891.* Oxford: Clarendon.

SAINT-MARTIN, Y.
1966   *Une source de l'histoire coloniale du Sénégal: les rapports de situation politique, 1874–1881.* Dakar: Faculté des Lettres et Sciences Humaines, Université de Dakar.
1967   *L'empire toucouleur et la France: un demi-siècle de relations diplomatiques, 1846–1893.* Dakar: Faculté des Lettres et Sciences Humaines, Université de Dakar.

STEWART, C. C., E. K. STEWART
1973   *Islam and social order in Mauritania: a case study from the nineteenth century.* Oxford: Clarendon.

SURET-CANALE, J. S.
1968   *Afrique noire occidentale et central: géographie, civilisations, histoire* (second edition). Paris: Editions Sociales.

WITHERELL, J.
1964   "The response of the peoples of Cayor to French penetration, 1850–1900." Unpublished Ph.D. dissertation, University of Wisconsin, Madison.

Changing Perspectives on African Resistance Movements and the Case of the Baule Peoples

TIMOTHY C. WEISKEL

TRENDS IN RESISTANCE STUDIES

For much of the colonial period observers of the African continent failed to recognize the historical significance of African resistance movements. Those who addressed the subject at all usually treated it as a mere sidelight to the creation of formal colonial administration. In military histories attention focused particularly upon European officers and the campaigns they undertook. African leaders like Samori, Rabah, and Ahmadu were mentioned as if they existed primarily as sparring partners against whom the European leaders eventually dealt crushing blows. As for the masses, it was thought that they did not really count: they had been led astray by tyrants and opportunists, and they were to be "delivered" from these false prophets with the arrival of the Europeans. In both instances their role was assumed to be essentially passive. After the capture of outstanding chiefs the issue was presumed to be settled.

In the case of French West Africa, most of the major Islamic resistance leaders had been captured by 1895, and, as one French historian phrased it with reference to the Ivory Coast, "from then on the military operations that took place in the Ivory Coast have only a local interest; they are no longer linked as clearly as the previous ones to the general history of French West Africa" (Deloncle 1934:248–249). The author then went on to assure his readers that an enumeration of subsequent resistance incidents would simply bore them, and in this fashion he blithely skipped over some of the most significant events of early Ivory Coast colonial history.

By the 1930's Europeans' confidence and pride in their accomplishments came to dominate their perceptions of the past to such an extent that some managed to convince themselves (and tried to convince others) that resistance had never taken place. No less a scholar than the noted social anthropologist Diedrich Westermann — otherwise a sensitive and acute observer — could write (1949:159):

> The European's position as a dominant power in Africa has been made easy by the fact that he was since his first arrival an object of admiration to the African. He was looked upon as a superior being, possessing every desirable object and being capable of doing almost anything, a man by nature a ruler to whom one willingly submitted.

Such an observation, written initially in 1934, would not have been made twenty years previously. Nor could it have been made twenty years later. By the mid-1950's modern nationalist movements were well on their way to mobilizing mass support for independence, and in this context the phenomena of "primary resistance" began to take on a new significance for historians of Africa.

The emergence of Sékou Touré as leader of the nationalist movement in Guinea dramatized the issue for the student of African politics. Sékou Touré was a militant anticolonial organizer with particular experience in labor-union work. Perhaps more significantly, however, his mass appeal was in part based upon the fact that he was reputed to be the great-grandson of Samori Touré, the famed nineteenth-century resistance leader who had succeeded in eluding French control for nearly fifteen years before he was finally captured in 1898.

When political scientists brought this to the attention of the public at large (Hodgkin and Schacter 1960:377), historians began to reexamine earlier resistance struggles in the light of modern nationalism. In most instances it was not possible to trace direct genealogical links between primary resisters and modern nationalists, as in the case of Samori Touré and Sékou Touré, but early resistance was important in a more indirect way. As one Nigerian historian summed it up in the mid-1960's (Tamuno 1965:294):

> these earlier movements of resistance . . . provided a favourable psychological climate, assisted by later events such as two world wars, for the work of later-day nationalists. The victims of earlier unsuccessful opposition . . . kept alive for later generations the feeling that British rule was "imposed" and not voluntarily accepted. . . .

From this perspective, then, modern nationalist leaders were but part of a continuing tradition to which they were expected to contribute. "The later-day nationalists were . . . left with an unfinished task bequeathed to them by their predecessors" (Tamuno 1965:294). By the end of the 1960's, studies by Ranger (1968, 1969) drew further attention to the large variety of connections between the "primary resistance" move-ments and the "later-day nationalists," and it became apparent that henceforth resistance studies were to be the cornerstone of any serious examination of modern nationalism (Davidson 1968:177). Simultaneously, the study of resistance phenomena became important from yet another perspective. If political scientists valued resistance movements essentially as a preface to modern nationalism, students of European expansion began to consider them as crucial for understanding nineteenth-century imperialism. In an effort to transcend Eurocentric theories of imperialism, Robinson and Gallagher (1962) focused attention upon what they called the "proto-nationalist" movements in the peripheral areas of Europe's informal empire. They argued that it was these resistance movements that provoked the process of imperial conquest, rather than any intrinsic pressure for expansion within European economies themselves. Indeed, Europeans were seen to have been only reluctantly drawn into imperial expansion as a result of the "proto-nationalist" initiatives (1962:632, 620).

> In the 1880's the policy makers had intended nothing more ambitious than building diplomatic fences around these territories and hamstringing their rulers by informal control. But such methods would not work with the proto-nationalists. . . . Dragged ever deeper into reactions which their own coming had provoked the powers were forced in the 1890's to occupy the claims which they had papered on the African map in the 1880's. The spectacular expansion that resulted has often been called imperialism. But at a deeper level it was a reflex to the stirrings of African proto-nationalism.

Clearly, then, a careful examination of resistance movements came to be as essential to the study of nineteenth-century imperialism as it was to the study of twentieth-century nationalism. Not all scholars agreed with the "excentric" or "peripheral" theory of imperialism forwarded by Robinson and Gallagher, but even those, like Kanya-Forstner (1969), who challenged it had to do so on the basis of a reexamination of the resistance movements themselves.

The revived interest of both political scientists and imperial historians in African resistance phenomena led to an enormous outpouring of case studies during the 1960's and early 1970's. In North Africa, attention centered on the nineteenth-century movement in Algeria led by Abd el-Kader and upon the early twentieth-century resistance struggles in Morocco (Roughton 1973; Burke 1976). In West Africa several studies reexamined the role of major Muslim resistance movements in the Sudan (Griffeth 1968; Ọlọruntimẹhin 1973; Person 1968–1975, 1970, 1971; and Echenburg 1971). Other studies devoted attention to peoples nearer the coast in Senegal, Sierra Leone, the Gold Coast, Dahomey, and Nigeria (Roche 1972; Witherell 1964; Crowder and Denzer 1970; Saffell 1965; Cornevin 1960; Ikime 1968; Igbafe 1971). Eastern African studies included an examination of movements in Tanganyika, Kenya, Uganda,

Somalia, and Ethiopia (Jackson 1970; Hodges 1971; Steinhardt 1971; Geshekter 1972; Rubenson 1970). In Southern Africa, movements were described in Malawi, Southern Rhodesia, South Africa, and South West Africa (Linden 1971; Ranger 1970; Marks 1970; Freislich 1964; and Wallenkampf 1969). In addition, two anthologies of collected case studies were particularly useful in bringing the resistance phenomena to the attention of scholars in general (Rotberg and Mazrui 1970; Crowder 1971).

In the light of these studies, scholars made a number of important advances in understanding resistance phenomena, and some of the common misperceptions about them were corrected. In the first place, the sheer number of case studies firmly established the point that resistance was not an isolated or marginal phenomenon in African history. On the contrary, virtually all African societies, or segments within them, proved themselves ready and willing to resist at least some aspects of European domination (Ranger 1969:304; Hargreaves 1969:206). Societies experienced European demands at different times and under different circumstances, and this accounted for the diversity of their responses. Some resisted European military intrusion prior to formal annexation, while others protested taxation, land alienation, or trade regulation only after the bureaucratic apparatus of empire was established. This fact led some scholars to distinguish between "resistance," on the one hand, and "rebellion," on the other, but, as they acknowledged, such an arbitrary categorization was not always useful (Rotberg and Mazrui 1970:xviii–xxi). Basically African societies resisted the loss of control over their own destinies implied by European intrusion, whether this intrusion occurred before or after formal annexation.

A second affirmation to emerge from the bulk of the studies on resistance was that African military prowess was by no means negligible. During the colonial period, the ultimate outcome of the resistance struggles left successive generations with the impression that European intrusion was somehow effortless. Even those with profound sympathy for the emergence of African nationalism tended by the early 1960's to underestimate the importance of African military resistance. As one writer summarized the late nineteenth-century situation (Davidson 1963:68):

The armies and expeditions of Europe could now do pretty well whatever they liked in Africa, and go more or less wherever they pleased. Backed by their wealth and increasing mastery of science, the European kings and soldiers carried all before them. In doing so they found it easy — and convenient — to treat Africans either as savages or as helpless children.

Such an image of European invincibility was impossible to sustain in the face of detailed studies of African military resistance. Time and time again, the armies of African states surprised European military officers with the tenacity and determination of their resistance. What they lacked in comparable armaments they often made up for in superior military strategy and knowledge of the terrain. Engagements that Europeans had estimated would take days or weeks frequently lasted months and even years, and the expense incurred in subduing African populations surprised and irritated colonial officials and metropolitan parliamentarians alike (Crowder 1971:1–2). In most cases it was not until well into the twentieth century that European administrators could "go where they pleased" within their own colonies.

Perhaps the most important general observation to emerge from the multiple resistance studies concerned the political character of African resistance leadership. In their stimulating synthetic study of the "Partition," Robinson and Gallagher (1962:640) suggested that primary resistance movements were essentially "romantic, reactionary struggles against the facts, the passionate protest of societies which were shocked by the new age of change and would not be comforted." To these movements Robinson and Gallagher contrasted what they called the "defter nationalisms" exemplified by those who chose to collaborate with the Europeans at least initially until fullfledged national movements could be formed in a later era. In a similar vein, Oliver and Fage (1966:203) distinguished the "far-sighted and well-informed" collaborators from the "less far-sighted, less fortunate, or less well-advised" resisters.

Each of these characterizations sounded reminiscent of the assessments made by earlier colonial administrators, and both proved inadequate as evidence from case studies became available. Resisters were by no means always "romantic reactionaries"; some generated support through explicitly modern reformist programs. Nor were collaborators necessarily more progressive in their outlook; indeed, it was often their essential conservatism that encouraged them to accommodate themselves as quickly as possible to the European presence in order to preserve their positions of privilege. Judgments about the political outlook of the African leaders could not be correlated consistently with decisions to resist or collaborate.

More fundamentally, historians began to realize that the entire attempt to divide "resisters" from "collaborators," as if they were mutually exclusive categories, was in many instances a meaningless exercise. As Ranger (1969:304) phrased it: "A historian has indeed a difficult task in deciding whether a specific society should be described as 'resistant' or as 'collaborative' over any given period of time. Many societies began in one camp and ended in the other." Hargreaves (1969:206) extended the observation to the leaders themselves, dismissing the earlier tendency to impute to these categories progressive or reactionary overtones: "In West Africa, as in East and Central Africa, it cannot be said that those who opted for resistance were less far-sighted or forward-looking than the 'collaborators.' In fact they were often the same men."

The emerging consensus by the end of the 1960's was that patterns of resistance and collaboration had to be studied jointly in any given society and that both needed to be examined in the light of local political traditions. Special attention was given to the diplomatic and political skills of African leaders from this perspective. Resistance and collaboration came to be viewed as alternative strategies available to any African leader at particular moments in his struggle to retain autonomy or obtain privilege. Even when the ideological appeal of particular leaders was couched in religious or millennial terms, historians emphasized the political implications of these movements, viewing them essentially as necessary solutions to the practical problems of extending resistance sentiment beyond the limits of ethnic boundaries (Ranger 1969:314).

Judgments had clearly shifted from the early 1960's. No longer were African kings and chiefs mere representations of vague principles of "reaction" or "progress." Instead they had come to be viewed as the kind of calculating political figures that historians were accustomed to writing about in other areas of the world. In this respect, resistance studies had accomplished a great deal, for they opened the way for historians to examine the politics of colonial rule on a much more sophisticated level than previously possible.

Despite these advances, there remain several glaring gaps in our understanding of resistance movements. The most obvious omissions have had to do with the resistance movements of acephalous or stateless societies. In part, the problem is simply a reflection of African historical studies in general (Horton 1972). State systems frequently preserved their own history, whereas stateless societies often lacked the institutional mechanisms for doing so. In terms of European documentation the problem is compounded. Centralized states usually faced European forces with armies of their own in well-defined campaigns, and these encounters frequently became the subject of published journals, memoirs, or official histories by the European participants. Stateless societies, by contrast, often skirmished with European soldiers in intermittent and inconclusive guerrilla activity, and these engagements were much less glamorous material for subsequent autobiography or government publications. Detailed accounts were sometimes compiled, but they lie buried in local or regional archives. The historian is faced with an extensive and expensive research task simply to unearth them, and so far this kind of work has remained beyond the resources of most doctoral research candidates.

Perhaps equally important, however, is the fact that in their effort to portray the subtlety and sophistication of African resistance leaders, scholars have gravitated toward those societies in which political leadership was well defined and particular personalities played salient roles. The result has been to concentrate on centralized political structures and present resistance history as if it could be understood primarily in terms of the biographies of its leaders. Davidson (1968:186) warned of the pitfalls of this approach:

> the biographical *genre* is fraught with great danger. In concentrating on the personality it is possible to miss the laws of social development. It must not be forgotten that in African countries as all over the world the motive force of history was the people. It was the people that rose in rebellion against colonialism. And any ruler or a chief was able to bring out his people in rebellion only if the idea of the struggle was congenial to the people, and if this idea had matured in their consciousness. That is why the restoration of the picture of the liberation struggle cannot be limited to the biographical form.

By examining resistance movements in stateless societies the preoccupation with biography can be overcome. Studies of this kind necessarily call for a different kind of focus — one that centers less upon the qualities of leadership than upon the pervasive mood of discontent.

A second striking deficiency in resistance studies to date is closely related to the first. With their concentration on military and then political aspects of resistance, scholars have not yet fully developed an understanding of the economic context of resistance movements. The need for this has been recognized, particularly in approaching resistance struggles of stateless societies (Hargreaves 1969:207), but more work is required to illumine the economic adjustments implied by colonial control and the ways in which these changes contributed to sentiment for revolt. Colonial rule imposed new trading relationships, new price structures, new cash crops, and different labor arrangements. All of these changes had to be mediated through local elites. The fact that some chose to resist these changes and others to accommodate themselves to them is no longer surprising. What needs to be examined in greater detail is the micro-economic context within which their respective decisions were made.

A third weakness of some resistance studies might be best described as a tendency toward episodic narrative, leading to a general perspective on the African past that emphasizes categorical breaks or ruptures in historical continuity. The dramatic quality of resistance incidents lends itself naturally to this form of writing, particularly since most primary documentation highlights the unprecedented nature of each revolt and the definitive character of European repression. Colonial administrators tended to view their experience in Africa in terms of a "before-and-after" explanatory framework. Historians would do well, however, to guard against the distortions of their sources, for it is often the case that resistance incidents obscured more fundamental and enduring types of encounters between Europeans and Africans. In studying individual incidents the continuous pattern of relations needs to be kept clearly in mind. Dramatic events may be of less significance than relatively minor incidents in illuminating the fundamental encounter between Europeans and Africans under colonial rule.

THE CASE OF BAULE RESISTANCE

The study of Baule resistance to French intrusion over the period from 1893 to 1911 provides a useful starting point for considering some of the new approaches to resistance studies. The Baule are Akan-speaking peoples occupying the area of what is now the central Ivory Coast. Although they have traditions of origin from the kingship systems of the more centralized Asante and Denkyira peoples, the Baule are a stateless society, formed from an amalgamation of immigrant Akan and preexisting communities of Dyula, Kru, and Voltaic peoples during the course of the seventeenth and eighteenth centuries (Weiskel 1976).

Initially the Baule were integrated into circuits of exchange with groups to the east in the Akan heartland as exporters of gold, woven cloth, and captives. During the nineteenth century, with the rise of palm-oil production along the coast, Baule exchanges focused increasingly in a north-south direction as the demand for gold, woven cloth, and captive labor developed among the coastal peoples. Thus, as the coastal peoples were adapting their productive economy to provide the cheap agricultural produce demanded in European commodity markets, the Baule economy continued to flourish on the commodities of the "royal" or "luxury" trade — gold, expensive fabrics, and slaves. Groups of Baule settlers began to move southward from about 1840 on to facilitate exchange with the coastal groups, but the Ebri, Alladan, Adiukru, and Avikam prevented the Baule from entering the offshore trade. Insulated from direct exposure to European demands by the intervening groups of palm-oil producers, the relatively archaic economic organization of the Baule continued to be viable well into the colonial period.

In the course of the two centuries prior to European contact, the Baule had developed a highly flexible social structure based on localized cognatic descent groups (aulo bo). Political power was decentralized and depended ultimately upon one's capacity to mobilize a loyal following rather than upon ascribed criteria. This led to a pattern of muted competition among household heads and village chiefs for the effective support of mutually available personnel. On the eve of European penetration this competition often expressed itself as well in the form of trade rivalries between villages linked in exchange relations in a north-south direction. These rival "trading chains" transcended ethnic boundaries and provided avenues for the flow of commercial goods to and from the coast in a relay system of exchange. One of the most important rivalries during the precolonial period was that between Tiassalé and its associates, on the one hand, and Ahua and its allies, on the other. The antagonism between these two rival trading chains was to prove crucial in the pattern of European intrusion in the area.

For most of the nineteenth century the French remained uninterested in their Ivory Coast possessions, but in 1889, when Binger succeeded in reaching the coast from the French Sudan, the potential of the Ivory Coast as a natural avenue to the Niger Bend began to attract French official attention. The government consolidated its holdings in 1889 and established customs posts along the coast, but this policy provoked a series of revolts that had repercussions far beyond the immediate range of the customs enclaves. Several French attempts to penetrate inland ended disastrously until Marchand led an expedition against the troublesome town of Tiassalé in 1893. With the help of collaborators from Ahua and its allied villages, Marchand was able to subdue Tiassalé resistance and replace its chief.

In the wake of this expedition Marchand entered Baule territory to the north of Tiassalé. There he witnessed Baule prosperity and reported on the commercial potential of the region as well as the apparent Baule receptivity to the idea of commercial relations with Europeans. More significantly, however, Marchand learned of Samori's advance in the northern part of the Ivory Coast, and he cabled the Ministry of Colonies, requesting an urgent expedition to defeat Samori and preserve French interests in the area.

The ministry responded by sending an expedition under Monteil with instructions to reach and defend Kong. Monteil, on Marchand's advice, chose to advance toward Kong through Baule territory. The Baule, however, were reluctant to provide the porters necessary for the expedition. In effect, the French proposal to take Baule slaves as porters northward toward their areas of origin seriously threatened Baule control over their newly acquired labor, and they turned on the French forces in open revolt. In January and February of 1895 the Baule succeeded in bringing the expedition to a standstill, and Monteil cabled the ministry that a full-scale operation against the Baule would be necessary. The ministry, wanting to avoid the embarrassment of further military commitments at the time, recalled Monteil and eventually removed the troops from Baule territory altogether. It appeared to the Baule, and indeed to many French critics as well, that in their first resistance struggle against the French the Baule had won a clear victory.

Following Monteil's departure, the Baule experienced a period of unparalleled prosperity from 1895 to 1898. As a result of Samori's conquests to the north of them, the Baule were able to obtain captives in exchange for guns, munitions, and provisions. The influx of new captives

swelled the ranks of Baule households, increasing their productive potential in the traditional industries of gold mining, refining, and cloth manufacture. Commercialization of these products increased with the arrival of
Apollonian traders, who began to penetrate the Baule region from the
south and east in search of wild rubber. The effect of economic prosperity
was to increase the decentralized character of Baule political structures.
The absorption of massive new slave populations obtained in trade with
Samori made it possible for the Baule to practice kin-group endogamy
through various forms of marriage with slave dependents. This in turn
increased the autonomy of the localized cognatic descent group, because
the alliances which would normally have been formed through exogamous marriages with neighboring groups were no longer being forged.

   Samori's retreat and capture in 1898 had profound consequences for
the Baule economy and social structure. Captives recently obtained in
trade began to escape in an effort to return to their homelands, no longer
threatened by Samori. Furthermore, the French created a military post at
Buaké, and its commander, Benoît, seemed intent upon "liberating"
Baule captives to obtain a work force for French administrative needs and
eventually to resettle the areas recently recaptured from Samori. In
response to this policy the Baule attacked the Buaké post in December
1898. The situation deteriorated further during 1899 and came to the
point of open revolt when Maurice Delafosse tried to settle a trading
dispute involving a local chief named Kuadio Oku. Unable to capture
Kuadio Oku on his own, Delafosse appealed for military reinforcements
to establish immediate order and reassert French control. The troops
eventually arrived, but their heavy-handed intrusion had the effect of
alienating the Baule on a massive scale, triggering the second major phase
of Baule resistance.

   French engagements with the Baule continued sporadically throughout
1900, 1901, and 1902. Baule guerrilla tactics proved highly successful in
keeping the French forces at bay, and the French were forced to concede
that despite their superior weaponry it was likely that their Senegalese
troops had incurred more casualties than the Baule. At the end of
November 1902, François-Joseph Clozel was named acting governor of
the Ivory Coast, and after consultations with Governor-General Roume
in Dakar he initiated a major change in official policy toward the Baule.
He called a halt to aggressive military conquest and began instead to
prepare the way for a more pacific commercial penetration of Baule
country by European trading firms.

   During Clozel's governorship the expansion of the colony's commerce
was remarkable, largely because of the massive increase in exports of wild
rubber. Total trade figures for the colony jumped from 12,400,000 francs
in 1901 to 25,200,000 francs in 1907, the final year of Clozel's administration, and over the period from 1902 to 1907 wild rubber came to

represent nearly two-thirds of the total value of the colony's exports (Weiskel 1977). The Baule remained only peripherally engaged in this trade, but Clozel gradually drew them into expanded exchange with European firms. His strategy was to establish a series of collaborative arrangements with Baule chiefs by granting them tax rebates, judicial functions, and commercial privileges. In doing so he was able to increase significantly the level of taxation of the rural population without provoking open revolt.

Clozel's collaborative system worked remarkably well from 1903 to 1907, but by the end of this period its weaknesses were becoming apparent. The creation of the budget for the Government General in 1904 had the effect of increasing taxation on the rural masses. In the long run these taxes would be forthcoming only if these populations could earn an income in the colonial economy. Up until 1907 the Baule had been able to earn enough to pay taxes either by exporting small amounts of wild rubber themselves or by providing goods and services to those who collected it in their midst. The trouble came when destructive tapping techniques gradually destroyed the vines and made wild rubber more and more difficult to obtain. At the same time prices for wild rubber on the European markets began to falter in the face of competition from Malaysian plantation rubber, and the future of this export commodity looked precarious indeed.

Gabriel Angoulvant succeeded Clozel as governor of the Ivory Coast in April 1908, and to avert the impending economic crisis he introduced tax measures, land-tenure reforms, and forced-labor directives to induce the rural population to accept new cash crops and increase their production of previous export commodities. At first the Baule reacted evasively to this attempt to reorganize their productive relations, but when the French continued to pressure them they entered into armed revolt in June 1909. In the face of this third phase of Baule resistance, Governor-General Ponty decided to authorize Angoulvant's plans for the complete conquest of the Baule.

The resulting battles were devastating. Militarily, the Baule continued to hold their own, but ultimately they could not prevail for logistic reasons. Located in the forest zone, the Baule depended upon an annual crop of yams to sustain themselves. In contrast with the rice- or cereal-based cultures in the Sudan, the yam-based culture of the Baule put them at a crucial military disadvantage. Rice and cereals could be stored from year to year with minimum spoilage, but yams could not. Thus, it was impossible for the Baule to lay up stores for a sustained struggle. They were tied to an annual cycle of planting and harvesting with little room for manoeuver. In addition, yams, unlike rice or cereals, contained a high component of water, making them too heavy and too bulky to transport. Unable to stockpile sufficient provisions over a period of years and hampered in transporting available supplies quickly to areas of acute need, the Baule found their capacity for sustained resistance severely limited.

The French strategy was as simple as it was brutal. Frustrated with their failures in previous limited encounters with Baule guerrillas, the military adopted a full-scale search-and-destroy policy culminating in the destruction of the homes, possessions, and crops of the rebels. By pursuing the Baule through two successive rainy seasons and systematically destroying their newly planted crops, the French brought the rebels to the brink of starvation. Many fled to neighboring groups; others submitted. By the end of 1911 Baule armed resistance had come to an end. In the aftermath of defeat, Baule armaments were confiscated and destroyed, heavy war fines were imposed, taxes were increased, and rebel "leaders" were exiled. The population of the region appears to have been diminished by hundreds of thousands as a result of the military engagements and the famine and epidemics that swept the region in their wake.

TOWARD A NEW FRAMEWORK FOR RESISTANCE STUDIES

When the three phases of Baule resistance are considered as a whole, several general observations can be made which may be of use in understanding other resistance phenomena. In the first place, the Baule case amply demonstrates that resistance could be effectively mounted in a stateless society. Indeed, acephalous societies had distinct advantages over centralized kingdoms in several respects. Since political power was decentralized, it was impossible to crush the rebellion by the simple capture of a few alleged leaders. To the extent that it is useful to make a distinction, as Iliffe has suggested (cited in Ranger 1968:446–447) between "soldiers' wars" and "people's wars," the struggles in stateless societies would seem to be "people's wars" from the outset. Under these circumstances a formal ideology of resistance was largely superfluous, for people were galvanized to action from a common sense of grievance rather than through an independent loyalty to an elaborate belief system. Militarily, stateless societies were capable of doing quite well. The guerrilla tactics employed by the decentralized Baule proved every bit as successful as the resistance fighting of more centrally organized armies. Defeat cannot be attributed to weaknesses of political or military organization or to the lack of an articulated ideology so much as to the underlying constraints of the productive cycle of Baule agriculture.

The Baule case further emphasizes the necessity of examining resistance and collaboration as related phenomena. As one might expect in a factionalized society, not all Baule resisted. From the beginning the French were able to find collaborators. Some sought new positions of advantage; others hoped to settle old scores with traditional rivals. In any case, the decision to resist or collaborate at a particular point was a complex political choice, and leaders frequently alternated their strategies over time, opting to collaborate when such a policy furthered their interests and resist when circumstances changed.

The major question that needs answering is: in what way did circumstances change so as to motivate large numbers of chiefs to resist in three successive stages of revolt? The answer can only come from an examination of the economic context of the encounter between the French and the Baule. In the precolonial era the Baule were by no means what anthropologists might call a "primitive isolate." On the contrary, their very existence was predicated on trade. As the westernmost extension of the Akan peoples, they formed a frontier zone between the heartland Akan and the Kru, southern Mande, and Voltaic peoples. Throughout the seventeenth and eighteenth centuries active trading took place along these frontiers as the Baule channeled gold, woven cloth, and captives toward the Akan circuits of exchange. In the nineteenth century the focus of trade shifted to a north-south direction, as the Baule continued to export gold, woven cloth, and captives to the coastal palm-oil producers in exchange for guns, powder, and European manufactures.

The crucial point, however, is that while the Baule were a highly monetarized and trade-oriented society in the precolonial period, they had not begun to shift their production to agricultural commodities for European industrial markets as their coastal neighbors had in the nineteenth century. Instead the Baule derived their trading profits either from buying and reselling captives or from putting them to work in local mining and craft production in order to sell these goods to their southern neighbors. The basic unit of production was the cognatic descent group with assimilated slaves, and the objects of production and exchange remained those of the "luxury" or "royal" trade — goods with high value-to-weight ratios. Because the coastal palm-oil producers were eager to purchase these goods, the somewhat archaic structure of the Baule mode of production remained viable long after other societies had shifted to producing cheap agricultural commodities.

French intrusion represented a direct challenge to the Baule mode of production. The crux of the problem centered on the social control of labor. Each of the three periods of revolt was precipitated by French demands that threatened the Baule's control over their captives. In the first two periods of resistance, the French were deliberately provocative toward the Baule to the extent that they sought to "liberate" Baule slaves. Just prior to the third phase, Angoulvant made it clear that he intended to transform the entire rural population into peasant producers for the world commodity markets. In economic terms alone, it is understandable that the Baule would have rejected participation in the emerging colonial economy, for their traditional forms of production and exchange remained highly profitable.

In addition, however, there was something else at stake. Angoulvant's programs undermined the social relations that had grown up to support and sustain Baule traditional production. By converting everyone into a cash-crop producer, Angoulvant collapsed significant social distinctions, placing slave and freeman alike on a potentially equal footing before the demands of the world market. Henceforth, status and reward depended upon performance — performance in an arena over which the Baule no longer had any control. Not surprisingly, the Baule rejected the cash-crop production that Angoulvant tried to implement, because by obliterating the operative distinction between themselves and their slaves, Angoulvant's programs aimed to destroy their entire social formation. It did not take charismatic leaders to arouse Baule resistance sentiment. Pervasive discontent emerged from objective shifts in the demands placed on Baule economic and social institutions.

The Baule case suggests that, in the future, resistance studies with an economic focus might serve as a useful bridge between two important schools of African historiography: the "trade-and-politics" school of precolonial history, on the one hand, and the "political-economy-of-colonialism" school, on the other. Studies of this kind can perhaps help us avoid the tendency to regard African resistance movements as if they were discontinuous episodes in Africa's past. In the Baule case the continuities are apparent. Primary resistance flared up over the issue of who would ultimately control the disposition of available labor. Similarly, the modern nationalist movement mobilized support in the postwar era precisely because it focused mass discontent over the issue of "forced labor." Ironically, Félix Houphouët-Boigny, the Baule chief who emerged as the leader of the latter-day nationalist struggle, was a political heir to Kuassi Ngo, one of the closest collaborators with the French in the period of primary resistance. In the Baule case, then, it is the underlying continuity of conflict over labor rather than any particular genealogical link between primary resisters and modern nationalists that provides us with the means of understanding the latter-day political movements.

From this perspective it would seem that resistance movements can be most usefully analyzed as the political and military expressions of broader economic shifts implied in the expansion of the world economy — a process still under way today. As Legassick (1976:440) has suggested, "perhaps the colonial and precolonial activities of the 'masses' should be re-examined not, following Ranger, in terms of their contributions to 'nationalism,' but as premature and so far abortive struggles against the inequalities of world capitalist development." The development of this type of perspective on African resistance would mark an important departure from the "nationalist historiography" of the 1960's, but it would seem far more consistent with what we have come to recognize as the longer-term struggle of the African peoples for economic emancipation.

REFERENCES

BURKE, EDMUND, III
  1976   *Prelude to protectorate in Morocco: precolonial protest and resistance, 1860–1912.* Chicago: University of Chicago Press.
CORNEVIN, ROBERT
  1960   Les divers épisodes de la lutte contre le royame d'Abomey, 1887–1894. *Revue Française d'Histoire d'Outre-Mer* 47:161–211.
CROWDER, MICHAEL, LA RAY DENZER
  1970   "Bai Bureh and the 1898 Sierra Leone hut tax war," in *Protest and power in Black Africa.* Edited by R. Rotberg and Ali Mazrui. London: Oxford University Press.
CROWDER, MICHAEL, *editor*
  1971   *West African resistance: the military response to colonial occupation.* London: Hutchinson.
DAVIDSON, A. B.
  1968   "African resistance and rebellion against the imposition of colonial rule," in *Emerging themes of African history.* Edited by T. O. Ranger, 177–188. London: Heinemann.
DAVIDSON, BASIL
  1963   *Guide to African history.* London.
DELONCLE, PIERRE
  1934   *L'Afrique occidentale française: découverte, pacification, mise en valeur.* Paris: Leroux.
ECHENBURG, MYRON J.
  1971   "African reaction to French conquest: Upper Volta in the late nineteenth century." Unpublished Ph.D. dissertation, University of Wisconsin.
FREISLICH, RICHARD
  1964   *The last tribal war: a history of the Bondelswart uprising.* Cape Town: Struik.
GESHEKTER, CHARLES L.
  1972   "British imperialism in the Horn of Africa and the Somali response, 1884–1899." Unpublished Ph.D. dissertation, University of California, Los Angeles.
GRIFFETH, ROBERT T.
  1968   "Varieties of African resistance to the French conquest of western Sudan, 1850–1900." Unpublished Ph.D. dissertation, Northwestern University.
HARGREAVES, JOHN D.
  1969   "West African states and the European conquest," in *Colonialism in Africa, 1870–1960,* volume one: *The history and politics of colonialism, 1870–1914.* Edited by L. H. Gann and Peter Duignan, 199–219. Cambridge: Cambridge University Press.
HODGES, G. W. T.
  1971   African responses to European rule in Kenya. *Hadith* 3:82–102.

HODGKIN, THOMAS, RUTH SCHACTER
1960 *French-speaking West Africa in transition.* International Conciliation 528.
HORTON, ROBIN
1972 "Stateless societies in the history of West Africa," in *History of West Africa*, volume one. Edited by J. F. A. Ajayi and Michael Crowder, 78–119. New York: Columbia University Press.
IGBAFE, PHILIP A.
1971 Western Ibo society and its resistance to British rule: the Ekumeku movement, 1898–1911. *Journal of African History* 12:441–459.
IKIME, O.
1968 *Merchant prince of the Niger delta.* London: Longman.
JACKSON, ROBERT D.
1970 "Resistance to the German invasion of the Tanganyikan coast, 1881–1891," in *Protest and power in Black Africa.* Edited by R. Rotberg and Ali Mazrui, 37–79. London: Oxford University Press.
KANYA-FORSTNER, A. S.
1969 *Myths and realities of African resistance.* Canadian Historical Association, Historical Papers.
LEGASSICK, MARTIN
1976 Perspectives on African "underdevelopment." *Journal of African History* 17:435–440.
LINDEN, IAN
1971 *Catholics, peasants, and Chewa resistance in Nyasaland, 1889–1939.* London: Heinemann.
MARKS, SHULA
1970 "The Zulu disturbances in Natal," in *Protest and power in Black Africa.* Edited by R. Rotberg and Ali Mazrui, 213–257. London: Oxford University Press.
OLIVER, ROLAND, JOHN FAGE
1966 *A short history of Africa.* Harmondsworth: Penguin.
OLORUNTIMEHIN, B. O.
1973 French colonisation and African resistance up to the First World War. *Genève-Afrique* 12:5–18.
PERSON, YVES
1968–1975 *Samori: une révolution dyula*, three volumes. Dakar: Institut Fondamental d'Afrique Noire.
1970 "Samori and resistance to the French," in *Protest and power in Black Africa.* Edited by R. Rotberg and Ali Mazrui, 80–112. London: Oxford University Press.
1971 "Guinea — Samory," in *West African resistance: the military response to colonial occupation.* Edited by M. Crowder. London: Hutchinson.
RANGER, T. O.
1968 Connexions between "primary resistance" movements and modern mass nationalism in East and Central Africa. *Journal of African History* 9:437–454, 631–642.
1969 "African reaction to the imposition of colonial rule in East and Central Africa," in *Colonialism in Africa, 1870–1960*, volume one: *The history and politics of colonialism, 1870–1914.* Edited by L. H. Gann and Peter Duignan, 293–324. Cambridge: Cambridge University Press.
1970 *The African voice in Southern Rhodesia, 1898–1930.* London: Heinemann.

ROBINSON, RONALD, JOHN GALLAGHER
1962 "The partition of Africa," in *The new Cambridge modern history*, volume eleven. Edited by F. H. Hinsley, 593–640. Cambridge: Cambridge University Press.
ROCHE, CHRISTIAN
1972 Un résistant oublié: Sunkaru Kamara, chef Malinké de Casamance. *Bulletin de l'Institut Fondamental d'Afrique Noire* 34:51–66.
ROTBERG, ROBERT, *editor*
1971 *Rebellion in Black Africa*. New York: Oxford University Press.
ROTBERG, ROBERT, ALI MAZRUI, *editors*
1970 *Protest and power in Black Africa*. London: Oxford University Press.
ROUGHTON, RICHARD A.
1973 "French colonialism and the resistance in Central and Western Algeria, 1830–1839." Unpublished Ph.D. dissertation, University of Maryland.
RUBENSON, SVEN
1970 "Adwa 1896: the resounding protest," in *Protest and power in Black Africa*. Edited by R. Rotberg and Ali Mazrui, 113–144. London: Oxford University Press.
SAFFELL, JOHN EDGAR
1965 "The Ashanti war of 1873–1874." Unpublished Ph.D. dissertation, Case Western Reserve University.
STEINHARDT, EDWARD I.
1971 "Transition in Western Uganda, 1891–1901: resistance and collaboration in the Ankole, Bunyoro, and Toro kingdoms of Uganda." Unpublished Ph.D. dissertation, Northwestern University.
TAMUNO, TEKENA N.
1965 Some aspects of Nigerian reaction to the imposition of British rule. *Journal of the Historical Society of Nigeria* 3:271–294.
WALLENKAMPF, ARNOLD V.
1969 "The Herero rebellion in South West Africa, 1904–1906: a study in German colonialism." Unpublished Ph.D. dissertation, University of California, Los Angeles.
WEISKEL, TIMOTHY C.
1976 L'histoire socio-économique des peuples baule: problèmes et perspectives de recherche. *Cahiers d'Etudes Africaines* 16:357–395.
1977 "French colonial rule and the Baule peoples: resistance and collaboration, 1889–1911." Unpublished Ph.D. dissertation, Oxford University.
WESTERMANN, DIEDRICH
1949 *The African to-day and to-morrow*. London: Oxford University Press.
WITHERELL, JULIAN W.
1964 "The response of the peoples of Cayor (Senegal) to French penetration, 1850–1900." Unpublished Ph.D. dissertation, University of Wisconsin.

Nation Building, Ethnicity, and the New Imperialism: Dilemmas of Political Development in Liberia

HENRY S. WILSON

Historians frequently have sought to correct the shallow perspective adopted by some social scientists when discussing African nationalism. Certainly, the pedigrees of "pan-Negro patriotism" and pan-Africanism, along with notions of nation building and the African personality, reach far back — especially in the case of West Africa — into the precolonial past. Merely to trace the genealogy of such ideas and thus establish an affinity with the optimism of the enlightenment and abolitionism seemed a highly appropriate historiographical accompaniment to the "springtime of the nations," the brisk procession to independence in the early 1960's. As in precolonial times, the stage then seemed set for an era of partnership in development between Africans and outsiders, and the ideas of such eminent Victorians as Africanus Horton and Edward Blyden, David Livingstone and Samuel Ajayi Crowther were seen to have an oddly modern ring.

Yet such ideas were not simply preserved in books and archives to await rediscovery by latter-day scholars. No collective amnesia afflicted the West African intelligentsia at the turn of the century. Some of the great names from the first generation of African nationalists — Blyden, for example — survived as links with the precolonial past, and even in the heyday of imperialism the pulse of African patriotism was manifestly strong. It was axiomatic that a sharp awareness of group identity and a staunch preference for native rule persisted among the newly annexed peoples of the hinterlands. (The imperial administrators themselves, of course, deferred to such sentiments and sought to turn them to their advantage in systems of control based upon indirect rule.) The problem which, therefore, confronted West African writers and politicians, nurtured on the nationalist ideas of the founding fathers, was how to adapt

Administrative Divisions and Tribal Areas

Figure 1.   Map of Liberia. *Source*: Frankel *Tribe and class in Monrovia*

their notions of identity, autonomy, and nation building to changing constraints and opportunities.

This study is concerned with the working out of such ideas in the adjoining territories of Liberia and Sierra Leone in the early twentieth century. Specifically, it is concerned with President Arthur Barclay's efforts to modernize Liberia in order to make it conform to contemporary standards of good government and thus ensure its survival. With outside assistance, he embarked upon an ambitious program of economic development and administrative reform. He was engaged in conscious nation building. He remarked that Liberia, at the time of independence (1847), had been recognized by the powers as a nation "in *posse* rather than in *esse*"; once the peoples of the hinterland had been caught up in modernization and its resulting prosperity, however, they would cohere around the Americo-Liberian nucleus, thus transforming Liberia from a potential into an actual nation-state. Barclay's plans were only partially realized when they were overtaken by a fierce "reactionary" (his word) backlash from within the Americo-Liberian community. Highly nationalistic, it was specifically directed against his British advisers. Further, this study analyzes the contrasting fates of the Kru and Grebo peoples on the Liberian coast and the inhabitants of Luawa in the interior. Both groups reacted against the prospect of incorporation within the greater Liberian state by seeking partial autonomy under British protection. Luawa achieved this aim, whereas the Kru and Grebo failed. Finally, all these developments are reviewed from the differing perspectives of West Africans and others writing and speaking at the time they occurred and of modern historians and social scientists blessed with hindsight.

At the end of the nineteenth century, Africans found themselves incorporated into an international political system and world economy dominated by outsiders. It took varying lengths of time for the significance of this to be appreciated, even when the process was signaled by outright annexation. After all, loss of sovereignty, however momentous in its consequences, could be relatively painless. This was especially so if accomplished by the preferred European instrument, the promulgation of a protectorate, which allowed the colonial power to appropriate sizable territories for a minimal initial administrative down payment. Only afterward, as Africans were exposed to such aspects of the imperial presence as novel forms of taxation and forced labor, police and military brutality, and interference with established forms of trade, did the full force of what had happened strike home. Hence, mobilization for primary resistance frequently occurred after annexation, as in the case of the 1898 Sierra Leone insurrection two years after the protectorate was promulgated.

Shielded by international recognition and prideful of their Christianity, Americo-Liberians were inclined to ignore events beyond their borders. Barclay (1906a) cautioned that the Republic was caught in the same quickening currents of world history that engulfed "savage Africa" outside:

... the Americo-Liberians are possibly the greatest travellers of all the civilized people of West Africa. It is a pity however that they pay little attention to the contiguous Colonies and protectorates. If they did so they would probably have formed a correct idea of the great improvements and enormous development which have taken place around them, and would not be inclined to criticize, but rather applaud and assist the efforts of their Government to keep pace, however lamely, with the times.

It was essential, he warned, to keep a "finger on the pulse of International Public Opinion." Liberians whose contacts with the wider world tended to be through mission and church connections, he continued, failed to comprehend that the present was "essentially a material age" in which "the philanthropic wave which moved and influenced the European world for over half a century seems for the present to have almost entirely ebbed." Isolationism could be as fatal to the Republic, he argued, as it had proved to other, more traditional African polities.

EUROPEAN AND AMERICAN ATTITUDES TOWARD LIBERIA

Liberia had been founded in 1822 by the American Colonization Society primarily to alleviate United States racial problems but also with the hope that its settlers might evangelize hinterland Africa. In 1847 the small coastal settlements transformed themselves into an independent sovereign republic to win international recognition for their commercial regulations and thus cope with recalcitrant European merchants. By the end of the American Civil War, some 15,000 black Americans had settled in Liberia, along with 5,000 Africans liberated from slave ships and nearly 350 Afro-West Indians. After emancipation, immigration from the United States diminished to a trickle.

The question which Barclay posed to the legislature was quite simply how such a relic of the age of abolition could survive in a period of predatory European imperialism. Britain and France already had sliced sharply into Liberia's territorial claims, and with the Republic scarcely able to afford the expense of boundary demarcation, let alone "effective occupation," further losses seemed all too likely. Barclay advanced the ingenious proposition that because the Republic's relationships with hinterland Africans were contractual, not coercive — Liberia regarded "all native tribes in its borders as citizens rather than subjects" — it should not in logic be expected to manifest the apparatus of "effective occupation" appropriate to a European colony or protectorate. He warned his listeners, though, that such instant annexation by adroit manipulation of republican political theory was unlikely to prove internationally acceptable: "it is a fact that the Great Powers really settle the principles of International Law. Small states must conform."

Four great powers impinged upon Liberia: Britain, France, Germany, and the United States. With the significant exception of the United States, all were African colonial powers which viewed Liberia through imperial lenses. By this time they had rationalized their colonial experience and come to loose agreement on the norms of government appropriate to tropical Africa. As they saw it, precolonial Africa had been wracked by chronic tribal warfare which Africans, left to themselves, were unable to end. It was proper, therefore, that Europeans, who were especially qualified to rule by reason of their innate "racial" characteristics and long imperial traditions, should intervene. Such was the white man's burden: the duty of a superior race to impose "pax" and in its wake uncorrupt government, thus opening the way for commerce and, possibly, Christianity.

Racial determinism was central to such ideas: individuals could only develop successfully along lines predetermined by the genius of their race. This orthodoxy governed imperial and race relations. It even permeated the West African intelligentsia as they countered European claims to a monopoly of civic virtue by asserting that Africans had unique spirituality and a genius for personal relations. White Americans reinforced these stereotypes by lurid accounts of post-Civil War reconstruction and their diagnosis that it failed because of black unfitness for the Anglo-Saxon style of self-government. At the turn of the century in British West Africa, the imperial authorities gave effect to such ideas by de-Africanizing the upper echelons of the colonial bureaucracies. The switch in French territories from a policy of assimilation to one of association had similar results.

At the same time, ideas of cultural relativism began to emerge from the matrix of racial determinism. Only in the interior, it was believed, had the "Negro, pure and simple," been free to follow the dictates of his genius, uncorrupted by Western fashion. Travelers in search of the "noble savage" found not the much advertised unpredictable chaos, but well-ordered societies governed by strict codes of morality. African customs hitherto dismissed as bizarre and barbaric — fetish, secret societies, polygyny — were now explained by sympathetic writers, such as Blyden and Mary Kingsley, as fulfilling essential functions in maintaining highly moral, structured societies. Here were the germs of cultural relativism and functionalism, though few of the pioneers sought to disentangle their speculations for long from the racialist idiom of the age.

Ideas of this sort proved highly attractive to imperial administrators because they suggested that their own pragmatic experiments in indirect rule could be placed upon a sure, scientific basis. In a wider sense, these notions bolstered the self-esteem of European imperialism's local agents by casting them as the prime custodians of the integrity of traditional Africa, a role for which they were considered well suited by their presumed immunity to local special pleading on the part of commercial interests, missions, and Westernized Africans. In an age when Europeans increasingly deferred to the principle of national self-determination within their own continent, they succeeded in squaring imperial practice with their political conscience. Indirect rule and, paradoxically, de-Africanization constituted essential links in a chain of argument which culminated in equating the surrender of sovereignty with the conservation of African nationality.

To an international public opinion beguiled by such a paradigm of colonial government, Liberia could only seem a dangerous anachronism. As an African state parading an American-style constitution, in which Westernized blacks presumed to govern traditional societies, it breached every canon of contemporary imperial social science. Furthermore, through its inability to pacify the interior, Liberia failed the basic practical test of governmental competence in the Africa of the new imperialism. (Across the border, British rule in Sierra Leone had provoked widespread insurrection in 1898, but the colonial authorities could command the requisite force to suppress this, hence, ironically, reinforcing the legitimacy of Pax Britannica.)

"So-called" was the pejorative epithet most regularly applied to Liberia — "so-called state," "so-called government," "so-called African society." The country attracted the full force of early-twentieth-century racial prejudice. A. W. Clarke of the British Foreign Office African Department was much more sympathetic to the possibility of Liberian reform than most of his fellows, but he began his carefully considered memorandum on British aid — a gunboat — with the axiom "Negro Adminstrations are notoriously poor things, and that of Liberia affords no exception to the rule" (British Foreign Office 1907a). His spontaneous reactions, when confronted by what he considered Americo-Liberian pig-headedness, were liable to be much more crude: he denounced McCants Stewart, an adviser of Barclay, for example, "as an excellent example of the nigger windbag. . . . He is of the species negro for whom the only proper argument, if we could but apply it, is the horsewhip" (British Foreign Office 1908a). About the same time, the German ethnographer Leo Frobenius (cited in Ita 1973:312–313) expressed the European view: "Considered as a state, Liberia is such a miserable and imperfect object, such a wretched caricature of our northern cultural circumstances, that it seems completely unworthy of playing any role as a sovereign and administrative power alongside the European colonizing powers." Again and again, Liberia's critics consoled themselves with the thought that the Republic's days were numbered — that it would soon collapse, through a combination of bankruptcy and hinterland rebellion, as a prelude to painless annexation.

PRESIDENT BARCLAY'S REFORMS: CLEAVAGE BETWEEN COAST AND INTERIOR

Barclay attempted to disarm this hostility by his schemes for modernization and reform. In return for international goodwill and reasonable access to credit, he offered to transform Liberia into a prosperous, well-governed state, open to commercial penetration. In such a favorable environment, he promised, settlers and natives would eventually coalesce into a single nation. Given Liberia's poor reputation and the built-in pessimism with which both racial determinists and "cake-of-custom" relativists viewed its prospects, it was not an easy matter to convince international opinion that his ideas were viable.

Barclay, though, had some advantages. For a start, it was possible for Europeans to categorize him as not strictly an Americo-Liberian. That key British official, Consul Braithwaite Wallis, identified him as a "West

Indian not a Liberian" (British Foreign Office 1908b). He was born in
Barbados, landed in Liberia as a boy of eleven in 1865, and still retained
his distinct Barbadian brogue (H. S. Williams, quoted in Hooker
1975:97). Once divested of Americo-Liberian status, with all its negative
connotations, he could be recognized by Europeans as a statesman of
goodwill and talent. In particular, he was credited with transcending the
"very American" preoccupation with the politics of place, displaying real
sympathy with native aspirations, and, above all, being free from the
blancophobia thought to be characteristic of Americo-Liberians. (When
race relations worsened, each side rationalized its hostility in the light of
the presumed prejudice of the other, thus reinforcing polarization.) Many
Europeans supported Barclay not simply because they approved his
policies, but out of fear for the consequences of his defeat and replacement.

   He also had the support of two experts on race relations and African
affairs, his fellow Afro-West Indian Edward Blyden and Sir Harry Johnston, the British proconsul. In their different ways, each had helped to
shape the consensus on African government and society; equally each
maintained his reputation as a radical thinker, creatively adapting ideas
to circumstances. Given Liberia's unfortunate image, this double seal of
approval was highly valuable.

   What impressed visiting critics, as well as the Liberians themselves, was
the sharp cultural divide between the indigenous peoples and the
Americo-Liberians. Not even in neighboring Sierra Leone, where the
Creoles were frequently dubbed "Black Englishmen," was the cultural
cleavage between the Westernized coastal elite and the indigenes so
striking. Culture reflected demography. In the British colony, Liberated
Africans soon outnumbered the original black settlers from the New
World, with the result that Krio, which evolved as the medium for
everyday speech in the polyglot settler population, developed into a
full-fledged Creole language capable of absorbing indigenous culture
concepts. In Liberia, on the other hand, the black American settlers
predominated and continued to speak American English and to perpetu-
ate other American cultural traits which maintained their separation
from local African cultures.

   Blyden, so often dismissive of Liberian politicians, considered Barclay
the most likely to establish good relationships with the Africans of the
interior and the European powers as an accompaniment to essential
reforms. Johnston, in his massive two-volume *Liberia*, advertised the
country as possessing enormous economic potential; indeed, "properly
tilled and drained, cleared and cultivated [it] might easily sustain a
population of twenty millions" (Johnston 1906:vi). (His own overesti-
mate placed the current population at around two million.) Unlike many
contemporary British imperialists, Johnston sympathized with the aspira-

tions of the "educated, uneasy, touchy, suspicious people whom our role has called into existence." He believed that the chief defect of British rule was to prefer peasants and princes to the Western-educated middle class who, should the British disdain "to trust them gradually with sobering responsibilities," would be the leaders of nationalist revolt (Johnston 1912:282–283).

Johnston believed that he could fuse two of his prime concerns, the political advancement of the Western-educated coastal elite and the achievement of rational, economically advantageous frontiers for British West Africa, through his alliance with Barclay. Both Sierra Leone and Liberia were threatened with being reduced to coastal enclaves, with their traditional trade routes to the interior cut off by the expansion of the French in the Sudan. If they could combine in an informal English-speaking alliance, perhaps a *de facto* customs union, he reasoned, then together they would constitute a highly effective geopolitical unit. He attributed similar ideas to Barclay: "Sierra Leone, he believes is advancing . . . [to] a reasonable degree of self-government. Although he feels it would be very imprudent to openly express aspirations towards a common future . . . he feels . . . that with the common possession of the English language and more or less English laws and customs, there must be a parallel development on similar lines" (British Foreign Office 1907b).

Despite the entry of the United States into the colonial club after the war with Spain, American angles of vision on the Republic continued to be significantly different from those of Europe. Secretary of State Elihu Root forthrightly acknowledged Liberia as "an American colony" when justifying sending the 1909 commission to Liberia to develop suggestions for President Theodore Roosevelt on ways and means of helping the Republic (*Foreign Relations of the United States* 1909). Reinforcing such ties of history and kinship was the American sense of being a settler society which had tamed its own wilderness and its warrior tribes. Unlike the Europeans, Americans were prone to sentimental identification with the Americo-Liberians, all the more so because Americans classified anyone with a "drop of non-white blood" as "Negro." Hence, whereas Europeans — and Blyden — tended to blame the "mulatto republic" for bad relations with the interior peoples, Americans made no such racial distinction and attributed the troubles "largely to the existence of a mass of uncivilized blacks whom the Liberian government was unable to control." Finally, having involved themselves in rescuing the Dominican Republic, which had defaulted on bonds and other obligations in 1904, American officials believed that they had found a recipe for "negro Republics generally." It was Secretary Bacon's view (British Foreign Office 1908c, 1908d) that

constitutional government by negroes was an experiment which so far had failed but which should not be allowed to collapse altogether. With a little help and some tutoring we might help them to work out their own salvation. . . . Once secure to these countries a regular income, free them from the pressure of foreign debt, and establish them on a sound financial basis, and there was good hope that they might succeed in governing themselves.

Black American opinion was still riven over emigration at the turn of the century, but with the collapse of Bishop Henry M. Turner's last repatriation scheme in 1903 Liberia became a much less divisive issue. Booker T. Washington, a staunch opponent of emigration, offered influential support. Afro-Americans simply could not let the Republic slide into bankruptcy and annexation, for, as the *New York Age* put it in 1914, "Liberia is a mighty lens through which the world is looking at the Negro race."

White Americans also viewed Liberia from the perspective of American race relations. Bishop J. C. Hartzell, Methodist missionary bishop to all Africa, warned Liberians that their state was regarded as a crucial test in Negro self-improvement. He also drew attention to the Sierra Leone insurrection of 1898 and urged Liberians to learn from Britain's mistakes as they, too, began to develop a hinterland administration. He was perhaps most American, however, in his unabashed advocacy of the Open Door, reminding Liberians that the United States would only defend them against European imperial intrigue if they were prepared to admit freedom of entry for people, ideas, and commerce (*West African Mail* 1907).

Barclay was fortunate that his reform presidency coincided with the era of the "great rapprochement" between the United States and Britain, the colonial power most closely concerned with Liberian affairs. From the beginning of the century Britain had decided to support Liberian independence and sealed that policy by the Anglo-Liberian agreement of 1901, which Barclay himself negotiated, because annexation by either France or Germany would have been detrimental to British trade. But whatever the official view laid down by the Unionist Foreign Secretary, Lord Lansdowne, until 1906 and after that by his Liberal successor, Sir Edward Grey, difficulty and danger were inherent in the attitudes of the Foreign Office and Colonial Office bureaucrats and their "men on the spot," who were imbued with the settled view of imperialism which regarded Liberia as a doomed anachronism.

British officials in Sierra Leone were notoriously anti-Liberian, and in 1904 it seemed that their constant complaints had won Colonial Office support for the notion of an Anglo-French protectorate over Liberia's hinterland as a means of stopping the importation of arms through Liberia in contravention of the 1890 Brussels Conference (British Foreign Office 1904). This was smartly rejected by the Foreign Office because of the likely international complications, yet its own African

Department yearned for a perfect world in which Britain's policy toward Liberia would not be crushed into a framework established by relations with the great powers. As Clarke put it in 1908: "No one is better aware than myself that the Government of Liberia is absolutely rotten . . . and that the best thing for the Republic itself and for those unfortunate Europeans who have dealings with it would be its division between England and France. But this is impossible and we must work with the very feeble weapons with which we are armed" (British Foreign Office 1908e).

Liberian independence survived in the late nineteenth century because of what Hargreaves (1974:15) has termed the "Hobbesian fear" which led the British and French governments to restrain their expansionist agents in Sierra Leone and French West Africa. The Colonial Office proposal for partition emerged, however, in the wake of the Anglo-French detente of 1904. Fortunately for Liberia, the epoch of this colonial entente was also that of the Anglo-American rapprochement, and the balance of international forces still precluded Clarke's ideal solution.

Arthur Barclay emerged as the successful candidate of the True Whig party in the May 1903 election. With only a two-year term, he had to begin campaigning again almost at once. Although he had to live down the charge of not qualifying as a true "son of the soil" and was liable to be denounced as a "Black Englishman" likely to betray the country to the British, Barclay continued in office until 1912, winning elections in 1905 and 1907 along with an agreement to extend the presidential term from two years to four. He had made his way in public life as a successful civil servant. He had been secretary of the treasury and chairman of the True Whig party and had conducted important diplomatic negotiations. He was, therefore, strong in his practical knowledge of government and international politics, even if relatively weak in family connections.

THE SEARCH FOR FOREIGN CAPITAL

Barclay already had his eye on British commercial interests, which had acquired certain rights in Liberia, as sources of development capital. Moreover, Johnston, with his official contacts and skill as a publicist, was involved with two of them: the Liberia Rubber Corporation, which was to exploit wild and plantation rubber, and the Liberia Development Chartered Company, with concessions for mining, banking, railways, roads, and telegraphs. For the most part, the European powers had avoided risking substantial government funds in developing Africa. A common technique was the granting of charters to private syndicates which promised to provide the necessary infrastructure for development in return for monopolistic commercial privileges. It therefore seemed entirely appropriate to the British Foreign Office to reject the Colonial Office proposal of direct involvement through Anglo-French protection and work indirectly by providing "such unofficial encouragement and support as was possible" for Johnston's companies. On the strength of such proposals, the British expected that Liberia would be able to negotiate an international loan if British officials were brought in to supervise the customs in order to ensure sufficient revenue to service the proposed debt (British Foreign Office 1906, 1907a).

In 1906 a loan of £100,000 was negotiated with the international banking house of d'Erlanger and Company. The interest charges were to be secured by the customs revenue of Liberia. The Foreign Office arranged for William Lamont, assistant collector of customs in Sierra Leone, to be appointed controller of customs in Monrovia. There he joined Braithwaite Wallis, the ex-district commissioner, also from Sierra Leone, who had taken over as British vice-consul early in 1905 when Consul Macdonell, shaken with fever, had bolted his post and boarded the first warship home. In terms of personnel, Barclay's reform schemes seemed well founded. Lamont was an experienced customs official who succeeded in raising annual receipts from around £37,000 in 1905 to £55,000 in 1907, and this despite the fact that many ships evaded recognized ports of entry along the Liberian coast. Lamont asked the British government to supply an armed steamer to prevent such smuggling and, it was hoped, double the customs revenue (Haliburton 1971:23). Wallis, too, seemed a promising recruit. Ambitious to make his name as a writer, he had already published a grandly titled, highly colored account of his Sierra Leone service, centering on the 1898 insurrection (Wallis 1903). He had followed this with two articles packed with ethnographic detail on the Mende of Sierra Leone (Wallis 1905a, 1905b), and he was keen to get out another book. Seemingly, Barclay had acquired another publicist who might supplement the work of Blyden and Johnston.

Barclay expounded his ideas on modernization in messages to the legislature and people of Liberia (1905, 1906a, 1906b, 1907). He urged a systematic program of nation building as a matter of survival. He proposed a five-point plan: creation of a viable state structure, functioning according to recognizable bureaucratic norms; reform of the currency; economic development, especially in the hinterland; incorporation of the native population into the Liberian polity; and maintenance of friendly relations with the neighboring great powers. He was well aware that the recently built British and French railroads threatened to capture Liberia's hinterland trade for Sierra Leone and French West Africa. Repeated efforts by his predecessors to attract foreign capital for a Liberian railroad had failed. The automobile, however, seemed full of promise; motor roads could be built at a fraction of the cost of railways.

As soon as he became president, Barclay summoned a conference of chiefs from the interior at Monrovia and shortly afterward a similar meeting of Kru and Grebo chiefs from the east (Johnston 1906:300–301). He seems to have understood the factionalism of ethnic groups better than any previous president. From 1905 he began grouping local chiefs who had a previous history of interaction under district commissioners, and conferred the new title of "paramount chief" where that seemed warranted. There were some sharp setbacks. When Barclay decided to hold his first interior council at Bopolu, he aroused fears among the local Gola that he was reviving the old Monrovia-Mandingo axis against them. Some of his messengers were killed, others were stripped of their Western clothes and sent back in loincloths — the mark of a slave. Generally, however, his hinterland councils proved highly effective. He has been credited with "courage and astute diplomacy" by recent analysts for his patient, flexible application of indirect rule, and traditional tribal historians tend to date improved relations with Monrovia from his administration (d'Azevedo 1969:47–48).

Unfortunately, the Liberian Development Chartered Company operations, which were supposed to provide the economic infrastructure, failed abysmally. Major J. G. Baldwin, who replaced Wallis as consul in 1909, claimed that Liberia could make out "a fair moral case of what could be termed at the mildest, extortion. . . . [because] as a result of an expenditure of £33,000 by the company, Liberia has received a river boat whose outside value is about £1,200, a few miles of practically useless road, and a certain quantity of equally useless machinery and tools" (British Foreign Office 1909a). The company had encountered determined and diversified African resistance, native as well as Americo-Liberian. British officials, exponents of what Hopkins (1973:189) has called "the art of light administration" — postpacification government without much expense or *dirigiste* economic development — might be inclined to sentimentalize "the unspoiled native," but Braham, the company's resident manager, would have none of this. He warned against hasty stereotyping, by Europeans who never ventured inland, of Americo-Liberians as arrogant and natives as tractable: "the native in Monrovia is another creature to the native on his own dung hill in the interior." Braham's characterization of "insolent, indolent and savage natives" reflected the company's failures in labor recruitment and work discipline (British Foreign Office 1908f). The chiefs did not recognize the authority of Monrovia, and the company had to deal directly with road laborers who, in turn, felt free to leave the job, whereas in colonial Africa gangs of laborers usually were levied by mutual agreement between the chiefs and government. Similarly, the chiefs did not expect the company's agreement with the Liberian government to absolve it from paying transit duties to them. Sometimes sabotage amounted to virtual guerrilla warfare. Johnston reported, "Several times . . . bridges were partly blown up or otherwise injured in the night by 'patriotic' Liberians as a protest against white men carrying out any work in their country" (British Foreign Office 1909b). Confronted by such factions and by the hostility of many top politicians of the True Whig party who wished to wrest control of the d'Erlanger loan money from the company, Barclay and Johnston abandoned the device of a chartered company. Johnston's companies remained in being but were stripped of their quasi-governmental functions. In 1907 Barclay visited Europe, ostensibly to reach a settlement with France on Liberia's frontiers, but also to negotiate a new basis for the British-sponsored reforms. He and Clarke agreed that, now that the façade of the development company had been removed, the Foreign Office must play a much more direct role. A Liberian frontier force led by Major R. Mackay Cadell was established, and Lamont became financial adviser to gain control over the expenditure of the customs revenues he collected.

BLACK NATIONALIST AND PAN-AFRICANIST INFLUENCE

In the same year, Liberia was preparing for the diamond jubilee of independence. The celebration had been fixed for January 1908, and Barclay was determined that it bring both profit and publicity to the hard-pressed Republic. When he reached London, therefore, it was natural that Johnston's old friend, the Trinidadian lawyer Henry Sylvester Williams, should be recruited to help. As convener of the 1900 Pan-African Conference and well-known campaigner against injustices in British possessions in Africa and the West Indies, Williams brought luster to the Liberian cause. Impressed by what he learned from Barclay and Johnston, Williams broadcast the Republic's attractions in *The Jamaican* (Hooker 1975:97–99).

Williams went to the jubilee celebrations and intended to settle in Liberia. His speech to the Liberian Bar Association on "Experiences in South Africa with some general references to the Negro race" was considered a stirring exposition of "the disadvantages of the black man under white men's rule" (*African Agricultural World* 1908). Williams was no radical. Indeed, his biographer has aptly epitomized his political philosophy as "imperial pan-Africanism." Even when he criticized imperial practice, he accepted "the demonstrable superiority of British culture, and the unquestioned pre-eminence of British power in the world" (Hooker 1975:74). Yet in that place, at that time, his presence radicalized and polarized opinion.

To Wallis and Lamont, shaped by their Sierra Leonean service, Williams's critique of British colonial practice demeaned their professional integrity. It rankled all the more — seemed somehow treacherous even —

that these views, which the Americo-Liberians found so attractive, emanated from one who was preeminently a polished black Edwardian. Cadell remembered happier days, back in South Africa, when he had personally helped run the black barrister out of Johannesburg. Their prejudices were reinforced by Blyden, who dismissed Williams as one more "mulatto adventurer" of the type that had so often blighted promising developments in Liberian history: "They despise the pure Negro and his racial inspiration and aspiration, and hate the white man who they know who would encourage racial independence" (British Foreign Office 1908g).

Williams had identified with the struggles of "colored," rather than indigenous, South Africans, in line with his view that culture was more significant than pigmentation or race, and, as a professional man, his own problems tended to coincide with those of that intermediate group. To Blyden, of course, this was anathema. The ultimate comfort Blyden offered his disciples was that such men were temporary irritants: mulattoes were doomed to extinction by the inexorable rules of biology. The sad end to Williams's Liberian glory seemed to confirm this fatalism. He nearly died of blackwater fever and left the country. He died three years later at forty-two, a year before Blyden, who died at eighty.

The Williams controversy sharply revealed Barclay's predicament. No other Liberian statesman manoeuvered so adroitly in the margin for the measure of African initiative allowed by the new imperialism. Always sensitive to European opinion, he had warned Liberians in his inaugural address (1906b:15) to "have nothing to do with what is going on in Lagos, Nigeria, French Guinea or Sierra Leone" and to "avoid agitating for Negro West African Congresses and that sort of thing." Yet if the jubilee was to provide badly needed good publicity in the United States and the Caribbean as well as Europe, the Republic had to be invested with symbolic, pan-African significance. Nor, however "British" Williams's rhetoric might be, could Barclay control the slant put upon it by an Americo-Liberian audience.

LOCAL OPPOSITION AND RESISTANCE

The True Whig party had been continuously in power since 1877. Yet the enforced resignations of Gardner in 1883 and Coleman in 1900 sharply illustrated the limitations on executive power in a one-party situation. The opposition to unpopular presidential policies could function inside the ruling party to force the incumbent to change course or leave office. Furthermore, established foreign commercial interests, especially the Hamburg firm of Woermann, felt sufficiently threatened by the development company and Barclay's promise of customs reform to provide discreet sponsorship for his rivals.

Opposition to reform within the inner circle of theTrue Whigs, headed by Vice-President Dossen and Secretary of the Treasury Howard, found fresh popular support as a fiercely anti-British "Young Liberia" movement emerged. Barclay urged his British advisers to move slowly, holding that Americo-Liberian susceptibilities needed careful nursing, especially over the integration of the hinterland peoples. This enraged Blyden, to whom Barclay now seemed something of a lost cause. Blyden wanted the British to hasten the needed reforms. If Britain made a show of strength, then the true tribal Africans would claim their birthright and bring the Americo-Liberian regime crashing down.

Sustained by Blyden's advice, the trio of British officials — Wallis, Lamont, and Cadell — pressured Barclay for speedy implementation of the reform package. This, however, was counterproductive, weakening the president's position and strengthening Dossen and Howard. When Lamont brusquely approached Howard to discuss the appointment of more European customs officials, Howard lashed out: "Not another one. . . . This is a black man's country, not white man's. . . . I am fully aware of President Barclay's policy, but he will receive a check directly. . . . I shall die fighting rather than agree to any more Europeans in the government service" (British Foreign Office 1908h).

Cadell precipitated the final crisis. He alarmed the Liberians by enlisting men from the Sierra Leone protectorate in the frontier force and compounded this when, desperate for cash, he took over the Monrovia municipal police. A group of his men demonstrated against Barclay, and Cadell informed the president that if they were not given their arrears of pay he could not answer for the consequences. Meanwhile, Consul Wallis in some alarm telegraphed for a warship to safeguard British lives and property. On February 10, 1909, the *Mutine* reached Monrovia, but its fifty marines stayed aboard ship. When Barclay told Wallis that Cadell refused to vacate the frontier-force camp, the consul ordered him and all other British subjects out. They obeyed, and the frontier-force mutiny, "the Cadell incident," was over. In the backlash against all things British, Barclay and the legislature turned to the United States for aid (for diplomatic background, see Foley 1965).

Throughout the crisis, the British officials in Liberia constantly reverted to the attitudes of the contemporary colonial service toward Western-educated Africans when dealing with the leaders of an independent African state. Each envisaged reform in terms of what had happened in British West Africa — the replacement of Africans by Europeans. Yet the proponents of this policy of de-Africanization meant to demote from positions of authority not all Africans, but only those who had staffed the Western-style colonial bureaucracies. The corollary of de-Africanization was indirect rule. In terms of Liberia, this meant embracing Blyden's view that Americo-Liberian privilege must be ended and the energies of the "vigorous tribes" released. Every Americo-Liberian replaced was seen as both a victory for their white-man's-burden view of Anglo-African relations and a lightening of the load of oppression on the shoulders of the indigenous peoples. Such committed men were psychologically disabled from giving effect to the Foreign Office policy.

ETHNIC NATIONALISM AND SEPARATIST MOVEMENTS

Barclay expected his vigorous show of reform to buy Liberia enough time to embark on the necessarily slow and complicated process of building a nation-state. In two instances, however, along the Kru coast and far inland at Luawa, measures taken to transform Liberia into an internationally credible state provoked dangerous separatist movements.

Just when Liberians were required to demonstrate their competence as African rulers by subduing their hinterland, they were confronted by insurrection on the coast. Those intrepid maritime migrant workers, the Kru, whose labor was so crucial in the development of European commercial links with West Africa, came from the seaboard of Liberia. (Kru, Bassa, Dey, and Grebo were all conventionally labeled "Kru.") Monrovia attemped to confine Kru recruitment to six stipulated ports of entry so that it could take police action against gunrunning and levy a labor tax on the ships' captains. Such interference was bitterly resented by the Kru, who found willing accomplices in their evasion of Liberian control among the European skippers, especially those employed by Sir Alfred Jones's Liverpool-based Elder Dempster Line. A community of interest and sentiment developed which Kingsley (1901:47) recorded: "The Kruboy is indeed a sore question to all old Coasters. They have directed themselves to us English, and they have suffered, labored, fought, been massacred, and so on with us for generation after generation. Many a time Krumen have come to me when we have been together in foreign possessions and said 'Help us, we are Englishmen.'"

The celebration of the Kru as an ideal combination of noble savage and honest toiler became more marked toward the turn of the century (Brooks 1972:57). This image functioned in implicit — indeed, often explicit — contrast with the negative stereotype of the Western-educated African, particularly the Sierra Leone Creole and the Americo-Liberian. Such encapsulated prejudice refracted the subtle modulations of reality into patterns compatible with the imperial consensus. *Some* Western-educated Africans *were* acceptable, that is, when they were categorized "Kru" and identified themselves as such by hostility to Monrovia and friendliness to Britain. Among such were the missionized Grebo from the eastern Liberian seaboard.

American Protestant Episcopal missionaries had been active among the Grebo since 1836. They produced a substantial literature in the vernacular which so effectively promoted Grebo solidarity and modernization that the Liberian authorities eventually initiated a campaign of destruction against it (Haliburton 1971:12). The Grebo therefore quickly developed a Westernized elite conscious of the inferior educational qualifications of many of the Americo-Liberian ruling group and able to equip Grebo ethnic separatism with an appropriate nationalist symbolism and ideology. In 1875 Grebo had tried to establish the "G'debo Reunited Kingdom" in a rising which in the Cape Palmas area was called "the Protestant Episcopal War" because of the prominence of church members carrying a banner inscribed with the American motto "In God We Trust" and leading the anti-Liberian ranks into battle singing the *Te Deum* (Haliburton 1971:14). They were suppressed by the Liberians with American help, but Grebo nationalism was likely to explode whenever Liberia sought to be an effective revenue-gathering machine.

At the time of Barclay's reforms, William Waddy Harris, schoolmaster and catechist at Graway, had emerged as a leader of the Grebo. He had also been government interpreter but had lost that post because of his alleged antigovernment activity. In January 1909 he visited Monrovia to complain of his dismissal. He met Blyden and returned home. Shortly afterward he is said to have publicly desecrated the Liberian flag and raised the Union Jack in sight of the Americo-Liberian settlement of Harper, while his excited followers beat drums, played brass instruments, and shouted obscenities. Americo-Liberians believed that Harris had been recruited by Blyden to lead a Grebo rising timed to coincide with the "Cadell incident" in Monrovia (*African League*, June 13, 1909, cited in Haliburton 1971:31). As in Monrovia, the coup never materialized. Harris was jailed and languished in prison when the Grebo did revolt the following year. In prison he experienced the visions which led him, on his release in 1912, to forsake politics for the life of a wandering evangelist.

In the far northeast, Liberian territorial claims abutted on those of Britain and France. Here, in the prelude to European partition, Kai Lundo built up his Luawa kingdom, placing his capital, Kailahun, directly on the linguistic divide between Mende and Kissi and drawing his following from chiefs of both ethnic groups. His successor and erstwhile speaker, Fabundeh, followed Kai Lundo's policy of alignment with the British, demonstrating his friendliness by refusing to take part in the 1898 Sierra Leone insurrection. Unfortunately, although Fabundeh only gradually became aware of it, the delimitation of the Anglo-Liberian frontier already had partitioned Kai Lundo's old kingdom, with Kailahun itself falling on the Liberian side. Following the practice of traditional African factional diplomacy, Fabundeh's opponents within Luawa already had preempted the pro-Liberian and pro-French options. Fabundeh was stuck with his policy of loyalty to Britain; somehow, operating within it he had to maintain the integrity of his kingdom. The British were aware of the plight of this "friendly chief" but felt bound by the international settlement. Furthermore, they were wedded to the idea of governing indirectly through traditional rulers and assumed that the Africans they designated paramount chiefs would preside over ethnically homogeneous groupings. Kai Lundo's kingdom was very new and ethnically diverse, so its removal from Liberian control and reconstitution, in its essentials, under British auspices represented a *tour de force* of diplomacy and state rebuilding by Fabundeh (for a full account, see McCall 1975).

Meanwhile Sierra Leone officialdom had recovered from the shock of the 1898 hut-tax rebellion by selectively assimilating the findings of the Chalmers Commission and the new practical anthropology of Mary Kingsley, Edward Blyden, and the *Journal of the African Society*. The "native," "African," or "Negro, pure and simple," was henceforth institutionalized in a rough-and-ready system of indirect rule, "understanding being a pre-condition of control and control constituting adequate proof of understanding," as Achebe (1975:5) has dryly commented. For such a system to work well, though, conceptually and practically, the "native" had to understand what he was expected to do and say. Fabundeh of Luawa played his part to perfection, feeding British paternalism with his references to Edward VII as "my big father," listening deferentially to Governor Probyn's homilies on the art of chieftainship, and wringing maximum pathos from his role with loyal protestations against being consigned to Liberian rule. ("Poor Chief Fahbundeh," minuted Clarke dolefully.) He showed considerable resource, even collecting the unpopular hut tax from the areas given to Liberia and presenting it to an unsuspecting British district commissioner as a token of his own jurisdiction and British sovereignty.

In pursuit of international respectability by demonstrating their capacity for effective hinterland occupation, the Americo-Liberians established customs posts, backed by a small military force, in Luawa in 1907. This was deeply resented by the Luawa, and popular revulsion, with Fabundeh as spokesman, threatened to become an insurrection. The British in Sierra Leone sent a detachment of the West African Frontier Force which compelled the Americo-Liberians to withdraw. Before long, in order to rationalize their action, the British were parroting such points from Fabundeh's petitions as "Black man won't be ruled by black man" and that the significance of the Americo-Liberians' having to travel through the Sierra Leone protectorate to inspect Kailahun demonstrated their incapacity to secure order and transport. Reading through British Foreign and Colonial Office records, past Fabundeh's petitions, and seeing his very phraseology reemerge as part of the folk wisdom of the imperial consensus, one realizes that the question "who was manipulating whom?" has no simple answer (for example, see British Foreign Office 1907c)

The Americo-Liberians decided that their position in Luawa was too precarious, and in any case they needed British support for their boundary negotiations with the French, so they agreed to an exchange of territory which brought most of Kai Lundo's old kingdom within the Sierra Leone protectorate, under Fabundeh (for a good discussion of role-playing in a colonial context, see Ranger 1976).

CONTEMPORARY COMMENTS ON LIBERIA: E. W. BLYDEN AND F. STARR

The chief theoretical commentary on Barclay's reforms came from Blyden in two speeches. "The three needs of Liberia" was delivered at Grand Bassa on January 26, 1908, shortly after the jubilee celebrations. On January 18, 1909, as Anglo-Liberian race relations were already slithering toward the Cadell incident, he addressed the legislature and principal resident Europeans on "The problems before Liberia." Although the tone of the 1909 address betrays a greater urgency, as befits the heightening crisis, Blyden delivered essentially the same message on both occasions: the need for a radical change of direction (Lynch 1971:119–125; *Sierra Leone Weekly News* 1909).

The Republic, he argued, was an artificial amalgam of the "ostracized, suppressed, depressed, elements" of the southern United States and borrowed European ideas. He accepted the current notions of ethnography "that every race, every State . . . has a constitution existing in the nature of things, written in the 'manuscripts of God.'" Liberia was, therefore, "racially an unconstitutional State in Africa." To bring their political and social institutions into harmony with the "laws of African life," Americo-Liberians must heal their rupture "from the parent stock." Unfortunately, they had done their utmost to emphasize their differences. Here Blyden hit on the dilemma of the Americo-Liberians. Precisely because they were not obviously physically different from the surrounding Africans, the fear of "going native," which they shared with white colonials, was heightened. As racist theories of society and history became increasingly dominant in the later nineteenth century and were matched by more systematic racial discrimination in European colonies, Americo-Liberians were driven to ever more desperate assertions that their cultural commitment to Christianity and "civilization" must take precedence over their racial identity. Blyden roundly condemned such bifurcation: "We must learn to occupy the standpoint of our aboriginal brother, and to believe that in his place there is no man under the sun better than or equal to him."

He thought that Barclay had made a good start toward healing the breach when in a 1907 amendment to the constitution he substituted the word "Negro" for "colored" (Huberich 1947:1018–1021 discusses the background of this amendment). For Blyden, with his intense racial patriotism and respect for indigenous African culture, this semantic change had to be the prelude to the Africanization of Liberia. Barclay believed that Americo-Liberians had made ineffective use of the mission schools and the apprenticeship or ward system to attract African tribespeople to become loyal citizens of Liberia. To Blyden, such assimilationism was wrong in principle and, demonstrably, in practice. Cape Palmas was the scene of intense missionary activity and an episcopal see, yet it exhibited fiercer conflict between colonist and native than anywhere else in the Republic. Americo-Liberians, according to Blyden, were uneasy in the presence of "educated aborigines" (exactly the response of European colonists). The stripping of these recruits of their culture, he argued, had "degraded princes into slaves." (He instanced a descendant of "the great Prince Boyer" whom he had met aboard a ship, speaking good English, certainly assimilated, but in fact proletarianized: "He was a cook!")

Blyden proposed that Liberians merge through intermarriage, abandoning the Western ideal of monogamy, which had proved disastrous morally and politically. Monogamy as an ideal conflicted with practice and led the colonists to reject alliance overtures from powerful chiefs. The spurned tribespeople then regarded the Americo-Liberians not as "kith and kin," but as alien intruders. Once Americo-Liberians abandoned their doomed attempt to build a Christian state on the European model, they would cease to be "the most infertile and the most contemptible of beings — hypocrites." Liberia would become a Christian state "in the Biblical sense." African religion was not incompatible with Biblical religion, for Jehovah had been proclaimed under "different names — Jehovah, Zeus, Allah, Olorun. . . . Those who call him Jehovah or Allah know no more of him than those who approach him as Olorun. . . . To the philosopher and to the peasant He is equally inscrutable." Blyden's study of comparative religion, his prime intellectual concern in his last years, had taught him that African religion must be treated on terms of equality with the major world faiths (Blyden 1910).

He asserted that once Liberia became a truly African state, its national status would be advanced and its international relations strengthened. At the core of this was his belief that every nation had a distinct contribution to make. Liberia's independence would not be compromised by accepting temporarily aid from Britain: "We have *nolens volens* taken up the

White Man's Burden and we need his aid to enable us to bear it with dignity and success." Europeans would provide essential capital and technical assistance, but because of the climate "no European, whether merchant, planter or official, could ever dream of settling in Liberia."

Perhaps the most cogent defense of Liberia as it was against Blyden's belief that the pan-Africanist ideal must be achieved by reverse assimilation was mounted by a white American, Frederick Starr, professor and curator of anthropology at the University of Chicago. Expressing an old-fashioned American opposition to imperialism and his own commitment to African freedom, he first visited the continent in 1905. There he encountered the sneers of imperialists who repeatedly stigmatized Liberia as exemplifying African incapacity for self-government. Starr, therefore, visited the Republic in 1912, interviewing leading politicians, including Barclay, on the country's difficulties with the great powers and gathering material for a book to mobilize American support. He brilliantly exposed the double standard applied to Liberia, which was expected both to conform to European imperial standards and to constitute "an actual African state" (Starr 1914:13). In particular, he rebutted Maurice Delafosse, sometime French consul in Monrovia, who criticized the Liberians

for too closely following us. He believes they should have developed the native culture, have founded a Negro nation, different from European types. His demand is unreasonable, impossible of realization. The story of Liberia's origin demonstrates the impossibility. Liberia had to repeat us, even in our errors, because she came from us, is of us. Had she tried to do what Delafosse suggests, she would long since have been suppressed by hostile and jealous European powers. They would not permit such a nation to continue for a year upon the West Coast of Africa. Liberia must play the game as other nations play it — or get off the board.

No European social scientist in his time was capable of such empathy and insight, for it was grounded in shared experiences of Americanism and new-settler nationhood and in a Midwestern detachment from European ideology.

MODERN EXPLANATIONS OF AFRICAN NATIONALISM

Present-day historians and social scientists have produced their own explanations and insights into African nationalism. Some of these, even though they do not deal directly with Liberia, seem especially relevant to events there. Ajayi (1963) has analyzed the seeming paradox that African nationalists were preoccupied with the modernization of their region, through the mechanism of the nation-building state, before European rule had mapped out the boundaries of Nigeria. Of course, their Liberian contemporaries were operating within a sovereign state but one which, like the prepartition British enclaves at Sierra Leone and Lagos, aspired to a vast hinterland "sphere of influence" beyond its strict administrative limits. In Liberia, mid-century concern with nation building was institutionalized in presidential and Independence Day addresses. I have dealt elsewhere (Wilson 1969) with this long tradition from which Barclay's ideas derive. Ranger's (1969) speculations on the political consequences of uneven development and the interpenetration of primary, secondary, and even tertiary resistance in modern African nationalism are also relevant to the present study. The successful Liberian opposition to the European development company's road scheme, for example, particularly invites such analysis. Like Blyden and Casely Hayford sixty years earlier Ranger has deepened his understanding of Africa's encounter with the West by shifting his focus from political to religious history. Recent studies of African religion and the role of religion in African resistance movements (Ranger and Kimambo 1972) give perspective to Blyden's and Hayford's pioneer investigations.

Barclay's reforming presidency constitutes a case study in the political consequences of race relations. Brooks (1972) has suggested that the relationship between the Kru and the Europeans should be analyzed in the light of Mannoni's theories. Curtin (1964), Cairns (1965), and Bley (1971) demonstrate how fruitful an analysis of the relations of stereotypes to reality can be. Anglo-Liberian relationships abound in instances of stereotyping and role playing which cry out for similar analysis.

The Republic's problems, as Bishop Hartzell warned, transcended race relations. He reminded Liberians of "what Paul Kruger and the Dutch of South Africa learned in the loss of their nationality, that no people of any race can claim an absolute right to any section of the world as their own entirely, and to govern it as they please and succeed" (*West African Mail* 1907). Wallerstein's analysis of the incorporation of local communities into the world economy offers another appropriate theoretical perspective here (Gutkind and Wallerstein 1976). Barclay's attempt to create a viable state structure which would satisfy international public opinion and withstand incorporation into the world economy, and the reactions this provoked, foreshadowed some of the most crucial problems of Africans in the postindependence decade.

REFERENCES

ACHEBE, CHINUA
1975   *Morning yet on creation day*. London: Heinemann.

African Agricultural World
1908   *African Agricultural World.* January.
AJAYI, J. F. A.
1963   Ninteenth-century origins of Nigerian nationalism. *Journal of the Historical Society of Nigeria* 2:196–210.
BARCLAY, H. ARTHUR
1905   *Annual message.* Monrovia: Government Printing House.
1906a *Annual message.* Monrovia: Government Printing House.
1906b *Inaugural address.* Monrovia: Government Printing House.
1907   *Annual message.* Monrovia: Government Printing House.
BLEY, HELMUT
1971   *South-West Africa under German rule.* London: Heinemann.
BLYDEN, EDWARD W.
1910   *The Arabic Bible in the Soudan: a plea for transliteration.* London: C. M. Phillips.
BRITISH FOREIGN OFFICE
1904   Antrobus to Clarke, June 21, 1904. 2/880.
1906   Foreign Office to Crown Law Officers, April 24, 1906. 367/187/4588.
1907a Clarke's memorandum, January 21, 1907. 367/65/3537.
1907b Johnston's memorandum, March 27, 1907. 367/65/97127.
1907c Wallis to Grey, March 25, 1907. 367/65/12213.
1908a Clarke's minute, January 1908. 367/113/3281.
1908b Wallis to Foreign Office, Feburary 4, 1908. 367/113/7296.
1908c Bryce to Grey, June 5, 1908. 367/113/20403.
1908d Howard to Grey, July 21, 1908. 367/113/20403.
1908e Clarke's minute, February 1, 1908, in Wallis to Grey, January 14, 1908. 367/113/3287.
1908f Braham to Wallis, January 29, 1908, in Wallis to Grey, February 7, 1908. 367/113/7297.
1908g Blyden to Wallis, March 10, 1908, enclosed in Wallis to Grey, March 28, 1908. 367/113/13640.
1908h Lamont to Wallis, January 11, 1908. 367/113/3287.
1909a Baldwin to Grey, May 19, 1909. 367/162/21504.
1909b Johnston to Foreign Office, September 22, 1909. 367/163/35487.
BROOKS, GEORGE
1972   *The Kru mariner in the nineteenth century.* Newark: Liberian Studies Association.
CAIRNS, H. A. C.
1965   *Prelude to imperialism.* London: Routledge and Kegan Paul.
CURTIN, PHILIP D.
1964   *The image of Africa.* Madison: University of Wisconsin Press.
D'AZEVEDO, WARREN L.
1969   A tribal reaction to nationalism. *Liberian Studies Journal* 2:43–63.
FOLEY, DAVID M.
1965   "British policy in Liberia, 1862–1912." Unpublished Ph.D. dissertation, University of London.
Foreign relations of the United States
1910   *Foreign relations of the United States.* Washington, D.C.: Government Printing Office.
GUTKIND, PETER C., IMMANUEL WALLERSTEIN, *editors*
1976   *The political economy of contemporary Africa.* Beverly Hills: Sage.
HALIBURTON, GORDON M.
1971   *The prophet Harris.* London: Longman.

HARGREAVES, JOHN D.
1974   The price of independence. *Odu*, n.s., 6:3–20.
HOOKER, J. R.
1975   *Henry Sylvester Williams: imperial pan-Africanist.* London: Rex Collings.
HOPKINS, A. G.
1973   *An economic history of West Africa.* London: Longman.
HUBERICH, CHARLES H.
1947   *The political and legislative history of Liberia*, volume two. New York: Central Book.
ITA, J. M.
1973   "Frobenius, Senghor, and the image of Africa," in *Modes of thought.* Edited by Robin Horton and Ruth Finnegan. London: Faber and Faber.
JOHNSTON, SIR HARRY
1906   *Liberia*, volume one. London: Hutchinson.
1912   "The rise of the native," in *Views and reviews.* London: Williams and Norgate.
KINGSLEY, MARY
1901   *West African studies.* London: Macmillan.
LYNCH, HOLLIS R.
1971   *Black spokesman.* London: Cass.
MC CALL, MALCOLM
1975   "Luawa under British rule." Unpublished Ph.D. dissertation, University of York.
New York Age
1914   *New York Age.* November 26.
RANGER, TERENCE
1969   Connexions between primary resistance movements and modern mass nationalism in East and Central Africa. *Journal of African History* 9:432–453, 631–642.
1976   From humanism to the science of man: Colonialism in Africa and the understanding of other societies. *Transactions of the Royal Historical Society* 5th series, 26:115–141.
RANGER, TERENCE, ISARIA KIMAMBO, *editors*
1972   *The historical study of African religion.* London: Heinemann.
Sierra Leone Weekly News
1909   *Sierra Leone Weekly News.* March 6 and 13.
STARR, FREDERICK
1914   "Introduction," in *Negro culture in West Africa*, by George W. Ellis. New York: Neale.
WALLIS, C. BRAITHWAITE
1903   *The advance of our West African empire.* London: T. Fisher Unwin.
1905a   The Poro of the Mendi. *Journal of the African Society* 4:183–189.
1905b   In the court of the native chiefs in Mendeland. *Journal of the African Society* 4:397–409.
West African Mail
1907   *West African Mail.* March 22.
WILSON, HENRY S., *editor*
1969   *Origins of West African nationalism.* London: Macmillan.

Long-Term Structural Change in the Economy of Central Niger

STEPHEN BAIER

This paper examines long-term change in patterns of interaction between major sectors of a Sahelian economy, in particular between sedentary agriculture, pastoral nomadism, and commerce. It summarizes research on the economic history of central Niger between 1850 and 1960 by focusing on three major types of historical influences. In the first of these general categories is the adaptation of human society and economy to the natural environment and to long-term cycles of drought and recovery. The second derives from the growth of a larger region which included not only central Niger, but also the Sokoto Caliphate and, after the imposition of colonial rule, much of northern Nigeria. Both the caliphate and the desert edge to the north were linked to the world economy by trans-Saharan caravans plying trade routes between Tripoli and the Central Sudan, but this paper will treat trans-Saharan trade, its impact on the Sudan, and the effects of its ending only in passing (for more detail, see Baier 1977). The third group of historical influences includes the economic effects of colonial policies. All too often the impact of colonial rule on African economies has been viewed in isolation; this paper will attempt to view colonial rule as an overlay on deeper, long-term processes. These groups of influences will be discussed in turn; a fourth section of the paper will treat local methods used to recruit labor and accumulate capital in commercial enterprises in early colonial Niger.

THE PRECOLONIAL ECONOMY

The geographical focus of this paper will be Tuareg territory in the Aïr massif, the north-south corridor of trade and transhumance which connected the Aïr and surrounding desert with areas of dryland farming in

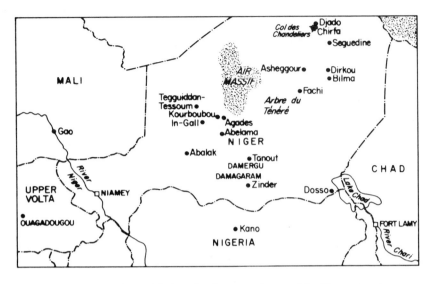

Figure 1.   Map of the Central Sudan, showing general area of the Taureg transhumance analyzed in this paper.

the Sahel and savanna to the south, and the eastern area of Hausa settlement in central Niger and northern Nigeria. For the purposes of economic analysis, this region can be divided into a northern sector, where pastoral nomadism prevailed, and a southern, sedentary sector, where most enterprises were heavily committed to farming. Of course, the southern sector included pastoralists and semi-sedentary people, most of whom were Fulbe. The vast majority of people in the savanna, however, had such an extensive commitment to agriculture as to preclude owning more than a few sheep, goats, cattle, or donkeys, since farmers could not properly tend crops and also take large herds to the best areas of rainy-season or dry-season pasture. Keeping large herds in the arid environment necessarily involved moving from place to place, whereas farming required sedentary life (Hopen 1958:17–40; Dupire 1962: *passim*).

In seeking to understand the structure of the Sahelian economy, the theoretical work of Barth (1973:11–22) on relationships between pastoral and sedentary groups in the Near East serves as an important point of departure. Barth argues that each of the principal productive regimes in arid environments should be analyzed within the common perspective of a regional economy including an area where nomadic pastoralism prevails and an area where farming is possible. This approach focuses attention not only on the characteristics of the pastoral and sedentary regimes, but also on interaction between them and on the interplay of production with ethnicity, stratification, and dominance within the region. Barth also calls attention to differences in the nature of pastoral and agricultural capital. In the pastoral sector, savings and investment were necessary, since herd capital was perishable and had to be replenished. Such investment took place in the enterprise as long as its managers did not actively intervene to kill animals for meat or sell them, thereby using up capital. In addition, investment took place automatically at the level of the enterprise, and public economic institutions to facilitate investment were not necessary. In contrast, in the agricultural regime land could not be increased by the reinvestment of its product except through elaborate economic institutions the function of which was to make conversion possible. Since land was the principal productive resource of the agricultural sector, conversion to still more land had to go through several stages. For example, in precolonial Africa, surplus agricultural production could be used to attract warriors or to buy slaves so that additional land could be conquered or brought into production, thereby increasing the productive capacity of the regime. If complex marketing systems existed, land could be converted directly into capital goods, but in the absence of institutions to facilitate conversion of one kind or another the agricultural regime was subject to stagnation. Thus the potential for growth in the two regimes was strikingly different; the tendency was for the pastoral sector to be volatile in comparison to settled agriculture, although this theoretical distinction need not apply in every real-life situation.

Differences in the potential for growth and in the nature of capital in the two sectors are especially important in the Central Sudan, where the influence of the natural environment was to reinforce these contrasts. Areas of desert and steppe where pastoral activities predominated have always been more severely affected by drought than farm land in the savanna because the variability of rainfall increased in marginal areas. Even in good years, rainfall was highly variable in time and space, and during drought this capriciousness was greater, with the percentage of deviation from long-term averages typically greater in arid regions than in fertile land in the savanna (Winstanley 1976:193–198). Not only has the risk of drought always been much more serious in the arid regions, but its effects on the productive capacity of the pastoral sector have always been greater. Herd losses undermined the productive capacity of enterprises in the pastoral sector in a way that deficient crop production in the agricultural sector did not. One or more bad years failed to alter the principal productive resource for farming, namely, the land, and most farmers survived all but the worst droughts. Therefore agricultural production tended to bounce back to its former level relatively quickly, whereas pastoral production did not, especially if herd losses were serious. Productive resources — water and pasture — were available after a drought, but reproductive resources, namely, breeding stock, were not. The growth of production in the regime was constrained by the number of surviving fertile female animals and the rate of growth of the herd, which in the conditions of the Sahel is estimated to have averaged something on the order of 5 10 percent per year (Dahl and Hjort 1976:28–76, 113–130). The rate was probably lower before veterinary medicine began to have an appreciable effect on Sahelian animal diseases. Thus pastoral enterprise was probably considerably more vulnerable to herd losses in the past than it is now, and consequently the level of risk from drought was greater.

With these analytical considerations as background, it is possible to proceed to a brief review of empirical evidence on the nature of the desert-edge economy. In the nineteenth century, the masters of the arid desert and steppe were noble Tuareg, warrior aristocrats who controlled dependent laborers occupying a number of status categories ranging from slaves to vassals (Baier and Lovejoy 1977). Tuareg could live on meat and milk from their herds, but most preferred to eat grain as well. As a result they traded salt, dates, animal products, slaughter animals, and beasts of burden for millet and other items from the south. They also received millet as payment of tribute from sedentary populations under their control — slaves or the descendants of people bought or enslaved by Tuareg and living on estates in the Sokoto Caliphate or in sedentary states to the north. The seasonal pattern of rainfall necessitated transhumance on the part of desert people, and some Tuareg groups evolved long cycles of transhumance which extended from the Aïr massif to dry-season pastures near Kano. While accompanying their herds on the journey to the savanna, Tuareg sold animals and desert products, using as an infrastructure the network of rural estates and also urban communities of formerly servile people who acted as brokers and intermediaries (Lovejoy and Baier 1975:554–571).

This far-reaching transhumance and trade allowed Tuareg nobles to develop a close involvement with sedentary areas and thereby to diversify the pastoral economy. They used diversification to cushion the risk of loss from drought by reinvesting the profits of rapid growth in the pastoral sector in farming and commerce in the savanna. In addition, Tuareg social stratification enabled those at the top to pass on most risk associated with life in the desert to the bottom levels of society. Skill and experience in warfare, the ability to make lightning raids using camels as mounts, and the vulnerability of both poor nomads and farmers to these raids enabled warrior aristocrats to dominate the desert and the Sahel. Supplies of dependent labor in turn allowed nobles to establish large firms involved in diverse economic activities. Nobles sometimes gave animals to groups of former slaves or to free but subservient people to raise on their own; they also provided trade capital and transport animals with which former slaves traded on their master's accounts.[1] Most dependent Tuareg enjoyed considerable freedom of movement, but they lacked a permanent claim on the productive resources with which they supported themselves. Consequently, if resources became scarce, for example, during drought, people at higher levels in society began to call in animals lent to those at the low end. If the size of herds fell below a minimum subsistence level, people of low status had to leave the desert to take up farming, as they did during the economic crisis of 1910–1920. Further, not all immigration to the savanna was in response to drought, as Lovejoy (1973:633–652) has shown; Tuareg of low status might also leave to reinvest modest profits in commercial opportunities in the south, and over time these immigrant communities took root in the savanna and came increasingly to identify with the predominant Hausa culture.

In short, the economic diversity of the precolonial Tuareg network contrasted sharply with the extreme specialization of many other pastoral societies. Military power in the desert and along the desert edge gave nobles access to dependent labor which in turn permitted them to reinvest the profits of animal husbandry in less risky enterprises in the savanna, such as agriculture, commerce, and craft industries. The network also functioned as a framework for emigration for the desert and the Sahel in case of drought.

REGIONAL ECONOMIC GROWTH

The second major group of long-term influences on the history of central Niger consisted of growth in the regional economy centered on the Sokoto Caliphate and its continued expansion under British rule. The vitality of the economy of Hausaland, as indicated by Hausa commercial expansion beyond its borders, antedated the jihad which formed the caliphate (Lovejoy 1974:565–567). Viewed from a perspective wider than that of socioeconomic change within the caliphate, the Fulbe jihad assumes the character of just another event in a larger process in which Islamization, economic growth, and increasing centralization of state structures were interrelated. Nicolas (1975:403–404) has called attention to an essential duality within Hausa society, and his analysis aids greatly in understanding these long-term forces. The original inhabitants of Hausaland, called Anna, Azna, Arne, or Asna depending on their location, once lived in clan villages which were largely self-sufficient, though trade in some commodities, notably salt and iron tools and weapons, was undoubtedly of great antiquity. Opposed to these non-

---

[1] For descriptions of Tuareg social stratification, see Rennell of Rodd (1926:136–138), Nicolaisen (1963:10–12), Bernus (1966), Clauzel (1962), Bonte (1975), and Baier and Lovejoy (1977).

Muslim villagers were what Nicolas calls the dynastic segment of Hausa society — the builders of Hausa states, who ruled villagers from their fortified towns. Nicolas correctly points out that to adopt current usage and call the two segments "Muslim" and "pagan" is to follow too closely the categories of thought of the segment which eventually won out and to ignore an important historical process. Over the centuries the dynastic segment grew at the expense of the Anna, aided by the growth of towns, increasing regional trade, and an expanding system of administration controlled by the ruling warrior aristocracy. The jihad of Usuman dan Fodio was possible because centralization and economic growth had proceeded to a point where the spark of religious fervor touched off a conflagration. The forces set in motion by the jihad, notably the formation of a large, economically vital state, with a peripheral reservoir of non-Muslim population which was continually raided for slaves, promoted in turn another round of centralization and conversion to Islam. First, slaves resettled in the economic heartland and had an incentive to acculturate by conversion; second, Islam provided the aristocracy with a workable overall plan for the control and taxation of an agricultural population. Trade increased because of peace in the heartland of the caliphate, a period of favorable climate, urbanization, and ready supplies of labor as slave trade relocated population from the periphery to the center (Lovejoy 1974:571ff.; Smaldone 1977:149ff.).[2] Hausa trading networks expanded to handle an increased volume of trade and to cover new territory, and the Tuareg system, which tied the caliphate to the desert sector, also expanded.

Economic growth in the center of the region had a dramatic impact on certain areas north of the caliphate. In the territory of Damagaram, a state ruled by a dynasty of Kanuri origin and its Hausa allies, the principal stimulus for change was the eastward shift of the major trans-Saharan route from Hausaland to Tripoli. In 1800 Zinder had been little more than a village and the headquarters of an obscure dynasty, but by mid-century it was an important trade city. It was also a point of contact between the desert sector and the economy of the savanna, since trans-Saharan trade brought with it the Tuareg groups who supplied camels and guides to trans-Saharan caravans. Tuareg involvement in Damagaram led to closer ties between nomadic nobles and the local ruling elite, and it led to the formation of a state within a state — one sedentary, territorially defined, and relying on revenue from agriculture and the other with a wider geographical scope, a marked seasonal fluctuation in the size of population as nomads came and went, and greater diversity of economic activities. The growth of the two sectors was mutually reinforcing, and both benefited from trans-Saharan trade, especially with the growth of

---

[2] Detail on plantation slavery in the Sokoto Caliphate is available in the recent work of Lovejoy (1976) and Hogendorn (1977 and this volume).

trade in local products after 1870 (Baier 1977:41–51). Trans-Saharan trade allowed Damagaram to attract farmers and craftsmen and to wage war successfully on its eastern and southern neighbors (Dunbar 1970:43–56; Salifou 1971:43–191). For the first time local Hausa-speaking farmers, who organized caravans during the dry season to take potash and animals to the caliphate, Nupe, and Yorubaland, participated in the general process of Hausa commercial expansion which had begun earlier (Baier 1974:13–19).

IMPACT OF COLONIAL RULE

A paramount consideration for the French colonial administration which was set up in Zinder in 1899 was the need to find sufficient revenue to finance their administration and to extend their military operations into the desert. The French had hoped to control and tax trans-Saharan trade, but they were restrained from placing too heavy a burden of taxation on the desert trade by the prospect that taxation would only speed its diversion to the new southern route through Lagos. Therefore they levied taxes on trade and markets in sedentary areas, but this policy was self-defeating; markets simply relocated across the border in Nigeria. Nor was the taxation of agricultural production an adequate source of revenue.

As the French extended their control into the desert, however, they found fewer initial obstacles to making the local economy pay for military operations and the administration which followed conquest. Pastoral wealth was highly visible and was concentrated in the hands of the nobles, and so when the French needed camels for remounts and for transport duties, they commandeered them from the Tuareg. The loss of camels, of course, struck at the heart of the desert economy and was compounded by bad climate and the effects of the collapse of trans-Saharan trade. With each French campaign in the desert, the need for transport animals increased because the supply lines lengthened. The French decision to occupy Tibesti in Chad in 1913 had especially grave consequences in Niger, in part because it coincided with the drought of 1911–1914 (Archives Nationales du Niger n.d.; Archives Nationales du Sénégal 1914, 1915). In 1916 Kaocen, a Tuareg exile from Damergu in central Niger who had taken part in Sanusi resistance in Chad and Libya, raised the banner of revolt among the Aïr Tuareg, and many joined him because of their desperate condition (Salifou 1971:55–157). The revolt in Aïr was the most serious of several Tuareg uprisings and required the efforts of sizable French forces and the better part of two years to put down (Fuglestad 1973).

Bitter fighting in the Aïr and the surrounding desert only worsened and prolonged the preexisting economic crisis. Both the rebels and the French took animals and supplies from noncombatants, filled in wells, destroyed crops in the valleys of Aïr, and laid waste the countryside. Much of the country became so barren as to be uninhabitable, and many Aïr Tuareg remained in exile in Nigeria until the mid-1920's, when they began to drift back to their homeland (Rennell of Rodd 1926:360–361). The Tuareg economy took nearly twenty years to recover, in part because camels, which calve only every second year, repopulate slowly.

While the natural antagonism of the French and Tuareg was greatest in the desert, where Tuareg represented the greatest danger to the colonizers, trouble at the northern end of the network was paralleled by developments in the savanna as the grain-producing estates of the fertile regions gradually slipped from the control of the nobles. Little detail is available on this process in Nigeria, but events near Zinder, where numerous estates and villages of newly sedentarized Tuareg were located, are probably representative. Here the French authorities, mindful of the threat to their rule posed by the nomads, systematically transferred the right to tax the inhabitants of estates from nomads to the sedentary political hierarchy (Gamory-Doubourdeau 1924). By the 1920's, most nomadic Tuareg retained only nominal ties with the people they once controlled or taxed. As time passed, even nominal ties grew weaker, so that nomads no longer could lay claim either to the produce of the estates or to rights to graze animals nearby.

An important result of this extended crisis in the desert economy was the permanent emigration of large numbers of low-status Tuareg to the farmland of the Sahel and the savanna, where they took up a sedentary life (Gamory-Doubourdeau 1924). The number of persons of servile Tuareg origin in Damagaram, most of whom trace their arrival to 1913–1918, indicates that permanent sedentarization removed many people from the desert economy. Although more research needs to be done on the size of the movement back to the desert as conditions improved, without doubt Tuareg nobles rebuilt their economy with a much smaller pool of dependent labor than they previously had at their disposal.

Meanwhile, in regions of sedentary agriculture, French colonial policy had produced another crisis of similar proportions. Besides levying heavy taxes on trade and markets, the French executed a local official responsible for collecting caravan taxes (Archives du Département de Zinder 1904; Muhamman Kane, personal communication, November 17, 1972). The availability of goods and services attracted settlement across the border, as did French policies concerning forced labor, recruitment during World War I, and requisitions of food and animals — all of which compared very unfavorably with life in Nigeria under British rule. The collection of trade taxes also resulted in innumerable inequities and opened the way for corruption among *chefs de canton* and *gardes de cercle.*

However, the French reserved the most detrimental and original form of corruption to themselves. Prevailing theory on the benefits of civilization required local people to use French currency in dealings among themselves and for payments into the treasury when at all possible, but current monetary theory dictated that token coinage for use in the colonies was impermissible.[3] Chronic shortages of French currency resulted, especially the forms of currency most in demand locally — silver coinage, especially coins of small denominations suited to local transactions. These shortages led to a series of unofficial exchange rates which deviated sharply from face values. It was possible to obtain a five-franc piece for as little as two and a half francs in coins of smaller denominations, and a five-franc bill could be obtained for four and a half francs in coins of large denominations. In other words, local people devalued silver of large denominations because of the scarcity of small coins, and they especially devalued paper because of the risks of storing it where termite infestation was common.

French administrators and military men exploited this black market freely. They had small coins sent to them in the mail, or they intercepted them as they were being introduced into circulation, and exchanged them for paper. They then took paper with them when they returned to France on leave. Local people suffered when they were forced, often at gunpoint, to accept five-franc bills in payment for goods sold to the French. On the local market these bills would be devalued by as much as half their face value, so that in effect local merchants or transporters received only half the nominal value of the payment given to them. The remnants of the North African trading community of Zinder, merchants who had had to adjust to the end of trans-Saharan trade in 1911, were especially hard hit by currency profiteering. Discrepancies between official and unofficial exchange rates lasted until the late 1920's, when the French were finally willing to introduce token coinage and shortages ended.

The net effect of the crisis in the pastoral sector, hardships in sedentary areas, and reaction to the drought of 1911–1914 was migration to the south. The railway which was completed to Kano in 1911 not only undermined trans-Saharan trade, which had once benefited both pastoral and sedentary sectors in the north, but also made possible large-scale exports of peanuts from the area surrounding the railhead. Since the decline of trans-Saharan trade was accompanied by continuing growth in the savanna economy, migrants were not only pushed from the north, but

---

[3]   For an excellent overview of monetary policy in the early colonial period, see Hopkins (1970). Many administrative reports document currency shortages in Niger (see, for example, Archives Nationales du Sénégal 1927). On speculation, see Abadie (1927), but most detail was supplied by Muhamman Kane (interview of December 4, 1972).

also attracted to the south. A small countercurrent of migration flowed northward against the main tide; Fulbe pastoralists arrived in the Niger steppe and southern desert in increasing numbers after 1900. Small numbers of pastoral Fulbe had ventured beyond the borders of the caliphate before the colonial occupation, but they stayed well clear of the territory controlled by the Tuareg. Vast areas of the Sahel and the southern desert are equally suited to use by camel nomads or by people who keep mostly cattle, but camels gave the Tuareg an incontestable military advantage, and they jealously guarded the land and water resources of the arid lands for their own use. After the arrival of the French, the Tuareg could no longer enforce this exclusivity, and soon Fulbe from Bornu, Gumel, Daura, Katsina, and Sokoto began to arrive in Niger. As these first arrivals moved north, they were replaced by waves of more recent migrants from Nigeria (Archives National du Niger 1940–1941, 1953; Archives du Département du Zinder 1953; see also Dupire 1962:21ff., 39, 130–132, and *passim).*

TUAREG AND HAUSA COMMERCIAL NETWORKS

From the early nineteenth century, central Niger, in particular the city of Zinder, was a crossroads for long-distance trade and therefore attracted merchants. Some were full-time traders of Tuareg origin who relied on Tuareg connections to trans-Saharan and desert-edge networks; others had begun by trading in the dry season and had linked up with Hausa networks extending south toward Nupe and Yorubaland. Participation in the Hausa and Tuareg commercial networks gave the people of central Niger experience and trade contacts, but the situation of these merchants changed drastically with the colonial occupation. The early colonial economic crisis, in particular the effects of the drought of 1911–1914, adjustments to the end of trans-Saharan trade, and the impact of wide-spread currency speculation, ruined a whole generation of these Zinder-based merchants. A new generation rebuilt, however, as conditions improved in the 1920's and as a peasant export economy developed in the 1930's. To the north in the pastoral regions, herders specialized in breeding and selling cattle into trading networks linking the desert-edge areas to regions near the coast where income from agricultural exports stimulated demand for beef (Baier 1974:145–178). As time passed, most large-scale professional traders, as opposed to farmers who engaged in trade during the dry season, left the countryside for Zinder, and by the 1950's urban traders and others from Nigeria handled most commerce in peanuts, cattle, cloth, and kola, leaving little scope for rural traders.

The traders of the new generation which rebuilt in the 1920's used preexisting models for the organization of firms.[4] The need to control the activities of client traders was crucial, because solving this problem allowed them to expand the scale of their activities beyond the dealings of a single merchant. The solution they adopted was to recruit clients from outside their immediate kinship group and start them out with menial tasks. As time passed and traders and their households became more familiar with their clients, a process of selection took place, those clients who appeared to be trustworthy being given more responsibility. Those who continued to inspire confidence were eventually allowed to trade on their own with the patron's goods. At early stages and especially when clients were on their own, the patron had to be able to prevent clients from stealing from him. In Zinder, ties of real or fictive kinship between patron and client fulfilled this function, with arranged marriages playing a key role. As young men in general relied on their father to arrange and pay for their marriages, clients relied on their patrons. Patrons arranged marriages and entered into relationships with their clients which resembled the interaction between father-in-law and son-in-law. They chose suitable marriage partners from their relatives and acquaintances. In Zinder between 1890 and 1940 the preferred marriage for a loyal and trusted employee was to the patron's own daughter. The next best was to his niece, and then came other classificatory daughters. If no relative could be found, the patron tried to arrange a marriage with a daughter of a close friend. In the case of young, unmarried clients, the prospect of an arranged marriage provided an incentive to remain honest and hardworking; after the marriage, this system allowed the patron to keep a hand in the domestic affairs of his clients and to integrate them as fully as possible into his own household.

This system provided not only a means for traders to control dependent labor, but also a framework for passing trade capital and accumulated wealth from one generation to the next. Inheritance in early twentieth-century Zinder was complex, but in general local custom and the overlay of Islamic law favored the division of estates in equal shares among sons and in lesser amounts to wives, daughters, and other relatives. In other words, the property of the deceased belonged in his patrilineage. Trading firms, however, often amassed working capital and wealth for their owners far in excess of the trivial sums ordinarily dealt with in customary

---

[4]   Most interviews recorded during field research in 1972 contain some information on commercial clientage, but see especially the accounts of Kasum Wurga (November 1, 1972), Sanda d'an Gayi (October 31, 1972), Abdu d'an Dabba (November 9, 1972), and Muhamman Kane (May 20, 1972, October 8, 1972, and November 24, 1972). Tape recordings of these interviews are on deposit at the African Studies Association Center for African Oral Data, Archives of Traditional Music, Indiana University, and at the Centre Régional de Documentation pour la Tradition Orale, Niamey. The best theoretical framework for interpreting commercial clientage comes from Meillassoux (1960) and focuses on means by which elder men control the access of younger men to women of marriageable age. For a more complete discussion, see Baier (1974:179–213).

inheritance. The accumulation of what was often considerable wealth raised the question of whether it properly belonged to the immediate lineage, as was the case in other circumstances, or to the firm and those who had helped build it. The second group was much smaller than the first, and, to make matters more complicated, often those with a claim on the resources of the firm did not belong to the lineage of the founder at all. Tension created by the prospect of the equal division of estates invariably embittered relations between fathers and sons in the Zinder merchant community, so much so that father-son continuity in trading enterprises was the exception rather than the rule.

A number of firms passed from father-in-law to son-in-law, that is, from patron to client, by the simple expedient of preinheritance. Clients who had been fully integrated into the patron's household gradually assumed the status of junior partners, and, as the senior partner retired, they gained complete independence. At the later stage of the relationship, when it assumed the nature of a partnership, it became increasingly difficult for the patron to keep his wealth separate from the trading capital of the junior partner. The result was that much of the capital attracted to commerce and built up over the years stayed within this sector rather than being dissipated among the heirs of the trader at his death. Although some "leakage" did occur, commerce was the only sector of the economy which had a mechanism for distinguishing the wealth of the firm from the property of the patrilineage.

However, merchants had great difficulty reinvesting wealth they had accumulated in commerce in productive activities in other sectors of the economy. From the 1930's, exports of peanuts from central Niger increased rapidly, and the rise of export-oriented production in agriculture might be expected to have created opportunities to reinvest commercial profits in agriculture. In fact, few merchants invested in land, and those who did produced little more than the needs of their family and clients. A few of the richest merchants had sizable networks of clients, but they used these networks to collect produce for sale rather than to mobilize labor on land they owned. Evidently hiring labor was not a workable solution, either because the costs of supervision were too great or because potential profits were not large enough to attract investment, but this is a subject for future research.

In a similar manner, other obstacles prevented investment in stock breeding. Because of seasonal variation in the availability of water and pasture, the only way to raise large herds was to move from place to place to take advantage of good pasture where it was available. Nomadism was the most efficient way to raise large herds, but sedentary farmers often owned a few animals and sometimes entrusted their cattle to nomadic Fulbe herders for several months or longer. This arrangement was less than ideal, because farmers often suspected herders of stealing from them

— reporting that animals had succumbed to disease when in reality the herders had sold them, substituting sickly calves for strong ones, or engaging in other underhand practices. These suspicions reflect the inability of outsiders to oversee the activities of nomads and therefore represent a major barrier to investment in stock.

CONCLUSION

The relationships between commerce, agriculture, and stock breeding are of course complex, but the material presented here suggests that in recent times scarce productive resources — labor and capital — have not moved easily between sectors. Large-scale urban merchants used commercial clientage to allow them to expand the scale of their activities and to arrive at a partial solution to the problem of distinguishing between the property of the firm and the property of the heirs of the founder. The presence of large firms in the commercial sector in the late colonial period contrasts with the situation in agriculture and stock breeding. Further research would be necessary to determine the reason for the failure of merchants to reinvest significant amounts of wealth in noncommercial activities. It is possible that the potential for profit is far greater in commerce than in other sectors, especially when large firms are involved. Another contributing factor is the lack of institutions for controlling and supervising labor in other sectors of the economy. If emphasis is placed upon difficulties involved in controlling labor, priority should be given to research on means of combining Western methods of organizing large firms, such as the use of accounting and legal sanctions, and local methods of the kind just described. Although very little scope was left for small-scale, rurally based traders, and therefore only a fraction of potential commercial opportunities remained open to them, flows of resources between commerce and agriculture may have been greater than in the case of the large urban firms; this is a topic which merits further investigation.

Whatever the relationships between commerce and agriculture, by the end of the colonial period large-scale Sahelian animal husbandry was almost completely isolated from other sectors of the economy. This isolation contrasts sharply with arrangements which once permitted nobles to shift productive resources in the precolonial Tuareg network. Tuareg nobles used military power to control dependent labor engaged in a variety of occupations including herding, farming, long-distance trade, commercial services in savanna towns, and craft production in the savanna. In the past, wealth accumulated in the relatively risky pastoral sector could be reinvested in savanna agriculture or in other forms of production in the south. The Tuareg network collapsed because colonial rule undermined the military power of the Tuareg and changed the rules of access to land for farming and grazing in the savanna; because the desert became a specialized periphery of a peasant export economy centering on northern and western Nigeria; and, most importantly, because the economic crisis brought on by early colonial rule coincided with a period of bad climate, the result being a cyclical downturn much deeper and longer-lasting than previous cycles of drought and recovery.

By 1950, the great half-century cycle of drought and recovery was complete, but it had moved the economy of central Niger to a far different position. The economic crisis of the early colonial period interrupted a pattern of precolonial economic growth in which desert and savanna were on more or less the same footing. Both Hausa and Tuareg trading networks had participated in a general expansion of internal commerce in the nineteenth century, and the Tuareg system had formed a link between desert and savanna. When southern demand for livestock increased in the twentieth century, however, Hausa merchants transmitted the pull of these southern markets into the Sahel by extending the capacity and geographical scope of their networks. Hence the main regional impact of the decline of the Tuareg network was to provide further stimulus to the Hausa commercial expansion which had been under way for a century and a half.

An important consequence of these changes was that the old reaction to drought, which removed people and animals from the desert during bad times and permitted expansion in good times, no longer functioned. The system had considerable drawbacks when viewed from the bottom of the social hierarchy rather than from the top, since it perpetuated an unequal distribution of wealth and power and caused suffering among those brought into the system as slaves. Whatever its drawbacks, however, it guaranteed its members, including those at the lowest levels of society, access to savanna resources. It is of course neither possible nor desirable to encourage stratification or the use of dependent labor to persist or reappear, but another and more fundamental principle of desert-savanna interdependence must be recognized: in the past, not only finished products, but also factors of production such as labor and capital moved between sectors of the economy.

REFERENCES

ABADIE, M.
  1927   *La colonie du Niger*. Paris: Editions Géographiques, Maritimes, et Coloniales.
ARCHIVES DU DÉPARTEMENT DE ZINDER
  1904   Rapport commercial, 2ᵉ trimestre 1904.
  1953   Brouin to Governor General of Niger, April 8, 1953.

ARCHIVES NATIONALES DU NIGER
1940–1941   Lafitte, Carnet monographique, cercle d'Agadez, 1940–1941.
1953   Geyer, Rapport annuel: contrôle des Peuls nomadisants, Agadez, 21 mai, 1953.
n.d.   TC 31, Loffler, Rapport sur les operations de Tibesti.
ARCHIVES NATIONALES DU SÉNÉGAL
1914   2G 14–4, Niger, Rapport agricole, 3ᵉ trimestre 1914.
1915   2G 15–11, Niger, Rapport d'ensemble 1915.
1927   2G 27–7, Niger, Rapport économique d'ensemble 1927.
BAIER, STEPHEN
1974   "African merchants in the colonial period: a history of commerce in Damagaram (central Niger), 1880–1960." Unpublished Ph.D. dissertation, University of Wisconsin, Madison.
1977   Trans-Saharan trade and the Sahel: Damergu, 1870–1930. *Journal of African History* 18:37–61.
BAIER, STEPHEN, PAUL E. LOVEJOY
1977   "The Tuareg of the Central Sudan: gradations in servility at the desert edge," in *Slavery in Africa: historical and anthropological perspectives.* Edited by Suzanne Miers and Igor Kopytoff, 391–411. Madison: University of Wisconsin Press.
BARTH, FREDERIK
1973   "A general perspective on nomad-sedentary relations in the Middle East," in *The desert and the sown: nomads in the wider society.* Edited by Cynthia Nelson, 11–22. Berkeley: University of California Press.
BERNUS, E.
1966   Les Toureg du sahel nigérien. *Cahiers d'Outre-Mer* 19:5–34.
BONTE, P.
1975   "Esclavage et relations de dépendance chez les Touaregs Kel Gress," in *L'esclavage en Afrique précoloniale.* Edited by Claude Meillassoux, 49–76. Paris: François Maspero.
CLAUZEL, J.
1962   Les hierarchies sociales en pays Toureg. *Travaux de l'Institut des Recherches Sahariennes* 21:120–175.
DAHL, GUDRUN, ANDERS HJORT
1976   *Having herds: pastoral herd growth and household economy.* Stockholm: Stockholm University Department of Anthropology.
DUNBAR, ROBERTA ANN
1970   "Damagaram (Zinder, Niger), 1812–1906: the history of a Central Sudanic kingdom." Unpublished Ph.D. dissertation University of California, Los Angeles.
DUPIRE, MARGUERITE
1962   *Peuls nomades: étude descriptive des Wodaabe du sahel nigérien.* Paris: Institut d'Ethnographie.
FUGLESTAD, FINN
1973   Les revoltes des Touareg du Niger (1916–1917). *Cahiers d'Etudes Africaines* 49:82–120.
GAMORY-DOUBOURDEAU, P.
1924   Etude sur la création des cantons de sédentarisation dans le cercle de Zinder, et particulièrement dans la subdivision centrale (arrondissement de Mirria). *Bulletin du Comité des Etudes Historiques et Scientifiques de l'Afrique Occidentale Française* 8:239–258.
HOGENDORN, JAN S.
1977   The economics of slave use on two "plantations" in the Zaria Emirate

of the Sokoto Caliphate. *International Journal of African Historical Studies* 10:369–383.

HOPEN, C. E.
1958   *The pastoral Fulbe family in Gwandu.* Oxford: Oxford University Press.

HOPKINS, A. G.
1970   The creation of a colonial monetary system: the origins of the West African Currency Board. *African Historical Studies* 3:101–132.

JOHNSTON, H. A. S.
1967   *The Fulani empire of Sokoto.* London: Oxford University Press.

LOVEJOY, PAUL E.
1973   The Kambarin Beriberi: the formation of a specialized group of Hausa kola traders in the nineteenth century. *Journal of African History* 14:633–651.

1974   Interregional monetary flows in the precolonial trade of Nigeria. *Journal of African History* 15:563–587.

1976   "The plantation economy of the Sokoto Caliphate." Paper presented at the annual meeting of the American Historical Association, Washington, D.C., December.

LOVEJOY, PAUL E., STEPHEN BAIER
1975   The desert-side economy of the Central Sudan. *International Journal of African Historical Studies* 8:551–581.

MEILLASSOUX, C.
1960   Essai d'interpretation du phénomène économique dans les sociétés traditionelles d'auto subsistence. *Cahiers d'Etudes Africaines* 1(4):38–67.

NICOLAISEN, JOHANNES
1963   *Ecology and culture of the pastoral Tuareg.* Copenhagen: Nationalmuseet.

NICOLAS, GUY
1975   Les catégories d'ethnie et de fraction ethnique au sein du système social hausa. *Cahiers d'Etudes Africaines* 15:399–442.

RENNELL OF RODD, FRANCIS
1926   *People of the veil.* London: Macmillan.

SALIFOU, ANDRÉ
1971   *Le Damagaram ou sultanat de Zinder au dix-neuvième siècle.* Etudes Nigériennes 27. Niamey: Centre Nigérien des Recherches en Sciences Humaines.

SMALDONE, JOSEPH P.
1977   *Warfare in the Sokoto Caliphate: historical and sociological perspectives.* Cambridge: Cambridge University Press.

WINSTANLEY, DEREK
1976   "Climatic changes and the future of the Sahel," in *The politics of a natural disaster: the case of the Sahel drought.* Edited by Michael Glantz, 189–213. New York: Praeger.

Biographical Notes

ADIELE E. AFIGBO (1937–   ) was born at Ihube in Okigwe, Nigeria. He received a B.A. in history from the University of London (1961) and a Ph.D. from the University of Ibadan (1964). He has taught at the Ahmadu Bello University, Zaria, the University of Ibadan, and the University of Nigeria, Nsukka, where he has been Professor of History since 1973. He has done his main research on the history of Nigeria.

BASSEY W. ANDAH (1942–   ) was born in Calabar, Nigeria. He received a first degree (B.A., University of London, 1964) in history at the University of Ibadan and then did graduate work at the University of London (M.Phil., archaeology, 1967) and the University of California, Berkeley (Ph.D., anthropology, 1973). He has taught at Berkeley, the University of California, Hayward, the University of Ghana, and the University of Ibadan, where he is currently Head of the Department of Archaeology. He has carried out paleoanthropological research in Upper Volta, Ghana, and Nigeria, with special focus on early man's cultural ecology and the achievement of food production.

ROBERT G. ARMSTRONG is Professor of West African languages, Institute of African Studies, University of Ibadan, Nigeria.

JOHN H. ATHERTON (1940–   ) was born in San Francisco, California. He received his B.S. (1964), M.A. (1966), and Ph.D. (1969) in anthropology from the University of Oregon and has taught since 1969 at Portland State University, where he is now Associate Professor of Anthropology. He has done archaeological work in West Africa (1967–1968), Oregon (1965–1966, 1973–1977), and Alaska (1964–1965). Most of his publications have been on West African archaeology, ethnohistory, and art history.

RONALD R. ATKINSON. No biographical data available.

STEPHEN BAIER (1944–   ) is Assistant Professor of History at Boston University and Assistant Director of the Boston University African Studies Center. He received his B.A. from Stanford University in 1966, served in the Peace Corps in Niger until 1968, and received his Ph.D. from the University of Wisconsin, Madison, in 1974. In 1971 and 1972 he was awarded a Fulbright-Hays Doctoral Dissertation Abroad Fellowship to carry out field research in Niger and archival research in Niger, Nigeria, Senegal, and Europe. In 1974 and 1975 he was employed at the University of Wisconsin Land Tenure Center. He has published articles on the interaction between pastoral and sedentary people in the Central Sudan, trans-Saharan trade to the region, and other aspects of Sahelian economic history.

LELAND C. BARROWS (1942–   ) is Associate Professor in African and European History at Voorhees College in Denmark, South Carolina. He spent the 1976–1977 and 1977–1978 academic years in residence at Harvard University as an Andrew W. Mellon Faculty Fellow in the Humanities. He has taught in the Program in Comparative Culture at the University of California, Irvine, and in the Department of History of Virginia Commonwealth University at Richmond. He has published several articles on aspects of the history of Senegal during the 1850's and 1860's. He was born in Washington, D.C., and earned his B.A. at Columbia University and his M.A., C.Phil., and Ph.D. at the University of California, Los Angeles. He has held three Fulbright-Hays Fellowships for research in France and in Senegal. His revised Ph.D. dissertation, *General Faidherbe, the Maurel and Prom Company, the French Expansion in Senegal,* is to be published by the Hoover Institution Press.

ROGIER M. A. BEDAUX (1943–   ), born in Tilburg, received his first degree in cultural anthropology from the University of Utrecht in 1968. After his final examinations in cultural prehistory at that university in 1970, he became scientific officer at the Institute of Human Biology, University of Utrecht, in 1971. He is specializing in the later prehistory of West Africa.

SYLVANUS J. S. COOKEY (1934–   ) was educated at University College, Ibadan, where he obtained a B.A. (honors, history, University of London) in 1961. He then pursued graduate studies at the London School of Economics and Political Science, obtaining a Ph.D. in 1964. He has since lectured at several universities in Nigeria, England, and the United States. He is now Professor of History and Africana Studies at

Rutgers University. His latest book, articles, and reviews cover various aspects of Nigerian history.

D. G. COURSEY (1929–   ) was born and studied in London. He joined the Colonial Agricultural Service and worked in Nigeria (1951–1964), most of his research being concerned with yams and cassava. His work was continued at the University of Ghana (1964–1966). where he extended his interests in root crops from the purely agricultural to the sociological and prehistorical aspects. In 1966 he returned to England, where he now works for the Ministry of Overseas Development and is mainly concerned with agricultural advisory work in the developing world. He is author of the standard monograph on the yam and of about sixty other papers.

NICHOLAS DAVID (1937–   ) was born in Cambridge, where he received his B.A. (1960) before doing graduate work at Harvard (M.A., 1962; Ph.D. 1966). He has taught at the University of Pennsylvania and at University College, London, and became Professor of Archaeology at the University of Ibadan in September 1974. Since 1967 he has carried out archaeological and ethnographic fieldwork in Cameroon, the Central African Republic, Nigeria, and the southern Sudan. His publications include papers in ethnoarchaeology and on central African culture history and man-land relationships from the early Holocene to the present.

OLIVER DAVIES (1905–   ), born in London, received his B.A. at Oxford University (1927). He was awarded a Litt.D. at the University of Dublin in 1946 for a book on Roman mines in Europe and an honorary Litt.D. at the University of Natal in 1979. He was Craven Fellow 1927–1929, Lecturer and then Reader at Queen's University, Belfast, 1930–1947, Professor at the University of Natal 1948–1951, and Professor at the University of Ghana 1952–1966. Since his retirement, he has been attached to the Natal Museum. He has done research in Ireland, mostly the excavation and surface survey of sites, and similar work in Ghana and Natal.

RAYMOND E. DUMETT (1931–   ) is Associate Professor of History at Purdue University, specializing in the history of Africa. His research fields of emphasis include the economic and social history of West Africa in the nineteenth and twentieth centuries and the economic history of Ghana (Gold Coast) during the precolonial and colonial periods. He received his Ph.D. from the University of London and has taught at The Ohio State University and the University of British Columbia. He has received a grant from the African Studies Association for the collection of oral data in Ghana and is now completing a book on the history of gold mining in that country. He is co-editor, with Lawrence J. Brainard, *Problems of rural development: Case studies and multi-disciplinary perspectives* (Leiden: Brill, 1975) and has published articles in a number of scholarly journals.

DAVID V. ELLIS (1950–   ), born in Wyandotte, Michigan, received his B.A. in anthropology from Ball State University in 1972. He has conducted fieldwork throughout the United States and served with the Arkansas Archeological Survey in 1975–1976. His primary interests are in the prehistory of West Africa and the Pacific Northwest, hunter-gatherer ecology, and visual anthropology. He is an M.A. candidate at Portland State University and a private archaeological consultant.

COLIN FLIGHT (1943–   ) was born in London and received his B.A. in Archaeology from the University of Cambridge in 1964. Between 1965 and 1969 he held a Lectureship in the Department of Archaeology, University of Ghana. He is now Lecturer in African Archaeology at the Centre of West African Studies, University of Birmingham, specializing in the later prehistory of Africa.

DONALD D. HARTLE (1923–   ) was born in Los Angeles, California, and received his B.A. in anthropology from the University of New Mexico (1949) and his Ph.D. from Columbia University (1960). He has taught at Hunter College of the City of New York, Queens College, New York City, and the American University. At present he is Professor of Archaeology at the University of Nigeria, Nsukka, where he has been since 1963. During the past fifteen years he has concentrated on the archaeology of Nigeria. Currently he is engaged in archaeological and ethnological research in southeastern Nigeria and the origin and diffusion of food crops in Africa.

T. R. HAYS (1940–   ) was born in Texas and received degrees from Southern Methodist University (B.A., 1966; M.A., 1969; Ph.D., 1971). His major area of interest concerns the transition to a sedentary way of life, primarily in the Sudan and Egypt. He has received research grants from the Smithsonian Institution, the National Science Foundation, and the National Endowment for the Humanities. He has taught at the University of Texas at Arlington and became Director of the Archaeology of the Institute of Applied Science, North Texas State University, in 1976.

EUGENIA W. HERBERT (1929–   ) received her B.A. from Wellesley College (1951) and her Ph.D. from Yale University (1957). She has taught at Yale and is currently Assistant Professor of African History at

Mount Holyoke College. The author of *The artist and social reform* (New Haven: Yale University Press, 1961) and co-author, with Claude-Anne Lopez, of *The private Franklin* (New York: Norton, 1975), she has also published extensively on African economic history. She is at work on an economic and cultural history of copper in precolonial Africa.

JAN S. HOGENDORN (1937–) was born in Lahaina, Hawaii. He received his B.A. in economics from Wesleyan University in 1960; his M.Sc. and Ph.D. are from the London School of Economics. Now Grossman Professor of Economics at Colby College, he specializes in the economic history of the slave trade. His books include *Managing the modern economy* (Cambridge: Winthrop, 1972) and, as co-editor with Henry A. Gemery, *The uncommon market: Essays in the economic history of the Atlantic slave trade* (New York: Academic Press, 1979).

JOHN O. HUNWICK (1936–) received his B.A. in Arabic from the University of London in 1959 and Ph.D from the same university in 1974. He lectured in Arabic and Islamic Studies at the University of Ibadan, Nigeria from 1960 to 1967. After a two-year period at the School of Oriental and African Studies, London he took up the post of Associate Professor in the Department of History at the University of Ghana, where he subsequently became Professor and Head of Department. Since 1977 he has been director of the Arabic Language Unit at the American University in Cairo. He has published extensively on Islamic West African history and on the Arabic writings of West Africa. He is currently Director of the *Fontes Historiae Africanae* project of the International Academic Union and editor-in-chief of its Arabic series.

RAY A. KEA (1935–) was born in Akron, Ohio, and received a B.A. in history from Howard University in 1957, an M.A. from the University of Ghana in 1967, and a Ph.D. from the University of London in 1974. From 1960 to 1968 he taught in Ghana. He is Assistant Professor of History at The Johns Hopkins University.

BRUCE L. MOUSER (1937–) received a Ph.D. in history from Indiana University in 1971. He is currently Associate Professor in the Department of History at the University of Wisconsin, La Crosse and was Visiting Research Scholar at the Institute of African Studies, Fourah Bay College, Freetown, Sierra Leone, in the spring of 1979. He has published articles on Sierra Leone and Guinea history in various periodicals and is the author of *Guinea journals: journeys into Guinea-Conakry during the Sierra Leone phase, 1802–1821* (Washington, D.C.: University Press of America, 1979).

PATRICK J. MUNSON (1940–   ), Associate Professor of Anthropology Indiana University, received his Ph.D. in Anthropology from the University of Illinois in 1971. His primary research interests are the prehistory of eastern North America and the later prehistory of West Africa and the southwestern Sahara, with particular emphasis on subsistence ecology and the origins of food production in those areas.

B. MARIE PERINBAM received her B.A. (honors) from the University of London (1954), her M.A. from the University of Toronto (1959), and her Ph.D. from Georgetown University (1969). She is currently Associate Professor of African History at the University of Maryland, College Park. She has taught at the Université d'Ottawa, Stanford University, and the School of Advanced International Studies of The Johns Hopkins University. Her publications include works on various aspects of precolonial African economic history and on the thought of Frantz Fanon, the Martinican psychiatrist and revolutionary. She has done fieldwork in North Africa and sub-Saharan Africa.

JOHN AUSTIN RUSTAD (1944–   ) was born in Seattle, Washington, and received his B.A. (1966), M.A. (1968), and Ph.D. (1976) in anthropology from the University of Washington. Under a Fulbright-Hays Fellowship, he conducted ethnographic research in Kenya 1974–1975. Currently he is a Research Associate of the Department of Anthropology, University of Washington, where he is involved with the construction of mathematical models for population analysis of contemporary, historically recorded, and archaeologically recovered societies.

B. K. SWARTZ, JR. (1931–   ) was born in Los Angeles, California, and received his B.A. and M.A. at the University of California, Los Angeles, and his Ph.D. in anthropology from the University of Arizona (1964). He is Professor of Anthropology at Ball State University. He was Visiting Senior Lecturer in the Department of Archaeology at the University of Ghana 1970–1971. He has done fieldwork in Ghana and North America and has published extensively on various archaeological topics. His African research interests deal with paleolithic archaeology and include analysis, classification, and terminology. He is editor of *Underground West Africa*, a newsletter for West African archaeologists.

TIMOTHY C. WEISKEL (1946–   ) received his B.A. from Yale University as a Scholar of the House in African History in 1969. The following year he undertook graduate training in social anthropology at Oxford on a Rhodes Scholarship and in 1970 received the Graduate Diploma of Social Anthropology. After further study at the Ecole des Hautes Etudes en Science Sociale in Paris and fieldwork on the Ivory Coast, he completed a Ph.D. dissertation in 1977 on the history of Baule resistance to French colonial conquest. His current work combines the approaches of economic anthropology and documentary history in an examination of the late precolonial and early colonial changes among stateless societies. He has taught at Williams College and is currently Andrew Mellon Fellow at Harvard.

HENRY S. WILSON (1928–   ), born in Newcastle upon Tyne, received a B.A. in history from the University of Durham (1949) and a B.Litt. from Oxford University (1955). He has taught at Fourah Bay College of the University of Sierra Leone, the University of Wales, and the University of Botswana, Lesotho, and Swaziland and is now Senior Lecturer in the Department of History and Centre of Southern African Studies of the University of York. His primary fields of interest are African nationalism, Anglo-Liberian relations, and United States relationships with southern Africa.

Index of Names

Index of Subjects

Patriclan, patrilineal system, 336, 337, 339, 469
Patronymics: jula, 291, 457, 464
Pawpaw, 169
Peanuts, 295; Niger, 596, 597, 598; Nunuz-Pongo region, 505, 506, 510; Senegal, 515, 519n, 520, 530, 537, 538, 540
Pearl millet, 164
Pebble tools, 12, 37
Pedology. *See* Soils
Pennisetum. See Bulrush millet
Phoenicians, 235, 236–237
Physic nut, 167
Plantain, 169, 282
Plantations, 293, 294, 375, 377, 490; Pongo region, 505, 510; Senegal, 520, 525
Plant remains, 61–63, 105, 106–107
Plants: protection, 72, 81–82, 83, 84, 85, 159, 168. *See also* Cultivation; Domestication
Pleistocene, 17, 19, 21, 23, 26, 28, 33
Pluvial periods, 25, 38, 82n, 84
Podocarpus milanjianus, 26
Podor, 527, 532, 533, 535
Political organization and institutions, 238, 241, 243, 279–280, 283, 287; Akwamu, 373; Igbo, 316, 334–335, 336–339; Nunez-Pongo region, 498, 499
Politics, 280, 299, 463–465, 471–472, 495, 501
Pongo, Rio, 495–510 *passim*
Populating, original, 12
Population(s), demography, 14, 112, 129, 133, 241; Dhar Tichitt, 107, 108; Igboland, 313, 314–315, 321, 322, 333, 339; North Cameroon, 141, 142, 143, 153–158, 171; Sahara, 116, 118, 125. *See also* Migration(s)
Portugal, Portuguese, 73, 294, 295, 438–441, 499–500
Potsherd pavements, 151, 234, 241
Pottery (ceramics), 7, 124, 124n, 125, 126, 127, 183–191, 384; Daima, 234; Dhar Tichitt, 103, 105; Igboland, 328, 330; Kintampo culture, 91, 92, 96, 208; Mali, 248–256; Nigeria, 129, 196–198, 199, 201–202; Nok culture, 228, 329; North Cameroon, 148, 149, 150–151, 153; Ntereso, 94–95, 208–214, 220, 221–223; Rim, 64, 65
Pottery kilns, 231, 232
Pouss, 150, 151
Precipitation. *See* Rainfall
Prehistory, 195–196
Priest-kingship, 400. *See also* Nri
Primary resistance, 298, 546, 549, 558, 565, 584

Protohistory, 10–11, 195
Public Record Office, London, 366n, 503, 503, 505, 505n, 507, 508, 509
Pulses, 167
Punpun phase. *See* Buobini culture

Quartz, 38, 64, 149, 219, 220, 248; Nok culture, 228, 231, 329; Sierra Leone, 262, 263, 264, 270
Quaternary, 3, 17–34
Querns, 199, 228

Race relations, 566, 569, 571, 581, 584
Racialism, 307–308, 566–567, 568, 569, 578, 581–582
Radiocarbon dates, 127, 129, 187, 201, 228–229
Railroads, 405, 448, 540, 573, 595–596
Rainfall (precipitation), 20, 47–48, 198, 589–590; Dhar Tichitt, 102, 104, 108, 109, 112; North Cameroon, 141, 142, 143; Ntereso, 206, 221; Sahara, 102, 115, 116, 125
Rasps. *See* Cigars
Regressions, Atlantic, 21, 24, 27–28, 29, 31, 32, 33
Religion, 393, 400, 582, 584; Igbo, 293, 306, 307, 316–317, 332, 341–342
Resistance, 295–298, 545–559, 565, 574, 584
Rice, 76, 101, 123, 164–165, 238, 497–502 *passim*
Rim, 4–5, 13–14, 41–65
Ritual and ceremonial, 80, 165, 200, 207, 253, 467; Igbo, 306–307, 316, 322, 336, 337; kingship, 396, 398, 399–404; protection of plants, 72, 80, 81, 83, 85. *See also* Burials
Rizga, 166
Rock shelters, 14, 95, 99, 199, 202, 263–264
Root crops, 123
Rop rock shelter, 127n, 149, 199
Royal Gazette and Sierra Leone Advertizer, 504, 509
Rubber, 554–555, 572

Safrap, 408
Sahara, 12, 14, 97, 102, 172, 194, 235; cultivation, 81–82, 114–116, 124–125, 130–132; desiccation, 132, 220, 239, 280, 328, 329; pottery, 183–188, 190–191, 238. *See also* Trans-Saharan trade
Sahel, 127, 147, 172, 432, 587–600; cultivation, 102, 116–118, 124, 130, 132
Saint-Louis, 296, 506, 517, 519n, 522, 523, 525, 530, 531, 534, 538, 540, 541